STUDIES IN PROVERBS

Laws from Heaven for Life on Earth

WILLIAM ARNOT

STUDIES IN PROVERBS

Laws from Heaven for Life on Earth

PUBLICATIONS

Grand Rapids, MI 49501

Library of Congress Cataloging-in-Publication Data
Arnot, William, 1808–1875.
    Studies in Proverbs / William Arnot.
        p.   cm.
    Reprint of the 1884 edition published by T. Nelson,
London under the title: Laws from heaven for life on earth.
    1. Bible, O.T. Proverbs—Criticism, interpretation, etc.
I. Title.
BS1465.A725   1978   223'.7'06—dc20   78-6014
                                                              CIP

ISBN 978-0-8254-2123-5

CONTENTS

PUBLISHER'S PREFACE

S eldom in life does one encounter a man or manuscript which inspires the thought, ''here is someone whose delight is in the law of the Lord.'' Such a valued volume is *Studies in Proverbs*. With the scriptural depth of a Spurgeon and the literary polish of a Robert G. Lee, Arnot discusses each proverb with a sacred savory touch.

Born in a farmer's home and apprenticed to a gardener, the Holy Spirit was preparing a chosen vessel for a very expressive task. Arnot accepts and acknowledges God's sovereign preparation. He draws upon his Lord's character training of him and shares it in practical application for the reader as you will see in the chapter, ''The Maker and the Breaker of a Family's Peace.''

Each God-breathed inerrant Proverb is surrounded with a commentary breathing forth the fresh aroma of one who has walked with the Rose of Sharon. Like a winter landscape on a sunny morn when each frost-flocked tree and bush sparkles with an ethereal radiance, these chapters capture the warmth of wisdom, the fire of conviction, and the beauty of reality.

As a student of the Scriptures and an intimate of God's presence, Arnot conveys with certainty and clarity to the reader the way of prosperous righteousness. Time has not diminished the truth or excellence of these concepts and instructions but has only served to enhance and enlighten their eternalness.

These illuminations of the Proverbs are not critical, continuous, or exhaustive. Arnot's thoughts on selected texts offer practical instruction and spiritual direction for a Christ-centered life built upon foundations in the doctrine of Grace. His aim was to be doctrinal, spiritual and practical.

Some allusion to passing events, as the reader will notice, bear reference to the date of the original publication, 1856-57.

It is with a most hearty commendation that we provide this

volume. Pastors will find it a spur to Biblical preaching. Teachers will find it a stimulation to practical guidance. Students will find it a storehouse of preparation for life. All will find strength for their Christian walk.

May all who read this volume be aware that "He who heeds instruction and correction is not only himself in the Way of Life, but is a way of life for others. And he who neglects or refuses reproof not only himself goes astray, but causes to err and is a path toward ruin for others" (Proverbs 10:17-Amplified).

THE PUBLISHER

The Preacher

(Proverbs 1:1)

"The Proverbs of Solomon the son of David, king of Israel."

GOD'S word is like God's world: it combines unity of pervading principle with endless variety in detail. The whole Bible, considered as one book, stands entirely apart from all other writings; and yet every several portion of it is distinguished from every other portion as much as one merely human writing is distinguished from another. This combination results from the manner in which it has pleased God to make known his will. One Divine Spirit inspires; hence the unity of the whole. Men of diverse age, taste, and attainments write; hence the diversity of the parts. Although the books are written by Moses, David, Solomon, they are all alike the word of God: therefore they exhibit a complete separation from all other writings, and a perfect consistency among themselves. Again, although they are all one as being the word of God, they are as much the genuine product of different human minds as the ordinary writings of men are the work of their authors: therefore there is in matter and manner an unconstrained, natural, life-like diversity. It was God who " spake unto the fathers," but it was " by the pro-

phets" that he spoke; not by their tongues only, but their understandings, memories, tastes; in short, all that constituted the men.
There is as much individuality in the books of Scripture as in any
other books. There is as much of Moses shining through the
Pentateuch as of Gibbon in the Decline and Fall. As are the
articulating lips to the soul whose thoughts they utter, so are the
prophets to the Holy Spirit, whose mind they reveal.

Every writer was chosen by God, as well as every word. He
had a purpose to serve by the disposition, the acquirements, and
the experience of each. The education of Moses as one of the
royal race of Egypt was a qualification necessary to the leader of
the exodus, and the writer of the Pentateuch. The experience of
David, with its successive stages, like geological strata, touching
each other in abrupt contrast, first as a shepherd youth, then as
a fugitive warrior, and last as a victorious king, was a qualification
indispensable to the sweet singer of Israel. God needed a human
spirit as a mould to cast consolation in for every kindred in every
age; and he chose one whose experience was a compound of meekness and might, of deep distress and jubilant victory. These,
when purged of their dross, and fused into one by the Spirit's
baptism of fire, came forth an amalgam of sacred psalmody, which
the whole church militant have been singing ever since, and
" have not yet sung dry."

Solomon did not, like David, pass his youth in pastoral simplicity, and his early manhood under cruel persecution. Solomon
could not have written the twenty-third psalm—" The Lord is
my shepherd;" nor the fifty-seventh—A psalm of David when he
fled from Saul in the cave. His experience would never have
suggested the plaintive strains of the ninetieth psalm—A prayer
of Moses the man of God—" Lord, thou hast been our dwelling-
place." But, on the other hand, Solomon went through a peculiar experience of his own, and God, who in nature gives sweet
fruit to men through the root sap of a sour crab, when a new
nature has been engrafted on the upper stem, did not disdain to
bring forth fruits of righteousness through those parts of the
king's experience that cleaved most closely to the dust. None of
all the prophets could have written the Proverbs or the Preacher;
for God is not wont, even in his miraculous interpositions, to
make a fig-tree bear olive berries, or a vine figs: every creature

acts after its kind. When Solomon delineated the eager efforts of men in search of happiness, and the disappointment which ensued, he could say, like Bunyan, of that fierce and fruitless war, " I was there." The heights of human prosperity he had reached: the paths of human learning he had trodden further than any of his day: the pleasures of wealth, and power, and pomp he had tasted in all their variety. No spring of earthly delight could be named, of whose waters he had not deeply drunk. This is the man whom God has chosen as the schoolmaster to teach us the vanity of the world when it is made the portion of a soul, and He hath done all things well. The man who has drained the cup of pleasure can best tell the taste of its dregs.

The choice of Solomon as one of the writers of the Bible at first sight startles, but on deeper study instructs. We would have expected a man of more exemplary life—a man of uniform holiness. It is certain that, in the main, the vessels which the Spirit used were sanctified vessels; " Holy men of old spake as they were moved by the Holy Ghost." But as they were all corrupt at first, so there were diversities in the operation whereby they were called and qualified for their work. There were diversities in the times, and degrees of their sanctification. Some were carried so near perfection in the body that human eyes could no longer discern spot or wrinkle; in others the principle of grace was so largely overlaid with earthliness that observers were left in doubt whether they had been turned to the Lord's side at all. But the diversity in all its extent is like the other ways of God; and He knows how to make either extreme fall into its place in the concert of his praise. He who made Saul an apostle did not disdain to use Solomon as a prophet. Very diverse were the two men, and very diverse their life course; yet in one thing they are perfectly alike,—together in glory now, they know themselves to have been only sinners, and agree in ascribing all their salvation to the mercy of God.

Moreover, although good men wrote the Bible, our faith in the Bible does not rest on the goodness of the men who wrote it. The fatal facility with which men glide into the worship of men may suggest another reason why some of the channels chosen for conveying the mind of God were marred by glaring deficiencies. Among many earthen vessels, in various measures purged of their filthiness, may not the Divine Administrator in wisdom select for actual use some of the least pure, in order by that grosser argument to force into grosser minds the conviction that the excellency of the power is all of God? If all the writers of the Bible had been perfect in holiness—if no stain of sin could be traced on their character, no error noted in their life, it is certain that the Bible would not have served all the purposes which it now serves among men. It would have been God-like, indeed, in matter and in mould, but it would not have reached down to the low estate of man—it would not have penetrated to the sores of a human heart. For engraving the life lessons of his word, our Father uses only diamonds: but in every diamond there is a flaw, in some a greater and in some a less; and who shall dare to dictate to the Omniscient the measure of defect that binds Him to fling the instrument as a useless thing away?

When God would leave on my mind in youth the lesson that the pleasures of sin are barbed arrows, he employs the experience of Solomon as the die to impress it indelibly upon my heart. I mark the wisdom of the choice. I get and keep the lesson, but the homage of my soul goes to God who gave it, and not to Solomon, the instrument through which it came. God can make the wrath of men to praise him, and their vanity too. He can make the clouds bear some benefits to the earth which the sun cannot bestow. He can make brine serve some purposes in nature which sweet water could not fulfil. So, practical lessons on some subjects come better through the heart and lips of the weary repentant king than through a man who had tasted fewer pleasures, and led a more even life.

Two principles cover the whole case: " All things are of God;" and "All things are for your sakes." We can never be sufficiently familiar with these two: 1. The universality of God's government; and, 2. The special use for his own people to which he turns every person and every thing. All Solomon's wisdom and power, and glory and pleasure, were an elaborate writing by the finger of God, containing a needful lesson to his children. The wisdom which we are invited to hear is divine wisdom; the complicated life experience of Solomon is the machinery of articulation employed to convey it to the ears of men. In casting some of the separate letters, the king may have been seeking only his own pleasure, yet the whole, when cast, are set by the Spirit, so that they give forth an important page of the word of truth.

The thought recurs that the king of Jerusalem was not, from his antecedents, qualified to sit in the chair of authority and teach morality to mankind. No, he was not; and perhaps on that very account the morality which he taught is all the more impressive. Here is a marvel; NOT A LINE OF SOLOMON'S WRITINGS TENDS TO PALLIATE SOLOMON'S SINS. How do you account for this? The errors and follies were his own; they were evil. But out of them the All-wise has brought good. The glaring imperfections of the man's life have been used as a dark ground to set off the lustre of that pure righteousness which the Spirit has spoken by his lips.

Proverbs - The Book

(Proverbs 1:6)

"To understand a proverb, and the interpretation; the words of the wise and their dark sayings."

I T is safer and better to assume that all men know what a proverb is, than to attempt a logical definition of it. As a general rule, the things that are substantially best known are hardest to define.

Proverbs are very abundant in all languages, and among all peoples. Many of them, though they seem fresh and full of sap on our lips to-day, have descended to us from the remotest antiquity. They deal with all manner of subjects, but chiefly with the broadest features of common life. The peculiar charm and power of the proverb are due to a combination of many elements. Among others are the condensed antithetic form of expression and the mingled plainness and darkness of the meaning. Often there is something to startle at first; and yet, on closer inspection, that which seemed paradox, turns out to be only intenser truth. Like those concentrated essences of food, which explorers carry in their knapsacks, the proverb may not present to the eye the appearance of the wisdom that it was originally made of; but a great quantity of the raw material has been used up in making one, and that one, when skilfully dissolved, will spread out to its original dimensions. Much matter is pressed into little room, that it may keep, and carry. Wisdom, in this portable form, acts an important part in human life. The character of a people gives shape to their proverbs; and again, the proverbs go to mould the character of the people who use them. These well-worn words are precious, as being real gold; and convenient, as being a portable, stamped, and recognised currency.

As a general rule, proverbs spring from the people at large, as herbage springs spontaneously from the soil, and the parentage of the individual remains for ever unknown. Very few proverbs are attached, even traditionally, to the name of any man as their author. From time to time collections of these products are made, and catalogued by the curious; and the stock is continually increasing as the active life of a nation gives them off. In other cases, books of proverbs have an opposite origin. Persons who appreciate the proverbial form cast their own thoughts in that mould, and so make a book of sentences, which are proverbs in their nature, although not, in point of fact, generated by casual contact of mind with mind in miscellaneous human life. It is altogether probable that, as to its construction, the Book of Proverbs partook of both kinds. It is probable that Solomon gathered and recast many proverbs which had sprung from human experience in preceding ages, and were floating past him on the tide of time; and that he also elaborated many new ones from the material of his own experience. Towards the close of the book, indeed, are preserved some of Solomon's own sayings, that seem to have fallen from his lips in later life, and been gathered by other hands.

Even in this one book the proverb appears under considerable diversity of form. Both in the beginning and towards the close, occur arguments, more or less lengthened, of continuous texture. But even in these the several links of the connected chain are cast in the proverbial mould; and the great central mass of the book consists of brief sayings, more or less arranged, indeed, but almost entirely isolated.

Considering how great a place proverbs hold in human language, and how great a part they act in human life, it was to be expected that the Spirit would use that instrument, among others, in conveying the mind of God to men. Proverbs, like hymns and histories, are both in human life and in the Bible—in the Bible, because they are in human life. If you wished to convey a message to a number of common people in France, you would not speak in Latin in order to display your own learning; you would speak in French in order to accomplish your object. God's will to man is communicated by means of instruments which man already uses, and therefore understands.

A greater than Solomon spoke in proverbs. He who knew what was in man sometimes took up that instrument, to probe therewith the secrets of the heart. Some he gathered as they grew in nature, and others he created by his word; but the old and the new alike are spirit and life, when they drop from the lips of Jesus.

Of the proverbs current in the world many are light, and some are wicked. Those of this book are grave and good. God's words are pure, whether he speaks by the prophets of old, or by his own Son in the latter day. " More to be desired are they than gold, yea, than much fine gold; sweeter also than honey, and the honeycomb. Moreover, *by them is thy servant warned*" (Ps. xix. 10, 11). The book from which the following studies are selected is peculiarly rich in "warnings," and the age in which we live peculiarly needs them. "Speak, Lord, for thy servant heareth."

The Root of Knowledge

(Proverbs 1:7)

"The fear of the Lord is the beginning of knowledge: but fools despise wisdom and instruction."

THE royal preacher begins his sermon at the beginning. He intends to discourse largely of knowledge and wisdom in all their aspects, and he lays his foundation deep in "the fear of the Lord." This brief announcement contains the germ of a far-reaching philosophy. Already it marks the book divine. The heathen of those days possessed no such doctrines. Solomon had access to a Teacher who was not known in their schools.

"The fear of the Lord" is an expression of frequent occurrence throughout the Scriptures. It has various shades of meaning, marked by the circumstances in which it is found; but in the main it implies a right state of heart toward God, as opposed to the alienation of an unconverted man. Though the word is "fear," it does not exclude a filial confidence, and a conscious peace. There may be such love as shall cast all the torment out of the fear, and yet leave full bodied, in a human heart, the reverential awe which creatures owe to the Highest One. "There is forgiveness with thee, that thou mayest be feared." "Oh, fear the Lord, ye his saints; for there is no want to them that fear him!" "I am the Lord thy God;" behold the ground of submissive reverence: "which brought thee up from the land of Egypt;" behold the source of confiding love. What God is inspires awe; what God has done for his people commands affection. See here the centrifugal and centripetal forces of the moral world, holding the creature reverently distant from the Creator, yet compassing the child about with everlasting love, to keep him near a Father in heaven. The whole of this complicated and reciprocal relation is often indicated in Scripture by the brief expression, "The fear of God."

" Knowledge" and "wisdom" are not distinguished here; at least they are not contrasted. Both terms may be employed to designate the same thing; but when they are placed in antithesis, wisdom is the nobler of the two. Knowledge may be possessed in large measure by one who is destitute of wisdom, and who consequently does no good by his attainments, either to himself or his neighbours. A lucid definition of both, in their specific and distinct applications, is embodied in a proverb of this book, xv. 2, "The tongue of the wise useth knowledge aright." The two terms taken together indicate, in this text, The best knowledge wisely used for the highest ends.

What is the relation which subsists between the fear of the Lord and true wisdom? The one is the foundation, the other the imposed superstructure; the one is the sustaining root, the other the sustained branches; the one is the living fountain, the other the issuing stream.

The fear of the Lord is the beginning of knowledge: the meaning is, he who does not reverentially trust in God, knows nothing yet as he ought to know. His knowledge is partial and distorted. Whatever acquisitions in science he may attain, if his heart depart from the living God, he abides an ignorant man. He who in his heart says "No God," is a fool, however wise he may be in the estimation of the world, and his own.

But how does this judgment accord with facts? Have not some Atheists, or at least Infidels, reached the very highest attainments in various departments of knowledge? It is true that some men, who remain willingly ignorant of God, who even blaspheme his name and despise his word, have learned many languages, have acquired skill in the theory and application of mathematics, have stored their memories with the facts of history, and the maxims of politics—this is true, and these branches of knowledge are not less precious because they are possessed by men whose whole life turns round on the pivot of one central and all-pervading error; but after this concession, our position remains intact. These men possess some fragments of the superstructure of knowledge, but they have not the foundation; they possess some of the branches, but they have missed the root.

The knowledge of God—his character and plans, his hatred of sin, his law of holiness, his way of mercy—is more excellent than all that an unbelieving philosopher has attained. If it be attainable, and if a Christian has reached it, then is a Christian peasant wiser than the wisest who know not God. It is a knowledge more deeply laid, more difficult of attainment, more fruitful, and more comprehensive, than all that philosophers know.

What right has an unbelieving astronomer to despise a Christian labourer as an ignorant man? Let them be compared as to the point in question, the possession of knowledge. Either is ignorant of the other's peculiar department, but it is an error to suppose the astronomer's department the higher of the two. The Christian knows God; the astronomer knows certain of his material works. The Christian knows moral, the astronomer physical laws. The subjects of the Christian's knowledge are as real as the heavenly bodies. The knowledge is as difficult, and perhaps, in its higher degrees, as rare. It reaches further, it lasts longer, it produces greater results. The astronomer knows the planet's path; but if that planet should burst its bonds, and wander into darkness, his knowledge will not avail to cast a line around the prodigal and lead him home. He can mark the degrees of divergence, and predict the period of total loss, but after that he has no more that he can do. The Christian's knowledge, after it has detected the time, manner, and extent of the fallen spirit's aberration, avails further to lay a new bond unseen around him, soft, yet strong, which will compel him to come in again to his Father's house and his Father's bosom. The man who knows that, as sin hath reigned unto death, even so grace reigns through righteousness unto eternal life by Jesus Christ our Lord, possesses a deeper, more glorious, and more potential knowledge than the man who calculates the courses of the planets, and predicts the period of the comet's return.

Men speak of the stupendous effects which knowledge, in the department of mechanical philosophy, has produced on the face of the world, and in the economy of human life; but the permanence of these acquisitions depends on the authority of moral laws in the consciences of men. If there were no fear of God, there would be no reverence for moral law in the bulk of mankind. If moral restraints are removed from the multitude, society reverts to a savage state. Inventions in art, though once attained, are again lost, when a community feed on venison, and clothe themselves with skins. So, "the fear of the Lord" is a fundamental necessity, on which high attainments, even in material prosperity, absolutely depend. True knowledge in the spiritual department, as to the authority, the sanction, and the rule of morality, is a greater thing than true knowledge in the material department, for the moral encircles and controls the economic in the affairs of men.

The man whose knowledge begins and ends with matter and its laws, has got a superstructure without a foundation. In that learning the enduring relations of man as an immortal have no place, and the fabric topples over when the breath of life goes out. But this beginning of knowledge, resting on the being and attributes of God, and comprehending all the relations of the creature, is a foundation that cannot be shaken. On that solid base more and more knowledge will be reared, high as heaven, wide as the universe, lasting as eternity.

The knowledge of God is the root of knowledge. When branches are cut from a tree and laid on the ground at a certain season, they retain for a time a portion of their sap. I have seen such branches, when the spring came round, pushing forth buds like their neighbours. But very soon the slender stock of sap was exhausted, and as there was no connection with a root, so as to procure a new supply, the buds withered away. How unlike the buds that spring from the branches growing in the living root! This natural life is like a severed branch. The knowledge that springs from it is a bud put forth by the moisture residing in itself. When life passes, it withers away. When a human soul is, by the regeneration, "rooted in Him," the body's dissolution does not nip its knowledge in the bud. Transplanted into a more genial clime, that knowledge will flourish for ever. Eye hath not seen, nor ear heard, what it will grow to.

The Family

(Proverbs 1:8)

"My son, hear the instruction of thy father, and forsake not
the law of thy mother."

THE first and great commandment is the fear of God;
and the second, which is next to it, and like to it, is
obedience to parents. Wherever the root is planted,
this is the first fruit which it bears.

The teaching of the Decalogue, and of the Proverbs, though
circumstantially different, is essentially the same. On the one
hand we have the legislator formally recording a code of laws;
on the other, the aged, prosperous, and witty monarch collecting
the best sayings that had been current at his court in that
Augustan age of Hebrew literature. The cast of the writings
corresponds with the position of the men; yet there are evident
marks of the same Spirit as the teacher, and the same truth as
the lesson. The ten commandments are divided into two tables.
The first lays the foundation of all duty in our relation to God,
and the second rears the superstructure in the various offices of
love between man and his fellow. In the Decalogue the fear of
God lies deepest as the root; and of the manifold duties which
man owes to man, the branch that springs forth first is filial love.
It is precisely the same here. The beginning of the commandment is, " Fear the Lord;" and the earliest outcome is, " My son,
hear the instruction of thy father." This verse of the Proverbs
flows from the same well-spring that had already given forth the
fifth commandment.

God honours his own ordinance, the family. He gives parents
rank next after himself. Filial love stands near, and leans on
godliness.

God is the author of the family constitution. He has conceived the plan, and executed it. Its laws are stamped in nature,

and declared in the word. The equal numbers of the sexes born into the world, the feebleness of childhood at first, and the returning frailty of age, are so many features of the family institute left by the Creator indented on his work. They intimate not obscurely the marriage of one man with one woman, the support of children by parents, and the support of decayed parents by the children grown. There are many such laws deeply imprinted in nature; and in nature, too, a terrible vengeance is stored up, which bursts with unerring exactitude on the head of the transgressor.

One of the wonders of that little world in the dwelling is the adaptation by which all the powers of the elder children are exerted for the protection of the youngest. A boisterous and impulsive boy, able and willing to maintain his rights by force of arms against a rival older than himself, may be seen to check suddenly the embryo manhood that was spurting prematurely out, and put on a mimic motherliness, the moment that the infant appears, bent on a journey across the room, and tottering unsteady by. A condescending look, and a winning word, and a soft arm around,—all the miniature man is put forth in self-forgetting benevolence. How exquisitely contrived is this machinery in nature, both for protecting the feeble thing that receives the kindness, and softening the rude hand that bestows it! There is fine material here for parents to watch and work upon. The stem is soft, you may train it; the growth is rapid, you must train it now.

In proportion as men have adopted and carried out the ordinance in its purity, have the interests of society prospered. All deviations are at once displeasing to God and hurtful to men. The polygamy of Eastern peoples has made the richest portions of the earth like a howling wilderness. The festering sores opened in the body of the community by the licentiousness of individuals among ourselves, make it evident that if the course, which is now a too frequent exception, should become the general rule, society itself would soon waste away. It is chiefly by their effects in deranging the order of families that great manufactories deteriorate a community. Though the Socialist bodies, being so sickly and diseased in constitution, have never lived much beyond infancy amongst us; yet, as they are founded on a reversal of the family law, their effects, in as far as they have produced effects, are misery and ruin. The Romish priesthood, abjuring the divinely provided companionship of the household, and leaving no alternative between solitude and sin, have ever been like a pin loose in the circling machinery of society, tearing every portion as it passes by. In the constitution of nature there is a self-acting apparatus for punishing the transgression of the family laws. The divine institute is hedged all round. The prickles tear the flesh of those who are so foolish as to kick against them.

In practice, and for safety, keep families together as long as it is possible. When the young must go forth from a father's house, let a substitute be provided as closely allied to the normal institution as the circumstances will admit. Let a sister be spared to live with the youths, and extemporize an off-shoot family near the great mart of business, with a dwelling that they may call their own. The cutting, though severed from the stem, being young and sapful, will readily strike root, and imitate the parent. This failing, let a lodging be found in a family where the youths will be treated as its members, participating at once in the enjoyments and restraints of a home. When the boy must needs be broken off from the parental stem, oh, throw him not an isolated atom on the sea of life that welters in a huge metropolis. Nor pen him up with a miscellaneous herd of a hundred men in the upper flat of some huge mercantile establishment, a teeming islet lapsed into barbarism, with the waters of civilization circling all around. If you do not succeed in getting the severed branch engrafted into some stock that shall be an equivalent to the family, and so exercise the natural affections, the natural affections checked, will wither up within, or burst forth in wickedness. The youth will be ruined himself, and the ruined youth will be an element of corruption to fester in the heart of the society that neglected him.

Honour thy father and thy mother. This is the pattern shown in the mount. The closer we keep to it, the better will it be both for the individual and the community. God is wiser than men.

Children, obey your parents in the Lord, for this is right, and all right things are profitable. To violate the providential laws is both a crime and a blunder.

Love to parents ranks next under reverence to God. That first and highest commandment is like the earth's allegiance to the sun by general law; and filial obedience is like day and night, summer and winter, budding spring and ripening harvest, on the earth's surface. There could be none of these sweet changes and beneficent operations of nature on our globe if it were broken away from the sun. So when a people burst the first and greatest bond—when a people cast off the fear of God, the family relations, with all their beauty and benefit, disappear. We may read this lesson in the fortunes of France. When the nation threw off the first commandment, the second went after it. When they repudiated the fear of God, they could not retain conjugal fidelity and filial love. Hence the wreck and ruin of all the relations between man and man. As well might they try to make a new world as to manage this one wanting the first and second, the primary and subordinate moral laws of its Maker.

Filial Love a Blossom of Beauty
(Proverbs 1:9)

"For they shall be an ornament of grace unto thy head, and chains about thy neck."

IT seems an instinct of humanity to put ornaments upon the person. It is greatly modified in its development by circumstances, but it is certainly a uniform tendency of our nature. It does not rank high among the exercises of the human faculties, yet it is quite above the reach of all inferior creatures. The propensity is fully developed in tribes that lie lowest in the scale of humanity; yet no germ of it can be traced in species that form the culminating point in the brute creation. By so many and so various marks may be known the abrupt and absolute separation between men who have fallen the lowest, and other sentient beings that occupy the summit of their scale.

Ornaments on the fallen, like many other innocent things, become the occasions of sin, but they are not in their own nature evil. It is probable that the pleasure which we derive from them springs originally from some association with moral qualities. There is some connection between sensible beauty and moral goodness, although the instances of deception are so numerous as to deprive that connection of all value as a rule of life. To deck with external beauty that which is morally corrupt within, is a cheat which men practise on themselves and others; but adornment of the person, modest in measure, and adopted instinctively by an innate sense of propriety, is conducive to virtue, and consistent with Scripture.

Ornaments, however, are mentioned here not for their own sakes, either to commend or forbid them, but as a form of expression to convey emphatically the truth that moral qualities, after all, are the true adornments of a human being. All the graces of the Spirit are lovely; but here the foremost of relative duties, a child's reverential regard for a parent, is recommended as an ornament of surpassing beauty. Young men and young women, put that ornament on your heads—twine that chain of gold around your necks! These jewels from heaven, set deep within your souls, and glancing at every turn through the transparency of an unaffected life, will do more to make your persons attractive than all the diamonds that ever decked a queen.

The world and its history teem with types of heaven. Beauty, and the love that fastens on it, are types, and they have their antitypes on high. The ransomed Church is the bride of the Lamb, and she is adorned for her husband. When the adorning is complete, she is all glorious, and the King greatly desires her beauty. When he presents unto himself a church without spot or wrinkle, or any such thing, then shall he see of the travail of his soul and be satisfied.

Put on now, O son! daughter! put on these beautiful garments; love, obey, cherish, reverence your parents. These are in God's sight of great price. They are valued not only by the spiritually minded disciples of Jesus, but even by every man of sense around you. They are thought becoming by all but fools. These ornaments will not be out of date when time has run its course. They will be worn on the golden streets of the New Jerusalem, when the fashion of this world shall have passed away.

Over against this beaming beauty, of similar shape and size, a dark shadow stands. Whithersoever that comely body turns, this ghastly spectre follows it. It is a daughter, emerging into womanhood, with ruddy cheek and sparkling eye—with beads on her neck and bracelets on her arms—who has so crushed a mother's heart by constantly trampling down its desires, that the disconsolate mother never utters now the reproof which she knows would be despised. Personal beauty, aided by costly ornaments, cannot make that creature gainly. The deformity within will make itself felt through all the finery. The evil spirit that possesses the heart will glance from the eye, and tinkle on the tongue, in spite of every effort to act the angel. Every mind that retains in any measure a healthful moral tone, will, in close contact with such a character, infallibly be sensible of a discord. Felt repulsive, she will be repelled. The disobedient daughter will gravitate down to the companionship of those who, having no sense of harmony, recoil not from a spirit out of tune. She is miserable, and knows not what ails her. She has broken that commandment which holds a promise in its hand, and been thrown over on the barbs of the counterpart curse. Those who see her impaled alive there, should learn that the moral laws of God have avenging sanctions, even in the powers of nature. Godliness is profitable unto all things. The first commandment is fruitful, even in this life ; and the second is like it : like it in its heavenly origin—like it in its holy character—like it in its glad results. Honour thy father and thy mother ;—this is an ornament of solid gold. Unlike the gilding of superficial accomplishments, the more rudely it is rubbed, the more brightly it glows.

The Foe and the Fight

(Proverbs 1:10)

"My son, if sinners entice thee, consent thou not."

THIS verse, in brief compass and transparent terms, reveals the foe and the fight. It is a Father's voice. It speaketh unto us as unto children. With a kindness and wisdom altogether paternal, it warns the youth of the *Danger* that assails him, and suggests the method of *Defence.*

The three preceding verses determine for us the character of the persons whom Solomon has here in his eye. They are not the ignorant, the outcast, the profligate. The stages over which he travels before he reaches this warning, show that he addresses the well-conditioned and hopeful portion of the community. In the seventh verse we have "the beginning of wisdom" laid in the fear of God ; in the eighth, the earliest outcome from that unfailing source,—the obedience of children to their parents ; in the ninth, the beauty of this filial obedience, as the most winsome ornament that the young can wear. We have wisdom presented first in its sustaining root, next in its swelling buds, and last in its opening bloom of beauty. The preacher fastens upon persons who have had the fear of God early implanted in their hearts, who have reverently obeyed their parents during childhood, and who in youth have been observed by others as adorning the doctrine of the Saviour. To these, as they are passing out of youth into the responsibilities of manhood, and from a father's house to the wide theatre of the world, he addresses this plain and pungent exhortation, " My son, if sinners entice thee, consent thou not."

The DANGER is, " If sinners entice thee." There are enticers and enticements ; the fowler and his snare.

The *enticers* of youth may be divided into two great classes, the *internal* and the *external*. There are a multitude of evil thoughts in the little world within, and a multitude of evil men in the great world without.

The sinners that entice from *within* are the man's own thoughts and desires. There is quite an army of these sinners in a young man's breast. Thoughts have wings. They pass and repass unobserved. They issue forth from their home in the heart, and expatiate over every forbidden field, and return like doves to their windows, through the air, leaving no track of their path. These thoughts become acquainted with sin. They are accustomed to visit the haunts of vice without detection. They revel unchecked in every unclean thing. They open up the way, and prepare a trodden path on which the man may follow. A gossamer thread is attached to an arrow, and shot through the air unseen, over an impassable chasm. Fixed on the other side, it is sufficient to draw over a cord ; the cord draws over a rope ; the rope draws over a bridge, by which a highway is opened for all comers. Thus is the gulf passed that lies between the goodly character of a youth fresh from his father's family, and the daring heights of iniquity on which veteran libertines stand. The sober youth stands on the solid platform of religious and moral worth. No one can think it possible that he should go over to the other side. But from the brink on this side he darts over a thought which makes itself fast to something on these forbidden regions. The film no one saw, as it sped through the air ; but it has made good a lodgment in that kingdom of darkness, and the deeds of wickedness will quickly follow when the way has been prepared. "Out of the heart," said He who knows it (Matt. xv. 19), "proceed *evil thoughts.*" Yes—that is what we expected ; but what come out next ? "Murders, adulteries, fornications, thefts, false witness, blasphemies." A horrible gang ! How quickly they come on ! How closely they follow their leaders ! Murders and adulteries march forth unblushingly ; but they follow in the wake of *evil thoughts.* Oh, if the fountain were cleansed, the streams of life would be pure ! So thought David, when, in an agony of grief, despairing of his own efforts, he cried, "Create in me a clean heart, O God !" This is the root of the evil, and no cure will be thorough or lasting that does not reach and remove it.

The sinners that entice from *without* are fellow-men, who, having gone astray themselves, are busy leading others after them. The servants of Satan seem to be diligent and successful. When a society, associated for economical or benevolent purposes, desires to enlarge the number of its members, a common method is to request every one to bring in two others. Thus the membership is tripled by a single effort. This seems to be the principle of administration adopted by the god of this world. All his subjects are busy. " Ye are of your father the devil, and the deeds of your father ye will do." The deed most characteristic that the father of lies ever did, was to lead others after him into sin. To entice into sin is specifically "the deed" of the devil, and that deed his children will instinctively do. An evil-doer has a craving for company in his wickedness. He cannot enjoy solitary crime. He is impelled to seek company, as a thirsty man is impelled to seek water. It is his vocation to draw others after him into sin. By a natural necessity, the licentious recruit among the ranks of the virtuous ; the drunken among the ranks of the sober. An enemy is amongst us : let the inexperienced beware.

How great the danger that every youth incurs as he issues forth from his parents' control, to take his place in the race of life, and on the stage of time! A dreadful conspiracy is organized against him. It is designed and directed by spiritual wickedness in high places ; its agents swarm unseen in his own heart, a legion of evil spirits, as it were, possessing him already. Co-operating with these intestine foes, are the whole host of evil-doers who come in contact with him in the world. Young man, this life is not the place to walk at ease in. If you slumber there, the Philistines will be upon you. Though you have a Samson's strength, they will put out your eyes, and make you grind in meanest slavery, and triumph in your misery and death.

It is a power of nature that is taken and employed to enslave men. The disposition in youth to go together is a law of the human constitution. Men are gregarious. The principle of association is implanted in their nature, and is mighty according to the direction it gets, for good or evil. This great power generally becomes a ready agency of ill. How faithfully a youth clings to a companion who has obtained an influence over him!

It often happens that the more vigorous mind has been imbued with wickedness. The very abandonment of that leading spirit adds to his power. There is a reckless hardihood attained, where the restraints of conscience are unknown, that acts like a charm on softer minds. One bold, bad spirit often holds many gentler natures, as it were, in a mesmerized state. They are not masters of themselves. They have been drawn into the vortex of the more powerful orb; destitute of an independent will, they flutter fascinated around him.

The *enticements*, like the enticers, are manifold. As addressed to well-educated, well-conducted youth, they are always more or less disguised. The tempter always flings over at least his ugliest side some shred of an angel's garment. An enemy who desired to destroy you by your own deed, would not lead you straight to a yawning precipice, and bid you cast yourself down. He would rather lead you along a flowery winding path, until you should insensibly be drawn into a spot which would give way beneath you. Enticements to moral evil will generally take that form. You will not be persuaded all at once to plunge into deeds of darkness, knowing them to be such. Few young men who have enjoyed a religious education come to a sudden stand, and at once turn their back upon God and godliness. Most of those who fall, diverge at first by imperceptible degrees from the path of right-eousness. When it is intended, by a line of rails, to conduct a train off the main trunk, and turn it aside in another direction, the branch-line at first runs parallel with the trunk. It goes alongside for a space in the same direction; but when it has thus got fairly off, then it turns more rapidly round, and bounds away at right angles to its former course. As engineers avoid the physical, so the tempters avoid the moral difficulty. An abrupt turn is not attempted in either case. The object is far more surely attained by a gently graduated divergence. The import-ance of the ancient rule, *Obsta principiis* (resist the beginnings), can never be over-rated. The prize is great. Everything is at stake. Life is at stake,—both the lives. Time and eternity, body and soul; all that you have or hope, is to be lost or won. Watch the begin-nings of evil. "Watch and pray, that ye enter not into tempta-tion."

We must name and briefly describe some of these snares

Their name is Legion. They cannot be numbered. We shall uncover and expose two from among the multitude of betrayers that lurk beside your path,—one peculiar to large towns, the other common to all places.

High in the list of dangerous enticements to the young stands *the theatre.* We shall not waste time in a dispute regarding the possibility of obtaining innocent and harmless dramatic entertainments. Enough for our present purpose is the fact that there are none such. The idea wherewith some would fain excuse their indulgence, is a stage managed in accordance with pure morals. It is a vain imagination. Those who build and manage theatres do so with the view of a good investment and profitable employment. They know the tastes of their customers. They must either conform to these tastes, or lose money by opposing them. A theatre conducted on such principles as would make it safe to the morals of youth would not pay its proprietor. There are many enlightened and benevolent citizens who rear and maintain institutions which do not bear their own charges. They submit to loss from zeal for the public good: but these men never choose theatres as the instruments of elevating the community.

We scarcely know anything that would make us fear more for a young man than to hear that he was in the habit of attending the theatre. We know that the practice, besides its own proper evil, would not long stand alone. A man cannot take fire into his bosom without being burned.

Does the impatient spirit of youth attempt to ward off our word, by averring that we would smother the joys of the young under the gloomy cloud of religion? Oh, for a balance that could nicely discriminate the degrees of happiness that each enjoys! We would enter the competition with the merriest frequenter of the stage. We would set any sensible, God-fearing youth in competition with him, and show that, even as to present gladness, the theatre is a cheat and a lie. Once, on a Sabbath morning, as the writer was going to church through the streets of a large city, he saw, flaunting gaudily on the walls, the stage placards of the preceding Saturday evening. In large, lying letters, they announced, "A Cure for the Heartache." Avaunt, deceivers! Ye often inoculate your victims with the poison of that disease, but ye have no power to take it away. Can the company of rakes and courtesans minister consolation to a mind distressed? Will they parody the griefs that wring a human heart? Will they make sport of that deep-set disease that Jesus died to heal? When a sinner's heart is aching, he must bend his steps to another place—he must seek the skill of another Physician! We have sometimes thought the matter of attending the theatre, and similar scenes of midnight merriment, might be profitably put in the form of a dilemma, thus:

The unconverted (having other work before them) have no time to be there.

The converted (having other joys within them) have no inclination.

The *customs* of society encouraging the use of *intoxicating drinks* constitute one of the most formidable dangers to youth in the present day. All are aware that drunkenness, in our country, is the most rampant vice. How broad and deep is the wave whereby it is desolating the land! It is not our part, at present, to register an array of facts tending to show how many are held helpless in its chain, and how deeply that chain cuts into the life of the victim. The extent and the virulence of the malady we shall not prove, but assume to be known. Our special business is to remind the young of the *enticements* by which they are led into that horrible pit. It is specially true of this potent enemy, that it makes its approaches unsuspected and by slow degrees. We have known many drunkards. We have witnessed scenes of wretchedness which haunt our memory in shapes of terror still. We have seen a youth brought down by it from a place of honour and hopefulness, laid upon his bed uttering hideous groans, twisting himself, in mingled bodily and mental agony, like a live eel upon a hook. We have seen an old man, who knew that drink was making his life-springs fail fast away, yet, in spite of threats and persuasion, going drunk to bed every night. We have heard that man, when sober, say, "If there is one place of hell worse than another, it must be mine, for I know the right, and do the wrong;" and yet he drank himself to death. We have seen a female, with a gentle air and a tender frame, stand and tell that she had a batch of demons within her, uttering loud voices, and declaring that they had her surely bound over to hell. Reason had fled. Drink had brought madness on. And yet, whenever the delirium abated, she returned to the drink again. What need of cases? We have seen drunkenness in most of its stages, and forms, and effects; but we never yet met a drunkard who either *became a drunkard all at once*, or who *designed to become one*. In every case, without exception, the dreadful demon vice has crept over the faculties by slow degrees, and at last surprised the victim. The sinners with whom he kept company did not entice him to become a sot in a single night. They only invited him to go into cheerful company. They suggested that religion, when rightly understood, did not forbid a merry evening. He went, and the evening was merry. Strong drink contributed to its merriment. He was sober. He had no intention of becoming a drunkard, either then or on any subsequent occasion. A drunkard, however, he now is. He is in the pit, and who shall pull him out! May God have mercy on the lost immortal, for he is beyond all help of man!

Let young men, as they value their souls, beware of these Satan-invented customs prevalent in society, which multiply the occasions of tasting strong drink. These habits of sipping so frequently, on every occasion of joy or sorrow, of idle ease or excessive toil, in freezing cold or in scorching heat—these habits of a little now and a little then, seem to have been invented with fiendish ingenuity, to beget at last, in the greatest possible number, that fiery thirst which, when once awakened, will mercilessly drag its subject down through a dishonoured life to an early grave.

Leaning on the bank of the majestic river a few miles above Niagara, a little boat was floating on a summer day. A mother plied her industry in a neighbouring field. Her daughter, too young yet for useful labour, strolled from her side to the water's edge. The child leaped into the boat. It moved with her weight. The sensation was pleasant. Softly the boat glided down on the smooth bosom of the waters. More and more pleasant were the sensations of the child. The trees on the shore were moving past in rows. The sunbeams glittered on the water, scarcely broken by the ripple of the stream. Softly and silently, but with ever-growing speed, the tiny vessel shot down the river with its glad unconscious freight. The mother raised her bended back and looked. She saw her child carried quickly by the current toward the cataract. She screamed, and ran. She plunged into the water. She ventured far, but failed. The boat is caught in the foaming rapids—it is carried over the precipice! The mother's treasure is crushed to atoms, and mingles with the spray that curls above Niagara. This is not a fiction; it is a fact reported in the newspapers of the day. But, though itself a substantive event, it serves also as a mirror to see the shadow of others in. The image that you see glancing in that glass is real. It is not single. It may be seen, thousand upon thousand, stretching away in reduplicating rows. Pleasant to the unconscious youth are the merry cup and the merry company. Lightly and happily he glides along. After a little the motion becomes uneasy. It is jolting, jumbling, sickly. He would fain escape now. Vain effort! He is rocked a while in the rapids, and then sucked into the abyss.

If many thousands of our population were annually lost in Niagara, the people, young and old, would conceive and manifest an instinctive horror of the smooth deceitful stream above it, which drew so many to their doom. Why, oh, why do the young madly intrust themselves to a more deceitful current, that is drawing a greater number to a more fearful death?

Such, young men, are some of your dangers. You should be ready to consider earnestly the means of escape. Even this cursory glance over the battle-field, and the array of the foe, should stir us up to "prove" both the armour that we wear, and our aptitude in using it. If the result of such survey should be a sense of utter weakness in presence of the adversary, and a cry from the helpless to the Lord God of hosts, it will be well: our labour will not be lost.

The DEFENCE prescribed is, "Consent thou not." How may one successfully contend against these formidable foes? Observe the form of the Scripture injunction, "If sinners entice thee, *consent thou not.*" It is a blunt, peremptory command. Your method of defence must be different from the adversary's mode of attack. His strength lies in making gradual approaches; yours in a resistance, sudden, resolute, total. For example, let a man who is now a drunkard look back on his course. He will find that he came into that state by imperceptible, unsuspected advances. But if ever he get out of that state, it is not by slow degrees that he will make his escape. It is not by lessening gradually the quantity of strong drink till he wean himself from the poison, and creep back from madness into himself again. The enemy can play at the graduated system better than he. His only safety lies in an abrupt, resolute refusal.

The same method that is best suited for recovery is also best for prevention. It is not by partial compliance and polite excuses that you can successfully repel enticements to sin. This is an adversary with whom you are not obliged to keep terms. Gather from Scripture the attitude you should assume, and the language you should hold : " Get thee behind me, Satan!" " Save your-selves from this untoward generation." " Come out from among them, and be ye separate, and I will receive you." Much depends on the round, blunt refusal,—the unfaltering, undiluted, dignified " No" of one who fears God more than the sneer of fools. Many stumble from neglect of this principle. They intend to refuse. They will not go all the way into sin ; but they will resist politely— they will keep terms with the enticers. They are not willing to let it be known that they are so timid about their own integrity. It might not be reckoned manly. They are like those who were disciples secretly for fear of the Jews. Your enticers are honour-able men, and they would be hurt if you should meet their invitation by a prompt negative, and give your reasons. Well : and is it not enough for the disciple to be " as his Lord ?" He was in the same position : " Master, in so saying thou condemnest us also." Out with it unreservedly, whenever and wherever com-panions would wile you into evil. If you begin to pare away the edges of your declinature, lest it should bear too hardly upon your tempters—if you make excuses that are not the real reasons, in order that under cover of them you may glide out of the way without the disagreeable shock of a direct collision—you may escape for that time ; but some day your excuse will fail, and your foot will be taken. " If sinners entice thee, consent not." The shortest answer is the best.

They speak of consecrated places ; we believe there are con-secrated spots on this earth, and desecrated spots too. That spot is consecrated in the eye of God and all the good, where a con-demned transgressor has been born again, and taken into the number of God's children : that spot is desecrated which has been the turning-point where an immortal chose death rather than life. Many such places there are, both in rural lanes and in the city's thoroughfares. A youth is leaving his place of business in the evening, and making his way homewards. At a crossing he meets a knot of companions, who hail and stop him. They are convening to a place of danger, and deeds of sin. They invite him to go. He replies that he is going home. They insist—they cannot go without him. As he hangs back and hesitates, a leading spirit of the club suddenly cries out he knows the reason: " Our friend is going to set up for saint—he is going home to pray." A loud laugh runs round the ring. The youth is not prepared for this. He desired rather to go home, but he is not yet a good soldier of Jesus Christ. He cannot endure hardness. He gives way at this last thrust, and goes with them. That night he parts with a good conscience; and it is but another step to make shipwreck of his faith. That spot where evil spirits embodied formed a circle round the youth, and won him—that spot is desecrated. The blood of a soul is there. The writer was standing one day lately among a crowd of visitors under the dome of St. Paul's in London, gazing upward in silence on its grandeur, when a gentleman touched him, and requested him to remove his foot; he then pointed to a small cross mark made by a mason's chisel on the marble pavement, informing the by-standers that a person who cast himself from the dome aloft, had fallen there and died. The group of living beings who had gathered round our informant stood instinctively back and sighed. The living were awed in spirit when they found themselves standing on the spot that had been stained by the blood of a self-murdered man. Oh, if there were marks made in the ground at every place stained by the suicide of a soul, how thickly dotted the world would be with the startling symbols ! how fearfully and tremblingly would the living thread their way between !

How much of the low spirits, the moody mind, the miserable incapacity, which abound, has been induced by violation of God's laws—both the natural marked in our constitution, and the moral revealed in the Bible !

Appetites indulged grow strong. Beware lest the cub which you fondle and feed, insensibly become the lion which devours you.

Friendship sealed by companionship in sin will not last long. It is not worth having. It deserves not to be known by that noble name. Friends that are glued together by the slime of their lusts will be torn asunder soon; and these foul exudations that seem now to bind them into one, will become the fuel to a flame of mutual hate, when first a spark of disagreement falls. They will bite and devour one another. The degree of their privacy to each other's wickedness will be the measure of their dislike and distrust.

After all, above all, including all, a reason why you should not consent to go with sinners is, you thereby displease God, crucify Christ, grieve the Spirit, and cast your own soul away.

The means of resisting.—We address those who have obtained a religious education. We do not speak here of the first and best means, the word of God and prayer. We assume that you know all that we could tell you regarding these, and only offer some suggestions on subordinate topics—such as *refinement of manners, profitable study, benevolent effort*, and *improving company*.

Refinement of manners.—I know well that it is the state of the heart within that decides the outward demeanour; but I know also that the outward demeanour has a reflex influence back upon the heart. I do not say that politeness will do as a substitute for religion; but politeness is of use as the handmaid of religion. Indeed, rude speech and manners are both the signs of moral evil already existing, and the causes of increasing it. In many districts of the country, and among certain classes, rude habits are the open inlets to great crimes. To cultivate a refined and tasteful form of speech and manners would become a shield to protect from many prevailing temptations. Christianity, with its living power in the heart, will produce refinement in the manners; and outward refinement will throw a shield round inward principle, and keep it out of harm's way. We do not mean to encourage show and fashion. The fop is most wretched himself, and most repulsive to an onlooker; but we would not avoid this extreme by leaping into the extreme of vulgar rudeness. We would not like a youth to be gilded; but neither would we like him to be rough and foul with rust. We would have him *polished;* that is the medium. Some people are rusty: their harsh, ungainly manners eat out whatever is good in their own character, and saw the very flesh of those who come near them. Some people, again, are gilt: a very brilliant exterior they present, but the first brush of hard usage rubs off the gilding, and reveals the base material beneath. A third class are polished; the polish, indeed, is on the surface, but it is a polish on the surface of solid worth; and in the multifarious crosses of human life, the more it is rubbed the brighter it grows. This is the thing: not a gilding to hide the baseness, but a polish to set off and make more useful the real substantial excellence of the inner man. Even when the material is sound to the core, a polish on the surface both fits it for use and protects it from injury. If we have two youths equal as to strength and soundness of Christian principle within, but unequal as to habits of refinement in intercourse with others, he who has outward politeness added to inward worth will be the more useful and the more safe.

Profitable study.—Occupation goes far as a means of safety. Add every day something to your store of knowledge. Study alternately books, and men, and things. Mere book-reading is not enough, without reflection and observation. Again, mere observation is not enough, if you do not enlarge your resources by the treasures which books contain. Both are best. You have many opportunities. You need not at any time be in want of a useful book. From experience we are able to say that a book perused intelligently, and with appetite in youth, will retain its hold better than information acquired at a later day. The few books to which we had access when we were young are fresh in our memory still, both the good and the bad. The "Pilgrim's Progress" was greedily devoured, and indelibly impressed; but so also were other books in which a like genius glowed, without a like baptism of holiness. The young of this generation may always have a book to read, and may choose a book that is worthy. Never let the machinery of your mind become rusty. The way to keep it sweet is to keep it going.

We have two opposite experiences to look back upon. In our retrospect are times of intellectual idleness, and times of intellectual diligence. We remember precious hours spent by a circle of youthful companions in silly, useless conversation,—a sort of slang which was directly vulgarizing, and indirectly demoralizing. We remember, too, times devoted to useful study,—we mean the

leisure hours of a labour-day. The writer remembers the days
when, as the dinner-hour was announced, and all gladly threw
their work aside, he satisfied a fresh appetite during the first five
minutes, and stretched beneath the shade of a tree, occupied the
remaining fifty-five reading the wars of Cæsar, and the songs of
Virgil, in the language of ancient Rome. It made his afternoon's
toil lighter. It made his neighbours respect him; and what is
more, young men, *it made him respect himself.* In virtue of that
employment, the enticers did not so frequently assail him; and
he was supplied with an auxiliary means of defence. There are
many branches of useful knowledge, easily accessible, from which
you may choose, each according to his taste. We earnestly counsel young men to scour up, and keep in use all the powers of
understanding and memory which God has given them. It will
sweeten your labour. It will be something softer to lean on
between your flesh and the iron instruments of toil. How great
the privileges of youth in this country, and at the present day!
How great is the waste, if the museums, libraries, and public
reading-rooms be not turned to good account!

Benevolent effort.—Every one, young and old, rich and poor,
should always be trying to do some good. There is abundant
opportunity, if there be the willing mind. Try to live in the
world so that you will be missed when you leave it.

More especially if any young man trusts in Jesus, and loves
souls, these affections will supply the impulse, and keep him
going. Providence on God's part, and prudence on his, will soon
shape out some useful work that he is able to do. You have not
the gifts and graces to conduct with effect missionary work among
the godless and ignorant? Well, if you have not the ten talents,
are you willing, without the shame of pride, to labour in the laying out of one? Will you become librarian, and distribute a few
soiled books into more soiled hands in a needy district, at a stated
hour on a Saturday evening? You are not clever enough to teach
a school of destitute children, nor rich enough to pay another?
Well, will you be the whipper-in of the ragged parliament for a
given lane, and see that none of the honourable members be absent
from the lesson? If there were but the willing mind, every
volunteer could be put into harness, so that his strength would
not be overtasked on the one hand, nor wasted on the other.

Over on the enemy's side all hands are called out, and every one is made to contribute to the mass of evil: the children of light should be wiser than they.

Improving company.—It is of great practical importance that young men have friends who will encourage and direct them. Union is strength. In the battle of life the want of a sympathizing companion may be the very point on which an otherwise brave combatant may at last give way. In this fight as well as others, "shoulder to shoulder" is a most potent principle, both for the defence and the onset. Here and there in history you may read of some hero, who single-handed has foiled an army; but, taking the common standard of humanity, even a brave man is easily overpowered by numbers when he stands alone. There are some points of analogy between that warfare and ours. To most men the sympathy of tried friends is a substantial support in the conflict with moral evil. Right-principled, true-hearted companions are often "the shields of the earth," which the all-ruling God has at his disposal, and throws around a youth to protect him from the fiery darts of the wicked one.

But though the society of the good is an instrument of protection not to be despised, it is still subordinate. There is another Companion. There is a Friend that sticketh closer than a brother. "Call upon me in the day of trouble: I will deliver thee, and thou shalt glorify me" (Ps. l. 15). That He might get into communion with us, and we with him, God was manifested in the flesh. The man Christ Jesus, God with us,—this is the companion by whose side a young man will be infallibly safe. We believe never youth could be more strongly assailed than Joseph in Potiphar's house. A sinner enticed him,—and oh, how many things conspired to give force to the temptation, as if Satan had concentrated all his strength, to break through the chain of purposed mercy for Israel in the fall of Joseph!—a sinner enticed him, but *he consented not.* How? Whence did this stripling derive strength to defy and repel such a cunningly-devised and well-directed onset? He was weak like another man, but he had help at hand. He had a companion whom he had chosen, and with whom he walked. God was not far from Joseph; Joseph was not far from God. His answer was, "How can I do this great evil, and *sin against God?*" There—there is Joseph's strength. Young man, you will be as strong as he was, if you lean on the Arm that supported him.

The best way of moving a young heart is to please it. The surest way of turning a person from one pleasure is to give him a greater pleasure on the opposite side. A weeping willow, planted by a pond in a pleasure-garden, turns all to one side in its growth, and that the side on which the water lies. No dealing, either with its roots or with its branches, will avail to change its attitude; but place a larger expanse of water on the opposite side, and the tree will turn spontaneously, and hang the other way. So it is with the out-branching affections of the human heart. Follies and vices on this side are sweet to its depraved nature. The joys are shallow at the best, but it knows no other, and to these it instinctively turns; to these it grows forth. It acquires a bent in that direction which no human hand can turn. It will never be turned unless you can open a rival joy, wider and deeper, on the other side. And, blessed be God, greater are those joys that are for us, than all that are against us ! The *enticements* on the side of holiness and safety are in themselves greater than all that Satan can spread out; and when a distracted mind can see, and a ladened heart can feel them as they are, it is forthwith won. "The love of Christ constraineth us." It is pleasure that can compete with pleasure. When you are entangled by the allure-ments of sin, and oppressed by the terror of wrath, "the joy of the Lord is your strength."

The lowliness of the prodigal's place, the hunger he endured, the loathsome appearance of the husks and the swine,—these things, doubtless, made some impression; but, alone, they could not save him. They might have crushed him in despair to the ground, but could not have borne him home in hope. It was the yearning of his father's love, it was the image of his father's open embrace, it was the presentiment of his father's weeping welcome, that drew the prodigal at once from his miseries and his sins.

Even the truth of God entering the heart, and fastening on the conscience, has not power to turn a sinner from the error of his ways, while it comes in simply as a terror. What the law could not do, God did by sending his Son. What naked righteousness, with vengeance at its back, failed to do, manifested mercy in Christ achieved. Righteous mercy—justice satisfied by Em·

manuel's sacrifice, and divine compassion flowing free upon the lost—this is the thing of Christ which the Holy Spirit wields as the weapon to win a human heart.

This heart, young man, is a space that must and will be occupied. It is the battle-field between Satan and Satan's manifested Destroyer. Within you this holy war must be waged. How long halt ye between two opinions? Who is on the Lord's side? let him come. Unless Christ dwell in your heart by faith, the enemy will return, or abide, in triumph. You cannot fight the *enticements* of sinful pleasure in your own strength. These iniquities, like the wind, will carry you away; but under the Captain of your salvation you may fight and win. The deceits and corruptions of your heart, which your own resolutions cannot overcome—bring forth these enemies and slay them before Him. Drag forth these enticements of sinners that seemed so fresh and sweet to the carnal eye—drag them forth and expose them there; —their root will become rottenness, and their blossom will go up like dust. The faces of these tempters that beamed with mirth in the glare of kindled passions, will, when seen in the light of His love, appear hideous as spectres of the night.

His entrance into the heart will turn the tide of the conflict; and He is willing: "Behold, I stand at the door and knock. If any man open, I will come in." "Even so: come, Lord Jesus!"

Filthy Lucre

(Proverbs 1:19)

"So are the ways of every one that is greedy of gain; which taketh away the life of the owners thereof."

THESE "ways," as described by Solomon in the preceding verses, are certainly some of the very worst. We have here literally the picture of a robber's den. The persons described are of the baser sort: the crimes enumerated are gross and rank: they would be outrageously disreputable in any society, of any age. Yet when these apples of Sodom are traced to their sustaining root, it turns out to be *greed of gain*. The love of money can bear all these.

This scripture is not out of date in our day, or out of place in our community. The word of God is not left behind obsolete by the progress of events. "All flesh is as grass, and all the glory of man as the flower of grass. The grass withereth, and the flower thereof falleth away; but the word of the Lord endureth for ever" (1 Peter i. 24, 25). The Scripture traces sin to its fountain, and deposits the sentence of condemnation there,—a sentence that follows actual evil through all its diverging paths. A spring of poisonous water may in one part of its course run over a rough rocky bed, and in another glide silent and smooth through a verdant meadow; but, alike when chafed into foam by obstructing rocks, and when reflecting the flowers from its glassy breast, it is the same lethal stream. So from greed of gain—from covetousness which is idolatry, the issue is evil, whether it run riot in murder and rapine in Solomon's days, or crawl sleek and slimy through cunning tricks of trade in our own. God seeth not as man seeth. He judges by the character of the life stream that flows from the fountain of thought, and not by the form of the channel which accident may have hollowed out to receive it.

When this greed of gain is generated, like a thirst in the soul,

it imperiously demands satisfaction : and it takes satisfaction where-
ever it can be most readily found.   In some countries of the world
still it retains the old-fashioned form of iniquity which Solomon
has described : it turns freebooter, and leagues with a band of
kindred spirits, for the prosecution of the business on a larger
scale.   In our country, though the same passion domineer in a
man's heart, it will not adopt the same method, because it has
cunning enough to know that by this method it could not succeed.
Dishonesty is diluted, and coloured, and moulded into shapes of
respectability, to suit the taste of the times.   We are not hazard-
ing an estimate whether there be as much of dishonesty under all
our privileges as prevailed in a darker day : we affirm only that
wherever dishonesty is, its nature remains the same, although its
form may be more refined.   He who will judge both mean men
and merchant princes requires truth in the inward parts.   There
is no respect of persons with Him.   Fashions do not change
about the throne of the Eternal.   With Him a thousand years are
as one day.   The ancient and modern evil doers are reckoned
brethren in iniquity, despite the difference in the costume of their
crimes.   Two men are alike greedy of gain.   One of them being
expert in accounts, defrauds his creditors, and thereafter drives
his carriage ; the other, being robust of limb, robs a traveller on
the highway, and then holds midnight revel on the spoil.   Found
fellow-sinners, they will be left fellow-sufferers.   Refined dishonesty is as displeasing to God, as hurtful to society, and as
unfit for heaven, as the coarsest crime.

This greed, when full grown, is coarse and cruel.   It is not
restrained by any delicate sense of what is right or seemly.   It
has no bowels.   It marches right to its mark, treading on everything that lies in the way.   If necessary in order to clutch the
coveted gain, " it taketh away the life of the owners thereof."
Covetousness is idolatry.   The idol delights in blood.   He demands and gets a hecatomb of human sacrifices.

Among the labourers employed in a certain district to construct
a railway, was one thick-necked, bushy, sensual, ignorant, brutalized man, who lodged in the cottage of a lone old woman.   This
woman was in the habit of laying up her weekly earnings in a
certain chest, of which she carefully kept the key.   The lodger
observed where the money lay.   After the works were completed

and the workmen dispersed, this man was seen in the gray dawn of a Sabbath morning stealthily approaching the cottage. That day, for a wonder among the neighbours, the dame did not appear at church. They went to her house, and learned the cause. Her dead body lay on the cottage floor: the treasure-chest was robbed of its few pounds and odd shillings, and the murderer had fled. Afterwards they caught and hanged him.

Shocking crime !—to murder a helpless woman in her own house in order to reach and rifle her little hoard, laid up against the winter and the rent! The criminal is of a low, gross, bestial nature. Be it so. He was a pest to society, and society flung the troubler off the earth. But what of those who are far above him in education and social position, and as far beyond him in the measure of their guilt? How many human lives is the greed of gain even now taking away in the various processes of slavery? Men who hold a high place, and bear a good name in the world, have in this form taken away the life of thousands for filthy lucre's sake. Murder on a large scale has been and is done upon the African tribes by civilized men for money.

The opium traffic, forced upon China by the military power of Britain, and maintained by our merchants in India, is murder done for money on a mighty scale. Opium spreads immorality, imbecility, and death through the teeming ranks of the Chinese populations. The quantity of opium cultivated on their own soil is comparatively small. The government prohibited the introduction of the deadly drug until we compelled them to legalize the traffic. Our merchants brought it to their shores in ship-loads notwithstanding, and the thunder of our cannon opened a way for its entrance through the feeble ranks that lined the shore. Every law of political economy, and every sentiment of Christian charity, cries aloud against nurturing on our soil, and letting loose among our neighbours, that grim angel of death. The greed of gain alone suggests, commands, compels it. How can we expect the Chinese to accept the Bible from us while we bring opium to them in return? British Christians might bear to China that life for which the Chinese seem to be thirsting, were it not that British merchants are bearing to China that death which the best of her people loathe.

A bloated, filthy, half-naked labourer, hanging on at the harbour, has gotten a shilling for a stray job. As soon as he has wiped his brow, and fingered the coin, he walks into a shop and asks for whisky. The shopkeeper knows the man—knows that his mind and body are damaged by strong drink—knows that his family are starved by the father's drunkenness. The shopkeeper eyes the squalid wretch. The shilling tinkles on the counter. With one hand the dealer supplies the glass, and with the other mechanically rakes the shilling into the till among the rest. It is the price of blood. Life is taken there for money. The gain is filthy. Feeling its stain eating like rust into his conscience, the man who takes it reasons eagerly with himself thus: " He was determined to have it; and if I won't, another will." So he settles the case that occurred in the market-place on earth, but he has not done with it yet. How will that argument sound as an answer to the question, " Where is thy brother?" when it comes in thunder from the judgment-seat of God?

Oh that men's eyes were opened to know this sin beneath all its coverings, and loathe it in all its disguises! Other people may do the same, and we may never have thought seriously of the matter; but these reasons, and a thousand others, will not cover sin. All men should think of the character and consequences of their actions. God will weigh our deeds; we should ourselves weigh them beforehand in his balances. It is not what that man has said, or this man has done; but what Christ is, and his members should be. The question for every man through life is, not what is the practice of earth, but what is preparation for heaven. There would not be much difficulty in judging what gain is right and what is wrong if we would take Christ into our counsels. If people look unto Jesus when they think of being saved, and look hard away from him when they are planning how to make money, they will miss their mark for both worlds. When a man gives his heart to gain, he is an idolater. Money has become his god. He would rather that the Omniscient should not be the witness of his worship. While he is sacrificing in this idol's temple, he would prefer that Christ should reside high in heaven, out of sight and out of mind. He would like Christ to be in heaven, ready to open its gates to him, when death at last drives him off the earth; but he will not open for Christ now that other dwelling-place which he loves—a humble and contrite heart. " *Christ in you*, the hope of glory ; " there is the cure of covetousness ! That blessed Indweller, when he enters, will drive out—with a scourge, if need be—such buyers and sellers as defiled his temple. His still small voice within would flow forth, and print itself on all your traffic,—" Love one another, as I have loved you."

On this point the Christian Church is very low. The living child has lain so close to the world's bosom that she has overlaid it in the night, and stifled its troublesome cry. After all our familiarity with the Catechism, we need yet to learn " what is the *chief* end of man," and what should be compelled to stand aside as a secondary thing. We need from all who fear the Lord, a long, loud testimony against the practice of heartlessly subordinating human bodies and souls to the accumulation of material wealth.

The Cry of Wisdom

(Proverbs 1:20-22)

"Wisdom crieth without; she uttereth her voice in the streets: she crieth in the chief place of concourse, in the openings of the gates: in the city she uttereth her words, saying, How long, ye simple ones, will ye love simplicity? and the scorners delight in their scorning, and fools hate knowledge?"

THE evil doers are not left without a warning. The warning is loud, public, authoritative. But who is this monitor that claims the submissive regard of men? WISDOM.—Wisdom from above is the teacher: the lesson that follows is not after the manner of men. We recognise already the style of that Prophet who came in the fulness of time, speaking as never man spake. It was in this manner that Jesus, in the days of his flesh, stood and cried to the multitude—to the simple who loved simplicity, and the scorners who loved scorning—" If any man thirst, let him come unto me and drink." Before He was manifested to Israel, His delights were with the sons of men. In the provisions of the well-ordered covenant, He had the means of sounding an alarm in human ears before He became incarnate. He found and used a willing messenger to preach righteousness to rebellious spirits in Noah's days. Neither did He leave Himself without a witness in the time of Solomon. The eternal Son of God is not only wisdom in himself, He is " made unto us wisdom." He who was seen by Abraham afar off was heard by Abraham's seed in later days. In the beginning was the Word, and the Word was God. The Word and Wisdom of God made Himself known to men at sundry times, and in divers manners, before He took flesh and dwelt among us.

In the Scriptures, Wisdom cried to men. " They testify of me," said Jesus. The prophets all spake of his coming, and prepared his way. The sacrifices offered year by year and day by day continually, proclaimed aloud to each generation the guilt of men, and the way of mercy. The history of Israel, all the days of old.

was itself Wisdom's perennial articulate cry of warning to the rebellious. The plains of Egypt and the Red Sea, Sinai and the Jordan, each had a voice, and all proclaimed in concert the righteousness and mercy that kissed each other in the counsels of God. The things that happened to them happened for ensamples; and the things were not done in a corner. In the opening of the gates, in the city's busiest haunts, the proclamation was made to unwilling listeners. The cry of Wisdom in those days of old, if it did not turn the impenitent, was sufficient to condemn them. It was so manifestly from God, and so intelligible to men, that it must have either led them out of condemnation, or left them under it without excuse.

But the wisdom of God is a manifold wisdom. While it centres bodily in Christ, and thence issues as from its source, it is reflected and re-echoed from every object and every event. There is a challenge in the prophets, " Oh, earth, earth, earth, hear the word of the Lord!" The receptive earth has taken in that word, and obediently repeats it from age to age. The stars of heaven and the flowers of earth, facing each other like the opposite ranks of a choral band, hymn, alternate and responsive, the wisdom of God. He hath made all things for Himself. He serves himself of criminals and their crimes. From many a ruined fortune Wisdom cries, " Remember the Sabbath-day, to keep it holy." From many an outcast in his agonies, as when the eagles of the valley are picking out his eyes, Wisdom cries, " Honour thy father and thy mother, that thy days may be long." From many a gloomy scaffold Wisdom cries, " Thou shalt not kill." Every law of nature, and every event in history, has a tongue by which Wisdom proclaims God's holiness, and rebukes man's sin.

But is there any prophet of the Lord besides these? Is there any other organ by which Wisdom cries to men? There is one. Giving force to all other intimations, there is a prophet of the Lord within every man—his own conscience. We are fearfully made. That witness within us is often feared and shunned more than armed men, more than gates and bars, more sometimes than the dungeon, the scaffold, and the drop. It is the case of the ancient king over again; he is a prophet of the Lord, " but I hate him, because he never prophesies good concerning me."

But conscience proclaiming God's anger against the man's evil, has not power to make the man good. All the instincts of the transgressor's nature are leagued in an effort to smother the disturber, and they generally succeed. It is the conscience sprinkled with the blood of Christ that at once speaks peace and works purity.

Three classes of persons seem to be singled out here, and to each is administered an appropriate reproof: 1. The simple who love simplicity; 2. The scorners who delight in scorning; 3. The fools who hate knowledge.

1. *The simple who love simplicity.* Probably we would not be far from the truth if we should accept this term in the Proverbs as intended to indicate that class of sinners whose leading characteristic is the absence of good rather than positive activity in evil. The root of bitterness has not shot forth in any form of outrageous vice, but it remains destitute of righteousness. They do not blaspheme God, indeed, but they neglect his salvation, and they cannot escape. Their hearts by a law of inherent evil depart from Him; He in judgment lets them go, and gives them over.

The simple for time are always a numerous class. They cannot be intrusted with money, for it will all go into the hands of the first sharper whom they meet. They will let the day pass, with no provision for the night, and never think it needful until the darkness has fallen down. They will let the summer come and go without laying up a store for the time to come; and when the winter arrives they have neither house nor clothing, neither money nor food. Somehow they did not think of these things; the sunshine was pleasant while it lasted; they basked in its rays; and it did not occur to them that a cloud might soon darken the face of the sky.

But the simple for eternity are more numerous still. While they have food and raiment they pass the time pleasantly, and never think of sin. As for righteousness, they do not feel the want of it, and form no high estimate of its worth. As to the judgment-seat of God, they have lived a long time, and have never seen it yet; they don't trouble themselves with anticipations of evil. The great white throne has always kept out of their sight, and they keep out of its sight. How many simple ones are going fast forward to death, with no life to triumph over it! How many are drawing near the border in utter listlessness, as if there were no sin, and no judgment—no God, no Heaven, no Hell!

2. *The scorners who love scorning.* This is another feature of the fallen—another phase of the great rebellion. This class meet the threatening realities of eternity not by an easy indifference, but by a hardy resistance. They have a bold word ever ready to ward solemn thought away,—a sneer at the silliness of a saint, an oath to manifest courage, or a witty allusion to Scripture which will make the circle ring again with laughter.

There have been scorners in every age. There are not a few amongst us at the present day. They may be found on both the edges of society : poverty and riches become by turns a temptation to the same sin. It is not only the shop of the artisan that resounds with frequent scoffs : the same sound is familiar in the halls of the rich. Many of the young men who have been educated in affluence belong to this class. They have large possessions, and larger prospects ; they wish to enjoy what they have. The triumph of grace in their hearts would dethrone the god of this world, and spoil his goods. The running fire of profane jests proceeds from advanced earth-works which Satan has thrown up around his citadel, in his earnestness not only to keep his goods in safety from the overthrowing power of conversion, but in peace from the troublesome assaults of conviction.

Scorners love scorning. The habit grows by indulgence : it becomes a second nature : it becomes the element in which they live. And what gives them confidence ? Have they by searching found out that there is no God ? or have they ascertained that He has no punishment in store for the wicked ? No ! they have not settled these questions at all, either to the satisfaction of mankind, or their own. These scoffs are generally parrying strokes to keep convictions away. These smart sayings are the fence to turn aside certain arrows which might otherwise fix their tormenting barbs in the conscience. The scorner is generally not so bold a man as he appears to be. He keeps the truth at arm's length : he strikes at it vehemently before it gets near him. All this betrays a secret sense of weakness : he cannot afford to come into close contact with the sword of the Spirit. These violent gesticulations against the truth indicate the unerring instinct of the old man resisting that which advances to destroy him. " What have we to do with thee, thou Jesus; art thou come to torment us before the time ?"

3. *The fools who hate knowledge.* By a comparison of various scriptures in which the term occurs, it appears that fools are those who have reached the very highest degrees of evil. Here it is intimated that they hate knowledge ; and knowledge has its beginning in the fear of God. All the branches springing from that root, and all the sweet fruit they bear, are hateful to fools. The knowledge has come to men, in as far as to be presented to their minds, and pressed on their acceptance. Some, the simple, never think of it at all ; and others, the scorners, bar its faintest approaches ; but these fools, after it has made its way into the conscience, exclude it from their hearts. They have not been able to keep Truth's heavenly form out of their minds, but they hate it when it comes in. Others only live without Christ, keeping Him at a distance ; but these are against Him, after He has been revealed in majesty divine. The emphatic " No God " of the fourteenth psalm indicates, not the despair of a seeker who is unable to find truth, but the anger of an enemy who does not like to retain it. It is not a judgment formed in the fool's understanding, but a passion rankling in his heart.

How long shall all this last ?

" How long, ye simple ones, will ye love simplicity ? " God is weary of your indifference ; how long will it cleave to you ? How long will a man continue to be regardless of his soul ? Till death ? It will certainly be no longer. He who would not cry in hope for mercy to pardon his sin, did cry without hope for a drop of water to cool his tongue.

" How long will the scorners delight in their scorning ? " Will they not cease from blaspheming God, until God, ceasing to be gracious, stop their breath, and take them away ? If you continue this scorning till your dying day, do you expect to continue it longer ? Will you make merry with the judgment-seat ? Will you be able to argue against the wrath of the Lamb ? " Depart from me, ye cursed"—that word will crush the scorning out of the boldest blasphemer. Would that the profane might make the discovery now ; for it will be too late to make it when the day is spent.

" How long shall fools hate knowledge ? " Unless they learn to love it soon, they will hate it for ever. They might learn to love it now ; for the same word that rebukes sin reveals mercy.

Well might the fool learn to love the knowledge which presents Christ crucified as the way of a sinner's return ; but if a man do not love knowledge revealing mercy, how shall he love it denouncing wrath ? The only knowledge that can reach the lost is the knowledge that the door is shut. How long will they hate that knowledge ? Evermore.

A Revival

(Proverbs 1:23)

"Turn you at my reproof: behold, I will pour out my Spirit unto you."

"TURN you at my reproof: behold, I will pour out my Spirit;"
—the command and the promise joined, and constituting
one harmonious whole. How strictly in concord are the
several intimations of the Scriptures ! " Work out your own salvation ; for it is God that worketh in you " (Phil. ii. 12). To him that
hath shall be given, and he shall have abundance. It is to those
who turn that the promise of the Spirit is addressed. These two
reciprocate. The Spirit poured out arrests a sinner, and turns
him ; then, as he turns, he gets more of the Spirit poured out.
The sovereignty of God and the duty of men are both alike real ;
and each has its own place in the well-ordered covenant. It is
true, that unless a man turn, he will not get God's Spirit poured
out ; and it is also true, that unless he get God's Spirit poured
out, he will not turn. When the dead is recalled to life, the
blood, sent circling through the system, sets the valves of the
heart a-beating; and the valves of the heart, by their beating,
send the life-blood circling throughout the frame. It would be
in vain to inquire what was the point in the reciprocating series
to which the life-giving impulse was first applied. The mysteries
of the human spirit are deeper still than those of the body. The
way of God, in the regeneration of man, is past finding out. One
part of it he keeps near himself, concealed by the clouds and
darkness that surround his throne ; another part of it he has
clearly revealed to our understandings, and pressed on our hearts.
His immediate part is to pour out the Spirit ; our immediate part
is to turn at his reproof. If, instead of simply doing our part,
we presumptuously intrude into his, we shall attain neither. If
we reverently regard the promise, and diligently obey the com-

mand, we shall get and do—we shall do and get. We shall get
the Spirit, enabling us to turn; and turn, in order to get more of
the Spirit. The command is given, not to make the promise
unnecessary, but to send us to it for help. The promise is given,
not to supersede the command, but to encourage us in the effort
to obey. Turn at his reproof, and hope in his promise; hope in
his promise, and turn at his reproof.

Religion, when it is real, is altogether a practical thing. It
disappoints Satan; it crucifies the flesh; it sanctifies the character; it glorifies God. It is a thing that acts, and acts mightily.
It is a thing, not of words, but of deeds. There is an enormous
amount of mere imitation religion amongst us. If there were as
great a proportion of counterfeit coin circulating in the kingdom,
we would be all on the alert to detect and destroy it. We would
feel the danger of being ourselves deceived, and losing the riches
for which we care. There ought to be greater jealousy of a
spiritless form, a gilded word religion, passing current in the
Church; for he who is taken in by this "name to live," though
he should gain the whole world, will lose his own soul.

A valorous hand to hand struggle with inherent corruptions is
distressingly rare in the wide-spread religious profession of the
day. You read and pray, and worship in the assembly, and complain that, notwithstanding, your souls do not prosper; you have
not comfort; you are not sensible of growth in grace. But all
this is mere hypocrisy, if you be not "turning"—tearing yourself
asunder from besetting sins, as from a right arm or a right eye.
The evil speaking, watch it, catch it on your lips, crush it as it
swells and germinates in the seed-bed of your thoughts within.
The equivocations, the half-untruths, down with them. Out with
the very truth, although it should break off the nearly completed
bargain—although it should freeze the friendship that seems
necessary to your success. Anger, malice, envy,—seize these
vipers, that twist and hiss in your bosom; strangle them outright
there. Your religion is nothing better than a cheat, if you are
not busy with the work of ceasing to do evil. "Herein do I
exercise myself," said Paul, "that I may have a conscience void
of offence." How can the feeblest learners of the truth attain, by
an idle wish, that actual progressive purification which its greatest
human teacher only strove after by incessant exercise ?

In the manifold diversities of sin there is such a thing as the pride of self-righteousness : you fall into this error when you pretend to turn from evil without trusting in God. You fall into the opposite snare of hypocrisy, when you pretend to trust in God, and do not turn at his command. Getting freely and doing faithfully, together constitute true religion. Get and do, do and get. Nor is it a partitioning of salvation between God and man, as if a part of it were his gift, and a part of it man's act. The turning which constitutes salvation is, supremely, all God's gift, and, subordinately, all the doing of the man. From the spring-head in the heart, to the outermost streams of life, he makes all things new ; and yet the man himself must, at God's bidding, turn from all iniquity.

We speak of a revival ; we pray for it ; perhaps we long for it. But all this, and an hundredfold more in the same direction, will not bring it about. God's arm is not shortened : his ear is not heavy. Our iniquities separate between us and him. The way to invite his presence is to put away the evil of our doings ; for he cannot dwell with sin. And if any one, conscious of his knowledge and jealous of orthodoxy, should say in opposition, it is God's presence, sovereignly vouchsafed, that makes the visited man put away his evil ; we answer, that is a glorious truth, but is not an argument against our injunction. That is the upper end of a revealed truth which reaches from earth to heaven : it is too high for us : if you put forth your hand to touch it at the top, it will consume you. That high thing is for God to handle, and not man. The end that leans on earth and lies to your hand is— " *Turn you at my reproof.*" The only safe way of moving the heaven-high extreme of the divine sovereignty for revival is, by throwing ourselves with our whole weight on this which is the visible, tangible, lower end of that incomprehensible mystery—this *turning* from our own evil in obedience to the command of God.

The grand hinderance to a revival by the Spirit poured out is the general conformity of Christians to the fashion of the world. The short road to a revival is to turn from the error of our ways. If there were more of the doing which religion demands, there would be more of the getting which it promises.

Turn *at my reproof.* God looketh on the heart : he measures the motive as well as the deed. There is such a thing as a proud, atheistic morality, which is as offensive to God as more vulgar vice. To abstain from common and gross transgressions, is not holiness : it is a partial process : it is to diminish the bulk of wickedness on one side, by directing all the stream of internal corruption to the other side. When a man turns from wickedness because God hates it, he will turn alike from every sin. If we reform ourselves, we will select despised and shameful lusts of the flesh to be sacrificed, but retain and cherish certain favourite lusts of the mind. If we permit God's word to search, and God's authority to rule, idols alike of high and low degree will be driven forth of the temple. If the turning be at his reproof, it will be a turning both complete in its comprehension and true in its character—a turning without partiality and without hypocrisy

When we turn at his reproof, he will pour out his Spirit : when he pours out his Spirit we will turn at his reproof ;—blessed circle for saints to reason in. He formed the channel wherein grace and duty chase each other round. He supplied the material alike of the getting and the doing. He set the stream in motion, and he will keep it going, until every good work begun shall be perfect in the day of Christ Jesus.

Hear that voice from heaven, " I will pour out." Yea, Lord ; then, we must draw away. We are placed at the open orifice in the lowest extremity of the outbranching channel : the fountain head is with God on high. When he pours out, we draw forth, when we draw forth, he pours out. It is because there is a pressure constant and strong from that upper spring of grace, that we can draw any here below for the exercises of obedience ; but the covenant is ordered so, that if we do not draw for the supply of actual effort, none will gravitate toward us from the fountain head. It is the still, stagnant, dead mass of inert profession, sticking in the lower lips of the channel, that checks the flow of grace, and practically seals for us its unfathomable fountain. If there were a turning, a movement, an effort, an expenditure, a need, a vacancy, at our extremity below, there would be a flow of the divine compassion to make up the want, and charge every vessel anew with fresh and full supply. Prove him now herewith ; exert and expend in his service, and see whether he will not open the windows of heaven and pour out a blessing, greater than the room made vacant to receive it.

Sowing Disobedience, Reaping Judgment
(Proverbs 1:24-28)

"Because I have called, and ye refused; I have stretched out my hand, and no man re-garded; but ye have set at nought all my counsel, and would none of my reproof: I also will laugh at your calamity; I will mock when your fear cometh; when your fear cometh as desolation, and your destruction cometh as a whirlwind; when distress and anguish cometh upon you. Then shall they call upon me, but I will not answer; they shall seek me early, but they shall not find me."

A T sundry times and in divers manners, the Omniscient Witness of men's wickedness has invited the evil doers to draw near, ere yet the judgment should be set and the books opened, that he may "reason together" with them on their state and prospects. One of those marvellous reasonings of the Judge with the criminal is recorded here.

I. *God in mercy visits a rebellious generation.*—Four terms are employed to describe this visit, and although they are arranged to suit the exigencies of Hebrew poetry, they follow each other in natural order, and issue in a climax. He calls, stretches out his hands, gives counsel, and administers reproof.

1. *The call.*—Men with one consent were departing from the living God. They had turned the back on him, and not the face. He does not leave himself without a witness, and he has many ways of uttering his voice. It is in the earthquake and in the storm: day unto day proclaims it, and night unto night: there is no speech nor language where it is not heard. Even where its only effect is to drive the scared culprit to superstitious observ-ances, it has been heard, and the superstitious are accountable. The call has come with more distinct articulation from the lips of prophets and apostles. It sounds with authority in a human conscience. Whether men obey the call or disobey it, they are secretly conscious that the call has reached them, and are left without excuse.

2. *The hands stretched out.*—When the call has come and startled the prodigal; when the prodigal, aroused, looks toward the quarter whence the voice proceeds, lo, a Father whom he has offended is opening his arms wide to clasp the outcast in the embrace of an everlasting love (Isa. lxv. 1, 2). When busy men lift up their heads from the dust to which their souls are cleaving, and listen to the voice of God, they find out that He is not yet against them a consuming fire. His hands are outstretched : there is a way, and the way is open unto the Father. There is no obstruction : there is no forbidding : there is no upbraiding. Chief sinners are even now entering in. Behold, they are arising and going to the Father. They are converging frequent and swift, as doves to their windows. They are neither kept back nor thrust down among hired servants ; they are welcomed as sons and daughters ; they are made heirs of God, and joint-heirs with Christ ; their sins are remembered no more.

3. *The counsel.*—Some who have heard the call and lifted up their heads and looked, and seen the door of mercy open, are glad, and take encouragement to continue a little longer far from God and righteousness. They see the arms of mercy stretched out all day long, although a people continue disobedient. Seeing this, they secretly feel, if they do not venture to say, that there is no cause for alarm. The door will remain open to-day, and to-morrow, and the next day : we shall run in before it be shut. What does God do for these deceivers ? He does not let them alone : He counsels them : "Flee to the stronghold, prisoners of hope ;" "Wherefore spend ye your money for that which is not bread ?" "Come unto me, ye that labour and are heavy laden, and I will give you rest." If they resist still, will He shut the door now, and shut them out ? No, not yet : He will administer,

4. *Reproof.*—Mercy interposes with the plea, Let them alone yet this once. There is One yearning over the callous, who have no mercy on their own souls. "How can I give thee up ?" He remembers mercy, and makes judgment stand back. He makes judgment his strange work, not permitting it to appear early or often to strike the decisive blow. He has yet another resource : when counsel is despised, He will bring forward reproof : if they will not be enticed by the promise of heaven, He will threaten them with the fear of hell. "The wicked shall be turned into

hell, and all the nations that forget God." " Except ye repent, ye shall perish." "Except a man be born again, he cannot see the kingdom of God." Inconceivably great is the weight of that wrath which is treasured up against the day of wrath, to be poured all on the impenitent then; but that reserved wrath is not left meantime lying useless in its treasure-house. Everlasting love needs a strong hard instrument wherewith to work out her blessed purposes on an unpliant race ; and mercy, in this the day of her reign, sovereignly seizing judgment before its time, works that mighty lever to move mankind. The terrors of the Lord are not permitted to sleep unnoticed and unknown, till the day when they shall overflow and overwhelm all his enemies : they are summoned forth in the interval, and numbered among the all things that work together for good. Though kept like a reserve in the rear, their grim hosts are exposed to view, in order that they may co-operate with kindlier agencies in persuading men to yield, and fight against God no more. " Him that cometh to me, I will in no wise cast out." Kindly plies the sweet promise next to a wounded heart : but the gentle promise is backed by a terrible reproof : *Cast out*—there it is ; judgment looming in reserve ; serving meantime by its blackness to make the invitation more winning; but there, unchangeable, omnipotent, to receive on its awful edge the crowds that rush reckless over the intervening day of grace, and fall into the hands of the living God.

He suffers long, and pleads : but even in Him compassions will not, cannot further flow. He calls, stretches out his hands, counsels, and, when men still refuse, He makes the threat of wrath mercy's instrument to compass them about, and compel them to come in : but He stops there. God will not put forth a hand to lift a man to heaven in his sleep ; or drag him in against his will. When counsel and reproof are rejected, then "there remaineth nothing but a fearful looking for of judgment and fiery indignation, which shall devour the adversary." Those who withstand all these means and messages, will be left like Esau without the blessing. " He cried with an exceeding great and bitter cry, and said unto his father, Bless me, even me also, oh, my father :" but the time was past, and the door was shut.

II. *A rebellious generation neglect or resist the gracious visitation of God.*—" I have called, and ye refused : I have stretched out my hand, and no man regarded: ye have set at nought all my counsel, and would none of my reproof." This is an appalling indictment uttered by the God of truth. Who are the guilty ? " Lord, is it I ? Lord, is it I ? "

" He that hath an ear to hear, let him hear what the Spirit saith." Men have ears and stop them. The Lord made the ear of man, and a wonderful work it is ; strange that it should be open to every voice but the entreaty of its Maker. In times when vile men held the high places of this land, a roll of drums was employed to drown the martyr's voice, lest the testimony of truth from the scaffold should reach the people. Thus they closed the ears of the multitude against the voice of the servants : not by a roll of drums at a single tyrant's bidding, but by a strong deep hum of business, kept up through common consent, is the ear closed now against the Master's own word. So constant is the noise of Mammon, humming day and night, that the partial silence of the Sabbath is felt an unwelcome pause. As arts advance, and more is crammed into the six days, so much the more eager are Mammon's worshippers to fill the Sabbath with the same confused noise. The word says, " Be still, and know that I am God :" those who don't want this knowledge are afraid to be still, lest it should steal in and disturb their peace. God's mighty hand sometimes interferes to quiet this hubbub in a heart, or a house. It is when the inmates are compelled to go about the house with whispers, that his voice is best heard. I know of nothing more fitted to touch a conscience than this tender complaint from our Judge. He stretched out his hands : no man regarded. What then ? He complains of the neglect, and addresses his complaint to the neglecters. Here is mercy full, pressed down, and running over. He whom men reject, pleads with men for rejecting him. When he so stretched out himself to us, how shall we answer if we turn our back on Him ?

III. *They shall eat the fruit of their own ways, and be filled with their own devices.*—This life is the spring time of our immortal being ; the harvest is eternity. Harvest is not the time for sowing ; we shall reap then what we sow now. This law is of God ; and it is like the laws by which He regulates all nature. If a

man sow tares or thistles in his field in spring, it is probable
that a bitter regret will seize upon him in the harvest day. He
will loathe the worthless crop that he gets to fill his bosom;
but he cannot, by a sudden and energetic wish, change all the
laws of nature, and make his field wave with ripened grain. As
certainly as a husbandman in harvest reaps only what he sowed
in spring, shall they who in life sow sin, reap wrath in the judgment. The provisions of his covenant are steadfast as the laws
of his world. His promises are sure as the ordinances of heaven,
and his threatenings too.

It is true that God destroys his enemies: but it is also true
that they destroy themselves. They throw themselves into the
fire, and by his laws they are burned. He has laws that are
everlasting and unchangeable; and He has not hidden them from
men: He has plainly declared them. " The soul that sinneth, it
shall die." Those who cast themselves on revealed wrath are
their own destroyers. These outstretched hands of his are clear
of a sinner's blood.

Judgment will be an exact answer to disobedience, as fruit
answers the seed, or an echo the sound. The strictness of retribution at last will correspond to the freeness of mercy now. There
would be no glory in God's present compassion, if it had not the
full terror of immutable justice behind it to lean upon. Even the
divine longsuffering would lose its loveliness if it did not stand in
front of divine wrath. You cannot paint an angel upon light : so
mercy could not be represented—mercy could not be, unless there
were judgment without mercy, a ground of deep darkness lying
beneath, to sustain and reveal it. That there may be a day of
grace pushed forward within the reach of men on earth, there
must be a throne of judgment as its base in eternity. When the
day of grace is past, the throne of judgment stands alone, and the
impenitent must meet it.

The anguish comes first within the conscience of the ungodly,
when the life course is drawing near its close. Desolation comes
like a whirlwind. The body is drooping : the grave is opening :
the judgment is preparing. He has no righteousness, and no
hope. Behold now the prospect before the immortal, when death,
like a rising wave, has blotted out the beams of mercy that
lingered to the last. It is now the blackness of darkness. Hope,

that flickered long, has gone out at length. And how rigidly strict must the retribution be ! They would not hear God in the day of mercy : in the day of vengeance God will not hear them. They laughed at His threatenings : He will mock their cry. This reciprocity is the law of his kingdom : it cannot be changed.

Let those who live without God in the world mark what it is that He counts the heaviest retribution upon sin : it is this— " They shall call upon me, but I will not answer." When, groping darkling on the shore of eternity, they cry in terror, " O God, where art Thou ? " only their own voice, mocking, will return from the abyss, " Where art *thou ?* " A man's life has a language which the Judge understands. The life utterance of the carnal, when divested of all its pretences, and gathered into one, is, " No God ! " That concentrated, intensified expression, issuing forth from time, has generated an echo in the receptive expanse of eternity. That echo meets the entrant on the border ; and conscience, not clouded now, is constrained to acknowledge it a truthful answer to the essence of his life. It is a fruit exactly after the kind of the seed which he had sown. " No God ! " was the meaning of his course in time : " No God ! " rebounding from the judgment-seat, at once fixes his place for eternity, and proclaims that it is the fruit of his own doing. Consider this, ye who live for your own pleasure, and leave the long-suffering Saviour stretching out his hands to you all day in vain : your life, thrown up, a sullen, bold, defiant *no*, from you to God in the day of his mercy, will rebound from the throne a *no* unchangeable, eternal, from God to you in the day of your need. Reciprocity runs through. When mercy was sovereign, mercy used judgment for carrying out mercy's ends : when mercy's reign is over, and judgment's reign begins, then judgment will sovereignly take mercy past and wield it to give weight to the vengeance stroke.

This terror of the Lord in eternity is clearly set forth in time, with the gracious design of persuading men to flee to the hope set before them.

At the close of this line of terrors there is a sweet and gentle word. It is a Father's voice, this still small voice that speaks when the storm and the thunders have passed by : " Whoso hearkeneth unto me shall dwell safely, and shall be quiet from the fear of evil." A safe dwelling-place ! There is now no condemnation to them that are in Christ Jesus. No plague shall come nigh them there. One would think this is enough. Himself our everlasting portion, if now we yield unto Him ; and a rest remaineth for the people of God. Enough, indeed : sinners saved could not of themselves expect more : but He provides and promises more. He will give them not only deliverance from death at last, but freedom from fear now ; safety from evil to come, and safety from the apprehension of its coming; justification at the throne of God, and peace within the conscience. When Christ came to work deliverance for all his own, he expressly provided both these blessings. It is not only to deliver them from death by receiving himself its sting; but also to deliver them from that fear of death, which otherwise would have held them all their lifetime subject to bondage (Heb. ii. 15). " Godliness is profitable unto all things." Eternal life secure in the world to come casts a beam of bright hope across, sufficient to quiet the anxieties of a fainting, fluttering heart, in all the dangers of the journey through. For his Redeemed Israel, who have already passed over the divided sea, he has provided a safe dwelling-place beyond the Jordan ; and under the shade of the Almighty, the pilgrims, even in the wilderness, will be *quiet* from the *fear* of evil.

Seek and Ye Shall Find

(Proverbs 2:4-5)

"If thou seekest her as silver . . . . thou shalt find the knowledge of God."

WISDOM continues still to cry unto men with the affectionate authority of a parent. The incarnation of the Son is God's grand utterance to mankind. The Word was made flesh, and dwelt among us. He came to make known the Father. "No man hath seen God at any time: the only begotten Son who is in the bosom of tne Father, He hath declared him."

Such is the speaker, and such the theme. Wisdom cries, " Incline thine ear unto wisdom." Christ calls on men to come unto Christ. It was He who opened the Scriptures; and He taught from them the things concerning himself. He is Prophet and Priest. He gives the invitation ; and the invitation is, " Come unto me." It is Christ offering Christ to sinners ; the teacher and the lesson alike divine. The preacher and the sermon are the same. He is the beginning and the ending. He is all in all.

The matter of the whole passage, ii. 1–9, consists in a command to seek, and a promise to bestow. The same speaker, at a later day, condensed his own discourse into the few emphatic words, " Seek, and ye shall find;" in this passage there is a needful expansion and profitable repetition of these two great pillar thoughts.

The seeking is in verses 1–4; the finding in verses 5–9. A Father speaks, and He speaks as unto children: He demands a reasonable service, and promises a rich reward.

In the fourfold repetition of the command there seems an order of succession; and the order, when observed, is both comely and instructive. It combines the beauty of the blossom and the profit of the fruit.

1. Receive my words,   and hide my commandments.
2. Incline thine ear,   and apply thine heart.
3. Cry after knowledge: lift up thy voice for under-
                          standing.
4. Seek her as silver: search for her as for hid
                          treasure.

1. " Receive my words." This is the first thing ; practical instruction must ever begin here. The basis of all religion and morality is the word of the Lord, taken into the understanding and heart. When the sower went forth to sow, some fell by the wayside, and the fowls came and devoured it. This is the first danger to which the published truth is exposed ; it does not enter the ground at all ; it tinkles on the surface of the mind, like seed on a beaten path, and next moment it is off, no one knows whither ; it never penetrated the soil ; it was never received. Corresponding to that first danger is the first counsel, " My son, receive my words ; " and if there should be any doubt about the meaning of the precept, the clause which balances it on the other side supplies the comment, " *hide* my commandments with thee." Our adversary the devil goeth about like a roaring lion, or ravening bird, seeking whom he may devour. He carries off the word from the surface of listless minds as birds carry away the seed that lies on the surface of unbroken ground. The word of God is a vital seed, but it will not germinate unless it be hidden in a softened receptive heart. It is here that providence so often strikes in with effect as an instrument in the work of the Spirit. Especially, at this point, bereaving providences work together for good. Even these, however, precious though they have been in the experience of all the saved, are only secondary and subordinate agencies. Sorrow is not seed. A field that is thoroughly and deeply broken may be as barren in the harvest as the beaten pathway. The place **and use** of providential visitation in the divine administration of Christ's kingdom, is to break up the way of the word through the incrustations of worldliness and vanity that incase a human heart and keep the word lying hard and dry upon the surface.

Every one is capable of perceiving the difference between merely hearing the word and receiving it. It is a blessed thing to have that word dwelling richly within you ; felt in all its freshness touching your conscience and enlightening your mind, during the busy day and in the silent night, giving tone to your spirit within, and direction to your course through life.

The Word was made flesh, and dwelt among us. Behold, He stands at the door and knocks ; if any man open, He will come in. To as many as receive Him, He gives power to become the sons of God.

2. " Incline thine ear." The entrance of the word has an immediate effect on the attitude of the mind and the course of the life. The incoming of the word makes the ear incline to wisdom ; and the inclining of the ear to wisdom lets in and lays up greater treasures of the word.

In practice it will be found that those who hide the word within them, feeding on it as daily bread, acquire a habitual bent of mind towards things spiritual. On the other hand, when the truth touches, and glances off again, like sunlight from polar snows, it is both a symptom and a cause of an inclination of the mind away from God and goodness. The great obstacle to the power and spread of the gospel lies in the averted attitude of human hearts. The mind is turned in another direction, and the faculties occupied in other pursuits. How hopeful the work of preaching becomes when the lie and the liking of the listener's soul is towards saving truth ! When the heart is applied to it, some portion of the word goes in, and that which has obtained an entrance prepares the way for more. To him that hath that little will be given much, and he shall have abundance. A man inclines his ear to those sounds which already his heart desires ; again to turn the ear, by an exercise of will at God's high command, to the word of wisdom, is the very way to inoculate the heart with a love to that word passing the love of earthly things. The lean of the disciples' hearts in the days of old drew them to Jesus ; and Jesus near, made their hearts burn with a keener glow. The ear and the heart !—precious gifts ! He that hath an ear to hear, let him hear what the Spirit saith ; he that hath a heart to love, let him love with it the altogether Lovely. The ear inclined to divine wisdom will draw the heart ; the heart drawn will incline the ear. Behold one of the circles in which God, for his own glory, makes his unnumbered worlds go round.

3. "Cry after knowledge." The preceding verse expressed the bent heavenward of the heart within and the senses without: this verse represents the same process at a more advanced stage. The longing for God's salvation already begotten in the heart, bursts forth now into an irrepressible cry. It is not any longer a Nicodemus inclined toward Jesus, he cannot tell how, and silently stealing into his presence under cloud of night; it is the jailer of Philippi springing in, and crying with a loud voice, "What must I do to be saved?" While the man was musing, the fire burned: now it no longer smoulders within; it bursts forth into a flame. He who gave Himself for his people loves to feel them kindling thus in his hands. Men may be offended with the fervour of an earnest soul—God never. "Hold thy peace," the prudent will still say to the enthusiastic follower of Jesus: but he feels his want, and hopes for help; he heeds them not: he cries out all the more, "Jesus, thou son of David, have mercy on me." Even disciples, apparently more alarmed by what seem irregularities in the action of the living than they were by the silence of the stiffened dead, may interpose with a frown and a rebuke; but compression will only increase the strength of the emotion struggling within. That word hidden in the heart will swell and burst and break forth in strong crying and tears, "Whom have I in heaven but Thee? and there is none upon earth that I desire beside Thee. My flesh and my heart faileth; but God is the strength of my heart, and my portion for ever" (Ps. lxxiii. 25, 26).

4. "Seek her as silver." Another and a higher step. The last was the earnest cry; this is the persevering endeavour. The strong cry is not enough: it is a step in the process, but the end is not yet. It might be Balaam's cry, "Let me die the death of the righteous," while in life he loved and laboured for the wages of iniquity. Fervent prayer must be tested by persevering pains.

Seek wisdom. Not only be inclined to spiritual things, and earnestly desire salvation, but set about it. Strive to enter in; lay hold on eternal life. Work out the salvation. "The kingdom of heaven suffereth violence, and the violent take it by force." The Christian life is a battle to be fought: the reward at last is a crown to be won.

More particularly, the search for wisdom is compared to another search with which we are more familiar. Seek her *as silver*

Those who seek the treasures that are at God's right hand are referred to their neighbours who are seeking treasures that perish in the using, and told to go and do likewise. The zeal of Mammon's worshippers rebukes the servants of the living God. We are invited to take a leaf from the book of the fortune-seeker. Besides the pursuit of money in the various walks of merchandise, there is, in our day, much of a direct and literal search for treasures hid in the earth. A prominent part of our daily public news, for years past, has been the stream of emigration from the settled countries of Europe to the western shores of America, and the great Australian Continent in search of hid treasure. The details are most instructive. Multitudes of young and old, from every occupation, and every rank, have left their homes, and traversed stormy seas, and desert continents, to the place where the treasure lies. Not a few have perished on the way; others sink under privations on the spot. The scorching sun by day, and the chill dews at night; labouring all day among water, and sleeping under the imperfect shelter of a tent; the danger of attack by uncivilized natives on the one hand, and by desperately wicked Europeans on the other,—all these, and a countless multitude more, are unable to deter from the enterprise, or drive off those who are already engaged. To these regions men flock in thousands, and tens of thousands. Those shores lately desolate are in motion now with a teeming population.

Search for her *as* for hid treasure ! He knows what is in man. He who made the human heart, and feels every desire that throbs within it, takes the measure of men's earnestness in their search for silver, and pronounces it sufficient for the object which he has at heart, the salvation of sinners. He points to it as a fit measure of the zeal with which a being, destitute by sin, should set out in the search for the salvation by grace : He intimates this will do—this earnestness, if directed upon the right object. How all this puts to shame the languid efforts of those who do seek the true riches ! There may be an inclination on the whole rather to the imperishable riches—a wish to be with Christ rather than left with a passing world for a portion. There may be the desire in that direction, but another question comes in,—what is the strength of that desire? That blessed portion in Christ is what you desire; well, but how much do you desire it? Will not the far-reaching plans, and heroic sacrifices, and long-enduring toil of Californian and Australian gold diggers rise up and condemn us who have tasted and known the grace of God ? Their zeal is the standard by which the Lord stimulates us now, and will measure us yet. Two things are required in our search,—the right direction, and the sufficient impulse. The Scriptures point out the right way; the avarice of mankind marks the quantum of forcefulness wherewith the seeker must press on.

But the search for hid treasure, which reads a lesson to the Church, is not confined to the gold regions, and the gold diggers. They dig as hard at home. It cannot be told how much of plan and effort, of head and hand, are expended in making money. It is no business of ours here to draw the nice distinctions between the rightful industry of a Christian merchant, and the passage through the fire of Mammon's child; this is not our present theme at all. What we want is to get our slackness in seeking a Saviour rebuked and quickened by the parallel movement of a more energetic search. Our question here is not how much is gold worth ? but is gold worth as much as the grace of God in Christ to a sinner ? You answer, No. This is our unanimous reply. It is true in its own nature; and sincerely it is uttered by our lips. Out of our own mouths then will we be condemned, if He who compasseth us about like air in all our ways, feels us striving with our might for the less, and but languidly wishing for the greater. Seek first the kingdom.

Those who seek thus shall not seek in vain; we have the word of the true God for it in many promises. Among the gathered multitudes in the great day, it will not be possible to find one who has sought in the right place for the right thing, *as other men seek money*, and who has nevertheless been disappointed. No doubt there are some who seek after a fashion, and gain nothing by it; who vent a wish to die the death of the righteous, and never attain to the object of their desire : but none fail who seek according to the prescription of the word, and after the example of the world. Many people proceed upon a principle the very reverse of that which the word inculcates : they search for money as if it were saving truth, instead of searching for saving truth as if it were money. These must be turned upside down ere they begin to prosper.

Perils in the Deep

(Proverbs 2:12-19)

" To deliver thee from the way of the evil [man], from the man that speaketh froward things ; who leave the paths of uprightness, to walk in the ways of darkness ; who rejoice to do evil, and delight in the frowardness of the wicked ; whose ways are crooked, and they froward in their paths: to deliver thee from the strange woman, even from the stranger which flattereth with her words ; which forsaketh the guide of her youth, and forget- teth the covenant of her God: for her house inclineth unto death, and her paths unto the dead. None that go unto her return again, neither take they hold of the paths of life."

"THE wicked are like the troubled sea when it cannot rest." Here an arm of that sea is spread out before us, and we are led to an eminence whence we may behold its raging. We must one by one go down into these great waters. We see many of our comrades sinking beneath the surge. It is good to count the number and measure the height of these ranks of raging waves, that we may be induced to hold faster by the anchor of the soul, which is sure and steadfast.

The dangers are delineated here in exact order, continuous succession, and increasing power. They come as the waves come when the tide is flowing; they gradually gain in strength until they reach their height; then, when Satan has done his worst, he retires sullenly, leaving all who have not been overwhelmed, high, and safe, and triumphing.

1. "The way of the evil." Whether they be persons or principles, whether they be men or devils, the word does not expressly say. The announcement, in the first place, is couched in terms the most general; the particulars are enumerated in the verses following. The way of the evil is the way which Satan trod, and by which all his servants follow. It is the way whereon all the wicked travel to their doom.

2. But more specifically, the first item of the evil is "the man that speaketh froward things." "The tongue can no man tame; it is an unruly evil, full of deadly poison." This little fire kindles

a flame which spreads and licks up all that is lovely and of good report in a wide circle of companionship. The man who speaks froward things is one of the foremost dangers to which the young are exposed at their first start in life. In a workshop, or warehouse, or circle of private friendship, there is one who has a foul tongue. It is difficult to conceive how quickly and how deeply it contaminates all around. There may be much specific variety in the forms of frowardness. In one case, the pollution assumes the shape of profane swearing : in another, it is the frequent injection of obscenities amidst the conversation of the day, feathered with wit to make them fly : in a third, it is infidel insinuation : in a fourth, it is one huge mass of silliness, a shapeless conglomerate of idle words, injuring not so much by the infliction of positive evil, as by occupying a man's heart and his day with vanity, to the exclusion of all that is substantial either for this world or the next.

It is hardly possible that one who is much in contact with these froward words should come off unscathed. Even when a person does not sympathize with the evil, and imitate it, his conscience gets a wound. Only One has ever appeared on earth who was entirely safe under the fiery darts of the wicked : "The prince of this world cometh, and hath nothing in Me" (John xiv. 30). If there were perfect purity within, these onsets from without would leave no stain ; but upon our impure hearts, even when the temptation in the main is resisted, and the tempter put to flight, the marks are left behind : some of the filth sticks, and will not off, to the dying day. For us, even in our best estate, it is not good, in that experimental way, to know evil. The foul tongue of the froward is one grand cause of dread to godly parents in sending their youths to a business, and even in sending their children to school.

How good are pure words ! Set a watch upon your mouth. "Let your speech be always with grace, seasoned with salt." Bad as it is to hear froward words, it is inconceivably worse to speak them. It is more cursed to give temptation than to receive it.

3. "Who leave the paths of righteousness." When the imagination is polluted, and the tongue let loose, the feet cannot keep on the path of righteousness. Thinking, and hearing, and speak-

ing evil, will soon be followed by doing it. The world is startled from time to time by the report of some daring crime; but if the history of the criminal were known, however much grief there might be, there would be no surprise at the culmination of his wickedness. When you see a mighty tree in the forest, you assume that it did not leap into maturity in a day, although you saw not its gradual growth: you may as confidently count that full-sized crime did not attain its stature in a day. In all of us are the seeds of it, and in many the seedlings are growing apace. The ways follow the thoughts and words, as trees spring from seeds. He who would be kept from the path of the destroyer must crucify the flesh with its affections and lusts. Out of the heart proceed evil thoughts, and soon after murders and adulteries follow. In the matter of watching for one's soul, as in all other matters, the true wisdom is to take care of the beginnings.

4. "To walk in the ways of darkness." There is a strictly causal and reciprocal relation between unrighteous deeds and moral darkness. The doing of evil produces darkness, and darkness pro- duces the evil-doing. Indulged lusts put out the eye-sight of the conscience; and under the darkened conscience the lusts revel unchecked. "From him that hath not, shall be taken away."

5. "Who rejoice to do evil." This is a more advanced step in guilt. At first the backslider is ashamed of his fall. He palliates, alleges the strength of the temptation, and promises amendment. As the hardening process goes on, however, he begins to feel more easy: he ceases to make excuses, and at last he glories in his shame. "Were they ashamed when they had committed abomi- nation? Nay, they were not at all ashamed, neither could they blush" (Jer. vi. 15). This is a measure of evil which should make even the wicked tremble. A man has become the very essence of antichrist, when it is his meat and his drink to oppose the will of our Father who is in heaven.

6. Profligacy can yet one step further go. They who "delight in the frowardness of the wicked" are more abandoned than the wicked themselves. To take pleasure in sin is a characteristic of fallen humanity; to delight in seeing others sinning is altogether devilish. Some monsters in human form have presided over the process of torture, and drunk in delight from a brother's pain; but it is a still clearer evidence that a man is of his father the

Devil, when he lays snares for a brother's soul, and laughs at his own success. There are not a few amongst us who have reached this stage of depravity, and yet have no suspicion that they are in any way more guilty than others. They have so drunk into the spirit, and been changed into the image of the first tempter, that they relish as dainty food the pollution of a neighbour, and yet never perceive that there is anything out of the way. " Blessed are they that hunger and thirst after righteousness, for they shall be filled:" cursed are they that hunger and thirst after wickedness, for *they shall be filled too;* they shall be filled with food convenient for them. It is the Lord's way both in mercy and judgment to provide for every creature in abundance that which it loves and longs for. This principle is announced with terrific distinctness in the prophet Habakkuk (ii. 15, 16). Those who have a relish for the sin of others, will be filled with the food they have chosen; and although the horrid sweet pall upon the taste by reason of its abundance, there is no variety, and no diluting of sin by fragments of good in the place of the lost. The same—the same that they loved on earth, the lost must abide for ever; sin —nothing but sin, within and around them.

To complete the picture of the danger, one other peril of the world's deep is marked on the chart which is mercifully placed in the voyager's hands—it is " the strange woman." Thanks be to God for his tender care in kindling these beacon-lights on the rock to scare the coming passenger away from the quicksands of doom.

The deceiver is called a " strange" woman. Whoredom is distinguished from marriage, which God appointed and approves. When man and woman are given to each other, as helps meet from the Lord, they become " one flesh:" they are not only known to each other, but, in an important sense, they lose their individual personality, and are merged into one. " A man shall leave father and mother and cleave unto his wife." To follow the " strange woman" is the Satanic reversal of this divine ordinance. There is no love, no holy union, no mutual helpfulness; but wild, selfish passions, followed by visible marks of God's vengeance. For it is not his word only; with equal clearness his providence frowns on licentiousness. That vice eats like a festering sore into the body of society. If all should act as libertines do, the race would dwindle away. We are fearfully and wonderfully made; we are fearfully and wonderfully *governed*. It is in vain that the pot-sherds of the earth strive with their Maker: his anger will track lust through all its secret doublings: he makes sin generate its own punishment. Vengeance against that evil thing circulates through the veins, and dries up the marrow in the heart of the bones. Verily, there is a God that judgeth in the earth. Of the strange woman it is said, " Her house inclineth unto death, and her paths unto the dead." Mark well this description, ye simple ones who are enticed to follow her. There is an " incline on the path ;" it goes *down*. She leads the way, you follow. It is easy to go down—down a slippery, slimy path ; but its issue is death. What death ? The death of the soul, and the body too. It leads to " the dead." It brings you to the society of libertines ; and they are dead while they live. This lust is a cankerworm that quickly withers the greenness of spring in the soul of youth. We have no trust in the patriotism, the truth, the honesty, the friend-ship of licentious men. When you get down into their company, you are among the dead : they move about like men in outward appearance ; but the best attributes of humanity have disappeared —the best affections of nature have been drained away from their hearts.

Wisdom Received and Retained

(Proverbs 2:10-11; 3:1)

"When wisdom entereth into thine heart, and knowledge is pleasant unto thy soul, discretion shall preserve thee, understanding shall keep thee."
"My son, forget not my law; but let thine heart keep my commandments."

CHRIST'S prayer for his disciples was not that they should be taken out of the world, but that they should be preserved from the evil that is in it. Life is a voyage on the deep: there are perils which we must pass; how shall we pass them safely? The grand specific is the entrance of wisdom into the heart. As already explained, you may understand by Wisdom either the Salvation or the Saviour. The entrance of the word gives light, and chases away the darkness. If the truth as it is in Jesus come in through the understanding, and make its home in the heart, it will be a purifier and preserver. "Sanctify them through the truth." The word of God and the way of the wicked are like fire and water; they cannot be together in the same place. Either the flood of wickedness will extinguish the word, or the word will burn and dry up the wickedness.

If we understand the Word personally of Christ, the same holds good. Where He dwells the lusts of the flesh cannot reign. Evil cannot dwell with Him. When the Light of the world gets entrance into the heart, the foul spirits that swarmed in the darkness disappear. His coming shall be like the morning.

The other strand of the two-fold cord which keeps a voyager in safety amid all these perils is, "when knowledge is pleasant to thy soul." The pleasantness of the knowledge that comes in, is a feature of essential importance. Even the truth entering the mind, and fastening on the conscience, has no effect in delivering from the power of evil, while it comes only as a terror: what the law could not do by all its fears, God did by sending his Son. The love of Christ constraineth us, when all other appliances have been tried in vain. The Spirit employs terror in his pre-paratory work ; but it is only when the redemption of Christ begins to be felt sweeter than the pleasures of sin that the soul is allured, and yields, and follows on to know the Lord. It is pleasure that can compete with pleasure ; it is "joy and peace in believing" that can overcome the pleasure of sin. Felix trembled under Paul's preaching, yet offered to sell justice for money; and, to curry favour with the multitude, kept the innocent in bonds. Although the word of God ran through him like a sword in his bones, it left him wholly in the power of his lusts. A human soul, by its very constitution, cannot be frightened into holiness. It is made for being won; and won it will be, by the drawing on this side, or the drawing on that. The power on God's side is greater than all on the side of sin. As long as that power is felt to be repelling, the sinner creeps still further and further from the con-suming fire ; but whenever the love of God in the face of Jesus becomes "pleasant" to his soul, that love keeps and carries him, as the central sun holds up a tributary world.

But after Wisdom has been received, it is also necessary that it should be retained. Wisdom accordingly continues to cry ; and the cry now is, "My son, forget not." Such pity as a father hath, like pity shows the Lord. Throughout his dispensations, the Eternal wears the aspect of a Father to his creature man. In the Bible, the parental regard is seen glancing through at every opening. When Jesus taught his disciples how to pray, Father was the foremost word of the inspired liturgy. With this tender name is the arrow pointed that is expected to penetrate the heavens. Those who have skill to read the hieroglyphs of nature, will find many a parallel text in earth and sea. The world is full of his goodness : the fatherliness of the Creator is graven on all his works.

The matter thus tenderly commended to the pupil's regard, is nothing less than "my law." He who made us knows what is good for us. Submission to his will is the best condition for humanity. What shall be the guide of our life—our own de-praved liking, or the holy will of God ? Our own will leads to sin and misery : the law of the Lord is perfect, converting the soul, and making wise the simple. The two rival rules are set before us : choose ye whom ye shall serve. His servants ye are whom ye obey, whether of sin unto death, or of obedience unto righteousness.

"Forget not my law;" another evidence that the Inspirer of the word knows what is in man. Silently to forget God's law is amongst us a much more common thing than blasphemously to reject it. To renounce God's law because your reason condemns it, is the infidelity that slays its thousands : to forget God's law because your heart does not like it, is the ungodliness that slays its ten thousands. The deceitfulness of the heart is a form of sin's disease much more widely spread and much more fatal than the hostility of the understanding.

"Let thine heart keep my commandments;" another step in the same direction—another stage in the process of dissecting the spirit, in order to reach the seat of sin. What the heart cleaves to is not readily forgotten. As a general rule it may be safely laid down, that what you habitually forget you do not care for : so true is it that love is the fulfilling of the law. If you do not love it, so far from obeying it, you will not even remember that there is such a thing. It is often given as an excuse for evil doing, that it was done without thought—that the evil of it was not present to the mind ; if you had observed at the time the real character of your action, you would have done otherwise. What is this but to tell that your heart does not keep God's commandment ? If that law had been at hand, in God's name forbidding the word or the deed, you would have refrained. No thanks to you ; that is as much as to say you would not of set purpose oppose the Almighty to his face. But you did what He complains of; you forgot Him and his law. You had extruded these from your heart as unwelcome visitors, and now you say, if they had been within, the mischief would not have happened. But why were they not within ? Why was the word not dwelling richly in you ? Why was your heart not its hidden home ? The house was full of the company that you liked. The law of the Lord, weary waiting on outside, had slipt away unnoticed. It was not there—it was not in sight, with its holy frown, when the temptation pressed suddenly, and prevailed. If it had been there, the enemy would not have gained an advantage over you ; and this is an excuse or palliation ! What you put forward as an excuse, God marks as the very essence of the sin. The heart keeps what it loves; what it dislikes it lets go. The very soul of sin is here; "an evil heart of unbelief in departing from the living God."

One ever-ready excuse of those who live without God in the world is "a bad memory." Where there is real imbecility in the nature, the excuse is good; but then it is never pleaded as an excuse. The skill which can plead a treacherous memory as an excuse for not knowing the truth, would have charged the memory with the truth if it had been so applied. Those who intend to plead a short memory at the judgment-seat of God, would need to see to it that other things should slip as quickly and as cleanly off from the mind as the word of Christ. When Saul averred to Samuel, "I have performed the commandment of the Lord, I have destroyed all that belonged to Amalek," Samuel replied, "What meaneth, then, this bleating of the sheep in mine ears, and this lowing of the oxen which I hear?" The king was confounded when his pretence was laid bare. What confusion must cover those who pass through life with scarcely a conception of how a sinner may be saved, when they put in the plea, "We had a treacherous memory," and are met by the question, "What mean, then, all those rules, and numbers, and events concerning the world, that crowded your memory through life, and clung there undefaced in your old age?"

Let us not deceive ourselves. When there is a hungering for the truth, the mind takes it in; when the heart loves divine truth, the memory retains it. Turn the excuse into an aggravation, while yet there is time. Plead no more a feeble memory; begin to grieve over an evil heart.

The Art of Printing
(Proverbs 3:3)

"Let not mercy and truth forsake thee: bind them about thy neck; write them upon the table of thine heart."

T HE matter to be recorded is "mercy and truth:" the tablet for receiving it is the human heart; and here we have some instructions on the art of printing it.

Look first to the legend itself—"mercy and truth." These two, meeting and kissing in the Mediator, constitute the revealed character of God himself; and He desires to see, as it were, a miniature of his own likeness impressed upon his children. As we cannot have any printing without a type, we cannot have mercy and truth in holy union raised on the life of a human being, unless we get the exemplar brought from above, and transferred to man.

What God desires to see in man, he showed to man. He who dwelleth between the cherubim, merciful and true, shone forth upon his creatures, that those who look might be transformed into the same image, as by the Spirit of the Lord.

It is only in Christ that we can know God. As manifested there, He is just and forgiving: mercy and truth meet in the person and sacrifice of the Son. Without the Saviour, we can conceive of mercy *or* truth being displayed by God to the rebellious. We could at least conceive of mercy without truth; but then it would admit the unclean into heaven: we could also conceive of truth without mercy; but then it would cast mankind without exception into hell. In order that there might be mercy and truth from the Judge to the sinful, Christ obeyed, and died, and rose again. "God so loved the world, that He gave his only-begotten Son;" but God so hated sin, that He gave Him up to die as an expiation to justice. Mercy reigns, not over righteousness, but through righteousness.

"Be ye followers [imitators] of God as dear children" (Eph. v. 1). If we receive grace reigning through righteousness, a corresponding result will appear in our life. The reception of these into the heart is, as it were, the sowing of the seed; and that seed will bring forth fruit after its kind. If, conscious of guilt and condemnation, you accept and rejoice in free grace from God, this doctrine will not lie barren within you. It will burst forth in meekness, gentleness, pity, love, to all the needy. If you mark, as you get pardon, how it comes—pardon through Christ crucified; if you take it as it comes,—bought by His blood; you will never make light of sin, either in yourselves or others. In all religions, true and false, there are an original and a copy. Either God manifested leaves the impress of his own character on the receptive heart of a believing man, or man unbelieving transfers his own likeness to the gods whom he makes in his imagination or by his hands. "Mercy and truth"—there is the type let down from God out of heaven; are our hearts open, soft, receptive, to take the impression on?

"Let them not forsake thee: bind them about thy neck." These injunctions indicate that there is a fickleness which makes the printing difficult, and the impression indistinct at the best. This command to bind them about the neck (Deut. vi. 8) was adopted by the Jews in the letter, and neglected in spirit. It degenerated into a superstition; and hence the phylacteries, the amulets worn by the Pharisees. The command here is more specific—"Write them upon the table of thine heart:" the reference obviously is to the writing of the law on tables of stone. These tables were intended to be not a book only, but also a type. From them we may read the law, indeed; but by them also an impression should be made on our own hearts, that we may always have the will of God hidden within us. This idea is with marvellous fulness expressed by Paul: "The epistle of Christ, written not with ink, but with the Spirit of the living God: not in tables of stone, but in fleshly tables of the heart" (2 Cor. iii. 3). Men can easily read the word from the old table of stone; but they are slow to learn "the art of printing" it on their own nature, so that it may be legible in all their life. This impression can be effectually taken only in the melting down of the regeneration, as Paul expresses it, Rom. vi. 17: "Ye have obeyed from the heart that mould òf doctrine into which ye were delivered."

This fleshly table of the heart lies open, and it is continually receiving impressions of some kind. It seems to harden after youth has passed, so that what it has previously received it tenaciously keeps; what is afterwards applied, it does not so readily take on. Of great moment it is, therefore, that right impressions should go deeply in, while the mind is still in a receptive state. But in this promiscuous life, the table of a young man's heart lies open for all comers; it is often seen indented deeply and crowded all over with "divers lusts and pleasures," so that no room is left whereon the things of God may mark themselves.

At places of public resort, such as the summit of a lofty mountain, or the site of some famous monument, you may see tables of wood or stone or level turf. All over them inscriptions have been chiselled so thickly, that you could not now find an unoccupied spot to plant a letter on. The characters are various: some old, some new, some well formed, some irregular scrawls, some mere scratches on the surface, which a winter's storm will wash out, some so deep that they will be legible for ages. As to matter, some are records of personal ambition, others a spurt of thoughtless jollity, others the date of some great event; some are profane, and some political. The table lies there, the helpless recipient of ideas, good or bad, that stray comers may choose to impress on it.

I have thought, as I looked on the Babel-like confusion, that the heart of a man, which the Bible calls a "table," is like one of these common public receptacles. In youth it is peculiarly soft, and affords an inviting material for every adventurous sculptor to try his hand upon. It often lies exposed, and receives the accidental impressions of ever passer by. Many legends of mere emptiness have been written on it, and were thought innocent; but there they are, at life's latest day, taking up room, and doing no good. Some impure lines have been early carved in, and now they will not out, even where the possessor has been renewed, and learned to loathe them. Parents, set a fence round your children; youth, set a fence round yourselves. Perhaps you may have seen one of these monumental tablets suddenly enclosed, and a notice exhibited over the gateway, doing all men to wit, that "whereas some evil disposed persons have imprinted vain and wicked words on this table, it has been surrounded by a strong fence, and henceforth no person shall be admitted to write thereon except the owner and his friends." Go thou and do likewise. Warn, ward the intruders off. Reserve that precious tablet for the use of the King its owner, and those who will help to occupy it with His character and laws.

Take these three in the form of practical observations.

1. The duty of parents is clear, and their encouragements great. Watch the young. Stand beside that soft receptive tablet. Keep trespassers away more zealously than ever hereditary magnate kept the vulgar from his pleasure-grounds. Insert many truths. Busily fill the space with good, and that too in attractive forms. This is the work laid to your hand. Work in your own subordinate place, and the Lord from above will send the blessing down.

2. Afflictive providences generally have a bearing on this printing process. God sends what will break the heart: nay, sometimes a fire to melt it like water within you; and this, in wise mercy, to make it take on the truth. When the pilgrims compare notes in Zion at length, it will be found that most of them learned this art of printing in the furnace of affliction. " Before I was afflicted I went astray, but now I have kept thy word" (Ps. cxix. 67). The heart, in contact with a busy world, was rubbed smooth and slippery; the type, when it touched, glided off the surface, and left no mark behind; this bruising and breaking opened the crust, and let the lesson in.

3. Whether in youth or in age, whether in sickness or in health, it is not an effort from within or a providence from without that will make the heart new and the life holy. It is the type, by the Spirit's ministry impressed on the prepared page; it is the mercy and truth united in Christ crucified for sin,—embodied love let down from heaven and touching the earth; it is Christ clasped to a softened heart, that will reimprint the image of God upon a sinful man.

Trust

(Proverbs 3:5)

"Trust in the Lord with all thine heart; and lean not unto thine own understanding."

FAITH is not fear, and fear is not faith. The terrors of the Lord beaming in upon the conscience, using guilt as fuel for the flame of a premature torment, do not constitute conversion. Christianity is not a dark ground, with here and there a quivering streak of light thrown in; blessed hope is the basis of it all. Many dark spots deface it, at the best; but the ground is a bright ground. It is a positive, and not a negative thing. It has many diseases and pains, but it is in its nature a life, and not a death. It flies to God, not from him. It is not a slave's struggle to escape from divine vengeance: it is a dear child's confidence in a Father's love. Christ is the way; but it is unto the Father that the prodigal returns. The only method of reconciliation is the looking unto Jesus, and looking on until confiding faith spring up; but the religious act of a soul saved is a trust in God.

This is an unseen thing, and it is misunderstood by those who look toward it from without. The reason why those who are wedded to their pleasures count religion to be dull and painful seems to be this:—they see religious people really renouncing the pleasures of sin and sense: they know, they feel what that renunciation would be to themselves; but they do not know, they cannot conceive the consolation which the peace of God gives even now to a human heart. They see what a religious man lets go; but they do not see in that other region the worth of the equivalent which a religious man gets; for it is spiritually discerned, and they are not spiritual. In their conception Religion is a grim tyrant, who snatches every delight from the grasp of a youth, and gives him nothing in return. The servant of the man of God sees on the one side an host of enemies pressing round, and on the other side no help at hand. "Alas, my master!" he cried, "how shall we do?" (2 Kings vi. 16, 17). "Fear not," said Elisha; but it was not until the young man's eyes were opened to see the mountain full of horses and chariots of fire round about Elisha that he could be confident, or even composed. We need the same re-creating Spirit to open the blind eyes of the carnal, ere they can see that the joys which God in grace gives are more than the pleasures of sin, which his presence drives away. The green apple does not like to be twisted and torn from the tree; but the ripened fruit, that has no more need for the root's sap, drops easily off. Trust in the Lord, when a soul attains it, loosens every other bond, and makes it easy to let go all which the world gives. When you feel your footing firm in the peace of God, you will not be afraid though the earth should sink away from beneath you.

Trust is natural to the creature, although trust in the Lord be against the grain to the guilty. It is our nature to be dependent: it is our instinct to lean. In regard to the unseen, man has an innate consciousness of his own frailty, and in general it is not difficult to persuade him to lean on something beyond himself. Ever since sin began, gods many and lords many have invited men's confidence, and offered them aid. It is easy to persuade Papists to lean on priests and saints, on old rags and painted pictures—on any idol; but it is hard to get a Protestant really to trust in the living God. It is a common remark that Papists have more devotion in their way than we have in ours. The fact is obvious: the reason of it is not always seen. Popery sails with the stream when it bids men trust, for this falls in with a tendency of nature; but it puts forward to receive the confiding soul a dead idol, whose presence is no rebuke to indulged sin. Among Papists you will find real devotion in all who are conscious of nature's weakness, and willing to trust; but among Protestants you can find real devotion only in those who are prepared to crucify the flesh—who, at enmity with their own sins, bound forward to meet the offered embrace of "our God," and so plunge their bosom lusts into "a consuming fire."

"With all thine heart." God complains as much of a divided allegiance as of none. A double-minded man is unstable in all his ways. In cleaving to Christ the effort to reserve a little spoils all. It endangers ultimate safety, and destroys present peace. The soul should grow into Christ, as grows the branch on the vine; but the reserved part is dead matter lying between the two lives, preventing them from coalescing into one. The somewhat which the soul refuses to surrender sticks in between, so that you cannot have your life hid in Christ; Christ cannot live in you. Your hope cannot find way into his heart, his peace cannot flow into yours. "Except ye be converted and become as a little child, ye cannot enter into the kingdom."

"In all thy ways acknowledge him, and he shall direct thy paths." Observe the universality of the command. There is no hardship in this; the commandment is holy and just and *good*. If we keep back any of the conditions, we lose all the promised return. This injunction is aimed, not at the speculative atheism which denies that there is a God, but at the much more common practical ungodliness which keeps Him at a distance from human affairs. Few will refuse to acknowledge a superintending Providence at certain times, and in certain operations that are counted great. If the commandment had been, "Acknowledge God in the uncertain and difficult ways of life," it would have met with a more ready compliance. To uphold the world and direct its movements, to appoint the birth and the death of men, to provide redemption from sin, and open the way into glory—in these grand and all-comprehensive operations men would be content to acknowledge God, provided they were allowed to retain all minor matters under their own management. They will treat God as subjects treat a king, but not as a wife treats her husband. The large, and the formal, and the public, they will submit to his decision; but the little, and close, and kindly, they will keep to themselves. Let him compass you about, as the atmosphere embraces the earth, going into every interstice, and taking the measure of every movement. "Trust in the Lord at all times; pour ye out your hearts before him."

The command is encouraging as well as reproving. It is not merely the promise that is encouraging, but also the command which precedes it. Does God claim to be acknowledged in all my ways? May I trouble the Master about everything, great or small, that troubles me? May I lay before the Almighty Ruler every care of my heart, every step of my path? Yes, everything. The great and glorious sun shines down from heaven upon the daisy, and the feeble daisy sweetly opens its breast, and looks up from earth upon the sun. God is the maker of them both; both equally enjoy His care, and equally speak His praise. The genuine spirit of adoption may be best observed in little things. The distant and unconfiding will come on occasion of state formalities to the sovereign; but the dear child will leap forward with everything. The Queen of England is the mother of a family. At one time her ministers of state come gravely into her presence to converse on the policy of nations: at another her infant runs into her arms for protection, frightened at the buzzing of a fly. Will she love less this last appeal, because it is a little thing? We have had fathers of our flesh to whom we came confidingly with our minutest ailments: How much more should we bring all our ways to the Father of our spirits, and live by simple faith on Him?

The Health of Holiness

(Proverbs 3:7-8)

"Fear the Lord, and depart from evil. It shall be health to thy navel and marrow to thy bones."

BY a striking and strongly figurative expression, which can be perfectly comprehended by readers of any age or clime, it is intimated that a religious rectitude preserves mental and physical health, and gives fullest play to all the human faculties. All God's laws come from one source, and conspire for one end. They favour righteousness and frown on sin. The law set in nature runs parallel, as far as it goes, to the law written in the word. It is glory to God in the highest, as governor of the world. Vice saps the health both of body and mind. Every one of us has seen monuments of this awful law, almost as deeply blighted as the warning pillar on the plain of Sodom, only they stalk about, and so publish their lesson more widely. When the brain has been dried, and the eye dimmed, and the countenance bleared, and the limbs palsied, and the tongue thickened by drunkenness, and other vices that march in its company or follow in its train, what remains of the man should be to us as dread a warning against his course, as if he had been turned into a salt statue, and stood upon the wayside to scare the solitary passenger. It behoves us to walk circumspectly, and not as fools. All around us, sin is withering the bloom of youth, and wasting manhood's strength—is shrivelling the skin upon the surface, and drying up the marrow in the heart of the bones. Verily we are in the hands of the living God: in Him we live, and move, and have our being: we cannot elude His observation, or break from his grasp.

Dreadful though its results be, I rejoice in these providential arrangements. The law by which disease and imbecility closely track the path of lust, is of God's own making, and, behold, it is very good. It is righteous, and merciful too. The link which connects the suffering with the sin, I would not break though I could : even so, Father ! for so it seemed good in thy sight. These wastings of the marrow are the terrors of the Lord set in array against evil ; if they were wanting, human governments could not withstand the tide of universal anarchy. These providential arrangements clog the wheels of evil, and so secure for the world a course of probation. If the Creator had not fixed in nature these make-weights on the side of good, the tide of evil that set in with sin would have soon wrought the extinction of the race. It is especially those sins that human governments cannot or will not touch, that God takes into his own hands, and checks by the stroke of his judgment. He has bowed his heavens and come down. He concerns Himself with the details of human history. He who does the great things, neglects not the less. He who makes holiness happy in heaven, makes holiness healthful on earth. Gather up the fragments of his goodness, that none of them be lost : set them all in the song of praise.

Capital and Profit

(Proverbs 3:9)

"Honour the Lord with thy substance, and with the first fruits of all thine increase."

THE two terms, "substance" and "increase," exist, and are understood in all nations and all times. They correspond to capital and profit in a commercial community, or land and crop in an agricultural district. Although the direct and chief lesson of this verse be another thing, we take occasion, from the occurrence of these terms, first of all, to indicate and estimate a grievous malady that infests mercantile life in the present day. It manifests itself in these two kindred features 1. A morbid forwardness to commence business without capital, that is an effort to reap an increase while you have no substance to reap it from ; and, 2. A morbid forwardness to prosecute business to an enormous extent, upon a very limited capital ; that is an effort to reap more increase than your substance can fairly bear.

In former, and, commercially speaking, healthier times, those who had no money were content to work for wages until they had saved some, and then they laid out to the best advantage the money which they had. That method was honourable to the individual, and safe to society ; but in our day an unfair and unsafe standard of estimating men has been surreptitiously foisted upon the community. Practically by all classes, the chief honour should be given, not to the great merchant, but to the honest man. A man who has only five pounds in the world, and carries all his merchandise in a pack on his shoulder, is more worthy of honour than the man who, having as little money of his own, drives his carriage, and drinks champagne at the risk of other people. A full discussion of mercantile morality under this text would be unsuitable and therefore we now refrain ; but a note of warning was demanded here on the one point which has been brought up. We must have truth and righteousness at the bottom as a foundation, if we would have a permanently successful commerce. Let men exert all their ingenuity in extracting the largest possible increase from their substance ; but let them beware of galvanic efforts to extract annual returns at other people's risk, from shadows which have no body of substance behind. This is the epidemic disease of commerce : this is the chief cause of its disastrous fluctuations : this is the foul humour in its veins that bursts out periodically in wide-spread bankruptcy. If all merchants would conscientiously, as in God's sight, confine their gains to a legitimate increase of their realized substance, the commerce of the nation would circulate in perennial health.

When the increase is honestly obtained, honour the Lord with its first fruits. To devote a portion of our substance directly to the worship of God, and the good of men, is a duty strictly binding, and plainly enjoined in the Scriptures : it is not a thing that a man may do or not do as he pleases. There is this difference, however, between it and the common relative duties of life, that whereas for these we are under law to man, for that we are accountable to God only. For the neglect of it no infliction comes from a human hand. God will not have the dregs that are squeezed out by pressure poured into his treasury. He depends not, like earthly rulers, on the magnitude of the tribute. He loveth a cheerful giver ; he can work without our wealth, but He does not work without our willing service. The silver and the gold are His already ; what He claims and cares for is the cheerfulness of the giver's heart.

A Fatherly Word on Fatherly Correction
(Proverbs 3:11-12)

"My son, despise not thou the chastening of the Lord; neither be weary of his correction: for whom the Lord loveth he correcteth; even as a father the son in whom he delighteth."

THIS passage is taken entire out of the Old Testament, and inserted in the New (Heb. xii. 5, 6).

I have seen the crown of our present Sovereign. It is studded all over with jewels, bright jewels of various hue. The eye can scarcely rest upon it for radiance. Some of these jewels have been found and fashioned in our own day; others have been taken from the crowns which English monarchs wore in ancient times; but the gems that have been taken from an ancient crown, and inserted in the newest, are as bright and as precious as those that were never used before. Jewels are neither dimmed by time, nor superseded by fashion. A prince will wear an old one as proudly as a new.

Such are these words, these tried and pure words, spoken of old by the Spirit in Solomon, and recalled for use by the same Spirit in Paul. This word of God liveth and abideth for ever. The king who uttered it at first has passed away with all his glory like the grass. The kingdom which he swayed is blotted out from the map of the nations. The temple where they may have been read to the great congregation has been cast down. Jerusalem became a heap. But these words of Solomon remain at this day bright and pure like the jewels on the crown he wore. The very gems that sparkled in the diadem of David's son, appear again reset in a circlet of glory round the head of David's Lord. Heaven and earth shall pass away, but none of these precious words shall fail.

In quoting the words from the Old Testament, Paul perceived, and pointed out a tender meaning in the form of the expression,

" my son." That formula occurs often in the Proverbs, and a careless reader would pass it as a thing of course. Not so this inspired student of the Scripture : he gathers a meaning from the form of the word before he begins to deal with its substance; the exhortation, he says, "speaketh unto you as unto children." Incidentally we obtain here a lesson on the interpretation of Scripture. Some would confine themselves to the leading facts and principles, setting aside, as unimportant, whatever pertains merely to the manner of the communication. By this method much is lost. It is not a thrifty way of managing the bread that cometh down from heaven. Gather up the fragments, that none of them be lost. We give no license to the practice of building precious doctrines upon conceits and fancies, while there are solid foundations at hand laid there for the purpose of bearing them. We do not want any of your word ; but we must have all that is the Lord's, great and small alike. We need every word that proceedeth out of the mouth of God to live upon. Take and use all that is in the word, but nothing more.

"My son." The Spirit in Paul recognised this as a mark of God's paternal tenderness, and used it as a ground of glad encouragement to desponding believers. Of design, and not by accident, was the word thrown into that form, as it issued at first from the lips of Solomon. God intended thereby to reveal Himself as a Father, and to grave that view of his character in the Scripture as with a pen of iron and the point of a diamond, that the most distant nations and the latest times might know that as a father pitieth his children, so the Lord pitieth them that fear Him.

Some men raise a debate about inspiration, whether every word be inspired, or only some ; but there was no such idea in Paul's mind. Not only the main propositions, but the incidental tone and cast of the language is understood to express the mind of God. We should not allow one jot or tittle of this word to pass away through our hands as we are using it.

Turning now to the matter of this text, understand by chastening, in the meantime, any affliction, whatever its form or measure may be. The stroke may fall upon your own person,—your body, your spirit, or your good name ; it may fall on those who are dearest to you, and so wound you in the tenderest spot ; it may fall upon your substance to sweep it away, or on your country to waste it. Whatever the providence may be that turns your joy into grief, it is a chastening from the Lord. Taking, in the first place, this more general view of chastening or rebuke, we observe that the command regarding it is twofold : 1. Do not despise it ; 2. Do not faint under it. There are two opposite extremes of error in this thing, as in most others ; and these two commands are set like hedges, one on the right hand, and another on the left, to keep the traveller from wandering out of the way. The Lord from heaven beholds all the children of men. He sees that some, when afflicted, err on this side, and some on that ; the stroke affects those too little, and these too much.

1. "Despise not." It means to make light of anything ; to cast it aside as if it had no meaning and no power. The affliction comes on, and the sufferer looks to the immediate cause only. He refuses to look up to the higher links of the chain ; he refuses to make it the occasion of communion with God. The disease comes upon him : it is a cold or a bruise ; it has been neglected, and so aggravated ; but the doctor has prescribed such a remedy, and he expects it will soon give way. The loss in business comes : he feels the uneasiness—it may be, the affront. He has grief for his own loss, and indignation against others ; but he was in a fair way, and might have succeeded, if such an article had not suddenly fallen in price, or such a man had not become bankrupt. The bereavement comes : nature sheds bitter tears a while, and nature by degrees grows easy again. All this, what is it, and what is the degree of its guilt ? It is specifically atheism : it is to be " without God in the world." The Father of our spirits touches us by certain instruments which are at his command ; and we refuse to look up and learn from the signs on his countenance.

We forbid not the consideration of instruments and secondary causes. Let them be observed, and the remedies which they suggest applied ; but do not stop there. Do not finish off with these dumb messengers whom the Lord sends ; they are sent for the very purpose of inviting you to a conference, secret and personal, with himself. When you smart under the chastening, acknowledge the Lord. He is not far from every one of us. He speaks to us as to children. He means thereby to represent himself as a Father. In that character he alternately visits us with mercy and judgment. He gives us life, and breath, and all things ; he also at other times rebukes and bereaves. He takes it ill to be overlooked in either capacity. He is a jealous God. He will not allow idols to intercept the homage of his creatures; so also he is jealous, and his jealousy will burn like fire, if you give to his servants, whether diseases, or stormy winds, or mercantile convulsions, the regard which is due to himself—your regard when success makes you happy, or when grief weighs you down. Do not meet sorrow by a mere hardihood of nature. Let your heart flow down under trouble, for this is human: let it rise up also to God, for this is divine.

2. " Faint not." This is the opposite extreme. Do not be dissolved, as it were—taken down and taken to pieces by the stroke. Do not sink into despondency and despair. You should retain presence of mind, and exercise all your faculties. Both extremes, when traced to their fountain-head, spring from the same cause— a want of looking to God in the time of trouble. If the bold would see God in his afflictions, he would not despise; if the timid would see God in them, he would not faint. As in other cases, the two opposite errors branch off originally from the same path, and converge upon it again. Truth goes straight over the hill Difficulty between. Godliness is profitable unto all things: it humbles the proud, and lifts up the lowly; it softens the hard, and gives firmness to the feeble.

The middle way is the path of safety. Be impressed by the stroke of the Lord's hand, but not crushed under it. Let your own confidence go, but lay hold on the arm of the Lord, that you may be kept from falling. Let the affliction shut you out from other helps, and up to the help that is laid on the Mighty One.

" Whom the Lord loveth he chasteneth." We must not suppose from this that the trouble which a man endures on earth is the mark and measure of God's love. It is not a law of the kingdom of heaven that those who suffer most from God's hand are furthest advanced in his favour. Hitherto we have considered the afflictive stroke simply as a suffering; but it is specifically in " chastening" that the love lies, and all suffering is not chastening. It means fatherly correction for the child's good; the word indeed signifies " education."

God, the ruler of the universe, permits suffering to fall on all men indiscriminately : but the God of mercy stands by to make the suffering love's instrument in training every dear child. The same stroke may fall on two men, and be in one case judgment, in the other love. "In vain have I smitten your children : they received no correction" (Jer. ii. 30). All were "smitten," but they only obtained paternal correction who in the spirit of adoption "received" it as such. You may prune branches lying withered on the ground, and also branches living in the vine. In the two cases the operation and instrument are precisely alike; but the operation on this branch has no result, and the operation on that branch produces fruitfulness, because of a difference in the place and condition of the branches on which the operation was performed.

In his comment on this text, Paul charges the Hebrew Christians with having "forgotten" it. He lays it expressly at their door as a fault, that this word of God was not hidden in their hearts, and ready in their memories. It is expected of Christians, in New Testament times, that they know, and remember, and apply the lesson of the Old Testament. When they forgot it, He who spoke it at first, repeated it again, accompanied with a complaint that their forgetfulness made the repetition necessary.

The warning has often been given, and it is needed yet, that terror in time of trouble may be no true repentance. The profligate, the vain, or the worldly has been laid low on a sick-bed. So near has death come, that the very shadow of the judgment-seat fell cold and dark over his heart, and took all the light out of his former joys. He grieves now that he has sinned so much. He resolves that if he recover he will fear God, and seek a Saviour. After quivering for a time between death and life, he gets the turn toward the side of time, and enters on another lease of life. The breezes of summer, and the exercise of returning strength, refresh again his pallid cheek, and rekindle his sunken eye. The affliction is over. The fear of death departs, and with it the repentance which it had brought. He returns to his pleasures again. He brings disgrace upon the holy name of Jesus, and provokes God to give him over. He deals by the Almighty as little children do by ghosts—cower down in breathless terror of them at night, and laugh at them when the daylight returns. He "will mock when their fear cometh !"

But unspeakably precious to dear children are the corrections of a Father's love, all these abuses notwithstanding. It is one of the finest triumphs of faith, when, in time of affliction, a Christian gets fresh confidence in a Saviour's love. How sweet it is to lay your besetting sins and characteristic shortcomings beneath the descending stroke, and count it so much gain when they are crushed! It may well encourage a believer to be patient in the furnace, to see that some of the dross is separating, and coming away. Not a drop too much will fall into the cup of the redeemed, and it will all be over soon. Lord, pity our weakness! Lord, increase our faith!

Making a Fortune
(Proverbs 3:13-15)

"Happy is the man that findeth wisdom, and the man that getteth understanding. For the merchandise of it is better than the merchandise of silver, and the gain thereof than fine gold. She is more precious than rubies: and all the things thou canst desire are not to be compared unto her."

WISDOM and understanding should be received here in the same sense as that in which they occurred and were expounded in the second chapter. It is wisdom in its highest view; wisdom in regard to all the parts of man's being, and all the periods of his destiny. This wisdom is embodied in the person of Christ, as light is treasured in the sun, but thence it streams forth in all directions, and glances back from every object on which it falls. He is the wisdom of God, and by the Spirit in the Scriptures, he is made unto us wisdom. In him the glory that excelleth is; and when our eyes are opened we shall behold it there, as the glory of the Only-begotten of the Father, full of grace and truth.

Saving wisdom is a thing to be "found" and "gotten:" it is not required of us that we create it. We could not plan. we could not execute a way of righteous redemption for sinners. We could not bring God's favour down to compass men about, and yet leave his holiness untainted as it is in heaven. This is all his own doing; and it is all done. All things are now ready. When we are saved, it is by "finding" a salvation, already complete, and being ourselves "complete in him." But while we are not required to make a salvation, we are expected to seek the salvation which has been provided and brought near. The command of God is attached to his promise, and together they constitute his blessed invitation, "Seek, and ye shall find." It will be a fearful thing to come short of eternal life, thus completed and offered, from sheer want of willingness to seek. "How shall we escape if we neglect so great salvation?"

Understanding is a thing to be gotten. It comes not in sparks from our own intellect in collision with other human minds. It is a light from heaven, above the brightness of this world's sun. The gift is free, and an unspeakable gift it is. Bear in mind that religion is not all and only an anxious fearful seeking: it is a getting too, and a glad enjoying. It is blessed even to hunger for righteousness; but a greater blessing awaits the hungerer, he shall be filled. The seeker may be anxious, but the finder is glad. " Happy is the man that findeth." It is a great glory to God, and a great benefit to a careless world, when a follower of Christ so finds salvation, as to rejoice in the treasure. When the new song comes from the mouth of the delighted possessor, many shall observe the change, and shall fear, and trust in the Lord (Psalm xl. 3). The joy of the Lord becomes a disciple's strength, both to resist evil and to do good. Those who, by finding a Saviour, have been themselves admitted into peace and joy, have the firmest foothold, and the strongest arm, to " save with fear " when it becomes needful to pull a neighbour out of the fire (Jude 23).

Wisdom is compared and contrasted with other possessions; it is "merchandise." There is a most pleasant excitement in the prosecution of mercantile enterprise; it gives full play to all the faculties. Those who prosecute it as a class have their wits more sharpened than other sections of the community. The plans are contrived, and the calculations made; the goods are selected, purchased, loaded, and dispatched; and then there is a watching for favourable winds. After all is clear at the custom-house, and the ship beyond his view, the owner left on shore may be seen to turn frequently round as he walks leisurely in the evening from his counting-house to his dwelling. He is looking at the vane on the steeple, or the smoke from the chimneys, or any object that will indicate the direction of the wind. His mind is fixed on the probable position of the ship, and his imagination vividly pictures its progress down the channel. He strains mentally after it, as if he could thereby aid its speed. If a photograph of his soul could be taken at the moment, it would be found that his spirit bent towards the distant ship, as the keen curler seems by his attitude to direct the course of the stone that he has launched until it reach the mark. Next day he scans the newspapers to learn whether similar exports are flowing to the same market. Every succeeding day some new aspect of the object presents itself, until the result of the adventure is known. He makes much of it, and so he should; whatever a man does, he should do well.

But meantime, what of the merchandise for a more distant country than that to which his goods are going—what of the traffic for eternity? Are there no careful calculations, no instinctive longings, no vivid imaginings, as to its condition and progress? Are your minds never filled with glad anticipations of its success, or anxious fear of its miscarriage! Do you watch those symptoms which indicate its prosperity or decay? This merchandise is better and more gainful than any other. The world contains not any such promising field for speculation. It opens up a richer and surer market than any port of time. In that region there is never any glut. He to whom you make consignment is ever faithful. What you commit to him he will keep until that day. He is wise that winneth souls; his own first, and then others. There is no gain to be compared with this: it is a treasure that cannot be taken away. Thieves cannot penetrate its storehouse; moth and rust do not corrupt the goods of those who are rich towards God.

It often happens that a merchant amasses a large fortune by the labour of many years, and then loses all by a single unfortunate speculation. Some dark tales hang on these catastrophes—too dark for telling here. When such a crash comes, the wonder of the neighbourhood, passing from mouth to mouth, is, why did he not lay up his fortune, when it was realized, in some place of safety? But, alas, where is that place? It lies not within the horizon of time. All the riches that can be laid up here will soon take wings and fly away. If we do not invest in heaven, we shall soon be poor; for the earth, and the things therein, will be burnt up. The prosperous merchant must soon put on "the robe which is made without pockets;" and he is destitute indeed, if he have not the true riches in eternity before him, for all other possessions he must leave behind.

By our own lips, and our own deeds shall we be condemned; if, being all energy for time, we be all indolence for eternity—if we fill our memory with mammon, and forget God.

A Lengthened Day and a Pleasant Path
(Proverbs 3:16, 17)

"Length of days is in her right hand. . . . . Her ways are ways of pleasantness, and all her paths are peace."

I T is certainly not a uniform experience, that a man lives long in proportion as he lives well. Such a rule would obviously not be suitable to the present dispensation. It is true that all wickedness acts as a shortener of life, and all goodness as its lengthener ; but other elements enter, and complicate the result, and slightly veil the interior law. If the law were according to a simple calculation in arithmetic, "the holiest liver the longest liver," and conversely, "the more wicked the life the earlier its close ;" if this, unmixed, unmodified, were the law, the moral government of God would be greatly impeded, if not altogether subverted. Wickedness shortens life; but God's government is moral—it is not a lump of mere materialism. He will have men to choose goodness for his sake and its own ; therefore a slight veil is cast over its present profitableness. Some apparent anomalies are permitted to try them that are upon the earth. Here is an example that often occurs. A stray drunkard lives to a great age: all the neighbourhood know it: it is trumpeted at every carousal: the hoary debauchee, who has survived all the saints of a parish, is triumphantly pointed to by younger bacchanals as evidence that a merry life will keep death long at bay. On the supposition that a certain measure of power were conceded to Satan, he could not lay it out in any way that would secure a greater revenue to his kingdom, than to give a long term of life to one profligate in every county. By means of that one decoy, he might lure a hundred youths to an early grave and a lost eternity. Individual cases of long life in wickedness are observed, and fastened on, and exaggerated by the vicious, to prove to themselves that their course is not a shorter road to the grave ; and yet it is a law—a law of God—in constant operation, that every violation of moral law saps, so far, the foundations of the natural life.

It is most interesting, and at the same time unspeakably sad, to observe how much more easily satisfied men are with evidence when they are about to risk their souls, than when they propose to risk their money. Investigations have been made of late years into the effect of intemperate habits on the length of life, not with a view to moral lessons at all, but simply in search of a basis for pecuniary transactions. It is expressly intimated that occasional drinkers are included in the calculations as well as habitual drunkards, and the tables exhibit among them a frightfully high rate of mortality. Out of a given number of persons, and in a given number of years, where 110 of the general population would have died, there died of the drinkers 357. Of persons between the ages of twenty-one and thirty, the mortality among drinkers was five times greater than that of the general community.* Life Assurance Societies proceed upon these facts and laws. A young man will risk his life and his soul on the lie that his fast life is consistent with a long life; but let him try to effect a life assurance on himself, and he will find that the capitalist will not intrust his money on such a frail security.

Drunkenness is selected by the agents of assurance societies for their calculations, and mentioned here for illustration, not that it is more sinful before God, or more hurtful to life than other vices, but simply because it is of such a palpable character that it can be more easily observed and accurately estimated. Others, if human eyes could trace them, would give the same result; but they are trackless, like a serpent on the rock, or an eagle in the air.

We are accustomed to the idea that the end of a good man's course is happy. We are well aware that when the pilgrim gets home he will have no more sorrow; but does not the journey lie through a wilderness from the moment when the captive bursts his bonds till he reach the overflowing Jordan, and, in the track of the High Priest, passing through the parted flood, plant his foot firmly on the promised land? It does; it traverses the desert all its length, and yet the path is pleasant notwithstanding. To the honour of the Lord be it spoken, and for the comfort of

* Paper by Mr. Neison, in "Athenæum."

his people, not the home only, but also the way thither, is pleasantness and peace. Those who have not trod it count it dreary. Those who see what it wants, and have not tasted what it is, naturally think that however safe the home to which it leads the traveller at last, it must make him in the meantime of all men most miserable. Those who abide in Egypt, by its flesh-pots and its river, may pity the host of Israel marching through a land not sown ; but Israel, in the desert though they be, get their bread and their water sure from day to day; all the more sweet to their taste that the water leaps in their sight at the Father's bidding from a barren rock, and the bread is rained from heaven around their tents. The pilgrim who flees from Egypt at God's command, and closely follows then the guiding pillar, will go safe and sweetly over. The young lion may suffer hunger, but they who wait upon the Lord shall not lack any good. In the keeping of his commandments there is great reward. The path is peace, although storms rage all around it, if there be peace in the heart of the traveller. The peace of God keeping the heart within will beam out on the untrodden way, and gild its jagged sides with gladness. The path of the justified is like the shining light: from the first struggling twilight it grows in beauty until it culminate in day. The path is peace: eye hath not seen, nor ear heard, what the home will be.

Wisdom Making and Managing Worlds
(Proverbs 3:19-20)

"The Lord by wisdom hath founded the earth ; by understanding hath he established the heavens. By his knowledge the depths are broken up, and the clouds drop down the dew."

THESE are specimens of Wisdom's mighty work on worlds,—these are the well-known tracks of God's goings in creation. There is a closer connection between creation and redemption than human philosophy is able to discover, or unbelieving philosophy is willing to own. The breach that sin has made in the moral hemisphere of the duplicate universe hides from our view the grand unity of the Creator's work. It is one plan from the beginning. The physical and the moral departments are the constituent parts of the completed whole. Throughout the present week (a thousand years is with the Lord as one day) creation labours painfully, by reason of a rent that runs through its spiritual side : provision has been made for healing it; and even now the process is going on. These labour days sprung from a preceding holy rest, and they will issue in another Sabbath soon. Creation is groaning now for its promised rest : when it comes, the material world will again be a perfect platform for the display of its Maker's goodness. When the earth is made new, it will be the dwelling-place of righteousness. The material and the spiritual, like body and soul, each fearfully made, and together wonderfully united, will be the perfect manifestation of divine wisdom and love.

A glance is gotten here into the circulation of the world. "The depths are broken up, and the clouds drop down dew !" He has instituted laws whereby the deep is divided. One portion rises to the sky, and thence drops down again to refresh the earth. " How wonderful, O Lord, are thy works; in wisdom hast thou made them all !"

By his knowledge, too, another depth is broken up. The wicked, a whole worldful, lie outspread beneath his eye, "like the troubled sea, when it cannot rest" (Isa. lvii. 20). What wisdom can separate the pure from the impure, and draw from that unholy mass a multitude, whom no man can number, to be fit inhabitants of heaven? God's wisdom has done this. Christ, set in the firmament of revelation, pours his beams of love upon the lost, and thereby wins them out from their impurity, and upward unto himself. There is a double upbreaking of these depths, and a double separation of the pure from the vile; the one is personal, the other public.

In an individual there is a great sea of sin. When the love of Christ comes in power, it dissolves the terrible cementing by which the soul and sin were run into one. Forthwith there is a breaking up and a separation. The man throws off himself; the new man puts off the old, and the old man puts on the new. The ransomed soul is severed from what seemed its very being, sin, and tends upward toward the Head. Sins trouble him still, and keep him low, but he is delivered from the law of sin.

In the whole community of the fallen there is a breaking up. The wisdom of God is rending asunder things that sin had pressed into one. The word of invitation is, "Come out of her, my people;" and there is power with the word. A separating process is going on over all the surface of sin's sea. This kingdom cometh not with observation. It is now an unseen thing within the separated; but a time is coming when the separation shall be as manifest, and the distance as wide, as that which now divides these raging waves of the sea from the white sunlit clouds of glory that have been lifted up, and now congregate and culminate in majestic beauty, as if around the throne of God. The white-robed multitude that do in very deed stand round it, were drawn from a sea of sorrow and sin; for they came out of great tribulation, and their robes were not white until they were washed in the blood of the Lamb.

Confidence in God the True Safeguard
from Temptation
(Proverbs 3:26)

"The Lord shall be thy confidence, and shall keep thy foot from being taken."

BEWARE of mistakes here. Let us not deceive ourselves by words without meaning. Do not say God is your confidence, if he be only your dread. An appalling amount of hypocrisy exists in Christendom, and passes current for devotion. He who is in Himself most worthy, and has done most for us, is often more disliked than any other being ; and, as if this ingratitude were not enough, men double the sin by professing that they have their confidence in Him.

I have observed that seagoing ships do not trust to themselves in the windings of a river. Where they are hemmed in between rock and quicksand, grazing now the one and now the other, they take care to have a steam-tug, both to bear them forward and guide them aright. They hang implicitly upon its power ; they make no attempt at independent action. But I have also observed, that as soon as they get clear of the narrows—as soon as they have attained a good offing and an open sea, they heave off, and hoist their own sails. They never want a steamer until they come to narrow waters again.

Such is the trust in God which the unreconciled experience. In distress they are fain to lean on the Almighty. While they are in the narrows, death seeming near on every side, conscious that they have no power and no skill, they would hang on the help of a Deliverer. " My God, we know thee " (Hos. viii. 2), is then their cry. Most devout they are, and most earnest. At every hour of their day and night they are exercised in spirit about pleasing God, and gaining his help in their need. The line of their dependence seems ever tight by their constant leaning. But when they begin to creep out of these shoals of life—when the path opens up wide and clear and safe again, they heave off, and throw themselves on their own resources. They become a God unto themselves, whenever dangers are out of sight. Forthwith and henceforth they live without God in the world, until they are driven into straits again. Then they remember God and pray, as a distressed ship makes signals for help when she is entering a tortuous channel (Isa. xxvi. 16 ; Ps. lxxviii. 34–37). This is not to have confidence in God ; this is to provoke Him to anger. He deserves a soul's confidence, and desires it.

Confidence in God is not to be attained by a wish whenever you please. You may, when you like, say, " Lord, I trust in Thee," but to make the just Judge his confidence, does not lie in the power of a sinner's will. There is a way of reaching it ; and the way is open, and all are welcome, but no man can reach it except by that way. Coming through Christ, and being accepted in the beloved, you will indeed confide in God ; but this is to be turned from darkness to light, to pass from death unto life. When any man enters by this way into favour, he will be ready to confess that it is the Lord's doing, and marvellous in his eyes.

It is this confidence that has power for good on the life. It is not terror, but trust, that becomes a safeguard from the dominion of sin. It is a peculiar and touching promise that God, when He becomes your confidence, " will keep your foot from being taken." Here incidentally the terrible truth glances out, that snares are laid for the traveller's feet in all the paths of life, in all the haunts of men. Our adversary, like a roaring lion, goeth about seeking whom he may devour. Alas, multitudes are entrapped, like birds in the fowler's snare. Many who set forth hopefully in the morning of life are caught ere they have gone far in some of these pit-falls, and bound over unto the second death. It is a fearful thing to pass by and hear their screaming, and have no power to help.

In my childhood, I sometimes saw rabbits that damaged the corn-fields, caught in snares. My first experience of the process melted me, and the scene is not effaced from my memory yet. The creature was caught by the foot. It was a captive, but living. Oh the agonized look it cast on us when we approached it ! The scared, helpless, despairing look of that living creature sank deep in the sensitive powers of my nature. As a child, I could not conceive of any more touching thrilling appeal than the soft rolling eyes of that dumb captive ; but " when I became a man," and entered both on the experience of the world and the ministry of the word, I met with scenes that cast these earlier emotions down into the place of " childish things." Soon after I began to go my rounds as a watchman on my allotted field, I fell upon a youth (and the same experience has been several times repeated since) who but lately was bounding hopefully along, bidding fair for the better land, and seeming to lead others on, caught by the foot in a snare. I went up to him, surprised to find him halting so ; but, ah, the look, the glare from his eyes, soon told that the immortal was fast in the devil's toils. He lived ; but he was held. All his companions passed on, and soon were out of sight, while he lay beating himself on the ground. He lives ; but it is in chains. The chains have sunk into his flesh. They ran through the marrow of his bones, and are wrapped around his soul, filthy as firm, firm as filthly. Oh, wretched man, who shall deliver him ? Not I ; not any man. We must pass on, and leave him. The same voice that wrenched from Death his prisoner is needed to give liberty to this captive. Only one word can we utter in presence of such a case : " Nothing is impossible with God." Having uttered it, we pass on with a sigh.

Cure in such a case is difficult—is all but impossible ; is there any method of prevention ? Yes : the Lord thy confidence will keep thy foot from being taken ; the Lord your dread will not do it, almighty though He be. Many who have an agonizing fear of a just God in their conscience, plunge deeper even than others into abominable sins. It is the peace of God in the heart that has power to keep the feet out of evil in the path of life. " He that hath this hope in Him, purifieth himself even as He is pure." " Sin shall not have dominion over you ;" and the reason is added—" for ye are not under the law, but under grace" (Rom. vi. 14). A son has wantonly offended an affectionate father, and fled from his face. After many days of sullen distance, the prodigal returns, and at nightfall approaches his father's dwelling. He is standing outside, shivering in the blast, yet afraid to enter, and meet the frown of an injured parent. Some abandoned youths, companions of his guilt, pass by, and hail him. By a little coaxing, they break his resolution of repentance, and carry him off to their haunts of vice. It was easy to sweep him off when they found him trembling in terror outside. He was like chaff; and iniquities, like the wind, carried him away. But if the youth had entered before the tempters came up, and the father, instead of frowning or upbraiding, had fallen on his neck and kissed him, setting him in the circle of brothers and sisters, and showering on him the manifold affections of a united family and a happy home—and if the same godless band had been passing then, and had beckoned him to join their revelry, they would not have succeeded so easily. The soul of this youth is like a ship at anchor now, and the current does not carry him away. Specifically, it is "the God of peace" who will bruise Satan under our feet (Rom. xvi. 20). Those who stand outside, with just as much religion as makes them afraid, are easily taken in the tempter's snare : the reconciled whom the Father has welcomed back with weeping, has now another joy, and that joy becomes his strength : " his heart is fixed, trusting in the Lord " (Ps. cxii. 7).

The Right Thing Done at the Right Time

(Proverbs 3:27, 28)

"Withhold not good from them to whom it is due, when it is in the power of thine hand to do it. Say not unto thy neighbour, Go, and come again, and to-morrow I will give; when thou hast it by thee."

IT is in general the law of righteousness between man and man; do justly to all, and do so now; pay your debts, and pay them to-day, lest you should lack the means to-morrow.

But it is probable that the precept has special reference to the law of love. Every possessor of the good things, either of this life or the next, is bound by the command of the giver to distribute a portion to those who have none. To withhold from any one that which is due to him, is plainly dishonest. But here an interesting inquiry occurs ; how far and in what sense the poor have a right to maintenance out of the labour and wealth of the community ? The answer is, the really poor have a right to support by the law of God, and the debt is binding on the conscience of all who have the means ; but it is not, and ought not to be, a right which the poor as such can make good at a human tribunal against the rich. The possessors of this world's good are not at liberty to withhold the portion of the poor : it is not left to their choice : it is a matter settled by law : disobedience is a direct offence against the great Law-giver. But the poor have not a right which they can plead and enforce at a human tribunal. The acknowledgment of such a right would tend to anarchy. The poor are placed in the power of the rich, and the rich are under law to God. It is true that in heathen and other degraded countries the poor perish, but it does not follow that any other principle would place them in a better condition. Whatever may be the law, the possessors in every country must administer it ; and so there cannot, in the nature of things, be any other law laid upon them than the law of love. They are made answerable to God in their own conscience for their conduct to the poor; and if that do not prevail to secure kindness, nothing else will. If they make light of a duty that may be pleaded at the judgment-seat of God, much more will they make light of it as against the poor who cannot enforce their own demands. The assessment for the poor, in a highly artificial state of society, is not the concession of their right to maintenance exigible against the rich by the laws of men: it is a mere expedient by those who give to equalize and systematize the disbursement of charity.

It seems to be the purpose of God in the present dispensation to do good to his creatures, by the inequality of their condition. The design of the providential arrangement is to produce gentle, humble, contented thankfulness on the one side, and open-hearted, open-handed liberality on the other. If God had not intended to exercise these graces, he probably would have made and kept men, as to external comforts, all in a state of equality. But this would not have been the best condition for human beings, or for any portion of them. Absolute equality of condition may do for cattle, but not for men. It appears that the same all-wise Disposer has arranged that there shall be great and manifold diversities of elevation in the surface of the material earth, and in the condition of its intelligent inhabitants. For similar purposes of wisdom and goodness have both classes of inequalities been introduced and maintained. Levellers, who should propose to improve upon this globe, by bringing down every high place and exalting every low, so that no spot of all its surface should remain higher than another, would certainly destroy it as a habitation for man; the waters would cover it. In attempting to make a level earth, they would make a universal sea. But the mischief cannot be done; the mountains are too firmly rooted to be removed by any power but that of the world's Maker.

We suspect that the other class of levellers aim at a change as perilous; and our consolation is, that it is equally impossible. We believe that for the present dispensation, the inequalities in the condition of individuals and families is as needful to the general prosperity of the whole, as the diversity of hill and valley in the surface of the globe; and we believe, also, that the arrangement is as firmly fixed. It would be as easy to level the world as its inhabitants. What may be in store for the earth and man in the future we know not ; there may be a time when the globe shall be smooth like an ivory ball, but then there must be no more sea : and if ever there come a time when all men shall be and abide equal, it must be that time when there shall be no more sea of sin to overflow them. If ever there come a time when there shall be no more masters and servants, it must be the time when all shall serve one Lord.

In many ways society is consolidated and strengthened by inequalities. He who made man, male and female, receptive weakness on one side and protecting strength on the other, welding both by the glow of love into a completer one, has thereby made the mass of humanity hold more firmly together. He has also provided diagonal girders running in a different direction—the relations of rich and poor, master and servant, in order to interlace the several portions of humanity more firmly into each other, and so make society as a whole strong enough to ride out the hurricanes of a tempestuous time.

" When it is in the power of thine hand to do it ;" a touching memorial this. Many who have cherished sound principles, and desired to do good, have permitted the time irrevocably to pass. When they had it in their power to do good they procrastinated, and now the means have fled. This is a bitter reflection in old age. There is only one way by which any man may make sure that such a bitterness shall not be his, and that is by doing now what his hand finds to do. If it is in the power of your hand this year to do good, it may not be so next year. The abundance may be taken from you, or you taken from your abundance. The secret of a happy life is to set the house in order, and keep it in order. Above all, keep as few good intentions hovering about as possible. They are like ghosts haunting a dwelling. The way to lay them is to find bodies for them. When they are embodied in substantial deeds they are no longer dangerous.

But there is yet another way in which it may be beyond the power of thine hand to do a duty to-morrow which has been deferred to-day. The hand has much power and skill, but it cannot move except at the command of the will. If the willingness of the heart were conclusively frozen up within, the hand, which is merely the heart's servant, can do nothing. When the rich refuse to do the duties of the day with their means, they are in danger of falling into the miser's madness. When you have contracted a diseased love of money which you do not use, it is not in the power of the hand to do the plainest duty. The man who loves money cannot part with it : he has let his opportunity pass. On the one side, there may be lavishness without generosity—the mere habit of letting money run out like water : on the other hand, there may be close carefulness without the virtue of frugality —the mere habit of holding the grip. Both conditions are most dismal. There is a tendency to fall into the one snare or the other. The way in the midst is a strait way : it is not easy to walk in it. If we begin early, and keep going, the work will become easy at length.

Observe how remarkably specific is the command not to postpone a gift. We ought to make up our minds, and act. Those who have the means of doing good in the community at the present day, are much tried, and should look well to their path. There are many good objects pressing, and as in all such cases, the very multitude of the good notes suggests and makes room for the circulation of bad ones, caution and discrimination are not only permitted, they are peremptorily required. The injunction of the text is a most useful rule in one department of this difficulty. If we have not the means, or if the object be unworthy, there ought to be a distinct declinature. A clear, unambiguous negative is, in many transactions, of incalculable worth. It is no man's duty to give to every one who asks, or to any all that he asks. There is such a thing as giving when you should not, from lack of courage to say No. Further, when the object is not worthy, and your mind is clear, and you determine to do nothing, it would be profitable both to yourself and others to say so at once. It is not altogether straightforward to another, or safe for yourself, to announce a postponement if you have resolved on a refusal. Softness may lead to sin. But the worst of all is when the cause is good, when you are convinced of its goodness, when the means are in your power, and yet you put the pleader off. Even though you should afterwards give, you have lost the blessing. God loves a cheerful giver; and though you have given, you gave with a grudge. When the fruit needs a violent pulling to wrench it from the tree, the tree itself is torn in the process.

The Curse and the Blessing upon the House
(Proverbs 3:33)

"The curse of the Lord is in the house of the wicked: but he blesseth the habitation
of the just."

W E have often, in the course of these expositions, had occasion to point out the effects of sin upon the person
who sins. Here is yet another of its bitter fruits : it
brings a curse on the house. Our interests are more closely connected with each other than we are able to observe, or willing to
allow. The welfare of one is largely dependent on the well-doing
of another. Let every wicked man learn here, that over and above
the ruin of his own soul, his sins bring a curse on his wife and
children, his neighbours and friends. Such is God's government,
that you cannot live in sin, any more than in smallpox or the
plague, without involving others in the danger. For wise purposes, it has been so ordained. This law is calculated to lay an
additional restraint upon a wayward spirit. A man, reckless of
his own character and fate, might be ready to act out the daring
maxim, "Let us eat and drink, for to-morrow we die." When
pity for himself did not arrest him, he might be arrested when he
saw that his own abandoned life would curse his dwelling. Doubtless this law of the Lord has been bit and bridle to hold in a man,
who would have burst through all other restraints. In blind,
despairing rage, he might pull down the pillars upon his own
unhappy head : yet when he feels his little ones clinging to his
knees, and his wife leaning on his breast, he may stand in awe,
and turn and live. "Fear and sin not :" the providence of God
gives terrible momentum to that sharp word. In addition to the
weight of divine authority upon the conscience, all the force of
nature's instincts is applied to drive it home. When the fear of
perdition to himself has not power enough, the laws of Providence
throw in all his house as a make-weight to increase the motive

He is held back from evil by all that he ever felt of tenderness in his youth, or feels of compassion still : and if, in the last resort, these weights avail not to keep him from sinning, they will be effectual in adding to his punishment.

This dark curse hanging over the dwelling of the wicked, is balanced by the blessing that falls on the habitation of the just. Here is pleasant work, and plenty of wages. Trust in Christ, and serve Him ; besides the saving of your own soul, you will be a blessing to your habitation. How sweet the privilege of being the parents of your children both for this life and the life to come ! And not only the parents—every one in the house may become the channel of blessing from on high. If God has a child in a family, he will have many an errand there. You who are fathers know how frequently you find occasion to visit the house where your own dear child is boarded out for education. Our Father in heaven so visits his own, in whatever habitation their education is going on; and all the house will get the benefit. The disciples of Jesus are a preserving salt, even when the mass preserved by their presence are unconscious of the boon. To be good is the shortest and surest way to do good. Jonathan in his lifetime was dear to David; and therefore Jonathan's son, an orphan and a cripple, sat daily at the royal table. If you be the King's friend, your children will get the benefit in some hour of need. It is a noble position, and should encourage one to bear trials with patience, to be the channel between a house and heaven, bearing them up to God, and getting down from him the blessing.

Precept and Example

(Proverbs 4:10, 11)

" Hear, O my son, and receive my sayings. . . . . I have taught thee in the way of wisdom: I have led thee in right paths."

IT is a great matter for a parent, if he is able to say to his grown son, "I have taught thee in the way of wisdom; I have led thee in right paths." Teaching and leading are closely allied, but not identical. It is possible, and common, to have the first in large measure, where the second is wanting. They are two elements which together make up a whole. With both, education in a family will go prosperously on: where one is wanting, it will be halting and ineffectual. Many a parent who acquits himself well in the department of teaching his children, fails miserably in the department of leading them in the right path. It is easier to tell another the right way, than to walk in it yourself. To lead your child in right paths implies that you go in them before him. Here lies the reason why so many parents practically fail to give their children a good education. Only a godly man can bring up his child for God. It is not uncommon to find men who are themselves vicious, desiring to have their children educated in virtue. Infidels sometimes take measures to have Christianity taught to their children. Many will do evil; few dare to teach it to their own offspring. This is the unwilling homage which the evil are constrained to pay to goodness.

Great is the effect when parents consistently and steadfastly go before their children, giving them a daily example of their daily precepts; but to teach the family spiritual things, while the life of the teacher is carnal, is both painful and fruitless. A man cannot walk with one leg, although the limb be in robust health; more especially if the other limb, instead of being altogether wanting, is hanging on him, and trailing after him dead. In this case it is impossible to get quit of the impediment; it will not off. The only way of getting relief from its weight is to get it made alive. An example of some kind, parents must exhibit in their families : if it be not such as to help, it will certainly hinder the education of the young. God, in the providential laws, permits no neutrality in the family : there, you must either be for or against him.

One of the broadest and best defined experiences that passed under my observation, and was imprinted on my memory in early youth, was that of a family whose father stood high above all his neighbours in religious profession and gifts, and yet returned from market drunk as often as he had the means. The sons of that family all turned out ill. Nothing is impossible with God ; but it would have been indeed a miracle of mercy if these young men, who were accustomed from childhood to see in their own father a lofty spiritual profession wedded to the vilest vice, had themselves, as they grew up, lived soberly, and righteously, and godly in the world.

Hold Fast

(Proverbs 4:13)

"Take fast hold of instruction; let her not go; keep her, for she is thy life."

OFTEN a ship's crew at sea are obliged suddenly to betake
themselves to their boats and abandon the sinking ship.
The case of an American whale ship in the South Seas,
lately reported, will serve as the basis of our parable. The huge
leviathan of the deep, wounded by the art of man, ran out the distance of a mile by way of getting a run-race, and thence came on
with incredible velocity against the devoted ship. Such was the
shock that she instantly began to fill, and was gradually settling
down. The sea was calm: there was opportunity for effort, but
not time for delay. They were not only far from land, but far
from the usual track of ships on the sea. In the dreary region of
the antarctic circle, they might wander a whole year, and see no
sail on the desolate horizon. There was little probability of rescue
until they should regain those latitudes through which the thoroughfare of nations runs. The word was given; all hands went to
work, and soon all the sea-worthy boats were loaded to the gun-
wale with the prime necessaries of life. The deck was now nearly
level with the water, and the boats shoved off for safety. After
they had pulled a hundred yards away, two resolute men leaped
from the boats into the sea, and made towards the ship. They
reach it while still afloat, and disappear down a hatchway. In
a minute they emerge again, bearing something in their hands.
As they leap into the water the ship goes down; the men are separated from each other and their burden, in the whirlpool that gathers
over the sinking hull. They do not seem to consult their own
safety. They remain in that dangerous eddy, until they grasp
again the object which they had carried over the ship's side.
Holding it fast, they are seen at length bearing away to their comrades in the boat. What do these strong swimmers carry, for they

seem to value it more than life? It is the compass! It had been left behind, and was remembered almost too late. Now they have taken fast hold of it, and will not let it go. Whatever they lose, they will at all hazards keep it, for "it is their life."

When shall we see souls, shipwrecked on the sea of time, take and keep such hold of the truth as it is in Jesus, because it is their life? When will men learn to count that the soul's danger in the flood of wrath is as real, as the body's danger on a material ocean? When will men begin to make real effort for the eternal life, such as they make to preserve the present life when it is in danger? There is not an atom of hypocrisy about a man when he is in instant danger of drowning or starvation. He lays about him with an energy and a reality that brook no delay, and regard no appearances. If we could truly believe that the life of our souls is forfeited by sin, that they must be saved now or lost for ever, and that there is none other name given under heaven among men to save them, than the name of Jesus; then there would be a corresponding reality in our cleaving to the Saviour. Although, in a sense, we seek the right things, all may be lost by reversing the order in which, by divine prescription, they should be sought. The rule is, Seek first the kingdom of God, and then it is intimated that other things may be innocently "added." Those who seek first these other things as their heart's portion, may also strive earnestly to attain the kingdom; but their labour is lost, because they do not "strive lawfully." "Lord, what wouldst thou have me to do," and how wouldst thou have me to do it? "Send out thy light and thy truth: let them lead me."

The Path of the Just

(Proverbs 4:18, 19)

" The path of the just is as the shining light, that shineth more and more unto the perfect day. The way of the wicked is as darkness: they know not at what they stumble."

THE essentials of a just man's character have been in all ages the same. The just in every dispensation have lived by faith, and walked with God: they have hoped for his salvation, and done his commandments (Psalm cxix. 166) : they believe, and obey ; they are bought with a price, and glorify God.

The path, the life course of such a man, is like the shining light. I do not think that the path of the justified is compared to the course of the sun, from the period of his appearance in the morning to the time of his meridian height. The sun is an emblem, not of the justified, but of the Justifier. I have always felt uneasy in hearing the life of a believer likened to the sun's course from horizon to zenith. The comparison does not fit. An effort to adjust the analogy either spoils its beauty, or gives a glory to man which is not his due. That grandest object in the visible creation is used as an emblem of the Highest One, and for his service it should be reserved. Christ alone is the source of Light: Christians are only its reflectors. The just are those whom the Sun of Righteousness shines upon. When they come beneath his healing beams, their darkness flies away. They who once were darkness are light now, but it is " in the Lord."

The new life of the converted is like the morning light. At first it seems an uncertain struggle between the darkness and the dawn. It quivers long in the balance. At one moment the watcher thinks, surely yonder is a streak of light: the next, he says with a sigh, it was an illusion: night yet reigns over all. When the contest begins, however, the result is not doubtful, although it may for a time appear so. The first and feeblest streaks of light that come mingling with the darkness, have issued from the sun; and the sun that sent these harbingers, though distant yet, is steadily advancing. Ere long the doubt will vanish, and morning will be unequivocally declared. Once begun, it shineth more and more unto the perfect day; and it is perfect day when the sun has risen, as compared with the sweet but feeble tints of earliest dawning. Sometimes there are irregularities and backgoings. Clouds deep and dark creep in between the sun and the world's surface. After the morning has so far advanced, the darkness may increase again; but, even in this case, the source of light is coming near without any faltering. The impediment which has partially intercepted his rays, is moveable, and will soon be taken out of the way. There are similar irregularities in the progress of a just man's course. Sometimes he halts, or even recedes. After experiencing the light of life, and exulting in a blessed hope, he again comes under a cloud, and complains of darkness. But the source of his light and life will not fail. He changeth not; and therefore that seed of Jacob, though distressed, will not be consumed (Mal. iii. 6). The breath of his Spirit will drive the intercepting clouds away, and the law of the kingdom, relieved from hindering exceptions, will yet have free course: the path of the just will be like the morning; it will increase until dawn break into day. If a thousand years may in the Lord's sight be accounted one day, much more may the life course of a disciple from the first throes of the new birth, to the moment when faith is lost in sight. That day is an high day in the eternal life of the saved. It is a day much to be remembered in the circle of victors that surround the throne. Now that the Lord God and the Lamb are their light, they will think of the time when the earliest dawn began to struggle faintly in their breasts. The remembrance of its mysterious birth out of primeval darkness, and its gradual growth into perfect light, will make them say and sing of that day, in adoring wonder, What hath the Lord wrought!

The analogy holds good more exactly still, if we take into view the actually ascertained motions of the planetary system. When any portion of the earth's surface begins to experience a dawn diminishing its darkness, it is because that portion is gradually turning round toward the sun, the centre of light fixed in the heavens. While any part of the earth lies away from the sun, and in proportion to the measure of its aversion, it is dark and cold: in proportion as it turns to him again, its atmosphere grows clearer, until, in its gradual progress, it comes in sight of the sun, and its day is perfect then. The path of the just is precisely like this. Arrested in his darkness by a love in Christ, which he does not understand as yet, he is secretly drawn toward Him in whom that love in infinite measure is treasured up. As he is drawn nearer, his light increases until at last he finds himself in the presence of the Lord. Day is not perfect here in a believer's heart, and yet the light of the knowledge of God from the face of Jesus shines into a believer's heart while he sojourns here. The dark get light, the dead get life from the Lord—in the Lord before his glorious appearing. They who thus get light from a Saviour unseen, shall, at his appearing, be like Him, and see Him as He is. The machinery of the everlasting covenant is meantime going, softly and silently, as the motion of the spheres ; and they that are Christ's here, whatever clouds may dim their present prospect, are wearing every moment further from the night and nearer to the day.

There follows a counterpart intimation fitted to overawe the boldest heart. " The way of the wicked is as darkness; they know not at what they stumble" (iv. 19). "If the light that is in thee be darkness, how great is that darkness?" (Matt. vi. 23). Its greatness consists chiefly in this, that it is " in you." A dark place on the path might be got over; but darkness in his own heart, the traveller carries with him wherever he goes. To the blind, every place and every time is alike dark. It is an evil heart of unbelief. Because of this they stumble upon that very Rock which has been laid in Zion to sustain a sinner's hope. He who is a sanctuary to others, is a rock of offence to them. " He shall be for a sanctuary; but for a stone of stumbling and for a rock of offence to both the houses of Israel " (Isa. viii. 14). Even when they fall they know not at what they stumble. Dreadful thought! to be crushed against Him, who has been given as a Refuge and a Rest to weary souls escaping from a sea of sin. The way to get light is to turn from evil. "The pure in heart shall see God."

The Fountain and its Streams

(Proverbs 4:23-27)

" Keep thy heart with all diligence; for out of it are the issues of life. Put away from thee
a froward mouth, and perverse lips put far from thee. Let thine eyes look right on,
and let thine eyelids look straight before thee. Ponder the path of thy feet, and let
all thy ways be established. Turn not to the right hand nor to the left: remove thy
foot from evil."

FIRST the fountain, then the streams: first the heart, and
then the life-course. The issues of life are manifold :
three of their main channels are mapped out here—the
" lips," the " eyes," and the " feet."

The corruption of the heart, the pollution of the spring-head,
where all life's currents rise, is a very frequent topic in the Scriptures. It occurs in many places, and in many forms. In proportion to the opposition which it is fitted to excite, is the doctrine
reiterated and enforced. The imaginations of man's heart are
only evil, and that continually. The heart is deceitful above all
things, and desperately wicked. As a fountain casteth out her
waters, Jerusalem casteth out her wickedness. God foreknew that
a deceitful heart would be unwilling to own its deceitfulness, and
therefore the truth is fortified beyond most others in the word.

" Keep thy heart with all diligence ; for out of it are the issues
of life." This precept of the Proverbs sounds very like some of
the sayings of Jesus. The king's ear caught prophetically before the
time, what we have heard historically after it, as if the word had
echoed either way. You may stand in the morning on a height so
great that you see the sun's disc emerging from the eastern
horizon some time before he has risen upon the plain. Solomon,
as a teacher of righteousness, was elevated far above the common
level of humanity. By special gift, and by the Spirit's interven-
tion, he was exalted much above other men in all knowledge, and
especially the knowledge of divine truth. So high was the mountain-top he stood upon, that, like Abraham, he saw Christ's day

afar off, and felt a beam from the Sun of Righteousness long before he had personally arisen upon the world.

A greater than Solomon has said, " Out of the heart proceed evil thoughts, murders, adulteries." Keep therefore according to Solomon's precept,—keep with all diligence that prolific spring. Here, as in all other cases, prayer and pains must go together. We cry to God in the words of David, Create in me a clean heart; and He answers back by the mouth of David's son, Keep thy heart. We must keep it, otherwise it will run wild. The Almighty Lord will bruise Satan; but it is "under *your* feet:" yourselves must tread on his writhing folds.

" Keep it with all keepings" is the word. Leave no means untried. Out of our own conduct will we be condemned if we do not effectually keep our own hearts. We keep other things with success as often as we set about it in earnest—good things from getting, and bad things from doing, harm. One who loves his garden, keeps it so well that travellers pause as they pass and look admiring on. You keep your family, your house, your money, and you keep them well. Even your clothes are kept, so that no stain shall be seen upon them. On the other side, dangerous creatures are kept with a firm hand and a watchful eye from doing evil. We keep in the horse or mule with bit and bridle. Even the raging sea is kept back by the skill of men, and ripening fields bask safely in the autumn sun below the level of its waters, and within hearing of its roar. In other keepings man is skilful and powerful too; but in keeping his own heart, unstable as water, he does not excel.

Keep it with all keepings. Keep it from getting evil, as a garden is kept; keep it from doing evil, as the sea is kept at bay from reclaimed netherlands. Keep it with the keeping of heaven above, and of the earth beneath—God's keeping bespoken in prayer, and man's keeping applied in watchful effort. Keep it with all keepings, for out of it are the issues of life. The true principle on which an effectual restraint can be put upon the issues of the heart is indicated in the 21st verse—" Keep" my words " in the midst of thine heart." The same prescription for the same disease occurs in that great hymn of the Hebrews (Psalm cxix. 11)—" Thy word have I hid in mine heart, that I might not sin against thee." The word of life is the salt that must be cast into these bitter springs of Jericho, to save the surrounding land from barrenness.

1. The first of the three streams marked on this map as issuing from an ill-kept heart is "a froward mouth." The form of the precept, put it away, reveals a secret of our birth. The evil is there at the first in every one: he who is free of it was not born free. We have not a clear ground to begin upon. When a man would erect a temple to God within his own body, the first effort of the builder is to clear the rubbish away. Of the things from the heart that need to be put away, the first in the order of nature is the froward mouth. Words offer the first and readiest egress for evil.

The power of speech is one of the grand peculiarities which distinguish man. It is a wonderful and precious gift; wanting it, and all that depends on it, man would scarcely be man. While we use the gift, we should remember the Giver, and the purpose for which he bestowed it. While we speak, we should never forget that God is one of the listeners. Men sin in comfort when they forget God, and forget God that they may sin in comfort. If the Queen were present, hearing every word, on a given day, in a given company, a restraint would be put upon every tongue; gravity and gentleness would breathe in every sentence: yet that same company is not refined and sobered by the presence of the King Eternal. Like Israel, in a backsliding time (Mal. i. 8), we bring unto God the blind and the lame, sacrifices that we would not offer to our sovereign; and that she would not accept at our hands. He who has a tongue to speak should remember that the bestower of the gift is listening, and keep back whatever would displease Him. Take the principle of Hagar's simple and sublime confession, accommodated in form to the case in hand, "Thou God, *hearest* me." If our words were all poured through that strainer, how much fewer and purer they would be! If all the words of our week were gathered and set before us at its close, the boldest head would hang down at the sight. When all the words this tongue has uttered are written and opened in His sight on that day, how shall I appear, if the dark record remains still mine? While for that reckoning we must trust all and only in the blood of Christ, that taketh sin away, we should diligently set about the business of watching and restraining the perverseness of

our own lips. The work is hopeful. They who try it in the right
way will be encouraged by seen progress. A vain, a biting, an
untruthful, a polluted, a profane tongue cannot be in the family
of God, when the family are at home in the Father's presence. The evil must be put away; the tongue must be cleansed;
and now is the day for such exercises: that which remaineth for
the people of God is a Sabbath on which no such work is done,
in a heaven where no such work is needed.

2. The next outlet from the fountain is by the "eyes." The
precept is quaint in its cast—" let thine eyes look right on;" and
yet its meaning is not difficult. Let the heart's aim be simple and
righteous. No secret longings and side glances after forbidden
things: no crooked bye-ends and hypocritical pretences. Both in
appearance and reality let your path be a straightforward one.
In a mercantile community especially this is the quality that
should be chiefly in request. Much mischief is done when men
begin to look aside instead of straight before them. A manufac-
turer glances to the side one day, and sees a neighbour making as
much by a lucky speculation in an hour as he has won by the regular prosecution of his business in a twelvemonth. He throws
for a prize, and draws a blank. In the speculation the capital
which sustained his business has disappeared: his legitimate
creditors are defrauded, and his family ruined.

Deviations from the straight line have become so many and so
great, that the deviators, keeping each other in countenance, begin
to defend their own course, and whisper a desire to establish a new
code of laws which may coincide with their practice. We have
here and there met with an appalling measure of obtuseness in
comprehending the first principles of justice, which should regulate
all commercial transactions. Men may be found amongst us holding
their heads high, and conducting business on a large scale, who
have not gotten the alphabet of honesty yet. It is ground of
thankfulness, indeed, that these are the exceptions. The body
politic of commerce is in a much sounder state than it appears to
a superficial observer, judging from instances whose abnormal
criminality has thrust them more prominently into view. If the
life were not on the whole robust, it could not bear diseased
tumours so many and so great; but the body whose beauty they
mar, and whose strength they waste, should, for its own health's

sake, be ashamed of the deformities, and intolerant of their growth. With this view, let every man, besides joining in the general condemnation of full-grown detected dishonesties in other people's transactions, search for and crush incipient secret abberrations in his own.

When the eye is single, the whole body will be full of light. Straightforwardness is the fairest jewel of our commercial crown. Those who spend their life in traffic should be jealous of themselves, and lean hard over from the side on which sly, sinister selfishness lies. Anything on the right side; uprightness, even downrightness, if you will; but let us keep far away from every form and shade of duplicity. It is true that mercantile pursuits tend to develop some noble qualities of humanity; but let it not be forgotten that some noxious weeds can thrive in the riches of its soil. Love and cultivate, by all means, the generous plants; but carefully watch the weeds, and resolutely cast them away.

3. The last of these issues is by the "feet." Ponder, therefore, their path. The best time to ponder any path, is not at the end, not even at the middle, but at the beginning of it. The right place for weighing the worth of any course, is on this side of its beginning. Those who ponder after they have entered it, are not in a position either to obtain the truth or to profit by it. Those who rush headlong into a path of conduct because they like it, and then begin to consider whether it is a right one, will probably either induce themselves to believe a lie, or refuse to follow discovered truth.

The injunction applies to every step in life, great and small. Ponder well what family you will be a servant in, what trade you will learn, what business you will engage in, what colony you will emigrate to. Every step is great, because it affects the destiny of an immortal soul. More particularly, by way of example, ponder your path at that great step which binds you for life to another human being as one flesh. God has made marriage a weighty matter—let not man make it a light one. Weigh well itself and all its accessories. Those who take this leap in the dark, may expect to find themselves in a miry pit. Those who weigh it in thought, until they find the burden all too heavy for their strength, and cast it therefore on the Lord, will be led out of their temptations, and through their difficulties. Most true it is that "marriages are made in heaven;" for the dear children refer the matter implicitly to their Father there, and he undertakes for them.

But the value of weighing anything depends all on the justness of the balance and the weights. Many shamefully false balances are in use and in vogue for weighing paths and actions. "Fashion," and "use and wont," are the scales into which most people throw their intentions, before carrying them into fact. These are the instruments which quacks supply, and fools employ. They are mean and contemptible cheats; and yet the multitude trust them. If nothing valuable were risked, one might be content to smile at their silliness, and pass on; but the path which these false balances induce their dupes to take, leads to perdition. Although the acts be transparent folly, we cannot afford to turn them into mirth. We dare not laugh at the stupidity of the entrance whose issue is in woe. These false balances are ruin to men, and abomination to the Lord! Cast them away. Here is a standard weight stamped as true by the imperial seal of heaven. By the word of God paths and actions will be weighed in the judgment: by the word of God, therefore, let paths and actions, great and small, be pondered now.

Family Joys

(Proverbs 5:15)

"Drink waters out of thine own cistern, and running waters out of thine own well."

A PAINTER lays down a dark ground to lean his picture on, and thereby bring its beauty out. Such is the method adopted in this portion of the word. The pure delights of the family are about to be represented in the sweetest colours that nature yields,—wedded love mirrored in running waters, and in order to relieve more boldly these "apples of gold" the Spirit, in the preceding portion of the chapter, has stained the canvas deep with Satan's dark antithesis to the holy appointment of God. An instance of the same high art you may see in the work of another master; Paul sets forth, in Eph. v. 2, his favourite theme, the love of Christ, in terms of even more than his usual winsomeness ; and you may see, in the verse that follows, how dark a ground he filled in behind it. Such fearful contrasts, under the immediate direction of the Spirit, make the beauty of holiness come more visibly out. But it is only at a great distance, and with extremest caution, that we dare to imitate this style in our expositions. The danger would be great, if the attempt were rashly made, of staining the pure by an unskilful handling of the impure. A reverent look towards the depths of Satan, as they are unveiled in the word of God, may alarm the observer, and cause him to keep further from the pit's mouth; but we fear to touch them in detail, lest our well-meant effort should be snatched, and used as another fiery dart by the wicked one. All round, this region seems infected. We have known some who, in venturing near to rescue others, fell themselves ; as miners, descending the pit to bring out a suffocated neighbour, have been known to perish with him. It is meet that even those who, from fear of God and love to men, run to the rescue, should hold in their breath, and pull hastily out of the fire whatever brand they can lay their hands on, and come back with all speed from the opening mouth of those descending "steps that take hold on hell." Indeed this is the substance of all these warnings which occur in the fifth chapter, and are repeated in the seventh ; the key note of the whole is, " remove far from her." The word assumes that men are weak, and warns them off from the edge of the whirling stream that sucks the unwary in. It is the same lesson that Jesus himself gave, when he taught that in this matter a look is already sin. In wise tenderness, He would keep the fluttering bird clear beyond the reach of the vile charmer's fascinating eye. "Hear ye Him," young men, as you love your life, and value your souls. We protest that we are clear from the blood of those that perish there, although we stand no longer near the deadly spot to warn them back.

The Lord condescends to bring his own Institute forward in rivalry with the deceitful pleasures of sin. The pure joys of a happy home are depicted in the fifteenth and subsequent verses The saying of Cowper, " God made the country, man made the town," although it contains no poetic brilliance, has obtained a wide currency for its pithy expression of a great and obvious truth. We may be permitted to use the poet's mould in giving form to our own conceptions, which we believe to be equally true, and more urgent; " God made the family, man made the casino, the theatre, the dramshop, the ball-room." The list might be largely extended, of Satan-suggested, man-made things, which compete with God's institute, the family, and drain off its support.

How beautiful and how true the imagery in which our lesson is infolded! Pleasures such as God gives to his creatures, and such as his creatures, with advantage to all their interests, can enjoy— pleasures that are consistent with holiness and heaven, are compared to a stream of pure running water; and specifically the joys of the family are "running waters out of thine own well." This well is not exposed to every passenger : it springs within, and has a fence around it. We should make much of the family, and all that belongs to it. All its accessories are the Father's gift, and He expects us to observe and value them. It is no trifling to apply the microscope to the petals of a flower, in order to magnify and so multiply its beauties : in like manner, it is worthy employment for the greatest to scan the minutest objects that are the genuine parts of the household apparatus, for, as the Lord's works, they are all very good.

But remember, although the stream is very pure—nay, because it is very pure, a small bulk of foreign matter will sensibly tinge it. You may have observed that if a drop of coloured matter be poured into pure water, it makes its polluting presence very widely felt. Had the water been discoloured from the first, the effect of another drop would not have been discernible. Thus the very purity of the family joys in themselves magnifies the effect of any infringement. Perhaps the drop that discolours for days the waters of his own well, may fall in an unguarded moment from the lips of the husband and father himself. A biting word, reflecting on the wife and mother in presence of the children, when something in her department is found out of order, will stir the mud at the bottom, and make the stream run turbid for many days. His absence, frequent or unnecessary, in the evening, till the children have gone to bed, and the wife feels that much of her labour in making everything neat has been thrown away, without an eye to see, or a tongue to applaud it—this will soon change "your own well" into the appearance of a river in flood. From the other side also the disturbing element may come. Even little neglects on the wife's part will damp the joys of the house, as a very small cloud may suffice to take all the sunlight out of the landscape. A slovenly dress for the husband's home-coming, made tidy only when strangers are expected, may be sufficient to tinge the whole current of conjugal intercourse. Something is felt to be wrong, and yet neither may know what the ailment is, or where it lies. Sharp, discontented words, a continual dropping from a woman's lips, whether with or without cause, will be a poisonous acid in the well, and all joy will die around its borders. The children, too, have much in their power both for good and evil. Heavy cares are strong temptations to the parents. Their spirits are burdened, and the burdened spirit is apt to give way. If the children, by ready obedience, and mutual love, would contrive to sit light as a burden on their parents' shoulders, the lightened parents might rejoice together, and the beams of glad contentment on the faces of father and mother would radiate through all the house. Children are sometimes little peacemakers, blessing their parents, and blessed by God.

But careful abstinence from evil is only one, and that the lower side of the case. There must be spontaneous outgoing activity in this matter, like the springing of flowers, and the leaping of a stream from the fountain. The command is peremptory, v. 18, " Rejoice with the wife of thy youth." It is not only feed and clothe her, and refrain from injuring her by word or deed. All this will not discharge a man's duty, nor satisfy a woman's heart. All the allusions to this relation in Scripture imply an ardent, joyful love. To it, though it lie far beneath heaven—yet to it, as the highest earthly thing, is compared the union of Christ and his redeemed Church. Beware where you go for comfort in distress, and sympathy in happiness. The Lord himself is the source of all consolation to a soul that seeks Him; yet nature is His, as well as redemption. He has constructed nether springs on earth and supplied them from his own high treasuries; and to these he bids a broken or a joyful spirit go for either sympathy. " Drink waters out of thine own cistern," is the express command. " Rejoice with the wife of thy youth "—this is not to put a creature in the place of God. He will take care of His own honour. He has hewn that cistern, and given it to you, and filled it; and when you draw out of it what He has put in, you get from Himself, and give Him the glory. Husband and wife, if they are skilful to take advantage of their privileges, may, by dividing, somewhat diminish their cares, and fully double their joys. They twain shall be one flesh, and when the two are one, it will be a robuster life, as two streams joined become a broader river.

But we must take care lest the enjoyments of home become a snare. God is not pleased with indolence or selfishness. When He gives that fountain, He expects it will " be dispersed abroad." To keep all to yourself will defeat your own end: to hold it in will make it stagnate. The only way of keeping it sweet for ourselves is to let it run over for the good of others. If the family is well ordered, ourselves will get the chief benefit; but we should let others share it. Those especially who are in providence deprived of this inestimable blessing, a home—those who have no parents, or whose parents are far away, should be admitted to taste of these pleasures. This is a charity which God-fearing families might distribute without cost to a class who need no material alms, and are therefore liable to be neglected in schemes of ordinary benevolence.

The Method of Providence for Restraining Evil

(Proverbs 5:21, 22)

" The ways of man are before the eyes of the Lord, and he pondereth all his goings. His own iniquities shall take the wicked himself, and he shall be holden with the cords of his sins."

GOD announces Himself the witness and the judge of man. The evil-doer can neither elude the all-seeing eye, nor escape from the Almighty hand. Secrecy is the study and the hope of the wicked. This word booms forth like thunder out of heaven into every human heart where evil thoughts are germinating into wickedness, proclaiming that the ways of man are before the eyes of the Lord. A sinner's chief labour is to hide his sin: and his labour is all lost. Darkness hideth not from God. The Maker of the night is not blinded by its covering.

He who knows evil in its secret source is able to limit the range of its operation; and there is a special method by which this is done. It is a principle of the divine government that sin becomes the instrument of punishing sinners. Both for restraint in this life, and final judgment at last, this is the method employed. It is not only true in general that the wicked shall not escape, but also in particular that his own sin is the snare that takes the transgressor, and the scourge that lashes him. The Maker and Ruler of all things has set in the system of the universe a self-acting apparatus, which is constantly going for the encouragement of good and the repression of evil. The providential laws do not, indeed, supply a sufficient remedy for sin and its fruits; another physician undertakes the cure; but these laws, notwithstanding, exert a constant force in opposition to moral evil. The wind may be blowing steadily up the river, and yet a ship on the river's bosom, though her sails are spread and filled, may not be moving up, but actually dropping down the stream. Why? Because the stream flows so rapidly down, that the breeze in the sails, though a force in the opposite direction, cannot overcome it. The wind does not, in spite of the current give the ship momentum upward, but it makes the ship's progress downward much more slow. That force does not make the ship move upward, but it prevents the ship from rushing down with such a headlong velocity as to dash itself in pieces. The providential laws are directed against the current of man's sinful propensities, and tell in force thereon. They do not, however, overcome, and neutralize, and reverse these propensities. They were not so intended. They impede the stream's velocity, and restrain its fury. The providential laws prevent the present system from dashing itself into chaos, but they do not supersede the redemption by Christ, and the renewing by the Spirit.

" His own iniquities shall take the wicked." This is an evident and awful truth. Retribution in the system of nature, set in motion by the act of sin, is like the " Virgin's kiss" in the Romish Inquisition. The step of him who goes forward to kiss the image touches a secret spring, and the statue's marble arms enclose him in a deadly embrace, piercing his body through with a hundred hidden knives. Verily a man under law to God would need to " ponder his path," for the ground he stands on is mined beneath his feet, and the first step from virtue's firm footing aside into the yielding slough of vice, sets unseen swords in motion which will tear his flesh, and enter the marrow of his bones. " The Lord reigneth, let the earth rejoice." Praise Him for his righteousness; his judgments will go into a song as well as his mercy.

Seven Hateful Things

(Proverbs 6:16-19)

" These six things doth the Lord hate: yea, seven are an abomination unto him: A proud look, a lying tongue, and hands that shed innocent blood, an heart that deviseth wicked imaginations, feet that be swift in running to mischief, a false witness that speaketh lies, and he that soweth discord among brethren."

S OME of these hateful things are characteristics of particular members in the body, and some are characteristics generally of the man. I do not perceive the principle of arrangement in the nature of the things; perhaps the order is modified by the exigencies of Hebrew poetry.

It is a claim which the Lord puts forth as the Maker and Giver of all our faculties. These are some of the marks by which his wisdom is visibly manifested in creation. He is displeased when they are plunged into lusts, and employed as tools in the service of Satan. These eyes, this tongue, these hands and feet, are instruments of surpassing skill and beauty. They declare God's glory as articulately as the stars of heaven or the flowers of earth. Who shall dare to corrupt the allegiance of these tributaries, and enrol them rebels against the King of kings? The Maker cares for all his works. To pervert any part of them provokes Him to anger. Every purpose to which the members of our body are put is noticed by the All-seeing. If we are in spirit his dear children, we have opportunity to please God as often as we exercise any faculty of our mind, or member of our frame.

There is one parallel well worthy of notice between the seven cursed things here, and the seven blessed things in the fifth chapter of Matthew. In the Old Testament the things are set down in the sterner form of what the Lord hates, like the " thou shalt not" of the Decalogue. In the New Testament the form is in accordance with the gentleness of Christ. There we learn the good things that are blessed, and are left to gather thence the opposite evils that are cursed. But, making allowance for the difference in form, the first and the last of the seven are identical in the two lists. "The Lord hates a proud look," is precisely equivalent to "blessed are the poor in spirit;" and "he that soweth discord among brethren," is the exact converse of the "peace-maker." This coincidence must be designed. When Jesus was teaching his disciples on the Mount, he seems to have had in view the similar instructions that Solomon had formerly delivered, and while the teaching is substantially new, there is as much of allusion to the ancient Scripture as to make it manifest that the Great Teacher kept his eye upon the prophets, and sanctioned all their testimony.

Mother's Law

(Proverbs 6:20-24)

"My son, keep thy father's commandment, and forsake not the law of thy mother: Bind them continually upon thine heart, and tie them about thy neck. When thou goest, it shall lead thee; when thou sleepest, it shall keep thee; and when thou awakest, it shall talk with thee. For the commandment is a lamp; and the law is light; and reproofs of instruction are the way of life: To keep thee from the evil woman, from the flattery of the tongue of a strange woman."

A FATHER'S commandment is the generic form, and is usually employed to signify parental authority; but here, in addition to the general formula, "the law of a mother" is specifically singled out. The first feature that arrests attention in this picture is, that effects are attributed to the law of a mother which only God's law can produce. The inference is obvious and sure; it is assumed that the law which a mother instills is the word of God dwelling richly in her own heart, and that she acts as a channel to convey that word to the hearts of her children. To assume it as actually done, is the most impressive method of enjoining it. Parents are, by the constitution of things, in an important sense mediators between God and their children for a time. What you give them they receive; what you tell them they believe. This is their nature. You should weigh well what law, and what practice you impress first upon their tender hearts. First ideas and habits are to them most important, for they give direction to their course, and tone to their character through life. Your children are by nature let into you, so as to drink in what you contain; the only safety is that you be by grace let into Christ, so that what they get from you, shall be, not what springs within you, but what flows into you from the Spring-head of holiness. To the children, it is the law of their mother, and therefore they receive it; but in substance it is the truth from Jesus, and to receive it is life. It is the law which converts the soul and makes wise the simple, poured through a mother's lips into an infant's ears.

It is a sweet employment, and an honourable place, to be mediators for our own children, bearing up to God their need, and bringing down to them God's will. This is a kind of mediation not derogatory to Christ. It is not a presumptuous priesthood; it is a humble ministry, appointed and accepted by himself. It belongs to the structure, both of the kingdom of nature, and of the covenant of grace. There is in the spiritual department something corresponding to the birth, when the parent travails again until the child be born to the Lord; and there is here also something corresponding to the nursing. Great must be the delight of a mother, herself renewed, when she becomes the channel through which the "milk of the word" flows into her child (1 Peter ii. 2); more especially when she feels the child desiring that milk, and with appetite drawing it for the sustenance of a new life.

The injunction is in form addressed to a grown son, that he forsake not in manhood his mother's law. It has often been repeated that mothers have much in their power, in virtue of their position beside the nascent streams of life, where they are easily touched and turned. The observation is both true and important. It is this weight, cast into woman's otherwise lighter scale, that turns the balance, and brings her to equality with man, as to influence on the world. In spite of man's tyranny on one side, and her own weakness on the other, woman has thus in all countries, and even in the most adverse circumstances, vindicated her right to a place by her husband's side, and silently leaves her own impress as deeply stamped as his upon the character of the coming generation.

In the pliant time of childhood, the character is moulded chiefly by the mother. Many melting stories are told on earth, and, I suppose, many more in heaven, about the struggle carried on through youth and manhood, between present temptations and the memory of a mother's law. Almighty grace delights to manifest itself in weakness; and oft the echo of a woman's voice, rising up in the deep recesses of memory, has put a whole legion of devils to flight. Oh, woman, if it cannot be said, great is thy faith,—even although it should be small as a grain of mustard seed, yet great is thy opportunity! The spring season and the soft ground are thine: in with the precious seed: sow and hope, even though it be also sometimes in tears; a glad harvest will come, here or yonder; now or many days hence.

If parents give to their children a law which they get not from God, their influence will be great for evil. As to form, the law of evil, like the law of good, distils chiefly in small dew-drops through the temper and tone. Few parents have the hardihood directly to teach wickedness to their offspring.

The mother should be much with the children herself. Wherever that is impracticable, it is either a calamity through the visitation of Providence, or a great fault on the part of the parents. The difficulties, the mistakes, and the transgressions of mothers are different according to their position in society, and the character of their employment. Working-men should take care not to lay too much on their wives. The mother, as a general rule in this country, undergoes not the out-door labour whereby the bread is won; but her hours are longer, and her task equally outwearing. Let the husband and father do his utmost by every contrivance to lighten her labour, and cheer her heart. The wounded spirit of a neglected wife cannot bear its own weight, far less sustain with buoyant, smiling countenance, the continual tension of several children hanging about her, with all their wants and all their quarrels, from morning till night. A father, whatever the effort might cost him, would not permit his infant child to suck a fevered nurse; he should beware, as far as it lies with him, lest the child's spirit should sustain a greater damage, by drawing its mental nourishment from a mother fretting, desponding, despairing.

In the case of mothers who live in affluence, perhaps trifling is the most pressing danger. Don't cram your children with unreal forms, like blown bladders, which occupy all the room, and collapse at the first rude rub on real life. In pity to your children, put something into them that will last and wear. Don't expend all your energies in tying ornaments on them, to attract the gaze of the curious on the street; get into them, if you can, some of that ornament which is in the sight of God of great price (1 Peter iii. 4). Mothers, if your hearts have been quickened by the Spirit, take your fashions from the word of God. Occupy yourselves mainly in moulding the heart and life of your children, after the pattern which Jesus showed and taught. This will give you most enjoyment at the time, and most honour afterward.

Hitherto we have been sketching from the reflection a parent's duty, but the command of this passage is directly addressed to the child. Very graphic and memorable is the advice here tendered to a son;—bind a mother's laws continually upon thine heart, and tie them about thy neck. The idea no doubt refers to the Mosaic precept about binding the law of the Lord on the person, which in practice degenerated into the phylacteries of the Pharisees. From this strong figure the moral meaning stands out in bold relief. If a piece of dress or a bag of money hangs loosely upon you, in the jolting of the journey it may drop off and be lost. Life is a rough journey. The traveller must crush through many a thicket, and bear many a shake. If that law of truth, which you get in childhood through a mother's lips, be loosely held, it may slip away. "Therefore we ought to give the more earnest heed to the things which we have heard, lest at any time we should let them slip" (Heb. ii. 1).

It is intimated in the 22nd verse that this law will be a close and kind companion to you all your days, if you treat it aright. It will be with you when you lie down to rest, and when you awake it will be there still, ready to talk with you. It is beyond expression valuable to have this law, impressed with all the authority of God who gave it, and all the tenderness of a mother who taught it, adhering to the memory through all the changes of life. A friend in need, it is a friend indeed. Although it be neglected for flatterers at night, when you awake it meets you at the moment, and talks over its saving truth again. Several kind offices of that true friend are enumerated here, and a crowning one is recorded at the close. Bound and kept in the heart as a friend, that law will prevail to keep the youth "from the strange woman." Observing a great swelling wave rolling forward to devour him, this faithful teacher imparts to the young voyager on life's troubled sea, a principle which will bear him buoyant over it. A slender vessel floats alone upon the ocean, contending with the storm. A huge wave approaches, towering high above her hull. All depends on how the ship shall take it. If she go under it, she will never rise again: if she is so trimmed that her bows rise with its first approaches, she springs lightly over it, and gets no harm. The threatening billow passes beneath her, and breaks with a growl behind, but the ship is safe. The law and love of the Lord, taught by his mother in childhood, and maintaining its place yet as the friend of his bosom and the ruler of his conscience, will give the youth a spring upward proportionate to the magnitude of the temptation coming on. Saved as by fire, with reference to the greatness of the danger, yet surely saved, the victor, as he leaps over the last wave and enters into rest, will cry out to the welcomers who line the shore, " I am more than conqueror through Him that loved me."

There must be many joyful meetings in the better land; but when a son, saved by the truth his mother taught him, enters into rest, and meets his mother there, the joy—oh, one would think that ministering angels must reverently stand back from it, as one too deep for them to intermeddle with!

The Worth of Wisdom and the Fear of the Lord
(Proverbs 8:10-13)

" Receive my instruction, and not silver : and knowledge rather than choice gold." .....
"The fear of the Lord is to hate evil."

I T is not necessary to inquire whether the wisdom that cries here be an attribute of God, or the person of Emmanuel. We may safely take it for both, or either. The wisdom of God is manifested in Christ, and Christ is the wisdom of God manifested. The cry, concentrated in the Scriptures, and issuing forth through manifold providential ministries, is public, "She crieth at the gates, at the entry of the city;" impartial, " Unto you, O men, I call, and my voice is to the sons of men ;" perspicuous, "They are plain to him that understandeth."

The very first warning uttered by this wisdom from above is the repetition of a former word, " Receive my instruction, and not silver ; and knowledge rather than choice gold." The repetition is not vain. Another stroke so soon on the same place indicates that He who strikes feels a peculiar hardness there. The love of money is a root of evil against which the Bible mercifully deals many a blow. There lies one of our deepest sores : thanks be to God for touching it with " line upon line " of his healing word. When a man is pursuing a favourite object with his whole heart, it is irksome to hear a warner's word continually dropping on his unwilling ear, telling that the choice is foolish. A father who is merely fond will discontinue the warning, that he may not displease his wilful child. Not so our Father in heaven. He is wisdom as well as love. He wields the same sharp word until it pierce the conscience and turn the course. It is only while you kick against this warning that it pricks you : when you obey it, you will find it very good.

A ship bearing a hundred emigrants has been driven from her course, and wrecked on a desert island far from the tracks of men.

The passengers get safe ashore with all their stores. They know not a way of escape; but they possess the means of subsistence. An ocean unvisited by ordinary voyagers circles round their prison, but they have seed, with a rich soil to receive, and a genial climate to ripen it. Ere any plan has been laid, or any operation begun, an exploring party returns to head-quarters reporting the discovery of a gold mine; thither instantly the whole company resort to dig. They labour successfully day by day, and month after month; they acquire and accumulate heaps of gold. The people are quickly becoming rich; but the spring is past, and not a field has been cleared, not a grain of seed committed to the ground. The summer comes, and their wealth increases, but the store of food is small. In harvest they begin to discover that their heaps of gold are worthless. A cart-load of it cannot satisfy a hungry child. When famine stares them in the face, a suspicion shoots across their fainting hearts that the gold has cheated them; and they begin to loathe the bright betrayer. They rush to the woods, fell the trees, dig out the roots, till the ground, and sow the seed. Alas, it is too late! Winter has come, and their seed rots in the soil. They die of want in the midst of their treasures.

This earth is the little isle, and eternity the ocean round it. On this shore we have been cast, like shipwrecked sailors. There is a living seed; there is an auspicious spring-time: the sower may eat and live. But gold mines attract us: we spend our spring there—our summer there: winter overtakes us toiling there, with heaps of hoarded dust, but destitute of the bread of life. Oh, that they were wise, that they understood this, that they would consider their latter end! Seek first the kingdom of God, and let wealth come or go in its wake. He who, in the market of a busy world, gains money and loses his soul, will rue his bargain where he cannot cast it.

He formally defines here the fear of the Lord. The definition is needful, for the subject is often grievously misunderstood. I know not an emotion more general among men than terror of future retribution under a present sense of guilt. To vast multitudes of men, this life is embittered by the fear of wrath in the next. To dread the punishment of sin seems to be the main feature in that religion which under many forms springs native in the human heart. This is the mainspring which sets and keeps all the machinery of superstition agoing. It was a maxim of heathen antiquity that "Fear made God." It is chiefly by the dread of punishment that an alienated human heart is compelled in any measure to realize the existence of the Divine Being. In proportion as that terror is diminished by a process of spiritual induration, the very idea of God fades away from the mind.

To fear retribution is not to hate sin ; in most cases it is to love it with the whole heart. It is a solemn suggestion that even the religion of dark, unrenewed men is in its essence a love of their own sins. Instead of hating sin themselves, their grand regret is that God hates it. If they could be convinced that the Judge would regard it as lightly as the culprit, the fear would collapse like steam under cold water, and all the religious machinery which it drove would stand still.

All the false religions that have ever desolated the earth are sparks from the collision of these two hard opposites—God's hate of sin, and man's love of it. As they strike in the varied evolutions of life, strange fires flash from the point of contact—fires that consume costly and cruel sacrifices. In Christ only may this sore derangement be healed. It is when sin is forgiven that a sinner can hate it. Then is he on God's side. The two are agreed, and " He is our peace" who hath taken away sin by one sacrifice. Instead of hating God for his holiness, the forgiven man instinctively loathes the evil of his own heart, and looks with longing for the day when all things in it shall be made new. Such is the blessed fruit of pardon when it comes to a sinner through the blood of Christ.

Rank and Riches

(Proverbs 8:18, 21)

"Riches and honour are with me; yea, durable riches and righteousness. . . . . That I may cause those that love me to inherit substance: and I will fill their treasures."

WISDOM from above cries in the gate, and enters into competition with the world's most powerful attractions. In the matters of rank and riches, the two strong cords by which the ambitious are led, the two reciprocally supporting rails on which the train of ambition ever runs,—even in these matters that seem the peculiar province of an earthly crown, the Prince of Peace comes forth with loud challenge and conspicuous rivalry. Titles of honour! their real glory depends on the height and purity of the fountain whence they flow. They have often been the gift of profligate princes, and the rewards of successful crime. At the best the fountain is low and muddy: the streams, if looked at in the light of day, are tinged and sluggish. Thus saith the Lord, " Honour is with me;" and He who saith it is the King of glory. To be adopted into the family of God,—to be the son or daughter of the Lord Almighty,—this is honour. High born! we are all low born, until we are born again, and then we are the children of a King.

The riches which this King gives to support the dignity of his nobles are expressly called " durable riches." This is spoken to place them in specific contrast with those riches that make themselves wings and fly away. They are also said to be coupled with righteousness for company. Surely the Spirit who dictates this word knows what is in man, and the wealth which man toils for. Its two grand defects—the two worms that gnaw its yet living body—are the unrighteousness that tinges a part of it, and the uncertainty that cleaves to it all. The riches which the King of saints imparts along with the patent of nobility to support its dignity withal, are linked to righteousness, and last for ever. Anointed by the Spirit, they are secure from both the rust spots that eat into the heart of the world's wealth; pure and imperishable, they have been by a double metaphor called "the silver springs of grace, and the golden springs of glory."

The Lord will cause those that love him to "inherit substance." Here is a withering glance from the countenance of the Truth himself at the cheat which the world practises upon its dupes. Those who are rich in grace inherit substance; this is obliquely to say that those who give themselves to the pursuit of wealth are chasing a shadow. They are ever grasping at it; and it is ever gliding from their grasp. Such is the dance through which Mammon leads his misers. It is kept up throughout all life's vain show, until the dancers drop into the grave, and disappear in its darkness. They who seek the substance shall find it; and as to the amount of their gain, the promise is precise—"I will fill their treasures." This is a great promise : it is made in a kingly style : there is no limit. It will take much to fill these treasures; for the capacity of the human spirit is very large. God moulded man after his own image, and when the creature is empty, nothing short of his Maker will fill him again. Although a man should gain the whole world, his appetite would not be perceptibly diminished : the void would be as great and the craving as keen as ever. Handfuls are gotten on the ground, but a soulful is not to be had except in Christ. "In him dwelleth all the fulness of the Godhead bodily, and ye are complete (that is, full) in him." Hear ye him : "I will fill their treasures." "Even so, come, Lord Jesus."

The Redeemer Anticipating Redemption
(Proverbs 8:22-31)

"The Lord possessed me in the beginning of his way, before his works of old. I was set up from everlasting, from the beginning, or ever the earth was. When there were no depths, I was brought forth; when there were no fountains abounding with water. Before the mountains were settled, before the hills was I brought forth: while as yet he had not made the earth, nor the fields, nor the highest part of the dust of the world. When he prepared the heavens, I was there: when he set a compass upon the face of the depth: when he established the clouds above: when he strengthened the fountains of the deep: when he gave to the sea his decree, that the waters should not pass his commandment: when he appointed the foundations of the earth: then I was by him, as one brought up with him: and I was daily his delight, rejoicing always before him; rejoicing in the habitable part of his earth; and my delights were with the sons of men."

HITHERTO, in this chapter, we have found it possible to speak of wisdom alternately as a property and a person; but henceforth the terms compel us to keep by the personal view. At the beginning something may be understood as applying to divine wisdom in general; but toward the close, the wisdom incarnate, in the person of Emmanuel, stands singly and boldly out. If the terms are not applied to Christ, they must be strained at every turn. On this subject, we who enjoy the fuller revelation, should remember that the Old Testament institutes were necessarily shadows. Before Christ came in the flesh, He could not be so clearly declared as now. Of design He was presented to faith under a vail. More could not have been done in consistency with the purpose of God, and the nature of things. In the book of Proverbs by Solomon, it could not be written that Jesus was born in Bethlehem, and died upon the cross. One might profitably put the question to himself, if the Spirit designed to make.known something of the personal history of Christ before His coming, how could He have done so in plainer terms than this chapter contains?

Regarding this divine person, we learn here, that being with God before creation, He looked with special interest upon the preparation of this world as the habitation of men, and the scene of redemption. This gives us a sketch of cosmogony, with the Eternal Word as spectator, and for view-point the throne of God. Here is the genesis of the world, as it appeared to Him, who even then longed to redeem it from sin. Out of previous indefinite water-depths the mountains were lifted up and settled. Out of a moving chaos the solid earth arose, one grand step in the process of providing a domicile for man. The heavens were prepared as a circle, by setting a compass on the face of the deep. The clouds were established above, and the home of the sea beneath was strengthened to keep its raging inmate. By the same law He established the clouds in the upper air, and fixed the ocean in the nether caverns of the earth. If a heap of solid water were poised on pillars over our heads, how dangerous would our position be, and how uneasy our life! But no such precarious propping is needed, when the Omniscient would construct a habitation for man. By heat, portions of the water are made lighter than air, and forthwith the same law which keeps one part beneath the atmosphere raises another into its higher strata. During this process of creation, the Son was with the Father, and already taking his place as Mediator between God and man. In verses 30th and 31st, these three things are set in the order of the everlasting covenant (1.) The Father well pleased with His Beloved, " I was daily His delight." (2.) The Son delighting in the Father's presence, "rejoicing always before him." (3.) That same Son also looking with prospective delight to the scene and subjects of his Redemption work, " rejoicing in the habitable parts of his earth, and my delights were with the sons of men." On that early morning of time, you see on the one side the High and Holy One, and on the other the sons of men, with Jesus already in the midst laying his hand upon both.

It is a touching view of the Saviour's love. When He saw the earth undergoing the process whereby it was furnished as a habitation for man—the mountains upheaving, the valleys subsiding, the vapour arising, and the clouds moving in the sky— He rejoiced in the prospect of being man, for behoof of the fallen, on that emerging world, and never flagged in his regard until He had borne back many sons and daughters into glory.

The exhortation which follows could not come from any other

lips than His own. None but Christ is able to say, "Whoso findeth me findeth life." From the New Testament we know that He only is the Light, and that the Light is the life of men. The counterpart, terror, is equally His own :—" he that sinneth against me wrongeth his own soul; and all they that hate me love death." There is no salvation in any other, and they who refuse or neglect Him cast themselves away. The perdition of the lost is their own doing, for redemption is nigh. " Ye have kindled a fire in mine anger," said the prophet (Jer. xvii. 4), "which shall burn for ever." A child or an idiot may kindle a fire which all the city cannot quench. In spite of their utmost efforts, it might destroy the homes of the poor and the palaces of majesty. So a sinner, though he cannot do the least good, can do the greatest evil. The Almighty only can save him, but he can destroy himself.

The Marriage Supper for the King's Son
(Proverbs 9:1-6)

" Wisdom hath builded her house, she hath hewn out her seven pillars; she hath killed her beasts; she hath mingled her wine; she hath also furnished her table. She hath sent forth her maidens: she crieth upon the highest places of the city, Whoso is simple, let him turn in hither: as for him that wanteth understanding, she saith to him, Come, eat of my bread, and drink of the wine which I have mingled. Forsake the foolish, and live; and go in the way of understanding."

IN the preceding chapter, Wisdom appears, forming worlds, and peopling them; anticipating the need of man, and covenanting a sufficient remedy. There Wisdom stood, and spoke from the high stage of the heavens; here we get a nearer view. The Word has come nigh. His habitation is among men. The colours for the picture here are taken from things that we know. The head of her own family, sovereign of her own realm, builds her house, provides her feast, sends out the invitation, and presses the invited guests to come. From the same materials, and with the same design, the Word of God framed similar parables, when He " was made flesh, and dwelt among men."

1. *The house.*—The frame is set up from everlasting, well ordered in all things and sure. The tried foundation is the Lord our righteousness. The temple which Solomon built, and the altar within it, whereon he sacrificed, were emblems of this house eternal. The seven pillars indicate, in oriental form, that its supports and ornaments are perfect in strength and beauty. The seven things (vi. 17–19) which the Lord hates seem to be the clearing of the rubbish away from the foundations; and the seven beatitudes (Matt. v.) the pillars of positive truth which the great master builder erected there. He removes the first, that He may establish the second. He takes the curse away, and brings the blessing in its stead, sevenfold each. • Both the curse which Jesus bears away, and the blessing which He brings, are measureless.

2. *The feast prepared.*—The provisions of God's house are wholesome, various, plentiful. Whatever the covenant provides, the true Church diligently sets forth in the ordinances before the people. The word, preaching, prayer, the sacraments, the service of song: a feast of fat things is provided. " Blessed are they that hunger, for they shall be filled." In the Father's house there is enough and to spare, in the Father's bosom a weeping welcome: prodigals perishing, arise and go.

3. *The inviting messengers.*—These correspond to the servants sent forth by the King in the New Testament parable. To keep up the idea of a matron householder, the messengers are here called maidens, but obviously in both cases they are the ambassadors whom Christ employs to carry the message of his mercy to their brethren. They have no strength, and no authority. All the power they wield lies in the Spirit that moves them, and the good news which they bring. Gentleness and purity are the qualifications most in request for those who bear the invitation from Divine Wisdom to a thoughtless world.

4. *The invited guests.*—The message is specially addressed to the simple. Those who are conscious of ignorance are ever most ready to learn the wisdom from above. Empty vessels fill best when plunged into the fountain. Those who are filled already, with their marrying and giving in marriage, their cattle markets, and their landed estates, send their excuse for absence, and do not themselves come to wisdom's feast. From hedges and lanes of conscious nakedness and need, the marriage festival is furnished with guests. To the poor the gospel is preached, and the poor in spirit gladly listen, whether they are clothed in purple or in rags.

5. *The argument by which the invitation is supported is positive,* " Come, eat of my bread, and drink of the wine which I have mingled;" *and negative,* " Forsake the foolish and live."—The bread and the wine are the provisions of our Father's house, the plenty on a Father's board, every word of God for the prodigal to feed on when he returns; but the grand turning point is to get the prodigal to break off from that which destroys him. Forsake the foolish,—the foolish place, and the foolish company, and the foolish employments; and what strong reason do you employ to induce the slave of lust to wrench himself away, although he should leave his right arm behind him? Reason! It is his life.

Life and death eternal hang in the balance of this decision. The Lord by his prophet in the time of old, uttered in the ears of men the brief command, "Turn ye," and followed it up with the awful argument, "*Why will ye die?*" The same Lord, in his own person, breathed from his breaking heart the tender plaint, "Ye will not come unto me *that ye might have life.*" There, from His own lips, you have a command to come, and a reason for coming. The argument to enforce his invitation is life—from Himself, in Himself, life that will never die. This Scripture, too, speaks from Him and like Him. It is the resound of his own words, afar on these heights of ancient prophecy, "Forsake the foolish and *live.*" By line upon line throughout all the Bible He is saying, Ye must be separate from them, or Me.

Reproof

(Proverbs 9:7, 9, 12)

" He that reproveth a scorner getteth to himself shame: and he that rebuketh a wicked
man getteth himself a blot. Reprove not a scorner, lest he hate thee: rebuke a wise
man, and he will love thee. Give instruction to a wise man, and he will be yet
wiser: teach a just man, and he will increase in learning. If thou be wise, thou shalt
be wise for thyself. but if thou scornest, thou alone shalt bear it."

THE subject is obvious, interesting, important, urgent.
The supposed case is of frequent occurrence; and it is
seldom well met. We need wise counsel to guide us in
this difficult step of the daily life-course. The lesson here is about
Reproof; how to give it, and how to take it. Reproofs are like
sharp knives, very needful and very useful; but they should not
be in the hands of children. Those who handle them rashly will
wound both themselves and their neighbours. We are all, by the
constitution of nature, much in contact with others. We see their
faults: they see ours. Reproofs are often needed and often given.
Sometimes they are unskilfully administered, and sometimes un-
faithfully withheld. This is a matter that bulks largely in life.
Great practical difficulties surround it. It is a subject on which
we need to be instructed. Some of its chief regulating principles
are concisely given here.

It is not difficult to realize the character of the scorner, who is
the principal figure in the scene. The man is in a state of nature.
He has no spiritual life or light. He is ignorant, but thinks himself knowing, and is proud of his skill. He has no modesty, and
no tenderness for others. He is a blusterer. He is hollow
sounding brass: a tinkling cymbal. He is surrounded by a knot
of companions who ignorantly applaud, or, at least, silently listen
to him. Thus encouraged, he speaks great swelling words of
vanity : he magnifies himself. As he proceeds with his display,
he affects a superiority to scruples of conscience. He laughs at

the good, and at goodness : he boasts of evil. Accustomed to
exaggerate everything, he exaggerates even his own wickedness.
He scatters blasphemies, and is intoxicated by the wonder wherewith the circle regards his boldness. He rejoiceth in iniquity.
He glories in his shame. You are a spectator of the scene: you
have heard the blasphemer. You fear God, and are jealous for
his honour. You observe, moreover, that some youths are there,
ignorantly wondering after this beast, and in danger of learning to
count such conduct manly. You grow warm—indignant. At
last, after some daring and foulmouthed sally from the scorner,
you break silence, and interpose a reproof. In God's name, and
out of God's word, you charge him with his sin, and challenge
him to the judgment. You have reproved a scorner, and you
will probably then and there get to yourself shame. You have
trampled on a snake, and it is his nature to spurt forth his venom
on you. But the circumstances are even more formidable than
the nature of the man. His place as ringleader is at stake. Unless he retrieve his honour in their presence, the ring of ruffians
will melt away. He is a god among them; but if his thunders
are silent now, they will lay no more incense on his altar. Your
stroke has stirred up every motive within the scorner, to redouble
his blasphemy. He is shut up either to submit to you as a conqueror, or to assault you as a foe. The first he will not, and
therefore the second he must do. He raises the laugh against
you, and against that blessed name which you invoked. Such is
the filthiness of the weapons employed, that you cannot maintain
the combat ; to reply would be to defile your own tongue. You
are obliged to be silent, because if you should follow him, you
could not maintain your footing on the slimy path. Truth is
silent before falsehood and filth, not from her weakness or their
strength, but from the place and circumstances in which the challenge was given and the battle accepted. His pride is touched :
he knows that his chieftainship is conclusively forfeited, if he is
seen to quail before a saint. Expressly, he will " hate thee." You
have struck a piece of wood while it is lying hollow, and instead
of cutting it, yourself will be injured by the rebounding blow.
There is a possibility of approaching it carefully and turning it
skilfully, and getting it laid solid before you strike. Then both
you will sever it, and it will not rebound on you.

If you could find the scorner alone, his courage would not be so great. Conscience makes cowards of us all. Whisper softly into his ear your solemn reproof. Tell him that he is trampling under foot that blood of the covenant which alone can wash his sin away; and if you tell him this weeping, your word will go the deeper in. There are many arts by which a wise reprover might approach the man on the unguarded side. Find a soft spot about him, or make one by deeds of kindness. Touch him so as not to stir the evil spirit at the first, and perhaps the evil spirit may not be stirred at all. If you gain a brother thus, it is a bloodless victory. The joy is of the purest kind that lies within our reach on earth. It brings you as closely into sympathy as a creature can be, with the satisfaction of the Redeemer when He sees of the travail of his soul.

But in all this we have in view chiefly the scorner himself. A witness for Christ may be so situated that he ought to reprove the scorner, although he knows that the scorning will be redoubled by the reproof. It may be more important, for the sake of others, to strike in, although the evil-doer should in judgment be more hardened. These principles regarding the blasphemer's tendency are most important. We should be aware of the laws that regulate all cases, and the circumstances that modify them in each; but no absolute rule can be laid down. We must get daily direction, as well as daily bread. Two things are needful—the swelling spring, and the well-directed channel for the stream to flow in. There should be jealousy for the Lord's honour, and compassion for men's souls like a well-spring ever in the heart; and then the outgoing effort should be with all the wisdom of the serpent, and the harmlessness of the dove; and "if any lack wisdom, let him ask of God."

Hitherto we have handled only the half of the lesson, and that the harsher half. Its complement is a kindlier thing: "rebuke a wise man, and he will love thee." There is a double blessing; one to him who gets reproof, and one to him who gives it. Is it, then, the mark of a wise man that he loves the reprover who tells him his fault? Judging by this test, we are forced into the conclusion that there are not many wise men amongst us. To tell a friend his fault is too often the signal for a breach of friendship. On both sides error is frequent, and wisdom rare; but wisdom here is precious in proportion to its rarity. It will repay all the labour of seeking and striving for it. The wisdom may be possessed on either side alone, or on both together. The Lord's meek and poor afflicted ones may get good from a reproof, although the reprover sinned in giving it : on the other hand, the witness of evil may rightly reprove it, and so keep his own conscience clear, although the evil doer have not grace to profit by the reproof. On both sides the wisdom is difficult; but when it is found, it is very gainful. " Harmless as doves ;" that is the word of Him who knows what is in man. The froth of human passion swells and spurts out, and impudently calls itself faithfulness. When Samuel was instructed to reprove Saul for his sin, " he cried unto the Lord all night," and uttered his faithful reproof in the morning (1 Sam. xv. 11). Such a preparation would take none of its strength away, and greatly add to its softness. For rightly receiving reproof, the short and simple rule is, be more concerned to get the benefit of the reproof, than to wreak vengeance on the reprover. He who should habitually act on this plain maxim, would grow rich by gathering the gold which other people trample under their feet.

" Give instruction to a wise man, and he will be yet wiser," is an interesting fact under the great gospel law, " To him that hath shall be given, and he shall have more abundance." Some of the true wisdom is a nucleus round which more will gather. A little island once formed in the bed of a great river, tends continually to increase. Everything adds to its bulk. The floods of winter deposit soil on it. The sun of summer covers it with herbage, and consolidates its surface. Such is wisdom from above, once settled in a soul : it makes all things work together for good to its possessor.

The principle involved in the parable of the Talents (Matt. xxv.) is embodied in the intimation, " If thou be wise, thou shalt be wise for thyself." The talents are, in the first instance, not won by the servant, but given by the master. So wisdom is specifically the gift of God (James i. 5). Those servants who use the talents well are permitted to retain for their own use both the original capital, and all the profit that has sprung from it ; whereas he who made no profit is not allowed to retain the capital. Thus the Giver acts in regard to the wisdom which is His own to bestow.

The wisdom, with all the benefit it brings, is your own. Every instance of wise acting is an accumulation made sure for your own benefit. It cannot be lost. It is like water to the earth. The drop of water that trembled on the green leaf and glittered in the morning sun seems to be lost when it exhales in the air unseen, but it is all in safe keeping : it is held in trust by the faithful atmosphere, and will distill as dew upon the ground again when and where it is needed most. Thus will every exercise of wisdom, although fools think it is thrown away, return into your own bosom when the day of need comes round.

Equally sure is the law that the evil which you do survives and comes back upon yourself : " If thou scornest, thou alone shalt bear it." The profane word, the impure thought, the unjust transaction—they are gone like the wind that whistled past, and you seem to have nothing more to do with them. Nay, but they have more to do with you. Nothing is lost out of God's world, physical or moral. When a piece of paper is consumed in the fire, and vanishes in smoke, it seems to have returned to nothing. If it bore the only evidence of your guilt, you would be glad to see its last corner disappear ere the officers of justice came in. All the world cannot restore that paper, and read those dreaded lines again. The criminal breathes freely now; no human tribunal can bring home his crime. But as the material of the paper remains undiminished, in the mundane system, so the guilt which it recorded abides, held in solution as it were, by the moral atmosphere which encircles the judgment-seat of God. Uniting with all of kindred essence that has been generated in your soul, it will be precipitated by a law; and when it falls it will not miss the mark ; thou alone shalt bear it. Those who have not found refuge in the Sin-Bearer, must bear their own sin. Sins, like water, are not annihilated, although they go out of our sight. They fall with all their weight either on the sin-doer, or on the Almighty Substitute. Alas for the man who is " alone" when the reckoning comes !

The Pleasures of Sin
(Proverbs 9:13-18)

"A foolish woman is clamorous; she is simple, and knoweth nothing. For she sitteth at the door of her house, on a seat in the high places of the city, to call passengers who go right on their ways: whoso is simple, let him turn in hither: and as for him that wanteth understanding, she saith to him, Stolen waters are sweet, and bread eaten in secret is pleasant. But he knoweth not that the dead are there; and that her guests are in the depths of hell."

WE have heard Wisdom's cry, and learned what are his offers to men: the next scene exhibits Wisdom's great rival standing in the same wide thoroughfare of the world, and bidding for the youth who throng it. The evil is personified that it may be set more visibly forth in all its deformity over against the loveliness of truth. All that is contrary to Christ, and dangerous to souls, is gathered up and individualized, as an abandoned woman lying in wait for unwary passengers, baiting her barbed hook with the pleasures of sin, and dragging her victims down the steep incline to hell. One of the foul spirits that assail and possess men is singled out and delineated, and this one represents a legion in the background.

The portrait is easily recognised. We have met with it before, both in the pages of this book, and in other places of the Scripture. It is no fancy picture,—it is drawn from life. Neither is it a peculiarity of Eastern manners, or of ancient times. It concerns us, otherwise it would not have met us here. The plague is as rampant in our streets as it is represented to be in the Proverbs. Mankind have sat for the picture: there is no mistake in the outline; there is no exaggeration in the colouring. It is a glass held up for the world to see itself in. Dark as the lines are in which the importunate, shameless solicitations of a wanton woman are drawn on this page, they are not darker than the reality, as seen in our crowded thoroughfares by day and by night

The vulture, with unerring instinct, scents the carrion, and flutters round the place where it lies until an opportunity occur of alighting upon it and satiating her appetite on the loathsome food. These vultures would not hover around our exchanges, and banks, and warehouses, and manufactories, unless the carrion that feeds them were scented there. While we have cause to thank God for the measure of truth, and love, and purity, that His word and Spirit have transfused through our families, we have cause also to weep in secret that so many whited sepulchres glitter pharisaically in the sun of the world's prosperity, while rankest corruption revels within. We again cry, " with a great and exceeding bitter cry," to all that is morally sound in society, resolutely to withdraw their countenance from the impure, however great their wealth may be, and however high their position in the world.

The specific occupation of the foolish woman is " to call passengers who go right on their ways," and persuade them to turn aside for " stolen waters." A multitude of the young, issuing from their parents' homes, where they have been trained in virtue, start in life's wide path, with the intention of going " right on ;" and of these, alas, how many are suddenly enticed aside, entangled in the net, and lost! Beware of the turning aside. Let not a youth ever once or for a moment go where he would be ashamed to be found by his father and his mother. " Forsake the foolish and live." Go not at her bidding aside ; " the dead are there."

But although the argument that stolen waters are sweet is, for the sake of vivid representation, put into the mouth of a " foolish woman," we must understand by the figure all evil—the devil, the world, and the flesh, whatever form they may assume, and whatever weapons they may employ. The one evil spirit dragged forth from the legion and exposed, is intended not to conceal but to open up the generic character of the company. From above Divine Wisdom cries (v. 4), " Whoso is simple, let him turn in hither ;" from beneath, a multiform lust, that is earthly, sensual, devilish, cries, " Whoso is simple, let him turn in hither." There they are, conspicuously pitted against each other, the two great rivals for possession of a human heart. No man can serve two masters. No heart can follow both of these drawings. No man can choose both death and life, both darkness and light. Every one must go this way or that. Every sinner must turn his back either upon his Saviour or upon his sin. In this life every human being is placed between these two rival invitations, and every human being in this life yields to the one or to the other.

The power of sin lies in its pleasure. If stolen waters were not sweet, no one would steal the waters. This is part of the mystery in which our being is involved by the fall; and it is one of the most fearful features of our case. Our appetite is diseased. If our bodily appetite were so perverted that it should crave for what is poisonous and loathe wholesome food, we would not give ourselves up to each random inclination : the risk of death would be great, and valuing life, we would set a guard on the side of danger. But in man fallen there is a diseased relish for that which destroys. Sin, which is the death of a man's soul, is yet sweet to the man's taste. There is much to appal us in this state of things : it should make us walk circumspectly, not as fools. When the redeemed of the Lord shall have come to Zion with songs of joy, they may indulge to the full unexamined, unrestricted, all their tastes. There will be no sinful things to taste there, and no taste for sinful things. There will neither be the appetite nor its food. Nothing shall enter that defileth. But here, and now it should make us tremble to know that there is an appetite in our nature which finds sweetness in sin. Oh wretched man that I am, who shall deliver me from myself ? God's children, while in the body, watch their sinful appetites, and endeavour to weaken and wither them by starvation. They who give rein to the appetite are daily more brought under its power: it grows by what it feeds on. If sin had no sweetness, it might be easier to keep from sinning. Satan might fish in vain, even in this sea of time, if he had no bait on his hook that is pleasant to nature. Beware of the bait, for the barb is beneath it.

It is only in the mouth that the stolen water is sweet : afterwards it is bitter. Sin has pleasures, but they last only for a season, and that a short one. On the side of sin that lies next a sinner, Satan has plastered a thin coating of pleasure : a deceived soul licks that sweetness, deaf to the warning that behind it an eternal bitterness begins. If a grand bazaar were erected, filled from end to end with sweetmeats of every form, and laid out in the most fascinating aspects, but all poisoned so that to swallow one were death ; and if it were a necessity laid on you to introduce your little child by a door at one end, and let him traverse the enticing avenues of death alone, till from without you should receive him at the other; you would warn your child with a voice of agony that would thrill through his frame, not to touch, not to taste, until, beyond the precincts of the pest house, he should be safe in your arms again. Notwithstanding all your warning, you would stand trembling, perhaps despairing, as you waited at the appointed door till your child emerged: you would scarcely expect that your little one would, all the way through, resist the attractions of the poisoned sweets. Such are the world's sweetened death-drops to us; and such, as to infantile thoughtlessness, are we in the world. Oh, for the new tastes of the new nature! " Blessed are they that hunger and thirst after righteousness." When you have tasted and seen that the Lord is gracious, the foolish woman beckons you toward her stolen waters, and praises their sweets in vain : the new appetite drives out the old.

One part of the youth's danger lies in his ignorance. He knoweth not, when he is invited to the place of pleasure,—" he knoweth not that the dead are there, and that her guests are in the depths of hell." What he knows not, Divine wisdom tells. He can tell us what is there, and He only. Who knoweth the power of God's anger ? Only Christ. None other can warn us what the guests of the strange woman suffer in the depths. The saved cannot tell, for thither they never go : the lost cannot, for they never return thence. Only He who bowed under wrath, and rose again in righteousness, can give warning as to the bitterness that lies behind the momentary sweet of sin.

That section of the Proverbs which closes here is characterized throughout by varied, pointed, unsparing rebuke of prevailing sins. We have gathered some lessons from this page of the Bible, and plied our lever to press them in. We desire humbly to cast the effort, as far as it has hitherto proceeded, on the quickening Spirit for power. Those who have escaped these corruptions, through the power of grace, will have their gratitude stirred anew by a backward glance on the bondage : the young and inexperienced may, by the forewarnings, be better forearmed ere the heat of their battle come ; but the objects of chief interest, while these reproofs are resounding from the word, are those who have been snared and taken—who have sunk, and are lying yet in the deep mire. Sins are sweet, and therefore men take them; they are soporific, and therefore those who have taken them are inclined to lie still.

A man has fallen into the sea and sunk: he soon becomes unconscious. He is living yet, but locked in a mysterious sleep. Meantime, some earnest neighbours have hastily made preparations, and come to the rescue. From above, not distinguishing objects on the bottom, they throw down their creeper at a venture, and draw. The crooked tooth of the iron instrument comes over the face of the drowning man, and sticks fast in the dress of his neck. It disturbs the sleeper, but it brings him up: it scratches his skin, but saves his life. The saved, when he comes to himself, lavishes thanks on his saviours, mentioning not, observing not, the hardness of their instrument, or the roughness of its grasp. Beneath the surface of society, sunk unseen in a sea of sin, lie many helpless men. Slumbering unconscious, they know not where they are. They dream that they are safe and well: they have lost the sense of danger, and the power of crying for help. Help comes, however, without their cry. Over the place where we know the drowning lie, we have thrown these sharp instruments down. We have been raking the bottom with them in all directions. If the case had been less serious, we might have operated more gently. If any be drawn up, they will not find fault with the hardness of the instrument that reached and rescued them. The slumbering may wish it were soft to slip over them, but the saved are glad that it was sharp to go in.

When a world of human kind lay senseless in a sea of sin, one wakeful eye pitied them, and one Almighty arm was stretched out to save. The Highest bowed down to man's low estate. He sent His word, and healed them; but the word was quick and powerful. The sleepers cry out when first they feel it in their joints and marrow. The evil spirit in them still resists the coming of Jesus as a torment; but when they are restored to their right mind, they sit at the Saviour's feet, and love Him for His faithfulness.

The Place and Power of a Son

(Proverbs 10:1)

" The Proverbs of Solomon. A wise son maketh a glad father : but a foolish
son is the heaviness of his mother."

"THE Proverbs of Solomon." Hitherto, although the
style has been in the main proverbial, there has been
a large measure of connection and continuity in the
argument. At this stage we enter a new section of the book.
Here we touch the edge of a vast miscellaneous treasure, contrived
or collected by Solomon, and transmitted in safe keeping down to
our own day. It is like a heap of wheat'; the grains are small,
but they are many ; they lie close together, and yet each is a
separate whole; they are fair to look upon, and good for food.

The first proverb is a characteristic specimen of its kind. Every
reader may see at a glance how its words and clauses are poised
upon each other, so as both to condense and reiterate the sentiment,—both to retain it on the memory and impress it on the
mind. " A wise son maketh a glad father." Do you hear this,
young man ? It is in your power to make your father glad, and
God expects you to do it. Here is an object for your ambition ;
here is an investment that will insure an immediate return. Come
now, make your choice. Whether will you try to please these
fools who banter you here, or to gladden your father's heart that
is yearning for you there ? He loved you in your childhood, and
toiled for you all the best of his days. He was proud of you
when you promised well, and clings fondly to the hope that you
will be something yet. These companions that come between
you and him—what have they done for you, and what would they
do for you to-morrow, if you were in distress ? They would
desert you, and mind their own pleasures. They have never lost
a night's rest by watching at your sick bed, and never will. But
your father—what has he done, and yet will do ? The command

of God to you is that you gladden that father, and not grieve him. Your conscience countersigns that command now. Obey.

In former lessons we found out where the root of wisdom lies —in the fear of the Lord : here is one of its sweetest fruits—**A son's wisdom is a father's joy !** Alas, how often do we see a son in manhood becoming a burden which a father must bear, instead of a support that his weary heart may lean upon ! A heavier burden this than was the helpless child.

" A foolish son is the heaviness of his mother." It is difficult to deal with this word. The conception is easy, and the examples manifold ; but though it is easy to comprehend, it is hard to express it. It is an almost unutterable thing. A son who breaks his mother's heart—can this earth have any more irksome load to bear ! Foolish son, do you ever allow yourself to think that you are bruising the bosom which you lay upon when you were a helpless infant ? It is not your mother only with whom you have to deal. God put it into her heart to love you, to watch over you night and day, to bear with all your waywardness, to labour for you to the wasting of her own life. All this is God's law in her being. Her Maker and yours knew that by putting these instincts into her nature for your good, he was laying on her a heavy burden. But He is just : He intended that she should be repaid. His system provides compensation for outlay. There are two frailties—a frailty of infancy, and a frailty of age. God has undertaken, in the constitution of his creatures, to provide for both. Where are his laws of compensation written ? The counterpart laws answer each other from two corresponding tablets, His own hand-work both, as the curse and blessing echoed and re-echoed alternate from the sides of Ebal and Gerizim, when first the Hebrews entered the promised land. One is written on the fleshly table of the heart, and the other on the table of the ten commandments—both, and both alike, by the finger of God. A mother's love ! You do not read in the Decalogue, " Mother, take care of your infant." So deeply is that law graven on a mother's heart, that God our Saviour compares to it His own everlasting love to His redeemed (Isa. xlix. 15). To that law the safety of infancy has been intrusted by the author of our being. The bed provided for the child is its mother's breast. There is the provision for humanity's first period of feebleness, and where lies the security for the next ? It is partly in nature too ; but it would appear that He who knows what is in man, would not confide to that instinct the care of an aged parent. He spoke the command from the mountain that burned with fire ; He engraved that command on the tables of the covenant, " Honour thy father and thy mother, that thy days may be long." There, foolish son, there is thy mother's title to her turn of cherishing. You dare not dispute her right, and you cannot withstand her Avenger. There will be compensation. All God's laws re-adjust themselves, and woe to the atoms of dust that are caught resisting, and crushed between their dreadful wheels ! How much more perfect and uniform is the parent's instinctive love than the child's commanded obedience, may be seen in all the experience of life, and is well embodied in the Spanish proverb, " One father can support ten sons, but ten sons cannot support one father."

I never knew a mother. I have been an orphan, almost from the first opening of my eyes. If at any time my mind breaks loose from sober submission to my lot, and wanders into wishes for what cannot be, the keenest longing of my heart is that I had a mother. One of the fountains of affection within me has been sealed up from my birth ; I would fain have an object to let it flow upon. Oh, how sweet it must be to a son in his manhood strength to be the gladness of his mother! Foolish sons are compassing sea and land to obtain pleasure, and trampling under their feet untasted a pleasure stronger, sweeter far, even to nature, than that which they vainly chase.

Let sons who are not prodigal—who seem to be fairly doing their filial duty, remember that their time for that duty is short and uncertain. Let those who now love and cherish a mother much, love and cherish her more. Occupy the talent, lest it be taken. Be yet more tender of your mother while you have her, lest you suffer by unavailing regret when it is too late—lest there should be thorns in your pillow the first night you lie down, after her voice is silent, and her eyes closed.

Diligent in Business
(Proverbs 10:4)

" He becometh poor that dealeth with a slack hand: but the hand of the diligent maketh rich."

THIS rule applies alike to the business of life, and the concerns of the soul. Diligence is necessary to the laying up of treasures, either within or beyond the reach of rust. The law holds good in common things. The earth brings forth thorns, instead of grapes, unless it be cultivated by the labour of man. This is an infliction because of sin, and yet it has been turned into a blessing. Even human governments have learned so to frame the necessary punishment as to make it a benefit to the culprit. The Governor of the nations did this before them. A world bringing forth food spontaneously might have suited a sinless race, but it would be unsuitable for mankind as they now are. If all men had plenty without labour, the world would not be fit for living in. The fallen cannot be left idle with safety to themselves. In every country, and under every kind of government, the unemployed are the most dangerous classes. Thus the necessity of labour has become a blessing to man. It is better for us that diligent application is necessary to success, than if success had been independent of care and toil.

That diligence is necessary to progress in holiness, is witnessed by all the word of God, and all the experience of His people. Indeed, it would be a libel on the character of the Divine economy to imagine that the tender plant of grace would thrive in a sluggard's garden. The work is difficult; the times are bad. He who would gain in godliness, must put his soul into the business; but he who puts his soul into the business will grow rich. Labour laid out here is not lost; those who strive, and strive lawfully, will win a kingdom. When all counts are closed, he who is rich in faith is the richest man.

Posthumous Fame

(Proverbs 10:7)

"The memory of the just is blessed: but the name of the wicked shall rot."

SOME are remembered for good, some are remembered for evil, and some are forgotten soon. This is a feature which is set in the machinery of God's moral government, as a power impelling to righteousness. How many motives to good doing are in providence brought to bear upon man! Besides all that pertain to our own life on earth, and the higher hopes that look up to heaven, a power from the future of this present world is directed now upon a human heart to aid in keeping it from wickedness. It seems an instinct of humanity to desire honour and dread disgrace to the memory after death. Like other good things, it may be overlaid and smothered by a great excess of vice; but its operation is very general, and all in some measure are sensible of it. Few are entirely indifferent to the reputation in which they shall be held among men after their departure. The desire to diminish the depth of the stigma on their name, is found in the greatest criminals when their end is near. To observe the memory of a bad man execrated by the people, is, as far as it goes, in favour of goodness. "Jeroboam, the son of Nebat, who made Israel to sin," is an expression that occurs frequently in the Old Testament, but the repetition is not vain. By many strokes on the same place the Spirit in the word at last stamped very deep upon the heart of Israel a detestation of the idolatry which Jeroboam introduced.

As it is not pleasant to the living to think that their bodies after death shall be torn by dogs, so it is not pleasant to the living to anticipate that their names shall be infamous in the generation following. Although David's sins are faithfully recorded, David's name was savoury in Israel for the good that predominated in his history. This memory of the just must have stimulated many an Israelite to emulate the spirit and the deeds of the Shepherd King.

As skilful men, finding wind and water and steam, powers existing in nature, have combined and directed them so as to make them all help in propelling useful machinery; so the Supreme Ruler has directed many streams from different quarters, and made them converge upon the wayward will of man, to impel it in the direction of righteousness. This curious appetite for a good name to abide in the world behind us, is not left like a mountain stream to waste its power. It is let into the system of Providence, and plays its own part in palliating the results of the fall. No man would like his name to "rot" among posterity. This motive is not strong enough to make a bad man good; but, along with others, it contributes to diminish the force of wickedness, and so to avert the absolute extinction of the race.

The Wise are Teachable, the Upright Strong
(Proverbs 10:8, 9)

"The wise in heart will receive commandments: but a prating fool shall fall. He that walketh uprightly walketh surely; but he that perverteth his ways shall be known."

WE have already learned what wisdom is, and whence it comes, and here is one of its most valuable results,—not what it gives, but what it receives;—it receives commandments. Receptiveness is a characteristic of the new heart; the new-born babe desires the sincere milk of the word, that it may grow thereby. The good well-broken ground took in the seed, while other portions kept it lying on the surface; and this was the chief cause of the great difference in the result.

As the thirsty ground drinks in the rain, so the wise in heart long for and live upon God's word. They are glad to get commandments. "It is not in man that walketh to direct his steps." "O send out thy light and thy truth: let them lead me." "What I know not teach thou me." This is a wise man, and he will soon be wiser. To him that hath shall be given. Blessed are they that hunger, for they shall be filled.

"A prating fool shall fall." All his folly comes out. Every one sees through him. The fool, being empty, busies himself giving out, instead of taking in, and he becomes still more empty. From him that hath not shall be taken. He is known, by the noise he makes, to be a tinkling cymbal. People would not have known that his head was so hollow if he had not been constantly ringing on it. If ever he become wise, he will begin to receive commandments; and when he receives them, he will grow wiser thereby. To receive a lesson and put it in practice implies a measure of humility; whereas to lay down the law to others is grateful incense to a man's pride and self-importance. The Lord himself pointed to the unsuspecting receptiveness of a little child, and said that this is the way to enter the kingdom.

The term upright, as applied to character, seems eminently direct and simple; yet in its origin, it is as thoroughly figurative as any word can be. It is a physical law declared applicable to a moral subject. When a man's position is physically upright, he can stand easily or bear much. He is not soon wearied; he is not easily broken down. But if his limbs are uneven, or his posture bent, he is readily crushed by the weight of another; he is soon exhausted even by his own. There is a similar law in the moral department. There is an attitude of soul which corresponds to the erect position of the body, and is called uprightness. The least deviation from the line of righteousness will take your strength away, and leave you at the mercy of the meanest foe. How many difficulties a man will go through, whose spirit stands erect on earth, and points straight up to heaven! How many burdens such a man will bear!

There is evidence enough around us that righteousness presides over the government of the world. Although men are not righteous, yet righteousness is in the long run the surest way to success even among men. As an upright pillar can bear a greater weight than a leaning one, so moral rectitude is strong, and obliquity weak. The world itself has observed this truth, and graven it in a memorable proverb of its own—" Honesty is the best policy."

A true witness will bear an amount of cross-questioning which is sufficient to weigh twenty false witnesses down. Truth stands longer, and bears more among men than falsehood. This law, operating in the world, is a glory to God in the highest. It visibly identifies the moral Governor of mankind with the Maker of the world. A lofty spire bears its own weight, and withstands the force of the tempest, chiefly because it stands upright. If it did not point plumb to the sky, it could not stand—it could not even have been erected. Wonderful likeness between material and moral laws! Like body and soul, they are joined for parallel and united action. In trying times, the safety of a man or a tower lies mainly in uprightness. For want of it, many mighty are falling in our day, and great is the fall of them. Many confiding families are crushed under the ruins of one huge speculation that has been reared without the plummet of righteousness.

The Well of Life and the Treasures of Wisdom
(Proverbs 10:11, 14)

"The mouth of a righteous man is a well of life. Wise men lay up knowledge."

SEE what the Lord expects, and the world needs, from Christians. The mouth is taken as the principal channel by which the issues of life flow out for good or evil. It is a well. If it be full, it flows over; and if the overflow be sweet water, the border will be fresh and green.

The well's supply falls in rain from heaven, and secretly finds its way by hidden veins to the appointed opening. The overflow fringes the well's brim with green, although the surrounding soil be barren. As the world is a wilderness, and the righteous are wells in it, there is urgent need that they should get supply for themselves in secret from above, and that the outcome of their conversation should be the means of reviving to all around.

In a hot summer day, some years ago, I was sailing with a friend in a tiny boat, on a miniature lake, enclosed like a cup within a circle of steep bare Scottish hills. On the shoulder of the brown sun-burnt mountain, and full in sight, was a well, with a crystal stream trickling over its lip, and making its way down toward the lake. Around the well's mouth, and along the course of the rivulet, a belt of green stood out in strong contrast with the iron surface of the rock all around. "What do you make of that?" said my friend, who had both an open eye to read the book of nature, and a heart all aglow with its lessons of love. We soon agreed as to what should be made of it. It did not need us to make it into anything. There it was, a legend clearly printed by the finger of God on the side of these silent hills, teaching the passer-by how needful a good man is, and how useful he may be in a desert world.

Let your heart take in by its secret veins what comes pure from heaven in showers of blessings; so shall itself be full, and so shall its issues, as far as your influence extends, contribute to fertilize the wilderness. The Lord looks down, and men look up, expecting to see a fringe of living green around the lip of a Christian's life-course. If we get good, we shall be good: if we be good, we shall do good. This comes by a law of nature; for every creature acts after its kind, and the new creature amongst the rest.

The wicked have a power similarly exerted, but in an opposite direction, and with an opposite effect. The wicked are like the sea—the troubled sea. It is always heaving from its depths, and casting up refuse and salt spray upon the shore; a belt of barrenness, therefore, runs all round. It scalds the life out of every green thing within its reach. The sea cannot rest, and herbs upon its border cannot grow. Thus the ungodly act constantly, inevitably by a law. The evil get evil, and do evil: sin propagates sin, and produces death.

In our great cities there are many such restless salt seas. There are many clubs of corrupt men who, by the law of their nature, corrupt their neighbours: there are men of false principles, of foul tongues, of callous hearts, of vicious lives. These cannot lie still. They swing to and fro, and clash upon each other, and fling their own bitterness all round. Alas for unsuspecting youths who saunter careless on the edge! Each tender shoot of grace that may, in kindlier exposures, have begun to spring, is scorched out by these corrosive drops. All the borders of that sea are barrenness. Linger not within its tide-mark. Escape for your life.

Wise men lay up knowledge; another brief definition of true wisdom. Many get knowledge, and let it go as fast as they get it: they put their winnings into a bag with holes: they are ever learning, and never wiser. The part of wisdom is to treasure up experience, and hold it ready for use in the time and place of need. Everything may be turned to account. In the process of accumulating this species of wealth, the wonders of the philosopher's stone may be more than realized. Even losses can be converted into gains: every mistake or disappointment is a new lesson. Every fault you commit, and every glow of shame which suffuses your face because of it, may be changed into a most valuable piece of wisdom. Let nothing trickle out, and flow away useless.   After one has bought wit at a heavy price, it is a double misfortune to throw it away.   As a general rule, the dearer it is the more useful it will be.   The wisdom which God gives his creatures through the laws of nature is of this sort.   The burnt child has, at a great price, obtained a salutary dread of the 'fire. None of the wisdom comes for nothing, either to old or young. Our Father in heaven gives us the best kind: and the best kind is that which is bought.   The saddest thing is when people are always paying, and never possessing.   Some men gain very large sums of money, and yet are always poor, because they have not the art of keeping it: and some learn much, yet never become wise, because they know not how to lay up the treasure.

The cleverest people are in many cases the least successful. A man of moderate gifts, but steadfast acquisitiveness, lays up more than a man of the brightest genius, whether the treasure sought be earthly substance or heavenly wisdom.   It is often found that the meek and quiet spirit, whose life casts no glare around him, has a supply of oil in his vessel which will keep his lamp from going out in seasons of sudden surprisal, or long continued strain.   Men, looking on the outward appearance, make great mistakes in judging of men.   Those who give out little noise may have laid up much wisdom.   There is great encouragement; in the Fountain Head is exhaustless supply, and " He giveth liberally."   It is a form of wealth that lies in little bulk ; one contrite heart will hold more than the world's balances are able to weigh.

The Money Power

(Proverbs 10:15)

"The rich man's wealth is his strong city: the destruction of the poor is their poverty."

HERE he is describing what is, rather than prescribing what ought to be. The verse acknowledges and proclaims a prominent feature in the condition of the world. It is not a command from the law of God, but a fact from the history of men. In all ages and in all lands money has been a mighty power; and its relative importance increases with the advance of civilization. Money is one of the principal instruments by which the affairs of the world are turned; and the man who holds that instrument in his grasp, can make himself felt in his age and neighbourhood. It does not reach the divine purpose; but it controls human action. It is constrained to become God's servant; but it makes itself the master of man.

It is an interesting and remarkable fact, that the Jews wield this power in a greater degree than any other people. Other channels of effort have been shut up from them, and consequently the main stream of the nation's energies has turned in the direction of money. This circumstance explains at once how their position has been acquired; but the ultimate design of Providence in the riches of the Jews cannot be seen as yet. Already the germs of vast power are in possession of the Jews, but in the meantime, the want of a country of their own effectually checks its exercise. The mighty lever is in their hands, but they are comparatively powerless for want of a fulcrum to lean it on. The proposal to buy the land of Canaan has often been mooted among them. They could easily produce the price; but other difficulties interpose. The power that "letteth" may, however, be taken out of the way sooner and more suddenly than politicians deem. In those eastern countries in our own day the angel of the Lord is doing wondrously; it is our part, like Manoah and his wife, rever‐ ently to look on. All powers, and the money power among them, are in the hands of our Father; nothing can happen amiss to his dear child.

Over against this formidable power stands the counterpart weakness,—" the destruction of the poor is their poverty." This feebleness of the body politic is as difficult to deal with as its active diseases. If pauperism be not so acute an affection as crime, it is more widely spread, and requires as much of the doc‐ tor's care. Besides being an ailment itself, it is a predisposition to other and more dangerous evils. All questions have two sides, and so has this. On one side the rich ought to help the poor: on the other, the poor ought to help themselves. By both efforts, simultaneous and proportionate, pauperism may easily be managed: under either alone it is utterly unmanageable. It is the part of those who have strength without wealth, to labour diligently for daily bread, that those only who have neither strength nor wealth may be cast for support upon the rich. If the community are obliged to support the poor only, the exertion will be healthful; but if they are compelled to bear also the profligate, they will sink oppressed themselves beneath the load. The poor we have always with us: this is the appointment of the Lord, to support them will do us good: it is more blessed to give than to receive. The vicious we have also with us, but to support them is pernicious both to them and us. We should correct and train them. But let it be known and reverenced as a providential law, that no pos‐ sible amount of rates or contributions can relieve the poverty that is caused by idleness and intemperance among the population. The disease is in its own nature incurable by that species of ap‐ pliance. All such appliances feed the disease, and nourish it into strength. Though all the wealth of the nation were thrown into the jaws of this monster, it would not be satisfied : the lean kine would eat up all the fat ones, and be themselves no fatter. To supply the children by increased poor-rates, while every enticement is offered to the wretched parents to spend their wages in dissipa‐ tion, is like pouring water into a cistern which has not a bottom, and wondering why it is never filled. When you have poured in all your substance, it will be as empty as when you began.

We are under law to God. The wheels of his providence are

high and dreadful. If we presumptuously or ignorantly stand in their way, they will crush us by their mighty movements. We must set ourselves, by social arrangements, to diminish temptations, and by moral appliances to reclaim the vicious, if we expect to thrive, or even to exist as a community. Vice, positively cherished by erroneous legislation, and neglected by a lukewarm religion, threatens to produce a poverty, such in magnitude and kind as will involve rich and poor in one common destruction. Money answereth all things in its own legitimate province of material supply; but when beyond its province you ask it to stop the gaps which vice is making, it is a dumb idol—it has no answer to give at all.

The struggle between manufacturers and mechanics in the form of strikes, a kind of intermittent fever to which this country is eminently subject, offers a luminous commentary on this text. In these conflicts, the rich man's wealth is his strong city, and the destruction of the poor is their poverty. The masters have most money, and fewest mouths to fill; therefore they hold longer out, and generally gain the victory, as the Russian army captured Kars, by starving the garrison. The men have little capital, and many thousand hungry wives and children. Poverty makes them weak, and the weak go to the wall. Their defeat is a great calamity: perhaps their victory would have been a greater.

A large proportion of the penniless are in agreater or less degree reckless. Partly their recklessness has made them poor; and partly their poverty has made them reckless. There is a reciprocal action in the process which enhances the result. When a multitude, who are all poor, combine for united action, rash and regardless spirits gain influence and direct the course. Such a spirit, powerful by the numbers whom it wields, is dangerous to every interest of the community. In this country, working men might take possession of the strong city as well as their masters; they might make this "unrighteous mammon" their own friend. Money, though a bad master, is a good servant. Money to the working men would answer all the ends which the strike contemplates, if each, by patient industry and temperance, would save a portion for himself. If a thousand men, of a district or a class, possessed on an average a free capital of fifty pounds each, the fruit of their own savings, they could maintain their own ground in a conflict with employers. Their success would be sure, as far as their claim might be legitimate; and their success would be salutary, both to themselves and their neighbours.

Any great community of men is like a body; all members have not the same office, but each is useful—each is necessary in its own place. In virtue of their union, if one member suffer, all the members suffer with it. Thus, by the constitution of things, each has an interest in the welfare of all. In arranging the laws of his universe, the Creator has given a bounty on the exercise of charity, and imposed heavy taxes for the discouragement of quarrels be-tween man and man, or between class and class.

The whole community of rich and poor, linked together in their various relations, may be likened to a living body. Suppose it to be the body of a swimmer in the water. The limbs and arms are underneath, toiling incessant to keep the head above the surface ; and the head, so supported, keeps a look-out for the interests of the whole. If the head be kept comfortably above the water, and no more,.the labour of the limbs will not be oppressive; but if a disagreement occur, and one member plot against another, damage will accrue to all.

If the head thoughtlessly and proudly attempt to lift itself too high, thereby and immediately a double effort is entailed upon the labouring limbs,—such an effort as they cannot long sustain. Wearied with the unnatural exertion, they soon begin to slacken their strokes, and, as a consequence, the head that unwisely sought to tower above its proper height sinks down beneath it. On the other hand, if the limbs beneath, jealous of the easy and honour-able and elevated position of the head, should intermit their strokes of set purpose to bring it down to their own level, they would certainly accomplish their object. When the limbs be-neath cease to strike out, the head helplessly sinks beneath the water. The head would indeed suffer, but the limbs which in-flicted the suffering would have nothing to boast of. When the head came down, the breathing ceased, and the blood got no re-newing. The heart no longer, by its strong pulsations, sent the life blood through its secret channels to the distant limbs, and a cold cramp came creeping over them. Glad were they therefore, if it were not too late, to strike forth again in order to raise the head above the surface, as the only means of preserving their own life

The promiscuous mass of human beings that are welded to-gether by their necessities and interests in this island is like a strong swimmer in the sea; and, alas! it is too often like "a strong swimmer in his agony." Easily might the huge but well-proportioned body lie on the water in a calm, and successfully buffet the waves when a storm comes on, if all the parts were willing to work in harmony. We have the knowledge and the power, and the material means, sufficient to maintain in comfort the whole population, without turning any into slaves; but half our productive capacity is lost by the want of concert and co-opera-tion. The head—and here we mean by that term merely those who have wealth and superior position—the head, in selfishness or silliness, unduly exalts itself. There is a competition in costly luxuries which throws heavier toil down on the labouring class. In the shape of long hours, and night-work, and diminished wages, it entails an agony in those members of the body which minister to its demands: in some poor garret, or in some dark cellar, the racking strain is felt, and the inmates know not whose weight has brought it on. In like manner, when the derangement begins below, the hurt is quickly thrown up to the head, and thence reverberates down to its sources, working reduplicated sorrow there.

Head and members are all on the water; and a great deep yawns beneath. Moderate exertion, if it be steady and uniform, will keep every part comfortably buoyant; but mutual animosities work common ruin. The stoppage of labour which brings down the head will soon paralyze the members: the inordinate uplift-ing of the head, which overtasks the toiling limbs, will rebound from the sufferings of the multitude a stroke of vengeance to lay the lofty low.

Two truths stand conspicuously out from all this confusion;—the world has a righteous Ruler, and the Ruler has a dislocated world to deal with. They speak of the progress and the perfection of the species: we are far from the goal as yet, even if we be in the way to it. The sign from heaven that most surely marks its neighbourhood is, *One is our Master, even Christ, and all we are brethren:* when we see that beauteous bud swelling and bursting and blooming all over our land, we may safely conclude that her millennial summer is nigh.

The Lips and Tongue
(Proverbs 10:18-21)

" He that hideth hatred with lying lips, and he that uttereth a slander, is a fool. In the
multitude of words there wanteth not sin: but he that refraineth his lips is wise.
The tongue of the just is as choice silver: the heart of the wicked is little worth. The
lips of the righteous feed many : but fools die for want of wisdom."

I T is not safe for a man or woman to open the lips and
permit the heart to pour itself forth by that channel
without selection or restraint. If the spring within
were pure, the stream could not be too constant or too strong :
but the heart is full of corruption ; and from a corrupt fountain
sweet waters cannot flow. It is the part of a wise man to set a
watch upon his own lips. This is a more profitable, though less
pleasant exercise, than to set a watch on the lips of our neighbours.
If we fling the door open, and allow the emotions to rush forth
as they arise, it is certain that many of our words will be evil,
and do evil. One who knows himself, if he cannot prevent evil
thoughts from swelling and swarming in his breast, will at least
lay a restraint upon his lips, and check their outgo. Weigh the
words : those of them that are allowed to take wing should be few
and chosen.

To refrain, that is, to bridle back the lips, is an exercise hard
and healthful to our spirits. It requires some practice to make
one skilful in it; but skill in that art will be very profitable in
the long-run. It is easier, and more natural, when one is full of
emotions, to open the sluices, and let the whole gush forth in an
impetuous stream of words. It is easy, but it is not right; it is
pleasant to nature, but it is offensive to God, and hurtful to men.
You must consider well, and pull the bridle hard, and permit no
false or proud words to pass the barrier of the lips. Strangle the
evil thoughts as they are coming to the birth, that the spirits
which troubled you within may not go forth embodied to trouble
also the world.

" The tongue of the just," that is, the stream of words that flows from it, "is like choice silver." Silver is bright, and pure, and not corrosive. It may safely be applied to the body, whether on a sound place or on a sore. Certain surgical instruments, that penetrate the human body, and come in contact with the blood, must be made of silver. Other materials would be liable to contract rust, and thereby inflame the wound. Silver, applied as a healing instrument, does not bite like an adder, and leave a poison festering behind. Thus, when an operation of faithfulness becomes necessary, the tongue of the just is a safe instrument wherewith to probe the sores of a brother's soul. Its soft, sweet answer turneth away wrath. The truth spoken will perform the needful operation; and spoken in love, it will not leave the seeds of fever behind. A biting, corrosive tongue is a curse alike to the serpent who wields it, and the victims whom it strikes.

There is another object, which in common language is constantly said, and in common understanding is instantly felt, to be like a belt of silver; it is a river, when it is seen from a great height following its graceful windings over the plain. All along its margin the watered ground is fresh and green. So would it be if we could obtain a heaven-high viewpoint, whence the eye could trace the stream of love and truth which flows from a good man's lips as he plods over the plain of human life from the spring-head of his new birth to the place of his disappearance on the shore of eternity. Softly and sweetly it shines, like a silver stream, on the dark ground of life, and like it too is fringed on either side with a growth of goodness.

" The lips of the righteous feed many." Themselves satisfied from the Lord's own hand, they will feed others. This bread of life which the disciples distribute is not like common bread: the more you give of it to the needy, the more remains for your own use. It is the bread which Jesus blesses in the wilderness—the bread from heaven, which Jesus is; and when from his hand, and at his bidding, you have fed three thousand on five loaves, you will have more bread remaining in your baskets than the stock you began with. Christ's miracles had a body and a soul. The inner spirit was embodied in sensible act, and the sensible act enclosed an inner spirit. In the act of feeding hungry thousands, through the ministry of the twelve, he was training them in the elements of their apostolic work. As their hands then distributed bread to the body, so their lips fed many souls, by the bread of life which came down from heaven, and dwelt richly within them. It is a high calling to be stewards of these mysteries. The Lord's disciples are made mediators between the source of life and those that are perishing. He blesses, He breaks, He is the bread of life, but all the disciples stand round Him, getting from His hands, and giving to those who will receive. A Christian's lips should keep knowledge; in the heart a precious store, through the lips a perennial flow for the feeding of many.

Behold the mutual relations of faith and love—of trust in Jesus the Saviour, and active effort for the good of men. Getting much from Him, you will feel the necessity of giving to others; giving much to others, you will experience more the necessity of drawing ever fresh supplies from the fountainhead. They who abide in Christ will experience a sweet necessity of doing good to men ; they who really try to do good to men will be compelled to abide in Christ, as a branch abides in the vine.

"Fools die for want of wisdom." So far from being helpful to others, they have nothing for themselves. They have taken no oil in their vessels, and the flame of their lamp dies out.

The Blessing of the Lord Maketh Rich
(Proverbs 10:22)

" The blessing of the Lord, it maketh rich, and he addeth no sorrow with it."

THE truth here is twofold. The cord, as it lies, seems single, but when you begin to handle it, you find it divides easily into two. It means that God's blessing gives material wealth; and also, that they are rich who have that blessing, although they get nothing more.

1. The silver and the gold are his, and he gives them to whom soever he will. A business may prosper at one time, and decay at another, while no one is able to detect the cause. It is not by accident: He who rules in the highest, reaches down to the minutest concerns of this world, and controls them all. Long ago, a certain people diligently plied their agricultural labours, and carefully watched over their household affairs; and yet misfortune succeeded misfortune, and general poverty was closing round the commonwealth. They could not read on earth the causes of their failure, but a voice from on high proclaimed it:—
" Ye have sown much, and bring in little; ye eat, but ye have not enough; ye drink, but ye are not filled with drink; ye clothe you, but there is none warm; and he that earneth wages, earneth wages to put it into a bag with holes. Thus saith the Lord of hosts, Consider your ways" (Hag. i. 6, 7). They had forgotten God, and he had withheld his blessing;—there is the religion of the case, and the philosophy of it too. Will a poor, short-sighted creature prate about the causes of things, to the exclusion of God's displeasure against sin, as if there were no causes of things which lie beyond our view? There are causes of things, which we have never seen yet. He is a sounder philosopher, as well as a better Christian, who owns that the blessing of the Lord has something to do with the prosperity of his business.

2. But his blessing makes rich—His blessing is riches, although the wealth of the world should all flee away. " Godliness, with contentment, is great gain ;" here is a mixture prescribed by the All-wise, for satisfying a soul, and attaining success in life.

" He addeth no sorrow with it." The word seems to imply that there are two ways of acquiring wealth; some people grow rich without God's blessing, and some grow rich by it. It would appear that the god of this world gives riches to his subjects sometimes, when neither giver nor getter owns the supremacy of the Almighty, and that God himself gives riches to some who are his children. Wherein lies the difference, since both the godless and the godly have gotten wealth? It lies here: He does not add sorrow to the riches which he gives, but that other lord does.

When you are permitted to obtain wealth on which you do not seek and do not get God's blessing, that wealth becomes a sorrow. There is no more manifest mark of a righteous providence now seen protruding through into time, than the sorrow that comes with ill-gotten wealth. It lies like a burning spark on the conscience, which will not out all the rich man's days. Sometimes the wealth is scattered by means that the public, with one voice, pronounce to be retribution ; sometimes it becomes waters of strife, to desolate his family after the winner has been laid in the dust: there are many arrows of judgment in the Almighty's quiver. Men may well tremble, when they find themselves growing rich on a trade whose secrets they are obliged to hide in their own hearts, and dare not pour out before the All-seeing day by day: to heap up these treasures, is to treasure up wrath over their own heads.

If you take God into your counsels, and so grow rich, no bitterness will be infused into your gains. It is a common practice to constitute firms for trade, and exhibit their titles to the public with a single name, " and company." Most partnerships, indeed, appear to the world in that form : such a man, and company,—this is all about the business that the passing stranger learns from the sign-board ; but, under that indefinite and comprehensive addition, who are included ? What deeds and what doers does that mercantile formula conceal ? Ah ! what some do in the dark beneath that veil! Now and then the world is startled by its accidental rending, and the exposure of a nest of night-birds in the light of day ; but the full disclosure awaits another rending and another light. Reverently take the All-seeing into your commercial company and counsels : if you cast Him out, there is no security that the worst will not some day be taken in. When these counsels cease to be godly, they are "earthly and sensual ;" and a terrible experience tells that no effectual barrier lies between these and the next step—"devilish." More especially those who have once made a Christian profession, if they allow themselves to engage in transactions on which they dare not ask God to look—if they glide into a business, for its gain, which is incongruous with prayer for a blessing, will probably be left to go greater lengths in shame than other men.

One peculiar excellence of the riches made in a company from whose councils God is not banished is, that the wealth will not hurt its possessors, whether it abide with them or take wings and fly away. Riches cannot with safety be laid next a human soul. Admitted into direct contact, they will clasp it too closely. If they remain, they wither the soul's life away ; if they are violently wrenched off, they tear the soul's life asunder. Whether, therefore, you keep them or lose them, if you clasp them to your soul with nothing more spiritual between, they will become its destroyer. Certain tortures that savages have invented and applied to human bodies, bear an analogy to the process by which his money makes the miser miserable, alike when it abides with him and when it departs. They wrap the body of the living victim all round in a thick impermeable plaster, and then set him free. If the covering remains, all the pores of the body are clogged, the processes of nature are impeded, and the life pines away ; if it is torn off, it tears the skin with it—the pain is sooner over, but it is more severe. Thus the soul of a thorough worldling is either choked by wealth possessed, or torn by wealth taken away. Out of that dread dilemma he cannot wriggle ; the laws of God have shut him in.

Those who get riches should beware lest a sorrow be added to them, more weighty than all their worth. The Maker of the soul is its Portion ; He made it for Himself. When riches are clasped closest to the heart, He is slighted and dishonoured : an idol has usurped his throne. "Covetousness is idolatry." For this very end Christ has come that a man might take the Holiest into his bosom, and yet not be consumed. Put on Christ; seek first the kingdom of God and his righteousness, and these other things may be safely added outside. If riches be added outside, while Christ is taken closest in, the riches there will not hurt their owner while they remain, nor tear him asunder when they depart. When your "life is hid with Christ in God," you will live there, whatever amount of the world's possessions may be attached outside; and though, in some social concussion, all the world's thick clay should drop off, you will scarcely be sensible of a change. If you be Christians,—if you have put on Christ, great riches may come and go; you will not be clogged while you have them; you will not be naked when they leave: but if the wealth be the first and inner wrapping of the soul, how shall that soul ever get into contact with the Saviour, that life from its fountain may flow into the dead? Many disciples of Jesus prosper in the world: few who have courted and won the world in their youth, become disciples in their old age. It is easy for a Christian to be rich, but hard for a rich man to become a Christian.

A Fool's Sport
(Proverbs 10:23; 14:9)

" It is as sport to a fool to do mischief."
" Fools make a mock at sin."

COSTLY sport this! We are wont to wonder at the stupid despot who set fire to his capital that he might see the blaze; but there are many greater fools in the world than he. The fire that Nero kindled in Imperial Rome was soon put out; the flame which sin for sport lights up can never be quenched. " Ye have kindled a fire in mine anger, which shall burn for ever" (Jer. xvii. 4).

To do mischief is one evil; to make sport of the mischief which you have done is another and a worse. A swearer frequently pours out a volume of filth and blasphemy in a fit of exuberant mirthfulness. "The Lord will not hold him guiltless who taketh his name in vain." To be held guilty by the Judge of men in that day, is a heavy price for a moment's mirth. Besides offending the Divine Majesty, an oath offends also the little ones for whom our Father specially cares. The sounds fall upon a tender conscience like drops of scalding fire upon the flesh. The fool pays dear for his mirth, when he incurs on account of it the anger of the orphan's Almighty Friend. Another species of mischief often done in sport is to make a neighbour drunk by practising upon the inexperience of the young, or the depraved tastes of the aged. We have all seen some instances of this amusement, and heard of more. This is wickedness of the very worst kind. The crime of a robber who maims your body, is venial in comparison of his who by stealth lays a paralysis at once upon your soul within, and your limbs without. We sometimes hear of those who deal in strong drink giving it for money to children, until the children are laid helpless in the gutter : to do this for gain is a great crime, but to do it for sport is a greater. I cannot find a name for the man who deliberately makes amusement for himself by defacing God's image from a brother's soul. If any of these occupy the position, they have certainly forfeited the character of gentlemen : they are destitute alike of godliness and manliness : brutal would be an improper designation ; devilish is the most suitable that language can supply.

There is not so much of this in our day as there was in the past generation. Of late there has been some faithfulness and earnestness in dragging these abominations to the light ; and the light these deeds of darkness cannot bear.

Perhaps the arrow would more readily find a joint in the harness to penetrate by, if I should name some sins that seem really lighter, and more fit for sport. Some people tell lies to children, with the view of enjoying a laugh at their credulity. This is to make a mock at sin, and they are fools who do it. The tendency in a child to believe whatever it is told, is of God for good : it is lovely : it seems a shadow of primeval innocence glancing by. We should reverence a child's simplicity. Touch it only with truth. Be not the first to quench that lovely trustfulness, by lies.

It is emphatically the part of a fool to mock at sin. God counted it serious when, to deliver us from its power, he covenanted to give his Son to die. Christ counted it serious when he suffered for it. All holy beings stand in awe before it. Angels unfallen look on in wonder, and converted men who have been delivered from it, fear it with an exceeding great fear. Only the victims who are under its benumbing power, and exposed to its eternal curse, can make light of sin.

The laugh is a symptom of cowardice, rather than of courage. It is not in the power of a human being to laugh at sin, if he look in its face. The mirth of these mockers is a violent effort to shut their eyes or turn round. Sin is not a suitable subject of sport. He who mocks at it, expecting thereby to gain a character for courage, is a coward who dares not to confront its issues, and hysterically strives to stifle his fear.

To mock at sin now, is the way to the place of eternal weeping. They who weep for sin now, will rejoice in a Saviour yet. Blessed are they that so mourn, for they shall be comforted.

Those who make a mock at sin are obliged also to mock at holiness. This is the law of their condition ; " evil men and seducers shall wax worse and worse." To laugh at sin and to laugh at holiness are two sides of one thing; they cannot be separated. Those who make mirth of goodness persuade themselves that they are only getting amusement from the weakness of a brother: let them beware; if that in a Christian which affords you sport be a feature of his Redeemer's likeness, He whose likeness it is, is looking on, and will require it. Let the merrymakers see to it, when they are raising a laugh at the softness of a Christian, lest they be really scorning the gentleness of Christ, reflected in the mirror of a disciple's life-course. God is not mocked.

When Jesus looked down from the brow of Olivet upon a city full of sinning men, he wept. He is wise, and knows what is suitable to the case. He sees the end from the beginning. None who look unto Jesus can mock at sin; the Redeemer's tears would quench profane mirth.

Fears Realized and Hopes Fulfilled
(Proverbs 10:24, 25)

"The fear of the wicked, it shall come upon him: but the desire of the righteous shall be granted. As the whirlwind passeth, so is the wicked no more: but the righteous is an everlasting foundation."

WE must not understand from this verse that the wicked experience only fear, and the righteous only desire or hope : the wicked have hope as well as fear, and the righteous have fear as well as hope. Both characters experience both emotions. In this respect, one thing happens to all. The dread of evil and the desire of good tumultuate and struggle for the mastery in a human breast all through this present life, whether the person be a child of God or a servant of sin. The difference between the righteous and the wicked lies, not in the existence of these emotions within them now, but in their issue at last. In both, the same two emotions operate now; in each, at the final reckoning, one of these emotions will be realized and the other disappointed. The wicked in life both hoped and feared : at the issue of all things, his fear will be embodied in fact, and his hope will go out like a lamp when its oil is done. The righteous in life both hoped and feared : at the issue of all things, his hope will be satisfied, and his fear will vanish as imaginary spectres that terrified the benighted traveller disappear with the day. Fear and hope were common to the two in time : at the border of eternity the one will be relieved from all his fear, the other will be deprived of all his hope. The wicked will get what he feared, and miss what he hoped; the righteous will get what he hoped, and miss what he feared. Ah, how deep this difference is ! One has his hopes all realized, and his fears all disappointed; the other has his fears all fulfilled, and his hopes quenched in despair.

It is not very difficult to ascertain what are the chief fears and desires of a wicked man. Cleaving to his sins, he is in enmity against God. The terrors of the Lord glance from time to time like lightning in his conscience, and he trembles at every quiver of the light, lest it be a bolt of wrath sent to strike him through. When one flash has passed and not smitten him, he gathers breath again, and is glad he has escaped; but ere he is aware, he is wincing beneath another. The wrath of God and the punishment of sin,—this is his fear; but what does he desire or hope? His desire for time is the indulgence of his appetites; his desire for eternity is that there should be no God, or, at least, that he should not be just to mark iniquity. This desire shall not be gratified; for God is, and is the rewarder of them that seek Him. It is a desperate throw to risk your soul and its eternity on the expectation that God will turn out to be untrue, and that the wicked shall not be cast away. This is the desire of every unrenewed, unreconciled man, whether he confess it to himself or not; and this desire must be disappointed. The hope of the sinner will perish when Christ shall come in the clouds of heaven and sit upon the throne of judgment; but the fear of the wicked—what did he fear? In spite of all his hopes, he feared death, and judgment, and eternity. His fear shall come upon him. All that a sinner feared shall come upon the sinner—all that he feared, and more. The fruits of good and of evil are equal as they are opposite. Eye hath not seen, nor ear heard, neither have entered into the heart of man the terrible things which God hath prepared for them that hate Him. The men who heard Noah preaching righteousness, and refused to repent, would nevertheless sometimes be conscious of fear under the patriarch's denunciations; but even those of them who feared the most had no conception of such a flood as that which came and covered them. The terrors of wrath that sometimes work in a sinner's conscience are only drops from an ocean infinite. The fear of the wicked, when it comes, will be greater than all that the wicked feared—greater by the difference between time and eternity. The expectation of the wicked shall perish. If the master of a ship at sea should, through carelessness or wilfulness, in spite of warnings, deviate from his course and hold on, with all sail set, by a false reckoning; and if he should expect and say, when told of his error that he would escape—that there would turn out to be no rock to strike upon—that he would no doubt get safe into the desired haven—what would become of his expectation? It would perish when his ship struck on a stormy shore.

In the voyage over life to eternity there is, indeed, one difference; no one has gone over the voyage and returned to tell that the rocks are really there, and if men persist in refusing to believe whatever they cannot see, they must even be left to themselves. But a message has been sent out to us: we can make only one voyage over this sea, and the Lord of that better land has sent out directions and a chart to guide us in. Most certain it is, if heaven and hell, if sin and salvation, be real, the expectation of the wicked shall perish.

The desire of the righteous shall be granted; what, then, shall become of his fears? What becomes of the darkness when the daylight shines? It is gone. Such are the fears that agitate the bosoms of God's dear children here in the body: when Christ comes, His coming shall be like the morning. But, meantime, let it be carefully noted that the saints are subject to fears. The promise to believers is not that they shall never fear; it is that the thing feared shall never come upon them. What are their fears? They fear sometimes that God's anger will lie upon them yet; and sometimes they fear that, in time of temptation, they may fall away: but though these terrors disturb them, the thing they dread can never come. " There is now no condemnation to them that are in Christ Jesus;" and "they are kept by the power of God through faith unto salvation, ready to be revealed." Their desire shall be granted; and what is their desire? It is twofold: that they may be pardoned through the blood of Christ, and renewed after his image. When these are the desires of our souls, how safe we are! If these desires were left unfulfilled, God our Saviour would be disappointed in His plan, and stripped of His glory. These desires are the desires of the Almighty Redeemer of men, and He will do all His pleasure. When I fear what He hates, my fears will be driven away like smoke before the wind; when I desire what He loves, all my desires will be gratified even to the whole of the kingdom. Behold the golden chain on which a disciple's hope hangs down from heaven,—"All things are yours; and ye are Christs; and Christ is God's" (1 Cor. iii. 22, 23).

The course of the wicked through time is like the passage of a whirlwind over a continent. Life moves quickly, like the wind: when seen from eternity it is as nothing. A wicked life is like the wind in the violence and eccentricity of its movements. The soul that has no hope in Jesus is driven up and down like chaff in a tempest: it is dashed from side to side a while, and at last thrown into the sea or the flames. The righteous is an everlasting foundation: he cannot be moved. Though the mountains should be cast into the sea, the righteous man's standing remains unshaken, untouched: the heavens and the earth shall pass away, but he who has made the Eternal God his refuge will never be removed. "Neither death nor life, neither things present nor things to come," neither men nor devils, can ever drive or draw the feeblest disciple from his confidence. The Lord will "lay a sure foundation;" and "he that believeth shall not make haste" (Isa. xxviii. 16). These two promises lie together in the Scripture. When your heart's hope is fixed on that precious cornerstone, you need not be thrown into a flutter by the fiercest onset of the world and its manifold temptations.

The Greatness of Little Things
(Proverbs 10:26)

*" As vinegar to the teeth, and as smoke to the eyes, so is the sluggard to them
that send him."*

THE minor morals are not neglected in the Scriptures:
cleanliness and punctuality have their place in religion
as well as the weightier matters of the law. These
lesser features must be all filled in ere the beauty of the Lord be
seen upon us. There may be the main things that constitute the
backbone of Christianity, and yet the character may be imperfect
and ungainly. There may be faith, righteousness, and truth, and
yet little of the loveliness of the bride prepared to meet her husband. A Christian has much need to pray that the Lord would
perfect that which concerneth him. Even when the substantial
ground-work has been attained, you can do little to honour the
Lord, or to win a brother, until the minuter features of the
heavenly pattern be imprinted on your life.

You would not select activity and punctuality as the cardinal
tests of a man's condition before God: and yet these things are by
no means of trifling importance. Indolence is a great blemish in a
man's character. Such a spot may sometimes be on one who is a
child of God, but it is not the spot of God's children. " What
thy hand finds to do, do it with thy might." Sluggishness is a
continual injury inflicted on others: it is a cutting, vexing thing.
Those who are Christ's should crucify this self-pleasing affection
of the flesh. One of the Christian laws is to look, not every
man on his own things, but every man also on the things of others.
If we would adorn the doctrine of Christ, we must be active, early,
punctual. It is a sin to waste another man's time, as much as to
waste his property. " Whatsoever ye do, do all to the glory of
God." No doubt it is the natural disposition of some people to be
slovenly, and unexact; but what is your religion worth if it do not

correct such a propensity? A person who is nimbler in body and spirit than you may find it an easier thing to fulfil his appointments; but he has some other weak side which he must watch: "watch and pray," each at his own weak side, "that ye enter not into temptation." If any man be in Christ, he is a new creature; and if the new life is strong in the heart, it will send its warm pulses down to the extremest member. It should be the delight of a disciple, to be leaving the things that are behind, and pressing forward to what lies yet before: it should be like the meat and drink of a disciple to be making progress in bringing unto captivity to the obedience of Christ those thoughts that hitherto have been allowed to run wild. We "are God's husbandry;" and our effort should be to bring all the outspread field of life under cultivation—to leave no corner lying waste. In olden times when land in this country was not so much valued, many portions, a strip by the roadside here, and a corner beside a stream there, were allowed to escape notice, and to lie unsown; but as its value increased, and became better known, useless roads were broken up, and useless hedges pulled out, and every yard of soil turned to account. A man's life is the field that belongs to the great heavenly Husbandman; it is not enough to cultivate its middle; every corner should be turned up and occupied. Those who are bent on making rich, know well how much depends on taking care of small fragments. If we were wisely ambitious of becoming rich towards God, we would not cast anything away. The furthest advanced Christian may be known by his care to serve Christ in little things, which others leave to chance—by his care to cultivate for Christ those little corners of life, which others allow to be filled with weeds. When any portions of the field, even outside edges and corners, are left unsown, uncared for, the roots and seeds which grow on these, spread widely and injure all. It is sad to see the whole field damaged by the weeds that run to seed on its borders. Do we not often see a Christian life marred and made almost useless by certain minor outside parts of it not being Christianized? The smallest extremity should be occupied for the Lord as well as the heart. Although the heart is the chief thing as to acceptance with God, the smallest things of life often become the most important for his service in the world. It is precisely at the extremities of our life course,—those parts that run out into diminutive points, that we come into contact with others: if these little outside things which they feel be not baptized in the spirit of Christ, we have no means of letting them feel our Christianity at all. A Christian in the city may be called to make a bargain with a man, or keep an appointment with him, a hundred times for once that he is called to tell his views of the Gospel, and the ground of his hope. Therefore, unless in these common things,—these little outside points, we witness for Christ, we shall seldom have it in our power to witness for him at all. Let every one please his neighbour for his good to edification.

There is in your house a central cistern for containing water, and it is supplied from the river or the spring. Out from that cistern, at its lip, go many channels leading to all parts of the house, for the use of all the inmates. If the cistern be nearly full —filled in almost all its bulk, and yet not filled to the lip, so as to cover the mouth of the outgoing channels, all these channels will remain dry, and none of the inmates will get any supply of water. The cistern is almost full,—a little more would make it overflow,—and yet to the household, in their several departments of labour, it is very much the same as if it were empty. They get none. There is not an overflow. It is not so full as to go into these branching channels, and appear at their furthest extremities, with constant pressure, ready to burst out at a touch.

I think I see many Christians useless to the world in this way. They are almost full, but not overflowing. They are concerned about the great things of eternity, but not so completely possessed as to let the spirit of Christ flow over into the smallest, commonest things of daily life. These remain hard and dry like the world. But it is by these that he touches others, and therefore, real Christian though he be, he does little good to others; perhaps he does harm to others by misrepresenting Christ to them, and even misrepresenting himself.

He who is a Christian in little things, is not a little Christian. He is the greatest Christian, and the most useful. The baptism of these little outlying things shows that he is full of grace, for these are grace's overflowings; and they are ever the overflowings of the full well that refresh the desert. The great centre must be fully occupied before the stream can reach that outer edge.

Honesty is the Best Policy

(Proverbs 11:1)

" A false balance is abomination to the Lord ; but a just weight is his delight."

FROM my youth I have been better acquainted with this verse than any other in the book, because I was wont to read it with much interest when I was a little boy, engraved in antique characters on a mouldering stone over the gateway of a market in the city of Perth.   In the times immediately after the Reformation, when the word of God was new to the people, it was much valued.   Through the spread of that word the nation had been emancipated from a bondage of many generations, and after the long darkness, men rejoiced in the light.   They were not ashamed of their deliverer : all classes felt and acknowledged their obligations to the Bible.   In this respect our lot has fallen on worse times : direct appeal to the Scriptures seems to be counted a violation of taste in places of power.   When that writing from the law of the Lord mouldered away by age, the magistrates, I suspect, did not engrave it again in their restored market-place.   The motto of another city, " Let Glasgow flourish by the preaching of the word," has dwindled down to " Let Glasgow flourish."   The legend became curt when the age grew carnal.   These straws show how the current has been running ; but there is reason to hope that the tide has already turned.   In the palace of the International Exhibition at London (1862), perhaps the greatest scene of human concourse that has ever been known in the world, texts of Scripture, sublime in themselves and finely appropriate to the circumstances, are written where they may be read by every eye.   It is refreshing to observe how the early reformers appealed to the Scriptures as the supreme arbiter in human affairs.   It was an evil day for the nation when rulers began to ignore the Bible, and govern as if God had never spoken to men.   Rulers and subjects, buyers and sellers alike should love the Bible : no other law can keep the world right.

The precept is abundantly plain; it requires no exposition. One of the ways in which dishonest selfishness strives to attain its ends is to use false weights and measures in the market. As civilization advances, fewer opportunities occur of successfully accomplishing this trick, and therefore other forms of deceit have crept in and cast into the shade the old-fashioned dishonesty. The modern dealer finds it more possible to cheat in the quality than in the quantity of the article. Dishonesty of either kind,— of every kind, is abomination to the Lord. Justice is His delight, alike in the weight of the goods and their worth. Though an honest man should get no thanks from the world, he ought to count it an abundant reward for all his self-sacrifice that the world's Judge sees every righteous deed, and delights in it. God claims to be in merchandise, and to have his word circling through all its secret channels; and when this salt is wanting, forthwith they become corrupt. Many men would fain banish God from his world. They are not Atheists : they are willing to meet Him by appointment on the Sabbath, and in the church, on condition that they shall be allowed to buy and sell without Him all the rest of the week. You may as well expect to escape from the air as from His presence. "In Him we live and move and have our being." The only man who in merchandise is happy or safe, is the man who, while trying to please his customer over the counter, tries also to please God. We ought, in this bustling community, to be aware that unfair trickery in disposing of goods is a sin that "doth most easily beset us." When a practice becomes common, it ceases to attract attention ; and if it be evil, it escapes reproof, by reason of its prevalence. It would be our wisdom to suspect ourselves on our exposed side. It is in a crowd that you are apt to lose your purse, or your good conscience. When you have cleverly concluded a bargain by concealment and falsehood, the loss is not all on one side. The seller suffers more by that transaction than the buyer: he leaves the shop with a damaged article, you remain with a defiled conscience. It is more blessed to give than to receive; and the counterpart is a terrible truth,— it is more cursed to be an intake than to be taken in.

But there is much actual dishonesty where the parties have not a deliberate intention to deceive. A man's judgment secretly leans to the side of his own interest. He has a bias in his own favour, and unless he be both watchful and prayerful, he will enter ere he is aware into the temptation, and give a false tone to his statements without admitting to himself the design of telling lies. This kind of dishonesty is still dishonest. A man may indeed innocently make a mistake, but the innocent mistakes will, on an average, as frequently favour your customers as yourselves. If they are all on your own side, they are not innocent. There is a rule by which we may escape this danger. I have seen a mechanic working with the appropriate tools upon a piece of wood, in order to bring its surface to a perfect level. After he had wrought some time, he took a rule and laid it along his work, bending his head and looking, to ascertain whether the rule and the wood plied to each other along their whole length, or whether daylight appeared anywhere between them. When the work had so far advanced that the rule and the wood touched each other throughout their length, the workman, not yet satisfied, turned the rule round the other way, and looked again. Why? He did not trust the rule; there might, for aught he knew, be a slight bend in it; and though the plank and it agreed, both might be uneven. By reversing the rule, he removes all chance of deception. His object is not that the plank should appear, but that it should be straight. Go and do likewise. You lay your rule along the transaction, and the two agree. But one's heart is deceitful; perhaps it is inclined to yourself a little. Reverse the rule. Put yourself in the customer's place, and the customer in yours. Would you then like the same representation to be made, and the same price to be paid? This is a method for detecting an unfair bias in our bargains, which the Redeemer himself condescended to supply—"Whatsoever ye would that men should do unto you, do ye even so unto them."

If I speak plainly, even bluntly, against dishonest shifts, it is not that I have any prejudice against trade. I honour merchandise. I place merchants on equality with princes in my esteem. I think the time is coming when their position will be more honourable still. To a greater extent every year, the surplus produce of one country is required to supply the increasing wants of another. This is a great providential arrangement for bringing

and binding the nations into one. Merchants are the true ambassadors of nations, conducting their intercourse and interlacing
their interests. The longer the world lasts, it will become more
difficult for nation to go to war with nation. They are undergoing a dovetailing process, and every year interpenetrating each
other with deeper and deeper indentations. Merchants are the
engineers and artificers in that mighty process of providence for
binding the peoples of the earth together by their interests, and
perhaps for preparing among them the way of the Lord. Between
east and west, north and south, barbarian and civilized, merchants
are the mediators accredited and sent by the Supreme. As the
atmosphere touching both, mediates for blessed purposes between
the sea and the earth, relieving the sea of its surplus water, and
pouring it over the thirsty ground ; so the class of merchants
mediate between the different countries of the world, making the
produce of all the property of each, and the produce of each the
property of all.

It is because I see the greatness of merchandise that I strive
for its purity. When the truth of God, as a preserving salt, shall
pervade the fountain in the merchants' hearts, the outgoing streams
of traffic will be pure, and the whole landscape will wave with the
blossoms of love and the fruits of righteousness. Though dishonesty be concealed, its effects cannot be diminished. The world
is under law to God. Falsehood, in proportion to its amount,
poisons and paralyzes the whole mercantile system. It is a
bitterness in the spring which, according to its extent, will infallibly tell in scorching the land with barrenness. The system
of nature is constructed so as to fit into truth. The world has
been made for honest men ; the dishonest rack and rend it, like
gravel among the wheels of a machine. But if lies impede the
motions of the social system, the social system in its slow and
solemn revolutions brings down heavy blows upon the liar's head.

Assorted Pairs

(Proverbs 11:2, 3)

" When pride cometh, then cometh shame: but with the lowly is wisdom. The integrity of the upright shall guide them: but the perverseness of transgressors shall destroy them."

IN morals, things go in pairs as rigidly and regularly as living creatures in nature. The Bible contains the history and the rules of God's government, and therefore the unions that exist in providence are written in the word. Here is one of them. Pride and shame constitute a pair : they must go together whether they will or not. All the wriggling of the victims cannot break the chain that binds them. For wise and righteous ends, they have been made twins by the Author and Ruler of the world. As well might you try to tear away the shadow, so that it should not haunt the body, as to prevent shame from dogging the steps of pride. The laws of nature cannot be overturned by the power, or overreached by the cunning of men. It is not only that shame will appear as the punishment of pride on some future day : " Pride cometh ; then cometh shame." There is always something at hand to gall pride, where there is pride to be galled. A proud man is never at ease : he is always apprehensive of danger, and always on the watch. It is certain that no man has good ground for being proud ; and to have ideas at variance with your circumstances, is to steep your life in misery. A proud man, having nothing to be proud of, is like a boy trespassing in a field not his own : the pleasure is all embittered by the fear of being caught. In this life, the condition of humanity at the best is one of suffering ; but pride adds other irritants of its own. Two men are confined in cells of equal capacity : neither habitation can be reckoned roomy ; neither inhabitant can be altogether content. But if one meekly submit, and make the best of it, his lot will be endurable ; whereas the other, if he dash himself continually on the sides of his prison, will make his life miserable while it lasts, and soon bring it to a close. Both the humble and the proud man are in a low confined condition ; but the one, by bowing his head, escapes the blow; the other, by stretching aloft, brings his body into destructive collision with the barriers which the Omnipotent has set round the sinful.

Pride ? what is the man proud of ? Money ? It will not procure for him one night's sleep: it will not buy back a lost friend: it will not bribe off approaching death. Land ? a very little bit of it will serve him soon. Birth ? what has he inherited, but sin and corruption ? Learning ? if he is equal to Newton, he has gathered one little pebble on the ocean's shore, and even that one he must soon lay down again. It would be better that shame should come now on the proud, like a flood, to cover them, that their hearts may melt in godly sorrow : for if shame come first when mercy has finally passed away, how dreadful will its coming be ! Then it will be " shame and everlasting contempt."

With the lowly is wisdom—the wisdom from above. The lowest parts of the land are warm and fertile; the lofty mountains are cold and barren. The secret of the Lord is with them that fear him. " Blessed are the poor in spirit, for theirs is the kingdom of heaven."

All obliquity and trick in the intercourse of men is a libel on providence. Every recourse to falsehood is a direct distrust of God. Truth is both the shortest and the surest road in every difficulty. How much labour is lost by adopting tortuous paths. A great part of life's labour consists in following a crooked course, and then trying to make it appear a straight one. The crooked line is far more difficult at the first, and the defence of it afterwards doubles the labour. The intercourse of nations with each other, designated by the general term diplomacy, is proverbially a game of dexterity. We do not certainly know what goes on, for we have never been admitted into their secrets ; but if diplomatists be not much maligned, there is a great deal of double dealing in their art. It seems to be understood that a man of transparent and scrupulous truthfulness is not fitted to be a diplomatist. It is a prevalent idea among politicians, that though truth is best in the abstract, yet in some cases it is not safe to depend upon it, while others are endeavouring to circumvent you. You are in difficulty and danger; you must fortify to the uttermost; you must do the best; therefore you will twist together a few lies in order thereby to defend your position, and foil your adversary! That is, when there is a stress you cast aside the straight line of truth, and trust to the crooked course of hypocrisy. The cripple, at a rocky part of the road, throws away his sturdy oak-staff, and grasps a bruised reed, by way of making sure that he will get safely over. Vain hope! "Truth is great, and it will prevail." Truth is the most potent weapon of attack, and the surest covering for the head in the day of battle. Each party throws the blame of lying on his adversary, and continues himself to lie. The ever-recurring justification of diplomatic trick is, Though we were willing to be true, we have lying rogues to deal with. What then? The question remains entire; in dealing with them, what is your strongest weapon and surest defence? Is it truth, or a lie? Meet them with transparent truthfulness. Your truth will, in the long run, be stronger than their lie, and you will overcome. We are confident that if a nation, in all its intercourse with neighbours, were transparent and true like sunlight, that nation would soon be in the ascendant. Truth is God's law, as well as gravitation. Those who conform to these laws, in their several departments, are safe; those who contravene them are crushed by their self-acting vengeance-stroke. Their own act brings down the retribution; "the perverseness of trangressors shall destroy them."

Hypocrites and Talebearers

(Proverbs 11:9-13)

"**An** hypocrite with his mouth, destroyeth his neighbours. A talebearer revealeth secrets: but he that is of a faithful spirit concealeth the matter."

AN untrue man is the moral murderer, his mouth the lethal weapon, and his neighbour the victim. Horrid employment! For what purpose have we been placed in the world? Look unto Jesus, and learn in His life what is your own errand here. He came to seek and save the lost. He went about doing good. Let no man deceive himself with words. Nothing in nature is surer and truer than this, that Christians are like Christ; and they who are not in some measure like Christ are not Christians. Let that mind which was in Him be also found in you. He has left us an example that we should follow His steps. The destroyers of a neighbour are as far from the track of Jesus as men in this life can be. Beware of carrying lethal weapons. For what end did God give to man and to man alone, a speaking mouth? The Maker of that tongue meant it not to be a dart to pierce a brother with. Remember every morning who gave you that wonderful instrument, and how he intended it to be used. When a kind parent sends to his distant child a case of curious mechanical instruments, he takes care to send along with them printed "directions for use." Even such a set of directions has our Father in heaven sent to us along with the case of cunning instruments which our living body contains. Look into the directions and see what is written opposite the mouth and tongue; for "speaking the truth in love" (Eph. iv. 15). Every dear child will do what his Father bids him. He tries the edge of the weapon on truth to honour the giver God, and on love to soothe the sorrows of brother men. The tongue is one, and that not the least, of the ten talents. "Occupy till I come," is the condition of the loan; near, though unseen, is the day of reckoning.

A talebearer [double tongued] is an odious character. He takes in all your story, if you are weak enough to give it to him, and then runs off to the next house, and pours it into the greedy ears of jealous neighbours. His character is a compound of weakness and wickedness. He is feared less than bolder criminals, and despised more. If he were not weak, he would not act so wickedly; but if he were not wicked, he would not act so weakly. He breeds hatred, and spreads it. He carries the infection from house to house, like a traveller, from city to city, bringing the plague in his garments. Families soon begin to mark him as a dangerous man ; and, in the exercise of sovereign authority within their own borders, they prescribe a rigid quarantine: they prescribe for him an offing wide enough to ensure their own safety. The true antithesis to the talebearer is a "faithful spirit." Poets have often sung the sweetness of true friendship, but they can never reach the bottom of it. It is a spring in the desert: without it the weary pilgrim would not get forward at all. Beyond computation precious is the friend who, instead of the weakness and wickedness of a talebearer, possesses the opposite qualities of strength and goodness,—who is soft enough to take in your sorrows, and firm enough to keep them. It is a substantial help to suffering humanity, when a being of the same nature with yourself goes into your very heart, and yet will not divulge the secrets which he has witnessed there. The Lord, who knows what is in man, takes notice of these things. He provides helps meet to us in our griefs : he provides human sympathy for human sorrow to lean upon. He approves when any one, for his sake, and at his bidding, acts the part of a friend to a needy brother : he gives, indeed, to his own people such duties as these to exercise their graces on. "Without spot or wrinkle, or any such thing," is their ultimate acquirement, and should be their present aim. They are glad to be employed by Him, and like Him. Apprentices learning a trade, they do not look for wages; rather they count themselves obliged, when subjects and opportunities are afforded to try upon, that by exercise they may grow more skilful in acting the part of faithful friends.

Debts and Sureties
(Proverbs 11:15; 6:1-5)

"He that is surety for a stranger shall smart for it; and he that hateth suretiship is sure."

RASH suretiship, and the ruin that follows it, seem to have been common in those days, as well as our own. The traffic of ancient times was small, in comparison with the vast system of exchange which now compasses the whole world, like network; but the same vices that we lament marred it, and the same righteousness that we desiderate would have healed its ailments. Neither the law of gravitation nor the law of righteousness has changed since the time of Solomon; both are as powerful now as they were then, and as pervasive. The things are different in form and bulk, but ancient and modern merchandise are of the same nature, and subject to the same laws. As to the laws, whether physical or moral, there is nothing new under the sun.

In those primitive times, it seems, as in our own, some men desired to get faster forward in the world than their circumstances legitimately permitted. They were determined to get up, although they had nothing to stand upon. Their ambition fretted at the slow and vulgar method of climbing up by patient industry; they would ascend by a bound. They must get a neighbour to become security for them, that they may get the use of money which is not their own. They will throw for a fortune to themselves at another's risk. There were also others, it appears, so simple as to become surety for the adventurers, perhaps because they could not command enough of courage to refuse a friend, although they thereby cast into a lottery the home and the food of their own families.

The warning does not of course discourage considerate kindness in bearing a deserving man over a temporary pressure.

When you have ascertained the character of the person, and measured the amount of his need; when you have balanced your own affairs, and discovered that they have buoyancy sufficient to bear both your yourself and your brother over the strait, then do a brother's turn, and enjoy a brother's love. No precept of the Bible demands that we should harden our hearts against the claims of the needy. The Bible permits and requires more of kindness to our brother than we have ever shown him yet; but it does not allow us to do a certain substantial evil, for the sake of a distant shadowy good. It condemns utterly the rash engagements which, under pretence of doing a kindness to one, inflicts injustice on a hundred. Righteousness, in all times, and all circumstances, reclaims against the blind effort which, for the sake of supporting a tottering fabric, incurs the risk of bringing your own house down about your ears, and crushing beneath its ruins many innocent victims.

We make no inquiry into the method of conducting pecuniary transactions in the days of Solomon: our object is not antiquarian research, but the rebuke of present wrong, and the establishment of righteousness. The most convenient method will be to apply what we count the straight line to a number of cases that are daily occurring in business. We shall thread them on like beads upon a string, and every one, with a Bible in his hand, and a conscience in his breast, may judge for himself whether they hang fairly.

1. If a merchant, possessing unencumbered twenty thousand pounds, desires to get the use of ten thousand more, he may legitimately obtain it in money or goods from bankers or brother merchants, if he do not misrepresent the real state of his affairs. But although he really possesses twenty thousand, and thinks himself safe, if he convey to others in any way the impression that he has forty thousand, in order to obtain more credit, he infringes the law of righteousness as certainly and sinfully as the trickster on a lower platform, and a smaller scale.

2. A man who has not more than ten pounds may legitimately borrow ten thousand, if he can get it, after revealing the whole case to the capitalist as thoroughly as it is known to himself. He may be such a man, that his character and ten pounds in hand are a better guarantee than another man can give who has

ten thousand pounds, but not a character. Let the whole truth be known—make a clear breast, and if another choose to take the risk, you may accept the money. The same principles would of course bind you to be at least as careful of the money so obtained as if it were your own.

3. A merchant is engaged in extensive business. He began it with a large capital, and good credit. In process of time he meets with heavy losses. He discovers from his balance that his assets will not cover his liabilities. What should he do? A common maxim in such a case is—take care not to change your house; on no account dismiss your coachman, or sell your horses; invite dinner parties more frequently this winter than you did the last, and see that the luxuriance be not in aught diminished,—all to keep up your credit. Measured by the line of God's law, all this is unmitigated dishonesty. It is to fence your position all round with a battery of lies. It is to keep money on false pretences. When you have nothing, if you keep up a show for the purpose of persuading your creditors that you are as rich as ever, you are cheating your neighbours. When the ground on which a man gave you credit has fallen away, you must let him know it. If, after revelation and explanation, he think it better on the whole that you should make another effort, it is well; let the effort be made, but concealment in these circumstances is sheer dishonesty.

4. A man has lost on his business this year. He hopes that he will make good the loss in another and better season. He borrows from his friends, and pushes forward. Again at the balance it is discovered that he is still sinking. He is below the horizon of solvency. He owes now more than all that he has. He borrows again, not revealing to the creditors the state of the case. Is he justified? No, verily. The act is dishonest, and there is a loathsome selfishness in the dishonesty; he is pushing forward, knowing that if he succeed the gain will be his own, if he fail, the loss will lie on his neighbours, for he has nothing to lose.

5. A man, honest and honourable, is conducting a legitimate business in a legitimate way. He is indebted to his customers, and his customers are indebted to him. The whole process goes regularly and fairly on. He gains a few hundreds every year for

the support of his family, and there is at all times a balance in his favour over the transactions in the mass. A friend not connected with him in business comes to this man, and requests the favour of his name to a bill by which he may obtain the use of ten thousand for a few months, to enable him to take advantage of a promising speculation—(speculations are always promising). He yields. In an evil hour he writes his name on that paper. Now his position in relation to his ordinary creditors is wholly changed. They knew him only in the transactions of business. They had, in the course of these transactions, given him credit to a legitimate amount, and for a reasonable time. When they gave it, he had the means of repaying all. Now he has contracted, without telling them, a liability which, if it become due, will swallow up all his substance, and leave his lawful creditors unpaid. To contract that liability was unjust.

6. One case more we shall adduce, connected like the last immediately and directly with suretiship, and selected as a specimen of the extravagant and dangerous excesses to which speculation runs in this feverish age. Suretiship, as distinct from money lending, has been converted into a business, and prosecuted for profit. A species of underwriters has sprung secretly up, who insure against losses, not on the sea of water, but on the more treacherous waves of gambling speculation. You are engaged in business, with large assets and heavy liabilities, but with the reputation in society of substantial wealth. Another man is struggling against the tide, and is no longer able to keep his head above water. He applies to a neighbour as needy as himself. A bill with both names attached is presented to the banker. The man of money shakes his head, and requests time to consider. But time is the very thing which the two adventurers cannot spare. Money they must have, and they must have it now. They present themselves with their bill in your counting-house. They want your name; you will never be troubled—all that they want is your name, to enable them to clear a pressing difficulty. You have no interest in them, and will not give them your name for love; but you have an eye to your own interest, and will give it for money. The terms are discussed—how much per cent. for your name; the terms are adjusted, and the bargain struck. If the applicant is needy, he will offer a large premium—not for the

loan of money, be it observed, for the poor borrower is obliged to pay the interest to the bank besides, and you do not give him a farthing, even in loan—he agrees to pay a large premium to you for the use of your name, to enable him to borrow in another quarter. If traffic becomes extensive, large profits may come in for a time ; but in the nature of things the medicine aggravates the speculator's disease. The traffic becomes more and more dangerous. The hollow principals fail to meet their engagements, and the liability falls back on you ; your capital is swallowed up, your family ruined, and your ordinary creditors defrauded.

Enough of these examples : now for the elucidation of the principles of truth and righteousness as applied to modern trade. We are met here by the old cry, that business cannot be conducted at all if these principles are closely insisted on. Let business perish if it must needs rise on downcast and dishonoured Truth ! Let business creep on the ground, in isolated acts of exchange, like the diminutive and simple transactions of children and savages, if its vast and symmetrical structure can be reared only upon the wreck of righteousness ! But we are not shut up to such a dire alternative. Business, in all its extent, and through all its complications, will stand more securely on a basis of perfect righteousness, and move more sweetly when every wheel turns in a bedding of transparent truth. The goodly machine needs no underhand dealing and false representation to keep it going. These are the things which make it jerk and creak, and break and rend those who handle it.

Specifically, as to sureties, the law of the Lord gives no harsh recommendation, and countenances no selfish neglect of a neighbour in need. Help him, if he is deserving and you are able ; but help him out of your own means, and do not mortgage for that object the money that really belongs to another man. You have a right to pledge your own money in the case, if you think the case is good ; but you have no right to pledge mine also in it, however good it may be : but you do pledge the money of other people, the moment that you bind yourself for more than you have of your own.

We are very far from saying or thinking that, in the intricate avenues of modern merchandise, a strictly conscientious man will always see his way clearly, and never meet with difficulties. We are well aware, that, in the evolution of circumstances, an honest man may suddenly find himself in an enclosure where it is exceedingly difficult to determine in what direction righteousness leads. Let it be supposed that he fears God and regards man ; that he would do justly at all hazards if he were sure what course would, on the whole, be most just. We grant readily that the line of duty may, in some cases, be involved in great darkness, and that with a pure purpose the man may sometimes take a step which involves himself and others in the direst disasters. Flesh and blood ourselves, and knowing that even when pure principle reigns in the heart, the path of practical duty, in any line of life, may be involved in many doubts, we would not proudly dictate to a brother on difficulties which beset his steps, and from which our different profession, not our superior probity, keeps us free. First, in the name of the Lord and in the cause of righteousness, we denounce all dishonesty and untruth, however large and intricate the transactions in question may be. And then, with human sympathy and in conscious weakness, we counsel all good men engaged in business to be aware of its dangers, and to watch and pray that they enter not into temptation. In this line of life as in every other, there are trials of faith and of other graces. All that we demand, and all that is needed, is that Christian merchants take their Christianity with them into merchandise, and keep it with them all the way. In every case seek the Lord's will and you will find it. Consult the honour of Christ and the safety of your soul as to what business you will go into, and how far in you will go. You have not fulfilled your duty when you are able to say that you did not of set purpose do any wrong. The question is, where the path is slippery and many falling, how painful and prayerful were you that you might not stumble unconsciously into evil. A Christian is not forbidden to go into business ; but if he look within and around, he will discover that his watchword there should be " Fear, and sin not."

As We Sow, We Reap
(Proverbs 11:17, 18, 20)

"The merciful man doeth good to his own soul; but he that is cruel troubleth his own flesh. The wicked worketh a deceitful work: but to him that soweth righteousness shall be a sure reward. They that are of a froward heart are abomination to the Lord: but such as are upright in their way are his delight."

"THE merciful man doeth good to his own soul : but he that is cruel troubleth his own flesh."

Blessed are the merciful ; all the good they do to others returns with interest to their own bosoms. "It is more blessed to give than to receive." In every act that mercy prompts there are two parties who obtain a benefit,—the person in need, who is the object of compassion, and the person not in need, who pities his suffering brother. Both get good, but the giver gets the larger share. In common life, the act of showing mercy to the needy is very good for the man who shows it. The good Samaritan who bathed the wounds and provided for the wants of a plundered Jew, obtained a greater profit on the transaction than the sufferer who was saved by his benevolence. It is like God to constitute his world so. Even Christ himself in the act of showing mercy, has his reward : when He sees of the travail of his soul He is satisfied.

Like other fixtures in nature, this principle has its counterpart. When light departs, darkness comes in its stead : when a human bosom is a stranger to the blessedness of the merciful, it tastes the misery of the cruel or the careless. As mercy blesses, cruelty torments both the parties,—the one who bears and the one who inflicts it. This is a law of God, set deep in the constitution of things—a law that magnifies his mercy. A man cannot hurt his neighbour, without hurting more deeply himself : the rebound is heavier than the blow. The man who chastises his brother with whips, will himself, by the movements of providence, be chastised with scorpions. Such is the fence which the Creator has set up to keep man off his fellow. This dividing line is useful now to check the ravages of sin ; but when perfect love has come, that divider, no longer needed, will be no longer seen. It is like one of those black jagged ridges of rock that at low water stretch across the sand from the edge of the cultivated ground to the margin of the sea, an impassable, an unapproachable barrier : when the tide rises, all is level and it is nowhere seen. This law of God, rising as a rampart between man and man, is confined to this narrow six thousand year strip of time : in the perfect state it will act no more, for want of material to act upon.

" The wicked worketh a deceitful work : but to him that soweth righteousness shall be a sure reward."

Wickedness is a work that deceives its performer; it may do the harm which he intended to a neighbour, but it cannot procure the good which he expected for himself. By necessity of his condition, every man's life, and every moment of it, is a sowing. The machine is continually moving over the field and shaking ; it cannot, even for a moment, be made to stand still, so as not to sow. It is not an open question at all whether I shall sow or not to-day ; the only question to be decided is, Shall I sow good seed or bad ? Every man always is sowing for his own harvest in eternity either tares or wheat. According as a man soweth, so shall he also reap : he that sows the wind of vanity shall reap the whirlwind of wrath. Suppose a man should collect a quantity of small gravel and dye it carefully, so that it should resemble wheat, and sow it in his field in spring, expecting that he would reap a crop of wheat like his neighbours in harvest. The man is mad ; he is a fool to think that by his silly trick he can evade the laws of nature, and mock nature's God. Yet equally foolish is the conduct, and far heavier the punishment, of the man who sows wickedness now and expects to reap safety at last. Sin is not only profitless and disastrous ; it is eminently a deceitful work. Men do not of set purpose cast themselves away : sin cheats a sinner out of his soul. The devil, man's great adversary, acts by deceiving : he is a liar from the beginning.

The same law sparkles brightly and beauteously in the counterpart : " To him that soweth righteousness shall be a sure reward." The reward is sure, because it comes in the way of natural law :

the reward follows righteousness as fruit follows the seed. The only righteous man that ever lived, the Righteous One, sowed in this desert world—sowed in tears ; but he sowed righteousness. Out of that sowing a great increase has already sprung, and a greater is coming. From that handful on the mountain top a harvest shall wave like Lebanon. "Come ye blessed of my Father, inherit the kingdom." Behold the husbandman returning home with joy, bringing his sheaves with him ! To his members in their own place the same law holds good. Sowing righteousness is never, and nowhere, lost labour. Every act done by God's grace, and at His bidding, is living and fruitful. It may appear to go out of sight, like seed beneath the furrow ; but it will rise again. Sow on, Christians ! Sight will not follow the seed far ; but when sight fails sow in faith, and you will reap in joy soon. More of the word of God is scattered over the world in our day than at any previous period of the Christian dispensation. The result, though unseen, is not doubtful ; in grace as in nature, things proceed by law, and the ultimate result is sure.

"They that are of a froward heart are abomination to the Lord : but such as are upright in their way, are his delight."

To think of God only as "angry with the wicked" is but half a truth; and half a truth sometimes becomes practically a falsehood. To picture our Father in heaven all in shade is to hide half His loveliness, and keep His creatures terrified away. There is another side of His character, and the two together make up the divine perfection : the righteous Lord loveth righteousness. It is an encouraging and not a presumptuous thought, that the Holy one delights in every good thing which grace has wrought in His children. "Ye are God's husbandry :" that field He watches and waters night and day. Many weeds grow there to grieve Him, and many spots lie barren; but our "Father is the Husbandman ;" the Husbandman is a Father, and he suffers long. He bears with the barrenness of His garden ; and, in as far as it thrives, he tastes the fruit and counts it pleasant. It was a wilderness until He, in sovereign mercy, took it in, and many things mar its fruitfulness yet ; but He does not therefore despise or desert it. He loves all that He recognises as His own there. That humble and broken heart becomes His dwelling-place.

A Jewel Ill Set

(Proverbs 11:22)

" As a jewel of gold in a swine's snout, so is a fair woman which is without
discretion."

T HE lines of this picture are few and bold. The details
are not elaborated; but by one stroke the likeness is
caught, and with unwavering hand it is held up to
public gaze. The conceptions and expressions here are peculiar
and memorable: they are remarkable alike for the unvarnished
homeliness of the allusion, and the permanent, palpable truth of
the picture. The very rudeness of the imagery is designed, and
serves a purpose. An analogy might have been found fitted to
convey a true sentiment on the point, and steering clear of
associations which affect the mind with a measure of disgust; but
that very disgust is an essential part of the impression to be conveyed. The words of the Lord are tried words : the comparison
is chosen for the purpose of setting before us an outrageous incongruity—the conjunction of two things whose union is palpably
and monstrously inappropriate. Both the judgment and the taste
must be educated. It is necessary that we should both see the
thing to be wrong, and feel it to be revolting : we need both to
have the understanding enlightened and the affections exercised.
A Christian's affections should be trained to strike out positive
and strong in both directions; he should love the lovely and hate
the hateful. Both emotions should start quickly, like instincts,
when their objects appear ; both should be hearty and effective.
A good man loathes evil as much as he loves good. The law that
action and reaction are equal and opposite holds good in morals
as well as in physics. The righteous Lord loveth righteousness,
and it is but the other side of that same glory that glances in the
rebuke of lukewarm Laodicea, " I will spue thee out of my mouth"
(Rev. iii. 16).

Personal beauty is not a thing to be despised: it is a work of God, and none of his works are done in vain. We do not count it a man's duty to be unimpressed by the grandeur of a lofty mountain, or the loveliness of a starry sky. It is obvious that human-kind are the chief of God's works on earth, and that in the human form is displayed the highest beauty of creation. Beauty is a talent, and has a power. Call it, if you will, a power like that of a sharp knife, dangerous in the hands of the weak or the wicked; but still it is a power the gift of God, and capable of being ranked among the all things that advance his glory. Like wealth or wisdom, or any other talent, it may be possessed by the humble, and employed for good. If the heart be holy and the aim true, personal beauty will enlarge the sphere and double the resources of beneficence. The same spread full sail may speed the ship on her course, or dash her on the rock of doom. If the beautiful be not also good, beauty becomes an object of disgust and a cause of ruin. For such a spread of sail, and such a breeze as it is sure to catch, a greater than ordinary amount of solid deep ballast is needed in the body of the character, not only for extended usefulness, but even for simple preservation from quick perdition.

The lesson on this subject appears in the word in a form of peculiar homeliness: we must beware, lest in straining after refinement, we let its strength slip through our fingers. If we would maintain congruity between the comment and the text, we must go to our object by a straight short line. Let a man beware of being tricked and caught and chained by a woman's beauty, so as to be dragged through the mire by the bewitching bond. When an impure character is clothed in corporeal loveliness, it is the spirit of darkness appearing as an angel of light, enticing to devour. A beautiful woman who is proud, flippant, selfish, false, is miserable herself, and dangerous to others. It is a combination to be loathed and shunned. A swine wallowing in the mire is not a creature that you would follow and embrace, although she had a jewel of gold in her snout! Such is the glass in which the Bible bids us see the sin and folly of the man who gives himself over to the fascination of a worthless heart, because it is covered by a fair skin.

Women who have beauty above the average should be peculiarly watchful on that side, lest they sin and suffer there. You have a jewel of gold; don't put it in a swine's snout. The misapplication will prostitute the gift; the incongruity will be repulsive to all whose tastes are true. It will attract the vain, and repel the solid. There are diversities of operation under the ministry of the same Spirit. For discipline to human souls in time, deformity is given to one, and beauty to another. The chief consideration for each is how she may best bear the trial, so as to get it enlisted among the workers for good, and instruments of saving. If both are saved, it will be a pleasant exercise to compare notes of their several paths and several burdens, when they meet in equal loveliness, without spot or wrinkle, in the presence of the Lord. If it were our part to judge, most of us would think it probable that beauty is the greater trial, and that under it a greater proportion stumble and fall. But we are not permitted to judge, for we are not able to judge aright. We do not see far. The Lord is judge himself; and the day shall declare whether beauty, in filling the soul with vanity, or deformity, in fretting it with envy, has been actually the more successful instrument of evil in Satan's hands. Meantime, those who on either extremity have a weight to bear, should watch unto prayer, and cast their burden on the Lord; while we, the mass of human-kind in the middle, who in that respect have neither poverty nor riches, should be humbly thankful to God for casting our lot in a safer place, and marking out for us an easier path.

The Desire of the Righteous
(Proverbs 11:23)

" The desire of the righteous is only good."

I N the preceding chapter we learned that "the desire of
the righteous shall be granted:" here we are told that
it is good. The fruit we gathered on a former page;
and now the tree that bore it is displayed. A good tree bringeth
forth good fruit: holy desires implanted in the heart will issue in
glad enjoyments. "Delight thyself also in the Lord, and he shall
give thee the desires of thine heart" (Ps. xxxvii. 4).

The new nature has new affections : every creature after its kind.
The desires of this new man which has been "put on" in conversion are "only good;" but the desires of the old nature are not
yet destroyed, and a life-long conflict is maintained between them.
In every Christian while he lives there is a warfare between two
opposite principles. Paul stands forth as the type of the truly
converted, but not perfectly sanctified disciple—" When I would
do good, evil is present with me" (Rom. vii. 21). There is a great
tumult in a human breast where these two contrary currents contend. It is like the meeting-place of the rising tide and the descending torrent. One stream, pure and transparent, is rising
mysteriously up; another, yellow and turbid, is rushing, according
to its constant nature, down. The contention is sharp, but it is
soon over. The pure overcomes the impure. That which rises
up, apparently contrary to law, overcomes that which flows down
obviously according to law : the ocean, entering that channel, over-
powers and beats back the mountain stream. It is thus that the
tide which issues from the Infinite, and acts against the law of the
carnal mind, arrests and throws back the carnal mind, notwithstanding its long possession and its impetuous flow. The tide that rises
is under law, as well as the stream that descends ; but the law lies
deeper among the things of God. That rising tide is not only pure

in itself, it has Omnipotence behind to urge it on. There will be a mixture at the point of contact, and while the conflict rages; but soon the unclean will be driven back, and the channel will be filled from brim to brim by a pure ascending stream.

Pure in character, and upward in direction, is the current of a righteous man's desire. This description is a standing rebuke of our poor attainments. How faintly is the attraction from heaven felt, how feebly flow the heart's emotions thitherward, how deeply tinged, even in their upward course, by the mingling remnants of the downward current! And yet there is encouragement here, as well as rebuke; this purity of desire is attainable in some measure, on the earth. The design of discipline is to increase it; and it will be perfect when the discipline is done. The hope of final and complete success is a powerful motive to present exertion. When the new man is perfect, his desires will be only good, with no admixture of evil; and when the desires are only good, they will all be gratified. When the last lust of the flesh is crucified, disappointments will cease. If my heart's desires were all and only good, they would be like God's; and when my will is God's will, it shall be accomplished, for he will do all his pleasure.

Scattering to Keep and Keeping to Scatter
(Proverbs 11:24)

" There is that scattereth, and yet increaseth; and there is that withholdeth more than
is meet, but it tendeth to poverty."

THE maxim, although in form approaching the paradox,
has become familiar by frequent use. If any of us
should hear it now for the first time, we would be startled by its boldness; but the proverb, like a well worn coin, has
become smooth by long continued handling, and it passes easily
from mind to mind, in the intercourse of life. To have undergone
so much wear, and yet to be accepted in the market-place for all
its original worth, is evidence both that the metal is pure, and that
the stamp of royalty is on it. Day by day this proverb of Solomon is offered and accepted on our streets, as a ground, legitimate
and authoritative, for giving freely of our means in behalf of objects
that are acknowledged good. By Christians, who labour for the
good of men, it is boldly applied; and wherever there is an enlightened conscience, and a sound understanding, it is felt to be
applicable. As the formal and authoritative expression of a fact
which may be observed in the history of Providence, it is a word of
great practical value. It is a sharp weapon, always at hand, by
which a man may deal a blow against incipient selfishness in himself or his neighbour.

The conception is similar to that of sowing righteousness, which
occurred before. In agriculture, to scatter corn is the sure and
only way to increase it. It is a species of faith that the cultivator
of the soil exercises when he casts good grain into the ground. In
point of fact, the exercise is easy, and the mind is not racked by
stretching far into the dark future for a pillar of truth to support
its trust; still, in its nature, it is faith in the unseen. The direct
design is to increase corn, and with that view the man who possesses it scatters what he has. His faith is rewarded by a mani·

fold return : if, in stupid, wilful, short-sighted penuriousness, he had withheld the seed, the hoarding would have tended to poverty.

To distribute portions of our wealth in schemes and acts of wise philanthropy, is like casting into the ground as seed a proportion of the last year's harvest. It goes out of your sight for the moment, but it will spring in secret, and come back to your own bosom, like manna from heaven.

An unwise man may indeed scatter his corn on barren rocks, or equally barren sands, and though he sow bountifully, he will reap sparingly there. So, in the moral region, the increase is not absolutely in proportion to the profusion of the scattering. When a man lays out large sums on unworthy objects, to feed his own vanity, or gratify his own whim, he neither does nor gets good : the outlay is in its own nature, and necessarily unprofitable. Sound judgment is as necessary in selecting the objects of philanthropy, and determining the proportion of effort that should be bestowed on each, as in deciding where and when the seed should be sown. To give money, for example, indiscriminately to street beggars, who tell a whining tale, and cunningly enact distress, is worse than to sow precious seed on the sand of the seashore. The seed cast on the sand will be lost : money given to the profligate is lost, and more. It is not barren ; it multiplies and replenishes the earth with vice. Many fields, both needful and promising, lie open for contribution and effort. In educating the young, in reclaiming the vicious, in supporting the aged poor, in healing the sick, and in making known the gospel to all, we have ample fields to cultivate, and the prospect of large returns to cheer us in the toil.

The law that judicious liberality does not impoverish, and selfish niggardliness does not enrich, may be seen in its effects by any intelligent observer. If one, not content with the homely evidence of experience, should demand how this can be, it would be sufficient answer simply to repeat that it *is*, and appeal to the history of the city or the generation. But, further, we may answer by another question, How does the material seed grow in the material ground ? In point of fact, it does grow; and this is the sum of our knowledge regarding it. Only the pride of the rankest ignorance imagines that we know how or why it grows. A step deeper, as was to be expected, are the ways of God in the moral processes, and on those borders where moral causes touch the material to produce sensible effects; but in both regions man must ever be speechless under the challenge, " Canst thou by searching find out God ?"

If we understand the maxim, we should act on it; and if we should act on it more, we would come to understand it better. Both as to our money and ourselves, it is better to wear than to rust. This is an earnest time. Seek a good investment; but lay it out. In the tides and currents of that commercial sea, which now as one connected ocean encircles all the earth, it is observed as a law that when many and great losses are incurred in one region, there is a flow of money into some other channel. Of late, investments in man's hands for time have not been secure. In that department we have heard many a heavy crash, and been called to pity the mangled victims as they crawled from beneath the ruins. Might we not expect that after these disappointments men would be seen streaming over to the other side, and hastening to invest in God's hands for eternity ? This lending to the Lord, when a surplus accrues, affords the best security, and insures the largest return. If the Son of Man should now come, would He find faith in the earth ? We think ourselves eminently a practical generation ; but we should beware lest we mistake the merely un- spiritual for the profitably practical. A carcass will not serve the purposes of a man. Action is useless or worse except in as far as it has true faith to energize and direct it. The material acquisi- tions of the age will become a heavier heap on the grave of humanity, if the Spirit of God be grieved away. The large and complicated body of our material prosperity will, if its soul goes out, only encumber us with a greater bulk of corruption. Faith is the animating soul of practice. Men cannot get forward even in things temporal unless they believe that God is, and that He is the rewarder of them that diligently seek Him.

The Waterer is Watered
(Proverbs 11:25)

" The liberal soul shall be made fat; and he that watereth shall be watered also himself."

IT is announced here that the bountiful shall be enriched; and that law is expressed in a simple, intelligible, and memorable figure—" He that watereth shall be watered also himself." How wisely and kindly God has bound his worlds into one, making all depend on each, and each on all! When we look up to the heavens, the moon and the stars which He hath made, we find there a law by which all the worlds of space are linked together. Our earth affects the moon, and the moon affects the earth; each planet influences all the rest : the removal of one would disturb the order of the whole. The well-being of all is concerned in the right working of each. This law pervades the works of God. Souls are linked to souls in the spiritual firmament, by a bond equally unseen, but equally powerful. One necessarily affects for good or evil all the rest in proportion to the closeness of its relations, and the weight of its influence. You draw another to keep him from error : the weight thus laid upon your shoulders keeps you steadier in your path. You water one who is ready to wither away ; and although the precious stream seems to sink into the earth, it rises to heaven and hovers over you, and falls again upon yourself in refreshing dew.

It comes to this : if we be not watering we are withering. There are only two things in time worthy of having the whole force of an immortal mind directed upon them, and these two are both here. The one is to be in Christ ourselves saved ; and the other, to be used by Christ in saving others. " None of us liveth to himself, and no man dieth to himself. For whether we live, we live unto the Lord ; and whether we die, we die unto the

Lord : whether we live therefore, or die, we are the Lord's " (Rom. xiv. 7, 8).

To water green flowers that they may not wither, or withered ones that they may revive, is one of the sweetest employments that fall to the lot of man. Moral and natural beauty are so entwined together in the act, that his spirit must be dull indeed who is not drawn by the double attraction. When the tastes of the spiritual life are kept keen by frequent exercise, it must be a keen and pure pleasure to be employed as a vessel to convey water from the well of life to souls which would wither for want of it. To be the instrument of keeping fresh a lively plant, or making fresh a drooping one, in the garden of God, is an occupation that angels might eagerly apply for ; but this work is all reserved for the children of the family : servants are employed in other and outer things.

There are diversities of occupation for the children, as well as diversities of operation by the Lord. To water flowers in a sheltered garden, at the going down of a summer's sun, is one work for man ; and to ply the hatchet on the hoary trunks of the primeval forest is another. The works are very diverse, and yet the same hand may do them both. The department of the Lord's work which this text commends is of the gentlest and most winsome kind. It differs as much from direct assault on Satan's stronghold for the first conviction of sinners, as that clearing of the first spot in the solitude which tries the strong arm of the emigrant differs from the watering of a garden-flower, which may be done by a woman's hand; but it is a work commanded by God, and needful for a brother. If we are his, and yield ourselves to him as instruments, he will at one time nerve us for rough work, and at another solace us with gentle occupation. He has both departments in his power, and in dividing he does all things well.

Opportunities and calls swarm at every turn. The blind may never see the case or the time in which he can do any good; but where the eyes are opened the willing man sees a mountain full of them.

Here is a young woman, into whose heart the word came with power in early youth. Through a storm of terrible conviction she emerged into peace. She sat down at the Lord's table in the church, and took the standing of the Lord's disciple in the world

She has grown up, and come out: perhaps by her parents she was ostentatiously brought out from the kindly shade of youthful retirement into the blaze of the world's hot light. Passions are kindled in her breast,—passions for dress, for company, for pleasure, which formerly she felt not and feared not. The sun has risen with a burning heat on the tender plant, not yet deeply rooted : forthwith it droops, and is ready to die. Run and water that weakling. Mingle faithful reproof with patient kindness. At the same moment touch her weakness with human sympathy, and her sin with God's awful word. When she feels that a disciple cares for her, she may be more easily convinced that the Lord cares for her too. Gently lead her to the beauty of holiness, that there she may lose relish for the pleasures of sin. She may be saved, and you may be the instrument of saving her. I have seen a plant of a certain species that had been exposed all day, unsheltered, unwatered, beneath a burning sun, bent and withered towards evening, and to all appearance dead ; but when one discovered its distress, and instantly watered it, the plant revived so suddenly and so completely as to strike inexperienced observers with astonishment.

Oh, it is sweet employment to be the waterer of a withering soul ! It is gentle work for tender workers. " Who is on the Lord's side let him come," and labour in this department. The work is pleasant and profitable. In the keeping of this commandment there is a great reward. To be a vessel conveying refreshment from the fountain-head of grace to a fainting soul in the wilderness is the surest way of keeping your own spirit fresh, and your experience ever new.

Raising the Market: The Practice and the Penalty
(Proverbs 11:26)

"He that withholdeth corn, the people shall curse him: but blessing shall be upon the head of him that selleth it."

T O keep up grain in order to raise the market is a practice of very old standing, and the world has not done with it yet. The manner in which this word deals with it is worthy of observation. This law bears no mark of having emanated from the ruling class of a nation. Here, as elsewhere, the Bible holds the balance even between the wealthy few and the needy many. Either class possesses its own peculiar power; one the power of wealth, another the power of numbers. The domination of any part over another is tyranny : liberty lies in the just balance of all interests. In this brief maxim no arbitrary rule is laid down to the possessor of corn, that he must sell at a certain period, and at a certain price : and yet the hungry are not left without a protecting law. The protection of the weak is intrusted not to small police regulations, but to great self-acting providential arrangements. The double fact is recorded in terms of peculiar distinctness, that he who in times of scarcity keeps up his corn in order to enrich himself is loathed by the people, and he who sells it freely is loved. This is all. There is no further legislation on the subject.

The wisdom of this course lies in its reserve. The history of some modern nations, especially that of France, reveals the disastrous consequences of forcing sales and regulating prices by arbitrary legislation. When a ruler rashly puts his hand to the wheel of providence to guide its movements, although it is done from the best of motives, he hurts both himself and his subjects. In the Bible no law is enacted, and no penalty prescribed. The evil doer is left under a penalty which legislation can neither abate nor enforce : " The people shall curse him." He becomes an object of detestation to the community in which he lives. No law and no government can shield him from that punishment : they might as well attempt to prevent the clouds from coming between his corn-fields and the sun. Nor is the punishment light. To be the object of aversion among his neighbours is a heavy infliction upon a human being. No man can despise it. What though I be lord of the land, as far as my eye can see on every side ; if the men and women and children who live on it loathe and shun me, I am miserable. When from the battlements of my castle I survey the landscape, and see the blue smoke from many a cottage curling up to the sky, the scene will to me have no sweetness, if I know that there rises with it a sigh to the Husband of the widow and the Father of the orphan for a judgment on my head. My barns may be full, but my heart will be empty. This, in the last resort, is the protection of the poor and the punishment of the oppressor. The mightiest man desires the blessing of the people, and dreads their curse. Wealth would be a weapon too powerful for the liberty of men, if he who wields it were not confined within narrow limits by the weakness of humanity, common to him with the meanest of the people. In the necessary dependence of man upon man lies the ultimate protection of the weak and the ultimate limit of the powerful.

In our country, and in our time, the scale of operations has been prodigiously enlarged, but they do not, in virtue of their magnitude, escape from the control of the providential laws. Latterly the contest with us has not lain between a single holder of grain and the labouring poor of the nearest village ; the whole nation was divided into two hostile camps. Agriculture and manufactures were ranged against each other. In the main it was a battle between those who sell bread and those who buy it. The bone of contention was not precisely whether corn should be hoarded or sold, but whether the buyers should be permitted to range the world freely for a market. The price of food in this country was formerly kept up, not by individuals withholding it from sale, but by the legislature preventing free importation. The land-owners held that peculiar burdens were laid on them, and claimed, therefore, corresponding protection in the form of a tax on foreign corn. Whatever amount of reality there might be in their plea, the form in which the issue was submitted was to their side altogether adverse. Their demand was, Close the foreign market from the people, that we may get a higher price. They believed that they had a right to compensation; but their position was most unfortunate. It was defended at a great disadvantage: its defenders accordingly were driven away before the onset of the multitude. All this was accomplished by peaceful moral means. It proceeded with utmost regularity under the great providential law or fact, "He that withholdeth corn, the people shall curse him." The tide of the people's displeasure, stimulated and directed by vigorous leaders, was steadily rising, and the opposing line, fearing that it should swell into a "curse," and burst into civil broil, gave way and submitted to defeat. The issue has been, not the triumph of one class and the prostration of another, but the equal benefit of all. Scarcely a remnant of party conflict, or even party feeling on that subject, now lingers within our borders. Buyers and sellers agree that corn shall not be withheld, come from what quarter of the world it may. The muttering curse has died away, and mutual blessings circulate from side to side of our favoured island home. "Bless the Lord, O my soul, and forget not all his benefits!"

The Tree and its Branch

(Proverbs 11:28)

"He that trusteth in his riches shall fall: but the righteous shall flourish as a branch."

S UPPOSE the world to be scorched by drought, as completely as it was deluged by water in Noah's day. Vegetable life disappears. Trees, shrubs, and plants remain where they were; but they are the sapless monuments of a former glory. Every root is rottenness, and the stiffened blossoms will at a touch of the finger go up like dust. The circulation is arrested, the life-sap is exhaled, and the vegetation of a world lies dead upon its surface. On hill or dale the observer's weary eye can find no green or growing thing to rest upon. On every side are the withered remnants of what once were trees, but no life. The branches are very many and very dry—dry as the bones of the unburied dead.

Can these dry branches live? No; *they* cannot. Moisture now would not restore them. Rain may preserve living plants, but cannot quicken the dead.

As you stand gazing on the desolation—weeping over a barren world, a new sight attracts your eye. From heaven a living tree descends. It is planted in the unmoistened dust—the living among the dead. It grows by its own life, in spite of the earth's barrenness. It spreads over the land. The hills are veiled by its shade. It stretches its boughs on the one hand to the sea, and on the other to the river. This heavenly plant is a root in a dry ground, but not a dry root. While all earth's own growth lies withered around, it is full of sap and flourishing.

But now another wonder: the withered branches begin to grow into that living root. One and another that have no life in themselves are successively grafted into it, and as soon as they are in it, live. No hand is seen to touch them, yet they move. Like the hewing of the stone out of the mountain, the process is accomplished " without hands." Branch after branch they begin to quiver where they lie, like the bones under Ezekiel's preaching, and by a mysterious power are drawn towards the tree of life and let in. The branches which abide on their own old stock continue dry, and at an appointed time are cast into the burning; but the engrafted branches are not dependent now on earth and air; they draw their life-sap from a fountain that never fails; they have life, and they have it more abundantly than any that this world's soil ever sustained.

The vision is of man's fall, and Messiah's mission. A native human righteousness flourished once on earth. The head of this material creation, like all its other parts, was very good as it came from its Maker's hands. Man was made in God's image. Trees of righteousness, the planting of the Lord, flourished in that garden which is now a wilderness : but the blight of sin came over it, and all moral life died ; " There is none that doeth good, no, not one." Is there any hope that this desert will revive and blossom like the rose ? No ; this is not the languor that will be refreshed by a shower. This is death. There can be no revival here, except by a new creation. These dry branches cannot of themselves live. Sin has cut sinners off from the Life, and a great gulf keeps the severed members away. We could not make our own way back to God, but he has come to us. He that is mighty has done great things for us. In amongst the dead came the living One. " In Him was light, and the light was the life of men." In Him the withered grow green, the dead become alive. " If any man be in Christ, he is a new creature." Standing within the circle of his own disciples, Jesus said, " I am the vine, ye are the branches" (John xv. 5).

Here lies the secret of spiritual life among men. The righteous —and some such there have been even in the darkest periods of the world's history—the righteous " flourish as a branch." They lean not on their own stem, and live not on their own root. From the beginning the same Jesus to whom we look was made known to faith. The manner and measure of making known truth to the understanding were in those days widely different; but the nature and the source of spiritual life were the same. They stood " afar off," but they looked unto Jesus. The medium of vision was diverse, but the object was identical. As to knowledge, the ancient disciples were children, whereas disciples now are grown men; but *life* was as true and vigorous in the Church's infancy as it is in the Church's age. There was in those ancient times a medium of union to the Redeemer: and blessed are all they that trust in Him. The branch will flourish when it is in the living tree.

But though all the real branches live, all do not equally flourish. Whatever girds the branch too tightly round, impedes the flow of sap from the stem, and leaves the extremities to wither. Many cares, and vanities, and passions warp themselves round a soul, and cause the life even of the living to pine away. When the world in any of its forms lays its grasp round the life, the stricture chokes the secret channels between the disciple and his Lord, and the fruit of righteousness drops unripe. It is only as a branch that Christians can flourish in this wilderness; they have no independent source of life and growth. It becomes them, therefore, to be careful above all things to keep clear the communion between themselves and the root of their new life in the Lord. Ivy has climbed from the ground, and gracefully coiled itself round a majestic bough. Beautiful ornament! you say; it would be barbarous to cut it through, and tear it off. We dispute not the beauty of the parasite, and we have no enmity to elegance: we only desire to keep everything in its own place. According to the order which the Scripture prescribes, let us have first the kingdom of God and his righteousness; and then, if we can get them, other things. Whether is its own life or the elegance of its ornament the chief thing for the branch? Let us not hear of any addition to its beauty, which may endanger its life. Granted that this adjunct adorns; the question remains, does it kill? If it strangles the living, I would ruthlessly tear off its tendrils: without compunction I would cast its green mantle in the dust. Let me have a flourishing and fruitful branch, although its stalk should seem bare, rather than a sapless stick within a wrapping of treacherous ornament.

By this short process should many questions be settled, which become the weapons of this world's god, and wound the consciences of incautious Christians. Gain, honours, accomplishments, company, are bought too dear, when they obstruct the flow of grace from its fountain. We speak not *against* the refinements of society, but *for* the preservation of the soul's life. When bodily interests are in the balance, we generally judge righteously between rival claims. The order of arrangement is *first* life, *next* health, and *last* adorning. The same principles faithfully applied to higher issues would carry us safely through. Life spiritual as an independent tree, is not possible: and seeing that we can have life only as a branch has it, the first care is to be in the living tree; the second is to let nothing warp round the branch which would diminish its freshness; and then ornaments, hung loosely on, may be allowed to take their place. The first thing is to be "found in Him;" the next is to cast off everything that hinders us from receiving "out of his fulness;" and when these two are satisfied, let the embellishments that pertain to the world be content with the fragments that remain.

Even those who are branches in the tree of life may be impeded in their growth; but those who are not in union with the tree cannot grow at all. "He that trusteth in his riches shall fall." I have seen a row of branches profusely covered with leaves and blossoms, stuck by children in the earth around a miniature garden. They appeared more luxuriant than those that were growing on the neighbouring trees, but they withered in an hour, and never revived. Behold the picture of a man who has gained the world and neglected the Saviour! The earth into which he plunges his soul has nothing to satisfy its craving, or sustain its life. All the gains and pleasures of time cannot contribute a drop of moisture to refresh a drooping soul in the hour of its greatest need. "The portion of Jacob is not like them" (Jer. x. 16).

The Wisdom of Winning Souls
(Proverbs 11:30)

"The fruit of the righteous is a tree of life; and he that winneth souls is wise."

TO win souls seems to be the chief fruit which the trees of righteousness bear in time. It is sweet and precious. It is pleasing to God, and profitable to men. It is an everlasting memorial. In monuments of marble we commemorate for a few years the deeds of the great; but a soul won through your means will itself be a monument of the fact for ever. It is thus that "the righteous shall be in everlasting remembrance" (Ps. cxii. 6). The righteous, we learn in a previous verse, "shall flourish as a branch;" this is the secret of his fruitfulness. "As the branch cannot bear fruit of itself, except it abide in the vine; no more can ye, except ye abide in me" (John xv. 4). Christ is the source of a Christian's fruitfulness. From Him it comes and to Him it returns. This branch bears fruit after its kind. It is the life work of the won, to win others.

A soul won is a bright conception, but it suggests inevitably its dread counterpart, a soul lost. From the night's darkness the daylight springs; there must be a sense of loss ere there can be a real effort to save. We must begin at the beginning. Our defect lies at the root. If we knew the ailment, the cure is at hand. Food is abundant; it is hunger that is rare. We seem to act as if men were safe in a competent hereditary portion, and might or might not lay themselves out for new acquisitions. The true state of the case is, all is lost already, and the soul that is not won shall perish. To realize this would embody theory in action, and change the face of the world. We would all labour more to win souls if we really believed them lost. "Fools" are "slow of heart to believe;" and therefore they are slack of hand to work. Faith knows the death by sin, and the life through

Jesus ; therefore the faithful work, and the workers win souls,— their own first, and then their neighbour's.

The charity that wins a soul begins at home ; and if it do not begin there it will never begin. The order of nature in this work is, " Save yourselves and them that hear you." But though this charity begins at home, it does not end there. From its centre outward, and onward all around, like the ripple on the surface of the lake, compassion for the lost will run, nor stop until it touch the shore of time. On this errand Christ came into the world, and Christians follow the footsteps of the Lord. He recognised the world lost, and therefore He came a Saviour. Those who partake of His spirit put their hand to His work.

To win an immortal from sin and wrath to hope and holiness —this is honourable work, and difficult. It is work for wise men, and we lack wisdom. On this point there is a special promise from God. Those who need wisdom, and desire to use it in this work, will get it for the asking. The wisdom needed is very different from the wisdom of men. It is very closely allied to the simplicity of a little child. Much of it lies in plainness and promptness. Those who try to win souls must not muffle up their meaning : both by their lips and their life they must let it be seen that their aim is not to make the good better, but to save the lost. Delays also are dangerous, as well as ambiguities. Get the word of life dropt on the conscience of the healthy, lest he be sick before another opportunity occur. Tell the whole truth to the sick to-day, lest he be dead before you return. None who try to win deal slackly, and none who deal slackly win, whether it be a fortune, or a race, or a battle ; those should throw their whole might into the conflict, who wrestle with a more powerful adversary, and for a greater prize.

A Bitter but Healthful Morsel
(Proverbs 12:1)

" Whoso loveth instruction, loveth knowledge; but.he that hateth reproof is
brutish."

REPROOF is not pleasant to nature. We may learn to value it for its results, but it never will be sweet to our taste; at the best it is a bitter morsel. The difference between a wise man and a fool is, not that one likes and the other loathes it; both dislike it, but the fool casts away the precious because it is unpalatable, and the wise man accepts the unpalatable because it is precious. It is brutish in a man to act merely according to the impulse of sense. We are not so foolish when the health of our bodies is at stake. When we were children, indeed, if left to ourselves, we would have swallowed greedily the gilded sweetmeat that sickened us, and thrown away the bitter medicine which was fitted to purge disease from the channels of life; but when we became men, we put these childish things conclusively away. Day by day, in thousands of instances that concern this life, we accept the bitter because it is salutary, and reject the sweet because it destroys. Would that we were equally wise for higher interests ! " I hate him; for he doth not prophesy good concerning me " (1 Kings xxii. 8): there, in the person of that ancient Israelitish king, is humanity in the lump and without disguise. Grown men lick flattery in because it is sweet, and refuse faithful reproof because it is unpleasant. The best of us has much to learn here : and yet we think that, by pains and prayer, Christians might make large and rapid progress in this department. No advancement will be attained without particular and painstaking trial; but such trial will not be labour lost. Paul reached his high attainments not by an easy flight through the air, but by many toilsome steps on the weary ground : smaller men need not expect to find a royal road to spiritual perfection

" Herein do I exercise myself," he said, " that I may have a conscience void of offence:" what he obtained only by hard exercise, we need not expect to drop into our bosom. Here is an exercise ground for Christians who would like to grow in grace. Nature hates reproof: let grace take the bitter potion, and thrust it down nature's throat, for the sake of its healing power. If we had wisdom and energy to take to ourselves more of the reproof that is agoing, and less of the praise, our spiritual constitution would be in a sounder state.

Some of the reproof comes directly from God by his providence and in his word. This, if there be the spirit of adoption, it is perhaps easier to take. So thought David ; when he found that a terrible rebuke must come, he pleaded that he might fall into the hands of God, and not into the hands of man. Still these chastenings are painful, and wisdom from above is needed to receive them aright. But although all are ultimately at the disposal of the Supreme, most of the reproofs that meet us in life come immediately from our fellow-men. Even when it is just in substance and kindly given, our own self-love kicks hard against it ; and, alas ! the most of it is mixed with envy and applied in anger. Here is room for the exercise of a Christian's highest art. There is a way of profiting by reproof, although it be administered by an enemy. It is in such narrows of life's voyage that the difference comes most clearly out between the wise and the foolish. A neighbour is offended by something that I have said or done ; he becomes enraged, and opens a foul mouth upon me. This is his sin and his burden ; but what of me ? Do I kindle at his fire, and throw back his epithets with interest in his face ? This is brutish ; it is the stupid ox kicking everything that pricks him, and being doubly lacerated for his pains. It is my business and my interest to take good for myself out of another's evil. The good is there, and there is a way of extracting it. The most unmannerly scold that ever came from an unbridled tongue may have its filth precipitated and turned into a precious ointment, as the sewage of a city, instead of damaging the people's health, may as a fertilizer become the reduplicator of the people's food. The process is difficult, but when skilfully performed it produces a large return. When Shimei basely cursed David in his distress, the counsel of a rude warrior was, "Let me go over and take off his head." This was merely a brutish instinct—the beam that lay not on the solid, rebounding, by the law of its nature, to the blow. But the king had been getting the good of his great affliction : at that moment he had wisdom, and therefore he got more. He recognised a heavenly Father's hand far behind the foul tongue of Shimei : he felt that the rebuke, though cruelly given, contained salutary truth. He occupied himself not with the falsehood that was in it in order to blame the reprover, but with the truth that was in it in order to get humbling for himself. " Let him alone," said the fallen monarch, meekly; " let him alone and let him curse, for the Lord hath bidden him." Here is wisdom. It is wise to receive correction from God, although it come through an unworthy instrument. Although the immediate agent meant it for evil, our Father in heaven can make it work for good.

A Husband's Crown

(Proverbs 12:4)

"A virtuous woman is a crown to her husband: but she that maketh ashamed is as rottenness in his bones."

WOMAN'S place is important; God has made it so, and made her fit for filling it. Man is incomplete without her; there is a blank about him which she alone can fill; it is here that her great strength lies. When she assumes an independent or rival place, she mistakes her mission and her power. Man, though made for the throne of the world, was found unfit for the final investiture until he got woman as a help. She became the completion of his capacity and title—she became his crown. Let woman ever be content with the place that God has given her; let her be what He made her, necessary to man, and not attempt to make herself independent of him. In her own place, her power has hardly a limit in human affairs; out of it, her efforts only rack herself, and reveal her weakness. Elsewhere in this book we learn that "a gracious woman retaineth honour, and strong men retain riches." The comparison intimates that what strength is to man in maintaining his wealth, grace is to woman for securing her position and influence. This is a finger-post directing woman in her weakness to the place where her great strength lies. If there be the fear of the Lord as a foundation, with wisdom, truth, love, and gentleness rising gracefully upon it, a queenly power is there. The winsome will win her way. Without the trappings of royalty, she will acquire the homage of a neighbourhood. The adaptation of the feminine character to be the companion and complement of man is one of the best defined examples of that designing wisdom which pervades creation. When the relations of the sexes move in fittings of truth and love, the working of the complicated machinery of life is a wonder to an observing man, and a glory to the Creator God

But what horrid contrast have we here, like the echo of a glad song given back transformed into despairing wails from some pit of darkness : "She that maketh ashamed is as rottenness in his bones !" We need not be surprised by this announcement. It is according to law; the best things abused become the worst. The picture is an appalling one, but it is taken from life. In many ways woman, when she is not virtuous, makes man ashamed. When she is slovenly and uncleanly in her person and her house ; thoughtless and spendthrift in the management of her means ; gaudy and expensive in her tastes for herself and her children ; company-keeping, gossipping, tale-bearing ; quarrelsome with neighbours or servants ; discontented, querulous, taunting, at home ; and last of all (for what abounds in the world should go down on this page, though it be a noisome thing), drunken : when the unclean spirit in any of these forms possesses woman, he contrives thereby to penetrate everywhere, and to poison all. Woman is the very element of home, wherein all its relations and affections live and move ; when that element is tainted, corruption spreads over all its breadth, and sinks into its core.

God did not take from among the creatures any help for man that came to hand, but made one meet for him. The Maker of all things took the measure of man's need, and constituted woman a suitable complement. This is God's part, and His work, in as far as it bears yet the mark of His hand, is very good. Every man on his part should seek an individual " help," " meet " for his own individual need. On that choice interests of unspeakable magnitude depend for time and eternity ; he who makes it corruptly or lightly is courting misery, and dallying with doom. Our Father loves to be consulted in this great life-match for his children, and they who ask His advice will not be sent away without it. If men were duly impressed with the vastness of the interests involved in the transaction, that alone would go far to bear them steadily through. Let a man remember that woman, by constitutional character, goes into all, like water : she should be clean who plies so close. Let a young man know, while he is adjusting the balance, what are the alternatives that depend on either side, and their weight will go far to keep his hand steady and his eyesight clear : in that act he is either setting a crown on his own head, or infusing rottenness into his own bones.

The Wicked are Cruel: The Liars are Caught
(Proverbs 12:10-13)

"A righteous man regardeth the life of his beast: but the tender mercies of the wicked are cruel. The wicked is snared by the transgression of his lips: but the just shall come out of trouble."

CONSISTENT kindness to brute creatures is one of the marks by which a really merciful man is known. When the pulse of kindness beats strong in the heart, the warm stream goes sheer through the body of the human family, and retains force enough to expatiate among the living creatures that lie beyond. The gentleness of Christ is one beauty of the Lord which should be seen on Christians. Over against this lovely light, according to the usual form of the proverb, yawns the counterpart darkness, habitation of horrid cruelty. Cruelty is a characteristic of the wicked in general, and in particular of Antichrist, that one, wicked by pre-eminence, whom Christ shall yet destroy by the brightness of his coming. By their fruits ye shall know them : the page of history is spotted with the cruelties of papal Rome. The red blood upon his garments is generally the means of discovering a murderer : the trailing womanish robes of the papal high priest are deeply stained with the blood of saints. The same providence which employs the bloody tinge to detect the common murderer has left more lasting marks of Rome's cruelty. The Bartholomew massacre, for example, is recorded in more enduring characters than the stains of that blood which soaked the soil of France. By the accounts of those who did the deed and favour Rome, 30,000 ; according to other estimates, 100,000 Protestants were slain. Such were the heaps, in some places, that they could not be counted. The Pope and his cardinals greatly rejoiced when they heard the news. So lively was their gratitude, that they cast a medal to commemorate the fact. There stands the legend, raised in brass and silver, *Strages Huguenot-*

orum ("the slaughter of the Huguenots"), in perpetual memory of the delight wherewith that wicked Antichrist regarded the greatest, foulest butchery of men by their fellows that this sin-cursed earth has ever seen. That spot will not out by all their washings. That monument, reared by the murderer's own hands, exhibits to the world now a faithful specimen of his tender mercies, and will remain to identify the criminal at the coming of the Judge. "Blessed are the merciful ;" but a curse lies on the cruel ever since Cain shed his brother's blood.

The Supreme has set many snares, in the constitution of things, for the detection and punishment of evil doers : the wicked are continually falling into them, and suffering. The liar's own tongue betrays him : in some of its movements, ere he is aware, it touches the spring which brings down the avenging stroke. It is instructive to watch with this view the progress of a criminal trial. In the faltering and fall of a false witness, you should see and reverence the righteousness of God. The first lie must be defended by a second, and that by a third. As the line of his defences grows in length, it grows in weakness. His fear and labour increase at every step. He is compelled at every question to consider what truth is like, and imitate it in lies. Ere long, when he is crossing his own path, he falls into a lie that he had left and forgotten there ; he falls, and flounders, like a wild beast in a snare. When a man is not true, the great labour of his life must be to make himself appear true ; but if a man be true, he need not concern himself about appearances. He may go forward, and tread boldly ; his footing will be sure. Matters are so arranged, in the constitution of the world, that the straight course of truth is safe and easy ; the crooked path of falsehood difficult and tormenting. Here is perennial evidence that the God of providence is wise and true. By making lies a snare to catch liars in, the Author of our being proclaims, even in the voices of nature, that he "requireth truth in the inward parts." All the labour of swindlers to dress up their falsehood, so as to make it look like truth, is Satan's unwilling homage to the true God. It is counted a glory to the Lord when his enemies feign submission unto Him (Ps. lxxxi. 15).

"The just shall come out of trouble ;" that is the word ; it is not said that he will never fall into it. The inventory which

Jesus gives of what his disciples shall have "now in this time," although it contains many things that nature loves, closes with the article "persecutions" (Mark x. 30). The recorded description, "These are they who have come out of great tribulation," belongs alike to all the redeemed of the Lord, when they come to Zion. These, who wave their palms of victory, and sing their jubilant hymns of praise, were all in the horrible pit once : they were held helpless by its miry clay, until the Mighty One lifted them up, and set their feet upon a rock, and established their goings.

Hope Deferred
(Proverbs 13:12)

" Hope deferred maketh the heart sick: but when the desire
cometh it is a tree of life."

THE rule, as expressed in the first clause, is universal; but in the second clause it is applied to a particular case. Hope deferred makes the heart sick, whether the person hoping, and the thing hoped for, be good or evil: thus far one thing happens to all. But the second member is a dividing word. The accomplishment of the desire " is a tree of life:" this belongs only to the hope of the holy. Many, after waiting long, and expecting eagerly, discover, when at last they reach their object, that it is a withered branch, and not a living tree. When a human heart has been set on perishable things, after the sickness of deferred expectation, comes the sorer sickness of satiated possession. If the world be made the portion of an immortal spirit, to want it is one sickness, and to have it is another. The one is a hungry mouth empty, and the other a hungry mouth filled with chaff. The cloy of disappointed possession is a more nauseous sickness than the aching of disappointed desire.

There is no peace to the wicked. They are all always either desiring or possessing; but to desire and to possess a perishable portion, are only two different kinds of misery to men. They are like the troubled sea, when it cannot rest. You stand on the shore, and gaze on the restless waters. A wave is hastening on, struggling, and panting, and making with all its might for the shore: it seems as if all it wanted were to reach the land. It reaches the land, and disappears in a hiss of discontent. Gathering its strength at a distance, it tries again, and again, with the same result. It is never satisfied: it never rests. In the constitution of the world, under the government of the Most Holy, when a soul's desire is set on unworthy objects, the accomplishment of the desire does not satisfy the soul. In the case here supposed, however, the desire must be pure, for the attainment of it is found to be a tree of life: it is living, satisfying, enduring. It has a living root in the ground, and satisfying fruit upon its branches.

Those who were enlightened by the Spirit before the incarnation, looked in faith, through the sacrifices, for Jesus; and they beheld his day, but it was afar off. They longed for Christ's coming as those that wait for the morning. While they waited for redemption in Israel, hope deferred made their hearts sick; but they waited on. Their desire, the Desire of all nations, came. The Word was made flesh, and dwelt among them, and they beheld his glory. That desire satisfied did not pall upon their taste. It was enough. "Lord, now lettest thou thy servant depart in peace, for mine eyes have seen thy salvation" (Luke ii. 29, 30).

The same experience is repeated in the personal history of disciples now. When a hungering for righteousness secretly rises in a human heart, the blessing is already sure; but it is not enjoyed yet. The hungerer "shall be filled;" but in the meantime, his only experience is an uneasy sensation of want. The craving of that appetite, while yet it is not satisfied, is a painful thing: the heart is sick of that love. Far-seeing friends delight to observe the symptoms of that sickness beginning in a youth, not for the sake of the suffering, but because of the glad enlargement to which it leads. In God's good time that desire will be satisfied. That longing soul will taste and see that the Lord is gracious. The peace of God which passeth all understanding will come in and keep that heart and mind.

In the tumults of these latter days, some earnest spirits greatly long for the second coming of the Lord. Their hope has been deferred, and their hearts are sick; but "when the Desire cometh" —and He shall come without sin unto salvation—the sorrow will no more be remembered in their joy of the Lord. To them that look for Him he will appear, and his coming will be like the morning. The redeemed of the Lord, when they come to Zion, shall sit under shadow of this "Tree of Life" with great delight, and the days of their mourning shall be ended. "The Lamb which is in the midst of the throne shall feed them, and lead them unto living fountains of waters; and God shall wipe away all tears from their eyes."

God's Word the Preserver of Nations
(Proverbs 13:13)

"Whoso despiseth the word shall be destroyed: but he that feareth the commandment
shall be rewarded."

THIS word has a private and personal, as well as a public
application; but it is in the providential government of
the nations that its truth has been most conspicuously
displayed. The kingdoms of the world in these days prosper or
pine in proportion as they honour or despise God's word. Show
me a land where the Bible is degraded and interdicted, and I will
show you a land whose history is written in blood and tears: show
me a land where the Bible is valued and spread, and I will show
you a country prosperous and free. Nor does the civil war
which has scourged the States of North America present any real
exception to this rule; for beyond doubt slavery is the ultimate
cause of the conflict, whatever the immediate and ostensible occasions may be; and, alas! in order to preserve that system, as it
exists in America, from destruction, the Bible must be either legis-
latively forbidden, or theologically explained away. Number the
nations over one by one, and see where property is valuable and
life secure; mark the places where you would like to invest your
means and educate your family; you will shun some of the sunniest
climes of earth, as if they lay under a polar night, because the
light of the truth has been taken from their sky. Traverse the
world in search of merely human good, seeking but an earthly
home, and your tent, like Abraham's, will certainly be pitched at
"the place of the altar." Scotland is a kindlier home than Con-
naught. The Irish Papist abjures the Bible as an unintelligible or
dangerous book, and implicitly submits to the spiritual guidance
of his priest: the British Protestant holds God's word in his hand,
at once the standard of his teacher's doctrine, and the rule of his
own life. Hence chiefly the difference, moral and material, between

the two peoples. They who despise the word are a prostrate race. A nation of beggars starves at our doors, on an island that might become a garden. The map of the world is sufficient evidence that God is, and that he has revealed his will to men.

This country has been preserved safe in many convulsions, while others have been rent asunder. It has grown great, while others have wasted. It has been gradually growing more free, while other nations are robbed of their liberty, or retain it at the price of their blood. We should know who makes us to differ, and what. The Bible has made us what we are; it is dark ingratitude to despise or neglect it. It is often observed that when a man rises in the world, he no longer knows the person by whom he rose. This is the mark of a low, ungenerous mind. Symptoms not a few of this vulgar vice may be seen in high places of our own land. The preserved do not care to know their preserver. A summer tour on the Continent does not afford a sufficient lesson: the power of Britain shields her subject during his travels, and the iron of Popish despotism does not enter into his soul. But a year of subjection to Roman rule, such as the Romans feel it, would teach politicians a truth which they are slow to learn. They might discover the worth of the Bible as the preserver of liberty, if they felt the want of it.

The Hard Way

(Proverbs 13:15)

"The way of transgressors is hard."

IS not the way of transgressors pleasant in its progress, though it ends in death? No. Sin barters away future safety, but does not secure present peace in return. Things are not always as they seem to be. The pleasures of sin are not only limited in their duration, they are lies even while they last. They are "for a season" as to endurance, and for a show as to their character. There is a bitterness in the transgressor's heart, which only that heart can know. The man in the gospel history, who wore no clothes, and lived among the tombs, did not lead a happy life. The rocky, thorny graveyard was a hard bed, and the dewy night air a cold covering for the naked man; but such was his will, or the will of the spirit that possessed him. It was the man's pleasure to take that way, but the way was hard. It is so still, and ever will be, for all whom the same spirit leads. It has neither the promise of the life that now is, nor of that which is to come. The race is torture, and the goal perdition. "Destruction and misery are in their paths, and the way of peace have they not known."

Here is a glory of God reflected from the experience of men. It is far-seeing mercy that makes the way of transgressors hard; its hardness warns the traveller to turn that he may live. Two mechanics work side by side all day, and receive equal wages at night. One goes home when his toil is over, and rests in the bosom of his own family, enjoying doubly all that he has won, because he shares it with those who love him there: the other having no home to love, or no love to home, goes into a public-house, and remains there as long as his money lasts. Late at night he is driven to the street, penniless, hungry, and without a friend. He falls at every turn. His clothes are besmeared with mud; his bones are bruised; his face streams with blood. In pity for his misery, rather than in vengeance for his crime, the officers of justice drag or carry him to a prison cell, and lay him on its floor till morning. The man followed the way of transgressors, and he has found it hard. Day by day his body is bruised and torn on the rugged sides of that crooked path; and yet he will not forsake it. If any one inquire after the name of this foul spirit, we answer, His name is Legion, for they are many.

Nor is this the only crooked path that tears the feet of the wretched passenger: they are all hard, however widely they diverge from each other—all that diverge from the line of righteousness. In some of them, the hardness is an iron that entereth into the soul, rather than the body, and therefore the wounds are not so palpable to others. The pain is not on that account, however, less pungent to the sufferer: " A wounded spirit, who can bear?"

But the right way is not a soft and silky path for the foot of man to tread upon; and, if one thing happens to all in the journey of life, what advantage have the good? Much every way, and specifically thus: The hardness which disciples experience in following the Lord, is righteousness rubbing on their remaining lusts, and so wasting their deformities away; whereas the hardness of a transgressor's way is the carnal mind, in its impotent enmity, dashing itself against the bosses of the Almighty's buckler. The one is a strainer, made strait to purge the impurities away, through which the purified emerges into peace; the other is the vengeance which belongeth unto God, beginning even here to repay. The stroke of discipline under which a pilgrim smarts, as he travels towards Zion, is an excellent oil which will not break his head: the collision between transgressors and the law of God, hardens the impenitent for completer destruction at the final fall. As the pains of cure differ from the pains of killing, so differs the salutary straitness which presses the entrants at the gate of life, from the hardness which hurts transgressors while they flee from God.

The Choice of Companions

(Proverbs 13:20)

" He that walketh with wise men shall be wise; but a companion of fools shall be destroyed."

LOVE of company is a steady instinct of the young; and it performs an important part in the economy of human life. Like many other forces under the control of a free moral agent, it is mighty for good or evil, according to the direction in which it is turned. It is the nature of certain plants, while they strike their own independent roots into the ground for life, to twist their tendrils round other trees for support to their branches. To this species in the animal department of creation belong the young of human-kind. Physically, the organization of each individual is separate and complete, but morally they interweave themselves into others; so that, though the growth of their bodies is independent, the cast of their characters is largely affected by the companions to whom they cling. At this point, therefore, there is room and need for much prayer, and watchfulness, and effort, both by and for the generation that is now tender, and taking the form of any mould that closes round and presses it.

The principle of reciprocal attraction and repulsion pervades all nature, both in its material and spiritual departments. Your character goes far to determine the company that you will keep; and the company that you keep goes far to mould your character. But while these two are hanging in the balance, it is the place and prerogative of man, for himself or his brother, to rush in and lay his hand upon the scales, and cast a makeweight into the side of safety. By the warnings of God's word, and the lessons of our own experience, we know before they begin what the end of certain companionships will be. The awful end is opened up to make us fear the beginning.

Your heart takes to a companion who has been accidentally

thrown in your way; you should not yield to that inclination merely because it works within you. The beasts that perish do so, and therein they never err: they associate with their kind, and are never corrupted by the company that they keep. Their instincts are perfect as they come from the Creator's hands: it is safe to trust them. But there is a bias to evil in a human heart; it must be watched and thwarted, if we would avoid error now and escape perdition at last. It is not for us to let our hearts have their own way in the selection of companions; on that choice depend interests too great to be safely left to chance. The issue to be decided is not what herd you shall graze with a few years before your spirit return to the dust; but what moral element you shall move in during the few and evil days of life, till your spirit return to God who gave it. I like this companion; he fascinates me; I cannot want him; an enforced separation would be like tearing myself asunder. Well, if that companion's heart be godless, and his steps already slipping backward and downward, why not tear yourself asunder? The act will be painful, no doubt; but "skin for skin, yea, all that a man hath will he give for his life." Your soul's life depends on that painful act. It is better that you enter into life maimed of that member, than that your tempter and you should perish together. In this way the young are put to the test, whether they will obey Christ's word or no. On this side there are right arms to be cut off, and right eyes to be plucked out. Young men and women, God and all the good are looking on, and watching to see whether you will throw off the chain of charms by which brilliant but wandering stars have led you, and cling to the skirts of the meek and lowly, who follow the Lamb whithersoever He goeth.

"He that walketh with the wise shall be wise." If he is wise he will walk with them, and to walk with them will make him wiser. To him that hath wisdom to choose the wise as his companions shall be given more wisdom, through their converse and example. Such is the blessed progress in the path of life, when fellow-travellers towards Zion help each other on; but, alas! what of him who "hath not" any wisdom to begin with? Let him who lacks wisdom ask of God, who giveth to all men liberally and upbraideth not. God takes peculiar delight in granting this request, when it comes up in earnest simplicity from the needy. Wisdom from above will be given to them that ask it for the purpose of selecting safe companions. No one, it may be safely affirmed, ever made this request in simplicity to God, and came away without an answer. No; when people cling to unprofitable and dangerous associates, it is because they take what they like without asking counsel of God, not because they asked counsel and failed to obtain it. This dashing, clever youth makes sport of serious things and serious persons. He quotes a text so dexterously, that the gravest of the circle are surprised into laughter. He sings merrily, and perhaps drinks deeply. He affects to be skilled in the mysteries of vice, and kindles the curiosity of a novice by knowing hints, which seem to leave the most untold. Here is a fool who will probably entice some to be his companions. Before the bargain be struck, while this leader and his dupes are arranging the terms of his lead and their following, a voice bursts out above them—"The companion of fools shall be destroyed." It is God's voice; He speaks in mercy; hear ye Him. Forsake the foolish and live."

The Father Who Hates His Son

(Proverbs 13:24)

" He that spareth his rod hateth his son."

Y OU indulge your child and do not correct him; you permit selfishness, and envy, and anger to encrust themselves, by successive layers, thicker and thicker on his
character : you beseech him not to be naughty, but never enforce
your injunction by a firm application of the rod ; and you think
the fault, if it be a fault, is a very trivial one : perhaps you appropriate to yourself a measure of blame for loving your child too
much. Nay, brother ; be not deceived ; call things by their right
names. Beware of the woe denounced against those who call evil
good. You do not love, you hate your child.

Love is a good name, and hate a bad one. Every one likes to
take to himself a good name, whether he deserve it or not. To
love one's own child, even though that love should run to excess,
is counted amiable : to hate the child in any measure, is reckoned
the part of a monster. In order to keep a fair character before
the world, a deceitful heart so shuffles in secret the two things,
that while hate is the real character of the deed, its outward
appearance shall be love.

It is obvious to any careful observer of human nature, that
even blame is pleasant to indulgent parents, when it is the blame
of loving their own children too much. They swallow the soft
reproof as a luscious flattery. The Scripture deals with them in
another way. It does not gratify them by the soft impeachment
of excess in parental love. It roundly asserts that they have no
love at all. It comes down upon them abruptly with the charge
of hating the child.

Sparing the rod is the specific act, or habit, which is charged
against the parent, as being equivalent to hating his son. The

child begins to act the tyrant : he is cruel where he has power and sulky where he has not : he is rude, overbearing, untruthful. These and kindred vices are distinctly forming on his life, and growing with his growth. The matter is reported to the father, and the same things are done in his presence. He tells the child to do better, and dismisses him with caresses. This process is frequently repeated. The child discovers that he can transgress with impunity. The father threatens sometimes, but punishes never. The child grows rapidly worse. By the certainty of escaping, acting in concert with a corrupt nature, the habit of intentional evil-doing is formed and confirmed. All the while this father takes and gets the credit of being, if not a very wise, at least a very loving parent. No; it is mere prostitution of that hallowed name to apply it to such ignoble selfishness. Love, though very soft, is also very strong. It will not give way before slight obstacles. To sacrifice self is of its very essence. If it be in you, it will quickly make your own ease give way for the good of its object. When a father gives the child all his own way, yielding more the more he frets, until the child finds out that he can get anything by imperiously demanding it, he yields not from love to his child, but from loathsome love of ease to himself. It is a low animal laziness that will not allow its own oily surface to be ruffled even to save a son. If there were real love, it would be strong enough to endure the pain of refusing to comply with improper demands, and chastening for intentional or persistent wrong-doing. Parents who are in the habit of giving their children what they ask, and permitting them to disobey without chastisement, may read their own character in this verse of Scripture. Such a father "hateth his son :" that is the word. To call it love is one of Satan's lies. It is unmingled selfishness. The man who gravely tells his child what is wrong, and, if the wrong is repeated, sternly chastens him,—that man really loves his child, and sacrifices his own ease for the child's highest good. It is enough to break one's heart to think how many young people are thrown off the rails at some unexpected turn of life by the momentum of their own impetuousness, for want of a father's firm hand to apply in time the necessary break. We need a manful, hardy love—a love that will bear and do to the uttermost for all the interests of its object.

Let it be remembered here, however, that every blow dealt by a father's hand is not parental chastening. To strike right and left against children, merely because you are angry and they are weak, is brutish in its character and mischievous in its effects. A big dog bites a little one who offends him : what do ye more than they ? Never once should a hand be laid upon a child in the hasty impulse of anger. The Koh-i-noor diamond, when it came into the Queen's possession, was a misshapen lump. It was very desirable to get its corners cut off, and all its sides reduced to symmetry : but no unskilful hand was permitted to touch it. Men of science were summoned to consider its nature and its capabilities. They examined the form of its crystals and the consistency of its parts. They considered the direction of the grain, and the side on which it would bear a pressure. With their instructions, the jewel was placed in the hands of an experienced lapidary, and by long, patient, careful labour, its sides were grinded down to the desired proportions. The gem was hard, and needed a heavy pressure : the gem was precious, and every precaution was taken which science and skill could suggest to get it polished into shape without cracking it in the process. The effort was successful. The hard diamond was rubbed down into forms of beauty, and yet sustained no damage by the greatness of the pressure to which it was subjected.

" Jewels, bright jewels," in the form of little children, are the heritage which God gives to every parent. They are unshapely, and need to be polished ; they are hard, and cannot be reduced into symmetry without firm handling ; they are brittle, and so liable to be permanently damaged by the pressure ; but they are stones of peculiar preciousness, and if they were successfully polished they would shine as stars for ever and ever, giving off from their undimming edge, more brilliantly than other creatures can, the glory which they get from the Sun of righteousness. Those who possess these diamonds in the rough should neither strike them unskilfully, nor let them lie uncut.

This boy placed in the dock before you, with his clothes torn, and his hair dishevelled, with an air of penitence put on, over a purpose of more mischief that gleams through the awkward covering, just one minute after your last lecture, has been caught up to the ears in another scrape. What is to be done with him ?

You have tried severity, and tried gentleness;—all in vain. He waxes worse in your hands. Do with him as the infant-school rhyme enjoins you, "try, try, try again." Don't let him alone, for he is all unshapely, and in this form he will have no loveliness in the sight of God or man : don't strike rashly, for in one moment you may start a rent of hatred and discontent through and through a soul that no after discipline will ever obliterate. Cautiously, firmly, perseveringly, lovingly, polish away at your jewel. Get a right estimate of its value impressed upon your heart, and you will not give up in despair, although you have made many unsuccessful efforts. The work is difficult, but the prize is great. If he is won, he is won to himself, and to you, and to society, and to God.

While there should be a strong manly love to wield the rod firmly, there should also be a far-seeing wisdom to judge, in view of all the circumstances, whether and when the rod should be applied. A parent must study carefully both his child's character and his own. If his own nature be now rigid, and incapable of going into sympathy with the impetuous playfulness of robust youth, he may with the best intention fall into a fatal mistake. He may chasten for that which is not a fault, and so crack the temper of his child for life. We must learn to measure the instincts of boyhood, and make allowance for the muscular exercise, amounting almost to perpetual motion, which nature demands. Love will give ample room for the effervescence of a buoyant spirit ; but, when it has separated so widely between sportiveness and sin, it will then all the more bring down the rod with the certainty and severity of a law of nature, for every discovered, definite, wilful wickedness. If a father on earth be like our Father in heaven, judgment will be his "strange work :" do not resort to it often, but let it be real when it comes.

I am disposed to set a high value on, not only the general principles of Scripture regarding this subject, but also its specific precepts. I would limit with jealous apprehension the application of the rule about duty changing with the change of circumstances. The only thing that I would leave open to be modified by circumstances is the mere instrument wherewith the chastening is administered. By all means let "rod" stand as a generic term, and under it let the most convenient implement be used, but the spirit of the text is abandoned, as well as the letter, when a parent abjures corporal chastisement altogether, and trusts exclusively to moral means. There is indeed no virtue in bodily pain to heal a moral ailment; it depends on the adaptation of punishment in kind and measure to the particular form of the child's waywardness. If a child so act as seldom to need the rod, or never, then seldom or never let the rod be applied; but beware of determining and proclaiming beforehand that you will not in any case resort to corporal chastisement, lest you be setting up your wisdom against the law of the Lord.

I have heard of some educators who, in public assembly, with much pomp and circumstance, cut the tawse in a hundred pieces, and scattered the fragments in the wind, proclaiming by way of contrast, the reign of love. There is more of quackery under this than the benevolent performers suspected. I suspect it is a mistake. The rod and love are not antagonist: it is not necessary to banish the one in order to submit to the reign of the other. Love keeps the rod, and lifts it too, and lays it on when needful. This is the very triumph of true love, over a spurious imitation. When a father puts forth his strength to hold the struggling victim, and applies the rod, although every stroke thrills through his own heart, this is love such as God commands and approves. Our Father in heaven chastens the children whom He loves, and does not spare for their crying. Genuine parental love on earth is an imitation of His own.

Although it is an important rule not to trifle with this work when it is begun, yet the effect does not depend on the number or weight of the blows. The result is determined more by the side on which the force is applied, than by the mere magnitude of the force. The stroke in which the operator suffers more than he inflicts, powerfully impels the child in the direction which you approve; but spurts of selfish anger drive him the other way. It is like admitting steam into the cylinder of an engine: if you admit it on this side, the machine goes forward; if you admit on that side, the machine goes backward.

One characteristic mark of genuine love is to chasten a child "betimes." To do it early is both easiest and best. It is cruel to let your son grow up without the correction which he needs.

If you who love him do not bend him while he is a child, those who do not love him will break him after he has become a man.

The word is specifically "son," and not generally "child." There is a reason for this selection of terms. Although there may be here and there individual exceptions, the common rule is that boys are more stubborn than girls. In proportion to the hardness of the subject, must be the heaviness of the blow. The child must be subdued into obedience at whatever cost. This is the most important of a parent's practical duties in life. He should not permit any other business to push it aside into a secondary place. The boy is your richest treasure, and should be your chief care. He is the greatest talent which the Master has placed in your hands; lay it out well, even though other things should be neglected. Exert all the wisdom and foresight and firmness that you can command in the cultivation of this field, no other will yield a return so sure or so satisfying.

Prayer and pains must go together in this difficult work. Lay the whole case before our Father in heaven: this will take the hardness out of the correction, without diminishing its strength.

Secularism

(Proverbs 14:6)

" A scorner seeketh wisdom and findeth it not: but knowledge is easy unto him that understandeth."

IT is the constant profession of those who reject the Bible that they are seeking truth. Their likeness is taken here from life. They seek wisdom, but do not find it. They want the first qualification of a philosopher, a humble and teachable spirit.

There is a race of men amongst us at the present day who scorn bitterly against faith's meek submission to God's revealed will. They desire to be free from authority. The papist, they say, submits to the authority of the church, and the protestant to the authority of the Bible: they count these only different forms of superstition, and cast off with equal earnestness both the bonds. They make a man's own feelings the supreme judge to that man of right and wrong, good and evil. The divinity, as they phrase it, is in every man; which means that every man is a god unto himself. It is, in its essence, a reproduction of the oldest rebellion: a creature, discontented with the place which his Maker has given him, strives to make himself a god.

If men really were independent beings, it would be right to assert and proclaim their independence; but as matters stand, this desperate kicking against authority becomes the exposure of weakness, and the punishment of pride. We are not our own cause and our own end; we are not our own lords. We are in the hands of our Maker, and under the law of our Judge. Our only safety lies in submission to the rightful authority, and obedience to the true law. The problem for man is, not to reject all masters, but to accept the rightful One.

Those who scorn the wisdom from above, seek laboriously for the wisdom that is beneath. The name " secularist" is adopted to indicate that they appreciate and study the knowledge that concerns the present world, and repudiate as unattainable, or useless, all knowledge that pertains to another. People sometimes lose their way in words as they do in mist; and then very vulgar objects seem mighty castles looming in the darkness. Let it be known, and remembered, that " secularism" is the Latin for *this-world-ism*, and means, Attend to the world that you are now in, and let the next alone. Perhaps this translation of the name into English may help us to take the measure of the thing signified. Before we adopt this philosophy we must be sure that there is no immortality for man; for, if there be another world, obviously our course here will affect our condition there, and the view that we take of eternity will decisively influence our path over time. Granting even that it is this world with which men have now to do, our present view of the world to come exerts a supreme control over the whole course of our conduct, and every step of our life. It is by faith in the unseen that men steer through this shifting sea of time. Cut us off from the future, and you have left the ship without a chart, and without a star: without a compass to steer by, and without a harbour to steer for; you have left the ship an aimless meaningless log lying on the water, to be tossed up and down by the waves, and driven hither and thither by the winds, until it fall asunder or sink unseen.

Those seekers of knowledge, who limit their search to the earth on which they tread, profess great zeal in the question of education. I am not aware that they do more in the work of education than others, but they say loudly, and oft, that the young of the nation should be educated according to their views. Children in the public schools, they say, should be thoroughly trained in secular knowledge, and religious dogmas should be left untouched. The public schoolmaster should be entirely neutral on the subject of religion: he should give no judgment for or against any of its doctrines. Verily, these men seek knowledge, and find it not: after all their efforts to learn, they are not yet very wise. They prescribe to the schoolmaster a task that is palpably impossible. Revealed religion has touched the world, and been the turning point of its history in all ages. The Scriptures of the Old and New Testaments, claiming as they do to be the inspired record of God's will, have in point of fact influenced the conduct and history of mankind more than all other books together. Jesus of Nazareth was, through the unwilling instrumentality of the Roman, put to death by the Jewish priesthood, because he made Himself equal with God; and this event has done more to cast the civilized world into its present mould, than any or all the revolutions of kingdoms since the beginning of time. How shall the teacher dispose of that book, and that event, in his complete course of secular instruction? Must he teach history and leave these things out of it? He may as well teach the elements of Euclid, omitting all the capital letters; he may as well weave without a warp, as exhibit the kingdoms of this world, without taking notice of the kingdom of God, and of his Christ. The religion of Christ has grasped the world, and penetrated human history through and through. If you exclude these topics, your disciple comes out of your hands a barbarian; and if you introduce them, you are compelled to take a side. For or against Christ the teacher must be, and the scholar too. God has, in providence, not left it possible simply to pass the Bible by without letting it be known whether you believe it or not. The question, "What think ye of Christ?" was of old pressed upon the Jews, though they desired rather not to commit themselves to an answer; and by the same sovereign Lord, who rules over all, it is in these latter days pressed upon men so as to force an answer out of them whether they will, or be unwilling. No man can teach the history and condition of this world without indicating expressly, or by implication, whether he counts Jesus of Nazareth a blasphemer, or the Son of God. No man can live where the gospel is known without accepting or rejecting Christ's claim to be the Redeemer of his soul, and the sovereign of his life. Such have been the effects of the Bible, and such is the place of Christ among men, that we must take a side. The decision cannot be avoided; all depends on making it aright. The liberty of having no Lord over the conscience is not competent to man. Submission absolute to the living God, as revealed in the Mediator, is at once the best liberty that could be, and the only liberty that is.

In these days, when the pendulum is often seen swinging from scepticism over to superstition, and from superstition back to scepticism again, we would do well to remember that there is truth between these extremes, and that in truth alone lies safety for all the interests of men. We must beware of confounding two questions that are totally distinct—the existence of truth, and our perception of it. Although all the men that live on the earth should awake to-morrow blind, that would not prove that the sun had ceased to shine. It is fashionable in high places to laud religious indifference, and stigmatize as bigotry all earnest belief. This is a great mistake. They who fall into it cannot read even profane history aright. Let politicians learn to apply the grand test, " By their fruits ye shall know them." To believe nothing will produce as rank intolerance as to believe all the legends of Rome. Look to the history of modern Europe, and you will see that those who believed all dogmas and those who rejected all are equally stained with the blood of the saints, and have equally impeded the progress of men. To have no belief, and to believe a lie, are seeds that bear only bitter fruits. The conceit of the sceptic that outside of himself there is no truth to believe in, projects into human life only an empty shadow of liberty; but if He who is the truth " make you free, ye shall be free indeed."

I see two men near each other prostrate on the ground and bleeding, while one man stands between them, with serenest aspect, looking to the skies; who and what are these? The two prostrate forms are Superstition and Unbelief. Superstition bowed down to worship his idol, and cut his flesh with stones to atone for his soul's sin. Unbelief scorned to be confined, like an inferior creature, to the earth, and was ever leaping up in the hope of standing on the stars. Exhausted by his efforts, he fell, and the fall bruised him, so that he lay as low as the neighbour whom he despised. He who stands between them neither bowed himself to the ground, nor attempted to scale the heavens; he neither degraded himself beneath a man's place, nor attempted to raise himself above it. He abode on earth; but he stood erect there. He did not proudly profess to be, but meekly sought to find God. This man understands his place and feels his need; to him therefore knowledge is easy. To him that hath shall be given. He has the beginning of wisdom, and he will reach in good time its glad consummation. " Blessed are the poor in spirit, for theirs is the kingdom."

Wisdom Modest and Folly Rash

(Proverbs 14:7, 16)

"Go from the presence of a foolish man, when thou perceivest not in him the lips of know-ledge......A wise man feareth, and departeth from evil: but the fool rageth, and is confident."

I N nature some creatures are strong and bold, having both instincts and instruments for combat : other creatures are feeble but fleet ; it is the intention of their Maker that they should seek safety, not in fighting, but in fleeing. It would be a fatal mistake if the hare, in a fit of bravery, should turn and face her pursuers. In the moral conflict of human life it is of great importance to judge rightly when we should fight and when we should flee. The weak might escape if they knew their own weakness, and kept out of harm's way. That courage is not a virtue which carries the feeble into the lion's jaws. I have known of some who ventured too far with the benevolent purpose of bringing a victim out, and were themselves sucked in and swallowed up. To go in among the foolish for the rescue of the sinking may be necessary, but it is dangerous work, and demands robust workmen.

The ordinary rule is, " go from the presence of a foolish man :" " forsake the foolish and live" (ix. 6). Your first duty is your own safety. But on some persons at some times there lies the obligation to encounter danger for the safety of a neighbour. Man is made his brother's keeper. It is neither the inclination nor the duty of a good man to be among the profane or profligate, but he sometimes recognises the call of God to go in among them for the purpose of pulling a brand from the burning. The specific instruction recorded in Scripture for such a case is, " Save with fear, pulling them out of the fire ; hating even the garment spotted by the flesh" (Jude 23). He who would volunteer for this saving work must " save with fear"—fear lest the victim perish ere he get him dragged out, and fear lest himself be scorched by the flame. We often hear of a miner going down a shaft to save a brother who has been choked by foul air at the bottom. It is a work of mercy: but the worker must beware; if he linger too long in the deadly atmosphere of the pit, instead of saving his neighbour, himself will share his fate. There may be—there ought to be an effort made to lay yourself along the drunken, the licentious, the profane, and so bear them out into safety: but it should be a rush in and a rush out again. When one begins to dally in the place of danger he is gone. When your earnest interference is resisted, fall back upon the rule of Scripture: " go from the presence of the foolish," lest your soul be polluted by contact with their blasphemy or vice.

A wise man fears sin, and distrusts himself. He knows that the enemy is strong, and that his own defences are feeble; his policy, therefore, is not to brave danger, but to keep out of harm's way: he seeks safety in flight. The character of the wise man may be read most distinctly in the dark but polished mirror that stands on the other side—" The fool rageth, and is confident." From the glossy surface of this intensified folly, the wisdom of modesty shines brightly out.

The fool's picture is truthfully sketched here, in few lines. His character is mainly made up of two features: he thinks little of danger, and much of himself. These two ingredients constitute a fool. He stumbles on both sides alike: that which is strong he despises, and that which is weak he trusts. The dangers that beset him are great, but he counts them nothing; the strength that is in him is as nothing, but he counts it great. Thus, he is on all hands out of his reckoning, and stumbles at every step.

The end of such a fool was described lately in the newspapers: many must have read and shuddered at the tragic tale. A certain man was employed by the Zoological Society of London, as a keeper in their collection of animals. His department was the care of the serpents. A separate building was appropriated to them, and stringent regulations laid down for their management. The keeper's wages were good, and his work was light. If he had been cautious and careful, his life would have been safe and his labour easy. Those of the serpents that are venomous must be closely confined and cautiously tended. The front of the cage is of strong glass. It is divided into two equal parts by a partition, in which there is a door. The serpents lie in one of these divisions, while the other is empty. It is the duty of the keeper, at certain times, to introduce an iron rod through a small opening, and therewith remove them by the door in the partition from the one compartment into the other. This done, he makes fast the door, and then enters the emptied cage, for the purpose of cleaning it and depositing food. One morning the keeper opened the door, before the serpents were removed, took one of them in his hands, hung it round his neck, and thus attired ran after his companions, sportively pretending to throw it upon them. He was warned that it might sting, and its sting might be death. He laughed at the warning. He then put the creature back into the cage, without having received any harm. Next he drew out a cobra capella, and placed it in his bosom beneath his coat, calling out, " I am inspired ; it will not hurt me." Waxing bolder by impunity, he grasped the deadly reptile by the middle, and held it up before his face pretending to speak to it. Drawing itself back to take aim, the creature made a sudden dart, and fixed its fangs in his nostrils. Sobered by fear, he screamed out, tore the fangs out of his flesh, and flung the serpent back into the cage. He was carried to an hospital, and died in fearful agony about an hour afterwards.

The fool raged and was confident; but he was drunk at the time, otherwise he would not have taken a venomous snake in his hand and held it up to his face. The man was not himself : it was strong drink that raged within him. Yes, he was drunk : his own act brought madness on, and then the snake plunged its poisonous fangs in the madman's blood. The snake did not abstain from stinging him ; the poison did not abstain from destroying his life because he was drunk : and will God abstain from judging him because he was drunk when he stumbled into eternity? How many in our land, every year, die as that fool died? They inflame their appetite by a little strong drink, and then blind the eye of reason by more. With reason laid asleep, and passions heated into sevenfold fury, they sally forth and get or give a mortal wound. Every man who even once maddens himself by drink is a fool of the same stamp with the serpent-keeper. He has allowed a snake to coil itself round his body : no thanks to him if it creep off without spurting death into his veins. The confidence of fools is their ruin: the safety of a wise man lies in that modest sense of his own infirmity, which makes him fear and depart from evil. Solomon's advice is, "Look not thou upon the wine when it is red, when it giveth his colour in the cup, when it moveth itself aright: at the last it biteth like a serpent and stingeth like an adder" (xxiii. 31, 32).

We seem as a nation to derive little benefit from the warnings which reach us through the newspapers by hundreds every year, in the form of frightful deaths caused by drunkenness. A man will readily resolve, as he reads these tragedies, that he will neither murder his neighbour nor walk over a quarry himself: but his resolution may avail him nothing if he dally with strong drink. This people are paying a heavy price, and yet they will get no wisdom in return, if they content themselves with punishing murder and loathing suicide, and continue to think lightly of drunkenness, which is the most prolific seed of both. He would be the greatest benefactor of his country, in all its interests, who should lodge in the public mind an adequate estimate of drunkenness, as a sin in the sight of God, an injury to the individual, and a crime against society. As long as public opinion makes light of this germ-sin, its fruits will work us heavy woe.

Sympathy

(Proverbs 14:10)

"The heart knoweth his own bitterness: and a stranger doth not intermeddle with his joy."

THE two extreme experiences of a human heart, which comprehend all others between them, are "bitterness" and "joy." The solitude of a human being in either extremity is sublime and solemnizing. Whether you are glad or grieved, you must be alone : the bitterness and the joyfulness are both your own : it is only in a modified sense, and in a limited measure, that you can share them with another, so as to have less of them yourself. We speak of sympathy, and sympathy means community of emotions between two human hearts. Doubtless there is a reality corresponding to that attractive name, but the share which another takes is a thin shadowy thing in comparison with the substantive experience of your own soul. A physical burden can be divided equally between two. If you overtake a weary pilgrim on the way, toiling beneath a load of a hundred pounds weight, you may volunteer to bear fifty of them for the remaining part of the journey, and so lighten his load by a full half. But a light heart, however willing it may be, cannot so relieve a heavy one. The cares that press upon the spirit are as real as the load that lies on the back, and as burdensome ; but they are not so tangible and divisible. We speak of sharing them by sympathy, and there is some meaning in the words, some reality in the act ; but the participation in kind and effect comes far short of the actual partition of material weight. The law of our nature in the last resort is, " Every man must bear his own burden." The weight that falls upon my body may be divided with you, but the weight that falls on my soul must lie all on my soul alone.

There are, indeed, some very intimate unions in human society as organized by God, and existing even yet in a fallen world. The family relations bring heart into very close contact with heart, and joys or sorrows that abound in one flow freely over into another. The closest of them all, the two "no longer twain, but one flesh," is a union of unspeakable value for such sympathy as is compatible with distinct personality at all; but when you estimate this union at its highest value, and take it all into account, there remains a meaning, deep and wide like the ocean, in this one touching word, "The heart knoweth his own bitterness." The wife of your bosom can indeed intermeddle with your joys and sorrows as no stranger can, and yet there are depths of both in your breast which even she has no line to sound. When you step into the waters of life's last sorrow, even she must stand back and remain behind. Each must go forward alone. The Indian *suttee* seems nature's struggle against that fixed necessity of man's condition. But it is a vain oblation : although the wife burn on the husband's funeral pile, the frantic deed does not lighten the solitude of the dark valley. One human being cannot be merged in another.

But the isolation of every man from his fellow in the hour of extremity may become the means of pressing the sufferer nearer another companion, who is able even then to remain. "There is a Friend that sticketh closer than a brother." Such is the person of Emmanuel, God with us, that the spiritual life of a believer is not a separate existence, but a part of His. As a branch in the vine, or a member in the body, so is a disciple in the Lord : the Christian is one with Christ in such a way as no human spirit can be with another. When the fangs of the persecutor vexed the life of his little ones, the pain throbbed that moment in the heart of Jesus : the Head on high cried out when the enemy hurt His member, "Saul, Saul, why persecutest thou me ?" Only Christ's sympathy is real and complete. He who suffered for our sins can make himself partaker of our sorrows. He who went through the wrath of God to make a safe path for his people, is able to keep them company in the swelling of Jordan. Long ago they saw His day, and rejoiced in His perfect sympathy. "Though I walk through the valley of the shadow of death, I will fear no evil, *for thou art with me*" (Ps. xxiii. 4)

A Man is Responsible for His Belief

(Proverbs 14:12)

"There is a way which seemeth right unto a man, but the end thereof are the ways of death."—xiv. 12

THE way seems right, but is wrong; and the result accords, not with the false opinion, but with the absolute truth of the case. Its issue in death proves that its direction was erroneous. A tree is known by its fruits, and a life-course by the end to which it leads. A man follows a path which he thinks right, but which really is wrong; if he persist he will perish. This case is of frequent occurrence in the world, both in its material and its moral departments. Your opinion that the path is right does not make it right: your sincerity in that erroneous opinion does not exempt you from its consequences, whether these affect more directly the body or the soul.

There is a mercantile company which bulks largely in the public eye, and turns over vast sums, and spreads its agencies widely over the world. You think the concern is solid, and court its alliance. You are accepted; your interests are bound to its fortune, and are ruined in its fall. Your favourable opinion of a hollow pretence did not prevent the loss of your means when the bubble burst. The law is universal. In the nature of things it cannot be otherwise. It is a hollow form of philosophy that deceives some men on this point. They say, surely God will not punish a man hereafter who conscientiously walks up to his convictions, although these convictions be in point of fact mistaken. They err, knowing neither the inspired Scriptures nor the natural laws. Do men imagine that God, who has established this world in such exquisite order, and rules it by regular laws, will abdicate, and leave the better world in anarchy? This world is blessed by an undeviating connection between causes and their effects; will the next be abandoned to random impulses, and run back to chaos? The idea is not only false, but impossible and absurd. It is not even conceivable that the direction of a man's course should not determine his landing-place.

But here an element is introduced into the calculation which, it is thought, essentially modifies the result. In morals the motive is an effective constituent of every transaction: and if a man endeavour to form a right judgment, and yet fall into error, will not his sincerity exempt him from the consequences of his mistake? This supposition is contrary both to the testimony of the word, and to the analogy of nature. It sets up wilful fancy against uniform fact. A man contracts and pays for a ship of first-rate material and workmanship. In due time a vessel is delivered to him of goodly appearance, but built of unseasoned material, and not water-tight in the joints. He embarks with his family and his goods in the treacherous bottom. When he is out of sight, and the storm has begun to blow, the truth begins to circulate from lip to lip among his former neighbours that the ship is not seaworthy, and the question is anxiously discussed whether she can accomplish the voyage. If one of them should reason that because the man did his best, and honestly believed the ship was good, a just God overruling all, would not permit the innocent to be drowned, while the guilty stood on dry land safe, the suggestion would be scouted by common consent as an unsubstantial dream. We all know that the laws of nature do not turn aside to shield a man from the consequence of his error, because his intention was good. Every man, also, may, by a little consideration, come to see that this arrangement is best for the interests of all. Such is the principle that operates with undeviating uniformity in all the region which lies within the view of man; and what ground have we for believing that order will be exchanged for anarchy in the government of God, whenever it steps over the boundary of things seen and temporal?

Perhaps the secret reason why an expectation, so contrary to all analogy, is yet so fondly entertained, is a tacit unbelief in the reality of things spiritual and eternal. We see clearly the laws by which effects follow causes in time; but the matters on which these laws operate are substantial realities. If there were a firm conviction that the world to come is a substance, and not merely a name, the expectation would necessarily be generated. that the same principles which regulate the divine administration of the world now, will stretch into the unseen and rule it all. On one of the latter days of a return voyage across the Atlantic, we paced the level deck beneath a brilliant sun, and on a placid sea, in earnest and protracted conversation with a benevolent and accomplished Englishman. He was sincerely religious in his own way: and a part of his confession was that every man's religion would carry him to heaven, whatever it might be in itself, provided he sincerely believed it. He accounted it rank bigotry to doubt the safety of any fellow-mortal on the ground of erroneous belief. His creed, although he would probably have refused to sign it if he had seen it written out, was, Safety lies in the sincerity of the believer, without respect to the truth of what he believes. We plied him with the analogy of nature in the form which circumstances most readily suggested. We are here coursing over the ocean at the rate of three hundred miles a day. We have seen no land since we left the shores of America, nine days ago. We are approaching the coast of Ireland, and will no doubt pass about a quarter of a mile on the safe side of Cape Clear. The captain and his officers have been carefully taking their observations, and calculating their course. We have confidence in their capacity and truth. But if they should commit a mistake, and cast up an erroneous reckoning, whether by their own ignorance, or by a false figure in their tables, or a misplaced mark on their quadrant—whether by their own fault or the fault of others whom they innocently trusted—will the sincerity of their belief that they are in the right course save them and us from the consequences of having deviated into a wrong one? If the ship is directed right upon a rocky shore, will the rocky shore not rend the ship asunder, because the master thinks he is in the accustomed track? Our friend was silenced, but he was not convinced. Argument alone will not remove such an error. It is not a clearer head that is needed, but a softer heart. When in conscious unworthiness and godly simplicity we are willing to have it so, we shall perceive that it is so. "Unto the upright there ariseth light in the darkness." Even so Father. for so it seemed good in thy sight.

It is fashionable, in some quarters, to deny responsibility for belief, on the ground that a man's opinion is not under his own control. There is precisely the same ground for affirming that a man cannot help his actions. His opinions do no doubt influence his actions, but his actions also influence his opinions. A bad life deranges the judgment, and a deranged judgment deteriorates still more the life. These two act reciprocally as causes, and emerge alternately as effects.

Truth shines like light from heaven; but the mind and conscience within the man constitute the reflector that receives it. Thence we must read off the impressions, as the astronomer reads the image from the reflector at the bottom of his tube. When that tablet is dimmed by the breath of evil spirits dwelling within, the truth is distorted and turned into a lie. It was because the man's deeds were evil that he missed the truth: he is responsible for his erroneous opinion as certainly as he is responsible for his un-righteous act.

It may be proved, by a large induction of facts, that among the multitude, those who become infidel in opinion have previously become vicious in conduct; and in other classes, where the experience seems to be opposite, the difference may be only in the outward appearance. Pride, and other forms of spiritual wickedness in the high places of the cultivated human intellect, are as hateful to God, and as adverse to right moral perceptions, as meaner vices in the low places of ignorant, unrestrained sensuality. There is no respect of persons with God.

There is a way which is right, whatever it may seem to the world, and the end thereof is life. "If any man be in Christ, he is a new creature." "I am the way, and the truth, and the life, no man cometh unto the Father but by me." God's way, of coming to us in mercy, is also our way of coming to Him in peace. Christ is expressly "the Apostle and High Priest of our profession" (Heb. iii. 1). He has come forth God's messenger to us, and returned as our advocate with the Father.

The Backslider
(Proverbs 14:14)

"The backslider in heart shall be filled with his own ways."

I F the secret history of backsliders were written, many startling discoveries would be made. Whatever the enormity it may end in, backsliding begins unseen in the heart. The Christian in name, whose fall resounds through the land, filling the mouths of scorners with laughter, and suffusing the faces of disciples with shame, did not descend to that depth by one leap from the high place on which he formerly stood. He does not by a sudden resolution of mind turn from virtue into vice. He does not even abandon his Sabbath school, or desert the prayer-meeting, by a deliberate judgment. A slipping begins secretly and imperceptibly in his heart, while appearances on the surface are kept unchanged. He ceases to watch and pray. He admits vain thoughts, and gives them encouragement to lodge within him. Having no hunger for righteousness, he neglects the bread of life. He grows weary of religious exercises and religious society. If he continue to attend them, it is a bodily service, endured for the purpose of maintaining the place which he has attained. Duties become more irksome, and forbidden indulgence more sweet.

There is a weighing beam exposed to public view, with one scale loaded and resting on the ground, while the other dangles high and empty in the air. Everybody is familiar with the object, and its aspect. One day the curiosity of the passengers is arrested by observing that the low and loaded beam is swinging aloft, while the side which hung empty and light has sunk to the ground. Speculation is set on edge by the phenomenon, and set at rest again by the discovery of its cause. For many days certain diminutive but busy insects had, for some object of their own, been transferring the material from the full to the empty scale. Day by day the sides approached an equilibrium, but no change took place in their position. At last a grain more removed from one side, and laid in the other, reversed the preponderance, and produced the change. There is a similar balancing of good and evil in a human heart ; the sudden outward change results from a gradual inward preparation.

All engineering proceeds upon the principle of reaching great heights or depths by almost imperceptible inclines. The adversary of men works by this wile. When you see a man who was once counted a Christian standing shameless on a mountain-top of open impiety, or lying in the miry pit of vice, you may safely assume that he has long been worming his way in secret on the spiral slimy track by which the old serpent marks and smoothes the way to death.

On the same branch of an apricot-tree that leant against the south side of a garden wall, I have seen two fruits, large and luscious, hanging side by side, and ripening apace in the sun. They were of equal size and equal loveliness. Their stainless bosoms peeped from beneath the leaves, to bask in the noonday heat. Nothing in nature could be more lovely to look upon, or more rich in promise. Yet, ere to-morrow's sun is hot, one of them grows black on the side, and bursts, and collapses, and becomes a mass of rottenness, while the other remains in undiminished beauty and fragrance by its side. Whence the diverse fates of these twin beauties ? Especially, why did the catastrophe happen so suddenly ? It happened thus :—yesterday, when you stood looking on the two, admiring their equal beauty, one of them was hollow in the heart. If then you had taken it in your hand, and turned it round, you would have seen corruption already pervading its mass. On the dark side, next the wall, it has been pierced and entered. Its inside has been scooped out and devoured, while it continued to present to the passenger as fair an appearance as ever ; and see, black, crawling, loathsome creatures are nestling and revelling in that hollow heart, beneath that beauteous skin.

Thus are fair promises in the garden of the Lord suddenly blighted. You have known two standing long side by side in a goodly profession, and labouring hand in hand for the kingdom of Christ. One of them falls headlong into a pit of vice, and next day the whole neighbourhood rings with the scandal. Diverse are the emotions, but all are moved. Christ's enemies sneer, and his members sigh. How sudden the fall has been, sorrowing disciples say to each other in a suppressed whisper, when they meet,—how sudden and unexpected! No, friends; it was not a sudden fall. In the heart, unseen, there has been a long preparation of backsliding. Vain thoughts have lodged within, and vile thoughts have been welcome visitors. Persons first vain and then vile have by degrees found their way into his presence, and charmed him, so that he cannot want them, though he knows they are stinging serpents. By such a process his heart has been hollowed out, and inhabited by creatures more loathsome than crawling vermin, while the skin of profession was kept whole, and its fairest side turned to public view. A cry of wonder rises from the crowd, when the hollow shell falls in, because they did not know its hollowness until the fall revealed it.

There is a warning, in such a case :—beware of backsliding in heart ; small beginnings may issue in a fearful end. But there is encouragement even here to disciples who are humble, and trustful, and watchful. There is no such thing as a sudden collapse of a sound heart. "They that wait upon the Lord shall renew their strength."

The Trustful and the Truthful
(Proverbs 14:15)

" The simple believeth every word; but the prudent man looketh well to his going."

"THE simple believeth every word;" and why not? If it were the universal rule, it would make a happy world. Trust is a lovely thing; but it cannot stand, unless it get Truth to lean upon. When its tender hand has been often pierced by a broken reed of falsehood, it pines away, and dies of grief. A man would find it easier to be trustful, if his neighbours were trust-worthy.

It is a well-known characteristic of little children to believe implicitly whatever you tell them. This is one, and not the least, of those features which make up their beauty, and draw forth our love. It remains a feature of the child until it is worn off by hard experience of the world. Perhaps we should recognise in it a remnant of our unfallen state. It is an obvious fact in nature, that the infant expects truth, until that expectation is burned out of him by many disappointments: suspicion does not appear until it has been generated by falsehood.

A great responsibility is attached to all our intercourse with children. Offences will come; but woe to him by whom the offence cometh. The child expects truth; let him have it. Be not the first to wring his simplicity out of him by double dealing. A lie told by seniors for their amusement threw a dark shadow over my childhood, and took much of the sunshine out of it. Some person in a military dress, interested in the child for his father's sake, took me fondly in his arms, when I was between four and five years of age, and slipped a shilling into my hand I either never knew, or have long since forgotten, what his name was, and what relation he sustained to the family ; but the instant he passed, older children and grown-up people told me, with an air of seriousness, that I was enlisted, and that whenever I should be old enough, the officer would return, and take me off to the wars. This intimation sank into me, and lay at my heart like lead, all the period of my childhood. I was afraid to speak of it, and suffered in silence. The terror was never taken off by a serious explanation, for no one knew how great it was. I obtained no relief until my understanding gradually outgrew it. That lie wrought grievous harm to me. Besides overclouding life at its very dawn, it left within me, when it departed, a general grudge against mankind for wantonly wounding the helpless. When the boy was big enough to shake off the phantom, he was full of indignation against the world for amusing itself by torturing a child. The Almighty has constituted himself the Helper or Avenger of the weak, whatever the form of their weakness may be; beware of hurting a little child by any untruth. The guilt is great when older children or servants torment the little ones by inventing false terrors. Stand in awe, and speak only sacred truth to the timid confiding infant, for the Almighty Friend of the feeble is looking on. Even in little things He will carry through the principle, "Inasmuch as ye have done it to one of these little ones, ye have done it unto me." God has made the infant trustful, and then cast him upon you : if you take advantage of that trustfulness to deceive, whether in great things or small, you are mocking its Author. The child is poor, and lying threats oppress it : "He that oppresseth the poor, reproacheth his Maker." "Vengeance is mine ; I will repay, saith the Lord." As the young of birds instinctively open their mouths for food, and their mothers never —not even once since the creation of the world—have thrown in chaff to mock their hunger ; so the trustfulness of children is the opening of their mouth for truth: if we fling falsehood in, and laugh at their disappointment, the Lord will require it. It is not amusement; it is sin. It is both a crime and a blunder. They are called Goths and Vandals who deface the precious remnants of Greek statuary that have descended to our times ; what name would fitly designate the barbarian who, in sheer wantonness, spoils the beauty of a finer, fairer form—who rubs off by vulgar lies the lovely trustfulness of a little child?

"The prudent looketh well to his going;" and good cause he has so to do. In this world a man is obliged to be suspicious.

Man suffers more from man than from the elements of nature or the beasts of the field. A time is coming when this species of prudence will be no longer needed. When the people shall be all righteous, there will be no deception on one side, and no distrust on the other. How sweet even this life would be, if there were no falsehood and no distrust. If every speaker were true, and every hearer trustful, already the new world would have begun. As yet, we must walk circumspectly at every step, lest a neighbour deceive us. In the new heavens and new earth, truth will pervade all like air. "They shall not hurt nor destroy in all my holy mountain, saith the Lord." Oh, that will be joyful, joyful, when there shall be no lie to generate suspicion, and no suspicion generated by a lie!

Witnesses

(Proverbs 14:25)

"A true witness delivereth souls."

"TRUTH is great, and it will prevail;" but truth in the abstract is like a disembodied spirit, and cannot exert a power upon the world. It must be incarnate in a living witness ere its effect be felt.

One witness, faithful and true, has appeared among men, and this witness delivers souls. He is the Truth in human nature, and the truth makes the captive free. If the Son make you free, ye shall be free indeed. Of the sin of men and the holiness of God, of the curse and the blessing, the fall and the rising again, He is witness. He is the way and the truth and the life. There is no salvation in any other. If we would see evidence either of God's anger against sin, or His mercy to sinners, we must look unto Jesus.

But in Him, and by Him, and for Him, Christians are witnesses too. In this respect, "as He is, so are we in this world" (1 John iv. 17). Every one whom Christ saves from the world He uses in it. Deserters from the powers of darkness are, one by one as they come over, incorporated in the armies of the living God, and sent back to do battle against their former lord. If you are a Christian, these two things are true of you: first, you have need of Christ, and, second, Christ has need of you. He saves you, and you serve Him. All things are in His hand. Those who are bought with His blood He loves, with a love that is wonderful, passing the love of mothers. He would call them home, and give them rest, if He had not some needful work for them to do in this outer world. The very fact of a Christian being here and not in heaven, is a proof that some work awaits him.

And the special work for which Christians are left in the world is to be witnesses. Himself told His disciples so when He was about to leave them: " Ye shall receive power after that the Holy Ghost is come upon you; and ye shall be witnesses unto me" (Acts i. 8). On high, whither he was then going, he does not need witnesses. There they behold his glory. The Lamb is the light of heaven, and they who bask in His rays need none to tell them that He is great and good; but in this outfield, where enmity and ignorance prevail, Christ has need of witnesses, and He has chosen to this office those who trust in His salvation and are called by His name.

He does not send angels to proclaim His message and wield His power. He does not command the thunders to pronounce His name, and the lightnings to write His character on the sky. The epistle in which He desires to be read is the life of His disciples. The evidence by which the Spirit will convince the world is His truth, uttered from the word, and echoed, still and small, from the meek and quiet life-course of converted men. It should be encouraging, stimulating, elevating to the humblest disciple to learn that the Lord who redeemed him has appointed his time and his path. It is required that we be witnesses unto Him wherever we are and whoever may question us. Two quali- fications are required in a witness, *truth* and *love* (Eph. iv. 15) : these are needed, but these will do. With these one will chase a thousand, and two put ten thousand to flight.

The place of a witness for Christ in the world is honourable, but arduous. A witness, in contested cases, after giving evidence in chief, is subjected to cross-examination. A Christian's profes- sion is, and is understood to be, his direct and positive testimony that he is bought with a price, and bound to serve the Lord that bought him: but as soon as this testimony is emitted, the cross- examination begins. If he be not a true witness, he will stumble there. Either or both of two persons, with very different views, may subject a witness to cross-examination—the judge or the adversary. It is chiefly done by the adversary, and in his interests. The Supreme himself puts professing disciples to the test before the public court of the world; but when He so tries his children, the truth comes forth purer and brighter by the trial. He who goes about as a roaring lion, seeking whom he may devour, tempts to destroy : he puts the witness to the question in order to break him down. An inquirer who saw you at the Lord's table meets you in the market-place : if he saw the solemnity of a trustful worshipper there, and feel the gripe of an overreacher here, he counts your testimony for Christ not true, and sets his conscience free from the restraints of begun conviction. The keen eye of an adversary, sharpened into more than natural intensity by the reproof which your profession administered, tracks you into the world, and questions you there. Every inconsistency raises a shout of triumph in the circle who will not have this Man to reign over them, and draws a sigh in secret from the broken hearts of the Lord's meek and poor afflicted ones.

They speak of the evidences of religion, and much has been done in our day to multiply and confirm them; but, after all, Christians are the best evidences of Christianity. Alas, we have for eighteen hundred years been printing books to prove Christianity true, and living so as to make men think we do not believe it. Living witnesses, if they be true, have far more power than dead letters of a book, however accurate they may be. The last words of Jesus on the earth were spoken to leave this charge upon his members, "Ye shall be witnesses unto me, both in Jerusalem, and in all Judea, and in Samaria, and unto the uttermost part of the earth ; and when he had spoken these things, while they beheld, he was taken up, and a cloud received him out of their sight" (Acts i. 8, 9). His last command is, In the place where ye happen to be, and in all the neighbourhood as far as your influence reaches, and when opportunity occurs to all mankind, be ye witnesses unto me. After this he departed in a cloud. He will come again in the clouds, and every eye shall see Him. Occupy till He come. At His coming we would like to be found faithful and busy in the very work which he prescribed. There is no other work worth living for, or fit for dying in. How much you have gotten from Christ, and how much you have done for needy men while passing through life—these are the only things that will be important when the closing hour has come. To be saved, and to commend the Saviour,—this is the double aim fit to fill a human heart and a human life.

" A true witness delivereth souls ; " and a false witness ? He is the stone over which they stumble. It is not in the power of any man to be neutral in the conflict between light and darkness. Good and evil in actual life are like land and sea on the globe; if you are not on the one, you must be on the other. There is no belt of intermediate territory for the irresolute to linger on. Let no man who bears Christ's name lay the unction to his soul, that that if he does no good he at least does no evil. One of the heaviest complaints made in the prophets against Jerusalem for her backsliding, is that she was a "comfort" to Samaria and Sodom (Ezek. xvi. 54); that those who had the name and place of God's people, so lived as to make the wicked feel at ease. If the salt retain its saltness, surrounding corruption will be made uneasy by the contact. If Christians live as like the world as they can, the world will think itself safe in its sin; and those who should have been the deliverers, will become the destroyers of their neighbours.

The Place of Refuge
(Proverbs 14:26)

"In the fear of the Lord is strong confidence; and his children shall have a place of refuge."

FEAR is confidence: the words sound strangely. They are like that blessed paradox of Paul, "When I am weak, then am I strong." They are strange indeed, but true: to fear God aright is to be delivered from all fear. "His salvation his nigh them that fear him:" to have such a neighbour is strong consolation to a human spirit in this howling wilderness. The fear which brings a sinner submissive and trustful to the sacrifice and righteousness of the Substitute is itself a confidence. The great and terrible God becomes the "dwelling-rock" of the fugitive. Those who went early to the sepulchre and looked into the empty grave where the Lord lay, departed from the place with "fear and great joy." A human soul, made at first in God's image, has great capacity still; in that large place fear and great joy can dwell together. There are different kinds of fear; there is a fear that "hath torment," and perfect love, when it comes, casts that kind out (1 John iv. 18). Like fire and water, these two cannot agree. The fear that hath torment by its very nature keeps or casts out confidence from a human heart; but the filial fear of the dear children may be known by this, that it takes in beside itself a great joy, and the two brethren dwell together in unity. When the fear of God, which a sinner feels, is plunged in redeeming love, the torment is discharged, and confidence comes in its stead.

"His children shall have a place of refuge." God is their refuge and their strength: they will not fear though the earth be removed. They "are kept by the power of God through faith unto salvation" (1 Pet. i. 5).

There are two keepings very diverse from each other, and yet alike in this, that both employ as their instruments strong walls and barred gates. Great harm accrues from confounding them; and therefore the distinction should be made, and kept clear. Gates and bars may be closed around you for the purpose of keeping you in, or of keeping your enemy out;—the one is a prison, the other a fortress. In construction and appearance the two places are in many respects similar. The walls are in both cases high, and the bars strong. In both it is essential that the guards be watchful and trusty. But they differ in this,—the prison is constructed with a view to prevent escape from within; the fortress to defy assault from without. In their design and use they are exact contraries : the one makes sure the bondage, the other the liberty, of its inmates. In both cases it is a *keep*, and in both the *keep* is strong,—the one is strong to keep the prisoner in, the other strong to keep the enemy out.

The fear of the Lord to those who are within, and have tasted of his grace, is the strong confidence of a fortress to defend them from every foe; to those who look at it from without, it often seems a frowning prison that will close out the sunlight from all who go within its portals, and waste young life away in mouldy dungeons. Mistakes are common on this point, and these mistakes are disastrous.

Life to the Christian is a warfare, all the way. He is safe, but his safety is not the peace of home; it is the protection of a strong tower in the presence of enemies. The children of the kingdom are safe though weak ; not because none seek their hurt, but because greater is He that is for them than all that are against them. This is the condition of all who have turned to the Lord, and have not yet entered into rest. They are out of the kingdom of darkness, but have not reached the presence of God. In all this middle region they are safe, but their safety cometh from the Lord.

Danger surrounds them : but they are kept in safety. Before they were converted they did not desire this keeping ; when they are glorified they will not need it. But in all this passage through the wilderness, after they have burst forth from Egypt, and before they have reached the promised land, " His children" need and get " a place of refuge."

This is their best estate on earth, His children though they be.

It is good to know precisely what we have a right to expect. If we carelessly count on advantages which have not been promised, and not provided for us, we shall be thrown off our guard, and suffer loss. The utmost request that Jesus made for his disciples was, not that they should be taken out of the world, but kept from the evil (John xvii. 15). This, therefore, is the utmost that will be given. Enemies swarm around—His children are feeble; the safety provided is confidence in Himself, the strong tower into which the righteous run.

But often a trembling fugitive mistakes the fortress for a prison, and refuses to go in. A single soldier in an enemy's country is crossing the plain in haste, and making towards a castle whose battlements appear in relief on the distant sky. A man, who appears a native of the place, joins him from a bypath, and asks with apparent kindness whither he is going. To yonder fortress, says the soldier, where my Sovereign's army lies in strength. The stranger, under pretence of friendship, endeavours to persuade him that it is a prison. He is an emissary of the enemy, sent to detain the fugitive until it be too late, and then cut him off. In this way many are turned back from the place of refuge after they seemed to have turned their faces thitherwards. Agents of the enemy, under various disguises, join themselves to the young, and insinuate that to be seriously religious is to throw their liberty away. Multitudes, whom no man can number, are thus cheated and lost. They would like to be safe, but cannot consent to go into a dungeon yet. When they grow old, and the appetite for pleasure is comparatively weak, they think they can submit to the sombre shade of those towers where the regenerate have taken refuge ; but as yet they love life too well to plunge into a living death.

A little religion is a painful thing. It destroys one pleasure, and supplies no other in its stead. In this land of light and of privilege, many go as far forward in a religious profession as to embitter the joy of the world ; few seem to advance far enough in the "new and living way" to reach a refuge in the joy of the Lord. Safety lies in drawing near to God ; and the distinguishing mark of an unbelieving heart is that it departs from Him. If the fortress were some pile of self-righteousness, or even a huge, unshapely heap of penances and fastings, men with their corruption all about them would be content to take shelter there; but since the offered resting-place is under the eye, and even in the bosom, of the Holiest, they will not and cannot go in, unless they are made willing to put off the old nature and leave it behind. " His children shall have a place of refuge;" and the refuge is such that only the children count it a boon. The Great Teacher told Nicodemus first about *seeing* the kingdom of God, and next about *entering* it (John iii. 3, 5). No man will go into the kingdom until he has some spiritual perception of what it is. Though the Refuge is provided, and the gate standing open, and the invitation free, poor wanderers stand shivering without, because a suspicion clings to the guilty conscience, that the "strong tower," offered as a safe dwelling-place, will turn out to be a place of confinement from genial society and human joys. We must take up Philip's simple prayer, " Lord, show us the Father:" if the prodigal could know the Father's love, he would arise and go to the Father's bosom.

Envy: The Disease and the Cure
(Proverbs 14:30)

" A sound heart is the life of the flesh; but envy the rottenness of the bones."

AN object is sometimes so situated that you can see it better by looking away from it to the surface of a mirror opposite than by attempting to look directly upon itself. If you want to know what is meant by a sound heart, look over to the other clause, and learn that envy is the rottenness of the bones. Soundness of heart is generous love to a brother, kindled there by Christ's love to us : "Love one another as I have loved you." When that grace of the Lord is transferred to a disciple, and written by the Spirit so deeply upon the fleshly table within, that it can be read by the passer-by on the man's outer life, the new creature is sound at heart and vigorous in action. "Perfect love casteth out fear" in relation to God, and envy in relation to fellow-men.

Among the many diseases to which the living body is liable, some are much more appalling and repulsive than others, though not more deadly. Perhaps there is not one of all the ghastly host that casts a deeper shadow of dismay before it over a human spirit than rottenness in the bones. The very conception of it in the imagination is enough to send a cold shudder through the frame. Such is the tried word chosen by the Spirit to designate envy, an evil disease which is endemic among mankind. Like other diseases that affect the spirit rather than the body, its nature is such that they who are most deeply tinged by the infection are least alive to the danger. To arouse the envious out of their indifference, that ailment of the soul is named after one of the most frightful maladies that preys upon the human frame, and wastes its life away. New creatures in Christ Jesus, if the spiritual life be in healthful exercise, dread every tincture of envy felt working within them as they would dread the symptoms of incipient caries in their bones.

Envy is called a passion; and passion means suffering The patient who is ill of envy is a sinner, and a sufferer too. He is an object of pity. It is a mysterious and terrible disease. The nerves of sensation within the man are attached by some unseen hand to his neighbours all around him, so that every step of advancement which they make tears the fibres that lie next his heart. The wretch enjoys a moment's relief when the mystic cord is temporarily slackened by a neighbour's fall; but his agony immediately begins again, for he anticipates another twitch as soon as the fallen is restored to prosperity.

No species of sensitive pleasure can be greater or purer than that of the convalescent when the disease has been cast out, and he walks forth without pain to breathe the fresh air, and look on the green fields again. Those who have long pined in disease, and been at last delivered, relish most keenly the blessing of health. Such is the delight of being delivered from the tormenting presence of envy, and emerging into love. It is the sensation of renewed health when rottenness has been purged out of the bones. They who are led into love walk at liberty. It is a large place. Your path would never be crossed, and your person never jostled, although all the world were beside you there. As to the room that is in him and about him, a disciple is, according to his capacity, like his Lord.

But the cure of envy, as it is wrought by the love of Christ, is not only a deliverance from pain; it is, even in the present world, an unspeakable gain. That man will speedily grow rich who gets and puts into his bag not only all his own winnings, but also all the winnings of his neighbours. Whenever love like Christ's takes possession of a man, and drives the rottenness from his bones, the capital of his enjoyment is increased by all his own prosperity and all the prosperity of others. His peace, according to the simple and sure imagery of Scripture, is like a river. A river that follows its own course in solitude does not grow great. The Nile, contrary to the analogy of other great streams, flows more than a thousand miles without receiving the waters of a single tributary; the consequence is, that it grows no greater as it courses over that vast line. Other rivers are every now and then receiving converging streams from the right and left, and thereby their volume continually increases until it reach the sea. The happiness of a man is like the flow of water in a river. If you enjoy nothing but what is your own, your tiny rivulet of contentment, so far from increasing, grows smaller by degrees, until it sinks unseen in the sand, and leaves you in a desert of despair; but when all the acquisitions of your neighbours go to swell its bulk, your enjoyment will flow like a river enriched by many affluents, growing ever greater as life approaches its close. It is some such river that makes glad the city of our God. Envy will be unknown there. " Faith, hope, charity, these three ; but the greatest of these is charity." Charity is very pure, and very great. When the rottenness that mingled with it shall be all cast out, and charity without spot or wrinkle shall be the element of heaven, the redeemed will be the happy inmates of a happy home. If there were no envy, but only love—if each should count and feel his neighbour's good to be his own gain, this earth would already be a heaven.

To have constituted the world so that envy is as rottenness in the bones, and love is felt like the glow of health permeating the frame, is a glory to the world's Maker. Every sensation of glad enlargement enjoyed by a loving heart, at the sight of a neighbour's prosperity, is a still small voice, announcing to him who hath an ear, that God is good ; and every pang that gnaws the envious, like rottenness in his bones, is the same word, *God is good*, echoed unwillingly back from the suffering of sin.

The Merciful
(Proverbs 14:31)

F AITH in God is the foundation that sustains the goodly superstructure of relative duties. A greater than Solomon imparted the same instruction to the apostle who leant on His breast. This commandment have we from him : " That he who loveth God, love his brother also " (1 John iv. 21). The Almighty casts his shield over those who have no other help. He espouses the cause of the poor. To oppress them is to reproach Him. In the arrangements of His providence, the poor we have always with us, as tests to try our love, and objects to exercise it on. Love of God is the root of the matter in a human heart : but the root, though the chief thing, is from its nature unseen. It is known by its fruit, and its fruit is philanthropy. The necessary dependence of human duty upon divine faith is laid down by Solomon as clearly as by John : " He that honoureth Him hath mercy on the poor." If the heart is right with God, the hand will be open to a brother ; but a profession of faith by a merciless man the Most High will repudiate as hypocrisy. The ancient Church possessed in full the glorious truth, that of all the real compassion which flows through human channels, the fountainhead is on high. He who gets mercy shows it.

In His own teaching on this subject, Jesus said, " These things have I spoken unto you, that my joy might remain in you, and that your joy might be full ;" and immediately added, " This is my commandment, that ye love one another" (John xv. 11, 12). The connection between these two intimations is interesting and obvious. First, his own joy ; next, that joy flowing into his disciples, so that they shall be full ; and then these full vessels flowing over in streams of Christ-like love on all the needy within their reach. It is this union to the Head that will enable—that will compel a disciple to love his brother. From this fountain, through this channel, a love-stream will flow of volume sufficient to carry down before it a whole legion of obstructing jealousies.

These are the principles ; and now, some suggestions as to the practice of mercy to the poor.

1. We must not confine our aim either to the sins of the soul on the one hand, or to the sufferings of the body on the other. You cannot effectively or permanently help your poor brother, if you treat him merely as a body with life in it : the laws of Providence forbid. Whom God hath joined, no man can with impunity put asunder. Soul and body are so united, that the one cannot really be elevated while the other is left low. Those who attempt the material elevation of the species by material means alone, do and must fail. Soul and body are bound together for better and for worse. We cannot keep our brother's body and neglect his soul ; if we would rescue the falling, we must lay hold of the whole man. On the other side, we will not succeed in influencing the spirits of the wretched, if we are callous to their bodily sufferings. If we leave behind unnoticed the body's privations, we shall not reach the soul to deal with its sins. The avenue to the spirit lies, in part at least, through the bodily senses. If we do not approach in that way, we shall be kept out, and our spiritual counsels, however good, will strike against the closed door of an anguished heart, and rebound in our faces, like an echo that mocks us from a rock. The double rule for the whole case is—as to the supply of spiritual destitution, this ought ye to do ; and as to the healing of physical ailments, that ought ye not to leave undone.

2. Every one must do his part in the great work of helping those who cannot help themselves. To prescribe other people's duty, and neglect our own, is a foolish and mischievous habit. We must not suppose that philanthropists are a few eminent personages, standing out in high relief on the page of history—men born, like poets, to their destiny, whose office is to cure human ills on the stage of a continent, and in sight of an admiring world. Honour to the greatly good of every age and every country ; but the bulk of mercy's work must everywhere be done by the many thousands of kind hearts and busy hands that are never heard of

half a mile from home. Most of the light we work by on the surface of the earth, comes to us reflected from unnumbered objects near that get it from the sun ; and so the glimpses of compassion that fall in all directions on the poor, from every heart that basks in the love of Jesus, constitute, by aggregate of many little things, the bulk and substance of the effort that mitigates the sufferings of men. Let every man do his best in the place which he holds, and with the means at his disposal.

3. Mercy to the poor must be a law operating from within, and not a system adopted from without. Wherever genuine coin is going, counterfeits appear. There is a species of charity, got up according to the fashion, that flourishes in benevolent societies abroad, and comes home to snarl at a servant who is doing her best to please. ·You never find the law of gravitation acting on a steeple, and forgetting itself in the shaft of a coal-pit where it is out of sight. The laws of God never put on appearances, whether they be the laws that are stamped on creation, or those that are written by the Spirit on a renewed heart. If there be truth in the inward parts, the outward actions will be consistent. The legs of the lame are unequal, and he makes no progress in this race of benevolence. I would estimate at a low price the philanthropy of the man who has spent ten thousand on an hospital, and oppresses his own dependants in detail. The ills of life are real ; we must have a real love to cope with them. Mercy to man must have its spring in the heart, that its streams may be ever ready to flow, wherever there is an opening. The sufferings of humanity cannot be conjured away by a *name:* a *nature* is needed to secure a steady supply of mercy, and that nature must be new. Howard was a man of great mercy, but he was not a great man. He was not great, but he was true, and the secret of his power lay in his truth. It was conscious union to Christ as a sinner saved that animated, sustained, and directed him. Mercy in him acted by a law of the new creature, and it was steady like nature's other laws. It acted on every object and at every time, without partiality and without hypocrisy. If the unhealthful cottages of Cardington had been left wet above and wet below, while Howard screwed the rents from their squalid inmates, he would not have been able to have poured the balm of humanity on the barbarism of British and continental prisons. Inconsistency, if he had been

guilty of it, would have unnerved his arm and undermined his influence. Neglect of smaller oppressions near his own dwelling would have shorn the locks of his strength ; and the mighty Philistines whom he met abroad, instead of falling by his sling, would have put out his eyes and made sport of his blindness. It was love that led him forth, and truth that made him strong. If a man is not merciful all over, he is not merciful at all.

4. There must be regulating wisdom as well as motive power. There must indeed be an impulse in order to energetic action, but we must not act by impulses. We need all the power that we possess ; it is a pity that any of it should be wasted. To give alms to little children sent by profligate parents to enact misery on the street is money thrown away, and mercy too. Of late years much has been done to indoctrinate the public mind on this subject. Whether the public have learned the lesson yet, I know not ; but certainly they have been often taught that it is useless and mischievous to give pence indiscriminately to beggars on the street or the wayside. This doctrine is true, but it does not contain the whole truth in regard to that subject. One side of truth may become practically falsehood. We need the counsels which have of late been largely addressed to us from many quarters, to harden us against giving by sudden impulse to persons unworthy or unknown ; but we don't need any lecture to repress within our hearts the movements of mercy to the poor. I am jealous for myself and others, lest, in leaning hard over from the side of lavish expenditure on the unworthy, we should fall, on the other side, into a callous indifference to human sufferings. We must not check the impulse because counterfeit poverty has abused our compassion and wasted our gifts. Direct it upon genuine poverty, and stimulate it to the utmost. Such is the constitution of the world, and the condition of men, that if the relations are rightly managed, the rich may get more good from the presence of the poor than the poor get from the gifts of the rich. The flow of compassion is healthful ; obstruction in the channel breeds disease in the moral system. It is both health and happiness to a mother to have a helpless, little, living thing hanging on her breast, and drawing its sustenance from her body. To want it would be neither a pleasure nor a profit. The poor we have always with us, and it is a double blessedness to give.

The discovery of abuses should induce us not to seal the fountain, but to direct the stream. Where no water runs, no ships, with their precious burdens, navigate the interior of a country. Even where there is a stream constant and strong, it does not follow that you can have safe and profitable inland navigation. If the water turn sharply round a corner here, and leap white and frothy over a rock there, it will be better to intrust no ship to its impetuous movements. What then? Then neither intrust your floating treasures to that wayward stream, nor let the country lie lean for want of commerce. Dig a canal. Your canal will do nothing for you dry, and your river will do nothing for you although it is filled to the brim ; but let the river into the canal, and forthwith ply your traffic. The whole neighbourhood will be enriched. Let us beware of either checking or wasting any impulse of humanity; we need it all, and more. Direct it wisely, and let it flow.

5. Another important rule for the practice of mercy to the poor is, whatever share you may be able to take in the wholesale benevolence of organized societies, you should also carry on a retail business, by personal contact with the sufferers. Societies and pecuniary contributions are necessary in their own place; but even although they should satisfy the wants of the receiver, the greater blessing to the giver cannot come through these channels. Personal contact—face to face—heart to heart—hand to hand— this is the best way to do good, and get good. We are indebted to our Father in heaven for all the good that we enjoy ; and as our goodness reacheth not unto Him, He has made the account payable to the poor; no man has any right to lift himself up in pride; no man has any right even to count that he condescends, when he enters the houses, and listens to the tale of the sufferers. He is only owning, we cannot say paying, a lawful debt. It is simply the act of honouring his Maker. When he has done all he is an unprofitable servant.

The Two Departures:
The Hopeful and the Hopeless
(Proverbs 14:32)

"The wicked is driven away in his wickedness: but the righteous hath hope in his death."

THE peculiarities of the Hebrew proverb shine conspicuously in this specimen. The two arms of the sentence are nicely balanced, and move round a common centre. There is a mixture of similarity and difference, which makes the meaning perspicuous and the expression memorable. But if there is peculiar beauty in the words, there is terrible sublimity in the thoughts which they convey. Unspeakably great are the two things which the two balanced branches of this proverb hold in their hands. These two arms, outstretched and opposite, direct the observer, by their piercing finger-points, to Death on this side, and Life on that—endless both. Looking this way, you read the doom of the wicked; that way, you descry the hope of the just.

1. *The doom of the wicked.*—He "is driven away in his wickedness." As smoke is driven by the wind, so will the wicked perish in the day of wrath. I think I hear arguments fitfully muttering through pauses of the blast, that "God would not make creatures, and then torment them." The smoke complains that it is hard to be driven by the wind; and yet it is driven by the wind. This very word will justify the Judge, and shut the convict's mouth: it comes to warn the wicked, that he may turn and live. If he come out of his wickedness at God's invitation, he will not be driven away in it by His wrath.

We are not able to form a right conception of what it is to be and abide in wickedness: because it is so near us, we do not know it. If it were a body standing before us, we could examine its proportions, and describe its appearance; but because it is a spirit transfused through us, we remain ignorant of its character and power. To be in sin is a fearful condition; yet he who is in it may be at ease. A ship is lying in a placid river when winter comes, and is gradually frozen in. The process was gentle, and almost imperceptible. There was no commotion, and no crash. The ice crept round, and closed in upon the ship without any noisy note of warning. If it had been a foreign body brought by human hands to bind the ship withal, the operation would have been observed. If men, whether professing to be friends or foes, had carried trees or stones, and piled them round the ship, suspicion would have been aroused; the owners would have heaved their anchors, and worn her down to the sea for safety. As it was, no one approached the ship. Her own element, the water on which she lay, closed and held her. It was not possible to prevent that lockfast, except by taking the ship out of the river in time.

But what is the effect? The ship is not shaken. No creaking is heard—no strain is felt. She feels firm and easy. Even when the pines of the neighbouring forest are bending to the blast, she sits unmoved in her solid bed. That bed she has made for herself, and therefore it fits her. This is very like the wicked in his iniquity, and before he is driven away. When it closed round him, he was not afraid. It was not some danger threatening from without, and pressed forward by another. It was his own; it was what he had always been in. It was his element. Silently and surely, that which he lived in congealed and locked him fast. Nor is he in any way alarmed. In its closing embrace, it does not thwart him. It humours him all round. It yields to every feature of his character, only it holds him fast. He is more at ease now than others, or than himself was before. His neighbours may be sometimes agitated, but he is at peace. He stands steady in his element, and no ripple disturbs its surface.

When the ice of the river goes away, the imbedded ship goes with it. It is a dreadful departure. The rupture of the ice on a large river is one of the sublimest scenes in nature. The water swells beneath; the ice holds by the crooked banks a while; but after a period of suspense, the flood prevails, and the trembling rending mass gives way. Reeling icebergs and foaming yellow waves tumble downward in tumultuous heaps, and the ship is swept away like a feather on a flood.

If we had a sense for perceiving spiritual things, the most heart-rending sight in the world would be a sinner set fast in his element, and the flood of wrath secretly swelling from beneath. They speak of angels weeping, and the figure may in its own place be useful; but we do not need the aid of such a supposition here. The Lord of angels wept indeed, when he saw sinners fixed and easy in their sin, with the tide of divine vengeance rolling forward to drive them away. That same Jesus looks in pity now on the wicked in their wickedness, and continues sweetly calling, " Come unto me."

No remedy is possible to the wicked in his wickedness; and the remedy which consists in bringing him out, he is not willing to accept. For all who are sinners—that is, for all men—a rending is prepared. Every one must either be riven out of his wickedness, or driven away in it. This tearing or that every one must endure. The alternative is, Come out of her, my people; or, Be partaker of her plagues. Pain there must be; either the pain of the new birth, or that of the final judgment. A process is ready for drawing the victims out. The power is Christ's love; the means the gospel message. Some lie locked fast in wickedness, who know that wrath is coming, and yet refuse to let the line of that Almighty love be laid about their souls. Why do they choose death rather than life? Because they are so closely bedded in their element, that to be drawn out of it is to be torn asunder. Such is the feeling of the captive soul; and the answer which the possessing spirit suggests is, " What have we to do with thee, thou Jesus; art thou come to torment us before the time?" But the love of Christ, when a repentant sinner casts himself confidently upon it, melts the fastenings away, and makes the outcome easy. When from the iron icy bondage, hope, the anchor of the soul, goes out, and up, and into Jesus our Advocate within the veil, not only is ultimate safety secured, but present severance accomplished. Down the line of hope's hold flows a melting heat from the Sun of righteousness, which loosens the gripe of sin, and sets the soul at liberty. But the sentence remains sure; he who is not so drawn out of wickedness, will be driven away in it.

2. *The hope of the just.*—" The righteous hath hope in his death." Certain it is that the faithful in ancient times believed

God, and it was counted to them for righteousness; but at this distance of time we are not able to determine how far their faith was like an appetite of the renewed nature, and how far it attained to understanding also. The regenerate in the childhood state of the Church were alive, and lived upon the sincere milk of the word, and grew thereby, whatever the measure of their knowledge or their ignorance may have been. The righteousness that justified Abraham was the same as that which Paul put on. The righteous of those days knew that, by birthright and personal desert, he was on the same standing with the wicked, and that the difference was due to redeeming love. If Israel's first-born were not destroyed like Egypt's, it was because the Lamb's blood marked their dwellings. On the ground of a perfect righteousness imputed, an actual obedience begins: he is bought with a price, and therefore serves the Lord. By birthright he was a child of wrath: he has been " begotten again into a living hope " This man has hope at the time when humanity needs it most— when death draws near. A friend in need is a friend indeed. Stars are a grateful mitigation of the darkness; but we do not want them by day. Hope, always lovely, is then sweetest when it beams from heaven through the gloom that gathers round the grave.

There are diversities in this department of the Spirit's ministry. Some even of the children depart under a cloud, and others in sunlight, softer at the setting than it was at noon. Some are glad when they are passing through the flood, and others do not begin their song till they are safe on the further shore. The various notes of their varied experience, when the redeemed tell the story of their life, will give richer music to the hymns of heaven.

There is one class of experiences of which many examples occur. A youth who has been seeking first the kingdom of God with alternate hope and fear, but without violent emotions on either side, comes suddenly and unexpectedly in sight of death. There is at first, and for a time, a very great tumult of alarm. When that tumult subsides, a peace that passeth all understanding keeps the heart and mind, until the spirit is released from flesh, and darts away.

The ship has set sail, and kept on her course many days and nights, with no other incidents than those that are common to all.

Suddenly land appears; but what the character of the coast may be, the voyagers cannot discern through the tumult. The first effect of a near approach to land is a very great commotion in the water; for it is one of the coral islands of the South Pacific, encircled by a ring of fearful breakers at some little distance from the shore. The waves are higher and angrier than any they have seen in the open sea; but forward they must go. Partly through the surf, partly over it, they are borne at a bound; strained and giddy, and almost senseless, they find themselves within that sentinel ridge of crested waves that guard the shore, and the portion of sea that still lies between them and the land is calm and clear like glass. It seems a lake of paradise, and not an earthly thing at all. It is inexpressibly sweet to lie on its bosom, after the long voyage and the wild tossing of the barrier ridge. All the heavens are mirrored in the water, and along its edge lies a flowery land. Across the belt of sea the ship glides gently, and gently touches soon that lovely shore.

It is thus that I have seen a true pilgrim thrown into a tumult when the shore of eternity suddenly appeared before him. A great fear tossed and sickened him for some days; but when that barrier was passed, he experienced a peace deeper, stiller, sweeter, than any he ever knew before. A little space of life's voyage remained, after the fear of death had sunk into a calm, and before the immortal felt the solid of eternal rest. On life's sea, as yet, was the spirit lying, but the shaking had ceased; and when at last the spirit passed from a peaceful sea to a peaceful land, the change seemed slight. The righteous had hope in his death. " Blessed hope!"

The Truth in Love
(Proverbs 15:1)

" A soft answer turneth away wrath ; but grievous words stir up anger."

W E greatly need an instrument capable of turning away wrath, for there is much wrath in the world to be turned away. It is assumed here that the anger is sinful in character, or excessive in degree; but there are occasions in which a good man may do well to be angry. It is recorded of Jesus once, in the days of his flesh, that He was angry; but the explanation is immediately added, He was " grieved for the hardness of their hearts" (Mark iii. 5). It is safe for a disciple "to follow the Lamb whithersoever He goeth." If all our anger were grief for sin, and grief for sin our only anger, the emotion would neither displease God nor disturb men. If our love were like Christ's, our anger would be like his too. In the meantime, most of the anger that prevails is sinful and dangerous. On that side there is especial need for watching and prayer, lest we enter into temptation.

We are on dangerous ground when we are contending in our own cause. A man may, indeed, through divine grace, rule his spirit aright even there; but it is his wisdom to be jealous of himself. Self-love ties a bandage on the eyes of the understanding, and then leads the blind astray. A great part of the danger lies in the suddenness of the explosion ; to obtain a delay of a few moments is half of the victory. " He that is slow to wrath is of great understanding; but he that is hasty of spirit exalteth folly" (xiv. 29). Some knowledge of human nature is displayed in the advice once given to a passionate man, to count a hundred after he felt the fire burning within, before he permitted it to blaze forth by his lips. The monitor shrewdly calculated that in many instances the passion would cool down during the interval, and the explosion be altogether prevented. An improvement on that method might be suggested. Instead of securing merely an empty interval, fill it with an air that the flame of anger cannot live in—fill it up with prayer. Employ the same space of time in prayer for yourself and for the offender. Nehemiah adopted this method to subdue another passion. He was oppressed by fear. The Jewish captive betrayed his patriotism before the despot, and symptoms of the royal displeasure appeared: "then I was very sore afraid." Then and there, however, notwithstanding the monarch's presence, Nehemiah "prayed to the God of heaven." Courage came, and wisdom with it: he asked skilfully, and obtain his desire. (Neh. ii.) The same resource would afford deliverance when anger is the passion that suddenly assails. After praying to "our Father" for your offending brother and yourself, you may speak to him safely. "The Christian's vital breath" is fatal to all the spawn of the serpent. Pass your resentment through a period of communion with Him who bought you with his blood, and it will come out like Christ's, a simple grief for a brother's sin, and a holy jealousy for truth.

In some such way should we treat our own anger; but how shall we meet the anger of other people? Turn it away by a soft answer. In man as he is, a sally of wrath from another seems to produce a similar sally in return, as naturally as a mountain-side gives back an echo of the sound that strikes it. If you listen to the quarrel of two men or women who have neither been purified by Christian principle, nor smoothed by a liberal education, you will observe the working of the natural law. Wrath generates grievous words, and grievous words aggravate the wrath that produced them. The reciprocating series goes on, until some accident break the chain, or the sounds die away from the exhaustion of the combatants.

There is an instrument for receiving anger on, so as to make it harmlessly expend its force, like lightning led by a conducting rod into the ground; and even if there be a rebound at first, the force gradually melts away, like a dying echo from a single sound. That patent shield for warding off the sharp strokes of wrath, is "a soft answer." Christianity makes it of the solid metal, and education supplies at a cheaper rate a plated article, useful as long as it lasts, and as far as it goes. The principle of softness increasing the strength of a defence is common to the physical and moral departments of the world. The Roman battering-ram, when it had nearly effected a breach in walls of solid stone, was often baffled by bags of chaff and beds of down skilfully spread out to receive its stubborn blow. By that stratagem the besieged obtained a double benefit, and the besiegers suffered a double disappointment : the strokes that were given proved harmless, and the engine was soon withdrawn. In our department a similar law exists, and a similar experience will come out of it : if the person assailed hang out in time his soft answer, the first stroke will not hurt him, and the second will never come.

In the effort to avoid one extreme, however, we must beware lest we fall into another : mere softness will not do. The down beds of the besieged Jews within Jerusalem would have been no defence against the battering-rams of Titus, if there had not been a solid wall of masonry behind them. A glove of velvet should cover the hand of iron, but an iron hand should be within the velvet glove. Faithfulness naked, may in its effect be little better than vulgar obstinacy ; and gentleness unsupported, may, in the miscellaneous strife of time, count for nothing more than lack of courage ; but when faithfulness is gentle in its form, and gentleness faithful in its substance, these two meet helps, made one in a marriage union, constitute the best preparation which man's imperfect state permits, for meeting rough jostlings in the moving crowd of life. Truth alone may be hated, and love alone despised : men will flee from the one, and trample on the other ; but when truth puts on love, and love leans on truth, in that hallowed partnership lies the maximum of defensive moral power within the reach of man in the present world.

There is a contrivance to prevent the destructive collision of carriage against carriage in a railway train, which human beings might profitably imitate. On the outer extremities, where they are liable to strike against each other, there is a soft spongy covering. Within, and at the very centre, is a spring, strong, but yielding ; yielding, but strong. There is both a soft surface without, and an elastic spring in the heart. If the impact of another body were met by mere hard unyielding strength, both would fly into splinters at the first shock. On the other hand, if there were in one of the carriages softness only, with no recuperative spring, the others would soon drive it from the rails, or crush it to pieces. The destroyed carriage would be lost to the owners, and its debris would cause additional mischief. These machines move in company, like ourselves, and they move quickly, and jostle each other by the way. The managers have marked the danger, and made skilful provision for escaping it. They take advantage of the great pervasive law, that firmness and softness united in each is the best arrangement for the safety of all.

The apparatus employed to keep these mute racers off each other, in the swift course of life, might almost be counted a modification of our great law, "speaking the truth in love." Although the two departments lie so far asunder, a parallelism is plainly perceptible in their laws. One inventing mind is at the fountain-head of creation, and the so-called discoveries, in the various departments, are so many drops from its diverging streams. It seems a reversal of the usual order, and yet we are assured the rule is reasonable and useful;—observe how carriages on a railway keep their own places, kindly meeting, yet firmly repelling every blow from a neighbour in the rapid race;—observe how they do, and do likewise.

A little girl came to her mother one day and inquired, in a tone which showed that the words were not words of course, if every word of the Bible is true. " Yes, child; but wherefore do you ask?" " Because the Bible says, 'A soft answer turneth away wrath;' and when Charlotte spoke to me in a rage, I gave her a soft answer, but it did not turn away her wrath." It was a natural, but a childish thought. It is true that such is the tendency of a soft answer,—in that direction it puts forth a power; but, alas, that power is often exerted without effect on a callous heart. " The goodness of God," says the Scripture, "leadeth thee to repentance" (Rom. ii. 4); but many who distinctly feel its drawing refuse to follow it. The obstinate perish unrepentant, and yet the word is true.

The most important practical rule, for our guidance under provocation, is to consider, not how hard a blow we can deal in return, consistently with a character for Christian meekness, but how far we can yield, without being faithless to truth and to God. In view of our own corruption, and the temptations that abound, a leaning to this side seems the safest for a Christian man. But when all rules fail to reach the case, let us have recourse to the great Example. He walked over our life-path, in order that we might have his foot-prints to guide us. Alike in love of good, and resentment against evil, the Master's conduct is the disciple's rule.

"Be ye followers of God, as dear children" (Eph. v. 1). The word is "imitators," and we know what that means in the instincts and habits of a loved and loving child. Our Father in heaven has given us an example, and if we have the spirit of dear children, our constant impulse and tendency will be to do as He has done. This lifts our eyes at once to the deepest counsel of eternity—the greatest event of time. To the enmity against Himself, which reigned and raged in human-kind, God replied by sending His Son to seek and save them. Look unto Jesus, and learn the answer from heaven to the anger of earth. JESUS is God's answer to the wrath of man. The answer is soft, and yet it is the greatest power that can be applied—the only power that will prevail to turn the wrath away, and win the wrathful back to love.

The All-Seeing

(Proverbs 15:3, 11)

"The eyes of the Lord are in every place, beholding the evil and the good. Hell and destruction are before the Lord: how much more then the hearts of the children of men?"

THE omniscience of God is usually considered a fundamental doctrine of natural religion. Nobody denies it. Infidelity in this department is acted, not spoken. Speculative unbelievers are wont, in a free and easy way, to set down at least a very large proportion of the existing Christian profession to the credit of hypocrisy. Hypocrite is a disreputable name, and most men would rather impute it to a neighbour than acknowledge it their own : but it is one thing to repudiate the word, and another to be exempt from the thing which it signifies. That weed seems to grow as freely on the soil of natural religion as in the profession of Christian faith. A man may be a hypocrite although he abjures the Bible. Most of those who reject a written revelation profess to learn from the volume of creation that a just God is everywhere present, beholding the evil and the good ; but what disciple of Nature lives consistently with even his own short creed ?

The doctrine of the divine omniscience, although owned and argued for by men's lips, is neglected or resisted in their lives. The unholy do not like to have a holy Eye ever open over them, whatever their profession may be. If fallen men, apart from the one Mediator, say or think that the presence of God is pleasant to them, it is because they have radically mistaken either their own character or his : they have either falsely lifted up their own attainments, or falsely dragged down the standard of the Judge.

Atheism is the inner spirit of all the guilty, until they be reconciled through the blood of the cross. All image worship, whether heathen or Romish, is Atheism incarnate. The idol is a body which men, at Satan's bidding, prepare for their own enmity against God. The gods many and lords many that thickly strew the path of humanity over time, are the product ever and anon thrown off by the desperate wriggle of the guilty to escape from the look of an all-seeing Eye, and so be permitted to do their deeds in congenial darkness. When spiders stretched their webs across the eyelids of Jupiter, notwithstanding all the efforts that Greek sculpture had put forth to make the image awful, the human worshipper would hide, without scruple, in his heart the thoughts which he did not wish his deity to know. It was even an express tenet of the heathen superstitions that the authority of the gods was partial and local : one who was dreadful on the hills might be safely despised in the valleys. In this feature, as in all others, the Popish idolatry, imitative rather than inventive, follows the rut in which the ancient current ran. Particular countries and classes of persons are assigned to particular saints. With puerile perseverance, the whole surface of the earth and the whole course of the year have been mapped and appropriated, so that you cannot plant a pin point either in time or space without touching the territory of some Romish god or goddess. In this way the ignorant devotee practically escapes from the conviction of an omniscient Witness. " Divide and conquer " is the maxim of the enemy, when he tries to deaden or destroy that sense of divine inspection which seems to spring native in the human mind. When he cannot persuade a man that there is no such witness, he persuades him, as the next best, that there are a thousand. When a man will not profess to have no god, the same end is accomplished by giving him many.

We sometimes experience and express surprise that rational beings should degrade themselves by worshipping blind, dumb idols, which their own hands have made ; but it is precisely because the idols are blind and dumb that men are willing to worship them. A god or a saint that should really cast the glance of a pure eye into the conscience of the worshipper would not long be held in repute ; the grass would grow again round that idol's shrine. A seeing god would not do : the idolater wants a blind one. The first cause of idolatry is a desire in an impure heart to escape from the look of the living God, and none but a dead image would serve the turn.

From history and experience it appears that idolaters prefer to have an image that looks like life, provided always that it be not living. A real omniscience they will not endure ; but a mimic omniscience pleases the fancy, and rocks the conscience into a sounder sleep. In the present generation the Romish craftsmen have tasked their ingenuity to make the eyes of their pictured saints move upon the canvas. The eyeball of a certain saint rolled, or seemed to roll, in its dusky colouring within the dimly-lighted aisle, and great was the effect on the devotions of the multitude. In places where Protestant truth has not shorn their superstition of its grosser out-growths, the procession of the *Fete Dieu* is garnished with a huge goggle eye, carried aloft upon a pole, moved in its socket by strings and pulleys, and ticketed "The Omniscient." This becomes an object of great attraction in the crowd. In one aspect it is more childish than any child's play ; but in another aspect a melancholy seriousness pervades it. This hideous mimicry of omniscience is an elaborate effort to weave a veil under which an unclean conscience may comfortably hide from the eye of God. After all the darkening and distorting effects of sin, there lies in the deep of a human soul an appetite for the knowledge of God, which, when it can do no more, stirs now and then, and troubles the man. It is the art of Antichrist to lie on the watch for that blind hunger when first it begins to stir, and throw into its opening mouth heaps of swine-food husks, to gorge and lay it, lest it should seek and get the bread of life.

This is the grosser method, which grosser natures adopt to destroy within themselves the sense of divine omniscience. There is another way running off in an opposite direction,—more refined, indeed, but equally atheistic,—more manly, but not more godly, than the crowded Pantheon of ancient or modern Rome. This other road to rest is Pantheism. If there is speculation in an age, it becomes restive under the thick clay of image-worship. There is a spirit which will not endure a material idol, and yet is not the spirit of God. Dagon falls, and the philosophers make sport of his dishonoured stump. Instead of making a little ugly idol for themselves, they adopt a great and glorious one made to their hands. God, they say, is the soul of Nature ; and Nature therefore is the only god whom they desire or need. Sea, earth, air,—flowers, trees, and living creatures, including man,—the creatures in the aggregate,—the universe is God. In this way they contrive to heal over the wound which the sense of an omniscient Eye makes in an unclean conscience. It is the personality of God that stings the flesh of the alienated. It is easier to deal with Nature in her majestic movements than with the Self of the Holy One. Nature heaves in the sea, and sighs in the wind, and blossoms in the flowers, and bleats on the pastures. Nature glides gently round in her gigantic orbit, and stoops not to notice the thoughts and words of a human being; he may live as he lists, although Nature is there. Philosophy compels him to reject the paltry, tangible, local gods of all the superstitions. Reason constrains him to own the universality of the Creator's presence. The problem in his mind is, how to conceive of the Lord's eyes being in every place, and yet indifferent to sin. In order to accomplish this, the personal, with its pungency, must be discharged from the idea of God. This done, the great idol, though more sublime, is not a whit more troublesome than the little one. The creature, whether great or small, whether God's hand-work or man's, cannot be a god to an intelligent, immortal human soul. Neither the idolater's stock nor the philosopher's universe has an eye to follow a transgressor into those chambers where he commits his abominations in the dark; but in every place "our God is a consuming fire" upon a sin-stained conscience. The darkness and the light are both alike to him (Ps. cxxxix. 21).

"*In every place*" our hearts and lives are open in the sight of Him with whom we have to do. The proposition is absolutely universal. We must beware, however, lest that feature of the word which should make it powerful only render it to us indefinite and meaningless. Man's fickle mind treats universal truths that come from heaven as the eye treats the visible heaven itself. At a distance from the observer all around, the blue canopy seems to descend and lean upon the earth, but where he stands it is far above, out of his sight. It touches not him at all; and when he goes forward to the line where now it seems to touch other men, he finds it still far above, and the point which applies to this lower world is as distant as ever. Heavenly truth, like heaven, seems to touch all the world around, but not his own immediate sphere, or himself, its centre. The grandest truths are practically lost in this way when they are left whole. We must rightly divide the word, and let the bits come into every crook of our own character. Besides the assent to general truth, there must be specific personal application. A man may own omniscience, and yet live without God in the world.

The house of prayer is one important place on earth, and the eyes of the Lord are there when the great congregation has assembled, and the solemn worship has begun. He seeth not as man seeth. Thoughts are visible to Him. Oh! what sights these pure eyes behold in that place! If our eyes could see them, a scream of surprise would rend the air. "Son of man, hast thou seen what the ancients of the house of Israel do in the dark, every man in the chambers of his imagery? for they say, The Lord seeth us not; the Lord hath forsaken the earth" (Ezek. viii. 12). Take your place beside a hive of bees in a summer day at noon, and watch the busy traffickers. The outward-bound brush quickly past the heavy-laden incomers in the narrow passage. They flow like two opposite streams of water in the same channel, without impeding each other's motions. Every one is in haste: none tarries for a neighbour. Such a hive is a human heart, and the swarm of winged thoughts which harbour there maintain an intercourse with all the world in constant circulation, while the man sits among the worshippers, still, and upright, and steady, as a bee-hive upon its pedestal. The thoughts that issue from their home in that human heart, bold like robbers in the dark, overleap the fences of holiness, suck at will every flower that they reckon sweet, and return to deposit their gatherings in the owner's cup. The eyes of the Lord are there, beholding the evil.

The family is His own work, and He does not desert it. His eyes are open there, to see how father and mother entwine authority and love, a twofold cord, at once to curb the children's waywardness and lead them in the paths of peace; how children obey their parents in the Lord; how a sister employs that gentleness whereby God has made woman great, to soothe and win the robuster brother; how a brother proffers the arm that the Almighty has made strong, a support for a mother or a sister in her weakness to lean upon; how masters become fathers to their servants, and servants lighten their labour by infusing into its dull heavy body the inspiring soul of love. In the family, the place where all these bonds unite, and all these relations circulate, are the eyes of the Lord its Maker ; let all its members " walk as seeing Him who is invisible."

In the street, in the counting-house, in the shop, in the factory, these eyes ever are. God does not forget and forsake a man when he rises from his knees and plunges into business ; the man, therefore, should not then and there forget and forsake God.

In the tavern, when its doors are shut and its table spread,— when the light is brilliant and the laugh loud,—when the cup circulates and the head swims,—in that place are the eyes of the Lord, and they are like a flame of fire. It would be a salutary though a painful experience, if the eyes of these time-killers were opened for a moment to meet the look of their omniscient Witness, before he become their almighty Judge.

But the eyes of the Lord are bent on this world, to behold the good as well as the evil that grows there. Is there any place among its thorns and thistles which bears fruit pleasant to the eyes of its Maker? Yes; there are fields which he cultivates (1 Cor. iii. 9), and trees which he plants (Isa. v. 3). On these places his eye rests with complacency, beholding the growth of his own grace. One of the places that attract the Redeemer's eye is a shady avenue where a youth saunters alone on a summer eve, communing with his own heart, grieving over its detected backslidings, and breathing a prayer for reconciliation and renewing. That angular recess in the ivy-covered rock, dark in daylight by the thickness of the leafy shade,—that is a place to which the Lord's eye turns intent; for thither, when the fire burned, the penitent turned aside unseen; and there he " wept and made supplication, and *prevailed*," nor parted from the place, nor let the Angel of the Covenant go, until he had gotten a whole Saviour for his soul, and surrendered his whole soul to the Saviour. This tree of righteousness is the planting of the Lord. By its freshness and fruitfulness he is glorified. The new creation is at least as lovely in the Creator's eye as the old one was before it was marred by sin. In that ransomed captive the Redeemer " shall see of the travail of his soul and shall be satisfied."

" Hell and destruction are before the Lord ; how much more then the hearts of the children of men?" This terrible truth these hearts secretly know, and their desperate writhings to shake it off show how much they dislike it. The Romish confessional is one of the most pregnant facts in the whole history of man. It is a monument and measure of the guilty creature's enmity against God. We know authoritatively from their own books what Rome expects her priests to do in the confessional, and history gives some glimpses of what they actually do. We have felt the glow of indignation in our breast as we learned how the confessor fastens like a horse-leech on his victim; and how the victim, like a charmed bird, abandons itself to the tyrant's will. We have heard how a full-aged unmarried man explores at will the half-formed thoughts that flutter in the bosom of a maid, and rudely rakes up the secrets that lie the deepest in the memory of a matron. We have wondered at the blindness and stupidity of our common nature, in permitting a man, not more holy than his neighbours, to stand in the place of God to a brother's soul. There is cause for grief, but not ground for surprise. The phenomenon proceeds in the way of natural law. It is the common, well understood process of compounding for the security of the whole, by the voluntary surrender of a part. The confessional is a kind of insurance office, where periodical exposure of the heart to a man is the premium paid for fancied impunity in hiding that heart altogether from the deeper scrutiny of the all-seeing God. Popish transgressors have no particular delight in confession for its own sake. Confession to the priest is felt and dreaded as an evil. The devout often need spurring to make them come; and when they come, it is on the principle of submitting to the less evil in order to escape the greater.

The incoming of the Heart Searcher is feared and loathed, like a deadly and contagious disease. A quack comes up, and by dint of bold profession, persuades the trembler that voluntary inoculation with the same disease in a milder form will secure exemption from the terrible reality. The guilty, although he does not like to have his conscience searched,—*because* he does not like to have his conscience searched, submits to the searching of his conscience. The pretending penitent accepts the scrutiny by a man, in the hope of escaping thereby the scrutiny of God. The impudent empiric tells his patient that if he submit to inoculation the small-pox will never come. Behold "the human nature of the question;" behold the philosophy of the confessional.

It is in principle the old question of the heathen,—"Shall I give the fruit of my body for the sin of my soul?" (Mic. vi. 7.) It is not, however, the fruit of the body that is offered, for they do not make their children pass through the fire to Moloch now; the spiritual chastity of the soul is laid down as the price of impunity for sin. God made the human soul for himself; it is vilest prostitution to abandon it to the authoritative search of a sinful man. Yet this unnatural sacrifice is made, this galling yoke is worn, in the vain hope of shutting out the eyes of the Lord from one place of his own world.

But what fearful dilemma have we here? The Holiest changeth not when he comes a visitant to a human heart. He is the same there that he is in the highest heaven. He cannot look upon sin; and how can a human heart welcome Him into its secret chambers? How can the blazing fire welcome in the quenching water? It is easy to commit to memory the seemly prayer of an ancient penitent, "Search me, O God, and know my heart; try me, and know my thoughts" (Ps. cxxxix. 23). The dead letters, worn smooth by frequent use, may drop freely from callous lips, leaving no sense of scalding on the conscience; and yet, truth of God though they are, they may be turned into a lie in the act of utterance. The prayer is not true, although it is borrowed from the Bible, if the suppliant invite the All-seeing in, and yet would give a thousand worlds, if he had them, to keep him out for ever.

Christ has declared the difficulty, and solved it: "I am the way, the truth, and the life: no man cometh unto the Father, but by me" (John xiv. 6). When the Son has made a sinner free, he is free indeed. The dear child, pardoned and reconciled, loves and longs for the Father's presence. What! is there neither spot nor wrinkle now upon the man, that he dares to challenge inspection by the Omniscient, and to offer his heart as Jehovah's dwelling-place? He is not yet so pure; and well he knows it. The groan is bursting yet from his broken heart: "O wretched man that I am! who shall deliver me from the body of this death?" (Rom. vii. 24.) Many stains defile him yet; but he loathes them now, and longs to be free. The difference between an unconverted and a converted man is not that the one has sins and the other has none; but that the one takes part with his cherished sins against a dreaded God, and the other takes part with a reconciled God against his hated sins. He is out with his former friends, and in with his former adversary. Conversion is a turning, and it is one turning only, but it produces simultaneously and necessarily two distinct effects. Whereas his face was formerly turned away from God, and toward his own sins; it is now turned away from his own sins, and toward God. This one turning, with its twofold result, is in Christ the Mediator, and through the work of the Spirit.

As long as God is my enemy, I am his. I have no more power to change that condition than the polished surface has to refrain from reflecting the sunlight that falls upon it. It is God's love, from the face of Jesus shining into my dark heart, that makes my heart open, and delight to be his dwelling-place. The eye of the just Avenger I cannot endure to be in this place of sin; but the eye of the compassionate Physician I shall gladly admit into this place of disease, for he came from heaven to earth that he might heal such sin-sick souls as mine. When a disciple desires to be searched by the living God, he does not thereby intimate that there are no sins in him to be discovered: he intimates rather that his foes are so many and so lively, that nothing can subdue them except the presence and power of God.

A Wholesome Tongue
(Proverbs 15:4)

"A wholesome tongue is a tree of life."

NOT a *silent* tongue; mere abstinence from evil is not good. The beasts that perish speak no guile; what do ye more than they? The tongue of man is a talent given by God, and the commandment, "Occupy till I come," is deeply graven in its wondrous structure. He who hides his talent in the earth is counted slothful and wicked. The servant vainly pleads that it was not employed for evil: the Master righteously condemns because it was not employed for good. Idleness is evil under the administration of God.—Not a *smooth* tongue: it may be soft on the surface, while the poison of asps lies cherished underneath. "The mouth of a strange woman is smoother than oil." A serpent licks his victim all over before he swallows it. Smoothness is not an equivalent for truth.—Not a *voluble* tongue: that active member may labour much to little purpose. It may revolve with the rapidity and steadiness of manufacturing machinery, throwing off from morning till night a continuous web of wordage, and yet not add one grain to the stock of human wisdom by the imposing bulk of its weightless product.—Not a *sharp* tongue: some instruments are made keen-edged for the purpose of wounding. "There is that speaketh like the piercings of a sword" (xii. 18). The wrath of man worketh not the righteousness of God. A great apostle used sharpness, and so did his Lord before him; but unless we partake of their spirit, we cannot safely imitate their plan. He would need to have a loving heart and a steady hand who ventures to cut with a sharp tongue into the quick of a brother's nature.—Not even a *true* tongue: truth is the foundation of all good in speech, but it is the foundation only. Wanting truth, there is only evil: but even with it there may be little of good. Truth is necessary, but not enough; the true tongue must also be *wholesome*.

Before anything can be wholesome in its effects on others, it must be whole in itself. The tongue must be itself in health before it can diffuse a healthful influence around. But our tongue, as an instrument of moral agency, is diseased. It is in the human constitution the chief outgate from the heart, and the heart of the fallen is not in health. The scripture of the Old Testament quoted by Paul in the New, declares, with memorable pungency, that it is corrupt and corrupting: "Their throat is an open sepulchre; with their tongues they have used deceit" (Rom. iii. 13). Government, watching over the health of the nation, will not permit a grave to lie open. Because there is putridity in its heart, its mouth must be closed. The throat of a grave, if left open, would breathe forth pestilence. Alas! the moral disease is pouring out moral infection, and no government can stay the plague. Every corrupt heart is generating the poison, and every unwholesome tongue is a vent for its escape. The air is tainted. Men both give out and draw in corruption like breath.

Parents who wisely love their children greatly dread unwholesome tongues. Sometimes they are in great straits as to the path of duty. They cannot take the young out of the world, and yet they are afraid to send them into it. When a father hears a torrent of polluting words from a foul tongue on the street, or in a public conveyance, and returns home to look upon his little boy, ignorant as yet of full-grown wickedness, he could almost wish that his child were deaf, and so shielded on one side from the great adversary's onset. If the wish were lawful, you would be inclined to say, Let his ear be open to the song of birds and the murmur of streams, to the rushing of the winds and the roll of the thunder; but let him not hear the voice of man until he hear it new in the kingdom of the Father.

But this cannot be; we and our children are in the world, and the world teems with evil. In particular, it is like a lazar-house because of unwholesome tongues. "The tongue is a fire, a world of iniquity: it defileth the whole body, and setteth on fire the course of nature; and it is set on fire of hell. It is an unruly evil, full of deadly poison" (James iii. 6, 8). One would think that parents, in view of such a pestilence abounding, would not be in haste to "bring out" their children at a tender age into the infected region. True love would rather shield them as long as possible from the inevitable contact, and in the meantime move heaven and earth to have the shield of faith interposed between the conscience of the child and the fiery darts of the Wicked.

Dogs licked the sores of Lazarus as he lay at the rich man's gate, and the poor cripple reaped a benefit from their kindness. The dumb brute has a wholesome tongue, and an instinct that prompts him to use it. Would that his master's tongue were as soft, and its touch as soothing! The best things, corrupted and misapplied, become the most mischievous. Our tongue is fearfully and wonderfully made! Great is its capacity for hurt or for healing. If it were attuned to the praise of God, it would be a medicine for the sufferings of men. If Christians were like Christ, they would be more happy and more useful. He spake as never man spake. When men had sunk helpless in a deadly disease, "He sent his word and healed them." For a wounded spirit there is no medicine like love-drops distilling from a wholesome tongue: even where they fail to heal the wound, they will soothe the sufferer, and so lighten his pain. A high place in the sight of God and man has the physician who remains on the battle-field after the conquering host has passed on, tending indiscriminately wounded friends and wounded foes; or who plies his task in a plague-stricken city, entering every house where a chalk-mark on the door indicates that the infection is within. His is an honourable work. Angels, eyeing him as they pass, might well envy his employment and his reward. But every one of us might attain a rank as high, and do a work as beneficent. If broken limbs lie not in our way, broken spirits abound in our neighbourhood. Sick hearts are rife on the edges of our daily walk. Although we lack the skill necessary to cure a bodily ailment, we may all exercise the art of healing on diseases that are more deeply set. A loving heart and a wholesome tongue are a sufficient apparatus; and the instincts of a renewed nature should be ever ready to apply them in the time and place of need.

The tongue, when it is whole and wholesome, "is a tree of life." In a former chapter (x. 11) the similitude employed was a well; but whether the manner of the diffusion be like a well sending forth its streams, or like a tree scattering its ripened fruit, the influence diffused from a good man is "life." The product which issues by the tongue from a renewed heart is healthful in its character, and spreads as seed spreads in autumn from the plant on which it grew. "Winged words" have fluttered about in poetry and prose through all the languages of the civilized world from old Homer's day till now. The permanence and prevalence of the expression prove that it embodies a recognised truth. Words have wings indeed, but they are the wings of seeds rather than of birds or butterflies. We are all accustomed to observe in autumn multitudes of diminutive seeds, each balanced on its own tiny wing, floating past on the breeze. Some of these have fallen from useful plants, and some from hurtful weeds; but the impartial wind bears the good and the evil alike forward to their destiny. Some plants are prolific almost beyond the reach of arithmetic or of imagination, and their seeds in countless multitudes are scattered indiscriminately over all the land. Words are like these seeds, in their varied character, their measureless multitude, and their winged speed. They drop off in inconceivable numbers: they fly far: they are widely spread. It is of deep importance that they should in their nature be good, and not evil. The tongue is a prolific tree; it concerns the whole community that it should be a tree of life, and not of death. Considering the influence of our words on the world, what manner of persons ought we to be in all holy conversation and godliness!

In modern times the art of printing has given wings to human words in a measure that seems to vie even with the fecundity of nature. The quantity thus carried is such as to baffle all our powers of description or conception. But in the department of art, as in that of nature, there is great variety in the character of the seed, and a terrible impartiality in the law of diffusion. When the evil seed is permitted to grow, the wings are at hand to carry it across the world. It is the part of those who love their kind, and desire to see this sin-cursed earth become a paradise again, to keep down the growth of noxious seed, and cultivate the better kinds. The quantity of vain and hurtful words that are flying across the world on printed pages is enough to make us tremble for the coming generation; but to stand and tremble in presence of the danger is neither useful nor manful. When we hear of unwholesome words being sent week after week by the ton-weight to the principal reservoirs in the large cities, and thence by various channels distributed over all the land, we should indeed be aroused to take the measure of the crisis, but not lose heart or hand at the discovery of its magnitude. We have words and wings for them as well as those who are against us : we have precious seed in our hands, and a world to spread it on. Our Father in heaven expects us to labour on his field. We have a good Master and pleasant work. In the labour of laying the words on these pages we are cheered by the thought that we are attaching wings to the living seed of saving truth, that it may be cast on the winds at a venture, and borne away, under the direction of an all wise Providence, to some needy, desert place. As we frame these sentences, we are like a humble artisan in his workshop, fashioning wings for the word of righteousness. We are encouraged to pray, as they pass from our hands, that, borne on these wings far beyond our sight, that word may drop in Indian jungle, or Australian mine, or American backwood, on some lone exile, and find entrance into the weary broken heart which at home in prosperity had been always hard and closed.

Ye who love the Lord and the brethren, wing the seed and give it to the wind. It is God's gift, and in his keeping. When it goes out of your sight, plead with Him who employs the winds as his angels to guide it to some bare but broken ground. While you pray for the fruitfulness of what has already been scattered, work to scatter more. This or that may prosper; perhaps this and that too. The very mountain-tops shall wave yet like Lebanon with a harvest from the seed of " wholesome words." The earth shall yet be full of the knowledge of the Lord. The sowers may well wipe their tears away as they go forth, for they shall one day return rejoicing, " bringing their sheaves with them." The Lord gave the word—the Lord is the Word ; great should be the company of them that publish it. (Ps. lxviii.) The shortest and surest method of killing and casting out the mischievous weeds that infest a field, is to get the field covered from side to side with a closely growing crop of precious grain. Wholesome words are the true antidote to the unwholesome. When the enemy sows tares, Christ's servants have only one way of effectually counter-working him, and that is by sowing wheat. The best way of eradicating error is to publish and practise truth.

Mirth a Medicine

(Proverbs 15:13; 12:25; 17:22)

"A merry heart maketh a cheerful countenance: but by sorrow of the heart the spirit is broken."

"Heaviness in the heart of man maketh it stoop: but a good word maketh it glad."

"A merry heart doeth good like a medicine: but a broken spirit drieth the bones."

T HE emotions that thrill in the heart mark themselves in legible lines on the countenance. This is a feature in the constitution of man, and a useful feature it is. The wisdom of our Maker may be seen in the degree of its development. If there had been more of it or less, the processes of human life could not have gone on so well. If the hopes and fears that alternate in the soul were as completely hidden from the view of an observer as the action of the vital organs within the body, the intercourse between man and man would be far less kindly than it now is. How blank would the aspect of the world be if no image of a man's thought could ever be seen glancing in his countenance ! Our walk through life would be like a solitary march through a gallery of statues,—as cold as marble, and not nearly so beautiful. On the other hand, if all the meaning of the soul could be read in the countenance, the inconvenience would be so great as to bring the machinery of life almost to a stand still. Society could not go on if either all the mind's thoughts or none were legible on the countenance. That medium which actually exists in the present constitution of humanity is obviously the best. You have some power of concealing your emotions, and your neighbour has some power of observing them. He who made us has done all things well.

Great purposes in providence are served by this arrangement. If the veil which hangs between the outer world and our hearts' emotions were altogether opaque, we would be too much isolated from our neighbours: if it were perfectly translucent, we would be too much in their power. The soul within is a burning light, sometimes bright and sometimes lurid : the countenance is a semi-transparent shade, through which the cast and colouring of the inner thought can be seen, but not its articulate details.   A happy heart beaming through a guileless countenance is the best style of beauty : it is pleasant to look upon in the spring-time, and does not wither in the winter of age.

But joy in the heart can do more than make the aspect winsome : besides enlivening a dull countenance, it heals a diseased nature.   It " doeth good like a medicine;" whereas its opposite, " a broken spirit, drieth the bones."   Those who have watched the experience of themselves and their neighbours will acknowledge this in all its breadth as a practical truth.   I know nothing equal to cheerful and even mirthful conversation for restoring the tone of mind and body when both have been overdone.   Some great and good men, on whom very heavy cares and toils have been laid, manifest a constitutional tendency to relax into mirth when their work is over.   Narrow minds denounce the incongruity : large hearts own God's goodness in the fact, and rejoice in the wise provision made for prolonging useful lives.   Mirth, after exhaustive toil, is one of nature's instinctive efforts to heal the part which has been racked or bruised.   You cannot too sternly reprobate a frivolous life ; but if the life be earnest for God and man, with here and there a layer of mirthfulness protruding, a soft bedding to receive heavy cares which otherwise would crush the spirit, to snarl against spurts of mirth may be the easy and useless occupation of a small man, who cannot take in at one view the whole circumference of a larger one.

But it is as medicine, and not as food, that mirth is useful to man.   As well might the wild ass live and fatten by snuffing up the north wind, as a man's character become solid if merriment is its chief or only aliment.   To live on it as daily bread, will produce a hollow heart and a useless history.   But that which is worthless as food may be precious as medicine.   Administered in proper quantities and at proper times, it will make the staple of solid seriousness more productive of actual good.

Even a dull observer may see wisdom and goodness in the habitual cheerfulness of the young.   There is a time to laugh, and childhood is eminently that time.   A sad, sombre spirit in a child.

is both the effect and the cause of disease. Mirth in large quantities is needful as a medicine for the ailments of childhood, and our Maker has placed an abundant supply of it in their nature with a tendency to draw it day by day for use.

But some persons and some classes are all too ready to acknowledge the virtue of mirth as a medicine. There are quacks who take it up and vaunt its universal efficacy. In ignorance or bad faith they apply it in cases where it may kill, but cannot cure. Recognising the law that a broken spirit drieth the bones, these practitioners, when conviction of sin burns like fire in the patient's conscience, would deliberately pour in a stream of mirth to quench it. With equal zeal they prescribe the same medicine as a preventive, lest the wasting body should be still more enfeebled by an inroad of seriousness upon the soul. They will quietly push a novel beneath the pillow on which the too beauteous cheek of consumption lies. They will search the sick-room round, and carry off bodily *The Saints' Rest*, or *A Call to the Unconverted*, lest these books should arouse a slumbering soul, and so shake too roughly its frail tenement. In their own way they adapt and apply the maxim, " A merry heart doeth good like a medicine."

It is true that to maintain the patient's cheerfulness hastens the patient's cure: a bright hope within will sometimes do more to restore the wasted strength than all the prescriptions of the physician. A light heart, we acknowledge, is itself a potent medicine, and lends effectual aid in co-operation with other cures. If the restoration of the body's health were our only care, we would not examine scrupulously either the kind or the quantity of joyfulness that friends might infuse into a fainting heart. But while the healing of the body is a great thing, a greater lies beside it. For the chance of contributing to a corporeal cure, I would not cheat an immortal soul, as it fluttered on the verge of eternity. Is it true—yea or nay—that before death mercy is offered, and after it judgment is fixed ? Is it true that Christ is the way to eternal life, and that there is no other ? If it is, to divert a human soul from looking unto Jesus when the last sands of life are running, is the unkindest act which man can do to man. If you were Atheists and Materialists,—if you believed in no God and no hereafter,—there would be at least a melancholy consistency in occupying life's last hours with trifles, that the spirit, burdened with a decaying body, should have no other weight to bear; but it is both cruel and stupid for those who bear Christ's name to blindfold, at the very exodus of life, a brother's soul, in order to catch a chance of temporary benefit to his body.

Nor is this all : this effort to banish care does not always succeed. Through all these coverings the terrors of the Lord may burst in, and agitate the soul all the more fiercely, that you have tried so long to keep them out. When bodily pains or convictions of conscience rise to the full, your frivolous pleasures are driven away like smoke before the wind. A merry heart is a medicine for his ailment! Granted ; but who shall give him a merry heart ? Who shall give the guilty a merry heart when God is drawing near to judgment, and sin is lying heavy on his soul ? If you could introduce the peace of God which passeth all understanding, it would keep his heart and mind; but no inferior consolation can meet the case. Will any one dare to say that in nature's extremity those who neglect Christ are happier at heart than those who trust in his love ?

When a human heart is stooping and breaking beneath the heavy load of suffering and sin, "a good word maketh it glad ;" but if the man is dying, to assure him he will soon be better, is not a good word ; if the man is in sin and under condemnation, to assure him his sins are trivial and his Judge indulgent, is not a good word. A good word will gladden the grieved heart, but where shall it be found ? Hark! the Man of Sorrows lets it drop like dew from his own lips—"Peace I leave with you, my peace I give unto you : not as the world giveth, give I unto you. Let not your heart be troubled, neither let it be afraid" (John xiv. 27). Happy are they who have such a comforter in the time of need. David, like Abraham, saw his Lord's day afar off, and was glad. The presence of his Redeemer kindled a gladness in his heart which took the torment out of even dying pains : "Yea, though I walk through the valley of the shadow of death, I will fear no evil : for thou art with me." (Ps. xxiii.)

True Christians have two advantages over the men of the world : they are happier now, and safer at last. There is more gladness put by a gracious God in a believing heart, than all that the worldly know even when their corn and wine abound the most. It would be a great attainment for themselves, and a great means of good to others, if the disciples of Christ in our day could let the hope which cheers their hearts also shine in their faces. If the joy of the Lord, which really is a Christian's strength within, should sit habitually as a beauty on his countenance, his talent would be better occupied now, and his entrance more abundant at the last. When Stephen's short but quick career was coming to a close,—when the seventy elders had taken their places on the judgment-seat, full of enmity against the name of Jesus,—when the baser sort of the persecutors, at the instigation of their leaders, had dragged him violently into the council-hall,—when perjured witnesses, taking their cue from the keen and cruel eye of Saul, declared in concert that he was a habitual blasphemer of holy things,—when the meek martyr saw and felt from many signs that through a boisterous passage he must quickly go to another judgment,—his heart did not lose its hopefulness, and his countenance did not fall. At that moment, when the crisis of his fate had come, the joy that played about his heart shone through: "All that sat in the council, looking steadfastly on him, saw his face as it had been the face of an angel." Perhaps that heaven-like brightness held some of the spectators, and would not let them go until it led them into the arms of Stephen's Saviour. We have known a case in which the gleam of joy on a departing disciple's face feathered the arrow of divine truth, and sent it home with saving power to a heart that had hitherto kept its iron point at bay. If Christians could get living hope lighted within, and let it beam like sun-light all the day through an open countenance, their lives would be more legible as epistles of Christ, and more effectual to win souls.

Tastes Differ

(Proverbs 15:14, 21; 21:15)

"The heart of him that hath understanding seeketh knowledge: but the mouth of fools feedeth on foolishness. Folly is joy to him that is destitute of wisdom."
"It is joy to the just to do judgment."

TASTES differ widely. Water is the element of one creature, and air the element of another. The same material is to this poison, and to that food. Each species differs in nature from all others ; and Nature will have her own way.

Among men, viewed in their spiritual relations, there is a similar variety of tastes and pleasures. There is first the grand generic difference between the old man and the new. The change of nature is radical, and the change of appetite consequently complete; what things were gain to me, these I count loss,—so true was the observation of the heathen as to the effect of the gospel preached by the apostles. The world to Saul of Tarsus was turned upside down from the moment that he met the Lord in the way, and as a lost sinner accepted pardon through the blood of the cross. After that moment his tastes were not only changed ; they were absolutely reversed. What he had formerly chased as gain, he now loathed as loss.

Besides the first and chief distinction between the dead and the living, many subordinate varieties appear, shading imperceptibly away into each other, according as good or evil preponderates in the character. The best way to know a man is to observe what gives him pleasure. A good man may once or many times be betrayed into foolish words or deeds, but the indulgence makes him miserable. Folly, like Ezekiel's roll, was sweet in his mouth, but left a lasting bitterness behind. Fools, on the contrary, feed on foolishness; it is pleasant to their taste at the time, and they ruminate with relish on it afterwards. Two persons of opposite spiritual tastes may be detected for once in the same act of evil;

but they do not walk abreast in the same life-course. Sin becomes bitter to the taste of the renewed, and he puts it away with loathing; but the corrupt, who has never known a change, counts the morsel sweet, and continues to roll it under his tongue. Two young men, of nearly equal age, and both the sons of God-fearing parents, were seen to enter together a theatre at a late hour in a large city. They sat together, and looked and listened with equal attention. The one was enjoying the spectacle and the mirth; the other was silently enduring an unspeakable wretchedness. The name of God and the hopes of the godly were employed there to season the otherwise vapid mirth of the hollow-hearted crowd. One youth, through the Saviour's sovereign grace, had, in a distant solitude, acquired other tastes, and the profanity of the play rasped rudely against them. He felt as if the words of the actors and the answering laugh of the spectators were tearing his flesh. He breathed freely when, with the retiring crowd, he reached the street again. It was his first experience of a theatre, and his last. It is a precious thing to get from the Lord, as Paul got, a new relish and a new estimate of things. This appetite for other joys, if exercised and kept keen, goes far to save you from defilement, even when you are suddenly brought into contact with evil; as certain kinds of leaves refuse to be wet, and though plunged into water come out of it dry.

The gratification of appetite is pleasant. This law of nature bears witness that God is good. Food and drink are necessary to the maintenance of life. If, as a general rule, the act of taking them were painful, the duty would be neglected, and the race would become extinct. The Author of our being has made the performance sure by making it delightful. The pain of hunger is an officer of the executive under the supreme government of Heaven, ever on the watch, compelling living creatures to give the body its necessary support. This beneficent law, like all the other good things of God, is perverted by the fallen: this truth of God is profanely turned into a lie by the corrupt appetites of men. Appetite, and the pleasure of indulging it, is still a great force when it is turned in the wrong direction. That which among God's works is mighty to save life, is in Satan's hand mighty to destroy it. When the taste is depraved, the pleasantness of the poison supplies a power like gravitation, silently dragging down the slave with ever-increasing speed into the bottomless pit. If folly were not joy to the fool, he might soon be induced to forsake it. Nothing will produce a new life but a new nature.

The soul has an appetite, and needs food as well as the body. In this department too the tastes are various, and there is a corresponding variety in the provided supply. Fools feed on foolishness, and like it: they have no relish for more solid food. On the other hand, "it is joy to the just to do judgment." The Just One relished the doing of the Father's will as his meat and drink. Christians grow like Christ: those who hope in his mercy learn to fall in with his tastes. If we saw a hungry human being turning away from the finest of the wheat, and by choice satisfying himself with the husks that swine do eat, we should shudder in presence of the prodigy; we should weep over the low estate into which one of our kind had fallen. Such a perversion of the bodily appetite is rare—perhaps altogether unknown: but a greater derangement of the spiritual taste is not only possible in certain cases; it is the common condition of men.

It is sad to think how men run to what they like, with as little forethought and as great impetuosity as swollen rivers rush towards the sea. In the main the taste of the renewed leads them to the food which will sustain and invigorate the health of the soul; but even they need to watch and pray, lest they enter into temptation. He will not be a thriving, growing Christian, who partakes freely of joys as they come, on the right hand and on the left. Even a healthful man, if he is wise, will observe carefully the nature of his food, and watch the effects of each kind. If he discovers that any species, though pleasant at the time, hurts his health afterwards, he will carefully abstain from the tempting morsel. You may prove to him that it is not poison,—that it will not take away his life: that is not enough: if it is hurtful to his health, he will abandon it. Alas! the children of this world are wiser in their generation than the children of light. Men who, on the whole, value their spiritual life the most, lightly expose its health to injuries against which they would resolutely defend their bodies. If a man should eat unwholesome food from day to day, the mischief would soon become palpable both to himself and his neighbours: he would feel his own feebleness, and others would stare at him as a walking skeleton. But when the spiritual life is exposed to the action of a slow poison, the emaciation of the soul is a thing not so easily felt by the patient, and not so easily seen by his neighbours. It is written of Ephraim in a time of spiritual decay, " Gray hairs are here and there upon him, yet he knoweth it not" (Hos. vii. 9). Ah! if the soul's health and sickness were visible like those of the body, the old question, " Why art thou, being the king's son, lean from day to day?" would be appropriately addressed now to many of the royal family of heaven. The answer, if truly given, would in most cases be, They feed too much on foolishness, and do not satisfy themselves with that which was meat and drink to their Master.

In dealing with men for their reformation, they who do not begin at the beginning lose all their labour. If you assume that human nature is already good, and only needs to be helped forward to higher degrees of virtue, you miss the mark, and gain nothing. You are fishing with a bait for which the fishes have no taste: they do not like it, and will not take it. The corrupt are not naturally alarmed at their own corruption, and eager to leap into holiness.

You may have seen creatures living in the rankest material corruption, and shuddered to think that life of any kind should be imprisoned in such a horrid place. The instinct of compassion for wretchedness is stirred within you; but a second thought lays it to rest again. These worms do not loathe that which is at once their dwelling and their food. It is their nature it is their life to be there. These worms, to your taste so loathsome, are not ashamed of their condition, and have no desire to leave it. Although an opportunity is offered, they do not hasten to escape into cleanness, and wipe themselves from their filth. Such is moral corruption, and the life therein, if it is left to itself. The tenants of the mire do not grow ashamed or weary of it: they have been bred in it, and it is their delight. Sinners are not, of their own motion, weary and ashamed of sin: they do not desire to escape out of it. Although all intelligent beings, who are not themselves in the mire, look on with inexpressible disgust, whether they be the angels who never fell, or the saints who have been lifted up, those who are, and have always been in it, love their condition, and would not leave it. If in compassion for living creatures crawling in material filth, you should benevolently pick them out one by one, and lay them in clean dry beds, you would become their tormentor by taking them out of their element. Such, to the spiritually impure, God's word is felt to be: the unclean do not hail it as a deliverer. This is the most fearful feature of our case. It is not like that of a man who has fallen into the water, and instantly struggles to escape with all the energy of his being: sin is the element of the sinful. The cure is not another place, but a new nature.

Mahomet manifested great shrewdness in the conception of his paradise. If he mistook the kingdom of God, he comprehended well the appetites of men: he promised his followers as a heaven the fullest gratification of all their desires. But what if a foundation of eternal truth be found lying beneath all these abominations! The prophet's followers have a right principle in their hands, although, by turning it upside down, they make it the most destructive of errors. It is true that heaven will give unbridled scope to all the appetites of all its inmates. There will be no crucifying of the flesh there: no man will have his taste thwarted, or his supply stinted there. Mahomet is right, in as far as he says that in heaven every entrant will have all his passions gratified to the full. The difference lies in this: they expect that heaven's joys will be made to suit human appetites; we know that the tastes of the saved will be purified into perfect conformity with the joys that are at God's right hand. In heaven, indeed, there is no foolishness to feed upon; but there are no fools to desire it. Heaven denies no pleasure, and yet provides nothing impure. All the evil desires are left behind, and all the good are gratified.

It is time that we who seek that better country should be forgetting past attainments, and reaching forth after newer and higher measures of holiness: "Grow in grace." The night is far spent; the day is at hand; be ye also ready. There will be no crucifying of the flesh in heaven; it must be crucified now. The old man must be put off with his deeds and his desires; and for this salvation work, "now is the appointed time." Those who do not on this side of life's boundary-line acquire a taste for holiness, will not on the other side get an entrance into heaven. "To them that look for Him, He shall appear:" they who look now in the opposite direction shall not then behold His face in peace.

Humility Before Honour

(Proverbs 15:33; 16:18; 29:23)

"Before honour is humility."

"Pride goeth before destruction, and an haughty spirit before a fall."

"A man's pride shall bring him low: but honour shall uphold the humble in spirit."

"IF a man strive for masteries, yet is he not crowned, except he strive lawfully" (2 Tim. ii. 5). There is only one way of reaching honour, and the candidates who do not keep that way will fail. You must go to honour through humility. This is the law—the law of God. It cannot be changed. It has its analogies in the material creation. Every height has its corresponding depth. As far as the Andes pierce upward into the sky, so far do the valleys of the Pacific at their base go down into the heart of the earth. If the branches of a tree rise high in the air, its roots must penetrate to a corresponding depth in the ground; and the necessity is reciprocal. The higher the branches are, the deeper go the roots; and the deeper the roots are, the higher go the branches.

This law pervades the moral administration as well as the material works of God. The child Jesus "is set for the fall and the rising again of many in Israel:" but it is first the fall and then the rising; for "before honour is humility." Fall they must at the feet of the Crucified, before they can rise and reign as the children of the great King. No cross, no crown. "Blessed are the poor in spirit, for theirs is the kingdom." What are these, and whence came they,—they are in honour now, whatever their origin may have been,—these that stand before the throne and before the Lamb, clothed with white robes and palms in their hands? These are they which came out of great tribulation, and have washed their robes, and made them white in the blood of the Lamb, (Rev. vii.) Like Joshua the high priest (Zech. iii.), they were clothed with filthy garments, before they obtained that glorious change. If the unhappy guest at the King's table (Matt. xxii.) had gone first through the valley of humiliation, he would not have been cast at last into outer darkness; if he had owned his own garment worthless, he would have gotten a fit one, free, and not have been speechless at the incoming of the King. "Before honour is humility:" this is the organic law of the kingdom of heaven. The King is far from the proud, but dwells with him that is humble and of a contrite heart.

There are two mountains in the land of Israel, equal in height, and standing near each other, with a deep narrow valley between. At an interesting point in the people's history, one of these mountains bore the curse, and the other received the blessing (Deut. xi. 26–29). If you had stood then on Ebal, where the curse was lying, you could not have escaped to Gerizim to enjoy the blessing without going down to the bottom of the intervening gorge. There was a way for the pilgrim from the curse to the blessing, if he were willing to pass through the valley of humiliation; but there was no flight through the air, so as to escape the going down.

These things are an allegory. All men are at first in their own judgments on a lofty place, but the curse hangs over the mountain of their pride. Nature's hopes are high, but there is wrath from the Lord upon them, because they dishonour his law by expecting that it will accept sin for righteousness. All the saved are also on a mountain height, but God the Lord dwells among them, and great is the peace of his children. All who have reached this mountain have been in the deep. They sowed in tears before they went forth rejoicing, to bear home the sheaves.

Paul was high at first in nature's pride: "I was alive without the law once." But the commandment came, like a light from heaven above the brightness of the sun, and its instant effect was to cast him down to the ground: "When the commandment came, sin revived, and I died." He felt that he was altogether vile; he saw that he was lost. After he had been brought low in conviction of sin, he was raised again in the hope of mercy It was necessary that he should be brought down, but it was also necessary that he should rise again. Fear is the way to trust, but fear is not trust. You must, indeed, come down from the mountain that is capped with the curse; but you must then ascend the mountain where Jesus, transfigured and radiant with the glory of grace, makes his ravished disciples feel that it is good to be there, and desire to dwell for ever in the light of his countenance. It is not the going down that will make you safe and happy. It is not the putting off, but the putting on, that saves; and the preciousness of putting off the old man lies in this,—that it is the only way of putting on Christ. Before honour is humility; but after humility is honour. If our hearts are truly humbled, God has pledged himself to exalt us in due season. In proportion as we attain the contrite heart, we may count on his gracious indwelling. If we are led by the Spirit of the Lord down into humility, we may be assured the next thing is honour; as we confidently anticipate that the day will follow the night. The broken heart is the Lord's chosen dwelling place. When David was in the depths (Ps. cxxx.) he waited for the Lord: how? As those who are exposed to danger in night's darkness wait for the morning,—keenly feeling the want of it, but confidently counting that it will come. The Lord loves to be so looked for: to them that look for him he will come, and his coming will be like the morning. This humility—this honour have all the saints.

It is a part of the same divine law that "a man's pride shall bring him low." That which brings a creature furthest down is his own rebellious effort to exalt himself. It is with spirit as with matter,—the further it shoots upward from its own proper sphere into the heavens above, the deeper will it sink down, and the more will it be broken by its fall. That law operated on spirit, as the law of gravitation acted on matter, before man was made. Among the angels that excel in strength, there was a leap of pride in order to exalt itself, and a consequent fall into the lowest depths of the pit. When these morning stars fell from the very height of heaven, they fell into a deep from which even the power of God provides no rising. In the same way man fell. It was a leap upward that brought us down so low: it was the proud effort to be as gods that brought man down to the companionship of devils. Under this eternal law the Papacy now lies. It cannot glide gently down from its presumptuous height, and so save itself from destruction. It has flown too high for falling softly; it is fixed, and that by an unchanging law, that it cannot be re-formed, and must be destroyed.

This law will crush every one who dares to cross its path. Like the other laws of God, it touches the smallest, while it controls the greatest. An atom obeys the same impulses that guide a world. Oh, how jealously should a man watch the swellings of pride in his own breast! How eagerly should each desire to have his own pride purged wholly out! Pride remaining in us will bring us down, though we were in the highest heaven. When two things are weighed in the opposite ends of a balance, who can make both simultaneously descend? The crushing of the proud is but the other side of the exaltation of the lowly. Either pride must be cast out of me, or I must be cast out from the company of the blessed.

The seventy-third Psalm, like the seventh chapter of the Epistle to the Romans, is a specimen of spiritual autobiography. Cut out, at the crisis, a section from that self-history of a soul: " So foolish was I and ignorant: I was as a beast before thee. Nevertheless I am continually with thee: thou hast holden me by my right hand. Thou shalt guide me with thy counsel, and afterward receive me to glory." Extremes meet here; the lowest and the highest touch each other. Within the compass of a few lines recording one man's experience, we find a humility which depresses him beneath the level of man, and an honour which admits him into the presence of God. One moment the penitent feels himself to be brutish; another, his glad forgiven spirit rises buoyant toward the throne like a flame of fire, or a ministering angel. These are the footsteps of the flock. It concerns us to know that we are on the same track; for none other conducts to safety. It is when a man is so purged of pride as to count himself like a " beast," that he is best prepared for the company of a justifying God, and the spirits of just men made perfect. They who thus put off their own righteousness as filthy rags, are ready to put on Christ; and in Him they are counted worthy. Paul kept close on the track of the Psalmist: in one verse it is, " O wretched man that I am!" in the next, " I thank God, through Jesus Christ our Lord" (Rom. vii. 24, 25). If we get down into the " humility " through which these ancient disciples passed, we shall share the " honour " to which they have been raised.

The Maker and the Breaker of a Family's Peace
(Proverbs 15:16, 17, 27; 17:1)

" Better is little with the fear of the Lord, than great treasure and trouble therewith. Better is a dinner of herbs where love is, than a stalled ox and hatred therewith. He that is greedy of gain troubleth his own house."

" Better is a dry morsel, and quietness therewith, than an house full of sacrifices with strife."

T HESE are blessed words in a world of strife. They are welcome as a well of water springing in the desert. They drop on weary hearts like rain on the mown grass. The gift is good: we receive it with gladness, and thank the Giver.

The constitution of man and the law of God are fitted into each other, like lock and key. The capability of the subject corresponds to the rule which the Sovereign enacts. When the creature falls in with the Creator's will, all the machinery moves smoothly: when the creature resists, it stands still or is riven asunder. Truth sweetens the relations of life; falsehood eats like rust into their core. When they live in love, men meet each other softly and kindly, as the eyelids meet ; envy casts grains of sand between the two, and under each. Every movement then sends a shooting pain through all the body, and makes the salt tears flow. So good are peace and love for human-kind, that with them a family will be happy though they have nothing else in the world; and without them miserable, although they have the whole world at their command.

No creature can with impunity break any of the Creator's laws. He is not a man, that he should fail to detect or punish the transgressor. He depends not on the activity of police, or the speed of the telegraph. Sin follows the sinner, and finds him out, and inflicts the punishment. Sorrow comes on the heels of sin, as the echo answers to a sound, as the rebound answers to a blow. Let a family have abundant wealth, and all the luxuries that wealth can buy,—a commodious house and a sumptuous table, broad lands and a troop of attendants,—yet if strife enters the circle, it will act like leaven in the mass, and imbitter all their enjoyments. Being under law to God they cannot escape. When they sin they suffer. Strife makes them more miserable amidst all their wealth than a loving family who have not wherewith to buy to-morrow's food.

A dinner of herbs and a stalled ox indicate the two extremes, —humble poverty on the one side, and pampered luxury on the other. These brief expressions open for a moment the doors of the cottage and of the palace that we may obtain a glimpse of what is going on within. Look into the dwelling on this side: it is dinner time: the family, fresh from their labour, are seated round a clean uncovered table; there is no meat from the stall or the flock, no bunch of ripe grapes from the vine-yard, and even no bread from the corn-field. Some green herbs gathered in the garden have been cooked and set down as the meal of the house-hold. The fare is poor; but this poor fare and love together, make a more savoury mess than any that ever graced a royal banquet: the people thrive upon the precious mixture. Look into the lofty castle on the other side at the moment when this word throws open its doors. A rich feast is reeking in the hall. The stalled ox is there, surrounded by a labyrinth of kindred luxuries. A crowd of attendants must be in the room, observing every look, and hearing every whisper. The poor man's family dine in private; the rich man's in public. This is one point in favour of the poor. The servant at his master's back is a man with human feelings in his breast. If he has been treated un-kindly, anger rankles in his heart, while the smile that is paid for plays upon his countenance. If, moreover, there be jealousy between husband and wife, rivalry between brother and brother, in this great house, their meeting at a meal is misery; their polite-ness before strangers is the incrusted whitewash on a sepulchre's side, cracking and falling off at every movement, and revealing the rottenness within. When love leaves the family circle, it is no longer a piece of God's own hand-work, and there is no security for safety in any of its motions. Love is the element in which all its relations were set, for softness and safety; and when it has evaporated, nothing remains but that each member of the house should be occupied in mounting a miserable guard over his own interests, and against the anticipated contact of the rest. In that dislocated house each dreads all, and all dread each. The only distinction remaining is, that the one who is nearest you hurts you the most.

But mark well, it is neither said in the Bible nor found in experience that they are all happy families who dine on herbs, and all unhappy who can afford to feast on a stalled ox. Some rich families live in love, and doubly enjoy their abundance; some poor families quarrel over their herbs. Riches cannot secure happiness, and poverty cannot destroy it. But such is the power of love, that with it you will be happy in the meanest estate; without it, miserable in the highest. Would you know the beginning, the middle, and the end of this matter,—the spring on high, the stream flowing through the channel of the covenant, and the fruitful outspread in a disciple's life below,—they are all here, and all one,—Charity: "GOD IS LOVE;" "*Love is of God;*" "Walk in love."

In this book the greed of gain stands side by side with strife, as the twin troubler of a house. As a husbandman looks on a prevailing weed that infests his garden, as a shepherd looks on a wolf that ravages his flock, so our Father in heaven looks on that love of money which grievously mars the harmony of his own institute, the family. That instrument of torture points both ways. The miser, as we know by his name, is a torment to himself: he is also a thorn in the flesh of those who are nearest to him. Perhaps in our community, and in our day, more families are troubled by a lavish expenditure, than by an undue hoarding of money; but the prevalence of one evil does not make another evil good. Dealing with one thing at a time, the words give out a certain sound,—that if a man be himself a miser, he makes his house miserable. When God has given a man one of his choicest blessings, a family; and given him, too, means sufficient for their support; if the man intercept the flow of the Creator's bounty, and hoard that which was given for use, he displeases the Giver, and injures the gift, as surely as if he should impiously arrest the flow of the blood from its central reservoir, and prevent it from circulating through the frame. The hoarded blood would clot and stagnate and corrupt; while the body, for want of it, would pine away. The benefit of its circulation would be lost, and its accu-

mulation in one place would become an encumbrance dangerous
to life. Thus the man troubles his house who diverts the children's daily portion into the miser's corrupting hoard.

In my earliest years, as far back on the line of life as memory's
vision can distinctly reach, the nearest neighbour of our house on
the right, was an old farmer, very religious, and very rich. He
had three sons and seven daughters. Instead of employing the
increase of his fields to elevate the condition and enlarge the
minds of his numerous, winsome, and well-conditioned family, he
left them to nature, and laid up his money in the bank. The sons
and daughters all married in succession, and left him. Thereafter,
at the age of seventy-three, he married a servant-girl of exactly
the same age as his youngest daughter. The match supplied the
young people of the district with merriment for many months.
The young woman wrought upon the old man's failing faculties,
and, in order to secure the money for herself, persuaded him that
all his children were banded in a conspiracy against his life. He
made his will under this impression, bequeathing the bulk of his
fortune to his wife; and, with a refinement of cruelty which was
certainly not his own invention, devised small sums to each of his
sons and daughters,—to one five pounds, to another ten, to each
a different amount, reaching at the highest the sum of twenty-five
pounds. The sums were made to vary with the varying shades
of the children's guilt, as they were marked on the imagination of
the imbecile parent. The old man died. The widow enjoyed
her legacy unchallenged. But the daughters who had got the
smaller sums went to law with their sisters who had obtained the
larger sums, in order to have them equalized. After these miserable pittances had served to rend a whole family asunder in hopeless feuds, the worthless money itself was lost in law. The God
of providence taught me early, as they teach children now in
schools, by a picture, that " he who is greedy of gain troubleth his
own house."

But the teaching was still more specific and guarded and
fatherly than this; at the same time the other lesson was exhibited with equal vividness on the other side. Our nearest neighbour on the left—in this case half a mile distant, and in the former
case a quarter—was another old man, very religious and very
drunken. He had a light rent, a long lease, and an indulgent

landlord. Plenty of money passed through his hands, but none ever remained in them. He was not greedy of gain, and yet he troubled his own house. His spendthrift and intemperate life, aggravated by his religious profession, told with fearful effect upon a band of stately and intelligent sons. They were all clever, but all made shipwreck.

At this advanced period of my life I think still with interest and awe on the sovereign providence that placed me, while yet a child, in that middle space between two evils, opposite, yet equal, and in full sight of both. The lessons were given not in the thin profile of a single line, but in the full breadth and varied features of large family groups. The examples did not glance into sight and out again like visions of the night: they remained in view for a long series of years. I saw the beginning, and I have lived to witness the end. In my childhood they were sowing the seed beside me, and in manhood I saw them reaping in tears. When God gave the law to Moses, it was accompanied by the precise and significant intimation, "I have written that thou mayest teach." The same Lord continues writing still on the fleshy tables of human hearts, and on the same condition—that the lesson so engraved should not be a talent hid in a napkin, but published for the benefit of all whom it may concern. These lines, written by the Lord's own hand in the workings of providence, lie in sharpest outline in the lower strata of my memory, and are fixed like fossils in the rock: the tide of city life rushing over them during many successive years, instead of defacing the letters, seems only to make the matrix more transparent, and so bring the characters more clearly out. The possession of these manuscripts I recognise as the obligation to exhibit them.

The man who lavishly spent his money, troubled his own house; so also did the man who greedily hoarded it. Between these two extremes the path of safety lies in the scriptural rule, "Use this world as not abusing it" (1 Cor. vii. 31).

The house—the family is God's own work. He intends that it should be a blessing to his creatures. He framed it to be an abode of peace and love. He visits his hand-work to see whether it is fulfilling its destiny. Let the disturber beware ; an eye is on him that cannot be deceived, a hand is over him that cannot be resisted. Whether it be husband or wife, parent or child, master or servant, the disturber of a house must answer to its almighty Protector for abusing his gifts, and thwarting his gracious designs.

" Blessed are the peace-makers : for they shall be called the children of God." How shall we best bring peace into a family on earth, and keep it there, until the little stream that trickles over time be lost in the ocean of eternity ? Invite Christ into the house, and the hearts of its inmates. " He is our peace,"— with God and with each other. Invite Him to come in : constrain Him to abide.

The False Balance Detected by the True

(Proverbs 16:2, 3)

" All the ways of a man are clean in his own eyes; but the Lord weigheth the spirits
Commit thy works unto the Lord, and thy thoughts shall be established."

THE first of these two verses tells how a man goes wrong,
and the second how he may be set right again. He is
led into error by doing what pleases himself; the rule
for recovery is to commit the works to the Lord, and see that they
are such as will please him. If we weigh our thoughts and actions
in the balances of our own desires, we shall inevitably go astray :
if we lay them before God, and submit to his pleasure, we shall
be guided into truth and righteousness.

Such is the purport of the two verses in general; attend now
to the particulars in detail : " All the ways of a man are clean in
his own eyes." To a superficial observer this declaration may
seem inconsistent with experience ; but he who wrote these words
has fathomed fully the deep things of a human spirit. As a
general rule, men do the things which they think right, and think
the things right which themselves do. Not many men do what
they think evil, and while they think it evil. The acts may be
obviously evil, but the actor persuades himself of the contrary, at
least until they are done. There is an amazing power of self·
deception in a human heart. It is deceitful above all things.
It is beyond conception cunning in making that appear right
which is felt pleasant. Some, we confess, are so hardened, that
they sin in the face of conscience, and over its neck ; but for one
bold, bad man, who treads on an awakened conscience in order to
reach the gratification of his lust, there are ten cowards who drug
the watcher into slumber, that they may sin in peace. As a
general rule, it may be safely said, if you did not think the act
innocent, you would not do it; but when you have a strong inclination to do it, you soon find means to persuade yourself that it

is innocent. After all, the real motive power that keeps the wheels of human life going round is this :—Men like the things that they do, and do the things that they like. In his own eyes a man's ways are clean : if he saw them filthy, he would not walk in them. But when he desires to walk in a particular way, he soon begins to count it clean, in order that he may peacefully walk in it.

In his *own eyes :* Mark the meaning of these words. Be not deceived; God is not mocked. Eyes other than his own are witnessing all the life-course of a man. The eyes of the Lord are in every place. He does not adopt our inclination as the standard of right and wrong, and he will not borrow our balances to determine his own judgment in that day." The Lord weigheth the spirits."' Not a thought, not a motive, trembles in the breast which he does not weigh; more evidently, though not more surely, are the gross and palpable deeds of our life open before him ! He has a balance nice enough to weigh motives—the animating soul of our actions ; our actions themselves will not escape his scrutiny.

Before we proceed to any " work," we should weigh it, while yet it is a " spirit" unembodied, in the balances which will be used in the judgment of the great day. Letters are charged in the post-office according to their weight. I have written and sealed a letter consisting of several sheets ; I desire that it should pass ; I think that it will ; but I know well that it will not be allowed to pass because I desire that it should, or think that it will ; I know well it will be tested by imperial weights and imperial laws. Before I plunge it beyond my reach, under the control of the public authorities, I place it on a balance which stands on the desk before me—a balance not constructed to please my desires, but honestly adjusted to the legal standard. I weigh it there, and check it myself by the very rules which the Government will apply. The children of this world are wise for their own interests. We do not shut our eyes, and cheat ourselves as to temporal things and human governments ; why should we attempt to deceive where detection is certain and retribution complete ? On the table before you lies the very balance in which the Ruler of heaven and earth will weigh both the body of the act and the motive, the soul that inspires it. Weigh your purposes in this balance before you launch them forth in action. The man's ways are unclean, although, through a deceitful heart, they are clean in his own eyes; by what means, therefore, "shall a young man cleanse his way? By taking heed thereto according to thy word" (Ps. cxix. 9).

A most interesting practical rule is laid down as applicable to the case—"Commit thy works unto the Lord;" and a promise follows it—"Thy thoughts shall be established." It is a common and a sound advice, to ask counsel of the Lord before undertaking any work. Here we have the counterpart lesson equally precious —commit the work to the Lord, after it is done. The Hebrew idiom gives peculiar emphasis to the precept—Roll it over on Jehovah. Mark the beautiful reciprocity of the two, and how they constitute a circle between them. While the act is yet in embryo as a purpose in your mind, ask counsel of the Lord, that it may either be crushed in the birth or embodied in righteousness. When it is embodied, bring the work back to the Lord, and give it over into his hands as the fruit of the thought which you besought him to inspire; give it over into his hands as an offering which he may accept, an instrument which he may employ. Bring the work, when it is done, to the Lord; and what will follow?—"Thy thoughts shall be established." Bring back the actions of your life to God, one by one, after they are done, and thereby the purposes of your heart will be made pure and steadfast : the evil will be chased away like smoke before the wind, and the good will be executed in spite of all opposition for "when a man's ways please the Lord, he maketh even his enemies to be at peace with him."

A boy, while his stock of experience is yet small, is employed by his father to lend assistance in certain mechanical operations. Pleased to think himself useful, he bounds into the work with heart and hand ; but during the process, he has many errands to his father. At the first he runs to ask his father how he ought to begin; and when he has done a little, he carries the work to his father, fondly expecting approval, and asking further instructions. Oh, when will the children of God in the regeneration experience and manifest the same spirit of adoption which animates dear children as an instinct of nature towards fathers of their flesh ! These two rules, following each other in a circle, would make the outspread field of a Christian's life sunny, and green, and fruitful, as the circling of the solar system brightens and fertilizes the earth.

Perhaps this latter hemisphere of duty's revolving circle is the more difficult of the two. Perhaps most professing Christians find it easier to go to God beforehand, asking what they should do, than to return to him afterwards to place their work in his hands. This may in part account for the want of answer to prayer,—at least the want of a knowledge that prayer has been answered. If you do not complete the circle, your message by telegraph will never reach its destination, and no answer will return. We send in earnest prayer for direction, and thereafter go into the world of action ; but if we do not bring the action back to God, the circle of the supplication is not completed. The prayer does not reach the throne ; the message acknowledging it comes not back to the suppliant's heart. To bring all the works to the Lord would be in the character of a dear child : it would please the Father. A young man came to his father, and received instructions as to his employment for the day. " Go work in my vineyard," was the parent's command. " I go, sir," was the ready answer of the son. Thus far, all was well ; but the deed that followed was disobedience. The son went not to work in the father's vineyard : but we do not learn that he came back in the evening to tell his father what he had done. To have done so would either have kept him right, or corrected him for doing wrong.

But some of the works are evil, and how could you dare to roll these over on the Lord ? Ah ! there lies the power of this practical rule. If it were our fixed and unvarying practice to bring all our works and lay them into God's hands, we would not dare to do any except those that he would smile upon. But others, though not positively evil, may be of trifling importance, and the doer may decline to bring them to the King, not because they are impure, but because they are insignificant. The spirit of bondage betrays itself here, and not the spirit of adoption. They are small ; they are affairs of children; trouble not the Master. Ah ! this adviser is of the earth, earthy: he knows not the Master's mind. The Master himself has spoken to the point : " Suffer the little children to come unto me, and forbid them not." Be assured, little children, whether in the natural family of man or the spiritual family of

God, act in character. There is no hypocrisy about them. The things they bring are little things. Children speak as children, yet He does not beckon them away : He rebukes those who would. He welcomes and blesses the little ones. Nay, more ; He tells us plainly that we must be like them ere we enter his kingdom. Like little children without hypocrisy bring all your affairs to him, and abandon those that he would grieve to look upon. Bring to him all the works that you do, and you will not do any that you could not bring to him.

"When a man's ways please the Lord, he maketh even his ene-mies to be at peace with him" (ver. 7). There is, it seems, such a thing as pleasing God. If it could not exist on earth, it would not be named from heaven. Even to try this is a most valuable exercise. There would be more sunlight in a believer's life if he could leave the dull negative fear of judgment far behind as a motive of action, and bound forward into the glad positive, a hope-ful effort to please God. "Without faith it is impossible to please him" (Heb. xi. 6) ; therefore with faith it is possible. "They that are in the flesh cannot please God ;" therefore they that are in the Spirit can. In this aspect of a believer's course, as in all others, Jesus has left us an example that we should follow his steps: "I do always those things that please him" (John viii. 29). The glad obedience of the saved should not be thought inconsistent with the simple trust of the sinful. A true disciple is zealous of good works; it is a spurious faith that is jealous of them. Those who, being justified by faith, are most deeply conscious that their works are worthless, strive most earnestly to do worthy works.

This, like that which enjoins obedience to parents, is a com-mandment "with promise." When your ways please God, he will make even your enemies to be at peace with you. This is one of two principles that stand together in the word, and act together in the divine administration; its counterpart and complement is, "If any man will live godly in Christ Jesus, he must suffer perse-cution." They seem opposite, yet, like night and day, summer and winter, they both proceed from the same God, and work to-gether for good to his people. It is true that the mighty of the earth are overawed by goodness; and it is also true that likeness to the Lord exposes the disciple to the persecution which his Master endured Both are best: neither could be wanted. If the principle that goodness exposes to persecution prevailed everywhere and always, the spirit would fail before him and the souls which he has made. Again, if the principle that goodness conciliates the favour of the world prevailed everywhere and always, discipline would be done, and the service of God would degenerate into mercenary self-interest. If the good received only and always persecution for their goodness, their life could not endure, and the generation of the righteous would become extinct: if the good received only and always favour from men, their spiritual life would be overlaid, and choked in the thick folds of worldly prosperity. A beautiful balance of opposites is employed to produce one grand result. It is like the balance of antagonist forces, which keeps the planets in their places, and maintains the harmony of the universe. Temporal prosperity and temporal distress, the world's friendship and its enmity, are both formidable to the children of God. Our Father in heaven, guarding against the danger on either side, employs the two reciprocally to hold each other in check. Human applause on this side is a dangerous enemy, and it is made harmless by the measure of persecution which the godly must endure: on the other side, the enmity of a whole world is a weight under which the strongest would at last succumb; but it is made harmless by the opposite law,—the law by which true goodness conciliates favour even in an evil world. A Christian in the world is like a human body in the sea,—there is a tendency to sink and a tendency to swim. A very small force in either direction will turn the scale. Our Father in heaven holds the elements of nature and the passions of men at his own disposal: his children need not fear, for he keeps the balance in his own hands.

Mercy and Truth
(Proverbs 16:6)

"By mercy and truth iniquity is purged: and by the fear of the Lord men depart from evil."

N O object can well be more dull and meaningless than the stained window of an ancient church, as long as you stand without and look toward a dark interior; but when you stand within the temple, and look through that window upon the light of heaven, the still, sweet, solemn forms that lie in it start into life and loveliness. The beauty was all conceived in the mind and wrought by the hand of the ancient artist whose bones now lie mouldering in the surrounding church-yard; but the beauty lies hid until the two requisites come together,—a seeing eye within, and a shining light without. We often meet a verse on the page of the Old Testament Scriptures like those ancient works of art. The beauty of holiness is in it,—put into it by the Spirit from the first; and yet its meaning was not fully known until the Sun of Righteousness arose, and the Israel of God, no longer kept in the outer court, entered through the rent veil, and, from the Holy of Holies, looked through the ancient record on an illumined heaven. Many hidden beauties burst into view on the pages of the Bible, when faith's open eye looks through it on the face of Jesus.

One of these texts is now before us. There is more in it than met the reader's eye before Christ came. The least in the kingdom of heaven is greater than the Baptist. The feeblest of the faithful after the incarnation sees more meaning in the Bible than the eagle eye of the mightiest prophet could discern before it. " By mercy and truth iniquity is purged:" that line of the Scriptures becomes thoroughly transparent only when you hold it up between you and Christ crucified.

The subject is the expiation of sin. The term is the one which

Is employed in connection with the bloody sacrifices. It intimates that sin is purged by the sacrifice of a substitute. The two clauses of the verse, balanced against each other in the usual form, seem to point to the two great facts which constitute redemption,—pardon and obedience. The first clause tells how the guilt of sin is forgiven; the second, how the power of sin is subdued. The first speaks of the pardon which comes down from God to man; the second, of the obedience which then and therefore rises up from man to God. Solomon unites the two constituent elements of a sinner's deliverance in the same order that his father experienced them : " I have hoped for thy salvation and done thy commandments " (Ps. cxix. 166). It is when iniquity is purged by free grace that men practically depart from evil.

How then is iniquity purged ? By mercy and truth. The same two things are repeatedly proclaimed as the grand distinguishing fruit of Christ's incarnation by the disciple that leant on his breast (John i. 14–17). "Grace and truth came by Jesus Christ," whether you take the term "truth" in its most general sense, or in its specific application as the fulfilment of the types. The law, according to the thunders of Sinai, gives one of these; and the gospel, according to the imaginations of corrupt men, gives another: but only in Christ crucified both unite. The law from Sinai proclaims Truth without Mercy, and the unrenewed heart desires Mercy without Truth. The one would result in the perdition of men ; the other in the dishonour of God. Truth alone would honour God's law, but destroy transgressors : mercy alone would shield the transgressors, but trample on the law. If there were only truth, earth would no longer be a place of hope: if there were only mercy, heaven would no longer be a place of holiness. On the one side is the just Judge; on the other the guilty criminals. If he give them their due, there will be no mercy; if they get from him their desire, there will be no truth. You may get one at the expense of casting out the guilty multitude; you may get the other at the expense of putting to shame the Holy One; but apart from the gospel of Christ, both cannot be.

They meet in the Mediator. In Christ the fire meets the water without drying it up : the water meets the fire without quenching it out. Truth has its way now, and all the desert of sin falls on

Him who bears it : mercy has its way now, and all the love of God is poured out on those who are one with his beloved Son. Iniquity is punished in the substitute sacrificed, and so purged from the conscience of the redeemed. " There is now no condemnation to them that are in Christ Jesus." The blood of Jesus Christ cleanseth from all sin. This is the gospel. There is no salvation in any other. The Scriptures from beginning to end testify of Christ. All their promises are yea and amen in him. We shall never discover the meaning of " mercy and truth " until we "look unto Jesus." We shall never get our " iniquity purged " until we " behold the Lamb of God that taketh away the sin of the world." All the power lies in the great fact, that Christ died the just for the unjust ; and all salvation comes through the simple act, " Believe in the Lord Jesus Christ, and thou shalt be saved."

This purging of iniquity is the first and great constituent of the gospel ; and the second, which is like unto it, is, Let the pardoned depart from evil. Only " by the fear of the Lord " can this command be obeyed. In preceding expositions we have pointed out that the fear of the Lord means the mingled awe and confidence of a dear child. Fear of the Lord is a very different thing from *fright at the Lord.* The reverential love which keeps you near tends to practical holiness ; but the terror which drives you to a distance permits you to wallow there in everything that is unclean.

The fear which produces obedience is generated by mercy and truth united in the manifested character of God. Mercy without truth would beget presumption : truth without mercy would beget despair. The one manifestation would not touch the conscience of the transgressor, and therefore he would not obey; the other manifestation would crush him so that he could not. It is by the fear of him who is at once a just God and a Saviour that men depart from evil. The emotion that fills a disciple's heart is, like the atmosphere, composed mainly of two great elements in combination. These are love and hate. Together in due proportion they constitute the atmosphere of heaven, and supply vital breath to believers on the earth. Love of the Saviour who forgives his sin, and hatred of the sin that crucified his Saviour,—these two, in one rich and well-proportioned amalgam, make up the vital element of saints. Separated they cannot be : to dissolve their union is to change their essence. As well might one of the atmosphere's constituent gases sustain the life of a man as one of these emotions satisfy a saved sinner. The separation indeed is impossible,— perhaps we should say inconceivable. Hatred of sin is but the lower side of love to the Saviour, and love to the Saviour is but the upper side of hatred to sin. In the new nature there is a twofold strain or leaning, acting constantly like an instinct, although much impeded in its exercise,—a strain or bent of heart towards the Lord and away from sin. They who are near to God depart from evil; and they who really depart from evil draw near to God. The man in the Gospel (Luke xii. 45) " said in his heart, My Lord delayeth his coming;" and then began in his practice to " beat the men-servants and maidens, and to eat and drink, and to be drunken." At the two extremities stand the " Lord " and " evil ;" in the midst, this man. He cannot move nearer this side without departing further from that. If he draw near the Lord, he will depart from evil : if he draw near to evil, he must put the Lord far away. When a man determines on a course of actual transgression, he puts God out of all his thoughts : when he desires to escape the snares of Satan, he must walk closely with God. A people near to him is a people far from wickedness : a people far from wickedness is a people near to him. Absolutely and in origin, there is none good save one, and that is God : comparatively among men, the more godly, the more good. In their course over a parched land, those streams continue longest full which maintain unimpeded their union to the fountain. Our goodness will dissipate before temptation like the morning dew before the sun, unless we be found in him and getting out of his fulness.

Providence

(Proverbs 16:9; 19:21)

"A man's heart deviseth his way : but the Lord directeth his steps."
"There are many devices in a man's heart: nevertheless the counsel of the Lord, that shall stand."

T HE Bible throughout teaches the providence of God in theory, and exhibits the providence of God in fact. The prophecies are one continuous assertion of the doctrine; the histories one vast storehouse of its fruits. The works are manifest; the worker is withdrawn from view. "Thou art a God that hidest thyself," is one of the songs in which the trustful praise him. The clouds and darkness that are round his throne concealed him from the wisest of the heathen; and yet, at the cry of any Israelite indeed, he was wont to shine forth from between the cherubim, and make bare his holy arm as it wrought deliverance. When a stroke of judgment was about to fall, so heavy that its sound should echo for terror to the wicked down through all time, the Lord said, "Shall I hide from Abraham the thing that I do?" Yet, with all their philosophy, the Athenians in Paul's day were compelled to own that they worshipped an unknown God. The knowledge of his ways is hid from the wise and prudent, but revealed unto babes. "Even so, Father; for so it seemed good in thy sight." If, as to power, faith can remove mountains, as to perception it can see through clouds. "The secret of the Lord is with them that fear him ; and he will shew them his covenant " (Ps. xxv. 14).

" God executeth his decrees in the works of creation and providence." There are two psalms—the 104th and 105th—placed next each other in the collection, which correspond to these two departments of the divine administration. The one is a hymn to God in nature; the other a hymn to God in history. In the first he appears appointing their course to the rivers of water; in the second, turning whithersoever he will the hearts of men. This psalm deals with the habitation and its furniture ; that with the inhabitant and his history. These two songs exhibit an intelligence most comprehensive and a devotion most pure, circulating in the rustic community of the Hebrews, at a time when the conceptions of other nations on the same themes were grovelling and their worship vile. Both in the history that records the act, and the psalms that celebrate the Actor, the patriarch Joseph appears a most vivid portrait standing out of the canvas, and the Exodus stretches away like a landscape lying in the light. The persons and events that occupy that great turning-point in human history serve as specimens of the government which the Most High ever exercises over the children of men.

Providence is as far above us as creation. To direct the path of a planet in the heavens, and his own steps over time, are both and both alike beyond the power of man. God is as much a sovereign in appointing the bounds of my habitation now upon the earth, as in appointing the earth at the beginning to be a habitation for living creatures. Our shoulders could not sustain the government ; we should delight to know that it rests on His.

These two proverbs of Solomon announce in different yet equivalent terms that the two grand constituent elements which exist and operate in the divine government of the world, are man's free agency and Jehovah's supreme control. When it is said that a man's heart deviseth his way, but the Lord directeth his steps, we must not think that the purpose of the creature is condemned as an impertinence ; it is an essential element of the plan. Neither human purposes, the material on which God exercises his sovereign control, nor the control which he exercises on that material, could be wanted. If there were no room for the devices of a man's heart, Providence would disappear, and grim Fate, the leaden creed that crushes Eastern nations in the dust, would come in its stead. If, on the other hand, these devices are left to fight against each other for their objects without being subjected all to the will of a Living One, Faith flees from the earth, and the reign of Atheism begins.

The desires of human hearts, and the efforts of human hands, go into the processes of providence, and constitute the material on which the Almighty works. When God made man in his own

image, a new era was inaugurated and a new work begun
Hitherto, in the government of this world, the Creator had no
other elements to deal with than matter and the instincts of brutes;
but the moment that man took his place on creation, a new and
higher element was introduced into its government. The sphere
was enlarged and the principle elevated; there was more room
for the display of wisdom and power. The will of intelligent
moral beings left free, and yet as completely controlled as matter
and its laws, makes the divine government much more glorious
than the mere management of a material universe. For God's
glory man was created, and that purpose will stand; a glory to
God man will be, willing or unwilling, fallen or restored, throughout the course of time and at its close. The doctrine of Scripture
regarding providence neither degrades man nor inflates him. It
does not make him a mere thing on the one hand, nor a god on
the other. It neither takes from him the attributes of humanity,
nor ascribes to him the attributes of deity. It permits him freely
to propose, but leaves the ultimate disposal in a mightier hand.

When we seek for specimens of providential rule,—of devices
manifold in a man's heart, and the counsel of the Lord standing
accomplished either by or against them all, the Exodus is, and
ever will be, the richest mine. Let us look at one example, and
learn from it the character of all. The cruel decree, repeated in
two different forms, devoting to death all the male infants of Israel,
was one of the blows, dealt unconsciously by the oppressor's own
hand, which went to break the captive's chain and set him free.
It was an edict that could not be executed. Blinded by his own
eagerness to achieve his object early, Pharaoh grasped at too much,
and therefore obtained nothing. It is in this way generally that
our Father in heaven protects the poor from the wicked devices
of the powerful. Evil is kept within bounds by being permitted
to exceed all bounds. Its excesses make it barren. As well
might Pharaoh have commanded the Nile to flow upward. A
massacre of innocents, commanded by a tyrant, may be executed
by his slaves. The babes of Bethlehem may be slaughtered by
the decree of Herod,—a stroke against Christ in his own person;
the Protestants of France may be murdered in a night,—a stroke
against Christ in his members; but neither the Instigator of evil
nor any of his instruments can secure the execution of a decree

which permanently violates the instincts of nature. To murder day by day and year by year continually the infants of a whole people as soon as they are born, is impossible. By the power of Pharaoh the Nile might be dammed up for a day, but all the power of the world could not stem its flood for a season. So, although the instincts of nature may be held in abeyance till the sword has done its short work on the babes of Bethlehem or the Huguenots of France, they gather strength, like the river, from the impediment that crossed them, and at the next onset will sweep all impediments away. The decree must have fallen aside as a dead letter when a few infant corpses had been washed upon the river's brim. In point of fact, the history contains no trace of its existence after the childhood of Moses. It served to prepare the way of a deliverer, and then disappeared. God served himself of that cruel law, and then crushed it by the instincts which he has planted in human breasts. The people of Egypt were flesh and blood ; therefore the purpose of their stony-hearted ruler could not be accomplished : they had infants of their own, and therefore could not day by day continue to murder infants, whose struggling limbs felt soft and warm in the executioners' hands. The huge machine constructed for the purpose of keeping down the Hebrew population, having been set in motion, turned round once, and stopped to move no more ; but by its one revolution, it threw a foundling—a capacious Hebrew mind and a fervid Hebrew heart —into the palace of the Pharaohs, to be charged there with all the learning of Egypt, and employed in due time as the instrument to break the oppressor's rod, and set his suffering kindred free.

Although God's hand is in it, and all the more because his hand is in it, the history, as to its form, is intensely human. Everywhere throughout the details, the purposes of men's hearts protrude ; and yet God's hand fashions the issue for his own purposes as absolutely as it framed the worlds of the solar system, and gave to matter its laws. The history of ancient Israel is marked all over with the footprints of the Chief Shepherd as he led his flock, and teems with types or working plans for the conduct of the divine government to the end of time. Even the life of the Great Deliverer pointed now to one, and now to another feature of the Mosaic programme, as the needle quivers beneath the electric current. In the beginning of his life on earth he

went down into Egypt, and out of Egypt again God called his Son.
At the close of his ministry, when he showed the three disciples
a glimpse of his heavenly glory, Moses was his companion, and
Exodus his theme. Children understand and love that wonderful
story; it engraves itself on their memory, and abides there even
unto old age. The book is true to nature, and true also to grace.
Children never weary of the tale; the children of God can never
get enough of its spiritual lesson.

There is literally no end to the multiplication of impressions on
the current history of the world, from the types which the deep
fount of sacred Scripture contains. They are thrown off as days
and years revolve, in number and variety all but infinite. The
Angel is doing wondrously; it is our part reverently to look on.

Passing over providential arrangements on a small scale involving similar principles and leading to similar results, numerous as
reflections of sun-light from the dancing waves, we select as an
example one that in several features bears an obvious analogy to
the Exodus—the present bondage and prospective freedom of the
Negro race in the United States of America. The process is not
yet complete, and therefore we cannot fully understand what the
counsel of the Lord therein may be. We cannot yet predict all
the turnings that the course of events may take; but the issue is
not doubtful. We know that the Lord reigneth; we know also
certain great principles that run through his administration. We
wait confidently for the end of the Lord in that great conflict.

The device of many leading politicians in the United States has
been, and is, to maintain three millions of human beings in slavery,
to be bought and sold like cattle or any other species of property.
There are, indeed, in the laws some shreds of protection for human
flesh and blood, not accorded to other species of possessions; but
these proceed upon low grounds, and never rise to the recognition
of a brother's nature and a brother's rights. The citizens of that
country have probably an average share of humanity in their personal character; but the institution to which they cling chokes
up the channel through which the affections of nature ought to
flow. They make laws on the one side to prevent excessive cruelty
in the treatment of slaves, and on the other side to forbid the
dissemination of knowledge, lest it should emancipate the mind
while the body remains in bondage. These alternate struggles

this way and that way are painful to the community that makes them, and by no means effectual to accomplish the end desired. To treat a man as the property of man, is to fight against nature and against God. He who falls upon this stone shall be broken. The nation, accordingly, is broken, is rent asunder, by a wound that refuses to be healed. Action and reaction are equal and opposite, as well in morals as in physics. One person or one race cannot hurt another, without receiving a corresponding injury in return. If my brother and myself are standing both together on ice, and I push him violently away from me, I have thereby pushed myself as far in the opposite direction. I may succeed in driving my brother out of his place, but the same effort drives me also out of mine. The Americans are so situated with respect to their slaves. They cannot push the Africans aside from the best condition of humanity on the one hand, without pushing them- selves as, far from the best condition of humanity on the other. Man is not a fixture on the earth like the everlasting hills : the ground is slippery, and our foot-hold feeble at the best. It is not in our power to turn aside a neighbour from his right, and maintain our own standing and character as before. The master depresses and degrades his slave; but in that very act he has deeply wounded the tenderest part of his own nature. If the op- pressed race are necessarily mean, the oppressing race are necessarily arrogant. As far as the slave is sunk below the level into brutish insensibility, so far the master is forced up above it into an odious unfeeling pride. It is in vain that the potsherds of the earth strive with their Maker. His laws are even now silently operat- ing to adjust these inequalities. Some portions of their working may be already seen cropping out upon the surface.

Slaves, stung by injuries at home, and favoured by compassionate hearts abroad, were escaping in a strong steady stream to a land of liberty. A gradual exodus had begun, and the dominant power, by the instinct of self-preservation, adopted a device to arrest it. They passed an enactment, know as the *Fugitive Slave Law*, which requires that the citizens shall aid in delivering the fleeing African into his pursuers' hands, and imposes severe pun- ishment on all who shall dare to harbour him or facilitate his escape. This, it seems, is the best device which the powerful could employ to keep the feeble under the yoke. But it has failed, and will fail

Like Pharaoh's device to keep down his slaves, it contains within itself the elements of its own dissolution. The Legislature of the States has ventured to run counter not only to the principles of justice, but to that which in human breasts is a stronger thing —the instincts of nature. Fathers and mothers in the Free States cannot be compelled to deliver up a fugitive mother and her infant to the mercy of her pursuer. There is a law which lies underneath that shallow enactment, with power to hold it in check for a time, and to crush it at last.

That latest effort which the slaveholding power has put forth to secure their property has probably done more than any other single event to weaken their tenure, and ultimately wrench it from their grasp. The counsel of the Lord, that shall stand, whether the adversary opposed to it be an ancient despot or a modern democracy. The stroke which was intended to rivet the fetters of the slave more firmly, guided in its descent by an unseen hand, fell upon a brittle link, and broke it through. The newspapers announced that the cruel device had been enacted into a law. The intelligence fell like a spark on the deep compassion that lay pent up in a woman's heart, and kindled it into a flame. The outburst took the form of a book, the instrument of power usually employed in these later ages of the world. It is certainly true, and is widely known, that the enactment of the Fugitive Slave Law produced the book, and that the book caused a panorama of slavery to pass before the eyes of millions in America and Europe, inexpressibly augmenting the public opinion of the civilized world against the whole system, root and branch. Let no one imagine that we are elevating little things into an undue importance; we speak of Jehovah's counsel, and how it stands erect and triumphant over all the devices of men. He is wont to employ weak things to confound the mighty. Long ago He employed the tears of a helpless child and the strong compassion of a woman (Ex. ii. 6) as essential instruments in the exodus of an injured race; and it would be like himself if, in our day, while statesmen and armies contend in the senate and the battle-field, he should permit women who remain at home to deal the blow which decides the victory, and distribute the resulting spoil. " He sits King upon the floods." "All are His servants." "Stand still and see the salvation of God."

The exodus of the New Testament, the decease which Christ

accomplished at Jerusalem, when, by the shedding of his blood, and through a sea of wrath, he opened a way for his redeemed to pass over, teems even more than that of the Old Testament with studies of Providence. Caiaphas proclaimed him the sacrificed substitute for sinning men (John xi. 49–52), and Pilate recorded his kingly dignity (John xix. 19). Are Caiaphas and Pilate also among the prophets? They are, although they know it not. He who makes the winds his messengers, and the flaming fire his angels, can harness these untamed spirits, and yoke them to his chariot. He makes the tongue of Caiaphas preach the priesthood, and the pen of Pilate write the sovereignty of Jesus. When God has a message to declare, he is not limited in his choice of the angel who shall bear it. He can compel the servants of Satan to do his errands, without even putting off their dark costume. Their own hearts devise their ways, but the Lord directs their steps. In pursuing their own devices, they unconsciously become the instruments of accomplishing the purpose of God.

" Pilate wrote a title," in Hebrew and Greek and Latin, and fixed it aloft upon the cross. The title so composed and published was, " JESUS OF NAZARETH, THE KING OF THE JEWS." In the same spirit the governor had already said, " Shall I crucify your King?" This testimony from his view-point served two purposes. It gave vent to the conviction struggling in his own mind that the Sufferer was innocent and divine : at the same time it afforded him the opportunity of taking vengeance on the Jews for the blood-hound cruelty with which they had hunted him down, and compelled him, against his own judgment, to give up the Just One to be crucified. He held their shame aloft to heaven, and spread it in three languages across the world. Such is the object which Pilate "proposes" to himself; but this man's weak vindictive passion God "disposes" so, that it shall proclaim to Hebrews, Greeks, and Romans, that the crucified is the King of Israel Pilate's shaft was well aimed : it reached its mark, and rankled in the bones and marrow of those Jewish rulers. The governor, whom their policy had concussed, now overreached them. They were ashamed that a formal title, under the supreme civil authority, should publish to the indigenous multitude in their vernacular, and to strangers from the east and west in the languages of the empire, that the Nazarene on the accursed tree was their promised, expected King. They requested that the writing should be changed. Pilate rejected their request. It was now his turn to tighten the screw on the flesh of the victim. Revenge at that moment was sweet to his revengeful heart. " What I have written I have written!" and he pushed them aside with contempt. He determined to pillory these proud priests aloft upon the place of skulls, as the subjects of the Crucified: and yet God employed that fierce passion to print above the cross, and publish through all time, a testimony to the royalty of Emmanuel. Said not the Scriptures truly, " The wrath of man shall praise Thee?"

We have been contemplating the working of Providence in those great events which have nations for their actors, and a world for their stage. We have preferred to exemplify a principle by the larger specimens of its produce, as we are wont to illustrate the law of gravitation by the balancing of worlds: but that law may be seen as well in the drooping of a snow-drop, or the falling of a leaf. And in like manner our Maker's might and our Father's tenderness descend with us from great public events, and follow our private, personal interests, until they are lost to our view, but not to His, in the microscopic minuteness of a hair falling off or growing gray. In a storm at sea, when the danger pressed, and the deep seemed ready to devour the voyagers, one man stood composed and cheerful amidst the agitated throng. They asked him eagerly why he feared not,—was he an experienced seaman, and did he see reason to expect that the ship would ride the tempest through? No; he was not an expert sailor, but he was a trustful Christian. He was not sure that the ship would swim; but he knew that its sinking could do no harm to him. His answer was, " Though I sink to-day, I shall only drop gently into the hollow of my Father's hand, for he holds all these waters there." The story of that disciple's faith triumphing in a stormy sea presents a pleasant picture to those who read it on the solid land; but if in safety they are strangers to his faith, they will not in trouble partake of his consolation. The idea is beautiful; but a human soul, in its extremity, cannot play with a beautiful idea. Strangers may speak of providence; but only the children love it. Those who are alienated from God in their hearts, do not like to be so completely in His power. It is when I am satisfied with his mercy, that I rejoice to lie in His hand.

Wisdom and Wealth: Their Comparative Worth
(Proverbs 16:16)

"How much better is it to get wisdom than gold? and to get understanding rather to be chosen than silver?"

THE question only is written in the book; the learner is expected to work out the answer. We, of this mercantile community, are expert in the arithmetic of time; here is an example to test our skill in casting up the accounts of eternity. Deeper interests are at stake; greater care should be taken to avoid an error, more labour willingly expended in making the balance true. Old and young, rich and poor, should take their places together in the school, and, under the Master's own eye, work this pregnant problem out to its issue.

The question is strictly one of degree. It is not, Whether is wisdom or gold the more precious portion for a soul? That question was settled long ago by common consent. All who in any sense make a profession of faith in God, confess that wisdom is better than gold; and this teacher plies them with another problem,—*How much better?*

Two classes of persons have experience in this matter,—those who have chosen the meaner portion, and those who have chosen the nobler; but only the latter class are capable of calculating the difference suggested by the text. Those who give their heart to money understand only the value of their own portion: those who possess treasures in heaven have tasted both kinds, and can appreciate the difference between them.

When a man has made money his idol and his aim, he may be made to feel and confess that it is a worthless portion. He may understand well that a world full of it cannot procure for him one night's sleep when he is in pain,—cannot dispel the terrors of an unclean conscience,—cannot satisfy the justice of God,—cannot open the gate of heaven. The man, in his misery, can tell you truly and intelligently that gold, as the chosen heritage of an immortal, is worthless ; but how much better heavenly wisdom would have been he cannot tell, for he has never tried it. As the man born blind cannot tell how much better light is than his native darkness ; as the slave born under the yoke of his master cannot tell how much better liberty is than his life-long bondage ; so he who has despised the treasures that are at God's right hand cannot conceive how much more precious they are to a man in his extremity than the riches that perish in the use. A man knows both what it is to be a child and what it is to be a man ; but a child knows only what it is to be a child. He who is now a new creature has experience also of the old man ; but he who has not yet put off the old man has no experience of the new. Only those who have chosen the better portion can intelligently compare the two.

But even these cannot compute the difference : eye hath not seen, ear hath not heard it. Wisdom from above, like the love of God, passeth knowledge. Even those who are best instructed can stretch their line but a little way into the depth. How much better is wisdom than gold ? Better by all the worth of a soul, by all the blessedness of heaven, by all the length of eternity. But all these expressions are only tiny lines that children fling into the ocean to measure its depth withal : none of them reach the ground. It is like the answer of a little child when you ask him, How far distant is that twinkling star ? It is very, very far above us, he will say ; but with all the eagerness of his tone and gesture—with his outstretched finger, and twittering lips, and glistening eye, he has not told you how deep in the heavens that lone star lies. As well might you expect to find out God, as find out, here in the body, the measure of the goodness which he has laid up for them that fear him.

In a time of war between two great maritime nations, a ship belonging to one of them is captured on the high seas by a ship belonging to the other. The captor, with a few attendants, goes on board his prize, and directs the native crew to steer for the nearest point of his country's shore. The prize is very rich. The victors occupy themselves wholly in collecting and counting the treasure, and arranging their several shares, abandoning the care of the ship to her original owners. These, content with being permitted to handle the helm, allow their rivals to handle the money unmolested. After a long night, with a steady breeze, the captured mariners quietly, at dawn, run the ship into a harbour on their own shores. The conquerors are in turn made captives. They lose all the gold which they grasped too eagerly, and their liberty besides. In that case it was much better to have hold of the helm, which directed the ship, than of the money which the ship contained. Those who seized the money and neglected the helm, lost even the money which was in their hands. Those who neglected the money and held by the helm, obtained the money which they neglected, and liberty too. They arrived at home, and all their wealth with them.

Thus they who make money their aim suffer a double loss, and they who seek the wisdom from above secure a double gain. The gold with which men are occupied will profit little, if the voyage of their life be not pointed home. If themselves are lost, their possessions are worthless. It is much better to get wisdom ; for wisdom is profitable to direct, and the course so directed issues in Rest and Riches. When Christ is yours, all things are yours, and gold among them. The gold and the silver are His, and whether by giving them to you or withholding them from you, he will compel these his servants to attend upon his sons.

The ship may carry a precious cargo of this world's goods, but the main concern of the master is not the quantity and value of his freight. It is better to come home empty a living man, than to be cast away in company with your riches. Alas ! I think I see many men spending their days and nights down in the hold keeping their eyes on the coffers, permitting the vessel which carries both themselves and their treasures to drift at the mercy of wind and tide. Come up ! come up ! This is not your rest. This is a tempestuous and dangerous sea. Look to the heavens for guiding light ; keep your eye on the chart and your hand on the rudder. Immortal man ! let your chief aim and effort be to pass safely through these troubled waters, and arrive at last in the better land. As to wealth, if you carry little with you, plenty awaits you there. " We passed through fire and water, yet thou broughtest us to a wealthy place."

The Highway of the Upright
(Proverbs 16:17)

"The highway of the upright is to depart from evil: he that keepeth his way
preserveth his soul."

E VERY man has a highway of his own. It is formed, as
our forefathers formed their roads, simply by walking
often on it, and without a predetermined plan. Foresight and wisdom might improve the moral path, as much as they
have in our day improved the material. The highway of the
covetous is to depart from poverty and make for wealth with all
his might. In his eagerness to take the shortest cut he often falls
over a precipice, or loses his way in a wood. The highway of the
vain is to depart from seriousness, and follow mirth on the trail
of fools. The highway of the ambitious is a scramble up a
mountain's side towards its summit, which seems in the distance
to be a paradise basking in sunlight above the clouds, but when
attained is found to be colder and barer than the plain below. The
upright has a highway too, and it is to " depart from evil."

The upright is not an unfallen angel, but a restored man : he
has been in the miry pit, and the marks of the fall are upon him
still. Even when a sinner has been forgiven and renewed—when
he has become a new creature in Christ, and an heir of eternal
life—the power of evil within him is not entirely subdued, the
stain of evil not entirely wiped away. He hates sin now in his
heart, but he feels the yoke of it in his flesh still. His back is
turned to the bondage which he loathes, and his face to the liberty
which he loves. He hastens away from evil, and if he looks
behind him at any time, it is to measure the distance he has
already made, and quicken his pace for the time to come. In
this way the pilgrim walks unwearied, nor dares to rest until in
dwellings of the righteous he hear that "melody of joy and
health :" " Salvation to our God who sitteth upon the throne, and

unto the Lamb." Then at last he ceases to depart from evil; for there is no more any evil to depart from. He treads no more his chosen beaten highway, because he is now at home.

The man who has found this highway, and keeps it, "preserveth his soul." How necessary to each other reciprocally are doctrine and life! To sever them is to destroy them; and to sever them is a more common error in Christendom than most are able to perceive or willing to confess. Doctrine, although both true and divine, is for us only a shadow, if it be not embodied in holiness. Nothing more effectually serves Satan's purpose in the world than a strict creed wedded to a loose practice. This union secures a double gain to the kingdom of darkness; it keeps the man himself in bondage, and also exposes to shame the gospel of our Lord. The true doctrine is necessary to salvation, because it is the only way of reaching righteousness. The preciousness of revealed truth lies in this, that it teaches how we may please God, first by the righteousness of Christ, second and subordinately by personal obedience. He who keepeth his way preserveth his soul: conversely, he who departs from it shall perish.

There stands the word in all its simplicity and bluntness: the preserving of your soul depends on the keeping of your way. The way is obviously the life: no reader can mistake the meaning of the term. It was not the profession, but the "walk" of those Philippian backsliders that made Paul weep, and ranked them "enemies of the cross of Christ." The Lord himself, in the sermon on the mount, has settled this point with extraordinary precision and minuteness (Matt. vii. 21–27), especially in the parable of the two houses, that of the wise man built upon a rock, and that of the foolish man built upon the sand. He has graven as with a pen of iron, and the point of a diamond in the rock for ever, the lesson that a sound creed will not save an evil doer in the great day.

To contend for a high standard of doctrine, and be satisfied with a low standard of life, is a fatal inconsistency. It is a "damnable heresy," whoever brings it in; for it issues in the loss of the soul. At certain periods in the history of the Church, and among certain communities of professors, evangelical doctrine has prevailed, while morality has languished. This knowledge, dissociated from obedience, is a more melancholy object of contemplation than the idolatry of Athens, where the living God was un-unknown; as a blighted corn-field is a sadder sight than a bare unsown moor. In the early Christian culture some fields ran waste in this way, on which much labour had been expended; and to these the reproof of James is specially addressed: "But wilt thou know, O vain man, that faith without works is dead?" (ii. 20). It is as false in philosophy as in religion to assume that a knowledge of the way will lead those home who refuse to walk in it.

In our day and our country, the supreme and fundamental importance of truth in doctrine is generally acknowledged and inculcated in the religious education of the people. This is both right and necessary, but it is not enough. Why should men separate and set up as rivals the knowing of the right way, and the walking in the way that is right? You may as well pit against each other the seeing eye and the shining light, some declaring for this and some for that as the one thing needful. Shake off prepossessions and traditions; go in simplicity to the Bible; sit at the feet of Jesus, and listen to the Teacher sent from God; and you will find that a so-called right believing which does not clothe itself in right living, so far from being a passport to safety, is an aggravation of guilt. "To him that knoweth to do good and doeth it not, to him it is sin."

When a wanderer has been met, like Paul, in the way of death, and led into the way of life, the end is not yet. Let not him that putteth on his armour boast himself as he that putteth it off. Those who have found the way must keep it. There are many by-paths, and many enticers clustering round the entrance of each. "Watch and pray that ye enter not into temptation." "He that endureth to the end, the same shall be saved."

It is in the *way*, the *conduct*, the *life*, that the breach occurs whereby a soul is lost, that seemed to bid fair for the better land. It is probable that with nine out of every ten of our people in this favoured land, the enemy finds it easier to inject actual impurity into the life than speculative error into the creed. Danger to the soul is greater on the side of practice than on the side of faith. A shaken faith, I own, leads the life astray; but also a life going astray makes shipwreck of the faith. I do not teach that any righteousness done by the fallen can either please God or justify a man; but I do teach, on the authority of the Bible, that a slipping from the way of righteousness and purity in actual life is the main stay of Satan's kingdom—the chief destroyer of souls. When your conduct becomes impure, your belief will not continue sound. It is more common in the experience of individuals, if not also in the History of the Church, to find evangelical doctrine undermined by sinful practice, than to find holy practice perverted by a heterodox belief. A successful assault by the enemy on either side will ruin all, but in the battle of life the side of conduct is weaker and more exposed than the side of profession. If the spirits of darkness could be heard celebrating their success, while erroneous doctrines might, in their dreary pæan, occupy the place of Saul who slays his thousands, indulged lusts would certainly be the David who slays his ten thousands. Young men and women ! when you are in the place and the hour of temptation, look to that apostle who had sorely stumbled himself, and therefore, when confirmed by grace, was better fitted than others to have compassion on them that are out of the way; his eyes are red with weeping and his manly heart is breaking in his breast : he cries with an exceeding great and bitter cry, that should run through you like a sword in your bones : " Dearly beloved, I beseech you as strangers and pilgrims, abstain from fleshly lusts, which *war against the soul*" (1 Peter ii. 11).

Every one has a highway, and every one is a traveller. The whole human race are travelling, each on his own chosen track, across Time and toward Eternity. Every traveller has something very precious in his custody—the most precious of created things —his own soul. "What shall it profit a man if he gain the whole world and lose his soul?" You will lose it, pilgrim, if you go off the way. The miners in the gold fields of Australia, when they have gathered a large quantity of the dust, make for the city with the treasure. The mine is far in the interior ; the country is wild; the bush is infested by robbers. The miners keep the road and the day-light. They march in company, and close by the guard sent to protect them. They do not stray from the path among the woods ; for they bear with them a treasure which they value, and they are determined to run no risks. Do likewise, brother, for your treasure is of greater value, your enemies of greater power. Keep the way, lest you lose your soul.

The Well-Spring of Life
(Proverbs 16:22)

" Understanding is a well-spring of life unto him that hath it."

T HE well is deeper now than Solomon in his day was able to penetrate, and sends forth accordingly, a fuller, fresher, more perennial stream. Then, in ancient Israel it was much to learn from the lips of the king all that the Spirit taught him about understanding as a well-spring of life; but a greater than Solomon is here teaching us, and the youngest scholar who sits at Jesus' feet may in these high matters be wiser than the ancients. "Whosoever drinketh of the water that I shall give him shall never thirst; but the water that I shall give him shall be in him a well of water springing up into everlasting life" (John iv. 14). Behold the lessons of David's son, expanded and completed by David's Lord !

Understanding is a well-spring to him that hath it : but in me dwelleth no good thing. Every good gift and every perfect gift is from above. A rainless sky makes a barren land : as long as the heavens are brass, the earth will be iron. There are many living well-springs on the earth, but the fountain-head is on high. The earth gets all the good of the refreshing streams as much as if they were originally its own; and yet it is indebted to the sky for every drop that rises in its springs and flows in its rivers. The springs are *in* the earth for possession and benefit, though not *of* the earth as their independent source. It is thus with the understanding which becomes a well-spring of life to men. It is in them; they possess it, and enjoy all its preciousness : but it is not their own ; it is the gift of God. They have nothing which they did not receive.

Two things are necessary to the opening and the flow of well-springs—deep rendings beneath the earth's surface, and lofty risings above it. There must be deep veins and high mountains The mountains draw the drops from heaven; the rents receive, retain, and give forth the supply. There must be corresponding heights and depths in the life of a man ere he be charged as a well-spring with wisdom from above. Upward to God and downward into himself the exercises of his soul must alternately penetrate. You must lift up your soul in the prayer of faith, and rend your heart in the work of repentance; you must ascend into heaven to bring the blessing down, and descend into the depths to draw it up. Extremes meet in a lively Christian: he is at once very high and very lowly. God puts all his treasures in the power of a soul that rises to reach the upper springs, as the Andes intercept water in the sky sufficient to fertilize a continent; and when the Spirit has so descended like floods of water, the secret places of a broken heart afford room for his indwelling, so that the grace which came at first from God rises within the man like a springing well, satisfying himself and refreshing his neighbours.

Enlarging the germ of thought which Solomon infolded within the Old Testament Scriptures, the Lord intimated that this well, when charged and set a flowing, springeth up into everlasting life. There are many joys springing from the earth, and limited to time, —joys which God provides, and his children thankfully receive; but the characteristic defect of all these is, that those who drink of them shall thirst again. It is recorded of Israel in the wilderness, that they came one day to a place where were twelve wells, and seventy palm-trees. Here, then, were two of the pilgrims' chief wants amply supplied—shade and water; but we learn from the history that at another station in their journey, a few days afterwards, the people were reduced to extremities again by thirst. Such are all the temporary refreshments provided for pilgrims by the way. He who has solaced himself at these wells to-day will thirst again to-morrow. But the well-spring of life, the water that flowed from the Rock, will follow the weary all their way, and refresh them most when their thirst is greatest—in the final conflict with the latest foe. "That Rock was Christ."

"To him that *hath it*," said Solomon, will understanding be a well-spring. "Whosoever *drinketh* of the water that I shall give him," said Jesus, "shall never thirst." Both the Old Testament and the New distinctly teach that grace offered by God may only

increase the condemnation : it is grace accepted by man that saves
There is plenty in the fountain, for "God is love ;" and yet you
may thirst again, and thirst for ever. There is plenty falling, for
in Christ our Brother, and for us, all the fulness of the Godhead
bodily dwells ; and yet you may thirst again, and thirst for ever.
The Son of God came the Life of men, and yet many men live not.
The Son of God came the Light of the world, and yet whole nations
are sitting in darkness. " He that hath the Son hath life." He
is the wisdom of God. This wisdom is life "to him that hath
it ;" but the greatness of this salvation, and the freeness of its
offer, only aggravate the guilt of those who neglect or despise it.

Thirst and water, the appetite and its supply, are fitted into
each other like a lock and key in human art, or the seeing eye and
the shining light among the works of God. In these pairs, either
member is useless if it be alone. However exquisite in itself one
side of the double whole may be, it is barren if it want its counterpart. Water can no more nourish fruit alone than dust ; dust can
no more nourish fruit alone than water. Let the dust be refreshed
by water,—let water saturate the dust. The two apart were
both barren : their union will be prolific. Thirst without water
is merely pain : water without thirst is merely waste. It is when
thirst receives water, water quenches thirst, that a substantial
benefit accrues. We should carefully observe this inexorable law
of nature, and learn that it reigns with all its rigour in the spiritual sphere. Men who personally reject the gospel seem to expect
that the gospel will save them notwithstanding. Understanding
cannot be a well-spring of life to him that hath it not. The
terms are, "Whosoever will, let him take the water of life freely."
Even the love of God cannot offer more favourable terms than
these, and it remains true, that those who will not take the water
of life perish for want of it. At Jerusalem, in the course of his
ministry, on the last day of the feast, Jesus uttered a great cry. It
was a cry of fear and grief : it came from the breaking heart of
the Man of Sorrows. He feared, as the feast days were passing,
lest the time of mercy should run out, and those lingerers be
lost. He who knew what is in man and before him, was anxious :
they who knew neither themselves nor their Judge, were confident. He cried out : they kept silence. His cry was, " If any
man thirst, let him come unto me and drink " (John vii. 37)

He saw the water of life poured out and running waste : he saw, too, a multitude of lifeless, withered, perishing souls. What he desired to see in them was a thirst that should induce them to take the offered mercy. Alas ! now when the Giver cries, the needy sit silent : a time will come when the needy will cry, and the great Giver will refuse to answer ! The loss of a soul is an exceeding bitter thing at every stage of the process, from the beginning to the close. Now there is water, but no thirst : then there will be thirst, but no water. If these two be not joined in the day of mercy, they will remain separate through the night of doom. If God's cry, "Take, take !" be left echoing unanswered in heaven, man's cry, "Give, give !" will echo unanswered through the pit. If God's offer be barren in time for want of man's desire, man's desire in eternity will be barren for want of an offer to meet it from God. To him that hath it, this wisdom from above will be a well-spring of life ;—to those who refuse it life will never spring at all.

The Cruelty of Fools
(Proverbs 17:12)

" Let a bear robbed of her whelps meet a man, rather than a fool in his folly."

THE wrath of man is a dreadful thing. The mere recital of the havoc which it has wrought on the earth would sicken the stoutest heart. Who can calculate how many acts of cruelty, done by man upon his fellow, have accumulated for the inquisition of the great day, since the blood of Abel cried to heaven for vengeance against his brother ? The rage of wild beasts is short-lived, and their power is circumscribed within narrow limits. Man has more cause to dread his brother than all the beasts of the forest. It is easier to meet a bear robbed of her whelps, than a fool in his folly.

Cruelties are of a different species, owing their origin to diverse passions, and perpetrated with a view to diverse ends. Ambition has often steeped her hands in blood. Many sweet olive plants, especially of those that spring round royal tables, have been nipt in the bud, lest their growth should obstruct the path of a usurper hastening to the throne. Perhaps it is not strictly correct to say that war perpetrates, for it consists of cruelties. It is, rather than does, murder. Jealousy, too, leaves many victims on its track. And Superstition, Pagan, Mohammedan, and Popish has lighted the fires of persecution in every land, and relieved the world of those who had grown so like to God that the world could not endure their presence. These, and many other species of cruelties, have offended God and afflicted man ever since sin began ; but the cruelty specified in this text is of another kind. It is not the cruelty of the warrior in his thirst for glory ; nor the cruelty of the persecutor, in his blindness thinking to please God by destroying men : it is the cruelty of a fool in his folly.

Nothing so exactly answers to this description as a drunkard in his drink. Both the tree and its fruits correspond precisely to Solomon's report. The proverb fully characterizes the violence done by drunkards, and can be applied to nothing else that is done on a large scale in our country and our day. An instance may be found of a fool's cruelty, apart from the influence of intoxication, more terrible to meet than the rage of a bereaved wild beast; but this kind is not characteristic of the nation or the age. In the records of drunkenness, cases answering to the description of the text are piled in heaps like the hills; elsewhere they are either not found at all, or found so seldom as not sensibly to affect the general estimate. We are therefore not only permitted, but compelled, if we attempt an application of the proverb at all,—to gather our instances where they may be found,—among the fools who drive their judgment out by strong drink.

Instances of violence in this form seem to be increasing in number and atrocity in the present day: at all events it is certain that they attract the attention of statesmen and philanthropists much more now than in former times. Day by day, as our eye runs over the loathsome list of wife-beatings and wife-murders, by drunken husbands, we read at the same time, in the same columns, indignant denunciations of the dastard deeds, and peremptory demands for more stringent laws to repress the growing enormity. This species of crime, it is acknowledged on all hands, is the fruit of drunkenness.

The public journals are never long free from the details of some gigantic atrocity. Before one tragedy has passed through the usual three acts in presence of the public, another is announced, and begins to attain its run. First the curtain suddenly rises and reveals a new deed of blood. When the neighbourhood has wondered nine days at the cruelty of a fool, the solemnities of the trial succeed. The foreground is occupied by the public-house, and the process whereby a number of men divest themselves at once of the money they have toiled for and the judgment which God has given them. Many subordinate episodes adhere to the principal plot. Glimpses are gotten, through doors accidentally opened in the cross-examination, of the drunkard's naked children at home, or the coolness of the publican in the prosecution of his business. This act closes with the solemn answer of the jury's foreman, the black cap of the judge, and removal of the weeping prisoner to the cell of the condemned. The last short act opens with the sound of carpenters' hammers in the misty dawn, and closes soon with the dead body of the drunkard dangling on the gallows. A thrill runs through the crowd, and a sigh escapes from such hearts as retain some tenderness. The people return to their employment, the newspapers chronicle the event, and it glides away on the tide of time into the darkness of the past. But ere these harsh echoes have died away from the ear of the public, some other she-bear in human form meets and mangles her helpless victim. The public is put through the same process over again. So frequently do these shocking barbarities pass before our eyes, that they have, in a great measure, lost the power to shock us. We hear of them unmoved, as things that have been, and that will be, and that cannot be prevented. If a tenth of the accidents, assaults, and murders, with which the folly of drunkards is year by year desolating the land, were produced by any other cause, the community would rise as one man and put forth all its wisdom and might in an effort to pluck up the evil by the root. The nation bears with appalling patience the tearing out of its own bowels by the cruel madness of the drunkard.

Not long ago the local authorities of a certain district in India sent to the supreme government a representation that as many as sixteen persons within the territory had perished in one year by the bite of a small poisonous snake, and requesting permission to set a price upon the head of the reptile, with the view of uniting the whole population in an effort to exterminate their subtle and deadly foe. The government granted all their demands, and proclaimed a liberal reward for every dead snake that should be brought in. The people, thus encouraged by their rulers, entered heartily into the plan, and the work was done. Ah! in compassion for my country, I am tempted to wish that our scourge had come in the form of poisonous serpents. Sixteen lives lost by that plague within a year, in a population perhaps as great as ours, were sufficient to bind the rulers and the people together in a solemn league, and send them forth, as by the summons of the fiery cross, to root out their destroyer. Our annual loss in the ignoble battle is to be reckoned not by tens but by thousands, and yet we have neither head to contrive nor heart to execute any plan adequate to the emergency. We seem to be as helpless as the children that mocked Elisha in the paws of the bears that tore them.

But, great and numerous as the publicly reported atrocities of drunken folly are, they constitute only a small proportion of what the nation suffers from that single scourge. From the nature of the case and the position of the parties, most of the cruelties, inflicted in secret, are suffered in silence; most of the murders, done by slow degrees, escape the notice of the judicial authorities. To hurt a stranger once on the street brings a drunkard into trouble; but he may hurt his own flesh and blood a hundred times at home, and hear no reproof, except the sighs of the helpless sufferers. When the fool kills a companion outright at once, with a knife or an axe, the law lays its strong hand upon him: but although, by blows, and nakedness, and hunger, he wear out by inches the life of his wife and little ones, he escapes with impunity. From personal observation, within my own sphere, and the testimony of others similarly situated beyond it, I know that a great amount of crime in this form is left unpunished, unnoticed.

I have entered the house of a labouring man, at his own earnest request, and found in it besides himself an ill-clad wife and a sick daughter. On making inquiry regarding the girl's health, I have heard the wife and mother, in tones that had long lost all their softness, declare, " She is dying, and there," pointing to her husband, " *there* is her murderer." He made no effort to deny the charge, or even palliate his guilt, for he was sober and repentant at the moment. The appearance of the man, the house, the child, corroborated, by unmistakable symptoms, the woman's strong indictment. It was true: the daughter was dying, and the father was her murderer. But, fool though he was, he did not hate his child; he did not desire her death. When he was " in his folly," he treated her so as to waste her life away; and he returned to his folly as often as he earned a few pence with which he might purchase spirits in the nearest public-house. By long habit, and in consequence of the permanent effect which frequent inebriation had left upon his brain, he could not, or (what as to its effects on others is practically equivalent) would not refrain. Given a shilling in that man's hand, and a public-house within reach, and his intoxication follows as surely as any of the sequences of nature. It has done so for many years. All the neighbourhood knows it. Murder of the worst kind is done in that house in open daylight, and in sight of all. Murder is so done in many thousand houses—we say not homes—of this our beloved land, and, provided it be done slowly and without much noise, we abandon the victims to their fate, and permit the murderers to go free.

It is only "in his folly" that even the fool is more dangerous to society than a wild bear would be. Comparatively few of these outrages would be committed if the perpetrators did not destroy their judgment and inflame their passions by drink. It is demonstrable that the guilt of the resulting crime lies mainly in the inebriation from which it sprung. If the fit pass off without any act of violence, no thanks to the man who voluntarily deprived himself of reason for a time, and so exposed his neighbour's life as well as his own to serious risk. Every man who makes himself drunk, thereby places the limb and life of his neighbour in danger; to do so is unjust and injurious: it is a crime against society, and should, like other crimes, be restrained by punishment.

Morally and economically this nation suffers much from the lightness with which the act or habit of intoxication is viewed and treated, both by those who commit it and those who look on. In the public opinion it seems scarcely to be regarded either as a sin or a crime. Even where it is so regarded, the impression is trivial, and the prevailing tendency is either to palliate the guilt of the deed, or make mirth of it as innocent. When the crime of murder is committed by a drunk man, we would not remove any of the guilt from the perpetrator, but we would lay a large proportion of it on the act by which he bereft himself of reason. A man drinks all the evening, quarrels with his comrade at midnight, and in the quarrel sheds that comrade's blood. Although he was "in his folly," and scarcely knew what he did when he dealt the blow, we admit no palliation,—we hold him responsible to the full before God and before man. The guilt lies on the man who, being sober and intelligent, made himself drunk and unintelligent. He is guilty not merely of the indiscretion of taking too much drink, but of shedding his brother's blood. The deprivation of reason by his own hand was the guilty act, and the guilt of murder lay in it, as the tree within the seed. The crime that followed, in as far as the controlling reason was actually in abeyance, was the unconscious consequence of an act already done. A Guy Fawkes might fire a train calculated to creep along the ground in silence for an hour before it should produce an explosion; that train might explode a mine, over which stood, innocent and unconscious, a thousand men; he who lighted it might be at a distance,— might die and be in eternity before the explosion, but, notwithstanding, he was guilty of the blood of all these; and the blood of all these would ooze through the earth, and trickle into the pit, and find him out in "his own place," to be a make-weight in his doom. In the act of drinking to excess a man fires the match: for anything he knows the other end of that match may be dipt in murder; and when it is fired it will run its course: he cannot extinguish it.

We all abhor the deeds of cruelty which the "fool in his folly" so frequently commits; but, alas! we have not all an adequate estimate of the guilt attaching to the man at the moment and in the act of entering into his folly. Public abhorrence and indignation should be stirred up and directed upon the act whereby a man turns himself into a bear bereaved of her whelps, and not reserve themselves until it be ascertained how many children the ferocious animal has torn limb from limb.

I shall record here, for the reader's benefit, the leading features of one case. I know it well, and shall tell it truly. A young man, now the only son of a widow, the only brother of a virtuous sister, began active life with the best opportunities and the fairest prospects. In the social circle he contracted habits of intemperance, in the usual way. By degrees he drank himself into delirium tremens. The disease returned so frequently, and with such violence, that it became necessary to place him under restraint. When his mother and sister, after bearing long, were at length worn out, a warrant of lunacy was obtained at the moment when he was "in his folly," and the fool was confined in the lunatic asylum. There he got no whisky, and, in consequence, long before his term had expired, he was in his right mind again. At the expiry of the three months he was dismissed,—for there is no law by which his confinement could be prolonged. He soon drank himself back into madness. Another warrant followed, and another period of confinement. Again came a cure in the asylum and a consequent dismissal. Whenever his senses return, the law lets him loose; and whenever he is loose, he drinks away his senses. I have lost reckoning of the times, but for many years that young man's life has passed in regular alternations of madness produced by drink, and sanity produced by compulsory abstinence. He lives his alternate quarters at home and in the madhouse.

What has this youth done for his mother in her age and widowhood? He has lain a mountain of lead on her heart. Her burden would be comparatively light, if her only son were in his grave. He debased himself by his own free will at first, but he cannot now work his own cure. His softened brain and scorched stomach draw in strong drink as a dry sponge draws in water. He is in the grasp of a disease which is incurable, except by abstinence from the stimulant; and if the stimulant is within his reach he will not abstain.

I have heard of a torture invented by the Inquisition which correctly shadows that widow's suffering. The victim is laid on her back, and bound to a table, with her breast bared. A huge pendulum, fastened in the lofty ceiling, is set in motion over her. Silently, heavily, slowly, it swings from side to side of the gloomy chamber, right over the victim's breast. A sharp blade protrudes downward from the bulb below, and above, the machine is so constructed that each vibration lengthens the rod by a hair's-breadth. As the eyes of the sufferer become accustomed to the dim light of the prison, she observes the quivering glance of the polished blade as it is swinging past. Nearer it comes, and nearer to her bosom, tortured already before it is touched. At length the knife's point grazes the skin. By the law of nature, the pendulum continues pitilessly to wag to and fro, tearing deeper and deeper at each vibration, till at last it lets out the heart's blood, and sets the prisoner free.

That widow is so bound; that widow's breast is so torn. Her only son is the horrid engine, set in motion by possessing demons, and playing with helpless and awful regularity over her. His alternate movements are slowly cut-cutting into his mother's heart. Swinging obedient to that overmastering lust, he is tearing out her life by inches, heedless and heartless as the iron rod and bulb that wagged in the inquisitor's dungeon.

Thus the "fool in his folly" is tearing the flesh of the mother that bore him, more cruelly than a bereaved she-bear would, and the nation stands by indifferent or helpless, able neither to invent a cure nor to inflict a punishment.

I am witness of many murders, slow but sure. Some of the victims have broken limbs, and many have broken hearts. One class live on the wounds and bruises of another, while the majority of the public pursue their own business, caring for none of these things. I am weary of witnessing the triple wrong—the tortures of the writhing victims, the wild-bear ferocity of fools in their folly, and the culpable indifference of the world. "Arise and depart; for this is not your rest, because it is polluted." "A rest remaineth for the people of God." "They shall not hurt nor destroy in all my holy mountain." Those who have sailed aloft on the atmosphere, as ships sail on the sea, tell us that the upper side of the darkest thunder-cloud which threatens the earth, is like a vale of paradise basking in the sunlight. Thus, while the proclamation, "Drunkards shall not inherit the kingdom of God," is, in its aspect earthward, a terror from the Lord to alarm the guilty; it is, in its aspect upward, a consoling promise to the heirs that their home in heaven will not be disturbed by those wild bears that terrified or tore them in the house of their pilgrimage. When the Lord, and they who waited for him, had, in symbol, entered into the eternal rest, "the door was shut." The clang of the shutting door resounds in both directions, a terror, indeed, to those that are without, but a thrill of joy unspeakable through all who are within. "Nothing shall enter that defileth."

Friendship
(Proverbs 17:17; 18:24)

"A friend loveth at all times, and a brother is born for adversity."
"A man that hath friends must shew himself friendly: and there is a friend that sticketh
closer than a brother."

MUCH has been said and sung about friendship among
men. Even the broken fragments of it that remain
now on earth are sweet to weary wayfarers. The
glimpses of it which we get in life are like those little isolated
pools which stand in the deeper portions of a water-course in
summer, when the spring-head has failed, and the stream has
ceased to flow. Some broken bits of heaven are mirrored on
their surface, when all around is dull and earthy. The burning
eye gets some relief when it rests upon them; and the parched
lips are refreshed by the water, such as it is, which they still
contain. To creatures who are "but for a season," and have
never known the fresh, full flow of the living stream, these little
pools seem very pure, and cool, and deep. These, accordingly,
have become the theme of earth's most joyful songs. Here in
the desert they deserve all the praise that they get. We shall
not lose sight of these little pools until the river flows full again.
They will continue to cheer disciples on their pilgrimage through
the desert, and will not be forgotten until they disappear in the
river which makes glad the City of God. When the redeemed of
the Lord shall enter the kingdom, these remnants of true friendship, which were their rejoicing in the house of their pilgrimage,
will have no glory because of the glory that excelleth. A new
song will be sung about friendship when the new heavens and
the new earth shall appear. Many disappointments in the past
generate fear for the future, and "fear hath torment,"—a torment
which dilutes, if it does not positively imbitter, the joys of an
imperfect love; but perfect love when it comes casteth out fear

and the joy of the Lord from its fountain-head flows forth unimpeded, filling the chosen vessels to the brim.

In the Scriptures we learn where the fountain of true friendship lies, what is its nature, why its flow is impeded now, and when it shall be over all like the waves of the sea.

" A friend loveth at all times." This proverb might be employed, if not positively as a definition of true friendship, at least negatively as a test to detect and expose its counterfeit. Sternly applied, it would diminish the crowd of fair-weather friends that flutter round the prosperous, as much as the proclamation permitting cowards to return, thinned the ranks of Gideon's army when the foe was near. Love is a holy thing. It comes from heaven, and, according to the measure of its prevalence, changes the face of the world, and turns its desert into a garden. Men who are strangers to its nature frequently appropriate its good name. We flatter ourselves that we are loving, when we are merely selfish.

You love, and love much. You are distinctly sensible of that blessed emotion circulating, and circulating in great volume, through your being. It is directed upon certain objects, now one and now another. Here is a neighbour, for example, whom you love. Both according to the definitions of the Bible, and in the estimation of the world, he is worthy. Surely then your emotion is pure on both sides; in its character, and its object. Nay; the conclusion is too hastily drawn. A number of mirrors are set round a little child. He looks into them all in turn, and admires each. What then? does he think the mirrors beautiful? No; he sees and admires only himself, although, in his childishness, he is not aware that the beauty which draws him is all his own.

Alas! we often use our friends only as looking-glasses to see ourselves in. We imagine that we are loving them because we look towards them while we love; but it is the reflection of our own interest, all the time, that leads us captive. Apply this proverb to detect the spuriousness of such love ; the shining counterfeit grows black when you touch it with the word. A friend loveth at all times, and in all places. Love, while it remains essentially the same, appears tenfold more loving when its object has fallen from prosperity into poverty; as a lamp, lighted during the day, shines much more brightly when the darkness comes. Many will court you while you have much to give; when you need to receive, the number of your friends will be diminished, but their quality will be improved. Your misfortune, like a blast of wind upon the thrashed corn, will drive the chaff away, but the wheat will remain where it was. How very sweet sometimes is the human friendship that remains when sore adversity has sifted it!

Of the many steamers that ply with passengers on the Clyde through all the sunny summer, one only continues its course on the Lord's day. As no business is done on that day, the voyage is emphatically a pleasure-trip, and doubtless there are many professions of brotherhood and fellow-feeling among the joyous company. In the narrow river near Glasgow, when the air was bright with sunlight and the water's surface like a mirror, one of the passengers, who, finding the sail not sufficient of itself, had adopted other means to augment his pleasure, lost his balance and fell overboard. Although he struggled for some time on the surface, the poor man sank and perished, ere his friends, all dry and comfortable, reached, by a circuitous route, the fatal spot. If there had been one in all the crowd with the nerve of a man, not to say the love of a Christian in his heart, he would have leaped into that still water and held his brother up a few moments until help had come from gathering hundreds. While our Father in heaven reigns over all, we often need help from a brother's hand; and I pray that when I am in danger I may be surrounded by other friends than a company of Sabbath pleasure-seekers. I would not count much either on the pith of their arm or the compassion of their heart. That species of pleasure takes the manliness out of a man, and forces native selfishness up to its fullest growth.

Man in his weakness needs a steady friend, and God in his wisdom has provided one in the constitution of nature. Not intrusting all to acquired friendship, he has given us some as a birthright inheritance. For the day of their adversity a brother is born to many who would not have been able to win one. It is at once a glory to God in the highest and a sweet solace to afflicted men, when a brother or a sister, under the secret and steady impulses of nature, bears and does for the distressed what no other friend, however loving, could be expected to bear or do. How foolish for themselves are those who lightly snap those bonds asunder, or touch them oft with corrosive drops of contention! One who is born your brother is best fitted to be your friend in trouble, if unnatural strife has not rent asunder those whom their Maker intended to be of one spirit. In visiting the sick I am often constrained to exclaim in glad wonder, What hath the Lord wrought! when I see the friendships of nature supplying a ministry in sickness for the poor, such in tenderness and patience as the wealth of a world could not buy for the rich.

"There is a friend that sticketh closer than a brother." He must be a fast friend indeed; for a brother, if nature's affections have been cherished, lies close in, and keeps a steady hold. I know how closely a brother sticks, for I have been warmed and strengthened by the grasp; and have shivered as if alone in a wintry world when it slackened in death, and dropped away. I know by tasting, both the worth and the want of a brother's love. It seemed the chief earthly joy of my youth. Perhaps the stream flowed more strongly because it was all confined within one channel, and that a narrow one; for I had only one brother, and him I had not long. We grew up together in childhood, and at the softest period of life were run into one by kindred tastes inherited, and common objects pursued. While we were passing together through the tender but decisive stage of youth, he was smitten by his death-disease, and I was spared in health. One was taken, and another left: not so taken, however, or so left, as to make a sudden separation; for the malady besieged the tower of his strength three full years and a half ere its gates were opened and the life given up. Born of the Spirit, and having his new life hid with Christ in God, he was, and felt himself to be, beyond the reach of that enemy who was closing round the body, and cutting off its resources. As the outward man was perishing, the inward man, both as to intellect and faith, was renewed day by day. Through his weakness and my strength, we were let into each other much more deeply than if both had been feeble, or both robust. It was something analogous to that other work of God in his creatures—woman's weakness and man's strength, so arranged with a view to completer union. Such a fusion, whether accomplished by a general law or a special providence, is good for man.　We did stick closely together, till death divided us.　His pale brow was in my hands when its aching ceased. His grave in the village churchyard became a place of pilgrimage. The memory of that brother cleaving to my soul, after he had gone to rest, was God's own hand holding me back from enticing vanities, at the period of their greatest power, that, undistracted by the tumult of the world, I might better hear his own paternal voice.　Oh! when hindering things are taken out of the way of God's work, a brother lies very close to a brother!　He who comes closer must be no common friend.

And yet there is a Friend that comes closer than a brother.　I do not venture to give a judgment here on critical grounds, whether the text contains a specific and intentional prophecy regarding the Son of Man, the Saviour.　But this is not necessary. We reach the same object more surely in another way.　The affirmation in the text is, that close though a brother be, there is a friend that comes closer still.　It is the idea of a friendship more perfect, fitting more kindly into our necessities, and bearing more patiently with our weakness, than the instinctive love of a brother by birth.　From God's hand-work in nature a very tender and very strong friendship proceeds: from his covenant of mercy comes a friendship tenderer and stronger still.　Now, although in some sense the conception is embodied in the communion of saints, its full realization is only found in the love wherewith Christ loves his own.　When the Word became flesh, and dwelt among us, man found a Friend who could come closer to his heart than any brother.　The precious germ which Solomon's words infold, bore its fully ripened fruit only when He who is bone of our bone and flesh of our flesh gave himself, the Just for the unjust.　Thus, by a surer process than verbal criticism, we are conducted to the man Christ Jesus, as at once the brother born for our adversity, and the Friend that sticketh closer than a brother.　The brother and the friend are, through the goodness of God, with more or less of imperfection, often found among our fellows; but they are complete only in Him who is the fellow of the Almighty.　Whoever would prosecute the twin ideas to their utmost issue, must pass out through humanity, and settle down in "God with us" beyond.

In the day of your deepest adversity, even a born brother must let go his hold. That extremity is the opportunity of your better Friend. His promise, " Lo, I am with you alway," entering into your sinking spirit, kindles the light of life in its darkness, and your confiding answer is, " I will not fear, for thou art with me."

" A man that hath friends must show himself friendly." It is another example of the pervading law, action and reaction are equal. When love is received, it is reciprocated. It is one of the most repulsive features of fallen humanity, to take selfishly material good from another, and refuse to show kindness to a neighbour when an opportunity occurs. This phase of selfishness, pictured by the Lord's own lips, is held up for our reprobation in the Bible (Matt. xviii. 26–30). A man in his distress asked and obtained mercy on a large scale from his master, and then harshly refused a little grace, when a fellow-servant humbly besought it at his hands. The man had a friend, and yet would not show himself friendly.

Our best friendship is due to our best Friend. He deserves it and desires it. The heart of the man Christ Jesus yearns for the reciprocated love of saved men, and grieves when it is not given. " Where are the nine ? " he exclaimed with a sigh, when one only of the cleansed lepers came back to praise him. Who shall measure the strength of that longing for the friendship of his friends which drew from his loving heart the triple appeal, " Simon, son of Jonas, lovest thou me ? "

Recall now the idea with which our exercise opened, that we may gather another lesson from it in the close. The separated pools remaining in the deeper places of the river's bed, after the river has dried up from its source, become narrower, and shallower, and muddier as the season advances. If no new supply come down, they will soon be dry. Even before they are wholly dry, the water is hot and stagnant, unsatisfying and repulsive ; and after the water has exhaled, the place where it lay is noisome. Such are friendships of the earth, if they be of the earth merely. As life draws onward to age, one and another will fail you. The breadth and depth of your pool will diminish apace, as secretly and insensibly, but as surely, as a lake is reduced in bulk by evaporation, when the sources of its supply have failed. When friends become fewer, you have not the power which you possessed in youth, of forming new intimacies to supply the place of the old.

Not only does the absolute quantity of available friendship gradu ally decrease; your capability of enjoying the remainder decreases too. Disappointments in the course of life do more to make us distrustful than success to render us confiding. Friends grow fewer, and feebler grows your trust in friends. It is a desolate thing to grow old in this world, and have none but the world and the worldly to lean upon in the day of need. The last little pool that lay in nature's deepest place has vanished like the rest, and the weary has not a drop of consolation now to cool his tongue! He has always been without God in the world, and now he is without man. The nether springs are dry, and the upper springs he never knew. Woe is me for the friendless!

But for those who are in faith's union with the Fountainhead another experience is prepared. To them that look for Him he shall appear. In due season a stream will flow in the desert. The little pools in the river-bed of their life will be lost too; not by a drying up, but by an overflowing. In the spring-time of youth close with the sinners' Friend, and he will not leave you comfort less when age draws on.

> "One there is above all others:
>   Oh, how he loves!
> His is love beyond a brother's:
>   Oh, how he loves!
>
> "Earthly friends may pain and grieve thee,—
> One day kind, the next day leave thee;
> But this Friend will ne'er deceive thee:
>   Oh, how he loves!"

The Bias on the Side of Self

(Proverbs 18:17)

" He that is first in his own cause seemeth just ; but his neighbour cometh and searcheth him."

THIS proverb touches human life at many points, and human beings feel it touching them. It accords with common experience ; it is much noticed, and often quoted ; evidence of its truth flashes upon us from the contacts and conflicts of life at every turn. This word falling from heaven on the busy life of men, is echoed back from every quarter in a universal acknowledgment of its justness.

It is true to nature—nature fallen and distorted. It does not apply to humanity in innocence : it has no bearing on the new nature in a converted man. It does not describe the condition which the unfallen possessed, which the regenerated aim at, which the glorified have regained. This Scripture reveals a crook in the creature that God made upright. There is a bias in the heart, the fountain of impulse, and the resulting life course turns deceitfully aside. Self-love is the twist in the heart within, and self-interest is the side to which the variation from righteousness steadily tends.

" He that is first in his own cause seemeth just." The word refers to the most common form of contention in the world. A man's interest is touched by the word or deed of another : forthwith he persuades himself that what is against his own wish is also against righteousness, and argues accordingly. He states his own case ; but he leans over to one side, and sees everything in a distorted form. Matters on his own side are magnified : matters that are against himself are overlooked. Viewing the whole case from this position and in this attitude, he gives forth a representation of it, as it appears to his eye ; but the representation is false. His conduct is both a sin and a blunder ; it offends God, and will

not deceive men. We are not now dealing with a case of deliberate intentional falsehood : we are not describing the vulgar vice
of making and telling a lie : we speak of a sin that is much more
covert, and to some classes, on that account, much more dangerous.
There are amongst us lying lips and brazen faces not a few. There
are persons who invent a new lie to clear each turn of a tortuous
course, apparently with as much readiness and ease as you would
throw your arms out now to this side and now to that, to keep
yourself from stumbling in a rugged path. There are others who,
in a sense, speak the truth with their lips, and yet have lies hidden
in their hearts. The heart makes the lie, deceiving first the man
himself, and thereafter his neighbours. The bent is in the mould
where the thought is first cast in embryo, and everything that
comes forth is crooked.

In my early childhood—infancy I might almost say—a fact regarding the relations of matter came under my observation, which
I now see has its analogue in the moral law. An industrious old
man, by trade a mason, was engaged to build a certain piece of
wall at so much per yard. He came at the appointed time, laid
the foundation according to the specifications, and proceeded with
his building, course upon course, according to the approved
method of his craft. When the work had advanced several feet
above the ground, a younger man, with a steadier hand and a
brighter eye, came to assist the elder operator. Casting his eye
along the work, as he laid his tools on the ground and adjusted
his apron, he detected a defect, and instantly called out to his
senior partner that the wall was not plumb. " It must be
plumb," rejoined the builder, somewhat piqued, " for I have laid
every stone by the plumb-rule." Suiting the action to the word
he grasped the rule, laid it along his work, and triumphantly
pointed to the lead vibrating and settling down precisely on the
cut that marks the middle. Sure enough the wall was according
to the rule, and yet the wall was not plumb. The rule was
examined, and the discovery made that the old man, with his defective eye-sight, had drawn the cord through the wrong slit at
the top of the instrument, and then from some cause which I cannot explain, using only one side of it, had never detected his mistake. The wall was taken down, and the poor man lost several
days' wages.

It is on some such principle that people err in preparing a representation of their own case. They suspend their plumb, not from the middle, but from one edge of the rule, and that the edge which lies next their own interests. The whole work is vitiated by a bias in the rule which regulates the workman.

This is not a light matter. Perfect truth will be the consummation in heaven, and should be the steady aim on earth. Honesty sufficient to keep you out of prison is one thing, and honesty that will adorn the doctrine of Christ is another. He left us an example, and it is our part to follow his steps. The reproof of this proverb touches not the life of the man Christ Jesus. Guile was not found in his mouth. How calm and truthful is every statement! No one coming after and searching him could find any flaw. The disciples, though they loved and followed him, lingered far behind. Disciples now have abundant room for growth of grace in this direction. On this side there is a large field for progress in conformity to the example of Christ.

What do ye more than others? In the statement of your case, do you permit a selfish desire for victory to turn your tongue aside from the straight line of truth? He who is through Christ an heir of heaven has an interest in being true before God, infinitely greater than in appearing right before men. Why should he neglect the greater and follow the less? There is room for improvement here, and improvement here would tell upon the world. If we lived in heaven and walked with God, our bearing, when we were called upon to plead our own cause, would reveal our home and our company. If the whole tone and strain of our evidence, in a case that touched our own temporal interests, were cast in the pattern that Jesus gave, the world would readily observe the likeness and take knowledge of us that we had been with him. They would own the act as a fruit not indigenous on earth, and conclude that the tree which bore it was the planting of the Lord. In all this he would be glorified.

" His neighbour cometh and searcheth him." If a man can detect exaggerations on one side, and concealments on the other, amounting to untruthfulness in their general effect, it shows that the fear of God was not before the eyes of the witness when he emitted his evidence. To walk with God in the regeneration is the short and sure way to rigid truth in all our intercourse with men. Acquaint yourself with him before you speak, and then let all the world sift your testimony. To make certain that you shall never be put to shame for your words by the searching of a neighbour, submit your heart's thoughts beforehand to the searching of the Lord. In vain would your neighbour scrutinize your testimony, if your God and Saviour had at your invitation searched the germ, while it was a purpose forming within your heart. According to the rural proverb, " The rake need not come after the besom ;" an adversary will find nothing in you, if a more skilful searcher has been there before him.

A Wife

(Proverbs 19:14; 19:13; 21:19)

" Whoso findeth a wife findeth a good thing, and obtaineth favour of the Lord."
"A prudent wife is from the Lord."
"The contentions of a wife are a continual dropping."   " It is better to dwell in the wilderness, than with a contentious and an angry woman."

THESE three portions, scattered promiscuously over several chapters, contain three distinct but connected propositions. The *first* intimates that the marriage relation as the appointment of God, and without particular reference to the character of the persons, is good for man. The *second*, that when a man, upon entering that relation, obtains a wife who is in her individual character a prudent woman, he has obtained a blessing above all price. The *third*, that when the object chosen to occupy a relation so tender and close is personally unworthy, the calamity to the man is great in proportion to the preciousness of the divine institute which has in this case been perverted. The three announcements may be more briefly expressed thus: 1. A wife—the conjugal relation as such—is a good gift of God. 2. When the wife is a good woman, there is a double blessing, in the nature of the relation, and in the character of the person fulfilling it. 3. When the woman's own character is evil, her position as a wife indefinitely augments her power for mischief. Having thus once for all set forth the subjects in their order and relations, I shall not rigidly adhere to the logical arrangement, but permit the illustration in some measure to revert to the miscellaneous form which characterizes the original text.

Had the first text made the boon depend on the personal goodness of the wife, it would have been more easily understood; but the range is wider, and the meaning deeper, as it is. The word declares boldly, and without qualification, that a wife is a gift from God, and good for man. The text which intimates that a prudent wife is from the Lord tells a truth, but it is one of the most obvious of truths; the text which intimates that a wife is a favour from the Lord, without expressly stipulating for her personal character, goes higher up in the history of providence, and deeper into the wisdom of God. His Maker in the beginning said, " It is not good for man to be alone;" and after all the ill that came to him through that weaker vessel, the same word remains as true as ever. Although Satan tempted Eve, woman as she came from God's hand, is the meetest help for man. The catastrophe did not take the Omniscient by surprise; the event did not change his view.

" From the beginning God made man male and female." He knows what is in man whom he made. Of design he made neither complete. He left a want in each, that the two might coalesce into one—one flesh and one spirit. Woman, who becomes the filling up of the vacuum in man, balancing his defects, absorbing the excesses of his cares, and reduplicating his joys,—woman, by her constitution and her place, is a good thing, and should be devoutly sought as well as devoutly acknowledged, a favour from the Lord.

The Creator of man gives peculiar honour to this ordinance. He, has framed the world in accordance with it. The designed imperfectness of an individual runs through all life, vegetable as well as animal; and the same type meets us on every hand, even in inanimate nature. Duality is necessary to completeness. This feature runs down from units to fractions,—from persons to the subordinate members of which they consist. You meet it in the hands, eyes, ears, of your own body. The principle that two are better than one lies very deep, and spreads very widely in the works of God. Having set it thus in nature, he solemnly appoints it in his word, and guards it in his providence. When he made man in his own image, he gave great prominence to this principle by making him at first alone, and thereafter finishing the incompleted work. He defended the integrity of the institution in thunder from Sinai, and engraved it in the tables of stone. He chose it as the body in which his own spiritual relation to ransomed Israel might become, as it were, visible: " Thy Maker is thy husband." And when Christ came to make all things new, he expressly took the marriage union under his own protection; certified it as an original appointment of God for man; purged it of the corruptions wherewith Jewish tradition had overlaid it; and gave it over to his church in such terms, that his apostles ever after delighted to call himself the Bridegroom, and his people the bride prepared for his coming.

This union is greatly honoured by God, and much dishonoured by man. We should recognise this as one great cause of his controversy with us, when we lament the judgments that fall on the nation and the deadness that lies on the church. In treating lightly what he counts so grave, in defiling that which he desires to keep holy as a fitting emblem of Christ's union to the saved, the nation is provoking the Most High to jealousy, and suffering retribution, in the uneasy motion or abrupt rending of the various joints which bind society together. The extent to which this holy institution is profaned and disregarded, both in high places and low, is one of the abominations done in the land, for which those who seek a revival should sigh and cry.

Here is a presumptuous abuse which provokes the Lord to anger, and torments the community by infusing rottenness into its bones:—Among certain classes marriage is deliberately contemplated beforehand, and in the fulness of an evil time deliberately resorted to, as a cure to save a libertine in the last resort. In some quarters it seems to be scarcely regretted that a youth with large prospects should run riot in early manhood, seeing he has marriage to fall back upon when he is wearied with his own ways. The slight and measured reprobation of this course, not to speak of the positive approval, is a daring defiance of the Holy One. Vengeance is exacted by the awful machinery of his providential laws. The shallow trick is not successful. Man cannot cheat the Omniscient. The barbs of punishment are bedded in the crime, and infallibly run through the criminal. When a young man, deceived it may be, and encouraged by the opinion of those who surround him, throws the reins on the neck of his passion, he flatters himself that he has a good heart,—that at any moment, ere matters go too far, he has it in his power to marry, reform, and enjoy the staid, sober pleasures of wedded life. He flatters himself, indeed! He is laying a lying unction to his soul. Licentiousness takes out of a human heart the softness necessary to complete conjugal union. Although the wounds which a libertine's soul has ignobly gotten in the house of the strange woman may be healed, through mercy, to the saving of the soul's life, their effects never can be removed until the body crumble into dust. There is a hardness which for ever prevents the peculiar fusion of nature implied in two becoming one flesh. Consciousness of antecedent impureness, and mutual suspicion thereby generated, constitute an effectual bar to the full fruition of the good ordinance of God. They who have dared the *knowledge of evil*, are inexorably driven from the garden, and must maintain an uneasy conflict against wild beasts without and thistles within, all their days. You cannot enjoy the pleasures of sin, and when these have failed, turn round and take the pleasures which our Father in heaven has provided for the pure. A treaty of alliance you may have, like those which potentates frame to regulate the intercourse of nations; or a partnership, like that which constitutes a mercantile firm; but marriage, as God appointed it at creation, and Christ described it,—marriage you cannot have, if you profanely grasp it as a convenience to stop your own excesses and decently cover the disgrace which they have entailed. No; the real coalescence of two into one, which doubles the joys and divides the sorrows of life, is an inner Eden, from which the weary debauchee is debarred for ever, as if by an angel with a flaming sword.

" It is better to dwell in the wilderness, than with a contentious and an angry woman." Though the bond in itself be a blessing, an unequal yoke only galls the wearers. Every one has known some pair chained together by human laws, where the hearts' union has either never existed or been rent asunder. Two ships at sea are bound to each other by strong short chains. As long as the sea remains perfectly calm, all may be well with both; though they do each other no good, they may not inflict much evil. But the sea never rests long, and seldom rests at all. Woe to these two ships when the waves begin to roll ! There are two conditions in which they might be safe. If they were either brought more closely together, or more widely separated, it might yet be well with them. If they were from stem to stern rivetted into one, or if the chain were broken, and the two left to follow independently their several courses, there would be no further cause of anxiety on their account. If they are so united that they shall move as one body, they are safe; if they move far apart they are safe. The worst possible position is to be chained to-gether, and yet have separate and independent motion in the waves. They will rasp each other's sides off, and tear open each other's heart, and go down together.

See in this glass the different kinds of conjugal union which obtain in actual life, and the corresponding consequences. Let it be a real marriage,—let the two be no longer twain, but one flesh; and then, though the united pair may experience many ups and downs in the troubled sea of life, they will rise and fall together. Common troubles will never make them tear each other. The two in one will present a broader surface to the sea, and stand more steady when it rages. But when the two are not one— when the mysterious cement has broken, or never taken band— when they obey separate impulses and point in different directions, while yet they are tied together by a legal contract, their condi-tion is dreadful. How many wretched pairs, separate and yet bound, are tossing on the troubled sea of time ! It is now a racking check when the binding chain is suddenly tightened, and now a rasping of their sides when they come together. Such are the alternations of married life where hearts are divorced and legal bonds still hold fast. Now and then a faint shriek is heard through the whistling winds ; and when the spectators look in that direction, one of the labouring vessels has disappeared. "To him that hath shall be given, and he shall have abundance ; but from him that hath not shall be taken even that which he hath." This awful law is ever at hand to defend or avenge God's primeval institute. As becomes a great King, the rewards are great on the one side, the sanctions heavy on the other.

"The contentions of a wife are a continual dropping." Conten-tions are not pleasant in any circumstances, but the closeness of the parties, whether in moral relation or physical position, inde-finitely augments the discomfort. A man may pass through a sharp contention in the hall of legislation or the mart of commerce, and an hour afterwards mingle with an unburdened heart in the sports of his children. The conflicts which are waged abroad may be left behind you when you go home, if love unmixed be waiting there to receive you. But a man soon becomes distracted if he is tossed like a shuttlecock from the wearing cares of business to the biting strifes of home, and from the biting strifes of home back to the wearing cares of business. A quarrel between a man and his wife is, as to the torment which it inflicts, the nearest thing to a quarrel between the man and his own conscience. Next after himself, she lies closest to him, and the pain of a disagreement is proportioned accordingly. Specifically, this contention is a continual dropping. Let a wife note well that the resulting mischief does not depend on the degree of furiousness which may characterize the conflict. It depends on length rather than loudness. A perennial drop may do more to drive a man to extremities than a sudden flood. A little for ever is more terrible to the imagination than a great outpouring at once.

" A continual dropping " is said to have been one of the engines which the wit of man contrived when it was put upon the stretch for the means of torturing his fellows. The victim was so placed that a drop of water continued to fall at regular intervals on his naked head. With length of time, and no hope of relief, the agony becomes excruciating, and either the patient's reason or his life gives way. Let a wife, or a husband, beware. Don't make home miserable by gloomy looks and taunting discontented words. Don't deceive yourself with the plea that your complaints were never immoderate : if your moderate complaints never cease, they will eat through a man's life at last. Although no such disturbance should ever occur as would demand the presence of the police, or give you among your neighbours the character of a scold, the patience of a husband may be utterly worn out. Though words of discontent should never rise into the violence of a passion—although they should never be heavier than drops of water—yet, if they continue drop, drop, dropping, so that he sees no prospect of an end, his heart will either be hardened into indifference or broken into despair. Love cannot be sustained by dislike, administered in moderate quantities ; if it do not get positive, manifest, gleaming love to live upon, it will die.

It is the testimony of all who have in person probed the sores of society, that unfeeling, spendthrift husbands, and sullen, slovenly wives, are to a large extent correlatives. In a very great number of cases, the two are found together in the same dwelling. In all these, it is further manifest that the two act reciprocally on each other as cause and effect,—a drunken husband making a sullen wife, and a sullen wife making a drunken husband. How often the circulating train of connected evils is set in motion at first by the fault of the husband, and how often by the fault of the wife, cannot be precisely ascertained. One may, however, infer that the predominance of the evil lies on the side where there is predominance of power. But making all due allowance on this side, it remains sure and obvious, that the contentions of a woman, falling like water-drops on her husband's head, cause the drunkenness in many cases, and aggravate it in all. In illustration of another text, I have distinctly intimated, that if we had a greater number of sober husbands we would have a greater number of smiling wives : here, desiring to divide the word as one who must give an account, I say, on the other hand, if there were a greater number of smiling wives, there would be a greater number of sober husbands.

"Only in the Lord" (1 Cor. vii. 39), is the apostle's rule on this subject. In view of all the difficulties, it is sufficient, and it alone.

If these suggestions have been cast mainly in a negative rather than a positive form—if, like the Decalogue itself, their prevalent aspect be, "Thou shalt not"—there is a cause. Laws are made for the rebellious. The obedient find a great reward in the act of keeping the commandment, and the reproof which is aimed at presumptuous transgressors passes harmlessly over them. I would fain give the encouragement and the warning too; but, where the blessing and the curse lie so near each other, it is difficult to divide them aright. This divinely-appointed union is, in human life, like the busy bee returning laden home. The sweetest honey and the sharpest sting lie in it both ; and they lie not far apart. But for the honey it has been created, not for the sting : for the honey it lives and labours, not for the sting. The sting is there only to make the honey secure. That which is of the highest value is most sternly guarded. The armed sentinel keeps watch beside the jewelled crown. Every day, and all the day, the honey is gathered and stored and enjoyed : the sting lies idle in its sheath, and, except to ward off or punish violence, is never used at all.

Those who in marriage lawfully seek and enjoy the sweets wherewith God has charged it, complain not of the sting that never touches them. For thieves and robbers it has been planted there, and the honest have no desire to pluck it out.

Anger

(Proverbs 19:11, 19; 20:3)

"The discretion of a man deferreth his anger; and it is his glory to pass over a transgression."

" A man of great wrath shall suffer punishment: for if thou deliver him, yet thou must do it again."

" It is an honour for a man to cease from strife: but every fool will be meddling."

TELL me the specific rebukes that most thickly dot the pages of the Bible, and I will tell you the specific sins that most easily beset mankind. In that glass we may behold our own defilements and dangers. If any vice is often reproved in the word of God, you may be assured it springs prolific in the life of man.

In this book of morals anger is a frequently recurring theme. The repetition is not vain. If the evil did not abound on earth, the reproof of it would not come so oft from heaven. There is much anger springing secretly in human hearts, and its outbursts greatly imbitter the intercourse of life. It disturbs the spirit in which it dwells, and hurts, in its outgo, all who lie within its reach. It is an exceedingly evil and bitter thing. Its presence goes far to make this world a restless sea, and its absence will be a distinguishing feature of the rest that remaineth.

Anger cannot, indeed, be, and in a certain sense ought not to be, cast wholly out of man in the present state. On some occasions we do well to be angry; but in these cases both the nature and the object of the affection should be jealously watched. The only legitimate anger is a holy emotion directed against an unholy thing. Sin, and not our neighbour, must be its object : zeal for righteousness, and not our own pride, must be its distinguishing character. The exercise of anger, although not necessarily sinful, is for us exceedingly difficult and dangerous. It is like fire in the hands of children; although it is possible for them in certain cases to handle it safely and usefully, we know that in point of fact they more frequently do harm with it than good. Accordingly we are accustomed, as a prudential measure, to forbid absolutely its use among the children. If anger in the moral department is like fire in the physical, we, even the best of us, are like little children. Unless we have attained the wisdom and stature of " perfect men in Christ," we cannot take this fire into our bosom without burning thereby ourselves and our neighbours. Thus it comes about, that although anger be not in its own nature and in all cases sinful, the best practical rule of life is to repress it, as if it were. The holy might use it against sin in the world, if the holy were here, but it seems too sharp a weapon for our handling. Let any one who tries to crucify the flesh and to please God, scrutinize his own experience in this matter, and he will find that the less he has felt of anger, the better it has been for the peace of his conscience and the usefulness of his life.

As usual in these laws of God's kingdom, suffering springs from the sin, as the plant from its seed. " A man of great wrath shall suffer punishment," and he shall suffer, although no human tribunal take cognizance of his case. The impetuous tide of passion will listen to no counsel, and submit to no control. Although the flood springs within the man, it carries him away. The progeny, as soon as it is generated, is too strong for its parent. He who this moment produced it, is next moment a helpless captive in its hands. When the frenzy runs high the " man of great wrath" gores right and left, like a wild bull, all who are within his reach ; but, when the frenzy has subsided, he is tormented by a remorse from which the brute is free. More is expected from the man than from the brute, and when no more is gotten, heavy retribution is at hand. The conscience, bent aside by the force of passion, comes back rebounding when that force is spent; and then he who *acted* as a brute, must *suffer* as a man. A man of great wrath, is a man of little happiness. The two main elements of happiness are wanting; for he is seldom at peace either with his neighbour or himself.

There is an ingredient in the retribution still more direct and immediate. The emotion of anger in the mind instantly and violently affects the body in the most vital parts of its organization. Hot cheeks and throbbing temples follow the mysterious spark of passion in the soul, as thunder-peals follow the lightning's flash. In presence of this phenomenon, an unfathomable work of God within our own being, it behoves us to " stand in awe and sin not." When the spirit in man is agitated by anger, it sets the life-blood a-flowing too fast for the safety of its tender channels. By frequent commotions these organs are injured : under great excesses they sometimes break. Thus, even in the organs of the body, impediments are thrown across the path of passion, and the flesh smarts for the spirit's waywardness.

The best practical specific for the treatment of anger against persons is to " defer it." Its nature presses for instant vengeance, and the appetite should be starved. A wise man may indeed experience the heat, but he will do nothing till he cools again. When your clothes outside are on fire you wrap yourself in a blanket, if you can, and so smother the flame : in like manner, when your heart within has caught the fire of anger, your first business is to get the flame extinguished. Thereafter you will be in a better position to form a righteous judgment, and follow a safe course.

" To pass over a transgression" is a man's " glory." This is like the doctrine of Jesus, but not like the manners of the world. It is a note in unison with the sermon on the mount, and at variance therefore with most of our modern codes of honour. It has often been remarked that the Bible proves itself divine by the knowledge of man which it displays; but perhaps its opposition to the main currents of a human heart is as clear a mark of its heavenly origin as its discovery of what these currents are. The vessel which moves up the strong stream of men's desires does not get from that stream its motive impulse : the breath of heaven gives it direction and urges it on. The best law on that subject which springs on earth makes it a man's glory to obtain satisfaction, and counts it his disgrace to pass an injury unavenged. We may discover here how little civilization by itself can do for man. The rule regarding injuries which prevailed throughout Europe in the generation now passing away coincides precisely with the sentiment of savage tribes. The principle of the duel reigned so imperiously till of late, in military and semi-military circles, that the man who dared to pass over an injury was, by a very vulgar species of persecution, driven from his post and his profession. This sentiment, which happily is passing away in our day neither marked

the Christian nor made the gentleman. The same sentiment prevailed among the Highland clans of Scotland before the Bible
reached their hearts, or roads led soldiers and sheriffs to their
fastnesses. The most savage communities and the most refined
stood, in the matter of the duel, nearly on the same level, and
both were opposed alike to Scripture and Reason. "Looking
unto Jesus" is, after all, the grand specific for anger in both its
aspects, as a sin and as a suffering. Its dangerous and tormenting
fire, when it is kindled in a human breast, may be extinguished
best by letting in upon it the love wherewith he loved us. Let
Faith arise and make haste and open the doors of an angry
heart to the compassions which flow in Christ crucified; the incipient tumult will be quenched like a spark beneath a flowing
stream. If you abide in him, sinful anger will be kept or cast out,
and that which remains, being like his own, will neither trouble
you nor hurt a brother.

A Poor Man is Better Than a Liar
(Proverbs 19:22)

"A poor man is better than a liar."

THE imperial standard of weights and measures has been sent by the King into the market-place of human life, where men are busy cheating themselves and each other. Many of these merchantmen, guided by a false standard, have all their days been accustomed to call evil good and good evil. When the balance is set up by royal authority, and the proclamation issued that all transactions must be tested thereby, swindlers are dismayed and honest men are glad. Such is the word of Truth when it touches the transactions of men.

Although society has, in many important aspects, advanced in these later times, it is our wisdom to cast former attainments behind us, and press on for more. Public opinion greatly needs to be elevated and rectified in its judgment of men and things. Society is like a house after an earthquake. Everything is squeezed out of its place. No angle remains square ; every pillar is leaning ; all is awry. The whirling world of human intercourse is out of joint, and must undergo a grand operation of "reducing" ere its movements become safe or easy.

Although here and there an individual may courageously protest, the great public opinion of the nation practically sets the gentleman high above the man, without waiting to define very precisely what is a gentleman. Exact definitions in this matter would go far to set us right. In misty evenings sharpers get more than their own, and honest men less : day-light would put the parties upon a more equal footing. As long as any sharper, under favour of the thick haze that hangs over the public mind, may, by dint of a good coat, a gold ring, and a stock of impudence, pass himself off as a gentleman, and bear away the substantial benefits attached to that dimly defined rank, the people must lay their account by frequent suffering in purse and person. Every now and then the public is cheated and wounded; but for ourselves, we confess that we do not greatly pity the public. For most of its misfortunes on this side, it has itself to blame. You alighted fawningly on a scare-crow gentleman, guided by his costume and his equipage; and you are now impaled alive on his sharp fleshless arms of sticks and nails. You are suffering, we confess, but we reserve our tears; for if you had looked for a man, you would have found one, and been infolded now in the warm, soft embrace of a brother. A standard has been set up in the market-place to measure the pretences of men withal, and those who will not employ it must take the consequences. According to that standard "a poor man is better than a liar;" if, in the face of that sure index, you despise an honest man because he is poor, and give your confidence to the substance or the semblance of wealth, without respect to righteousness, you deserve no pity when the inevitable retribution comes.

Error in this matter is not confined to any rank: it is as rife in high places as in low. The tendency to trust in quacks seems to be an instinct in human nature, which education and experience can never wholly remove. We sympathize with the denunciations which the sufferers are accustomed to launch against the depredators, and make no effort to shield the delinquents from the blows that fall thick and heavy on their devoted heads. As that part of the business is done heartily, if not very wisely, by the public themselves, we shall step round to the other side, where we can see the castigators, and there endeavour to estimate what share of the blame lies at their own door. "There are two at a bargain;" in every one of these great frauds there are two parties. One alone, however evil in his own nature, could not bring forth any fruits of mischief. Swindlers would not produce much commotion in society if they found no dupes. Rogue and fool are a pair; either is barren if it do not meet its mate. Many are ready to lecture the swindler;—we have a word for the dupe.

"Do not cheat," is a needful and useful injunction in our day; and "Do not be cheated" is another. The trade of the swindler would fail if the raw material were not plentiful and easily wrought. The reckless life of a son is, indeed, a proof of his own wickedness; but it may be also a proof of his father's self-pleasing indulgence. Such is the homage paid to wealth, that any man who, with some degree of adroitness, puts on its trappings, will be followed by a crowd of worshippers. " Covetousness is idolatry." Not without cause is the definition written in that pungent form. Every species of idolatry begets a kind of sottish blindness: the idolaters lose their common sense: they are given over to believe a lie. The wide-spread sufferings that periodically rend the community, at the discovery of full-grown fraud, are the strokes which our own sin inflicts when it finds the sinners out. If the community would cease to value a man by the appearance of his wealth, and judge him according to the standard of the Scriptures, there would be fewer prodigies of dishonesty among us. When we learn practically to honour true men, although they labour for their daily bread, and turn our back upon liars, although they drive their carriages, we shall be less exposed to the depredations of unjust men, and more under the protection of a righteous God.

There is a most refreshing simplicity in the language of Scripture upon these points. This word speaks with authority: it is not tainted with the prevailing adulation of riches. A dishonest man is called a liar, however high his position may be in the city; and the honest poor gets his patent of nobility from the Sovereign's hand. The honest rich are fully as much interested in this reform as the honest poor. Make this short proverb the key-note of our commercial system, and these epidemic panics will disappear. Get this standard acknowledged in the exchange, and the reformation is accomplished. Let it become the fashion to frown on all falsehood, whether spoken or acted—all unrealities, however specious their appearance; let it become the practice, open and uniform, to honour the honest, as far as he is known, however poor he may be; and swindling will die out for want of food. After each catastrophe people go about shaking their heads and wringing their hands, asking, What will become of us, what shall we do? We venture to propose an answer to the inquiry: From the Bible first engrave on your hearts, then translate into your lives, and last emblazon aloft on the pediment of your trade temple, this short and simple legend–

" A POOR MAN IS BETTER THAN A LIAR."

The Deceitfulness of Strong Drink
(Proverbs 20:1)

"Wine is a mocker, strong drink is raging; and whosoever is deceived thereby is not wise."

FROM our point of view it seems strange that in the Proverbs we should not have met with a specific warning regarding the dangers of strong drink until now. The book is eminently practical. It was a book for the times: it rebuked impartially the vices and follies of every class. Covetousness, anger, falsehood, dishonesty—all the more common vices that infest society have, in the preceding portion of the book, been repeatedly exposed and reproved; but hitherto drunkenness has not found a place in the discourses of this ancient Hebrew preacher. I cannot account for this, except by the supposition that the vice was comparatively rare.

If Solomon had lived among us, and written a volume of lessons on life in the same style as the Book of Proverbs, he could not have reached the twentieth chapter without a word on drunkenness. This vice, with its causes and consequences, would have crossed his path in every movement, and forced itself upon his notice every day. It would have claimed a place at an earlier stage, and continued to protrude through almost every paragraph. If such a book in our day and land should proceed as far ere any allusion to strong drink appeared, it would indicate a bias in the writer's mind, and undermine the authority of all his teaching. Ah, it would be a blessed day for our poor beloved fatherland, if it were possible here honestly to compose such a sermon for the times, introducing intemperance at a late period, and saying little about it even then! Although the sin existed and produced its appropriate sorrows in those ancient days and those Eastern lands, it could bear no comparison with our experience, either as to its absolute extent or its proportion to other kindred ills.

In regard to the whole subject of intemperance, it is of the utmost importance to observe and remember the difference between wine-growing countries in ancient times and our own northern land now. The main points of distinction are these two :—1. The chief agent of intoxication among us is not wine at all, but a much more potent draught, which was entirely unknown to antiquity. 2. Even the wines which we use, partly imported from abroad, and partly manufactured at home, are, by admixture of spirits and other materials, much more powerful as intoxicants than the wines ordinarily used of old on the soil which produced them. I adjure all, as they fear God and regard man—as they would save themselves and their brethren, not to overlook these distinctions. I entertain a sorrowful and solemn conviction, which I have often spoken before, and speak now again weeping, that many among us wrest to their own destruction those scriptures which commend the use of wine. To quote these expressions and apply them, without abatement, to the liquors now ordinarily used in this country, is logically incorrect, and practically most dangerous. It is quite true that wines capable of producing intoxication were made and used in those days: it is also quite true that there were both drunkards and isolated acts of inebriation in those days: yet it is neither just nor safe to assume that what is said in the Scriptures of wine is applicable, without restriction, to our intoxicants. As to the measure of the difference, exact knowledge is probably not attainable, and it does not become any one to dogmatize; but if all were induced to acknowledge that there is a difference, and stirred up to seek direction for themselves, from Him who gives the word, as to how far a scriptural commendation of the weaker may be transferred also to the stronger stimulant, our object would be obtained; for they who seek shall find: the meek He will guide.

It would be out of place to agitate here the questions regarding the nature of ancient wines, and the meaning of the several different Hebrew and Greek words indiscriminately translated " wine " in the vernacular version of the Scriptures. I deem it my duty, however, to record at this place the indisputable facts: 1. That some of the wines of antiquity possessed the intoxicating property in various degrees, and some of them did not possess it at all. 2. That several terms, totally distinct from each other in etymology, are in the original Scriptures applied to the manufactured juice of the grape, and, as a general rule, rendered in our version indiscriminately by the term " wine." I take this opportunity further of expressing, sorrowfully and solemnly, my conviction that the questions arising out of these facts in our day, are in themselves as interesting, and in their bearing as important, as any questions of history or philology can possibly be. It may be that the unwise, attempting to solve them, fall into dangerous mistakes, and that the wisest cannot solve them fully; but the questions are grave and worthy of the most serious consideration. To ignore them as impertinent or trifling, and quote from the English Bible a text about ancient Judean wine in support of modern Scottish whisky, is not right, and cannot long be successful.

Avoiding the examination of particulars, as being, on account of its necessary length, unsuitable for these pages, I submit a general proposition, which I believe all my readers will feel to be safe and moderate: *The expressions in Scripture which commend wine and strong drink are* LESS *applicable to the liquors in ordinary use among us, and the expressions which denounce them,* MORE. How much less, and how much more, it is difficult precisely to tell. Each must judge for himself; as for me, I shall, God helping me, endeavour, in the difficulty, to lean to the safer side.

The characteristic of strong drink which this text singles out is its *deceitfulness*. In the illustration of it I shall exclusively regard our own day and our own circumstances. The warnings of Scripture may be intensified manifold when brought to bear on the power of our intoxicants to " mock " their victims. If the fruit of his own vine sometimes chastised the unwary Israelite with whips, the fiery products of our distilleries chastise the nation with scorpions. The little finger of strong drink in modern times is thicker than the loins of its father and representative in Solomon's day. The deceits which our enemy practises are legion; and legion too are the unwise " who are deceived thereby." I shall now enumerate a few of these lying devices.

1. A great quantity of precious food is destroyed in this country that strong drink may be extracted from the rubbish. Barley, the principal material, is a wholesome grain, and if it be unsuited to the taste of the community in the form of food, others might be cultivated in its stead. The fruit of the earth, there-

fore, which is fit for the food of man, is destroyed by man's own hand, to supply him with drink. As to the quantity so consumed, exact statistics are not necessary for our purpose; we can afford to leave a margin wide enough for all contingencies. On an average of ten years the quantity of barley converted into malt in the United Kingdom has been nearly six millions of quarters annually. When you add to this the unmalted grain consumed in the distillation of spirits in Ireland, you have an aggregate sufficient to feed between four and five millions of people throughout the year.

When I see cart-loads of dirty, brown, reeking rubbish passing along the streets, food for pigs and cattle, I gaze with melancholy interest on the repulsive object. The sight, though few would count it poetical, is more suggestive to my imagination than shady groves at noon, or moonlight on a rippling lake. I think of the yellow waving harvest field which reproduced its seed a hundred-fold—of the labourers who tilled it going home with heavy hearts to their half-fed children—of the *amen* that rose from many a cushioned pew when the prayer for daily bread was addressed to "our Father in heaven." If the question, "Where is the bread which I have given you?" should now peal in thunder from the throne, this nation must stand speechless, between those bounteous harvest fields on the one hand, and these steaming, fetid heaps of husks which the swine do eat, on the other.

So much we destroy of that which God commands the earth to bring forth for the life of man; and what do we obtain in return? A large quantity of malt liquors and distilled spirits. And is the gain not equivalent, or nearly equivalent, to the loss, in the material means of supporting life? Here lies another deceit:

2. The curative and strengthening properties of our strong drinks, which are so much vaunted, are in reality next to nothing. We except, of course, the infinitesimal proportion of them that is used as medicine. We speak of the ordinary use of these articles as a beverage by the people. A vague but influential notion is abroad that there is a good deal of nourishment in ale and spirits. The evidence of science is distinct and decisive on the other side; but it is not potential on the mind and conduct of the community. Ardent spirits contain no nourishment at all. If they contribute at any time to the quantity of force exerted by man, it

corresponds not to the corn which you give to your horse, but to the whipping. A master who has hired you only for a day, and desires to make the most of his bargain, may possibly find it his interest to bring more out of your bones and sinews by such a stimulus; but you certainly have no interest in lashing an additional effort out of yourself to-day, and lying in lethargy to-morrow. The ardent spirits put nothing in; whatever therefore they take out, is taken from your body. The inevitable consequence is, permanent feebleness and shortened days. Whatever gain it may be to the master, every atom of exertion drawn forth by the stimulant is a dead loss to the man. As to malt liquors the case is different, but the difference is small. When you go down among infinitesimals the calculation is difficult. Our strong drink is eminently a mocker. It successfully deceives the people as to the quantity and the kind of nourishment which it contains. How many gallons of porter an Englishman must drink ere he get into his stomach a quantity of food equal to a loaf of bread, I do not remember, and I fear readers would be incredulous if the figures were set down. Liebig has a pleasant notion about balancing on the point of a pen-knife, like a pinch of snuff, all the nourishment that the most capacious German swallows with his beer in a day; and it is chemistry that he is giving us, not poetry or wit. He is submitting the results of a scientific analysis. But people don't believe the chemists,—at least not with that kind of belief which compels a man to thwart his own appetite. We believe them when they detect by their analysis a few grains of arsenic in an exhumed body, and on the faith of their evidence we hang a man for murder; but we do not believe them when they tell us how little sustenance and how much poison is in our beer. Why? Because we like our beer. It takes a great deal of evidence to convince us, when our appetite is on the other side. Draymen may be seen in London, belonging to the breweries, living, as it were, at the fountain-head of drink, and showing an imposing bulk of body. If we judge men by the standard applied to fat cattle, they will bear away the prize. But apart from all moral considerations, and looking to the men as machines for doing work, the bulk damages the article. It will not last;—see the tables of mortality. It is not sound; if the skin is scratched, it cannot be healed again. How much better bodies these might have been,—how much better working machines,—if they had eaten as bread the grain which has been destroyed to supply them with porter ! How much tougher bodies—how much brighter souls !

3. Strong drink deceives the nation by the vast amount of revenue that it pours into the public treasury. It is a true and wise economy to tax the articles heavily for behoof of the community, as far and as long as they are sold and used; but it is a false and foolish economy to encourage the consumption of the article for the sake of the revenue which it produces. Drink generates pauperism, and pauperism is costly. Drink generates crime, and crime is costly. If the national appetite for stimulants should suddenly cease, and the stream of taxation which constitutes one-third of the imperial revenue should consequently be dried up, a smaller amount of money, no doubt, would pass through the treasury ; but we would find it easier to pay our way A comfortable balance is a healthier thing for a mercantile firm, or an imperial treasury, than mere magnitude of transactions, where the expenditure is continually threatening to rise above the income. They who are deceived into the belief that strong drink enriches the nation " are not wise."

There is a huge living creature with as many limbs as a Hindu idol, and these limbs intertwined with each other in equally admired confusion. The creature having life must be fed, and being large must have a great deal of food for its sustenance. One day, having got rather short allowance, it was rolling its heavy head among its many limbs, and felt something warm and fleshy. Being hungry, it made an incision with its teeth, laid its lips to the spot, and sucked. Warm blood came freely : the creature sucked its fill, and, gorged, lay down to sleep. Next day it supplemented its short rations in the same way. Every day the creature drank from that opening, and as this rich draught made up about one-third of its whole sustenance, the wonder grew, why it was becoming weaker under the process from day to day. Some one at last bethought him of turning over the animal's intermingled limbs, and found that all this time it had been sucking its own blood ! The discoverer proposed to bandage the spot, and not permit the continuance of the unnatural operation. The financiers cried out, " A third of the animal's sustenance

comes from that opening; if you stop it, he will die!" Behold
the wise politicians who imagine that the body politic would die
of inanition if it were deprived of the revenue which it sucks from
its own veins, in the shape of taxes on intoxicating drinks !

4. In as far as human friendship is, in any case, dependent on
artificial stimulant for the degree of its fervency, it is a worthless
counterfeit. No man who entertains a proper respect for himself
will accept the spurious coin in the interchange of social affections.
There is another sphere on which the deceiver sometimes operates,
—a sphere so high, that I am afraid to follow him thither and
contend with him there. I am in a strait betwixt two. I dare
not speak it out, lest the very mention of it should offend God's
little ones; and I dare not pass it in silence, lest some unwise
brother should stumble into the snare for want of the timely
warning. The priests of Israel were expressly prohibited from
tasting wine or strong drink before they approached the altar
(Lev. x. 9). When the redeemed of the Lord—a spiritual priesthood all—enter into the Holiest through the blood of Christ, no
spark of strange fire should be permitted in any degree to add
intensity to the flame of their emotions.

5. Perhaps, after all, the chief deception practised by strong
drink on the community lies in the silent, stealthy advances
which it makes upon the unsuspecting taster, followed, when the
secret approaches have been carried to a certain point, by the
sure spring and relentless death-gripe of the raging lion who goes
about amongst us seeking whom he may devour. All are not so
deceived into drunkenness: the majority are not so deceived. If
they were, the vessel of the State would soon go down bodily.
Even as it is, the drunkards, a sweltering inert mass of brutalized
humanity, lie so heavy in her hold, that a practised eye may
observe a sickly stagger as she yet boldly breasts the wave. How
came all these into that condition of shame and wretchedness?
Ask these many thousands of mindless, pithless, hopeless, inebri-
rates—ask them one by one; they will all tell, and tell truly, that
they did not intend to sink into that condition, but sank into it
beyond recovery ere they were aware of danger. You are strong;
you feel your footing firm: so did they. "Let him that thinketh
he standeth, take heed lest he fall." This Bible warns you that
wine is a mocker. The warning applies with greatly augmented

force to us. I implore the reader to observe that the caution to the sober, to beware of the deceiving, insnaring power of strong drink, is not the alarm of an enthusiast, but the word of God.

A deceiver is in the midst of us. He has many strongholds in our streets: he has free access to our homes. His victims are many; and his treatment of them is merciless. Like the old serpent, he fastens his chains always by guile, never by violence. His professions are friendly, and his approaches slow. He touches the taste, and pleases it: he is therefore invited to return. Every time he is admitted to the tongue he sends along the nerves to the brain an influence, as secret as the electric current along the wire, and as sure. The effect is distinctly felt each time, but it seems to go off soon: it does not all go off, however. Something remains, invisible, it may be, as the effects of light at first on the photographer's plate, but real, and ready to come out with awful distinctness at a succeeding stage. When the brain is frequently exposed to the comings and goings of these impressions, silent and secret as rays of light penetrating the camera, it acquires imperceptibly the susceptibility which an accident any day may develop into an incurable disease. Considering the power of this deceiver, —considering the number around us who are deceived thereby, —considering the wondrous delicacy and susceptibility of the human brain,—considering that in this life the soul can neither learn nor act except through the brain, as its organ,—considering that strong drink goes by a secret postern direct into the presence-chamber of the soul,—considering the satanic malignity with which it holds the struggling victim,—considering how few of those who have fallen into this pit have ever risen again, and how tenderly God's word warns us not to venture near its slippery brim, —surely it is the part of wisdom to lean hard over to the safer side. Brother! your immortal soul is embodied in flesh. You have in that body only one organ through which the soul can act, either in getting from God or serving him. That organ is refined and delicate beyond the power of words to express. If its eye is dimmed and its feeling blunted, your soul has lost its only avenue of access to the Saviour. As you hope to see God, beware of those mists that cloud the vision of the soul. As you hope to feel a Redeemer's love softly embracing you in a dying hour, beware of those drops that have turned so many hearts into stone.

The Sluggard Shall Come to Want

(Proverbs 20:4)

"The sluggard will not plow by reason of the cold; therefore shall he beg in harvest, and have nothing."

THE reproof of slothfulness often recurs: we may safely infer that it was a besetting sin in the Hebrew commonwealth. It is a vice to which primitive and pastoral communities, other things being equal, are more liable than merchants and artisans. You may expect to find more of it in the Scottish Highlands than on the wharves of Liverpool, or in the mills of Manchester. As a general rule, it is not the weak side of the Anglo-Saxon race; our history and position in the world prove that we possess in large measure the counterpart virtue. Other vices thrive on our busy industry, like parasites upon living creatures; but it cannot be said that we are nationally a slothful people.

Individual instances of sloth, however, occur amongst us; all the more inexcusable because of the industry which abounds. Short and sure is the process by which the sluggard's sin finds the sluggard out. If he does not plough, he cannot reap: if he is idle in the seed-time, he will be hungry in the harvest. The very alphabet of providential retribution is here; the simplest may read the law when it is written in letters so large, and so fully exposed to the light. We submit to the law as inevitable; and wherever reason is even moderately enlightened, we acquiesce in the law as just and good. No man who neglects his field in spring complains that it does nothing for him in autumn: we all know that such the law is, and most of us secretly feel that such it should be.

God's system of government is not to work for man, but to supply him with the means of working for himself. He gives rain from heaven; but if we do not till and sow on earth, our fields will not be fruitful, our hearts will not be glad. He gives seed, but he gives it to the sower.   Riches without limit are stored in His treasuries, but only the hand of the diligent can draw them forth.   No man expects a different arrangement of the providential laws, and no wise man desires it.   It is better for man, as man now is, that he is placed in circumstances to win his bread by the sweat of his brow, than if bread had dropped into his lap from heaven, or sprung spontaneously from the earth.   Our Father has graciously turned the very curse into a blessing: the rod that was lifted in anger to smite the alien, descends as discipline to correct the child.

There is a silent submission to the law, if not an intelligent acquiescence in its propriety.   All our habits of acting are formed in accordance with it.   A poor man honestly seeking work is everywhere respected: a sturdy beggar clamouring for alms is everywhere despised.   The common sense of men falls in with the express injunction of the gospel, that he who will not work should not be allowed to eat (2 Thess. iii. 10).

This principle lies deep in the nature of things, and pervades every department of the divine government.   Its operation is as sure and uniform in morals as in matter.   The Scriptures frequently employ the physical facts as types wherewith to print off for learners the spiritual law.   May " He that ministereth seed to the sower increase the fruits of your righteousness," was Paul's prayer for the Corinthians when he longed for their growth in grace (2 Cor. ix. 10).   He knew that God would give it; but he knew also that it would be given only as the increase of the field is given.   Writing at another time to the same people, he says, " We are labourers together with God; ye are God's husbandry"(1 Cor. iii. 9).   True, the Author and Finisher of their faith will not leave them in the greatest of all matters to their own resources ; God works in concert with men for their good, but he works in a special department and within well-defined limits.   He is a fellow-worker in promoting their spiritual progress, but it is as he co-operates with men in their " husbandry."   He does not relieve the husbandman from tilling.   God is a fellow-worker in giving him rain from heaven ; but if he does not till and sow he will beg in harvest, although the Almighty offers to be his partner in the work.   Such is the law by which the husbandry of the heart is regulated.   The promise, sufficient, yet not redundant, is, " Their soul shall be as a watered garden"(Jer. xxxi. 12). Notwithstanding the promise of an omnipotent co-operator, the garden well watered by the rain of heaven will be a fruitless waste if it be not tilled, fenced, sown, weeded. This is no abatement from the worth of the promise or the kindness of the Promiser. If He should so work with men, either in spirit or in matter, as that the fruit would be sure independently of the husbandman's labour, all distinctions between good and evil would be lost and government become impossible.

He is in this husbandry a fellow-worker; the industrious cannot fail: but He works only in his own department; the lazy cannot succeed. Your soul is the garden : it need not lie barren, for he will water it; but it will lie barren, if you do not work.

The watered field will fill no man's bosom in the harvest if it be not *tilled* in spring. " Break up your fallow ground " (Jer. iv. 3). When the heart is beaten hard by troops of worldly cares treading constantly over it, and not broken up or made small by exercises of self-examination and godly sorrow, the seed does not go beneath the surface, and, so far from reaping a golden harvest, you never see even the promises of spring. But although the field be tilled and broken from its depths, the labour will be unprofitable if it be *sown* with tares or not sown at all. " The seed is the word ;" and ourselves are the field to be cultivated. Put the good seed plentifully in. Hide the word in your heart diligently, hopefully, as the husbandman commits his precious seed to the ground. If we do not sow our own field, how shall we help to sow the field of our neighbour? Even a tilled and sown field may be rendered in a great measure unproductive for want of *fences*. If it be left exposed to every comer, its early sprouting will be trampled under foot, and the hopes which it kindled will be quenched in tears. If men would treat their souls as carefully as they treat their fields, all would be well. Draw defences round your soul: keep out those who would cruelly or carelessly tread down the buds of beginning grace. Leave not your heart open, like an exposed common, to the reckless tread of promiscuous passers. Tempters, like wild boars of the woods, prowl round about your garden : ward them resolutely off; keep it for the Master and his friends. Further still : the tilled, sown, fenced garden, may be overrun with *weeds*, and the full-grown fruit be choked before it reach the ripening. In the garden of your soul weeds spring up without any sowing: unless you labour daily to keep them down, they will gain upon the good seed and overtop it. As a man who loves his garden may be seen stooping down every now and then in his daily walk through it to pluck out and cast over the wall each weed that meets his eye as it is struggling through the ground; so a man that loves his soul and would fain see it flourishing, is ever on the watch for malice and envy and falsehood, and vanity and pride and covetousness,—for any and for all of the legion-species of bitter roots that are ever springing up, troubling himself and defiling his neighbours (Heb. xii. 15). They that are Christ's have crucified, and all their life long continue to crucify, their own lusts.

All these efforts for the garden will be useless if it is not watered: but, on the other hand, the plentiful watering of the garden with rain from heaven will not make it fruitful if any of these operations are neglected. These operations lie to our hand. God works with us, indeed, but he will not perform for us these works. He co-operates by giving us refreshing rain, and commands us to meet his gift by our industrious labour. He does for a soul what he does for a garden: it shall be watered. The grace of the Spirit shall not be wanting; yet, in the spiritual husbandry, the sluggard who will not plough shall not reap.

Not having any ripened grain to reap, he falls a-begging when the harvest comes: "Lord, Lord, open to us." But it is too late: the Lord does not give at that time, and in that way. He will give seed to the sower in spring, but not alms to the sluggard in harvest. He gave seed and rain, and saw them wasted. He pleaded with men to accept and use them, and they would not. At last, when they plead with him, he will not. In an accepted time they would not take the seed: in a rejecting time they cry for the fruit of eternal life, and are sent empty away. Alas! the sluggard begs in harvest, "and has nothing:" his soul was the only real treasure that he ever had, and now it is lost.

Wisdom Modest, Folly Obtrusive

(Proverbs 20:5, 6)

"Counsel in the heart of man is like deep water: but a man of understanding will draw it out. Most men will proclaim every one his own goodness: but a faithful man who can find?"

HERE are two twin misfortunes from which mankind suffer much,—the retiring bashfulness of true worth, and the chattering forwardness of empty self-esteem. The man who has something which would do good to his fellows, is apt to keep it within himself: the man who has nothing solid, is continually giving forth sound. The wisdom which we value we cannot obtain, for it lies in the heart of a modest man like water at the bottom of a deep well; the folly of which we are weary we cannot escape, for it babbles spontaneously from the fool's tongue on the crowded thoroughfares of the world. It would be a double benefit to society if the one man could be persuaded to say more, and the other to say less. In the heart of that man there is " counsel;" but it is like deep water, and " a man of understanding " is required to draw it out. On the lips of this man is vain-glory, which bursts out unbidden; and a " faithful man " is needed to keep it in. Who amongst us has not groaned under these afflictions, either separately or both together? Who has not felt, alternately or simultaneously, the counterpart twin desires, that the fountains of this wise heart were opened and the mouth of that fool shut? The two kindred sufferings generate two kindred desires; and these two desires should make us expert in the two useful arts of drawing out the good in conversation and keeping in the frivolous.

1. How to draw out the good. " Counsel in the heart of a man is like deep water: but a man of understanding will draw it out." Some men have the root of the matter within them, but no tendency spontaneously to give it out. Constitutional timidity, or the

grace of modesty, or both combined, may shut in any company the wisest lips. A stone lies on the well's mouth, and a man of understanding is the Jacob who rolls it off, that all the circle may draw and drink. It is a touching picture, and represents a frequently-recurring fact in actual life. A man who is at once wise and modest is compared to a deep well. Although a supply of water is within, neighbours may walk round the brim and get no refreshing, because it is deep and still. This is not a rare case. The conversation in a company is often frivolous, although the company is not destitute of solid, well-charged minds. When no one has skill to draw out the wisdom of the wise, the folly of the fools will rush out without any drawing, and inundate the circle. It is not to be expected that men of solid gifts will spontaneously exert themselves to bring out their treasures and press their instructions on unwilling ears. A righteous man may here and there be found so ardent in his love, and so zealous of good works, that his mouth is like "a well of life" (x. 11), spontaneously pouring forth a perennial stream; but many real wells are of the deep, still sort, which keep their water within themselves, until some one draw it out. There is a certain sensitiveness which often seals up within a man not only the treasures of useful information, but also the graces of the Spirit. He who has the tact to wait his opportunity, and gently draw the covering aside, and touch the vein, and make the treasures flow, has conferred, by a single stroke, a double benefit,—one on the company for whom, and another on the individual from whom, the instruction has been drawn. When water is drawn from a deep well, the thirsty who stand round its brim enjoy the benefit; but an advantage accrues also to the well itself. When much is drawn out the circulation sweetens the supply, and leaves it as large as before. One who values time, and watches for opportunities of improving it, may be as useful to society by drawing " counsel " out of others as by giving it himself.

2. How to repress the worthless. "Most men will proclaim every one his own goodness; but a faithful man who can find?" This humiliating description is more literally true, and more extensively applicable, than we in the present artificial state of society are able to perceive. There is so much of politeness on the surface, that it is exceedingly difficult to estimate how much

of real humility exists in the heart. Polish is a picture of grace, and pictures skilfully painted sometimes look very like life. Among uncivilized tribes or little children, the reality is more easily seen. Unsophisticated nature, when it has a good opinion of itself, frankly declares it. The complicated forms of refined society supply convenient folds where the sentiment which cannot creditably be confessed may be prudently concealed. To cover vain-glory under a web of soft phraseology is not the same as to crucify the lusts of the flesh. "This poor, worthless effort of mine," may in secret mean, "This great achievement which I have successfully accomplished." We would not, however, discard the idiom of modesty which refinement has infused into our speech; it is often true, and always comely. It is not that we love the garb of humility less, but its living body more.

It is easy to find a man who will proclaim his own goodness, but a faithful man, who will keep down such egotism, is more needful and more rare. This faithfulness, where it exists, develops itself in two branches, the one suppressing our neighbour's vanity and the other our own. The last mentioned is first in the order of nature, and in relative importance the chief. True faithfulness, like charity, begins at home. If you do not first successfully crush your own self-esteem, your efforts to do that service for others will provoke laughter or kindle wrath. Faithful reproof of another's foibles is a virtue which some can exercise without an effort. They deal a hearty blow on the head of a luckless brother egotist who stands in the way of their own advancement, and then expect to be praised for faithfulness. But it is Jehu's driving: the zeal which impels it is not pure. It is a spurious faithfulness that spares self-esteem at home and smites it abroad.

Most proclaim their own goodness; but a faithful man who can find? The ailment is prevalent, the remedy rare. But if faithfulness is seldom found, it is precious in proportion to its scarcity. When it is of the true, solid, authoritative kind, loquacious vain-glory flees before it like smoke before the wind. You may have seen a mighty boaster, self-constituted sole monarch in the centre of a gaping crowd, quenched in a moment by the entrance of one honest man who knew him. An honest man is indeed a noble work of God, and a useful member of the commonwealth. Happy is the society that possesses a few tall enough to be visible over all its surface, and stern enough to scare away the vermin of empty boasters that prey upon its softer parts.

A consistent Christian is, after all, the best style of man. A steady faith in the unseen is the safest guide through the shifting sands of things seen and temporal. When a man's treasure is in heaven, he is not under the necessity of courting popular applause. Those who have truly humbled themselves before God, experience no inclination falsely to magnify themselves in the sight of men.

Two Witnesses:
The Hearing Ear and the Seeing Eye
(Proverbs 20:12)

"The hearing ear, and the seeing eye, the Lord hath made even both of them."

TWO witnesses, the hearing ear and the seeing eye, are summoned forth to prove before the world that the Maker of all things is wise and good. These two palm branches, ever green, plaited into a simple wreath, are chosen from the whole earth as a diadem of glory for the Sovereign's brow. These words so gently spoken, these works so wonderfully made, challenge for their Author the homage and service of all intelligent created beings.

It is a well-known fact in human experience, that the nearer wonders are to the observer, and the oftener they occur, the less wonderful they seem to be. Perhaps the most powerful practical fallacy in life is to confound things that are common with things that are of little value. The counterpart and complement of this error is, to esteem a thing in proportion to its distance and rarity. Bread and water, light and air, are lightly esteemed and ungratefully wasted by those who would pass a sleepless night if a little sparkling stone were stolen or lost. God's word invites us to consider his works : He takes it ill when we blindly overlook the wisdom and goodness with which they are charged.

"This famous town of MANSOUL had *five gates*, in at which to come, out at which to go ; and these were made likewise answerable to the walls,—to wit, impregnable, and such as could never be opened nor forced but by the will and leave of those within. The names of the gates were these :—Ear-gate, Eye-gate, Mouthgate, Nose-gate, and Feel-gate." The reader would recognise in the picture John Bunyan's hand, although his name were not inscribed on the corner of the canvas. The ear and the eye are the two chief gateways through which the human soul, in its imperial palace, receives its knowledge from heaven or earth. They are suitable specimens of divine workmanship, for being submitted to the inspection and employed in the instruction of men.

The ear and eye are curious instruments fixed in the outer walls of the bodily frame, for receiving impressions from sound and light, and conveying corresponding sensations to the mind.*

The ear, as a complex mechanical apparatus, lies almost wholly within the body and beyond our sight : only a wide outer porch through which the sound enters is exposed to view. The mechanism within, like that of all the corporeal organs, exhibits abundant evidence of contrivance exerted intelligently with a view to a specific end. The sound passing successively through a suite of chambers each appropriately furnished, touches in the innermost the extremities of the nerves which bear the message to the brain. The eye, though more easily observed, is scarcely more wonderful in its structure, adaptations, and uses. It is a window in the wall of this house of clay, without which it would be comparatively a dark and dreary dwelling for the soul. It is supplied with a machinery in the form of eye-lids for washing and wiping the glass all day long, so that the window may never be dusty. It has an opening for receiving rays of light, which enlarges itself spontaneously when the light is scarce, in order to take in much, and contracts itself spontaneously when the light is plentiful, in order that less may be admitted. It has transparent lenses like a telescope, through which the rays pass ; and a white curtain on its inmost wall, like a camera, on which the pictures of external objects are painted. Into that canvas from behind nerves are introduced like electric wires, through which the soul receives in her presence-chamber instant intimation of all that is going on without. Sun pictures of the outer world were taken instantaneously upon a prepared plate, by an instrument of small bulk which a man can carry about with him, long before the invention of photography. Inventors are only discoverers of what already is, and has from the beginning been. They are hounds of keener scent, who track the secret footsteps of nature more stanchly than their neighbours ; and nature is nothing else than the method by which it pleases

* See a most interesting and instructive little treatise on the *Five Gateways of Knowledge*, by the late Professor George Wilson of the University of Edinburgh.

God to carry on his work. The rule applied to religion is, even in its terms, strictly applicable also to art, "Be ye imitators of God, as dear children."

The adaptation of each organ to its object, presents an additional evidence of wise design, perhaps even stronger than that which the mechanism of the instrument supplies. The ear would be nothing without sound : the eye, with all its curious and exact machinery, would be an elaborate abortion if light were not, or were subject to different laws. Whatever evidence of beneficent design may lie separately in the seeing eye and the shining light, it is multiplied a thousand-fold by the perfect reciprocal adaptation which subsists between them.

Philosophy has long puzzled its disciples with questions regarding the reality of the external world. Seeing that the human mind does not come directly in contact with earth and air and sea, but only receives pictures or notions of them through the organs of sensation, a doubt has been raised whether substances corresponding to these pictures have any real existence. As the picture of an object is not sufficient evidence that the object exists, it has been said, Sensations of the external world, which are only pictures conveyed to the brain through the senses, do not certainly prove that the external world really is. This question, though in itself an interesting one, is scarcely entitled to rank higher than a plaything. It is useful in calling our attention to the means by which we obtain a knowledge of things beyond ourselves, but it has not power to throw the slightest shade of uncertainty over the existence of these things. The eye and the ear are the chief instruments by which we ascertain the existence and qualities of external objects, and God is the maker of them both. For that very use he framed them and gave them to his creatures ; and he has done all things well. There are no deceptions in his plan, and no blunders in its execution.

Besides, our belief in the existence of things is confirmed by the mouth of many independent witnesses. To each object several of the senses, and to many all, bear concurrent testimony. The eye and the ear do not act in concert; they are as independent of each other as any two witnesses that ever gave evidence in a trial. If the eye should give a false testimony the ear would correct it. To suppose that all the senses were made for telling lies, and corroborating each other in their falsehood, is at once to magnify the wonders of the contrivance, and ascribe it to Satan instead of God. These gateways of knowledge were pierced in the body by its Maker's own hand, that the soul might not sit darkling within its house of clay. The hearing ear and the seeing eye, the Lord hath made even both of them. He, into whose hands believers commit the keeping of their souls, is "a faithful Creator" (1 Peter iv. 19).

On this subject, and in this point of view, the Popish doctrine of transubstantiation possesses a peculiar interest. We look at it in its philosophical rather than its religious aspect. It comes across our path here, not as a perversion of the word, but as a dishonour done to the works of God. Our cause of quarrel with it in this place is, that it pours contempt on the seeing eye, which the Lord has made and given to his creatures.

The belief, inculcated and professed throughout the mysterious spiritual commonwealth of Rome, that the bread and wine in the sacrament of the Supper are changed at the utterance of the consecrating word, and are no longer bread and wine, but the body and blood of Christ, is a great feature in the working of the human mind, and a great fact in the history of the human race. It sprung up in a dark age, and was irrevocably incorporated in a system which professes itself infallible and dares not change. The dogma of transubstantiation could not be cast out when an age of light returned, because to lose the prestige of immutability would be more destructive to Rome than to retain a belief which places her in contradiction to the laws of nature and the senses of men. Accordingly they retain it, and, with impudence on the one side, and ignorance on the other, manage to keep their heads above water in some way, notwithstanding the weight and awkwardness of their burden.

This doctrine brings the huge bulk of Popery right across the path on which we are now advancing. They teach that what I taste and see to be bread and wine, is not bread and wine at all, but the flesh and blood and bones of a human body,—the very body that was nailed to the cross on Calvary! They thereby repudiate the testimony of the senses, competently given, and disparage the work and gift of God. They concede that the senses, in as far as they give, or can give, a testimony on the subject report the elements to be bread and wine; but affirm that the senses are not in all cases trust-worthy, and specify cases in which erroneous inferences are sometimes drawn from the impressions of a single sense. Suppose we should commence the controversy on the other side, by showing that their position proves too much, and cuts away the ground on which they stand :—If the senses deceive, how can I be sure that my ear conveys to me the words of the priest? Under this pressure they select the sense of hearing, and affirm that it may be trusted, and it alone. The senses of seeing, tasting, smelling, and feeling, all take cognizance of the object, and all concur in representing it to be bread ; the sense of hearing does not take cognizance of the object at all, and has no testimony to give : this one they select as the only one that should be trusted! Five witnesses are called to give evidence regarding a certain fact. The question, "Were you present ?" is put successively to all the five. The first four answer, Yes; the last one, No. The next question is, " Did the prisoner commit the deed?" The first four answer, Yes; the last one answers, No. The jury return a verdict of acquittal. But they are perjured men. They have a purpose to serve. They have believed one witness who was not present, against four witnesses who were. Such is the state of the case when contemplated in the abstract, but it becomes much clearer and stronger when we refer to examples in Scripture.

After his resurrection, and before he ascended to heaven, Jesus showed himself alive, " by many infallible proofs," to the apostles whom he had chosen (Acts i. 3). And what were the proofs which he gave? The evidence of the senses, and that alone;— " being seen of them forty days, and speaking of the things pertaining to the kingdom of God ;" it was the evidence of sight and hearing. When it is proposed to prove the resurrection of Christ—the fact on which the world's redemption hangs—the hearing ear and the seeing eye are the two witnesses called to support it. They are competent and true, for "the Lord hath made even both of them." The evidence of the senses is either sufficient proof of a fact, or it is not. If it is sufficient, transubstantiation is not true, for the senses testify against it : if it is not sufficient, the resurrection of Christ is not proved, for it has no other evidence to rest on. Thus the foundation of a believer's hope and the foundation of the Popish system cannot both stand: thus is Popery proved to be Antichrist.

In this place, however, we enter the lists against that mysterious power, expressly in defence of the hearing ear and the seeing eye as the good gifts of a true God. He counts their evidence sure, for he has made it a link of the chain on which his great salvation leans, when it is let down to men. Through these inlets comes to us the knowledge, not only of earth, but also of heaven; not only of time, but also of eternity. It is by seeing and hearing that the word enters a believing heart; and the entrance of the word giveth life. The word, coming in and abiding is life—life for evermore; he that hath the Son hath life.

Man and his faculties are spoken of in Scripture as vessels or instruments, wherewith God works out his plans. Paul was a "chosen vessel" for containing and bearing to the nations Christ's name (Acts ix. 15). The Romans were enjoined to yield not only themselves in general, but specifically their "members as instruments of righteousness unto God" (Rom. vi. 13). He honours his own work in our bodies, although we blindly despise and abuse it. These eyes and ears which he has made, are, as instruments, worthy of his wisdom; they are capable of useful employment in his service; it is breach of trust to use them in another and adverse interest.

The Omniscient is not bound to us and the organs of our body for the accomplishment of his plans; with or without us, he will do all his pleasure. It is our surest safety to be on his side—our greatest honour to be employed as his instruments. The world which he works in is full of the tools which he works with. In trees and plants, every thorn, and leaf, and tendril, is a cunningly-contrived instrument fitted to conduct some delicate operation in the vegetable economy. In animals, every member of the body is a tool: the work-shop is full of materials and implements. Again, every part of creation is an instrument necessary and suitable for some department of the universal work. The internal fires of the globe are machinery for heaving up the mountain ridges, and causing the intervening valleys to subside. The clouds are capacious vessels made for carrying water from its great reservoir to the thirsty land. The rivers are a vast water-power in perpetual motion, slowly wearing down the mountains, and spreading the debris in layers on the bottom of the sea. The sun is an instrument for lighting and warming the world, and the earth's huge bulk a curtain for screening off the sunlight at stated intervals, and so giving to weary workers a grateful night of rest. Chief of all the instruments for the Master's use is man, made last, made best,—broken, disfigured, and defiled by sin, but capable yet, when redeemed and renewed, of becoming a vessel for conveying God's goodness down to creation, and creation's praises articulate up to God.

In our religious exercises we must not limit our view to the soul and its sins, so as to neglect the body and its organs; for, in acts of sin or of holiness, the body is related to the soul as the moving machinery to the water-stream which drives it. In spiritual matters we are accustomed to think with something like contempt of the senses and their organs. There is some risk of error and loss at this point. It is true that we deserve contempt when we waste them on vanity or cripple them by vice; but these members are worthy of their Maker. They are given to us for the noblest purposes. They are given in trust; we should highly esteem the talent, and diligently occupy it till the Giver come. He is not ashamed to own that hearing ear and that seeing eye as his. He who spread out the heavens, and sprinkled them with sparkling worlds, points to these members of our bodies as specimens that will sustain his glory. How warily should they walk upon the world who bear about with them these precious and tender jewels, the cherished property of the great King! How carefully should we preserve from pollution these delicate instruments, to which he is even now pointing as evidence of his skill and kindness!

Christian! these ears and eyes are the openings whereby light and life have reached your soul; occupy them henceforth with sounds and sights that will please Him. If I am Christ's, these ears and eyes have been bought for himself by the price of his own blood ; I must not employ them to crucify him afresh, and bring him to an open shame. Let me listen to those sounds and look at those sights which I would listen to and look at if he stood beside me listening and looking too : to other sounds let me be deaf,—to other beauties blind.

The subject is not a little one. Issues inconceivably great depend on the purposes to which we now apply these good gifts of God. Our time and our eternity both depend on their use or abuse. The conflict rages now: the victory will be decided soon. Through their ears and eyes disciples, like their Lord, are plied with strong temptations. To them as to him the kingdoms of the world and their glory are offered, on the same dark condition.

Sin waves its painted beauties and shakes its music-bells to win and enslave. Through unwary ears and eyes the adversary enters to drag the soul into captivity and death.

Hark! another voice! Behold another sight! "Hear, and your souls shall live." "Come unto me, all ye that labour and are heavy laden, and I will give you rest." Hear these words of life: behold that Lamb of God who taketh sin away. By these openings, which his own hand has made into our being, God our Saviour will send in light and life.

Soon these ears and eyes will be closed for ever against earthly sounds and sights; but they will open again for other entrants. The trumpet shall sound, and every ear shall hear it. "All that are in their graves shall hear the voice of the Son of man, and shall come forth." Nor shall the world's destiny be pronounced by an invisible Judge. He shall come as the lightning comes, and every eye shall see him; they also who pierced him. The voice of judgment will penetrate the ear that was deaf to the message of mercy. The outcast will have an ear to hear, but no word of hope will ever reach it: an eye to see, but no light will ever dawn to meet its straining.

Let my ears now hear the word, and my eyes behold the beauty of the Lord: then, at his appointed time, let them close in peace. When next they open, they shall see and hear, what eye hath not seen nor ear heard as yet,—"the things that God hath prepared for them that love him."

Buyers and Sellers
(Proverbs 20:14)

"It is naught, it is naught, saith the buyer; but when he is gone his way, then he boasteth."

A VERY large proportion of man's intercourse with man is occupied by the acts of buying and selling: nation buys from nation separated by the sea,—citizen from citizen separated by a street. In the progress of civilization the commercial relations of states are gradually rising above the political in importance and power. Fleets and armies may, by a sudden blow, derange the course of commerce for a time, but its accumulated waters soon acquire a momentum sufficient to carry away all artificial impediments, and clear or make a channel for themselves. The many rivulets of domestic trade obey the same laws as the majestic rivers of international commerce. Buying and selling on every scale, from the pennyworth of the poor widow to the precious cargo of a merchant prince, have in time past flowed like rivers, and like them will continue to flow. It is not in the power of men to stop or turn either class of streams. Those circulations that are necessary to the world's well-being are placed by the almighty Ruler beyond the reach of man's capricious will and meddling hands; neither our own body nor the body of the earth is dependent on our thoughtfulness for the flow and re-flow of its life-blood. In like manner, though in measure less complete, commerce holds direct of the universal Lawgiver, and spurns the behests of parliaments and kings. It determines its reservoirs in the interior, traces its own channel along the plain, curving now to this side and now to that without giving an account of its ways, and at last chooses its own outlet on the ocean. Each of these circulations maintains a life after its kind; and it is good for man that, alike in the momentum of their flow and the degree of their occasional deflection, they obey other laws than his.

The chief effort of the first Napoleon, in the latter years of the great war, was to intercept the flow of commerce into Britain by his celebrated Continental System, and so compel us to capitulate, like a garrison whose supply of water is cut off. The scheme failed, notwithstanding the vast resources employed in its behalf, and the extraordinary energy with which it was prosecuted. The commerce of nations is of the nature and dimensions of a mighty river,— no embankments made by man can arrest its course. The increase of commerce in our day is a happy omen for the future of the race. Next to the spread of the Truth in power, buying and selling are the best antidotes to the spirit and practice of war.

The passing and repassing of merchandise through some of the greater arteries of the world's commerce is a sight eminently fitted to arrest and occupy alike the imagination, the intellect, and the heart. The stream of carts and trucks and boats through the heart of a great commercial emporium, is as sublime as rushing rivers or floating clouds ; through its prosaic crust the true poet's eye can see a pure and healthful current witnessing the beneficence of God and bearing blessings to men. Some silly people of other countries have sneered at Britain as a nation of merchants ; they may as well sneer at the waters which bear our merchandise, or the winds which waft it on. We could sit easy under the taunts of strangers for the quantity of our buying and selling, if we had no cause to reproach ourselves on account of its character. The nation's trade is the nation's honour ; the dishonest tricks that mingle with it constitute in that matter our real, our only disgrace. Commerce is a noble occupation,—be it ours to keep its mighty current pure.

The exchange of commodities in its minuter details occupies a very large proportion of the time and attention of neighbours when they meet. Let a farmer, for example, take in this light a note of a week's transactions ; he will find that most of his meetings and conversations were connected with buying or selling. On the one hand are a numerous class from whom he obtains his supplies by purchase ; and, on the other, a smaller class to whom in larger transactions he disposes of his produce by sale. His business with each is a bargain. The community is not divided into two classes,—one of buyers and another of sellers ; the interests of all are much more completely interwoven than would be possible under such an arrangement. Each class and each individual is a buyer and seller by turns. He who sells bread buys clothes, and he who sells clothes buys bread. This intermixture binds society together. It is in some measure analogous to the chemical and mechanical admixture of constituents which secures the solidity and cohesion of stones or timber.

Buying and selling, then, constitute in a great measure the point of contact for individuals as the particles which make up society in the mass; and it is of the utmost importance that there should be softness and cohesiveness, not hardness and repulsion, on both sides at the meeting-place. If suspicion and dishonesty prevail there, the peace of each will be marred, and the strength of the whole diminished. Truth and trustfulness will bind us into one, and union is strength : the soundest commonwealth is a commonwealth of honest men.

Throughout the Proverbs reproofs frequently occur directed expressly against the unjust balances of the dishonest seller : the sentence now before us uncovers the disingenuous pretences of the untruthful buyer. The blame of existing evils does not all lie at the seller's door. Allowing, for the moment, that he is guilty of all the tricks which the public so readily and so indiscriminately impute to him, the question remains, To what extent did the community of buyers, by their own tortuous conduct, produce in the seller the vice by which they suffer and of which they complain ? The case by its very nature precludes the possibility of a precise analysis, but perhaps we would not greatly err if we should assume, in a general way, that nearly half of the mischief belongs to the buyer.

The counts of the indictment against the seller are numerous and varied, but the one with which we are more immediately concerned here is,—He asks for his article a larger price than it is fairly worth, and if he cannot get what he first demands, he will sell it at a much lower price, rather than not sell it at all. Well, this is your complaint : assuming it to be true, and not justifying his conduct, we raise the other question,—How far are you, the buyers, guilty of inoculating the sellers with that vice ?

By expecting dishonesty in the seller, you produce it. The piece of goods is displayed and examined; you desire to purchase it, and ask the price. If from your knowledge of the article you

think it too high, and determine not to give so much, it is perfectly competent and fair to offer a lower price ; but when you
demand an abatement, simply in order to bring the seller down,
not based on a judgment as to the worth of the goods, you endanger both his conscience and your own.   This kind of demand
will be made upon the seller equally whether he asks at first ten
shillings for the article or five.   It is not a legitimate judgment
regarding the bargain at all, but a morbid appetite to bring down
the price. This occurs not once or twice, but many times every day.
Conceive yourself in the seller's place.   This blind and uniform
demand for an abatement presses upon him from successive
customers, like the continuity of a stream.   He perceives that the
people who make it are not competent to form an opinion on the
value of the goods ; he perceives that their aim is to bring him
down from the price which he has first announced, whatever it
may be ; he perceives that the satisfaction of the buyer is not
regulated by the real advantage of his bargain, but by the difference between the price that was first asked and that which was
ultimately accepted.   The pressure thus brought to bear upon the
seller to turn him aside from the line of righteousness is very
strong.   It is true he ought to withstand the pressure ; but it is
also true that his customers ought not to subject him to its
dreadful strain.   If he yields to the temptation, his method is
short and easy : he asks a higher price than the goods are worth,
and then pleases the purchaser by letting it down.

The cunning buyer, when the price is named, addresses himself vigorously to the work of depreciating the article.   Proceeding by rhyme rather than by reason, he reiterates some unvarying
formula, like that which the text has preserved in a fossil state
since Solomon's day,—" It is naught, it is naught."   When he
has kept the dealer under the clack of this mill for a sufficient
length of time, he offers a price, perhaps the half or two-thirds
of that which was at first demanded.   His offer is accepted : he
shoulders his prize, believes the goods are excellent and cheap,
and goes home chuckling over his achievement.   He imagines he
has circumvented the dealer : the dealer, being one degree more
cunning, has circumvented him.   At every step of this miserable
process, buyer and seller are fellow-sinners, and fellow-sufferers.
If the public say to the merchant, Ask only one price, and we

will cease to beat down ; the merchant may reply to the public, Cease to beat down and I will ask only one price. Trust begets honesty, and honesty begets trust.

We are well aware that the art of higgling is in a great measure antiquated now: the mine has been well-nigh wrought out, and the diggers are trying other veins. The old, base, undisguised see-saw process of knaves and fools going into each other, the one asking a double price, and the other pleased with a bad bargain because he has screwed it down, has fallen now into the lower and more vulgar strata of commercial life. In the higher spheres of trade, sellers and buyers alike would be ashamed in the present day to begin, in this form, the reciprocating series of deceit. I rejoice over the advancement which has been made. I believe that a large proportion of it is a real gain, and is due to the diffusion of sound principles : I am not so sanguine, however, as to believe that the root of the evil has been destroyed. When the more healthful public opinion of the age prevents it from sending forth its branches in one direction, it will push them out in another. The forms of its manifestation will vary with time and circumstances, but a great amount of distrust and dishonesty, reciprocally generating each other, still hangs over the border line where men meet to make bargains, rendering it a comparatively waste and withered region—a region where grace finds it hard to live and grow.

In the days when England and Scotland were rival kingdoms, and their barbarous peoples animated by hereditary feuds, a traveller found, as he approached the border on either side, a wide, uncultivated, unproductive territory. The soil was as generous, and the sky overhead as fair, as in other portions of the country; but the inhabitants on either side occupied themselves with alternate raids, and each ruthlessly devastated his neighbour's land. The two parties contrived to make matters nearly equal one year with another: the balance was kept even by the impartial desolation of both. At this day, too, the interests of English and Scotch on both sides of the border line are maintained on a footing of perfect equality. Neither obtains any advantage over the other: yet waving corn-fields touch the separating rivulet on either brim There is no belt of barrenness. The labour of our forefathers in fighting against each other was more than lost. Peace can make neighbours equal as well as war, and give them all their crops beside.

A state of warfare makes a barren border. Mutual suspicion between buyer and seller makes the two equal by wasting both. Trust on the one side and Truth on the other would make bargaining morally as pleasant and as profitable as any other exercise in life. Righteousness at the point of contact would do for the parties what peace on the border has done for contiguous kingdoms: it would at once weld the two into one, and preserve intact the interests of each.

Might the analogy be pursued yet another step? The shortest and surest way of preventing a devastating hostility on the borders, is to embue the hearts of the borderers on both sides with loving loyalty to one rightful King. When independent and hostile tribes are brought under complete subjection to the prince, they cease to wage war against each other. Those who are under law to Christ, will not try to overreach their neighbours in a bargain.

A Good Name
(Proverbs 22:1)

"A good name is rather to be chosen than great riches, and loving favour rather than silver and gold."

WE are not good judges of value, in the public market of life. We make grievous mistakes, both in choosing and refusing: we often throw away the pearl, and carefully keep the shell. Besides the great disparity in value between the things of heaven and the things of earth, some even of these earthly things are of greater worth than others. The valuables in both ends of this balance belong to time; and yet there is room for a choice between them. There is a greater and a less, where neither is the greatest.

A trader at his counter has a certain set of weights which he uses every day, and all day, and for all sorts of commodities. Whatever may be in the one scale, the same invariable leaden weight is always in the other. This lump of metal is his standard, and all things are tried by it. Riches practically serve nearly the same purpose in the market of human life. Whether people are aware of it or not, riches become insensibly the standard by which other things are estimated. As the dealer mechanically throws his old leaden pound weight into one scale, whatever species of goods the other may contain; so in human life, by a habit so uniform that it looks like instinct, men quietly refer all things to the standard of gold.

This is a mistake. Many things are better than gold; and one of these is a good name. A good conscience, indeed, is better than both, and must be kept at all hazards; but, in cases where matters from the higher region do not come into competition, reputation should rank higher than riches in the practical estimation of men. If a man choose honour as the substantial portion of his soul, it flits before him as a shadow, and he is never satisfied; but, shadow though it be, and worthless alone, it is precious as an accompaniment of the substance. The shadows are not the picture, but the picture is a naked, ungainly thing without them. Thus the atmosphere of a good name surrounding it, imparts to real worth additional body and breadth. As the substitute for a good conscience, a good name is a secret torment at the time, and in the end a cheat; but as a graceful outer garment with which a good conscience is clothed, it should be highly valued and carefully preserved by the children of the kingdom. Robes rich in texture, and comely in form, would not make a wooden image gainly; but it does not follow that they are useless to the living human frame. An idol is vile, whether it be gold or a good name; but as articles in the inventory of our Father's gifts, gold is good, and reputation better.

The term "loving favour" serves to indicate the sweetness of being esteemed and loved by our neighbours. The Lord, who has made us capable of that enjoyment, does not set it down as sin. If we be "a people near unto him," he will take care that we shall not be spoiled by over-doses of loving-kindness from men. It is our part so to act as to deserve that love: then, if it be given, we may innocently enjoy it; if it be withheld, we should meekly submit. If in adversity even a brother turn his back, a Friend remains who sticketh closer.

I do not know any department of providence in which the hand of God is more frequently or more visibly displayed, than in maintaining before the world the good name of those who, before himself, maintain a good conscience. A small parenthesis of two words in the evangelic history serves, like a magnetic needle, to point out in this matter the way of the Lord. Among the twelve, there was a Judas, besides the betrayer, and he was faithful to the Lord. His fellow-disciple John (xiv. 22), having occasion in the course of his history to record a question which this Judas addressed to the Master, adds to his name the significant notandum, "Not Iscariot." "The shields of the earth belong unto God," and he is ever ready to throw one round the reputation of a true disciple, when danger is near. The Master knows who betrays him, and who proves faithful: he will not permit the two to be confounded. Eli made a mistake when he reckoned Hannah among the drunkards, but her righteousness came out as light. There will be no confusion in the current accounts of the world; for its Governor is wise and powerful. He will not spare the sins of his servants. Now by the stern rebuke, "Get thee behind me, Satan," and now by the silent look that melts the fickle denier's heart, he will take vengeance on their inventions; but he will encircle themselves in his own everlasting arms.

An interesting example of "particular providence" in this department has been recently brought to light. A brief entry was discovered in an authentic record, which seemed to leave a stain on the memory of Patrick Hamilton, the herald and first martyr of the Scottish Reformation. In the household accounts of the royal treasurer for the year 1543, a sum is entered for a gown to Isobel Hamilton, a lady of the queen's household, "daughter of Patrick, abbot of Ferne." This was evidently the martyr's daughter, in all probability a posthumous child. He died young. Hitherto no mention had ever been made of his marriage. In the silence of history it was assumed that he had not been married. Could it be that this youth, whom we have all along considered in every sense a holy martyr of Christ, had imitated in his life the licentiousness of the Romish dignitaries whom he denounced? Almost as soon as the question was raised, an answer was provided. Evidence the most incidental, undesigned, and certain, appears in time to shield the confessor's good name at the threatened point. The writings of Alexander Alesius, a contemporary Scotchman, a witness of Hamilton's death, and a convert of his ministry, have lately been brought to light on the Continent.* The affectionate pupil, all unconscious of the use that would afterwards be found for his testimony, records, in a treatise written while he was in exile for the truth in Germany, that Hamilton married a "lady of noble rank," in the interval between his return from the continent and his trial at St. Andrews. The letters of a true disciple's name were beginning to appear very like those of the traitor, and forthwith the writing, "*Not Iscariot*," beamed from the wall, as if emblazoned there by an angel's hand.

* Precursors of Knox—Patrick Hamilton. By Professor Lorimer of London.

The Rich and the Poor Meet Together
(Proverbs 22:2)

"The rich and the poor meet together."

IN observing and representing the relative position of these two, or of any two, much depends upon the view-point. When you stand among the crowd on the surface of the plain, the rich and the poor appear to move on lines far apart, and never once to approach each other from the beginning of life's journey to its close. In their birth they seem to be far asunder; one is exposed to hardship as soon as his eyes are opened to the light; the other is tenderly cared for, before he knows that he needs care. In their childhood, intercourse is forbidden, as if it would introduce infection. In maturity the divergence is still further increased; and distance is maintained even in the grave. This proverb briefly and bluntly affirms that the rich and the poor meet: but where, and when? If we look not to exceptional instances, but to the ordinary course of events, these seem to be the very two classes who are all their life-time most widely separated, and never meet at all.

Change the view-point, and the scene will change. When you lift your eyes from the earth and look on objects in the expanse of heaven, worlds that move in separate orbits appear to touch each other, and several, like water-drops in contact, merge into a larger one. Thus the spaces between rich and poor, which seemed so vast to themselves and other observers near them, disappear when eternity becomes the background of the view. They meet by appointment of their common Lord. There are many inevitable meeting-places and meeting-times; they meet in their birth and their death—in the cradle and the grave. At the beginning and at the end, and at many of the intermediate stations of life's pilgrimage, the two courses touch each other, and the two pilgrims walk side by side.

At birth they meet, answering each other by a cry. The one is animated dust, the other animated dust; and both have within themselves the seeds of many sorrows. In regard to the two grand distinguishing features of man's present condition, sin and suffering, they stand precisely on the same level; and if in some minor points there is a distinction, its amount is too insignificant to affect greatly the general result. Even in the periods of infancy and childhood the two paths converge more closely than superficial observers deem. If the rich man's infant gets more attention from servants, the poor man's child lies more constantly on his mother's breast. There is compensation here, arranged by Him who balanced so nicely the greater and the lesser orbs that circulate in space. Mother-love cannot be made by man nor hired for money. We do not undervalue the faithfulness and affection of domestics. We find no fault with gas light; it is inestimably useful in the absence of day. Such is a hired servant's care of an infant; it is excellent of its kind, but not to be compared with that love which is of God's own kindling in a mother's heart. It ought to be instructive to the rich and reassuring to the fainting, overburdened poor, to observe and remember that the welfare of an infant depends much more on the character than on the wealth of its parents. For this special object a good name is rather to be chosen than great riches.

Each sickness is a meeting-place between the rich and the poor, and these occur frequently in the path of life. A rich man's tooth is at least as liable to caries as a poor man's, and it aches as keenly. The best joys, too, as well as the sharpest pains, are common to the two conditions. Food, rest, sleep; light, sounds, odours; family affections and social intercourse,—these and other main arterial streams of sensitive enjoyment are at least as great, and pure, and sweet, in the ordinary experience of the poor as in the ordinary experience of the rich.

It would, however, be a defective, and therefore in so far an untrue, representation of the facts, to speak only of those meetings between rich and poor which nature and providence inexorably prescribe; there are meetings not a few in our day and our land, spontaneous in their character and beneficent in their effects. Some on both sides justly estimate the reciprocal relations of the parties, and honestly address themselves to the duties which these relations impose. This is one of the brightest features of the age,—a gleam of sunlight gilding a somewhat dusky landscape. Good intentions alone, however, will not gain this cause. It is an apostleship that demands the wisdom of the serpent at least as much as the harmlessness of the dove. There are precious rights on both sides that ought to be preserved. One must walk softly over that meeting-ground, lest he rudely tread on something that is dear to a brother. Those approaches only are safe and useful in which each man is both obliged to respect his neighbour and permitted to respect himself. Willing union of rich and poor for mutual benefit, is the true preventive of those revolutionary shocks which reduce all classes to a level beneath a despot's feet. Looking to the measure of our privileges in this respect, we have good cause to thank God and take courage. When cloud meets cloud in our skies, they seem, although charged with antagonist forces, to give and take gently until the equilibrium is restored; in other countries the same forces, more rigidly pent up, have found relief in the lightning's flash and the thunder's roar. The adjustment comes, but it is with the deluge.

Approaching very near each other at many stations on the way, the life-lines of rich and poor coincide completely towards their close. They meet, without a figure, in the grave. Unto dust both, and both alike, return. They meet at the judgment-seat of Christ. None may be absent when the roll of our race is called from the great white throne. At that bar there are no reserved seats, no respected persons.

The lesson is obvious, and it looks both ways. The poor need it as much as the rich, and the rich as much as the poor; here, too, there is equality. Let the one learn humility, the other contentment. If both be " bought with a price," and both, in their several stations, glorify God, yet another meeting awaits them at another meeting-place. In Christ Jesus now there is neither Greek nor barbarian, neither bond nor free, neither male nor female. That union avails to efface the distinctions that are most deeply marked in nature; much more those which lie on the surface of changing circumstances. There will be no rich men in heaven, for the sinful are all in utmost need; neither will there be any poor men there, for all who enter are " rich in faith, and heirs of the kingdom." The rich and the poor meet together in the Father's house ; the Lord is the Redeemer of them all.

Faith exercises a decisive influence on practice. The hope cherished now, of mingling on terms of complete equality with the whole family of God, when they assemble in the Father's house, would cast out corroding jealousies, and sweeten all the intercourse of life. Those who are bought by the same price, and called by the same name, should habitually look forward to the time, not distant, when the distinctions which now separate one from another will be lost in the equal perfection of all; and those who " have this hope in Him," that earthly distinctions will shortly terminate, should " purify themselves, even as He is pure," from that selfishness which, in various forms, turns the necessary inequalities of human condition into thorns for tearing human hearts.

Hiding-Places for the Prudent
(Proverbs 22:3)

" A prudent man foreseeth the evil, and hideth himself: but the simple pass on, and
are punished."

ONE main element of safety is a just estimate of danger.
Many of the great disasters that have occurred in war
are due to the rashness which springs from under-
valuing the enemy's power. He who foresees the evil, hides himself until it pass; and he who so hides himself escapes the storm
which lays lofty rashness low. There is much room for this
species of prudence to exercise itself upon, in relation both to the
present life, and to that which is to come. There are both encom-
passing dangers and safe hiding-places in the several regions of
our secular business, our moral conduct, and our religious hopes.

1. In the ordinary business of life there are evils which may
be foreseen by the prudent, and places of shelter in which he may
safely lie. When speculation is rife, for example,—when all that
a man has, and much that belongs to his neighbour, is risked
at a throw, and a fortune made by return of post,—when people,
made giddy by success, rush further and faster into the stream,—
evil is near and imminent. It hangs like a thunder-cloud overhead. The prudent in such an hour is on his guard. He seeth
the evil before the bolt has actually fallen. He seeks a place of
shelter. Nor is that shelter far away; his daily labour and his
legitimate business will be a sufficient defence against these foes.
A disciple who has his heart in heaven should beware of fretting
because his hands are full all day long with earthly business;
labour, when the Lord appoints it for his people, is a strong wall
built round them to keep dangerous enemies out.

2. Evils lie before us in the region of practical morality—evils
for which the prudent keep a sharp look-out. Frivolous and
licentious companions, theatres, Sabbath amusements, and a mul·

titude of cognate enticements, press upon a young man like wind ; if he be like chaff, he will be carried away. The wisest course is to go into hiding. In your father's house and in your sisters' company,—among sober associates and instructive books,—in the study of nature or the practice of art,—a multitude of hiding-places are at hand. Even there the enemy will seldom find you. But a deeper, safer refuge still,—a strong tower of defence, from which all the fiery darts of the wicked will harmlessly rebound, —is that "name of the Lord" into which the righteous run. All the power of the world and its god can neither drive a refugee forth from that hiding-place, nor hurt him within it.

3. But the greatest evils lie in the world to come, and only the eye of faith can foresee them. To be caught by death unready, and placed before the judgment-seat without a plea, and then cast out for ever, are evils so great that in their presence all others disappear like stars in the glare of day. But great though they are, the prudent may foresee, and the trustful prevent them. There is a refuge, but its gate opens into Time. If the prudent do not enter now, the simple will knock in vain at the closed door, when he has passed into eternity without any part in Christ. If the needy are numerous, the refuge is ample : if the exposed are in poverty, the admission is free : if the adversary is legion, the Saviour is God.

"The simple pass on, and are punished." "How long, ye simple, will ye love simplicity?" Although the saved are not their own saviours, the lost are their own destroyers. The reason why they perish is declared by Him who knows their hearts : "Ye will not come unto me." A man is passing on in the way which he has chosen ; he is eating and drinking, and making merry. Guilt is on his conscience, but he feels not its fiery bite ; wrath is treasured over him, but he fears not its final outpouring. The open door of mercy abuts upon his downward path, but he heeds it not : he passes on—he passes by it. As he passes, a voice falls upon his ear ; it is the voice of God's own Son conjuring him with strong crying and tears to turn and live. Startled for a moment by the sound, he pauses and looks ; but seeing nothing that takes his fancy, he passes on again. Again a voice behind him cries, in tones which show that life and death eternal are turning on their hinge, "Repent, lest you perish ! why will you die?" He stops and looks behind; it is a fit of seriousness, but it soon goes off. He heard a sound; but it must have been an echo in the mountains, or a call to some wanderer who has lost his way. Stopping his ears, and shutting his eyes, he passes on. Deaf to warnings from above, and blind to beacons reared before him, he still passes on, until, at a moment when he counts his footing firmest, he stumbles over the brink of life, and falls into the hands of the living God! This fall, the Bible tells us, "is a fearful thing." Fear it now, and flee, ye who are passing on through life in your sin, and without a Saviour. Surely it should be plain to any rational being, that though a man may live without God in the world, he cannot escape from God when he dies. Do those who are passing on with their backs to Christ, and their hearts full of vain shows, know where life's boundary-line lies, or what awaits themselves beyond it? Why will men pass on, if they are on such a path that another step may be perdition?

If there were no hope, the wanderers would have no resource but to go forward in despair until their doom declared itself : but here, and now, blessed hope abounds. Cease to go on neglecting the great salvation, and the great salvation is ready for you : seek and ye shall find. They are not the great, and the wise, and the good who escape, but the sinners who seek the Saviour,—the prudent who foresee the evil, and hide. The question is not, How great is your sin? or, How long have you been a sinner? If you are lost while another is saved, it is not because your guilt is greater than his, but because you neglected the salvation which he deemed precious. If the simple is punished at last, it is because, in spite of a beseeching, weeping Saviour, "he passed on" through the day of grace, and fell upon the day of judgment.

Education

(Proverbs 22:6)

"Train up a child in the way he should go; and when he is old, he will not depart
from it."

A T all times and in all places education is a matter of
first-rate importance; and in this country at the present time its importance is, in some measure, felt and
acknowledged. It has become, or at least is becoming, the question of the day. Out of it many difficulties spring; over it many
battles are fought. It should moderate our grief, however, and
silence our fretful complaints, to remember that our troubles grow
out of our privileges. This species of thistle is found only in fat
corn-fields; it is never seen in uncultivated moors. It is because
we have so much education that we complain so loudly of the deficiency, and cry so earnestly for more. Besides all the noise
which we make about the quantity of education, we quarrel energetically about the kind. Now, although this state of warfare is
not the optimism in which we should acquiesce as a final attainment, yet, as a symptom of progress, we might have worse.
The educational difficulties which trouble us do not agitate the
worshippers of Brahma or Mahomet. Few of them are felt in
Spain or Italy. These questions do not rise in those portions of
the world where superstition and despotism crush the intellectual
energies of the people. If an adventurous inquirer at any time
dare to raise them, he is silenced by a short and simple process.
Tyrants make a solitude, and call it peace. When they point with
scorn to the strifes which agitate Protestant communities, we sit
easy under the taunt. We love not the contentions for their own
sake, but we love liberty so much that we endure, with some
measure of equanimity, the troubles which, while men continue
imperfect, must follow in its wake. If the uneasy twisting and
groaning of the body politic prove that the nation, in matters of
education, is on a sick-bed, they prove also that she is not in the

grave. Granted that Britain educationally is ailing; other countries that might be named are dead. We would be glad to see the silent satisfaction of robust health, but, in the meantime, we like the cry which indicates life, better than the stillness that broods over the body when the spirit has gone.

This verse of the Bible is a pregnant utterance on our much-vexed question. It goes to the point at once, and goes through all the points in a very short space of time. Root and branch of the case are here. Adopting the terms of the English version, as conveying the sentiment of the original substantially and perspicuously, without the aid of critical remarks, we find in it three clearly distinguished yet closely related parts:

1. Whom we should educate—the material: " A child."

2. How we should educate—the process: " Train up."

3. Into what we should educate—the aim and issue: " In the way he should go."

In education, the *material* should be pliable, the *method* skilful, and the *pattern* divine. These three points correspond nearly to the philosophy, the art, and the religion of the question.

1. The material on which the educator operates,—" A *child.*" That childhood is the proper period for education is one of the most obvious of all general truths. In profession, at least, it is universally acknowledged. The law on which it is founded holds good in all countries and all times. Its range is not limited to human kind; it traverses the boundary of the animal kingdom, and determines the form of a branch as well as the character of a man. The world teems with analogies, both real and obvious, whereby the moralist may enforce the duty of educating in the comparatively pliable period of youth. You may, within certain limits, determine at will the direction of a river, a tree, a man, if you touch them near their sources, where they are tiny and tender; but none of the three when full-grown can be bent, except in very minute degrees, and at an expense of labour greatly disproportionate to the result. The belief universally diffused through society, and floating impalpable in the moral atmosphere, has at one spot been precipitated and solidified in the convenient mould of a rhythmical Scottish proverb:

> " Learn young, learn fair;
> Learn auld, learn sair."

In the horizon of the nation's future there is no more ominous cloud than the multitude of children that are advancing to maturity uneducated. We were slow to learn the danger; but we are in some measure aroused at length. The lesson has been lashed into us by the rod of correction, after gentler admonitions had been tried in vain. The aggregate of crime was becoming so great, that the vessel of the State was sensibly staggering under its weight. When we came to close quarters with full-grown criminals, we found that neglected children are the raw material out of which they grow. Efforts were put forth by individuals, societies, and the legislature, to mitigate or arrest the evil. Hence the ragged schools and kindred institutions which have of late years occupied a large share of the public attention, and which chracterize the philanthropy of the day. The opinion boldly proclaimed by some distinguished Christian patriots, That no man has a right to rear a young savage in his house, and let him loose when full-bodied to prey upon a civilized community, seems to be making its way toward general acceptance. It is conceded that when parents cannot, or will not educate their children, the nation may and should, in its own interest, effectually interfere : the disputes that have arisen respect not the principle, but the best method of carrying it into practice. Slowly and painfully the confession has been wrung from an afflicted and penitent people, that to ply the gallows and the penal colonies for the punishment of convicted malefactors is only the left-hand side of national duty ; while we permit careless or profligate parents to inundate society with a brood of young Anakim, a hybrid compound of animal strength and moral imbecility. The double conviction is taking possession of the popular mind, and already expressing itself in imperial legislation, that the nation in its collective capacity should come to the rescue, and that the rescue can be effected only by a thorough and universal education of the young. We live in an active and hopeful time. Life does not stagnate for want of movement. There is room for all—for the man of thought, and the man of labour—for all who have talents, and all the talents of each. We need a spark of truth from the head of the wise, and a push from the arm of the strong—one contribution to the direction of the movement, and another to its force. To draw the country out of the slough in which it has deeply settled down, we need a long pull, and a strong pull, and a pull all together.

We must not deceive ourselves by accepting a shadow for the substance ; a general confession that the thing ought to be done is not the doing of the thing. The kind of evil spirit that possesses the outcast, neglected youth of the kingdom, will not go out before a blast of words, whether spoken or printed. After all that has been said, the greater part of the work remains to be done. The number of children undergoing a training into evil, is at once the greatest disgrace and the greatest danger to the commonwealth. The most formidable barrier, however, which impedes practical reformation is neither the inertia of parliament nor the intolerance of sects, but the short-sighted selfishness of human hearts. It costs something to keep our outcast brother in a course of training from childhood into adolescence, and therefore under various pretexts we shuffle the obligation off. The sin most surely finds us out, and exacts a fourfold retribution, but we are not prudent enough to foresee the evil and hide from it betimes in measures of prevention. Even the machinery which has been erected for the accomplishment of this work is left in part unemployed, not for want of the raw material, but to save the expense of the operation. Corporations and communities, penny wise and pound foolish, save their money, and leave the lost little ones lying in the nation's skirts, like the cannon balls which they sew up in the hasty winding-sheet of those who die at sea, a dead-weight to make the body sink. The guardians of a union may stave off an assessment by making strait the gate of entrance to the industrial school ; * but out of the ashes of every such crushed request a sturdier applicant springs up, whose demands they will be compelled to grant,—whose heaviest drafts they will be compelled to honour. It is easy to abandon feeble infants, but when abandoned children have grown wicked men, their voice must be heard, and their weight will be felt. Crime and punishment constitute the awful Nemesis of our neglect. Train up a child in the way he should go, while he is a child.

---

* I have myself danced attendance on a police magistrates' court from day to day, according to successive appointments by the officials, provided with witnesses and the person of the culprit, in the hope of rescuing a fatherless child from a training in beggary by her own mother; and have been compelled to retire from the conflict baffled and disgusted, because agents of parochial boards protected successfully the cash-box of their constituents

For that specific work, now only is the accepted time; now is the day of salvation.

2. The process of education,—" *Train up* a child." Of late years much attention has been directed to the distinction between teaching and training. The effort was needed, and has been useful. The tendency in a former age to pile up reading, writing, and a few other kindred arts, and call them education, was superficial in its philosophy, and disastrous in its practical results. There cannot be training without teaching ; but there may be teaching without training. The various branches of knowledge which the teacher imparts constitute as it were the elements which the trainer employs. They are the types skilfully cast, and lying in the fount before him ; but they have little meaning, and less power, until they have been arranged in his frame, and submitted to his press. Moral training according to a divine standard, with the view of moulding the human being, while yet young and tender, into right principles and habits of action, and using up in its processes all kinds and degrees of information within its reach, is the only education worthy of the name. So much has of late been done in this department, and so familiar have all the intelligent portion of the community become with the subject, that though it comes most naturally in our way, we do not think it necessary in this place either to explain what moral training is, or to enforce its paramount importance in education.

The oldest training school is still the best : home is the best school-room, sisters and brothers the best class-fellows, parents the best masters. The chief value of those charitable institutions for the training of the young which characterize and honour our age, consists in supplying the lack of home education. These schools deserve all the praise that has been bestowed on them ; but it is on the principle that when the best has entirely failed, the next best is very precious. When limbs are broken, hospitals are excellent ; but it would have been better both for the patients and the community if hospitals had not been needed. To make well in the industrial school is good ; but to keep well in the home is better,—is best. We speak specifically of training, the highest department of education. As to its subordinate materials, the arts of reading and writing, and the like, parents even in the best state of society do well to avail themselves of professional aid ; but themselves should preside over the process, and with their own hearts and hands labour to get the whole, while soft, cast into a heavenly mould of truth and righteousness. Let any one and every one help in spreading a sail and catching a breeze, but let the parent keep the helm in his own hands.

Formidable obstacles, both intrinsic and extrinsic, prevent or impede parental training. In some cases personal deficiencies, in others the pressure of circumstances from without, and in many both barriers combined, stand in the way of the work. But in all these the beautiful law of Providence appears, that good principles and habits, as well as bad, count kin and help each other. Suppose a father and mother personally deficient, but desiring to have their children trained to truth and righteousness,—observe how the various portions of the machinery work together for good. In giving them children, and filling their hearts with parental love, God has supplied them at once with the best exercise for improvement and the most powerful motive to urge them on. Love to the little ones will make them try the training, and each trial will increase their capacity for the work. Every effort to train their children will elevate themselves ; and every degree of elevation to which they attain will be an addition to their power of doing good to the children. God's good gifts run in circles ; and an entrance into his family in the spirit of adoption secures for you the benefit of them all. If you should certainly know that in five years hence your boy, who is now a little child, would fall into a deep river all alone, you would not wait till the event should happen ere you prepared to meet it : you would begin now the process which would be safety then. Your child cannot swim, and you are not qualified to teach him ; but forthwith you would acquire the art yourself, that you might communicate it to him, and that he might be prepared to meet the emergency. Now beyond all peradventure your child, if he survive, will in a few years be plunged into a sea of wickedness, through which he must swim for his life. Nothing but right moral principles, obtained from the Bible, and indurated by early training into a confirmed habit, will give him the necessary buoyancy. Hence, as you would preserve your child from sinking through the sea of sin into final perdition, you are bound to qualify yourself for training him up in the way he should go.

In like manner when the obstacles are extrinsic, the necessities of his child supply the parent with motives to exert himself for their removal; and the effort which he makes for his child will rebound in blessings on himself. For example, if a parent has, through carelessness or a supposed necessity, adopted a line of life which demands Sabbath-day labour, or late hours all the week, he will discover, as his children grow up, that his business is incompatible with his duty to them. If, from love to his family and enlightened desire for their welfare, he successfully shake off the bondage, and obtain the means of living without giving the Lord's day or the evening hours to labour, he has thereby secured a double boon,—to his children and to himself.

Sabbath-school instruction, although good as far as it goes, does not supply adequate moral education for the juvenile hordes which infest the streets of our large cities. The interval between Sabbath and Sabbath is too wide. It is like spreading a net with meshes seven inches wide instead of one, before a shoal of herrings. By the great gap of the week, the little Arabs easily slip through, in spite of the stout string which you extend across their path on the Sabbath evening. Ply the work by all means, and ply it hopefully. Labour for the Lord in that department will not be lost: saving truth is thereby deposited in many minds, which the Spirit of God will make fruitful in a future day. Ply the work of Sabbath schools, but let not the existence and abundance of these efforts deceive us into the belief that the work is adequately done. The Sabbath-school cannot train up a child: the six days' training at home, if it be evil, will, in the battle of life, carry it over the one day's teaching in the school, however good it may be.

3. The aim and end of education,—" Train up a child *in the way he should go.*" This is the most important of the three. Wisdom in choosing the proper time, and skill in adopting the best method, would be of no avail if false principles were instilled into the mind, and evil habits ingrafted on the life. If you are in the wrong way, the more vigorously you prosecute the journey the sooner will disaster come. If we do not train the children in Truth and Righteousness, it would be better that we should not train them at all. Here, at the very outset, we meet full in the face the old question, " What is truth ? " The Teacher to whom Pilate petu-

lantly put the question will give us the answer, if we reverently sit at his feet: " I am the way, and the truth, and the life; no man cometh unto the Father but by me." Christ is the truth, and the Scriptures the standard by which truth may be known. This is not only religiously the best solution of the question, but philosophically the only solution that can be given. If we do not adopt the Bible as our standard in training the young, combined training is impossible. If in moral principles every man is his own lawgiver, there is no law at all, and no authority. You may train a fruit-tree by nailing its branches to a wall, or tying them to an espalier railing; but the tree whose branches have nothing to lean on but air is not trained at all. It is not a dispute between the Scriptures and some other rival standard, for no such standard exists or is proposed: it is a question between the Bible as a standard, and no standard at all. But training without an acknowledged standard is nothing—is an empty form of words, by which ingenious men amuse themselves. There are some who would borrow from the Bible whatever moral principles they have, and yet are unwilling to own the Scriptures in their integrity, as an authority binding the conscience; because, if it is binding in one thing, it is binding in all.

We assume, then, that if moral training has any substantial existence, it is a training according to the rule and under the authority of the Bible, as the revealed will of God. In efficient training these two things are absolutely necessary,—a *rule* to show the ignorant what the way is, and an *authority* to keep the wayward on it. A thread extended in the air between two points is a sufficient rule for those who need nothing but a rule, and by such a line, accordingly, the builder rears his wall; but an extended thread pointing out the boundary between your garden and your neighbour's is not sufficient where children and ripe fruit are brought into contact. Besides a mark to let them see where their neighbour's property is, a wall is needed to keep them out of it. In the Scriptures, received and revered as the inspired word of God for the whole duty of man, we have at once a conspicuous rule and a supreme authority. Those who practically neglect or theoretically oppose that word, have bereft themselves both of the knowledge and the power necessary in the moral training of youth: they have neither a line to let the honest see the right way, nor a sanction to prevent the dishonest from transgressing it.

The adverse argument of theorists, although it opens up an interesting field of speculation, does not in practice exert much power. The objection to scriptural doctrine in the training of the young proceeds upon the assumption that, if you imbue the mind with opinions before the judgment is capable of independently sifting the evidence, the ultimate issue cannot be a reasonable service. The difficulty so pressed emits an imposing sound, but its heart is hollow and its sides are thin : it collapses under the slightest rub. To leave the mind throughout childhood without prepossessions in regard to religious truth is simply impossible. The question does not lie between furnishing the mind with opinions in youth, and leaving it empty. Left empty it cannot be : we are limited to the alternative of filling it with the sifted wheat of truth, or abandoning it to be filled with the flying chaff of various error. If you do not employ the revealed doctrines of the Bible as an authoritative rule in the training of your child, you have not maintained neutrality : you have decided for your child against the authority of the Bible. When he has, under your training, grown up to manhood without God in the world, you cannot bring him back to the softness of childhood again, to correct the error, if error there has been. We are shut up to the necessity of making a choice for the moral training of our children, as certainly as we are shut up to the necessity of choosing the kind of food by which their bodies shall be sustained.

But further : the argument which proves that we should not commit the child according to our opinion, proves too much, and therefore proves nothing. The principle would compel you to leave the child untaught on many other points besides the doctrines of revealed religion. The youth whose intellect has been highly educated from childhood, may in maturity adopt the opinion that such education is an evil, and that he would have been happier if he had grown up a worse philosopher and a robuster man. But he is committed for ever by the choice of his parents. The effects of that choice cannot be removed. The same reasoning holds good even in matters more exclusively physical. On the same supposition you have no right to determine for your child the kind of food and clothing to which his frame shall be habituated, for that choice once made can never in its effects be reversed. The child could not judge; you judged for him; and the man is bound all his days by your decision. Some sort of training, both physical and moral, you must give the child, and you are bound to give him that which in your judgment is best, for he is incapable of forming a judgment for himself.

A Chinese parent compresses his child's feet, by shoes of peculiar shape and diminutive size. An African parent covers his child's face with fantastic markings, and stamps them indelibly in the flesh. Both operations are useless and cruel: they thwart the purposes of God, and leave a blemish on his beautiful work. These parents sin in thus disfiguring for life the bodies of their children. They err; but wherein does the error lie? Not in the fact of forming a judgment as to the treatment of their infants, but in forming a judgment that is false and injurious. In this enlightened community every parent, by aid of professional skill, performs a painful operation on the body of his infant. He makes a wound in the flesh, and into that wound insinuates a drop of poisonous fluid. The poison circulates through the blood. A fever ensues, and an unsightly sore grows over the wound, leaving a permanent mark in the skin. You find no fault with the parent for all this. Why? Because he thereby diminishes greatly the risk of a dangerous disease. The operation is useful; the judgment that dictated it was sound. This shows on what ground the Chinese and African should be condemned. If you say they went beyond their province when they took it upon themselves to judge for others to the effect of indenting indelible marks upon their flesh, you include in your condemnation those parents who, with the most enlightened affection, inoculate their children to preserve them from small-pox. Both in the physical and moral departments the error lies, not in forming a judgment and carrying it out, but in forming and executing an erroneous judgment. The court is competent, if the sentence be according to truth.

But the moral training of children is much more effectually obstructed by the dead-weight of indifference which will not do it, than by the theoretic opposition which argues that it should not be done. An erroneous principle may be met by argument

—may be neutralized by diffused truth; but what can argument do against the inertia of parents who, in thousands and tens of thousands, eat and drink and sleep, leaving their children to nature and chance, as trees of the forest or beasts of the field?

In this department much remains to be done. Our position, nationally, is not high in the godly upbringing of the young at present; but one good symptom is, that we have of late been in some measure awakened to observe and confess our defects. In the meantime three classes of persons amongst us should be supported by all the help that human arms can offer, and cheered by all the hopes that can be brought from heaven. These are, 1.) Those parents who devote themselves at home to the training of their own children in the way of truth and goodness; (2.) Those who prosecute household missionary work in lapsed and listless families; and (3.) Those who, by combined effort and on a large scale, gather outcast children into schools, whether on the Lord's day or throughout the week, and there nobly do their best to heal again the wounds which other hands have already made.

It is a blessed employment to be leading little ones to Jesus; we know that it is a service with which the Lord himself is well pleased. These neglected wanderers, when gathered in, constitute the kingdom, and satisfy the soul of the King. To gather them is honourable work: it is a "well-doing" of which Christians should never weary.

The Bondage of the Borrower
(Proverbs 22:7)

"The rich ruleth over the poor, and the borrower is servant to the lender."

THE law is laid down in general terms, that it may be freely modified in its application by the circumstances of each case. It is not written, Thou shalt not borrow; or, Thou shalt not lend. The text describes the practical consequences of the act, and leaves every reader to judge for himself whether his circumstances permit or require him to come under their influence. In some cases it may be right to borrow, and in others it is certainly wrong : this text does not cut the knot and make morality easy by an authoritative permission on the one side, or an authoritative prohibition on the other. It is an instance of the reserve which is a common characteristic of Scripture. Minute directions are not given for the conduct of daily life. Principles are laid down and tendencies indicated ; and from these every man must construct a working plan for himself, according to the analogy of faith and the testimony of conscience.

A book of medicine, emanating from the highest authority, distinctly describes the effects of a certain stimulant, when administered internally, upon the human body. It quickens the circulation, and stirs all the vital functions into a greater than their normal activity ; but when the effect of the potion has passed away, a lassitude supervenes, which brings down the patient's strength to a lower point than that at which it stood before the application of the stimulant. The medicine adds nothing to the permanent resources of the system, but gives you the command of a stronger impulse for a time, on condition of full repayment, and something to boot, as the price of the accommodation. Already we know certainly that this article of the pharmacopœia may in peculiar circumstances be useful as a medicine, but can never in any case be available as food. A man may be so situated that the power of making an extraordinary effort for an hour will be worth purchasing at the price of an exhaustion many degrees below his normal condition during the whole of the following day. In such a case temporary resort to the medicine may be a lawful expedient; but no circumstances can possibly make it wise or safe to administer or use it from day to day as an ordinary article of food.

The expedient to which the " borrower " resorts in his difficulty is precisely such a stimulant. It is not necessarily and in all cases evil. It is a medicine, but not food. It may sometimes be administered with good effect at the crisis of the pecuniary distress; but such is the character of this substance, that you cannot safely employ it as a curative agent at all, unless you secure the highest professional advice as to the prescription at first, and exercise the most scrupulous care afterwards in the actual administration of the dose. Thus prescribed and thus administered, it is lawful and useful. It is one of those good things of God which watchful disciples may receive with thankfulness, and use with profit. When you have taken into consideration the character and capacity of the individual who requires the stimulant, the kind and extent of the losses that have temporarily placed him in straits, and the prospects of trade at the time, generally in the community and particularly in his own department—when you have considered and compared all these elements, and found that the stoppage is only a momentary faint in a sound constitution, by all means administer the draught: but watch the patient while he is under its influence, and bring him back as soon as possible to his ordinary regimen. If he begin to like the stimulant, and the dreamy comfort which it supplies; if he manifest a tendency to resort to another dose as soon as the effects of the last begin to wear away,—the symptoms are alarming. The patient has acquired a morbid appetite for the medicine. The cure has become more dangerous to him than the disease.

There is a remarkably close analogy between the expedient of borrowing money in a temporary strait, and the expedient of borrowing for the moment from your own future store by means of ardent spirits. There is a likeness in the usefulness and power of the expedients when skilfully applied at the crisis of an ailment;

a likeness in the tendency to undue repetition of the stimulants, often begotten in the patient by their use ; and a likeness in the wretched life-long bondage to which the victim is reduced when that which at first was occasionally resorted to as a medicine has become necessary to him as daily food.

When an honest and industrious man has been thrown into pecuniary distress by a series of adverse circumstances which he could neither foresee nor avert, he may—he should cast about for some one who can, by a loan, help him over the chasm which has suddenly opened across his path and forbids his progress. When a man of worth has fallen into such a strait, he generally finds some one able and willing to do a brother's turn. In this lower sphere of temporal things, they who wait upon the Lord are often enabled to renew their strength. In this department, they who observe wisely the course of events, may often see and taste the loving-kindness of the Lord. Having frankly grasped in his weakness a brother's offered arm, he puts all his energies to their utmost stretch, in order to reach at the earliest moment an independent footing, where he can stand alone again. This done, he takes his own burden upon his own shoulders, and sets his benefactor free. It is well. He fell into distress ; he applied a remedy ; the remedy was successful ; he is thankful for the relief which it gave him, but he has no desire to continue the application of the remedy ; he casts it away as the convalescent casts away his drugs, glad that he had them in the time of need, but as glad to get quit of them when the time of need is past. This hearty, conclusive repudiation of the labelled bottles that stood in rows in his sick-room, is one symptom that the cure is complete. The tendency, wherever it is manifested, to continue sipping at the stimulant or narcotic draught, is evidence that if the patient has been relieved of one disease, he has in the process contracted a worse. The honest man who borrowed in a time of need, never breathes freely till he is standing on his own feet, and working his own way again. " Owe no man anything," sounded in his ears as long as he was in debt ; and he felt that he could not answer to the Lord, whose word it is, if he should indolently neglect any opportunity of reducing it. His fear of God and his regard for man conspire to strain every nerve in the effort to be free.

But there is in the community a numerous class whose normal condition is debt. If at the first they took borrowed money, as they might take opium, a medicine to relieve an acute disease which would not yield to other means, they chew it now every day and all day, as the staff of their life. The appetite has become like a second nature. Whenever real life touches the dreamer roughly, he opens his eyes languidly, takes another pill, and sleeps himself into the fool's paradise again, until the next jolt disturbs his ignoble slumbers. This disease is prevalent in the community. There are dealers of various grades who seem to count debt their element; they live in it; they do not expect to get out of it; they scarcely wish—at least they never energetically strive to get out. They borrow and spend, and borrow again, in a weary, unvarying circle. If they lose, the loss falls on others, for they never possess anything which is really their own. The disease is chronic, and the patient in some sense actually likes to be in it. To him the negative condition of debt affords fewer cares than would the positive possession of wealth. A community cannot thrive in which this habit of life largely prevails: a family is wretched whose daily supply is filtered through this unhealthy medium. A soul cannot grow in grace while the lower life is steeped in this stagnant element.

Beside the ravages which it commits in the higher sphere of commerce, this vice is spreading among the labouring poor, and weakening society by eating into its foundations. The difference between a workman who pays his way as he goes, and a workman who lives on credit, is in one aspect very small, and in another very great. A very small sum of money saved or squandered, and a very slight personal effort made or refused, will turn the balance and determine whether of the two conditions shall be yours; but though the antecedents of the two conditions lie so near each other, their consequences are far apart. A very little, in the way of cause, will place a man in this position or in that; but this position will produce to its occupant, in the way of effect, a life of comfort, and that position a life of misery. A little makes the difference; but the difference which that little makes is very great.

Morally and materially the habit of borrowing is to a working man and his family an incalculable evil. It is eminently a demoralizing habit. The man who indulges it loses by degrees the power to keep a shilling in his pocket. The winsome but delicate bloom of self-respect is soon worn off. By giving up the exercise, you soon destroy the power of foresight : the capacity of self-denial is destroyed and the reins flung loose on the neck of indulgence. Such is the blighting influence of this habit that no virtue can live in its atmosphere.

As it is morally a vice, it is economically a blunder. Here the truth of the text comes most clearly out, that the borrower is servant to the lender ; and a degrading service it is. If the workman borrows from his employer, he is enslaved to the capitalist, and has lost the power of maintaining his own rights : if he borrows from a shopkeeper, he has thrown away the privilege of buying in the cheapest market. The vice is reduced to a system in large communities, and cultivated as a trade. It is a wound received in life's stern battle, and left without a bandage to fester in the sun : it affords food and feasting to a horde of vermin, but wastes the poor soldier's life away.

Two mechanics are employed in the same factory, and live with their families in contiguous dwellings. From the one house, at certain stated seasons, the wife and mother issues forth with money in her hand to purchase necessaries for her household : from the other, the wife and mother steals out at irregular intervals and untimely hours to borrow the means of satisfying her children's hunger. Into both houses the same amount of weekly wages comes ; but twenty shillings laid out bring more comfort into this house than into that. The buyer goes to any shop that pleases her, and takes there the articles which she judges cheap and good : the borrower is led by an agent to the shopkeeper who is willing to part with his goods without receiving their price. The merchant who sells on credit to such a class of customers needs a large profit, and takes it. The article is dearer to the borrower than it is to the buyer, and not so good. The agent must be paid too for seeking out the customer, and it is the customer who pays for being sought out. The borrower is the lender's slave : the servant is impoverished, and probably in the long-run the master is not enriched.

When the system is fully elaborated, the agent prowls about during the day, when the wives are idle and the husbands absent baiting his hook, and getting its barb insinuated into the victim's mouth. He gives a showy article in hand, which the woman may wear to-morrow, although she has not a penny wherewith to pay for it. Her name is inscribed in his book under an obligation to pay one shilling every week, until the payments reach a pound,— this sum being considered sufficient to cover material, agency, risk, and interest. Ten or twelve weeks in succession the poor woman wends her way to the appointed place and deposits her shilling. Then the gaudy garment disappears from her shoulders : perhaps the pawnbroker's shelves could give some account of it. She has not now the comfort of possession. When the article is off her back, the shilling slips from her memory. The payments are interrupted one day—one hour beyond the stipulated time. At this opening a pair of pincers, diabolically prepared beforehand, are introduced, to tear out the pound of flesh according as it is in the bond. They are constructed thus : Certain messengers, or sheriff's officers, in league with the agent and sharers of the spoil, come in with a summons to the small debt court. Decreet, as a matter of course, goes against the defaulter, expenses and all. A large portion of the expenses consists of fees to these officers. If, in addition to the principal, the names of two securities have been attached to the bond, each is served with a summons, and a triple profit accrues. Business and pay are thus created for the company, and the miserable borrower serves the associated lenders as the worn-out camel serves the watchful vultures, when the caravan has passed and left it lying still living on the sand. One form of human vice suggests and sustains another. As long as men will fight and kill each other in thousands, creatures in human form will follow the trail of armies, and prowl on the battle-field at night, stripping the dead, and occasionally, perhaps, giving the finishing stroke to the dying. As long as the improvidence of multitudes shall provide the carcase, harpies will hover overhead, and make a bold swoop down for a morsel as often as an opportunity occurs : nor is it to be expected, considering their character and calling, that when the victim is helplessly prostrate, they will always be scrupulously conscientious in waiting till the breath go out. The rank corruption that has been allowed to creep over the economic condition of the people, allures and harbours these loathsome night birds. The evils are deeply seated and widely spread,—only one cure can fully meet the malady; but the evils lean on each other, and to cut the roots of one would impede the progress of the rest.

We have already said that a very small amount of money and effort would suffice to turn the scale, and give the borrower all the buyer's vantage-ground. Of time a week, of money twenty shillings sterling,—this is all external to the men, that constitutes the interval between them. In a fishing village, on the margin of an estuary through which one of our larger rivers pours itself into the sea, live two labouring men. On each is laid the task of pulling his boat with the produce of certain fisheries daily up the river, to a market town about fifteen miles inland. One starts with the flowing tide, and returns on its receding wave: the other delays his departure till the tide has turned. A single mistake insures a double misfortune: the sluggard must contend against the stream in his upward voyage, and the tide has set in against him again ere he is ready to return. These two men accomplish the same distance in a day, and over the same course; but the task of the one is easy, and the task of the other hard. Such is the difference between the workman who, having fallen behind the world once, remains behind it always, and the workman who begins by paying his way, and has always the means of paying it. One effort, one sacrifice, and instead of running hither and thither with your wages to pay the debts of the past, you have the money free in your hand to command the market for the time to come. This could easily be accomplished, but the character which would keep matters right when they are right is not so easily attained. Although you should give the borrower a sum of money sufficient to pay all his debts, he will soon be deeper in debt than ever. Unless the moral principle be implanted, and the provident habit formed, no amount of material contribution can improve the condition of the people. Wealth and charity in league cannot do it. Although mountains of gold and silver were thrown into the chasm, it would gape as dark and wide as before. In this matter as in others we must adopt the Lord's way, and employ his instruments. Train up a child in the way he should go, and when he is old, he will in no wise depart from it.

These things are more intimately connected with spiritual religion than the reader at first sight may suppose. If one should say in regard to the natural history of animals, Let us have the life of the living creature, and we care not what may be the constituents of the element in which it dwells,—you would not count him a discriminating observer. No less does he miss the mark who, in efforts for the regeneration of the people, concerns himself only with their faith in Christ, and neglects, as irrelevant, the economics of their homes.

Spiritual life, we confess, is the one thing above all others needful for the dead in sin; but that life will not thrive—that life cannot be in an alien element. The double difficulty of paying an old debt and contracting a new one is precisely "the care of this life" which will most effectually choke the word and make it unfruitful. When Moses proclaimed to Israel in Egypt the richest promises of God, it is expressly recorded that "they hearkened not unto Moses for anguish of spirit, and for cruel bondage" (Exod. vi. 9). The consolation which the lawgiver brought to them from the treasures of divine grace was the very medicine which their broken hearts needed; but these hearts were so crushed by oppression that they could not take the consolation in. The perplexity of the Hebrews when they were compelled to make bricks without straw could not be greater than that of a labouring man in one of our cities, with hungry children round him, and his wages all spent before they are won. The pawnbroker and his kin are harder masters than any Pharaoh that ever ruled in Egypt. When the borrower is conclusively subjected to the lender's yoke, his bondage is more irksome than that under which ancient Israel groaned. The perennial anguish which accompanies this economic dislocation forbids the approach of saving truth to the soul that needs it most. The new life, begotten by the Spirit and growing into strength, would prevail to cure the economic derangement; but reciprocally, an improved condition of the household economics would powerfully work together with more direct means to kindle and cherish the spiritual life.

Can these dry bones live? They may; but it is when the Spirit of the Lord breathes life into them. Reformation will not do: regeneration is needed.

Convenient Food

(Proverbs 23:1-3)

"When thou sittest to eat with a ruler, consider diligently what is before thee: and put a knife to thy throat, if thou be a man given to appetite. Be not desirous of his dainties: for they are deceitful meat."

FORTY years ago, on the banks of the river Earn, five or six miles above its confluence with the Tay, an elderly countryman, the tenant of a small farm, sat on a mossy bank beneath the shade of a beech-tree, and ate from his own knee the dinner which his boy, then playing beside him, had brought at the appointed hour to the field of labour. A gentle breeze fanned gratefully the branches of the sheltering tree, and the grizzled locks on the bared head of the labourer. Fleecy clouds were flying slowly over a background of blue sky, and answering shadows flitting across the waving fields of hay and corn. At that moment the lord of the manor passed by. Too kind-hearted to turn aside, and too polite to interrupt the meal of his tenant friend, he said without stopping as he passed, in tones as gentle as a mother's when she soothes her child to sleep,—" Well, Robert, you are dining." "Yes, my lord," replied Robert, elevating the hand in token of respect, and glancing upward through the beechen boughs to the glorious canopy beyond,—" Yes, my lord, and I have an elegant dining-room." A suppressed smile could be seen playing about his lordship's lips, as he stalked forward with stately step in his wonted solitary, silent roam. I was there the only witness. My memory faithfully records the scene and recalls the laconic colloquy. The facts were deeply planted in my mind at the time, but the philosophy did not begin to bud till long afterward. The only effect which the great man's approach produced on me was to make me leave the chased butterfly uncaught, and the coveted wild flower unplucked, and creep close to my protector, holding in my breath till " my lord " was out of sight. Since that period, and especially since both the interlocutors have passed away from the stage, I have often recalled that and similar interviews that passed under my observation, and thought with a sigh, how happy this country would be in its domestic condition, and how mighty in its foreign relations, if the several classes of society through all its borders were knit to each other by bonds as soft and strong as these. Two and thirty years these two lived in the relation of landlord and tenant. During that period the rent was never changed, and never in arrear. In their intercourse the superior was never haughty, the inferior never presuming. The one maintained all the dignity of the noble, the other all the self-respect of the man. When the tenant died in a good old age, the landlord, himself by that time advanced in years, mourned for the loss of a friend, and said with tears that his patrimonial fields were growing less lovely as the old occupiers were, one by one, departing.*

The dining-room was such as nature only could provide, and the dinner was all that nature needed. When an appetite such as hay-making begets in a healthful frame turns the plainest fare into a luxury, the maximum of both pleasure and utility in eating is attained. An ignoble warfare is waged, an ignoble race is run, when people strive to make up for the failing appetite of the indolent eater by elaborate refinements in the ingredients and preparation of the food. Luxury makes the senses dull, and then intenser luxury is needed to penetrate into the quick of these dull senses. On either side men strive to produce and maintain a right relation between the appetite and the food. On this side, rich fools strive by culinary art to raise the savour of the viands to such a point of pungency that they shall produce lively sensations of pleasure on a worn and weary palate : on that side, the wise, whether rich or poor, by exercise and temperance easily bring healthful hunger up to such a pitch that it finds sweetest luxury in the hardest fare. In this matter the multitude are not left to their own judgment : they are in better hands. Labour and open air are imposed upon them whether they will or not, for their good. Our Father in heaven cares for them as for children. Delicate

---

* As the facts are narrated with the most rigid accuracy, without either exaggeration or addition, and the persons have both been removed by death, there seems no longer any reason for veiling the name of that amiable and honoured proprietor, the late Lord Ruthven. of Freeland, Perthshire.

dishes, fitted to provoke into activity the languid desire, cannot be provided for the majority of men: the other alternative is the better of the two. Where there is not wealth to season the food, there is labour to invigorate the appetite. Here is yet another point at which the rich and the poor meet together; setting aside exceptional cases from both classes, it will probably be conceded by all dispassionate observers, that the poor on the whole enjoy as much pleasure through the sense of taste from their food as the rich.

The first specific warning on the subject which the proverbs contain, is given in these three verses. The case supposed is that of a ruler—a man of wealth and luxurious habits—who prepares a feast and invites his friends. The guests are enjoined to consider well the delicacies that are set before them, and beware of excess. The two elements which constitute the danger are both taken into account; these are, the weakness of the tempted and the strength of the temptation. Coarse fare tends to check the excesses of an inordinate appetite: and a subdued appetite makes you safe with the most luxurious food. The danger is doubled when both the elements meet—when a ruler spreads a tempting feast, and the guest is a man given to appetite.

It is of the Lord that hunger is painful, and food gives pleasure: between these two lines of defence the Creator has placed life, with a view to its preservation. If eating had been as painful as it is pleasant to our nature, the disagreeable duty would have been frequently forgotten or neglected, and the world, if peopled at all, would have been peopled by tribes of walking skeletons. The arrangement which·provides that the necessary reception of aliment into the system gives pleasure to the senses, is wise and good; it is an ungrateful return for our Maker's kindness when the creature turns his bounty into licentiousness. The due sustenance of the body is the Creator's end; the pleasantness of food the means of attaining it. When men prosecute and cultivate that pleasure as an end, they thwart the very purposes of providence. When the pleasure is pursued as an object, it ceases to serve effectually as a means of healthfully maintaining the living frame.

When the appetite is strong, and the food enticing, the danger of sinning and suffering is great,—greater than most of us care to observe, and acknowledge to ourselves. The warning here is strongly expressed, and all its strength is needed. "Put a knife to thy throat," is in form similar to the injunctions of the Great Teacher, to pluck out the offending right eye, and cut off the offending right hand. "Be not desirous of his dainties, for they are deceitful meat." They are of set purpose made deceitful : they are prepared by an artist of skill, whose whole life is devoted to the study. Resisting virtue in the guests must be strong indeed, for the temptation is as powerful as wealth and experience can make it.

Although there is much poverty in the community there is also much wealth. Wherever there is much wealth there is much luxury. Some forms of luxury are much more dignified and safe than others. We speak here of one form only, one that lies near the bottom of the scale. Great feasts are a ready outlet for great riches ; and in this way, accordingly, those who have much money and little refinement relieve themselves of their surplus. I am well aware that in this matter much depends on circumstances, and an absolute rule is not possible. I shall not, by descending into the details of the kitchen and the dining-room, give the culprit an opportunity of laughing down the reproof. I cannot come down to dispute with epicures about the number of dishes and the ingredients of each : with my footing firm on the higher platform, I can deal a more effective blow. "Whether ye eat or drink, or whatsoever ye do, do all to the glory of God." "Put a knife to thy throat, if thou be a man given to appetite." This is the authority on which we stand : these are the rules which we prescribe. Let these rules be applied to our feasts, and their dimensions will, in many instances, be curtailed.

In this department of practical duty, as in many others, innocence and guilt are not divided from each other by a visible partition-wall rising sheer up between them : they meet on each other's margin as the colours of the rainbow meet. In all cases it is a matter of degrees. The point of optimism is not fixed; it moves from side to side with the internal constitution of the individual, and the condition of society around him. If it were not so, there would be a defect in the moral discipline of men. The dividing line is not such as to force itself on the notice of those who do not look for it. They who seek shall find it; they who do not seek shall miss it. The law of the greatest good in the sustenance of our bodies is, like God its author, the rewarder of them that diligently seek it.

To sit two dreary hours, as if pinioned to your chair and your neighbour, in a room kept steaming with hot viands, chasing each other out and in,—to have so many dishes of diverse flavours placed under your nostrils in quick succession, that unless your gastric stability be above the average, you cannot comfortably partake of any one,—to have your ears filled meantime with matter not much more ethereal than that which occupies your other senses, —all this I would be disposed to shun as an endurance, rather than accept as a favour. The money is not well laid out: the time is not profitably spent. Unnecessary cares are laid on the heads of the house, and unnecessary labour on the servants. Worst of all, the mind is clogged by all that goes beyond the sufficient supply of nature's need. In greater or less measure, the dipping into these manifold and artfully-prepared meats impedes the soul in its flight, as when the feet of a winged insect are immersed in mud. We have need for all our mental power always. The soul needs all its buoyancy to bear home the precious freight, and should not be willingly weighed down by such vile ballast. Simplicity in these things both imparts the highest pleasure and brings in the richest profit. Simplicity is both godly and manly. Religion prescribes philosophy approves simplicity.

The Rights of Man

(Proverbs 22:22, 23; 23:10, 11)

" Rob not the poor, because he is poor: neither oppress the afflicted in the gate: for the
Lord will plead their cause, and spoil the soul of those that spoiled them."

" Remove not the old landmark; and enter not into into the fields of the fatherless: for their
Redeemer is mighty; he shall plead their cause with thee."

T HE margin of the Forth opposite Edinburgh is fringed
for several miles by a broad belt of trees, very lofty and
very luxuriant, as these matters go in this northern
clime. The line of the shore at the spot is partly a curving bay, and
partly a rocky, precipitous headland. A straight arched avenue of
beeches, dimly lighted in the day-time through the telescopic opening on the sky at its further extremity, might seem the vestibule
of some vast temple not made with hands of men, yet sacred to
the worship of the Creator. Labyrinths of shaded walks,—now
straight, now curving,—now closed on both sides by thickets, and
now exposing suddenly a solitary sail on the glittering sea, or the
spires of the distant city,—persuade the urban visitant that he is approaching the forbidden precincts of some feudal palace. Yet the
people of all ranks pass and repass unchallenged: no liveried warder
is seen watching for trespassers. At either end the visitor enters
by a breach in a substantial stone wall of recent workmanship. The
sides of the gateways are not squared by the tool of the mason:
both openings are ragged disruptions, as if the walls had been
blown up by gunpowder or breached by cannon shot, to make way
for an assaulting column. Why this mark of war in a scene over
which a perfect peace is brooding? Thereby hangs a tale; there
was a war, and the peace which now prevails is the fruit of vic·
tory.

A few years ago, the great proprietors of the neighbourhood,
believing that their rights were absolute, built the public out by
a massive wall of stone and lime. The people quickly burst the

barriers and regained possession ; but they did not stop there : they organized, procured funds, and tried the case in the courts of law. They were successful, and secured for themselves and posterity the unchallenged right to one of the finest marine promenades that the varied coast-line of our island supplies. Peasants, artisans, and merchants, mothers and children, young men and maidens, tread promiscuously these stately avenues, with the firm step and upward look of the free : the neighbouring nobles have not a surer right to their castles and estates. An attempt was made, in good faith, but in ignorance, to remove an ancient landmark ; it failed : the rights of the poor were defended successfully against the encroachments of the rich.

To whom did the feeble owe their victory over the strong ? A court of law, you will say, and no feudal superior, threw its broad shield over them. It did : but the real cause of the event lies deeper. A mightier Redeemer espouses the cause of the poor in this land. The liberty of the subject is secured by a more ancient charter than that which constitutes the Court of Session. The Bible is the true *Magna Charta* of British freedom. Courts of law were established in this land at a time when the Bible was under ban, and what did our forefathers gain by the privilege ? Courts of law did not then protect the property and person of the poor from the grasp of the powerful : they dispensed law, but not justice. The triumph of true religion brought in the era of equal rights : when the conscience was emancipated from the thraldom of the priest, the property was secure from the agression of the noble; when the people placed themselves under the law of God, they no longer suffered from the lawlessness of men.

There is a causal connection, and not merely a coincidence, between the spread of God's word and the security of men's rights in a land. This may be demonstrated either by examining the contents of the Book, or by reading its history. I know of no country really free in which the Bible is laid under restraint, and no country enslaved where the Bible is free. Some have zealously advocated the rights of man, and striven at the same time to throw discredit on the Scriptures. The double labour was labour lost. To undermine the foundation does not contribute to the stability of the superstructure : to blot out the first table of the Decalogue is not the best way of enforcing the second. If you teach that a man may have no god, or any god, or all gods, you cannot thereafter so effectually bring home the commandments, " Thou shalt not kill, Thou shalt not steal, Thou shalt not covet."

Living creatures, the most noxious and loathsome, have instincts ever true to guide them in their effort to preserve their own life. Such are systems of despotism: while they know not and do not good, they know unerringly what will destroy or preserve themselves: deceitful in all else, they may be trusted for one thing—for knowing surely, and warding off vigorously, whatever would endanger their own existence. With the true instinct of self-preservation, tyrants, great and small, cast or keep out Bibles from their territory. The operation of this principle has embodied in the history and jurisprudence of nations the most convincing evidence that the word of God is the true palladium of popular liberty: the Truth's chief enemies become the unwilling witnesses of the Truth. One obvious method of proving that the Bible favours spiritual, political, and social liberty, is to show that tyranny, spiritual, political, and social, sets itself with all the steadfastness of an instinct against the Bible.

1. The Bible and *spiritual* tyranny are, in their nature, reciprocally antagonist. If we show that spiritual tyranny instinctively fears and hates the Bible, we shall have proved that the religion of the Bible favours the spiritual emancipation of mankind. The Popedom is the most finished specimen of spiritual tyranny that the world has ever seen. It is not necessary to give evidence of this; both parties to our present argument will acknowledge it. It is known and acknowledged by all who are outside of the Pope's thraldom, that all who are within it are spiritually slaves. The right of private judgment is denounced as damnable heresy at Rome: " I believe as the Church believes," is lauded as the most perfect creed. The best Papist is the man who has no will and no opinion but that of his priest; and the best priest is the man who has no will but that of his superior. No man within the grasp of the Papacy is allowed to think for himself ; this is evident and notorious. But this most consummate spiritual despotism counts and treats the open Bible as its most dangerous foe. Popery has use for the Bible shut, perverting and employing it thus to enforce its own decrees ; but the Bible open—God's

word spoken to men, as shines his sun out of heaven upon the earth, it cannot endure. The advocates of Rome acknowledge that the use of the Bible is not freely allowed to the people : they confess that it is given only to such persons as the priest knows to be discreet, and as far as he permits them to use it. This is enough to show that the Bible is the acknowledged enemy of Rome. None but dangerous and dreaded books are so treated. In Italy, accordingly, and wherever Popery is supreme, the frontiers are more jealously guarded against the introduction of the Bible than against the inroads of armed men. In the circular letters of the Pope, in our own day, the Bible is denounced as the under-miner of his throne.*

Surely sceptics, who are zealous for human liberty, should see in this an evidence that the Bible comes from the Maker and Preserver of man.

2. As Rome serves for a specimen of spiritual, Russia may serve as a specimen of *political* despotism. Both kinds actually exist in each ; but the most outstanding characteristic of Rome is the spiritual, and of Russia the political slavery. The Pope is first and essentially a spiritual despot, and thereby he has reduced his subjects also into political bondage. The Czar is first and essentially a political despot, and thereby he has employed the material resources of the state to subjugate the souls of a nation. Rome has employed its despotism over the soul, to enslave also the body; Russia has employed its despotism over the body, to enslave also the soul. The religion of Russia is only a depart-ment of state administration. It is, like the religion of the old Roman empire, in the hands of the government, and used chiefly for the purpose of making the masses loyal. As in the pagan system of old, the Emperor becomes practically the object of attachment and religious reverence ; but it is on the basis of a material temporal authority that all this semi-spiritual superstruc-ture has been reared. Historically the Czar was a king before he became a god to Russia. Whereas it is the Pope's spiritual authority that procures for him money and armies: it is the Emperor's money and armies that obtain for him the super-stitious homage of his ignorant subjects.

* This chapter was written in 1856; and notwithstanding the beneficent changes that are in progress, it is left entire in this edition, that the portions which are inapplicable to the present may serve as a monument of the past.

This political tyranny, with the true instinct of self-preservation, casts out and keeps out Bibles and Christians. If the Bible be not the friend of liberty, why does the Emperor of Russia seize or turn every Bible at his frontier? The northern Pope, like his Italian brother, has no objection to a closed Bible. You may give his people a Bible if it be in a language which they do not understand; but the Bible in the Russian tongue is contraband. If any one doubts whether Russia proscribes the Bible, let him try to introduce it within her borders : at the border line he will feel an argument that will fully convince him.

To both these species of tyranny, and to both these archtyrants, our own country and our own Queen afford a blessed contrast. In this country, mind is free : in Italy it is enslaved by a blasphemous spiritual hierarchy. If any man doubts the double fact, let him change places with some of the Italian martyrs who are wandering in exile or lying in prison for the crime of being found in their own houses with open Bibles before them. But in Italy the Bible is proscribed, while it has free course here ; the inference is obvious and sure : no honest open mind can fail to take it in. Both Rome and Britain agree in the sure instinctive feeling that the Bible favours the freedom of the soul; therefore Rome keeps it out, and Britain lets it in. Rome wards it from her shores as she would the plague : Britain spreads it as sunlight over all her borders.

In Britain there is real political liberty for all classes—imperfect, indeed, but in such measure as is nowhere else seen on a large scale, except among our own sons and brothers who have planted our liberty in another soil : in Russia the government is the most absolute autocracy that it is possible to reduce to practice in human affairs : the Emperor of Russia is as strictly a despot as the limited capabilities of man will permit. Both Britain and Russia feel with unerring instinct that the Bible introduces, defends, consolidates political and civil liberty. Therefore Britain lets the Bible in, and Russia keeps it out. They know what they are doing : the creatures are acting after their kind.

3. The Bible is the enemy of *social* tyranny, and therefore the friend of social liberty. The most outrageous violations of human freedom in the social relations that have been known in modern times among civilized nations are the slave trade and slavery. It

was Christianity that first abolished the trade, and then emancipated the slaves. There were two long battles, and two glorious victories. The first secured that no more African men should be stolen from their homes and carried into bondage by British ships: the second procured the actual freedom of all who had been already bought, or born in bondage, throughout the dominions of the Crown. No fact in recent history is more certain than this, that it was the love of Christ that gave the impulse to that holy war, and the Scriptures that directed its course. The lives of its heroes are the biographies which Christians put into the hands of the young, in the hope of winning them to a Saviour, and without reference to the question of slavery. Clarkson and Cowper, Wilberforce and Buxton, the army that overcame slavery, the chiefs and the men, were a Christian army. The force that burst its bloody bonds was the force of truth, deposited from the Scriptures into human hearts, and becoming vital in believing men. The explosive energy which prevailed to heave up and cast away the mountain-weight of self-interest opposed, was the conviction in Christians that slavery is against the word and will of God.

Those who, in the present day, keep African negroes in bondage, have done more than cross the landmark and enter the fields of the fatherless: they do not permit their brother to possess a field—they do not permit their brother to possess himself. Those who carried them from their native land at first, robbed the poor because he was poor : those who now refuse to set them free, are oppressing the afflicted in the gate. The Redeemer of these orphans is mighty, and he will plead their cause.

But surely the slaveholders believe that the Bible is on their side, for they constantly appeal to it in their own defence. Why then do they frame laws to keep the negroes from knowing it ? Why do they cast citizens into prison whose only crime is that they have taught slaves to read the Bible ? When the slaveholders quote Scripture in support of their institution, the fact proves that they need its support, not that they have it. When they are really convinced that the word of God gives divine sanction to their right of property in the Africans, they will teach the Africans to read, and supply each with a Bible. The Pope and those Republicans have more in common than themselves suspect:

both are jealous of God's word, because both hold in bondage their fellow-men.

In our own country the most conspicuous example of removing ancient landmarks and robbing the poor of their heritage occurs in connection with the day of rest. "Remember the Sabbath-day, to keep it holy," is a very ancient landmark : the Father of our spirits set it up for the benefit of man, when man was first made. Some endeavour to tread it down, that they may rob the poor of their heritage, which lies safe behind it. How shall the poor man defend his patrimony, when his powerful neighbours are bent on adding it to their overgrown domains ? His only safety is to point to the ancient landmark, and appeal to his almighty Protector. If he give up the Lord's day to labour, he will plead in vain, This or that great man promised an equivalent. The day is his by an ancient charter from the King : it is his wisdom to fall back on that authentic instrument, and defy the aggressors. If the labourer hold his rest day on that authority, he will succeed ; if not, he will fail. What man gives, man can take away. The rich are rulers everywhere : the poor will go to the wall, unless he lean direct on the Omnipotent.

The command is, " Enter not into the fields of the fatherless." Orphans under age are the feeblest class of the community; in all countries they have been the peculiar prey of heartless oppressors. Because they have no help in man, God takes up their cause and makes it his own. If you have the prospect of leaving an orphan child behind you at your departing, you take care to assign your property for his use, but you do not place it in his power. Poor child ! the first sharper who passed would snatch it from his hands. You look for some one wise and great and good, and constitute him guardian of your infant's inheritance : you place the treasure under the guardian's authority, for behoof of your child.

So, " the Sabbath was made for man," but " the Son of man is Lord of the Sabbath." It is a precious legacy from the Maker of all things to poor, short-sighted, silly children. If it were in their own hands, they would barter the boon away to swindlers. But our Father in heaven, although he made it for our use, has not placed it in our power. Christ is constituted Lord of the Sabbath, and yet the Sabbath is a day for man. If it were in our power, it would soon be wrenched from our grasp : in his hands it is in safe keeping. If the poor know where their strength lies, they will keep their heritage. If these orphans appeal to their mighty Redeemer, the powers of the world dare not plant a foot within their fields. Let the fee-simple lie in the Trustee's hands, and come to him weekly for the usufruct. He will preserve the capital ; you will enjoy the life-rent.

So far has the law of God infused its spirit into the statute-book of this favoured land, and so complete is the supremacy of law, that we cannot point to an actual case of a rich man stepping with impunity over the ancient landmark and taking away the field of the fatherless. There is much of secret deceit which human laws can never reach ; but strong-handed oppression is among us impossible. While the poor have cause to rejoice in this, the powerful have no reason to repine; when a free Bible becomes the protector of right, the rights of all classes are protected equally. There is no respect of persons with God ; in as far as the principles of the Scriptures affect the jurisprudence and habits of a people, the balance is held even between conflicting interests and parties. When the common people, by a process of law, successfully maintained their own rights, they did not follow up their victory by a tumultuous assault upon the rights of the proprietors. Had they done so, law and public opinion would have conspired to repress the outrage. When the people gain a victory in a land where the word of God is not diffused and reverenced, they follow it up, and return the blow with interest; the oppressed become the oppressors. In as far as justice in our land prevails, and victors are moderate, we are indebted for the benefit to the free circulation of the Scriptures, and the hold which their doctrines have obtained upon the public mind. In proportion as the fear of the Lord pervades a community, the legislation will be wise and the executive impartial. If we accept the greater, we shall secure also the less : if a people seek first the kingdom of God, they will get it, and a kingdom on earth besides. A people religiously right, will not long remain politically wrong. As worship rises to heaven, justice radiates on earth. If faith go foremost, charity will follow.

A Faithful Father

(Proverbs 23:15-35)

"My son, if thine heart be wise, my heart shall rejoice, even mine,"

THE style of the composition has again changed. At this place the sayings are not isolated ; the discourse has become connected and continuous ; it is almost dramatic. It is a life-like sketch. Each feature stands out in strong relief, and in the perspective all blend easily into a congruous whole. The picture seems to move and speak. When the curtain rises, two persons are seen in close conversation on the stage. One is verging towards age, although his look is still fresh and his step vigorous ; his companion, though not yet of full stature, has turned his back on boyhood, and strives to look the man. They are a father and his son. They have stepped forth from their dwelling in the evening, to enjoy a walk together through the adjoining fields. For the moment they neither have nor need any other company. The senior has laid aside a portion of the austerity that belongs to his years, and the junior a portion of the levity that belongs to his. Each has approached the other, and notwithstanding disparity of age, they have met in the midst a well-matched pair. The father stooping to sympathize with the child, encourages the child to rise into sympathy with the father. There is wisdom in this method. If the instructor had been more forbidding, the pupil would have been more frivolous. A parent should spare no effort to make himself the companion of his boy : the victory is half won when the boy learns to like the company of his father.

To obtain a meeting,—to get the two minds really brought into kindly contact, is a great point, but it is not the whole : a platform to work upon is secured, but the work remains yet to be done. Notwithstanding the points of coincidence, these two are in many features diverse. The elder, for example, looks both behind and before; the younger, forward only. The objects lying in front of them for the time, are the wine-cup and the sumptuous feast, the loud song and the merry circle. These things seem bright in the boy's eye, and he bounds forward impatient to participate in their promised joys. The father sees the same things, but forms a different judgment regarding them. The experience of the past decisively modifies the promises of the future : rays from *above* and from *behind* converging on these painted pleasures, reveal a rottenness in their hollow heart. He sees the inside, and the end of them : he knows that they are vanity and vexation of spirit. He looks upon his boy, and grieves to see that his eye is glistening in a tumultuous hope of indefinite enjoyment. He knows that, unless these springs prove dry, they will be poisonous ; but from the youth's view-point, a rainbow beauty is painted on the spray that rises from their agitated waters. Fain would the affectionate father tear off the tinsel from these seducers, and reveal the cheat in time to his inexperienced child.

Meanwhile, in the pauses of the converse, some prayer rises from that father's heart, unheard until it reaches the ears of the Lord of hosts. Perhaps it is the ancient prophet's cry adapted to his own case: " Lord, I pray thee, open the young man's eyes, that he may see " (2 Kings vi. 17). In some sense a mediator, striving to lay his hand upon both, he plies with pains his own son according to the flesh, and with prayers his own Father in the Spirit. Here is a companionship—here an occupation on which angels may well desire to look. May the Lord hear this man when he cries in faith, and the youth hear him when he speaks in faithfulness.

The foremost word of the colloquy is gladsome encouragement: " My son, if thine heart be wise, my heart shall rejoice, even mine." A parent's brow should not always wear a frown when it is turned toward his child : there should be at least as much drawing as of driving in the discipline of the family. Reproof, however faithful, and punishment, however just, make up at the best only one side of a two-fold operation. The spirit of a child will bend and break under the dead-weight of monotonous, unrelieved objurgation : we should be as ready and forward to rejoice with him in his well-doing, as to be displeased with his faults. There is reason to fear that deficiency at this point is common and mischievous. It comes easier to nâture to launch forth successive rebukes, to chase each successive error of a boisterous child, than to watch, and discriminate, and cherish, and praise, whatever is good. If a parent sit in his easy chair enjoying his own reverie, taking no notice of the finer features of character that burst out thickly in the progress of the play, and never make his presence felt except by an angry bark when some naughty noise disturbs his dream, his children may grow up to something good, but they will owe very little of their moulding to him. It is probable that the only effects of his interference will be to make the young heartily dislike the reprover, and cling more closely to the faults.

It is worthy of remark, that in the two verses immediately preceding this tender, affectionate, encouraging address, the necessity and duty of corporal correction are reiterated in terms of even more than the usual pungency: " Withhold not correction from the child ; for if thou beatest him with the rod, he shall not die. Thou shalt beat him with the rod, and shalt deliver his soul from hell." The command is framed upon the supposition that parents often fail on the side of tenderness: the word is given to nerve them for a difficult duty. There is no ambiguity in the precept: both the need of correction and the tremendous issues that depend on it are expressed with thrilling precision of language. A parent is solemnly taken bound, as he loves his child and would deliver his soul, to enforce his lessons by the rod, when gentler measures fail. But the next moment, as if he were in haste to get into a more congenial element, that stern father stands with a smile lighting up his countenance, and a stream of winning words flowing from his lips, engaging the youth to goodness by foretastes of its glad rewards: " My son, if thine heart be wise, my heart shall rejoice, even mine." Iron is not penetrated, unless it is supported beneath as strongly as it is struck from above. On some such principle it is that blows only bruise, and leave the character more unshapely than ever, unless there be an effort of positive cheering to sustain, fully equal in power and continuity to the pressure of reproof that bears against evil from the other side.

But the youth, although he dutifully yields to the better judgment of his father, secretly thinks that in doing so he is depriving himself of many pleasures which others, not under similar restraint, freely enjoy. Parental experience anticipates the difficulty, and meets it: "Let not thine heart envy sinners." Their happiness is hollow; their prosperity short-lived. "Surely there is an end, and thine expectation shall not be cut off." It is as much as to say that their expectation shall not ripen into possession; the blossom is luxuriant, but the fruit is already blighted. The young look on life as little children look on a fine picture; the objects that lie in the fore-ground, bushes or cottages, fill the eye with their bulk, and the chief beauties of the landscape are neglected. Even the wisest of men never completely acquire the art of apportioning rightly their regard between the really small but apparently great things that fill up the fore-ground of time, and the apparently small but really great things that stretch away into the eternal. This lesson, in its higher stages, the parent is still learning day by day, while he teaches its rudiments to his inexperienced child.

But hard work lies before us here, and we must go into the heart of it: the rude battle of life is raging, and we must strike home. The lessons selected are those which the pupil needs; not those which may be pleasant to the master, or interesting to the audience. Life is real; the preparation for it must be regulated by its actual requirements. To educate a young man for his life voyage is stern work. To go about and cull the beautiful flowers is not enough; we must grasp the thorns and thistles with a resolute hand. The things that are amongst us must even be named amongst us, although the sound grate harshly on a disciple's ear. Let us follow this father over the course of lessons which he gives his child.

1. "Be not among wine-bibbers." Mark well where the teacher begins. He sees the first narrow point of the rail that leads life into a line of error, and runs forward to turn it aside, so that it may not intercept and destroy the precious freight that is approaching. This father sees a danger long before his son become a drunkard—before even he become a companion of drunkards. To be in the company of those who circulate and sip strong drink, he counts unsafe for the youth. That company and that employment this father dreads—this lesson teaches to shun. Our lessons to the young on this subject would be more successful, if, like this text, they should begin at the beginning. Keep out of harm's

way: go far from the entrance of the abyss;—this is the style of Scripture on that momentous theme.

On the principle of supplying the right, as well as forbidding the wrong kind of enjoyment, he gives a glimpse of a happy family circle, by way of contrast with the club of revellers: "The father of the righteous shall greatly rejoice: thy father and thy mother shall be glad." The enemy pleases the tastes of youth: those who are on the other side must countermine in that direction. A dirty or sombre home cannot compete with a brilliant club-house or tavern: a frowning father and a scolding mother cannot compete with a merry circle of boon companions. It is not enough to meet the smiles of vice with the frowns of virtue; we must meet enticement with enticement. Material comforts at home and glad looks from its inmates cannot, indeed, be in the place of God to renew an evil heart; but they will do more than any other human agency to save the youth, and, in the worst event, keep your own hands clean.

2. "Buy the truth, and sell it not." This teacher is skilful in the word of righteousness. He divides the truth aright: he knows that a soul cannot live on negatives. While with one hand he strives to purge the poison out, with the other he administers the bread of life. Although these twin devils, drunkenness and whoredom, with which he is grappling, were cast out of the youth's heart, if that heart remain empty, both will soon return with others worse, and take up their abode again in the empty house. After each stroke dealt to drive out the evil, there is an alternating effort to fill the vacancy with saving truth. Although you were able to chase out every foul spirit in succession by the pungency of your reproof, your labour is lost unless you introduce that peace of God which will keep the heart and mind against the subsequent assaults of the returning and reinforced foe. It is not the devil out of you, but Christ in you, that is the hope of glory (Col. i. 27). Buy the truth, whatever it may cost; sell it not, whatever may be offered. Accept the portion which has been bought by the Redeemer's blood, and is offered free to you. "I am the Truth," said Jesus: close with him, and trust in his salvation. When your heart is so occupied, these lusts will knock for admission in vain. "This is the victory that overcometh the world, even your faith."

3. " A strange woman is a narrow pit." That father's heart is burning within him as he talks with the youth by the way. He has told him of the wisdom from above, the way of mercy in the covenant; but he will not stop there. He returns to another gate of the city Mansoul, where the legions of the enemy are congregating for the assault. Having within the palace crowned the rightful King, he girds himself again for battle, and betakes himself to a threatened post. Well done, good and faithful servant! The work of presenting to a sinner the manifested salvation of God, thou hast done; and the work of loudly, plainly, particularly warning the professing disciple, to avoid every form of evil, thou hast not left undone.

One remarkable peculiarity of this chapter is the junction and alternation of these two kindred sins. There they stand, like two plants of death, growing, indeed, on separate but independent roots, nourished by the same soil, cleaving close to each other by congeniality of nature, and twisted round each other for mutual support. This word takes a sun-picture of these brethren in iniquity, as they combine their strength to dishonour God and enslave men. As if one green withe, growing rank on the sap of corruption, were not enough to hold the captive, the two, by an evil instinct, plait themselves into one. Woe to the youth who has permitted this double bond to warp itself round his body! A Samson's strength cannot wrench it away. The alliance, so generally formed and so firmly maintained, between drunkenness and licentiousness, is a master-stroke of Satan's policy. It is when men have looked upon the deceitful cup, and received into their blood the poison of its sting, that their eyes behold strange women; and when they have fallen into that "narrow pit," they run back to hide their shame, at least from themselves, in the maddening draught. Here is one father who is willing to take upon his lips some names which his heart loathes, rather than by silence permit his son to go forward unwarned, unarmed, into the ambush which the enemy has laid. Let sons who hear this alarm stand and start back, and keep far from the way of transgressors. These deep ditches yawn on every side for living prey. The youth who has inflamed his passion and dimmed his reason by stimulants, is most liable to stagger on the slippery brink, and fall. Turn from the dangerous place and the dangerous company; turn, and live.

4. " Look not thou upon the wine when it is red, when it giveth his colour in the cup, when it moveth itself aright. At the last it biteth like a serpent, and stingeth like an adder." This teacher does more than merely counsel the youth not to drink to excess: this father distinctly advises his son to turn his eyes away from the face of that cup, which has a charm in its visage and a sting in its tail. For my part, I shall endeavour to follow his example : I shall do what I can to persuade my son not to look at all upon any cup whose nature it is to sting those who take much, and to tempt to much those who taste a little. I shall keep close by the very words of Scripture ; I shall say to him, My son, " look not thou upon it ;" " it has cast down many strong men ;'' and " let him that thinketh he standeth, take heed lest he fall."

5. " Thou shalt be as he that lieth down in the midst of the sea, or as he that lieth on the top of a mast. They have stricken me, shalt thou say, and I was not sick ; they have beaten me, and I felt it not: when shall I awake ? I will seek it yet again." This remarkable description would prove, although it stood alone, that ancient brewers contrived to manufacture liquors of power sufficient to produce and sustain full-grown drunkenness, and that ancient drunkards contrived to make themselves thorough sots upon such drinks as they had. If the malady in its more advanced stages had not existed, this description would not have been written, and could not have been understood. There may have been, and there certainly were, differences between ancient and modern times, as there are now between vine-growing and grain-growing countries, both as to the power of the draughts used and the proportion of inebriates to the population ; but specimens of intoxicating drink and intoxicated men were not wanting in Solomon's kingdom in Solomon's day. Gross drunkenness is not a new thing under the sun, although its material resources have been greatly increased and its sphere greatly enlarged in these latter ages of the world.

" The love of the Spirit" appears in this faithful description of the oinomaniac. One would think that to unveil this loathsome madness in presence of the sane, would keep them for ever far from every avenue that might possibly lead to its precincts. But alas ! experience shows that a description of sin's doom is not sufficient to deter the corrupt from sin. To know the consequences, bodily and spiritual, of any vicious indulgence, will not by itself save, but it is a primary necessity among the means of saving; therefore in mercy and faithfulness it is given here.

It is as a lion that the devil goeth about seeking whom he may devour, and as a lion he devours his victims. It is a characteristic of the feline tribe to let go their prey when they are sure of it, and amuse themselves by clutching it again. Thus the drunkard becomes a plaything in the lion's paw. He is sober; he repents of his excesses; he intends to be temperate now; no man shall ever see him drunk again. Has he escaped? Has the wounded mouse escaped when the cat has opened her claws, and permitted it to creep forward? He is wearied with his own way; he was sick; he was like one that lay on the top of a mast; he loathes the enemy that overcame him, and himself for ignobly succumbing. But notwithstanding all this, when he awakes he will seek it yet again. Some false friend will put the cup to his mouth, and when the fire has again touched the membranes, all is in a blaze. I have seen many of my fellow-creatures in the grasp of that mysterious malady which is so graphically pictured on this page of the Scripture. Their despairing cries and haggard looks haunt my memory: the meaning that looked from the faces of their relatives when the grave had at last closed on the victim haunts me too. Dread of their destroyer has been burnt into my soul by the sights that I have seen. I adopt and repeat the twofold counsel of this wise and affectionate father: Feed on saving truth, and flee from the approaches of danger—flee from the approaches of danger, and feed on saving truth. I receive from the Bible and give to the young these two heavenly counsels: " Buy the truth;" " Look not on the cup." Get the treasure for your soul, and keep out of the robber's way.

The Prosperity of the Wicked

(Proverbs 24:1, 19, 20)

" Be not thou envious against evil men, neither desire to be with them. Fret not thyself
because of evil men, neither be thou envious at the wicked: for there shall be no reward to the evil man; the candle of the wicked shall be put out."

SIN is like sound, and it finds the moral nature of fallen
man, like the atmosphere, a good conducting medium.
The word or deed of evil does not terminate where it is
produced: it radiates all round; and besides the direct propa-
gation from a centre by diverging lines, it further reduplicates
itself by rebounding like an echo from every object on which it
falls.   Human beings may well stand in awe when they consider
the self-propagating power of sin, and the facilities which their
own corruption affords it.   Different persons are affected in different ways.   One is shaken by the example of wickedness in its
first outgo; another by its rebounding blow.   One is carried away
in the stream; another hurts himself by his violent efforts to resist it.   Some imitate the sin; others fret against the sinner.
Both classes do evil and suffer injury.   Whether you be im-
patiently " envious against evil men," or weakly " desire to be
with them," you have sustained damage by the contact.

Here, it is not the first and direct, but the secondary and circuitous effect of bad example, that is prominently brought into
view.   The reproof in this word is intended not so much for the
facile who glide with the current, as for the proud who betray a
sullen and discontented spirit in their struggle to oppose it.

To turn aside in company with the wicked is not the only
direction in which danger lies.   Those who resist the example of
evil most vigorously may fall into a deep pit on the other side.
Some who are in no danger of falling in love with their neighbour's sin, may be chafed by it into a hatred of their neighbour.
You do not weakly imitate the deed, but do you proudly despise

the doer? This is the snare which lies on a disciple's path; this is the warning which the Master gives them. The example of Jesus is peculiarly applicable here; it exhibits complete separation from sin in conjunction with the tenderest compassion for sinners. Those who hope in his mercy should be conformed to his image. When you detect in your own heart an impatient fretting against an evil-doer, consider where you would have been if the Holy One had so regarded you. The gentleness of Christ is the comeliest ornament that a Christian can wear.

But besides an impatient fretting against another because he is wicked, there is a discontented envying of his condition because, though morally evil, he is materially prosperous. This is the more presumptuous form of the sin. The other was a fretting against man; this is a fretting against God. It is directly to impugn the justice of the divine government. The seventy-third psalm contains a detailed record of Asaph's experience when he was in conflict with this temptation. He frankly confesses how far he fell: "My feet were almost gone; my steps had well-nigh slipped. For I was envious at the foolish, when I saw the prosperity of the wicked." He saw great wickedness and great prosperity meeting in the same persons: forthwith the presumptuous thought sprung up that nothing is to be gained by goodness: "I have cleansed my heart in vain." Knowing that this thought must be an error, he was, notwithstanding, unable to solve the difficulty until he went into the sanctuary of God. Then and there the mystery was solved: "Then understood I their end." The solution was obtained by getting a higher stand-point and a more extended view. The prosperity was but for a moment, and the sin of the prosperous was preparing for them tribulation without measure and without end. Successful ungodliness did not trouble this tempted disciple after he got, in the house of God, a glimpse of its awful issue. From that time forward he counted "affliction with the people of God" a better portion than "the pleasures of sin for a season."

At the present day those who desire " to live godly in Christ Jesus" are often exposed to this fiery trial. A neighbour who neither fears God nor regards man has been successful in business. You are struggling ineffectually against difficulties in trade, endeavouring in the meantime to do justly, and to love mercy, and to walk humbly with God. You have kept a good conscience and lost your money; he has kept his money and let a good conscience go. You are trudging along the road care-worn and wearied; he is whirled past in his carriage. Beware, brother, as your eye follows the brilliant equipage quickly diminishing in the distance before you,—beware of the feelings that glow at that moment in your weary heart. Envy of that rich man is rank rebellion against an overruling God. Your position is too low and too near; the range of vision is limited, and the little that may be seen is dim with dust. To elevate the observer gives him at once a wider compass and a purer medium: from a height he both sees more and sees it better than from the level ground. When Asaph met the prosperous scoffers in the crowded market-place, he saw only their condition for the time; but when he ascended the hill of God, and entered there the sanctuary, his eye from that elevation could run along their glittering life and descry its gloomy end. The same experience, described in figurative language, happened to John in Patmos: "After this I looked, and behold a door was opened in heaven: and the first voice which I heard was as it were of a trumpet talking with me; which said, Come up hither, and I will show thee things which must be hereafter" (Rev. iv. 1). In order to drive envy of the prosperous out of a disciple's heart, nothing more is needed than a window open in heaven, and an invitation from the angel, " Come up hither." A higher viewpoint and a clearer sky will enable you more intelligently to compare your own condition with his. When in the spirit of adoption, and from the place of a son, you look along the career of those who fear not God, you will learn to acknowledge that your lines have fallen in a more pleasant place, and that you have obtained a more goodly heritage.

Some heirs of the kingdom now in the body thank God fervently for causing the riches of their parents to take wings and fly away. They see some who have inherited wealth caught and carried away by the temptations which it brings, and tremble to think where and what themselves would now have been, had the world courted them at a time when they would have been most easily won by its fascinations. The world's cold shoulder in their youth was not pleasant to nature at the time, but they now know that it was the safer side. Instead of envying, they pity the people who are getting riches and forgetting God. By experience they have learned that their own hearts are not trustworthy; they think it likely that if they had been equally prosperous they would have been equally godless. They rejoice with trembling; they tremble with rejoicing, as they think how wisely their lot has been appointed by a Father in heaven, and how unwisely it would have been chosen if their own wishes had been granted.

If a Christian, whether rich or poor, envy any man's possessions, he is forgetting his place and his prospects. The heirs of a kingdom are inexcusable if they cast a longing eye upon a few acres of earth which a neighbour calls his own. A " lively hope" would effectually still these tumults in a believer's breast. They who walk by faith are not easily disturbed by the things which appeal to sight. The rest that remaineth, when kept full in view, makes the passing toils feel light. " Blessed are the poor in spirit, for theirs is the kingdom of heaven."

A Brother's Keeper

(Proverbs 24:11, 12)

"If thou forbear to deliver them that are drawn unto death, and those that are ready to be slain; if thou sayest, Behold we knew it not; doth not he that pondereth the heart consider it? and he that keepeth thy soul, doth not he know it? and shall not he render to every man according to his works?"

THE principle that God, our common Father, counts every man his brother's keeper, pervades the Scriptures as an animating spirit, and is here, in vivid language, expressly affirmed and defined. From the beginning it was so. Nowhere can this truth be more distinctly seen than as it glances reflected from the black, hard heart of the first murderer. Cain's sullen denial, when rightly read, is equivalent to a disciple's positive confession; for that carnal mind was in violent enmity against God. In the lie that flashes back from that guilty conscience you may read the heavenly truth that touched and tormented it. As from the beginning, so it is also at the end: he who closed the record of Revelation in Patmos, in character by that time as well as doctrine a contrast to the murderer of Abel, embodies the principle in the last words of inspiration, and disappears in the very act of stretching out his hands to save a brother who is ready to perish: " Let him that heareth say Come; and let him that is athirst come; and whosoever will, let him take the water of life freely" (Rev. xxii. 17). The prophets before Christ's coming, and the apostles after it, all conspired to teach, by their lips and by their lives, that a man liveth not to himself, and dieth not to himself. Ye who bear the Saviour's name, and trust in his love, ye are not your own; ye are bought with a price. Ye have talents to lay out, and a work to accomplish—a Master to serve and a brother to save. Look not every man on his own things, but every man also on the things of others. Whoso hath this world's good, or the next world's good, or both, and seeth his brother have need, and shutteth up his bowels of compassion from him, how dwelleth the love of God in him?

I know not any point in the whole circumference of duty on which the human mind makes a more obstinate stand than here, against the authority of God. The determination to be his own master, and do what he liked with himself, seems to have been the very essence of the sin which constituted man's fall, and still animates the fallen. "Who is lord over us?" is the watch-word of the life-long battle between an evil conscience and a righteous Judge. Here the commandment is exceeding broad: like divine omniscience, it compasses the transgressor before and behind. It checks his advance, and cuts off his retreat. Although a man should actually maintain, in relation to every brother, the neutrality which he professes, it would avail him nothing. Under God as supreme ruler, and by his law, we owe every human being love; and if we fail to render it, we are cast into prison with other less reputable debtors. Nor will anything be received in payment but the genuine coin of the kingdom; it must be love with a living soul in it and a substantial body on it. If it be a material gift thrown to a needy brother, wanting the fellow-feeling of a sympathizing heart, it is a body without a soul—a carcase loathsome to the living; if it be a sentimental emotion resembling pity, unaccompanied by any corresponding deed, it is a soul without a body—an intangible spirit. A pure emotion must animate the act: a substantial act must clothe the pure emotion. The great Teacher has so constructed the parable of the talents that on this point none can miss its meaning. No actual injurer of his neighbour is introduced into the picture at all; the heaviest sentence which the Bible contains, or the lips of Jesus uttered, is left lying on the "unprofitable servant"—the man who failed to do good with the means at his disposal (Matt. xxv. 30). But Christ's example prints this lesson in still larger letters than his preaching. By looking unto Jesus we may learn it better than by listening even to his own word. Where would we have been now, if he had satisfied himself with abstaining from inflicting injury on a fallen world? He did not let us alone in our extremity: as we desire to be like him we should not desert our brother in his need. Jesus bids us do good, and shows us the way. Listen to his teaching, and follow his steps.

The law which runs through the Scriptures on this point is laid down in these verses in copious, clear, and memorable terms. The distress of a neighbour, the indifference of a selfish man, the excuses which the guilty presents to his own questioning conscience, and the terrors which the Lord holds over his head, are marshalled all in order here, and made to pass before our eyes like a section of actual life.

First of all, what ails our brother, that he needs the compassion of a tender heart, and the help of a strong arm? He is " drawn unto death," and " ready to be slain." This is the very crisis which at once needs help and admits it. If the danger were more distant, he might not be sensible of his need; if it were nearer, he might be beyond the hope of recovery. He is so low that help is necessary; yet not so low that help now offered would be vain. He is " drawn unto death," and therefore is an object of pity; but his life is yet in him, and therefore he is a subject of hope. Such, in general terms, is the work which lies to our hands in the world.

The death into which a neighbour is gliding may be the death of the body, or the death of the soul, or both together. The example of Christ and the precepts of Scripture concur in teaching us to acknowledge either danger, and render either aid. A deaf ear, a blind eye, a palsied arm, a breaking heart, Jesus instantly owned as claims on his compassion; but he was grieved when men went away with the healed body, feeling not the death and seeking not the life of the soul. We should go and do likewise. Count disease and poverty a valid claim for help, but count not the cure complete when these wants have been relieved.

Disciples now are certainly like their Lord in this department of his experience: they find the sense of temporal want and the urgency for temporal relief much more common and more keen, than grief for guilt or desire for pardon. We direct attention to the disease which draws the soul to death; that which draws the body down directs attention to itself. The man is not yet in the death that is final and hopeless. He is sliding gradually into it; something is drawing him down, and that something is within him. If that ailment be not cast out, perdition is sure. The sting of death is sin, and already that sting is planted deep in the soul. It has not yet reached its issue, but it is running its inevitable course. When a poisonous serpent plunges its sting into the flesh and blood of a man, the man lives yet a while : the body does not instantly become cold. The poison mingles with the blood, and so permeates the frame. The fever rises, tumultuously but steadfastly, like the tide. The serpent's sting has taken hold of the life, and is drawing it surely to death. Like this uneasy interval is human life, until it is made new in Christ. The sting of the Old Serpent has gotten hold, and will not let go until it be taken out by a Stronger One. " Sin when it is finished bringeth forth death." If a gang of captured Africans, chained to each other, were in our sight driven from the interior to the shore for sale, there would not be a dry eye amongst us as the sad procession passed ; these chains, and that death to which they draw the victims, are things seen and temporal. Captives more numerous, and more firmly bound, are drawn along our thoroughfares to a greater death ; if we had spiritual perception to estimate the distress, our compassion would not be shut up within our own bosoms for lack of subjects to exercise it on.

Such are the objects and such their claim : how do those meet it who have themselves gotten help from God ? The form of the warning indicates the point at which the defect is anticipated : " If thou forbear to deliver." The Author of this word knows what is in man. The point of the sword goes to the joints and marrow : it does not assume that men, when they see a brother drawn unto death, will in mere wantonness give him a, blow to hasten his fall. Such a deed of gratuitous wickedness may here and there be found ; but it is an abnormal excrescence, and not the ordinary fruit which even fallen humanity bears. If the reproof had been aimed at that enormity, it would have missed the most of us ; the arrow, pointed higher, comes more surely home. The charge is not that we strike a standing brother down, but that we fail to raise a fallen brother up. The law under which we live is the law of love ; and whenever any doubt arises as to practical details, the Pattern is at hand to mould it on and test it by : " Love one another as I have loved you." A Christian doing good should be like an artist working from a model, looking alternately from the rude material in his hands up to the perfect example which he imitates, and down from that example to the rude material again.

The excuse, " We knew it not," will not avail us in as far as we might have known. " Seek, and ye shall find," applies to opportunities of saving them that are ready to perish, as well as to benefits which we may obtain for ourselves. Ignorance will not be reckoned for innocence, if He who pondereth the heart saw it selfishly keeping the disagreeable knowledge away. He that keepeth thy soul will ask one day what thou hast done for the keeping of others, and He will then render unto every man according to his works.

The conclusion of the whole matter may be expressed in these words of the apostle : " Let us not be weary in well-doing ; for in due season we shall reap, if we faint not. As we have therefore opportunity, let us do good unto all men, especially unto them who are of the household of faith " (Gal. vi. 9, 10). The two limits are, on this side " opportunity," and on that side " all men." Between these two lies the ample exercise-ground for a Christian, on which he is expected, like his Master, to go about doing good. Do more for the household of nature or of faith than you do for those who are distant from you or from God,—it is not sinful to respect these relations and permit them to influence the proportion of your efforts ; but the heart's compassion should acknowledge no limit to its flow short of the world's boundary, and the helping hand no limit to its stretch except the opportunity and the power.

The destinies of men are so closely interwoven together, that every one of us has a direct interest in delivering those who are now drawn unto sin and death. If we forbear to help him who is falling now, he and his may drag down with themselves our children when we are no longer here to prevent the calamity. That poor wretch who is drawn, like the Gadarene swine, by possessing spirits down a steep place into the abyss, has a number of young children littering in the hovel which they call their home. These children are growing up a brood much more dangerous than savages : in them the forces of civilization are under the control of barbarism. They are an ingredient which, in proportion to its bulk, darkens and pollutes the society into which it is poured. My children must be poured into the same great tide of time, and I cannot keep them from indiscriminate contact with its varied impurities. Thus, by my love to my own children, God binds me to do my best for my neighbours; and the rod which is lifted up for punishment will strike me on the tenderest place, if I neglect this salvation work.

A few miles above Montreal, the two great convergent rivers of British America, the St. Lawrence and the Ottawa, meet. The St. Lawrence is a pure stream, of a peculiar, light-blue colour: the Ottawa is dark, as if it were tinged by moss in its way. After their meeting the two rivers run side by side a few miles, each occupying its own half of one broad bed; but gradually the boundary line disappears, and all the waters are mingled in one vast homogeneous flood. Although the life of the inhabitants below depended on preserving the pure cerulean hue of the St. Lawrence, it could not possibly be preserved: all the might of man cannot prevent the Ottawa from tinging the united waters with its own dark shade: unless the darkness can be discharged from its springs, that great affluent will effectually dye the main river in all its lower reaches. Behold the picture of the process by which the neglected children of our unsaved brother, meeting our own at a lower point in time's rolling current, will blot out the distinction which is now maintained. Behold the rod lifted up in our sight to prevent the neglect now, or punish it hereafter! The dark cellars in which ignorant, vicious, godless parents, now pen their hapless brood, are the springs which feed a mighty river. Our little ones rise in cleaner spots, and in the meantime a solid bank separates the streams. But that turbid river lies within the same basin, and by the laws of nature must converge towards the central channel of society. It is an affluent; we must accept the fact, for we cannot change it. We dread that dark stream which, at a little distance, is flowing parallel with our own. Over the embankments, now not very lofty, we hear sometimes the ominous gurgle of its rapid flow. There is only one way of subduing that terrible enemy. If we cower timidly in our own hiding-place, the destruction which we thereby invite will quickly overtake us. In this warfare there is no armour for the back of the fugitive; safety lies in facing the danger. The evil which in its issue is a deluge, may in its origin be successfully neutralized. Below, you cannot keep the gathered volume out: above, you may do much to purify the rising spring.

Piety and Patriotism
(Proverbs 24:21)

" My son, fear thou the Lord and the king: and meddle not with them that are given to change."

"THERE are two kings and two kingdoms in Scotland," said James Melville to his royal master; and our forefathers sturdily maintained the maxim through a long series of troubles, until the tyrants fell and liberty triumphed. The supreme authority of God, and the subordinate authority of human government may both have fullest scope in the same country, and at the same time. Godliness and loyalty, like brethren dwelling together in unity, may possess the same heart, and the heart is all the nobler that these twin inhabitants have made it their home. Those who cherish both principles together fulfil best the specific duties which belong to each. The Covenanters and Puritans were not faultless men. By aid of the light which we now enjoy, some of their measures may be corrected and improved: but it is too late to make them better now, and it is a pity that our philosophers who see their faults so clearly when they are in their graves, had not been present in the conflict to give them counsel. In the main, those men were right, and God has blessed their labours. They were the honour of their country, and have proved the benefactors of their race. Those who laugh most loudly at their faults, have in secret no sympathy with their virtues. Looking outward at the present experience of other nations, and upward through the history of our own, patriots, rejoicing in achieved liberty, may well tremble yet as they try to picture what our condition might have been at this day, if God had not raised up rank after rank of religious and loyal men—a break-water to receive the waves of combined spiritual and temporal despotism, and ward them from our shores.

The fear of the Lord and the fear of the king are in themselves great and interesting subjects, but at present I ask the reader only to glance at their order and relations. I speak not of godliness and loyalty separately and in all their extent, but only of their mutual bearing upon each other. Submission of heart and life to the King Eternal overrides and controls, yet does not injure, a citizen's allegiance to an earthly ruler. This principle lies deep, and spreads far. It reaches all lands, and runs down through all generations. The word is, " Fear the Lord and the king ; " the fear of the Lord must go first, but the fear of the king may follow. The supreme does not crush, it protects the subordinate. Although the heart is full of piety, there is plenty of room for patriotism. Nay more, patriotism nowhere gets full scope except in a heart that is already pervaded by piety. These elements are like the two chief constituent gases of the atmosphere. The space which envelopes the globe is full of one gas, and it is also full of another. To discharge the nitrogen would not make the space capable of containing more of the oxygen. The absence of the one constituent destroys the quality but does not enlarge the quantity of the other. Take away godliness, and your loyalty, without being increased in amount, is seriously deteriorated in kind : take away loyalty, and you run great risk of spoiling the purity of the remanent godliness. God's works are all good : his combinations are all beneficial. If we attempt to amend, we shall certainly mar them.

Obedience to rulers is a positive command. It is binding everywhere and always, until it is taken off by the same authority that imposed it. Men are not permitted to determine for themselves how far they shall go in obedience to magistrates. Such a principle would produce universal anarchy, and is not found in the Bible. Go forward in your allegiance to " the powers that be," not until you think you have gone far enough, but until you come upon the law of God, claiming the space in front for Himself, and absolutely forbidding your advance. Go forward with the fear of the king, unless and until the fear of the Lord cross your path like a wall.

There is room for every effort by the citizens to get laws amended and grievances redressed, but no permission given in the Scriptures to rise in rebellion with the view of achieving any temporal good. Resistance is not prescribed as a remedy when the magistrate invades your rights; that terrrible resource is held in reserve for one terrible contingency—when the magistrate invades the rights of God. If any one, looking from the political view-point, should say this concedes only a limited measure of liberty; it is not my business to supply an answer. My duty is to point out what the Scriptures teach. To their authority I fondly cling; for the subject on independent grounds of philosophy is too deep for me. If I am cast abroad upon abstract speculation for the grounds and limits of a subject's obedience, I am in a sea where I can feel no bottom and see no shore. No feasible rule can be laid down, except that which the Scriptures contain. Let any man try to write down a scale showing when and wherefore private persons may lawfully resist public authority, and he will soon be convinced that the task is hopeless. Every attempt to define the liberty of rebellion will be found to open a door to anarchy.

In point of fact very little of the liberty that now exists in the world has been achieved by violent resistance to governments because of oppression in temporal things. Wherever civil liberty is large and lasting, it has grown slowly by successive accretions, the effect of peaceful effort: or, if it has been obtained wholesale, it will probably be found that the tyrant government fell and broke itself upon a resisting people in the effort to usurp the authority which belongs to God. Violent revolutions, although provoked by injustice and oppression on the part of princes, have seldom secured and consolidated the liberty of the people.

The condition of the European continent now, and its history during the last ten years, lead us back, in the interests of patriotism as well as religion, to the very letter of the scriptural rule, "Fear the Lord and the king, and meddle not with them that are given to change." It is true that the people have been oppressed by their rulers; but it is also true that they have gained nothing by rebellion. We can observe these two facts; but we cannot do much more. The subject is too deep for us. God in his word condemns all tyranny on the part of princes, but he does not there prescribe an armed rising of the people as the method of redressing their wrongs. He retains the retribution in his own hand, and permits it to fall in his own time on the head of the guilty. Men who intelligently fear God, and make his word their law, while they unite with every patriot in efforts to improve the condition of the people and the laws of the state, are disposed to bear wrong when their temporal rights only are invaded, and to reserve the ultimate remedy of resistance for those laws of man that would compel them to violate the law of God.

Among enlightened Christians loyalty is more than a negative principle. It is not enough for them that they refrain from resisting constituted authority; they learn from the Scriptures to be "subject not only for wrath but for conscience' sake." Fear of the king is comparatively a feeble sentiment; alone it cannot long withstand assailing temptations. The fear of the Lord is a mightier principle; it is its nature, wherever it lives and thrives, to strike its roots down into the deepest places of a human heart. In the Scriptures the feebler force is made fast to the stronger, and so carried through in trying times. Loyalty is most secure where it has godliness to lean upon.

The Popedom has appropriated these doctrines to itself, and employed them for its own ends. The principle of Melville is adopted at Rome : the priests teach most earnestly that allegiance to a temporal sovereign is limited, and controlled by a prior and superior spiritual claim. This truth perverted has become the main-stay of popish power. They adopt the divine revealed law, " Fear the Lord and the king," and foist an old Italian priest, the chief or the tool of a college of cardinals, into the place of the living God. The nations, with their eyes put out, grind like Samson in the mill of these lordly priests. The Romanists are accustomed to take up the arguments wherewith we defend the truth, and employ them to support their own lie. Hence, when the ancient war-cry of our forefathers, " We must obey God rather than man," began to rise in a crisis of our own day, the politicians recognised a wonted sound, and exclaimed, Here is Popery over again. Yes; the doctrine of the Covenanters and of the Papists is the same. Both maintain and teach that a supreme allegiance is due to One Supreme, and that obedience to human governments comes in under it, and only in as far as may be consistent with it. Up to this point they agree; but in one thing they differ. Those accord the supreme allegiance to God, according to the rule of the Scriptures; these accord it to the Pope, as advised by the dark and selfish counsels of the junto that surround him. If our legislators had an eye to take in the breadth and depth of that distinction, it would be better for themselves and the nation.

The popish doctors have a pleasant coating wherewith they cover their bitter pill; they teach that it is spiritual authority only that is claimed by the Pope, not temporal. Thus the shipmaster, with a leer in his eye and the helm in his hand, tells the remonstrant horseman on deck that he may mount his own steed and ride in any direction he pleases. When persons or peoples embark on board the Pope's ship, they may, like little children, play at temporal liberty, by chasing each other from side to side, or from stem to stern; but the wary pilot has them under his power, and will carry them and theirs into any port he chooses.

A British Christian owning God, according to his word, as supreme ruler of the conscience, and knowing no authority on earth superior to the Queen, is a safe subject and a useful citizen : a Papist, settled on our soil and enjoying the benefits of our constitution, sworn to yield primary allegiance to a foreign prince in all that relates to spiritual interests, and conceding absolutely to that prince the right to define what spiritual interests are, may be in his own character personally a good man, but cannot in any crisis be counted a loyal subject. The difference between these two is as great as the difference between light and darkness. If it were generally perceived, and practically acknowledged, it would go far to right the labouring ship of the State, and prepare her for meeting the baffling winds and deceitful currents of the times.

We do not, however, expect light to arise on the political horizon: we must look in another direction for the dawn. Although Popery is the greatest tyrant, and the chief support of other tyrannies, the love of civil liberty has not light enough to perceive the danger nor strength enough to strike the blow. Civil liberty is indeed in principle and practice against the Popedom, but it is like an infant in a giant's hands. The Popedom is a "spiritual wickedness in high places :" terrestial patriotism stands on a lower platform, and cannot reach its mighty foe.

Political liberalism, though it desire a good thing, has not strength to win it. It lacks pith and bottom. Popery is too many for it. The great victories over the world and its god are won, not by policy, but by faith. It is "not by might, nor by power, but by my Spirit, saith the Lord."

The Sluggard's Garden

(Proverbs 24:30-34)

"I went by the field of the slothful, and by the vineyard of the man void of understanding; and, lo, it was all grown over with thorns, and nettles had covered the face thereof, and the stone wall thereof was broken down. Then I saw and considered it well; I looked upon it, and received instruction. Yet a little sleep, a little slumber, a little folding of the hands to sleep: so shall thy poverty come as one that travelleth; and thy want as an armed man."

THIS section of the Book of Proverbs is wound up by a touching picture of sloth and its consequences. The description is true to nature, because it is taken from fact. The words need no paraphrase; the meaning all shines through. This observer has taken a photograph of the sluggard's garden, without asking the sluggard's leave. Copies may be multiplied to an indefinite extent, showing the condition of his home, and shop, and factory. From the same original you might even sketch with considerable accuracy the desolation that broods over his soul.

In this case, however, as in many others, good came out of evil. The idle man, without knowing it, gave the passenger a lecture on the virtue of diligence: "Then I saw and considered it well; I looked upon it, and received instruction." If the learner's own heart is in a right condition he may obtain a profitable lesson from every sight that meets his eye, and every sound that falls upon his ear. A teachable scholar will make progress under a very indifferent master, and in a very unlikely school. If a man has a clean conscience and a well-balanced mind, he is in a great measure independent of sorrounding circumstances. When a man's ways please the Lord, He will make even his enemies to be at peace with him; all things will be constrained to work together for good. If the rightous are in sight, he will follow their footsteps: if the evil cross his path, he will turn another way.

The learner and the lesson stand before us here in a picture which looks like life. A passenger is suddenly arrested by some object on the way-side: he stops short, seeks an elevated standpoint, and gazes earnestly through a gap in a broken wall. It is a field with a vineyard on its sunniest slope, the patrimonial farm of a Hebrew householder who lives in the cottage hard by. They were not the ripening clusters of a well-dressed vineyard, or the waving grain-fields of a thrifty husbandman, that drew the curious eye of the traveller in that direction. Thorns and nettles covered all the ground within, and the wall that once surrounded it was crumbling. There was no fence round the vineyard to defend the fruit, and no fruit within the vineyard to be defended. The owner did nothing for the farm, and the farm did nothing for the owner. But even this neglected spot did something for the passing wayfarer who had an observant eye and a thoughtful mind. Even the sluggard's garden brought forth fruit—but not for the sluggard's benefit. The diligent man reaped and carried off the only harvest that it bore—a warning. The owner received nothing from it; and the onlooker " received instruction."

Here is a principle which might be extended. The lesson read by one may be learned by a thousand. People complain that they have few opportunities and means of instruction; here is one school open to all; here is a schoolmaster who charges no fee. If we are ourselves diligent, we may gather riches even in a sluggard's garden. He who knows how to turn the folly of his neighbours into wisdom for himself cannot excuse defective attainments by alleging a scarcity of the raw material. If we were skilful in this kind of mining, we would find many rich veins in our own neighbourhood. There are many sluggards' gardens on either side of our path: if we consider them well, we shall receive instruction from each. If we obtain a little from each, a rich store of wisdom will soon accumulate in our hands.

Here is a sluggard's garden; the object is worthy of a second look, and will repay it. You observe the house into which that haggard, half-naked labourer entered; follow him and you will find a lesson written on the inside of his unhappy home. The house is empty and unclean; the wife is toiling hard in the heart of the confusion, and scarcely looks up as her husband comes in. There is not a seat on which he can rest his wearied limbs; and as no preparation has been made, an hour must pass ere food of any kind can be prepared to satisfy his hunger. He growls in anger, or groans in despair, according as he has been more or less inured to this species of misery. If you examine him, he will tell you that he came early home so often and found the house unready for him, that the motive was at last worn away: if you examine her, she will tell you that she prepared so often for his early return in the evening, and so often waited in vain, that the motive was at last destroyed, and she ceased to struggle. To determine precisely the origin of the evil, as between the two, seems a problem as difficult as to ascertain the sources of the Nile: but the result is abundantly plain. Their house is desolate,—their hearts are callous. The garden has been neglected, and now it is utterly waste. This garden produces no sweet fruit to its owner; but you may bear away a harvest from the stinging nettles that grow rank on its grave-yard corruption. Let a young man watch and pray that he enter not into temptation in his choice at first. Let a young woman, when a proposal is made to her, seek the consent of " our Father in heaven" ere she gives her own. Let the two, when united, bear one another's burdens, and so fulfil the law of Christ. Let a husband cherish and manifest a tender affection, strive to make his wife's burdens light, and be pleased with her efforts to please. Let the wife have a clean house, and a comfortable meal, and a blithe look, all ready for her husband when he returns from his toil. The inside of a loveless dwelling, the pen that shelters an ill-matched pair, teems with lessons for the inexperienced passenger: look on it, and receive instruction.

A youth, after having lain a heavy burden on his parents throughout the period of childhood, rebels and defies them as soon as he has acquired strength sufficient to win his own way in the world. Weary of listening to their counsels, he deserts them. While they were strong and he was weak, they stinted themselves to supply all his wants; when he became strong, and they in turn were feeble, he selfishly left them to sink or swim, and devoted all his means to the gratification of his own tastes. His parents have at last been brought with sorrow to the grave, and his pleasures have begun to pall. Now the prodigal would fain arise and go to his father; but he has no father and no home. His bursting heart would get relief if he could weep on the neck of those whom he has injured, and confess his sins; but this ma not be—it is too late. He is wretched, and his wretchedness stares out of his eyes upon every observer. Consider him well, young man; there is a lesson in him. He gives instruction, as Lot's wife gave it, free to all who pass. The sluggard has wasted his own garden, and starves; but the hand of the diligent may gather riches within its broken walls, and from its barren surface.

A young woman, with a fair countenance and a light heart, has listened to flattering lips, and, confident in her own steadfastness, has ventured to walk on slippery places. She has sunk in deep mire. Hope has perished now, and therefore effort has ceased. These rags cover a shrivelled frame, and that shrivelled frame conceals a broken heart. Look upon that vineyard. Consider well the rent wall that lays it open to prowling wild beasts; and the rank growth of nettles, the chosen cover of noisome night-birds. Look, young woman, on that once blooming garden, now a fetid swamp,—look on it, and receive instruction.

All things are new in the world without to those who are renewed in the heart within. If the eye is single, the whole body will be full of light. When the learner is a child of God, even the works of the devil will supply him with a lesson. When the record is complete of all the "schools and schoolmasters" that have in various departments contributed to educate "the whole family of God," it will be a wonderful miscellany. Its running title will be, "All things are yours, and ye are Christ's."

Monarchs, Under God and Over Men

(Proverbs 25:1-5)

"These are also proverbs of Solomon, which the men of Hezekiah king of Judah copied out. It is the glory of God to conceal a thing; but the honour of kings is to search out a matter. The heaven for height, and the earth for depth, and the heart of kings is unsearchable. Take away the dross from the silver, and there shall come forth a vessel for the finer. Take away the wicked from before the king, and his throne shall be established in righteousness."

SOLOMON spoke three thousand proverbs (1 Kings iv. 32). Whether they were all written we do not know, but they have not been all preserved. Some of them, though useful in their day, were not suitable or necessary in subsequent ages; others were selected by holy men of old whom the Spirit moved, and stored in the Scriptures as a treasury of practical instruction and reproof for all nations and all times. Inspiration obviously applies to the selection of what should be recorded, as well as to the utterance of that which is in itself true and divine. We need not be surprised to learn that many of Solomon's sayings, after serving " their own generation, fell on sleep," and were lost to the world; for a greater than he spoke many words of heavenly wisdom to His immediate disciples which were not recorded, and which we on earth will never know. The apostles drank in for their own life all that fell from the great Teacher's lips, but recorded only those portions which his Spirit directed them to preserve as the heritage of the Church.

" The men of Hezekiah" were not ordinary men. That godly King of Judah was surrounded by a band of kindred spirits, who co-operated with him in a great revival. It was a bright time at Jerusalem when Hezekiah reigned and Isaiah prophesied. It is evident that the king encouraged the prophets, and the prophets supported the king. The Seventy read, " The friends of Hezekiah." Solomon's words were counted precious in those days; and the associated patriots gathered up the fragments, that nothing which was permanently useful might be intrusted to tradition. This collection was made by inspired prophets, and admitted into the canon of the Jewish Scriptures from the first. It was recognised by the Lord and his apostles as part and parcel of the Scriptures which were given by God to teach the way of eternal life.

This portion opens with a contrast as to dignity and wisdom between the King Immortal and an earthly ruler: "It is the glory of God to conceal a thing: but the honour of kings is to search out a matter." God is the uncaused cause of all things. He is the centre and source of being. He knows the end from the beginning. In his knowledge there is no progress, because there is no imperfection. "His understanding is infinite." It is by slow degrees and by laborious effort that we work our way into the minute portions of creation that lie within our reach. It is the privilege and glory of man to search into the infinite above and beneath him; but he is not able to go far in either direction. Mines which we count deep have been driven by human hands into the earth's crust, and yet how short is the line that sounds them in comparison with the earth's radius! But this conveys no adequate idea of the difference between the depths of God's works and the line which limits men's researches. Between the shaft of a deep mine and the depth of the globe, from its surface to its centre, there is a definite and known proportion; but between what we know of God's work and that work in all its extent, there is no proportion which we can calculate at all.

"Thou art a God that hidest thyself," is one of the attributes of the Supreme. In nature he has, so to speak, two hiding-places, one above man, and another beneath him. Some things are hidden from our view by being too great, and some by being too small for us. Men search as far as they can in the one direction with the telescope, and in the other with the microscope, but beyond every depth attained lies a deeper still. How great the contrast between divine and human government! The one proceeds from within outwards, with perfect knowledge of the whole; the other feels its way laboriously upon the surface, and cannot fully comprehend even the small matters that lie within its jurisdiction.

These men of Hezekiah "feared the Lord and the king" in due

order and proportion : they were godly and loyal. In arranging their collection of Solomon's proverbs, they set in the fore-ground the supreme and unapproachable wisdom of God, and thereafter magnify the office of the prince: " The heaven for height, and the earth for depth, and the heart of kings is unsearchable." Though an earthly sovereign is feeble and short-sighted in contrast with the Supreme, yet, in comparison with other men, kings enjoy great honour and exercise great influence. There is a certain sublimity in the royal dignity: in every condition men expressly or tacitly own it : even those who in theory are adverse to regal government cannot be entirely stoical in a monarch's presence. There is grandeur in sovereign power, without respect to the justness of its title or the beneficence of its sway. We have seen all Europe watching the countenance of one man, and eagerly scanning every sign or syllable which might indicate the purpose of his heart. But the still, reverential regard of millions, does not imply a belief on their part that the man who is its object is endowed with superhuman wisdom; it is enough that in point of fact his single will can quench or kindle war over the area of two continents. This element of power possessed elevates monarchy, and sets it on the summit of earthly things. The constituents which compose Mont Blanc are not more heavenly than the earth of lesser hills, and yet the human spirit stands in awe before that regal mountain. In some such way are men affected by the presence of a king, although they know well that the person occupying the office for the time is nothing more than an average specimen of humanity. The Lord reigneth, and they who fear him should rejoice. He will set restraining bounds to the wrath of man. Although mankind have suffered much from the cruelty of despots, yet the race have derived an incalculable benefit from the tendency to venerate monarchy, which manifests itself so strongly, especially in a primitive state of society. Government, as compared with anarchy, is so great a blessing, that even after many heavy oppressions are deducted, a surplus of solid gain remains to human kind.

But seeing that a king by office wields a power so great, the law of God and the interests of men require that it shall be wisely directed towards beneficent ends. Kings have, in all times and all places, been more or less swayed by the counsellors who surround them. In our country, more than in any other monarchy, the people, in their collective capacity, have a potential voice in the selection of the persons who shall stand next the throne and influence the government; the precept is therefore directly applicable to us. We are commanded to take away the dross from the silver, that the forthcoming vessel may be pure. In as far as it is placed in our power, it is also laid upon our conscience to " remove the wicked from before the king," that his " throne may be established in righteousness." Here lies the duty, and here the danger of Britain. We need not expect that the supreme Ruler will support our sway in the world if we elevate the wicked to the high places of authority, and sustain them there. His law is, " Them that honour me, I will honour." If, by the united will of a God-fearing nation, God-fearing counsellors are planted round the throne, we may hope for the continuance and extension of our authority in the world. How shall we dare to pray that God would preserve to us the empire, in order that we may squeeze riches for ourselves from the sinews of subject millions? If our rule is such as to bless the nations, we may plead with the Lord to prolong our sway. We need not expect that God will give the world to us, if we do not count and make it our mission to bring the world to God. Wherever the Master imparts the ten talents, he accompanies the gift with the injunction, Lay them out for me. No counsel will prosper that rejects or ignores that highest law. If we permit the dross of ungodly selfishness to tinge the councils and control the government of the state, the goodly vessel will go to pieces in our hands.

In India, the noblest foreign possession of our own or any other crown, the policy of the government, sustained by the community, has been to maintain intact the variegated superstitions of the East, lest any religious commotion should interrupt the stream of gain in its homeward flow. The authorities have with smooth tongue flattered, and with strong hand defended, the hideous and cruel worship of devils, which in the name of religion possesses and torments the land. They have supported and propagated doctrines which they knew to be dishonouring to God and injurious to men, that the multitude so flattered might be more easily governed. They have exerted their influence against the introduction of Christianity among the natives, lest conversion should breed commotions and diminish our gains. Now God has with-drawn his protecting hand, and permitted an insurrection to burst forth to which the world's history cannot afford a parallel. Our policy has failed. We fawned on these hideous idols as if we had known no almighty Protector in heaven; and now these idols tear us limb from limb. We adopted the policy, and are suffering the chastisement of Ahaz, the weak and wicked King of Judah: " For he sacrificed unto the gods of Damascus, which smote him; and he said, Because the gods of the kings of Syria help them, there-fore will I sacrifice to them, that they may help me. But they were the ruin of him, and of all Israel" (2 Chron. xxviii. 23).

In the whole matter of Indian government, a counsel vicious to the core has predominated. We must " take away the dross from the silver, and there shall come forth a vessel for the refiner." We must no longer suppress revealed truth, and uphold the doc-trine of devils; we must fear God in the heathen's sight, and have no other fear.

A Faithful Messenger

(Proverbs 25:13, 19)

"As the cold of snow in the time of harvest, so is a faithful messenger to them that send him; for he refresheth the soul of his masters. Confidence in an unfaithful man in time of trouble is like a broken tooth, and a foot out of joint."

T HE art of cooling drinks in a hot climate by snow and ice preserved or imported seems to have been known and practised at an early period of the world's history. In our cool insular clime we cannot fully appreciate the worth of such a refreshment, because we never very keenly experience the want of it. Imagination must largely aid the senses ere we can rightly estimate how the eyes of a Hebrew husbandman sparkled at the sight of "snow from Lebanon" when a harvest sun was beating on his brow. Such a refreshment in time of difficulty is a faithful messenger who goes forth through the danger, and comes back with relief.

In a crisis, at an early stage of the Crimean war, the bearing of a message became the hinge on which success or disaster turned, and the messenger who bore it became the hero of the day. When the Russian army had been routed on the Alma, and the allied commanders had determined to march past Sebastopol and seize the port of Balaclava as a base of operation, a message to the fleet, charging it to meet the army in the morning there, was a vital element of the plan. The British officer who bore it proved a faithful messenger. When the army, after their inland night march, first crowned the heights that overlook the sea, the foremost ships of the fleet were steaming cautiously up the narrow inlet. When the commander of the army, with the responsibility of the manœuvre lying heavy on his heart, looked over those girdling hills and saw the admiral's flag waving in the harbour, the faithful messenger whom he had despatched across the enemy's country the evening before, must have been felt like snow in harvest refreshing his soul.

The American missionary Judson was imprisoned in Burmah and doomed to death. Alone in the hands of heathen savages, that Christian apostle could do nothing to preserve his own life. He learned in his prison that a British ship of war was in the Burmese waters. Both power and will to save were at hand, but all might have miscarried if no messenger had been found, or if the messenger sent had not been found faithful. God had given the missionary favour in the eyes of some who had access to the prison. Having intrusted the vital message to one of these, he intrusted himself to his Father in heaven, and awaited the result in patience. Next day the boom of a cannon fell on the ear of the missionary, as he lay in his dark, hot dungeon. It was evidence that a knowledge of his danger had reached the British captain. His messenger had been faithful, and that faithfulness then was like snow in summer to his weary heart. When the message was delivered all the rest was easy; the ship of war soon wrenched the Christian captive from the hands of the barbaric king.

A history might be written of such decisive messages borne by such faithful messengers, and a thrilling history it would be. But the position and power of the oppressor are sometimes such, that a mere messenger, however faithful, cannot in any measure contribute to the deliverance of the captive. When the enemy's hosts girdle the beleaguered city round, to bear a message forth would be to the bearer a baptism of blood.

Such is the condition of the world, and such the baptism which the " Messenger of the covenant" came through in his saving work. He is a brother born for the adversity in which we lay. He is faithful to bear tidings of the danger, and mighty to save from death. He delights to speak of himself as one who has been sent. " He that sent me," is the epithet by which he loves to designate the Father. This Messenger came into the world to make God's mercy known; and by his faithfulness the Sender was refreshed. The testimony came in a voice from heaven : " This is my beloved Son, in whom I am well pleased."

But Jesus is a messenger in another way. He is Mediator. He lays his hand upon both. He brings God's message to us, and bears our message back to God. If we in our low estate have any request to present before the King Eternal, he is ready to be its bearer. " We have an advocate with the Father." " He ever liveth to make intercession for us." Through him the meanest captive who pines in this distant prison and sighs to be free, may send his petition safely to the Lord God of Hosts. The Messenger is faithful, and will certainly refresh the souls of those who intrust their petitions to his hand. He bore the tidings of mercy to us, though the wrath due to a world's sin blocked up the way : how much more will he bear our request to the Father, now that his suffering is over and his everlasting joy begun! He carried God's message to us, when our ungrateful ears were shut against the sound : how much more will he carry our cry to God, who loves to hear of the prodigal's purpose to return! All ye that are weary and heavy laden, send in your requests by the hand of this faithful Messenger. For the purpose of presenting them with power Christ ascended. " It is expedient for you that I go away." He delights when we give him work; He is happy when his hands are full. He put his disciples on the way of pleading, like a master guiding his pupil's hand in writing the petition out. " Hitherto," he said, " ye have asked nothing in my name : ask and ye shall receive." This Messenger will be like snow in harvest to those who in their extremity send a message unto God by him ; He will refresh the souls of those who send him.

Our help is laid on One that is mighty : He is Messenger and Conqueror too. There is none other who is able and willing to save. He stands now at the door of a closed heart, ready to bear a message from the perishing to the throne of grace, and pleading for such a message to bear. Present always by his word and Spirit, he cries, and cries again, weeping, to the careless, " Here am I, send me." He promises to pray to the Father for us : and we know that his prayer prevails. Already as Prophet he has come, making known the way of salvation : now he enters as Priest within the veil, bearing his people's requests for grace : in the end he will come again as King, and bear his people into glory.

In contrast with the refreshment which a faithful messenger pours into a weary spirit, " confidence in an unfaithful man in time of trouble is like a broken tooth, and a foot out of joint" (ver. 19). It is worse than want. To expect support, and be, in consequence, pierced by a broken reed, is a greater calamity than the sternest refusal could inflict. The greatest disaster, in proportion to the number of men engaged, that has befallen our arms in the Eastern insurrection, was the direct result of confidence in an unfaithful man. At Arrah on the Ganges three or four hundred soldiers were sent to attack a body of the rebels, and relieve some British residents who were in danger there. A native was employed to ascertain the position of the enemy. In consequence of his report the men left the river and made a night march into the interior. The messenger was false. The little army fell into an ambush prepared for them in the jungle. Two-thirds of their number were shot down in the dark by unseen foes. The remnant escaped to their ships when the day dawned. As they lay in that fatal valley getting their death-wounds in the dark, and helplessly wishing for the day, how exquisitely bitter must have been the reflection that a too ready trust in a faithless man had wrought them all this woe!

When life is at stake there should be no softness or slackness in scrutinizing the character of a messenger; especially in matters which directly affect the life of a soul, the credentials of unknown mediators should be rigorously tested. What shall become of those who send their petitions for mercy from God through the saints of the Romish calendar? The messenger is unfaithful, and the message will never reach its destination. These old bones and pictures cannot carry your request to the throne, or obtain its answer there. The disembodied spirits whom these relics are said to represent are not more effectual mediators than the relics themselves; they have neither omniscience to hear your prayer on earth, nor merit to make it prevalent in heaven.

Christ is the faithful Messenger, and "now is the accepted time." There is a gulf which even Jesus will not cross to make a path for the prodigal's return. Although the separation which sin has made between us and God is inconceivably great, a living way stretches over it by which petitions go now for grace—by which the petitioners shall follow to glory. But the Messenger of the covenant will never traverse the chasm which the final judgment will leave between the good and the evil. Weary pilgrims! as you would have refreshment for your souls in your day of need, send your petition by a faithful messenger in an accepted time. "Come unto God by Him," for there is no other advocate with the Father: and come now, lest the door be shut.

The Fire that Melts an Enemy

(Proverbs 25:21, 22)

"If thine enemy be hungry, give him bread to eat; and if he be thirsty, give him water to drink: for thou shalt heap coals of fire upon his head, and the Lord shall reward thee."

THE germ of this most precious moral lesson was deposited in the earth at an early period of its history. In the laws of Moses it takes a form suited to the simplicity of primeval times: "If thou meet thine enemy's ox or his ass going astray thou shalt surely bring it back to him again" (Ex. xxiii. 4). Jesus in his day found it in the Pharisee's hands, covered over with an encrustation of Rabbinical traditions, which not only obscured, but utterly perverted its meaning; as corrupted by the Jews the precept ran, "Thou shalt love thy neighbour, and hate thine enemy." When the Lawgiver incarnate had stripped the encumbering glosses from his own command, the vital germ, released from the imprisonment of ages, budded and burst and blossomed in the Light: "But I say unto you, Love your enemies, bless them that curse you, do good to them that hate you, and pray for them which despitefully use you, and persecute you; that ye may be the children of your Father which is in heaven" (Matt. v. 44, 45). This is the ripened fruit which the simple Mosaic precept produces for our use in the new dispensation; for Christ came not to destroy the law and the prophets, but to fufil. In the lips of Jesus the lesson attained its fullest dimensions and divinest form. Paul, delighting in all things to follow his Master's footsteps, took up the ancient law, as Solomon had expressed it, and wove it for ornament and strength into his greatest treatise at its practical turning point: "Dearly beloved, avenge not yourselves, but rather give place unto wrath: for it is written, Vengeance is mine; I will repay, saith the Lord. Therefore if thine enemy hunger, feed him; if he thirst, give him drink: for in so doing, thou shalt heap coals of fire on his head. Be not overcome of evil, but overcome evil with good" (Rom. xii. 19–21).

But we have not reached the origin of this wonderful law when we have traced it up to Moses : his and all subsequent expressions of it are copies merely. The original is indeed a deep thing of God : that which he commands us to do to one another He had already done to us in the everlasting covenant. He saw mankind in active enmity against Himself. He visited his enemies not to condemn, but to save. He gave food to the hungry, and water to the thirsty. He gave all good in Christ. He gave that unspeakable gift to enemies. He gave it, as coals of fire, to melt the hardened. This is the pattern after which all true morality is fashioned : the soul of social duty is, " Love one another as I have loved you ! "

To love an enemy is a principle that comes from heaven; it is not indigenous on earth. Even after it has been planted in a human heart its growth is generally stunted, for want of a soft soil and a genial atmosphere ; it is a tender exotic, and its fruit seldom comes to perfection in the cold damp field of the world. Some who seem to excel in other graces, fall far short here. This is peculiarly the "grace of the Lord Jesus." One who knew it well represented it as the distinguishing feature of his work, that "while we were yet enemies, we were reconciled to God by the death of his Son" (Rom. v. 10). Those disciples, accordingly, who walk most closely with their Master will be found to excel the most in this rare attainment. It is only when the same mind is in us that was also in Christ Jesus, that we love our enemies and do them good. When he was lifted up on the cross he gave out the key-note of the Christian life : "Father, forgive them." The gospel must come in such power as to turn the inner world upside down ere any real progress can be made in this difficult department of social duty. When we learn like Paul to "long after" our neighbours "in the bowels of Jesus Christ" (Phil. i. 8), we shall like him long after them all without exception. It is in proportion as a disciple loses the sense of his separate identity, and realizes his union as a member in the body of Christ, that his charity is able to cover the high provocations of those who deliberately do him wrong. As water, though it be actually low within the distributing channel, will rise again to the height of its source, so when the compassion that flows through a believer in the body is the very compassion that flows into him from Christ, it is a good of sufficient power to overcome the most formidable manifestations of evil. Practice directly depends on faith : when duty is difficult, faith must be strong. Accordingly it was when the Master enjoined his disciples to forgive an enemy seven times a-day, that they cried out, " Lord, increase our faith" (Luke xvii. 4, 5). They felt the force of mercy in their own hearts utterly inadequate to the difficult work which was prescribed, and with the true instincts of the new creature, sought a remedy suited to their want—a sealed union of the empty channels with the upper spring of abounding grace.

This method of treating an enemy is prescribed, not merely because it is abstractly right in principle, but also as the best practical means of obtaining a specific beneficial result. Do him good in return for evil, "for thou shalt heap coals of fire upon his head." The idea of a furnace is introduced here with reference to the smelting of mineral ore, and not to the torture of living creatures. The coals of fire suggest not the pain of punishment to the guilty, but the benefit of getting his hard heart softened, and the dross removed from his character. Love poured out in return for hatred will be what the burning coals are to the ore : it will melt and purify.

In the smelting of metals, whether on a large or a small scale, it is necessary that the burning coals should be above the ore as well as beneath it. The melting fuel and the rude stones to be melted are mingled together, and brought into contact particle by particle throughout the mass. It is thus that the resistance of the stubborn material is overcome, and the precious separated from the vile. The analogy gives an impressive view both of the injurer's hardness and the power of the forgiver's love. Christians meet much obdurate evil in the world. It is not their part either peevishly to fret or proudly to plan revenge. The Lord has in this matter distinctly traced a path for his disciples, and hedged it in. It is their business to render good for evil; it is their business to pile forgiveness over injuries, layer upon layer, as diligently and patiently as these swarthy labourers heave loads of coals over the iron ore within the furnace; and that not merely in conformity with an abstract idea of transcendental virtue, but with an object as directly and as substantially utilitarian as that which the miner pursues. The Christian's aim, like the miner's, is to melt, and so make valuable, the substance which, in its present state, is hard in itself, and hurtful to those whom it touches.

The Americans have a tract on this subject, entitled *The Man who Killed his Neighbours*. It contains, in the form of a narrative, many useful practical suggestions on the art of overcoming evil with good. It is with kindness,—modest, thoughtful, generous, persevering, unwearied kindness, — that the benevolent countryman kills his churlish neighbour; and it is only the old evil man that he kills, leaving the new man to lead a very different life in the same village after the dross has been purged away. If any one desires to try this work, he must bring to it at least these two qualifications, modesty and patience. If he proceed ostentatiously, with an air of superiority and a consciousness of his own virtue, he will never make one step of progress; the subject will day by day grow harder in his hands. But even though the successive acts of kindness should be genuine, the operator must lay his account with a tedious process and many disappointments. Many instances of good rendered for evil may seem to have been thrown away, and no symptom of penitence appear in the countenance or conduct of the evil-doer; but be not weary in this well-doing, for in due season you shall reap if you faint not. Although your enemy has resisted your deeds of kindness even unto seventy times seven, it does not follow that all, or that any one of these has been lost. At the last, the enmity will suddenly give way, and flow down in penitence under some single act, perhaps not greater than any of those which preceded it; but every one that preceded it contributed cumulatively to the glad result. The miner does not think that his coals of fire are wasted, although he has been throwing them on for several successive hours, and the stones show no symptom of dissolving: he knows that each portion of the burning fuel is contributing to the result, and that the flow will be sudden and complete at last. Let him go and do likewise who aspires to win a brother by the subduing power of self-sacrificing love.

The practical effect of kindness in subduing the evil-doer, as well as its originating principle, is exhibited in the covenant of grace before it can appear in the life of believers. In this department as in others, Christians are not inventors,—they must be "imitators of God as dear children." If any one succeed in melting a neighbour's hard heart by undeserved love, he has borrowed the method whereby Jesus won his own. Led to repentance himself, when he was seared in sin, by the undeserved goodness of God, a renewed man instinctively repeats the process on a smaller scale wherever he can find a subject, as little children imitate in a diminutive sphere the actions of their father. The saved know the effect which goodness from God in return for evil has produced on their own hearts, and therefore are ever, according to their measure, trying the same process on their fellow-men.

Nor does this unmeasured mercifulness impede the action of righteousness either in God or in man : mercy to sinners, as it appears in the gospel, is totally diverse from indulgence to sin. God knows how to be both just and the justifier of them that believe in Jesus. The perfect adjustment of righteousness and mercy in the Pattern should be sufficient to keep the imitator right. It is possible to forgive freely a brother's sin, and yet thereby give him no encouragement to repeat it. No man can supply a directory which shall tell the learner, in every case that occurs, wherein and how far he should, in the interests of justice, maintain his rights against an evil-doer; and wherein and how far he should, in the interests of mercy, forgive. No such external rules exist; no such external teaching is possible. It is not lo here and lo there; the kingdom of God and its laws are within the hearts of its loyal subjects. When you love both righteousness and your erring brother as Christ loved both righteousness and you, the difficulties will vanish like mist as you go forward to meet them. If you get upon the traces of the Lord's goings, the way will be easy and the issue sure. If you are willing to follow him, he will lead you through. Your forgiveness of wrong, when you see your way to bestow it freely, will not embolden the transgressor to think lightly of the law ; your stand for righteousness, when you see meet to make it, will not detract from mercy's melting power upon the transgressor's heart. Be mercifully righteous, and righteously merciful, like the Lord; and as he has thereby won you, you will thereby win your brother.

The workman in this department is worthy of his hire, and he will get it. The Master who prescribes the task has promised the labourer his wages: "The Lord shall reward thee." Those who fulfil this "royal law" will receive from the King a royal recompense. The wages are not "corruptible things, as silver and gold;" the winner's reward is the brother whom he has won. The Lord himself expressly announced, as the profit accruing from a cognate labour, "Thou hast gained thy brother" (Matt. xviii. 15). No work is so well paid as this; and no efficient workman goes away discontented. Those who would not value this kind of reward are precisely the persons who never try this kind of work. To render good for evil without limit as to time and quantity, is a hard effort; and to turn a neighbour's hatred into love is all that can be made by it. He who does not value the pearl will not dive for it; but he who dives for it shows by the very act that he values the pearl. The same love that risks the outlay will count the return abundant. This is the way of the Lord; in the doing of his commandments is a great reward. Those who do his work cannot be deprived of their wages; for the work is wages and the wages is work.

A Time to Frown and a Time to Smile
(Proverbs 25:23)

"The north wind driveth away rain: so doth an angry countenance a backbiting tongue."

THERE is a use for everything. There is a use for the north wind, and for an angry countenance. Rough visaged, ungainly messengers both are; but when sent on necessary errands, they fulfil their mission well. When David wanted a weapon, Ahimelech, the peaceful priest of Nob, having no other than the sword of Goliath, which he kept as a relic, apologized as he offered it, thinking it not sufficiently slim and fashionable for a soldier from the court. "There is none like that," said David; "give it me." The man of war had seen hard service, and expected more: the sword that could deal a heavy blow was the sword for him.

According to the translation in the text, which is perhaps on the whole as free from difficulties as that in the margin, it appears that in the climate of Palestine the north wind carries the rain clouds away, and prevents them from discharging their burden on the land. The same phenomenon is to some extent observed in our own island. This meteoric fact is framed into a proverb, and employed to describe an analogous feature in the action of moral forces upon human life: "An angry countenance driveth away a backbiting tongue."

There is a place for anger as well as for love. As in nature a gloomy tempest serves some beneficial purposes for which calm sunshine has no faculty; so in morals a frown on an honest man's brow is, in its own place, as needful and useful as the sweetest smile that kindness ever kindles on a human countenance. A gentle, loving character, is much admired, and, where it is genuine, deserves all the admiration it has ever gotten yet. These features, however, constitute only one side of a man, and we must see the other side ere we can pronounce an intelligent judgment on his worth. If he has not another side, he will not leave his mark on the world. If he has not the faculty of frowning, I would not give much for his smile. A worthy matron once showed me her own portrait set in a massive frame, and suspended in the most conspicuous place of her best room. Her sons had secured the services of an eminent artist to fix their mother's features on the canvas that filial piety, in a future day, might have the double aid of sense and memory in the effort to recall the past. The old lady, after asking her visitor's opinion, frankly pronounced her own: " It is not in the least like me; I never had such great black blotches in the middle of my face." The artist's shade offended her. A shining disc of red and white would have pleased her better. She excelled more in the management of family economics than in judging a work of art. Such, in a more important sphere, is the taste that demands only gentleness in human character, and would dispense with virtues of swarthier hue.

We don't want a fretful, passionate man; and if we did, we would find one without searching long or going far. We want neither a man of wrath, nor a man of indiscriminating, unvarying softness. We want something with two sides; that is, a solid, real character. Let us have a man who loves good and hates evil, and who, in place and time convenient, can make either emotion manifest in his countenance. The frown of anger is the shade that lies under love and brings out its beauty. The wisdom that is from above, whether as doctrinally revealed in the Bible or practically operating in a Christian's life, " is first pure and then peaceable." Salt is worthless when it has lost its saltness. The double command of the Lord, corresponding to the two constituent elements of a disciple's character, is, " Have salt in yourselves, and have peace one with another" (Mark ix. 50). The gentleness which will have peace on any terms, is neither pleasing to the Lord nor beneficial to men; if there is no pungency there will be no purifying.

An angry countenance is a specific for taking the venom out of a backbiting tongue. The disease is painful and dangerous; the medicine which cures it worth its weight in gold. An angry countenance is not in itself and for its own sake a blessing to its possessor. Like some valuable medicines, it is a fiery and dangerous thing. It is not safe to harbour it in large quantities, or carry it about in company; there is imminent risk of explosion. But it is good to have a supply of the tincture always within reach, and wherever a backbiting tongue shows itself, resolutely to administer the dose.

A backbiting tongue would be comparatively harmless if it should never meet with itching ears. Alone, it would be like seed without a soil; the mischief would soon die out if it wanted the power to propagate its kind. To speak evil is, in this department, the first and great sin; but the second, which is like unto it, is to hear evil. Knit your brows at the backbiter's approach, and he will soon sneak away : if you do not take the venom in, he will not long continue to give it out. Frown like the north upon the parasite who flatters you by speaking evil of a neighbour : call up the angry countenance to chase the troubler from your presence, as you would unleash the gruff watch-dog to scare the robber from your garden.

In a subsequent proverb this principle is specifically applied to an actual case: " If a ruler hearken to lies, all his servants are wicked" (xxix. 12). Whether he be the ruler of a family, a shop, a manufactory, or a nation, it behoves him to lay to heart this plainly spoken and homely warning. The practice which this word exposes is very common and very mischievous. It is not enough that you abstain from telling lies to the prejudice of others; to listen to such lies is only one degree less guilty. There is an appetite in human nature for secrets clandestinely obtained : stolen waters are sweet. This tendency should be jealously watched and sternly repressed. It is a man's interest, as much as his duty, to starve this morbid curiosity out of his own heart. Like other abnormal appetites, if it is indulged it will increase; if you give it much, it will demand more. Nor will the supply of aliment fall short; he who listens to lies will always have plenty of lies to listen to. This habit in a ruler is disastrous directly to his dependants, and indirectly to himself. Those of the servants who tell lies to their master become sycophants; those of them against whom lies are told grow desperate. Confidence is destroyed, and fear has no power to hold the incongruous elements together. The servants are wicked, and the loss falls ultimately on the master.

From this side the responsible head of any large establishment is always exposed to danger. Backbiters are moving about like flies in the sunshine. Timidly at first, and tentatively, and one by one, they alight upon him. If they find him soft, they gather courage and sit down in swarms upon his body. Firmness is a fundamental requisite for the master who has many servants: without it, even genuine kindness will be practically thrown away. A man who has not a frown in reserve cannot turn his smiles to any good account. It is refreshing to see the vermin flying before an angry countenance. When once scared away, this kind do not so readily return. Those masters who give the tale-bearers their desert at first, are seldom troubled with them a second time. One master's weakness, although not so sinful in itself, may thus be as mischievous in its effects as another master's wickedness. Many grain-fields have rotted after they were ripe, for want of a sharp north wind to drive the clouds away; and many social blessings have been blighted in the bud, for want of a frown at the proper time upon the ruler's face.

Such anger, far from being antagonist to love, is the very instrument which love wields. If you have not a frown on your face wherewith to meet the backbiter, you cannot have true kindness in your heart towards the innocent whom he undermines. No man can serve these two masters: to obey the one is to despise the other. You cannot both maintain the cause of the innocent, and open your ear to the traducer's tale. Love of the true is, on its other side, a north wind that will drive a cloud of lies away. You may as well attempt to admit light into a chamber without expelling the darkness, as to retain affection for the good without becoming a terror to the evil.

Nor do the real interests of the injurer himself require a different treatment; love even to the backbiter demands that you should have an angry countenance ever ready to meet a backbiting tongue. You are cruel to him, and not kind, if by your softness you stimulate still further the growth of a thorn which is already choking whatever good seed has been sown in his heart. Give the devil that possesses your brother a blow, although your brother himself should feel the smart: when he comes to himself he will thank you.

Cold Waters to the Thirsty Soul
(Proverbs 25:25)

" As cold waters to a thirsty soul, so is good news from a far country."

WATER is a wonderful work of God. The consumption of it is great, but the supply is abundant. It is stored in the ocean, and distributed by clouds. For the preservation of its purity, it is laid up in salt; but each portion that is carried away for actual use is distilled in the process of removal, that it may be fresh and sweet when it is poured upon the ground. It is carried in clouds across the continents, and poured out on central mountain ridges, that the whole land may be refreshed by it as it returns to the sea. Both the chemical composition of the water, and the mechanical apparatus employed in its distribution, teem with wonders. Some hydraulic machines of vast power have been made by human hands, but the greatest of them sinks into insignificance before the self-acting engine which irrigates a world with fresh water from a salt sea, and brings back the used material as good as ever to the store again, without the loss of as much as a dew-drop in a thousand years.

The common rule in human affairs is, that things of great intrinsic value are possessed in diminutive quantities; whereas coarser stuffs are more abundant. The reverse is the law in the Creator's storehouses : they contain the largest stock of the best articles. Men ungratefully hide from their own minds the unspeakable worth of water, under the vast profusion of the supply. There is seldom a lively appreciation of the benefit until it be burnt into the memory by the pain of privation. If you would have cold water valued at its true worth, offer it to a thirsty soul. In our own country happily we must depend on the testimony of others for the full meaning of the figure. It is not in our moist climate that instances of severe suffering from thirst occur. We are familiar with the phenomenon as a matter of history, but not as a matter of experience. Certain touching episodes in the Scriptures have made us acquainted with the facts from our earliest years. The story of Hagar and her boy is one of those that go into the memory, as a legend goes into the rock from the pen of iron that writes it there; and what reader of the New Testament will ever forget the picture of the wondrous Man, sitting weary on the well of Sychar, asking common water of the woman to refresh his own parched lips, and giving her in return the living water which springs up into everlasting life!

Like that best of all bodily refreshments is the relief which good news from a far country brings to a spirit that has been chafed by many successive alarms, and worn out by long-continued apprehension of evil. During the present season British mothers not a few have had sons and daughters in the interior of India, shut up within frail walls with a scanty supply of food, while thousands of cruel heathens swarmed around thirsting like wild beasts for their blood. The bi-monthly message has reported, in its usual laconic terms, that the Europeans had taken refuge in the fort, that the treacherous enemy lay in force before it, and that help was still far distant. After these few pregnant words have been uttered, there is silence until the succeeding mail arrives. Fourteen times the sun goes down in the west and rises in the east again, and all that time these British mothers can see no sign from that distant land where their treasures lie. Imagination peoples the time and space with varied terrors. The massacres already perpetrated by the same faithless foe supply too readily a body in which fear's fevered dream may clothe itself. Bloody swords and ghastly corpses flit all night before sleepless eyes. These two weeks expand into years, and the expanded space is full of agony. The strain of the suspense is drying up the marrow in the heart of the bones. We have thirsty souls here, and lo, from the Eastern heaven cold water comes. The good news, travelling literally with the lightning's speed, falls in large cool drops on these burning hearts: A British army has swept across that sultry plain, driven away the hordes of cruel Asiatics, and borne the famished garrison away alive to a place of safety.

Another example of the principle presents itself by association before us here, and presses for a notice too. Better news, from a more distant country, has come to cheer a deeper gloom. " Good news " is the specific name by which God's mercy to men is known. The "peace on earth" which was proclaimed by angels and procured by Christ—which is offered in the word and enjoyed by the faithful, is like cold waters to a thirsty soul. An intelligent being, not of our race and nature, would expect that when the message came the whole world would be on tiptoe to receive it. But in point of fact very many silently neglect, and not a few openly despise it. Those who pant for it, as the hart for waterbrooks, seem to be in all ages a minority in the world. The message of mercy is to most men like cold water to a soul that is not thirsty. Where there is a burning thirst perhaps there is no material blessing that affords to a human being such a lively pleasure as cold water ; but, on the other hand, scarcely anything can be more insipid in the absence of thirst. When it is applied to the lips of a satisfied man, it is not indeed actively or violently offensive, but it is utterly tasteless, and is therefore set aside and forgotten.

Such precisely is the treatment which the " glad tidings " get at the hands of men. To " neglect the great salvation " is at once the sin of the greatest number, and the greatest sin. There is relish enough in the world for all sorts of news except the best.

> " Whene'er we meet you always say,
>   What's the news? what's the news?
> Pray, what's the order of the day ?
>   What's the news? what's the news?
>
> Oh ! I have got good news to tell,—
>   My Saviour hath done all things well,--
> And triumphed over Death and Hell:
>   That's the news, that's the news."

It has been said, although we have not been able to verify the report, that the writer of these lines was a lunatic; but if he was such a babe, a wisdom which is hidden from the wise and prudent had been revealed to him. If by some film on his brain the lower lights were excluded or distorted, his soul was open upward, and the " Light of Life " came in.

But there are many thirsting souls on earth, and many refreshing drops falling from heaven. " The Lord knoweth them that are his ; " and they who are his know the Lord. Thirst is a blessed thing, if cold water be at hand ; cold water is a blessed thing to those who thirst. Needy sinners get ; a gracious Saviour gives. When thirst drinks in cold water, when cold water quenches thirst, the giver and the receiver rejoice together. While the redeemed obtain a great refreshment in the act, the Redeemer obtains a greater ; for Himself was wont to say, " It is more blessed to give than to receive."

An Impure Appetite Seeks Impure Food
(Proverbs 26:11)

" As a dog returneth to his vomit; so a fool returneth to his folly."

THE natural tastes may be keen and tender, while the moral sense is blunt. Refinement may be dissociated from holiness. Some who live in spiritual impurity would shriek at the sight of material filth.

According to the usual method of the Scriptures, a known thing is employed here to teach an unknown. The taste which inheres in nature is used as an instrument to implant the corresponding spiritual sensibility : the revulsion of the senses from a loathsome object is used as a lever power to press into the soul a dislike of sin. The image suddenly thrown across our path in this text is reflected from one of the most disgusting sights that meet the passenger's eye on the promiscuous paths of life. The suggestion, acting through memory on a vivid imagination, makes the flesh creep. But this is not an oversight : he who knows what is in man seeks a tender place, and of set purpose touches him there. This word wounds the quick flesh in order to awaken sensibility in the dead spirit. Through the lively perceptions of nature an arrow of conviction is aimed at a callous heart.

Although the original is inexpressibly revolting, the image is boldly and broadly sketched. No graceful drapery shrouds the unseemliest features of the object : the figure is exhibited in its length and breadth. The plainness is all needed : the lines are strongly drawn that the lesson may be clear and cutting. There must be a rude, hearty blow, for there is a hard searing to be penetrated. Those who go back to suck at sins which they once repudiated, may see in this terse proverb the picture of their pollution ; only the Omniscient perfectly knows and loathes the vile original.

The apostle Peter, finding this reproof in the Bible, judged it a suitable instrument to be used in the coarser portions of his work. He was an earnest, outspoken man. His speech was more distinguished for strength than for polish. When called in the course of his ministry to deal with backsliders, he snatched this weapon from the old armoury of Solomon, which the men of Hezekiah had preserved, and used it without a word of apology for its serrated and trenchant edge. The whole passage in Peter's epistle is peculiarly interesting, as an example of the manner in which the writers of the New Testament sanction, adopt, embody, and expand, the inspired record of the older dispensation: " For if after they have escaped the pollutions of the world through the knowledge of the Lord and Saviour Jesus Christ, they are again entangled therein, and overcome, the latter end is worse with them than the beginning. For it had been better for them not to have known the way of righteousness, than, after they have known it, to turn from the holy commandment delivered unto them. But it is happened unto them according to the true proverb, The dog is turned to his own vomit again; and the sow that was washed to her wallowing in the mire" (2 Pet. ii. 20–22).

Some persons who had heard the gospel, abandoned their vicious courses, and been enrolled as members of the church, had after a while openly returned to their former sins. The apostle betrays no faltering in dealing with the case: he utters a certain sound. Although it was "the knowledge of the Lord" that induced them at first to reform their lives, they had never been in true faith united to the Saviour. The fear of the Judge had driven them for a time from their indulgences, but the love of the Redeemer had not conclusively won them to hope and holiness. They dreaded Christ's judgment-seat, but were not created again into his image. They fled in fear from the material food of their corrupt appetites, but carried their corrupt appetites away alive in their breasts. When the terror passed the tastes revived, and, by a resistless instinct, devoured again the very abominations which they had cast out as evil.

Peter supplies a graphic description of the process by which old lusts regain their dominion, and he who seemed emancipated is again enslaved; the man who fled from the pollutions of the world is " entangled" therein again, and thereby overcome. The term indicates that one thing is plaited into another, as the strands of a rope, or the branches and roots of contiguous trees. Where suitable substances are so interwoven, whether by art or nature, they cannot be severed from each other without being torn in pieces and destroyed. When the affections of a corrupt heart are by fre-quent gratification allowed to push their roots deeply into the pollutions of the world, and the pollutions of the world are allowed to warp themselves round the affections of a corrupt heart, a dread-ful process of "plaiting" is accomplished under ground unseen; and the insnared victim at last refuses to renew the struggle, be-cause he feels or fears that a violent separation would wrench out his life. A man's life has been partially reformed, while his con-science remains unclean. He flees from the sins which he fears, and yet loves the sins from which he has fled. Under the impulse of this unsubdued desire he steals back, when an opportunity occurs, to the neutral ground between good and evil, and dallies with the old impurities across the boundary-line. To him all seems level and safe; but he is on the brink of ruin, and his steps will "slide in due time." When thirst for the world's pollutions re-vives, he saunters on the edge of the world's territory, where by stretching over he can sip a little now and a little then of the abandoned sweets. Chafing under the self-imposed but unkindly restraint, he argues with himself that Christianity does not frown on harmless enjoyments. He intends to stand with his feet on the safe side, while with his hand he plucks a pleasure from the side which is not safe. The appetite and its gratification, both unchanged, grow into each other again. When the unrenewed heart and the pollutions of the world are, after a temporary sepa-ration, brought together again, the two in their unholy wedlock became "one flesh." The crash of a sudden judgment disturbs the long lethargic slumber: the Philistines be upon thee, Samson! The unconscious captive arises and shakes himself; but his locks are shorn and his strength is gone. Any green withe may bind and hold him now: his eyes will soon be out: he will grind dark-ling all his days in the prison for sport to his cruel foe.

Peter summons another witness of kindred character to corro-borate the testimony of the more ancient proverb. The apostolic supplement, though the same in kind, is in degree less caustic than the original germ. The appended proverb, though less pungent as a reproof, reveals a touching feature in the nature of spiritual declension. The sow was washed: the filth was wiped from the creature's skin, but the creature's instincts remained unchanged. She is as clean and white as the lamb that feeds beside her on the grass; but whenever an opening appears in the fence, she bounds towards the mire and bathes her body in it. It is not necessary to watch the lamb, and fence it round lest it should go and do likewise. It has no inclination to do so; it has another nature. Man's true need—God's sufficient cure is, "Create in me a *clean heart*, and renew a new spirit within me."

Now or Tomorrow

(Proverbs 27:1)

"Boast not thyself of to-morrow: for thou knowest not what a day may bring
forth."

T O-MORROW will come: on that point there is no doubt:
but will you be here to meet it? The day is sure, but
your interest in it is altogether uncertain. We have
faculties for knowing the past and experiencing the present, but
none for discerning the future. We know well, each in his own
immediate sphere, what was yesterday, and what is to-day, but
we know not at all what shall be to-morrow. The uncertain things
are not the day and its nearness, but our life and our condition
when it arrives.

To count on to-morrow so as to neglect the duty of to-day is
in many respects the greatest practical error among men. None
have a wider range, and none are charged with more dreadful consequences. Whether the work in hand pertain to small matters
or great,—to the sowing of a field or the redemption of a soul,—
for every one who deliberately resolves not to do it, a hundred
tread the same path, and suffer the same loss at last, who only
postpone the work to-day with the intention of performing it to-
morrow.

This proverb contains only the negative side of the precept; but
it is made hollow for the very purpose of holding the positive
promise in its bosom. The Old Testament sweeps away the wide-
spread indurated error; the New Testament then deposits its
saving truth upon the spot. The law declares that to-morrow is
the worst time for making the decisive choice, and the gospel proposes to-day as the best. For making the choice on which the
interests either of time or eternity depend, Solomon warns us to
distrust the future, and Paul persuades us to occupy the present
hour. "Behold, now is the accepted time; behold, now is the

day of salvation." "To-morrow" is the devil's great ally,—the very Goliath in whom he trusts for victory: "Now" is the stripling sent forth against him. A great significance lies in that little word; it marks the point on which life's battle turns. That spot is the Hougomont of Waterloo; there the victory is lost or won. Men do not often join issue against God on the person of Christ or the ministry of the Spirit, on the ground of acceptance or the necessity of faith; on all these points and many others the carnal mind readily acquiesces in the doctrine of Scripture, like willows bending to the breeze, but resists Christ's claim to be admitted now, as a rocky shore resists the onset of the waves. The worldly will freely agree to be Christians to-morrow, if Christ will permit them to be worldly to-day.

The *Now* which divine mercy presents to men, instead of their own false *To-morrow*, represents in one view a line running through all time, and in another a point touching only the present moment. One day is with the Lord as a thousand years, and a thousand years as one day. The two representations are congruous, and each is in its own place important.

1. Let Paul's *Now* represent time and Solomon's *To-morrow* represent eternity; in this aspect to-day and not to-morrow, is the day of salvation for mankind.

When we compare time with eternity in relation to the hopes of men, serious misconceptions sometimes steal in under the guise of a more advanced spirituality. People search for comparisons to indicate how very small this life is, and how very great is the life to come; imagination is put upon the stretch for the means of expressing how much eternity exceeds in importance the present time. In one point of view and for one purpose this is right; but in another point of view and for another purpose it is wrong. This life is in one aspect the least, and in another the most important period of our destiny : this life is in one sense the smallest, and in another sense the greatest thing to man.

When you separate the two, and look at them apart, as distinct and rival portions, time for an immortal is a very small thing, and eternity inconceivably great. No comparison can do justice to the difference between them; no imagination can measure how far the infinite future exceeds in importance this passing scene. But when you consider time and man's life on earth as the beginning of his eternity,—that part of it which gives direction and character to all the rest,—then, though it seems a paradox, it is nevertheless true, that the present life is the greatest treasure intrusted to man. This earth is a more important place for us than any that our feet will ever stand upon, for here all is lost or won.

Time, considered by itself as a portion, is very insignificant ; but in its own right place it is more important than eternity itself. In all the universe there is no spot so significant as this globe on which mankind dwell. On it the issues of eternity for all the human race are fixed. Here in our nature Emmanuel wrought deliverance; and here all his people are born and nourished and trained for his kingdom. This life is the germ of immortality; this earth is the nursery for heaven.

You have seen the tiny blossom of the fruit-tree opening in early spring. After basking a few days in the sun, it fades and falls. A germ is left behind on the branch, but it is scarcely discernible among the leaves. It is a green microscopic speck that can scarcely be felt between your fingers. If a hungry man should pluck and eat it, the morsel would not satisfy ; although he dreams of eating, when he awakes his soul is empty. The germ, as to present use, is a sapless, tasteless nothing ; grasped now as an object and end, it is the most worthless of all things: but left and cherished as the germ of fruit, it is the most precious ; according as it fades or thrives will the husbandman have joy or sorrow in the harvest.

This life is the bud of eternity; if it is plucked and used as the portion of a soul, that soul will be empty now, and empty for ever. If the husbandman should gather all the germs green, while they are tiny, tasteless atoms hidden among the leaves, he would be disappointed at the time, and destitute at last; he would gather worthless things in spring, and have nothing to gather in harvest. This life, taken and used as the portion of an immortal being, is green and sour and hurtful; if you pluck it at this stage, you will taste no real sweetness at the time, and possess no ripened store at last. But while the present world thus abused is worthless, rightly used it is beyond all price. Here is generated, cherished, ripened, the life that will never die. Time, from the creation of man to the final judgment, is in God's sight as one day, and that day is an high day in the calendar of heaven. On it, at early dawn, man was made in God's image, and lost that image by his own sin: on it, at high noon, the Son of God took human nature, and died the Just for the unjust: ere its evening close in darkness, "the whole family of God" will have been born and educated for glory. This day, in the midst of eternity, though it seems small like a lone star in the blue sky, is greater than human thought at its utmost stretch can measure. Man signalized it by making it a day of perdition; God signalized it by making it a day of salvation.

This view of the earth would make pilgrims at every stage tread it reverently as holy ground: this view of life would infuse a heavenly wisdom into the spirit and conduct of the living. Time's one great day begins with the creation of man, and ends with the coming of the Lord; but already in God's sight that expanse is nothing more than a point; and to ourselves, when from eternity we look back, it will seem a speck upon the infinite. As one star differeth from another star in glory, this day will shine more brightly than all the rest, for it is the bride's birth-day; it is the date attached to every name in the Lamb's book of life.

2. Let *Now* represent this moment, and *To-morrow* the next. The same object may appear at one time as a lengthened line, and at another as a single point, according as it is presented to the observer. The "now" of mercy's offer, which runs parallel with the human race over all the course of time, is also a moment which passes ere its name can be pronounced. Imagine the whole human race of all generations to be a moving row of living men, like a procession marching along the street; such, indeed, it actually is, almost without a figure. Conceive the "now" to be a fixed point on the route—a signal displayed from the palace of the King, and left to wave a welcome there throughout that great day, on which the procession is defiling past. From morning till night that same gladsome signal hangs at the same spot: but each man of the lengthened line is compelled to march quickly past, and to him it remains only a few moments in sight. One man marches forward; others follow, beholding the signal in their turn; but those who have passed cannot see it now, although the sight were their life. Suppose the six hundred thousand Hebrews in the wilderness, when stung by the fiery serpents, formed in one

vast column, and defiling, two or three deep, past the spot where the healing emblem hung. The movement occupies one whole day. The healing symbol is like God's present accepted "Now," and the march of the Hebrews past it is like the course of mankind over time. Mercy abides there all day long, but each passenger sees it only while he passes. If the wounded do not look when he is at the spot, he will go forward diseased, and perish beyond, although others coming after him are still getting life from the look.

Now is displayed from heaven, an invitation from its Lord to the generations of men, as they are gliding past it like a stream. He holds it out all the day, from the morning, when he made man in his own image, till that gathering night, when a mighty angel shall proclaim that time shall be no more. He has never drawn it up, although the provocation has been great; and will not draw it up till the last man shall heave in sight and look upon it. To the race it is a line stretching over all time: but to the individual it is only a point. For narrowness it is a point, but it is the point of the sceptre extended from the hand of the King; and the law of the kingdom is, that whosoever touches it shall live. Such and so winsome has Mercy made *to-day*, that men might be persuaded not to put their trust in an unknown *to-morrow*.

We know not what a day may bring forth. Behind the dark curtains of the future, to-morrow lies concealed. She is travailing in birth; and what shall her offspring be? Whether weal or woe, whether sickness or health, whether prolonged probation in this life or quick removal to the judgment-seat, is unknown and undiscoverable. "We all do fade as a leaf." And how does a leaf fade? Two main features characterize the manner of its fall—certainty and uncertainty. In one aspect nothing is more fixed, and in another nothing more fluctuating. All those myriads that now glitter in the sunshine or flutter in the breeze will be strewn on the ground ere the year die out; but when this one shall fall, and how long that one shall hang, no tongue can tell. One falls smitten by a mildew soon after it has burst from the bud in spring; a second is withered by a worm at its root in early summer; a third is shaken off by a boisterous wind; and a fourth is nipped by frost in autumn. In what part of the year any leaf will drop is wholly uncertain; that all will be down ere the year be over is absolutely sure. We may see in this fragile mirror the reflection of our own frailty. The generation now living will in a few years be all beneath the dust; but the departure of each is as uncertain as the dropping of the leaves. Some drop in childhood's spring, some in the bloom of youth, some in the maturity of manhood, and some hang on till the winter of age arrives. These two things are terribly clear—the time is short to all, and the short time is uncertain to each.

An artist solicited permission to paint a portrait of the Queen. The favour was granted—and the favour was great, for probably it would make the fortune of the man. A place was fixed, and a time. At the fixed place and time the Queen appeared; but the artist was not there,—he was not ready yet. When he did arrive, a message was communicated to him that her Majesty had departed, and would not return. Such is the tale: we have no means of verifying its accuracy; but its moral is not dependent on its truth. If it is not a history, let it serve as a parable; such a disappointment might spring from such a cause. Translate it from the temporal into the eternal; employ the earthly type to print a heavenly lesson.

The King Eternal consented to meet man. He fixed in his covenant and proclaimed in his word the object, and the place, and the time of the meeting. It is for salvation; it is in Christ; it is now. The "faithful Creator" has been true to his own appointment. He came, not to condemn, but to save; He came in Christ, God manifest in the flesh. He waits now to embrace returning prodigals. If they abide among their husks to-day, and come running and panting to-morrow, they may find that the door of mercy is shut, and the day of redemption past. Have you felt a fainting of heart and a bitterness of spirit when, after much preparation for an important journey, you arrived at the appointed place, and found that the ship or train by which you intended to travel had gone with all who were ready at the appointed time, and left you behind? Can you multiply finitude by infinitude? Can you conceive the dismay which will fill your soul if you come too late to the closed door of heaven, and begin the hopeless cry, "Lord, Lord, open to us?"

The Countenance of a Friend
(Proverbs 27:17)

" Iron sharpeneth iron: so a man sharpeneth the countenance of his friend."

WHEN an iron tool becomes blunt, an instrument of the same material is sometimes employed to restore its edge. In such a case, literally " iron sharpeneth iron." This process is compared to the quickening influence which a man's countenance may exert on the flagging spirit of his friend. As an instrument made of steel may, when blunted, be sharpened again by another instrument also made of steel; so a man, when cares oppress his spirit and cloud his face, may be brought to himself again by intercourse with a brother who has a more sprightly countenance and a more hopeful heart.

A man's mind is liable to become dull in the edge as well as the tool which he handles. The moral bluntness is as common as the natural, and springs from a similar cause. Much application, especially on hard and unyielding subjects, rubs off the sharp edge of the intellect, and renders it less capable of successful exertion. A man in this condition is like an artisan compelled to work with a blunted instrument ; the effort is painful and the progress is slow.

For a blunt tool or a weary spirit we are not limited to one application. Many whetstones lie within our reach, of various material and various virtue; and one of the chief is, " the countenance of a friend." Bring the downcast into the presence of a true friend ; let a brother's countenance beam upon the worn-out man ; let it sparkle with hope and speak encouragement ; forthwith the blunted mind takes on a new edge, and is able again to cut through opposing difficulties. Every one who knows what care is has experienced the process of blunting ; and every one who has a friend knows how much power there is in human sympathy to touch the soul that has become like lead,—as heavy and as dull,—and sharpen it into hopeful activity again. Saul of Tarsus, even after the quickening of grace was superadded to the natural intensity of his intellect, was himself beaten broad and blunt by many successive blows on coarse, cross-grained material, and burst into glad thankfulness when he felt the countenance of a friend touching his spirit and restoring its tone : "We were troubled on every side ; without were fightings, within were fears. Nevertheless, God that comforteth those that are cast down, comforted us by the coming of Titus." While he acknowledges God as the source of all consolation, he confesses with equal distinctness that the instrument which applied it was the face of a friend.

We are wonderfully made, both as individuals and as members of a community. Each man is a separate being, conscious of his own personality and continued identity, and amenable to the Supreme Judge for himself alone ; yet each has as many separate relations as there are persons with whom he holds intercourse in the various offices of life. We influence others, and are in turn affected by them. Man would scarcely be man if he were prevented from associating with his kind. It is not good for man to be alone ; solitude rigidly maintained and long continued produces insanity. One half of the human faculties are framed for maintaining intercourse with men, and one half of the divine law is occupied with rules for regulating it.

Although social meetings become frequently, in point of fact, the occasion of sin, they are not in themselves and necessarily evil. The concourse of numbers for social enjoyment affords an opening by which the tempter may come in ; but even in the face of such a danger, we dare not advise that the door should be wholly and for ever shut. Watch and pray against temptation on every side, but forbid not the meeting of man with man, whether in seasons of joy or of grief.

The countenance of a friend,—the mark of glad recognition after protracted absence,—the intelligence that looks out of every feature, and the love that kindles all into a glow,—the countenance of a friend, with all that is in it, is a wonderful work of God. It is a work as great and good as the sun in the heavens ;

and, verily, He who spread it out and bade it shine, did not intend that it should be covered by a pall. When the Creator had made a shining sun, he hung it in the midst of heaven that all the circling worlds might look on its beauty and bask in its rays : so, when he makes a " lesser light" of equal brilliancy, —a loving human countenance,—he intends that it should shine upon hearts that have grown dark and cold. Social, or, if you will, convivial parties, are the outgoing of instincts which our Maker has planted in our being. A convivial meeting is one where men eat their bread together, getting and giving reciprocally meantime rays as sweet as sunlight from the faces of friends. Why should not the sons of God meet thus, and bless each other as brothers, while they are fed by a Father's hand ? Alas ! when they meet, Satan still presents himself among them. When the avenues of the heart are fully opened to admit a brother's love an evil spirit glides in to possess and defile. But it is not the happy face of a friend that stings and kills. There is no evil in it: behold, it is very good. Let " Holiness to the Lord" be written on it, and then enjoy freely the society of men. We may eat our bread together, and look on each other's faces while we eat, and thank God for his goodness. Meetings are not evil ; social meals are not evil ; cheerful conversation is not evil ; kind looks are not evil. Christians ! here is a work to be done, a battle to be fought, a victory to be won : wrench these good things from Satan's hands, and let the children of God, for whom they are provided, enjoy their own again.

The human countenance !—receptacle of a thousand joyful impressions, that at a signal leap into their places simultaneously, and crowd and flit, and glow and glitter there, a galaxy of glory, a teeming, overflowing source of manifold and wide-divergent consolation ; the human countenance,—oh, thou possessor of the treasure, never prostitute that gift of God ! If you could and should pluck down these greater and lesser lights that shine in purity from heaven, and trail them through the mire, you would be ashamed as one who had put out the eyes and marred the beauty of creation. Equal shame and sin are his who takes this terrestrial sun,—a human countenance,—and with it fascinates his fellow into the Old Serpent's filthy folds!

In a certain Italian city, not many years ago, six men of diverse age, and rank, and attainments, were sitting late at night around the table, within the dwelling of one of their own number. Each had a Bible in his hands. Each man looked alternately down on that blessed book, and up on his brother's countenance. Both were beaming, and the light that shone in both was a light from heaven. As iron sharpeneth iron, so these persecuted disciples of Jesus sharpened mutually their own broken spirits by looking on each other's faces while they conversed upon the word of life. The spoiler came. The agents of a despot broke suddenly into the chamber, and dragged its inmates to prison. But a friendly countenance reached the martyrs there, and healed their broken hearts. The face of that Friend whose presence gave "songs in the night" to Paul and Silas in the inner prison at Philippi, bursts yet through every barrier to cheer the hearts of those who suffer for His sake.

This soul is obliged, in the conflict of life, to force its way through hardnesses which, sharp though it is, destroy from time to time its penetrating power. It strikes suddenly upon temptation, upon worldly cares, upon pains, upon bereavements; and, onward further in its course, it must strike upon the armour of the last foe. When the spirit is sorely blunted on all these, and turned into lead by contact with the last, how shall it acquire a keenness, whereby it will be able to go with a glance right through the armour of death, and gain the victory? The sharpener provided for this extremity is still the countenance of a Friend. As iron sharpens iron, a Man is provided to quicken in the last resort the sinking soul of man. For our adversity a Brother is born. It is this countenance lifted up, and looking love on a human being in the hour of his need, that will revive the downcast spirit, and put a new song into fainting lips. By the countenance of that Friend, falling with its holy light on the solitary pilgrim at the entrance of the dark valley, the spirit, in the very act of departing, has often been brought to a keener edge than it ever knew before; and then, conscious of power, and fearless of obstacles, it has leaped forth, and darted away like light, leaving the bystanders gazing mute on the illumined wake. When they regain their lost breath, and dare to break the silence in presence of the placid dead, it is to whisper to each other, through struggling tears,—"What hath God wrought!"

Conscience

(Proverbs 28:1)

"The wicked flee when no man pursueth; but the righteous are bold as a lion."

NO *man* pursueth; and yet a pursuer is on the track of the fugitive, otherwise he would not flee. Pursuit and flight are in nature correlatives, and constitute an inseparable pair. Pursuit follows flight, or flight precedes pursuit, as an advancing body casts a dark shadow forward or backward according to the direction of the light. His own shadow may be, and often is, the most terrible pursuer that ever dogged the steps of a criminal. A swift foot does not avail the man who is fleeing from himself. When Cain shed his brother's blood, no man pursued the murderer; yet he was pursued. He was hunted like a deer by dogs. His own apprehension was, "I shall be a fugitive and a vagabond in the earth; and it shall come to pass, that every one that findeth me shall slay me." Every bush that waved in the wind became the avenger of Abel, and made the life-blood curdle in Cain's heart. This was the Lord's doing in that early age; and the same method is still adopted in the government of the world. A man has committed murder, and successfully concealed his crime. No human eye but his own witnessed the deed; no other human ear heard the groans of the victim; no officer of justice arrested the perpetrator. Yet he is pursued and arrested: in some cases, his shadow-pursuers drag him in by force, and hand him over to the constituted authorities for trial: in other cases, they hold him in their own thin arms, and glare on him with their own fiery eyeballs, exacting, all his life long, a severer punishment than any that lies within the province of a human judge.

When they escape from man, God is the pursuer of the guilty. "If I say, Surely the darkness shall cover me; even the night shall be light about me." He bows his heavens, and comes down for vengeance as well as for mercy. The "invisible God" has a way of making his presence felt. A reflector fixed in the human constitution points ever to its Author, as the magnet points to its pole, whatever the windings of life may be. With more or less of distinctness, this mirror receives and reveals the frown or the smile that sits upon the Judge's brow. Thus, in effect, God is present in every human breast. Conscience within a man is one extremity of an electric wire, whose other extremity is fastened to the judgment-seat. This apparatus brings the Judge and the criminal terribly near to each other; and if peace has not been restored, enmity in such close contact is intolerable.

Unable to tolerate it, the guilty betakes himself to flight. No man pursues him, yet he flees as if from armed legions. Whenever and wherever the fugitive may halt to recover breath, his pursuer is still at his heels. The reflector which he carries within himself ever points in one direction, and ever reveals the face of God. Although he should flee from human abodes, and dwell in the heart of earth's deepest desert, the same sun would shine on him there, and the same mysterious tablet in his own soul would receive its burning beam. "Hast thou found me, O mine enemy!" "It is a fearful thing to fall into the hands of the living God."

A man may be saved from death by seeing the reflection of danger in a mirror, when the danger itself could not be directly seen. The executioner with his weapon is stealthily approaching through a corridor of the castle to the spot where the devoted invalid reclines. In his musings the captive has turned his vacant eye towards a mirror on the wall, and the faithful witness reveals the impending stroke in time to secure the escape of the victim. It is thus that the mirror in a man's breast has become in a sense the man's saviour, by revealing the wrath to come before its coming. Happy they who take the warning,—happy they who turn and live! The truth-teller is troublesome, and men besmear its bright surface with the thick clay of various pollutions, that the light which glances from it may no longer go like a sharp sword through their bones. You may dim the surface of the glass so that it shall no longer be painfully bright, like a little sun lying on the ground; but your puny operation does not extinguish the great light that glows in heaven. Thus to trample conscience in the mire, so that it shall no longer reflect God's holiness, does not discharge holiness from the character of God. He will come to judge the world, although the world madly silence the witness who tells of his coming.

Conscience is in many respects the most wonderful element in the constitution of man. It is the point of closest contact and most intimate communion between us and the Father of our spirits. None of the human faculties constitute so hard a problem in mental philosophy. It has never fully melted yet in the crucible of the metaphysical analyst. Considering its position and uses, we need not be surprised that it more thoroughly eludes our search than other faculties of our nature. Thereby chiefly God apprehends us: thereby chiefly we apprehend God.

By "the wicked" we must not understand only those who are reckoned criminals by human governments. If heathen darkness covers the people, or searing has gathered hard and thick round a man, nothing short of bulky crimes can disturb the conscience; but where the true light shines, his own sins may oppress the penitent while the neighbourhood rings with his praise. "We are all as an unclean thing, and all our righteousnesses are as filthy rags." He who uttered that confession was probably reckoned a saint in the city where he lived. Light from God's word without, and a quickened conscience within, revealed transgressions, like a cloud for number and for blackness, while the spectators saw nothing but virtue in the suppliant's life. He has looked in upon his own heart, and back upon his past life, and upward to the righteous Judge, and forward to the great day, and in all the horizon swept by his straining eye no spot appears where conscience can find a resting-place.

Who shall stand between the fugitive and his pursuer? Who shall settle the controversy between an unclean conscience and a just God? The question points, as John did, to the Lamb of God who taketh sin away. There is one Mediator between God and man. Terrors are sent as messengers of mercy to arouse loiterers, and compel them to flee. While Lot lingered in Sodom, the angels were urgent. The urgency of the angels was irksome to Lot; but when the saved man looked from his refuge in the mountain down upon the burning city, he was glad that the consuming fire passed before him as an image to terrify, before it fell from heaven in its substance to consume. The warning was troublesome, but it saved his life. It is better to be roughly awakened to safety, than to perish asleep. So think many now, in earth and in heaven, who in the day of mercy feared coming wrath, and fled from the wrath to come. The fugitive gets "boldness to enter into the holiest," when he enters "by the blood of Jesus" (Heb. x. 19).

Sin Covered and Sin Confessed
(Proverbs 28:13)

"He that covereth his sins shall not prosper: but whoso confesseth and forsaketh them shall have mercy."

T HIS verse is divided to our hand. The separating lines are very distinctly drawn : they mark at once the appropriate place of each portion, and the mutual relations of all. Two persons are introduced ; two opposite courses are ascribed to them ; and two correspondingly opposite results are predicted. The one covers his sins, and therefore shall not prosper : the other confesses and forsakes his sins, and therefore shall have mercy.

The two distinct yet closely related subjects are the *covering* and the *confession* of sin, with the consequences that follow either course. Two kinds of seed are sown in spring, and two kinds of fruit are gathered in harvest. As a man sows, so shall he reap.

1. "He that covereth his sins shall not prosper." Few people know what sin is ; and those few do not know it well. Both the name and the thing which it signifies are common ; and yet neither is well or widely understood. Men cover their sins because they know a little of them, and then the covering prevents them from learning more. They suspect that the knowledge would not be pleasant, and therefore keep it out of the way. They would call that prophet willingly, if they could be assured that he would prophesy good concerning themselves.

Sin is in a man at once the most familiar inmate and the greatest stranger. There is nothing which he practises more, or knows less. Although he lives in it—because he lives in it, he is ignorant of it. Nothing is more widely diffused or more constantly near us than atmospheric air ; yet few ever notice its existence, and fewer consider its nature. Dust and chaff and feathers, that sometimes move up and down in it, attract our regard more than the air in which they float ; yet these are trifles which scarcely concern us, and in this we live and move and have our being. The air which we breathe every day and all day affects our life and happiness more than those occasional meteoric phenomena which excite the wonder of the world. The air exerts a predominating power on life, independently of the thought or thoughtlessness of those who breathe it. Such, in this respect, is sin. It pervades humanity, but in proportion to its profusion men are blind to its presence. Because it is everywhere, we do not observe it anywhere : because we never want it, we are not aware that we ever have it. But to ignore its existence does not change its nature, or re- move its effects. Sin decisively affects the time and eternity of men, although they neither observe its presence nor dread its power. Our ignorance or indolence cannot change the law of God and the nature of things. Sin is sin in its character and conse- quences—in its present guilt and future doom—although the sinner die without discovering the element in which he lived. " Behold, I knew not," will neither arrest nor annul the sentence, " Depart from me." The true reason of the sinner's ignorance is the great- ness of his sin. If it had been some brilliant feather floating in the air, he would have followed it with his eye, and inquired into its origin : but the air itself—he lived in it, and therefore never became aware that there was such a thing.

Beware of the old, stolid, atheistic blunder, of counting that nothing exists which cannot be seen. Moral evil is invisible as the human soul, or God its maker ; yet it exists, and its effects are great. God unseen rewards the search of those who seek him ; sin unseen punishes the neglect of those who seek it not. If you diligently seek for God your friend, he will be your rewarder ; if you diligently seek for sin your foe, it will not be your destroyer. The acute and learned Saul of Tarsus, did not discover his own sin until his journey to Damascus, although it wrought constantly as a law in his members. It was because it lay so near that he failed to observe it. A scratch on the skin is more easily discovered than a poison circulating in the blood. Alas ! we know better every trifling accident that occurs in the world, than the enmity to God which reigns at first in all, and troubles even disciples to the last.

But the knowledge of sin, difficult by the nature of the thing, is rendered still more difficult by positive efforts to conceal it. Life has three sides like tablets, on which moral character, good or evil, is graven and displayed—an aspect inward, an aspect outward, and an aspect upward. The corresponding departments of duty, as expressed in Scripture, are, " to live soberly and righteously and godly ;" but when in any or all of these directions a man comes short, an evil heart of unbelief makes an effort to conceal the sin. Watchers and witnesses stand round the man on all the three sides : himself, his neighbour, and God, observe and condemn the various forms of transgression.

Criminals are not the only class who strive to hide their deeds from the sight of men : reputable citizens occupy much of their time, and expend much of their energy, in the task of making themselves seem better than they are. But after covering his sin from his neighbour the hypocrite must take up the more difficult task of concealing it from himself. A busy court is constantly in session within a human heart. Opposing parties are ever wrangling there. Nowhere is special pleading more cunningly employed to make the worse appear the better reason. No effort is spared to hide the ugly side of sin, and set off its more seemly parts as virtue. The imaginations of man's heart, evil themselves, are constantly employed like clouds of artisans in weaving webs to cover other evils.

But the chief effort of the alienated must ever be to cover his sins from the sight of God. The arts are manifold ; and they are practised in secret : it is not easy to detect and expose them. The strong man armed who maintains possession of the citadel puts forth all his strength to prevent the entrance of a stronger one. As long as a human heart is held by the prince of darkness, the human faculties enslaved are compelled to guard the gates against the Light of Life. The key-note of the carnal is given by the possessing spirit : " What have we to do with thee, thou Jesus ? art thou come to torment us ? " All the wiles of the tempter and all the faculties of his slave are devoted to the work of weaving a curtain thick enough to cover an unclean conscience from the eye of God. Anything and everything may go as a thread into the web ; houses and lands, business and pleasure, family and friends, virtues and vices, blessings and cursings—a hideous miscellany of good and evil—constitute the material of the curtain : and the woven web is waulked over and over again with love and hatred, joys and sorrows, hopes and fear, to thicken the wall without and deepen the darkness within, that the fool may be able with some measure of comfort to say " in his heart, No God ! "

But " he shall not prosper " in this effort to cover his sin. God cannot so be mocked: his laws cannot so be evaded. Although sin in its spiritual nature cannot be seen by human eyes and weighed in material balances, it is as real as the objects of sense. Although its essence is not palpable, its power is great. If it be not destroyed, it will become the destroyer. If it be not through grace cast out of a man in time, it will in judgment cast the man out from God and the good at last.

Certain great iron castings have been ordered for a railway-bridge. The thickness has been calculated according to the extent of the span and the weight of the load. The contractor constructs his moulds according to the specifications, and when all is ready pours in the molten metal. In the process of casting, through some defect in the mould, portions of air lurk in the heart of the iron, and cavities like those of a honey-comb are formed in the interior of the beam; but a whole skin covers all the surface, and the flaws are effectually concealed. The artisan has covered his fault, but he will not prosper: as soon as it is subjected to a strain the beam gives way.

The catastrophe, you reply, is due to the violation of physical laws, and we all know that they inexorably and impartially chastise transgressors. For that very reason has the example been taken from the domain of the natural laws. You know that it is foolish to hide a sin in the heart of the iron. It shall not prosper : laws which you see in operation will avenge the trick. The case belongs to matter and its essential properties; the senses take cognizance of the fact. We believe it, because we see it.

Well; sin covered becomes a rotten hollow in a human soul, and when the strain comes, the false gives way. If the hypocrite, through the merciful arrangements of Providence, be tried and tested in this life, the fair appearance will collapse, and a deceived heart, taught by terrible things in righteousness to know itself, may yet find God a Saviour. It is thus that the trial of faith " is much more precious than of gold that perisheth " (1 Peter i 7). The fall which reveals a fatal defect, before it is too late to obtain a remedy, is in form a calamity, but in essence and effect the best of blessings. If no severe pressure come to test the spurious goodness within the limits of this life, it may hold together until it be out of sight in the grave. But it is appointed unto men once to die, and after death the judgment. The strain which will try every man's work is put on there: the unsoundness caused by covered sin will be detected then. The assize and the condemnation are not visible; if men refuse to believe what they cannot see, they must even wait until they get their own kind of evidence. If a material generation in a material age will make sure that there is no flaw in the iron which spans the river and bears their goods, and go with the hollow which covered sin has left in their souls to meet the final judgment, they must even be left in unbelief to take in conviction when it can no longer lead to life. " Seeing is believing." That curt proverb will receive a terrible fulfilment. When the Lord comes the second time, " Every eye shall see him : " but they who are first convinced then shall " believe and tremble."

2. " Whoso confesseth and forsaketh his sins shall have mercy." The subject in the second member of the proverb is that genuine confession which stands opposed to the covering of sin. It tells us what such confession is, and what it obtains. Reformation is the test of its character, and pardon its blessed result. There is a relation of a close and interesting kind between confessing and forsaking sin. Confession is false, unless the confessed sin be also forsaken; and actual amendment is unsound at heart, unless the forsaken sin be also confessed. Neither can stand alone; they must lean on each other.

Confession is made to Him against whom the sin has been committed. All sin is sin against God; to God therefore confession of all sin should be made. Some acts offend also a brother; and in these cases confession should be made also to him.

The confessional system of Rome is false from the foundation. It blasphemously puts a man in the place of God. Its roots are rotten, and its branches cannot bear fruits of righteousness. Instead of securing that the sin confessed shall be forsaken, its natural tendency and common effect is to prepare the way for repetition. It is like a merchant's monthly clearance, leaving the room empty for another set of accommodation bills to be cleared out in turn when the next month is done. So violently did this abuse outrage even men's natural sense of right, that it became the hinge on which, in its earliest stage, the Lutheran Reformation turned.

True confession is made to God. The human spirit must come into direct contact with the Divine. The Father of our spirits permits the child to approach himself on such an errand: and the offspring man has faculties fitted for converse with God a spirit.

When confession is real, it is complete. The same conviction which shows a sinner that he ought to confess, shows him that he ought to confess all. If it is not a confession of all, it is not confession; it is the old trick of covering the sin. When the spirit of adoption is attained, the confesser, with the simplicity of a little child, gives the keys of his heart to God, and welcomes the Omniscient Searcher into all its secret chambers.

True confession will produce actual forsaking of sin, as a living root sends up branches, spreads out blossoms, and nourishes fruit. If a son, far separated in residence, and long alienated in heart, relent at length and humbly invite his father to forgive and visit him: and if evil men and evil works find harbour still in the son's dwelling, before the father's visit the place will be purged of its disreputable occupants. If the son is still wedded to these companions and these pursuits, he will not sincerely invite his father to come in; if he really desires that his father should come in, he will at the same moment and under the same impulse drive out the offenders. It is thus that true confession to God, in the nature of the thing, carries with it an abandonment of the sins confessed; and if the sins confessed are not effectively abandoned, the confession has been a lie. If the persons and things that displeased the father are not dismissed, the son, whatever he may have said, did not actually desire that the father should visit and inspect his dwelling.

There is also a relation between making confession of sin and obtaining mercy from God. Sin is confessed, forsaken, forgiven; so lie the links of this short chain. When sin is cast out of the heart, it neither works any more as a ruling power in the man's members, nor lies as condemning guilt in the book of God. It is sin hidden, and so made still the object of your choice, that has power either to pollute or destroy. Sin cast forth from the heart is harmless. It cannot then pollute the life; and it will not then remain an element of treasured wrath. Similar facts and laws may be found in nature. Some substances which on the surface of the earth cannot hurt a child, may, if pent up within the earth, rend the mountains or engulf a city.

If any one fear lest this representation should rob God of his glory, and ascribe the initiative to man, let him look again, and look more narrowly into the process.

First of all, the confession of the sinner did not provide the mercy of God: that mercy was complete before he confessed his sins, before he committed the sins which he confesses. First and last the mercy is divine. It is the Father's love; Christ's sacrifice; the Spirit's ministry. It was finished when Messiah died. Bought by the blood of the Lamb slain from the foundation of the world, it was waiting in full free offer when first man's need began. The penitence of sinners did not make God gracious. His mercy is all his own, and his glory he will not give to another.

Further: the confession and reformation of sinners did not open in the treasured fountain of mercy a channel which was formerly shut. Before the man confessed, not only was the fountain full, but the stream was flowing. It was beating on the door of his closed heart. It ran waste because he shut it out; but all the work of grace was done by God, and all the glory of grace due to God, before that callous nature opened to receive it. When at last the barrier gave way, mercy flowed in; but the man's confession neither made the mercy in its upper spring, nor charged therewith the channels which unite the earth to heaven.

But, once more and chiefly, confession, so far from being the cause, is the effect of divine mercy. You see on the surface of the word here that confession obtained mercy; but you must look beneath and learn what produced confession. It was mercy. The promise is, " Whoso confesseth and forsaketh his sins shall have mercy." That promise was in substance made before any sinner-confessed, otherwise there never would have been on earth any confession of sin. That promise has power. It touches a sinner while he is dead, and hard, and still as a stone—it touches and moves him. It touches his heart, and makes it flow down like water in confession; it touches his life, and leads him into the paths of righteousness. Had there been no such gracious offer from God, there would have been no such submissive surrender by man.

This is a circle, you say. The sinner who confessed obtained mercy, and that very mercy caused the sinner to confess. It is; and therein it is like God. All the worlds are globes, and all their paths are circles. His dispensations circulate. All good comes forth from himself, and all glory returns to himself. His mercy displayed, broke the stony heart, and caused the confession to flow; the confession flowing, opened the way for mercy to enter. If I have not a broken, contrite heart, God's mercy will never be mine; but if God had not manifested his mercy in Christ, infinite and free, I could never have a broken, contrite heart.

This principle may be seen reflected from the darkest event which has yet sprung from the war in India. Some hundreds of British men and women with their children were shut up within a hastily reared and imperfect fortification at Cawnpore. A numerous enemy swept round their crazy fort, and cut off all hope of escape. When heat and hunger had well-nigh done his work for him, the insurgent chief approached and offered terms to the enfeebled garrison. They surrendered on the heathen's promise, confirmed by his oath, that they should all be permitted to depart in safety to their friends. The promise was cruelly broken, and the broken promise has wrung the nation's heart and nerved her soldiers' arms; but the promise produced the surrender. The promise of life, when trusted, had power to open those gates, which the enemy could not have forced, as long as a living defendent stood within. Another garrison in a neighbouring city were surrounded afterwards in a similar manner by the same faithless foe; but they have not opened their gates, and certainly never will. No promise is held out to them, at least no promise in which they will confide. They will trust no white flag held up by those bloody hands. They will fight in hope as long as they can, and when hope dies, they will fight in despair; but fight they will to the uttermost and to the end.*

* When this page was first committed to the press, the whole nation was listening with bated breath for the next intelligence from India regarding the fate of a feeble garrison surrounded in the Residency of Lucknow by a savage and triumphant enemy. They held out within their frail fort until they were relieved by a British army.

So would sinners fight against an angry God, if he did not promise free pardon, or if they did not trust the promise made. It is the promise of life that makes the dying open their gates.

When we were unjustly suspecting the true God, as our countrymen justly suspect the heathen chiefs,—when we, like stupid children, were refusing to trust in redeeming love,—Jesus, who came to show us the Father, taught us, as they teach little children, by a picture. The picture is the prodigal son. We are all familiar with the scene. Its features, great and small, are graven on our memories from our earliest childhood, and maintain their place even to old age.

In upon the callous heart of the worn-out and weary profligate, when his pleasures were palling and his flesh was pining away from his bones,—in upon his dry, desolate heart darted the memory of a father's love; down into the depths of that long alienated spirit sank the conviction that his father's fondness was still unchanged. That power overcame: he said, "I will arise and go to my father:" he arose and went. These are the objects that loom dimly in the back-ground; but look!—hush! These figures full in the fore-ground,—who are these? Many false and foolish things are said of canvas paintings; but this picture, which Jesus gave in his word, of the Father's mercy winning a wanderer back,—of a wanderer so won, making full, frank confession of his sin, and getting instant free forgiveness,—this is the picture for me. See the figures! They move! they move! The Father ran and fell upon his neck and kissed him; and he, the worthless, lay upon the Father's bosom. It is all over: on this side there is no upbraiding, on that side no distrust.

A simple-minded disciple once said to Jesus, "Lord, show us the Father, and it sufficeth us." What that good man desired to see, surely our eyes have seen. God, as Jesus shows him to us,— "God is love."

The Fear of Man Bringeth a Snare
(Proverbs 29:25)

" The fear of man bringeth a snare: but whoso putteth his trust in the Lord shall be safe."

T HIS " fowler's snare" is spread at every turning in the path of life, and many " silly birds " are entangled in its folds. Shall I do what I know to be right, in order to please God; or what I feel to be wrong, in order to gain the favour of men? When the question is so put, the answer is easy. On this point the knowledge of the true is universal; but the practice of the right is rare. Few act the answer which all agree to speak. The men of this day would fain be accounted far-seeing, and yet in its leading principle their policy is emphatically short-sighted. That devoted missionary of the olden time, who "looked not at the things which are seen, but at the things which are not seen," was on a better tack for both worlds than those of our day who plume themselves on looking to what they call the " main chance." He who endeavours to secure his own interests by pandering to the prejudices of men " is blind, and cannot see afar off." Safety lies on the other side.

Neither the snare nor the victim is confined to one class. There are endless varieties in the character and the condition both of the fearing and the feared. At one time the material of the snare is a monarch, and at another time a mob. Either is in its own place suitable for the destroyer's purpose, and either becomes to those who stumble into it what the spider's web is to the flies. The victims, too, are various in character and rank. Little children and grown men, poor and rich, subjects and princes, are each in turn caught in this cruel snare.

The evil begins at a very early stage of life. For Infants, the snare is thoughtlessly spread, and infants thoughtlessly step in. Those who have charge of children very frequently teach them in words to speak the truth, and by deeds entrap them into false-hood. The fear of man is a dreadful thing to a little child. When you conjure up terrors before his eyes, and accumulate threats, in order to deter him from one transgression, you are digging a pit which will ensure his fall into a worse. When you utter exaggerated threatenings, by way of making an impression, you silently make allowances for your own exaggerations; but the infant, at least in the earliest stages of his experience, takes all for truth. He is filled with a great fear of you and your promised punishment. When he commits a fault, this fear rises up like a giant before him, and prevents him from confessing it. He invents a lie in order to escape the punishment, and another lie as a buttress to the first. The poor child is taken in the snare, but they are not guiltless who laid it across his path. Even when no previous threatenings have been uttered, children magnify in their own imaginations the pain of expected punishment; and the temptation to deceive is thereby proportionally increased. Early and earnest effort should be made to elevate the fear of God into potential predominance over the fear of man in an infant's mind. Severe punishments for trifling faults, on one extreme, demoralize as much as the utter abandonment of discipline on the other. Encourage to the utmost a truthful confession of the fault, by making it tell effectually in favour of the culprit. Adopt a policy that favours confession, and never throw artificial barriers in its way. In education let the chief aim ever be to make love of truth before the living God the power paramount in childhood's little busy life. Dethrone, as far as it lies in your power, the fear of man, and let the fear of the Lord reign in its stead. Dread of punishment by a parent or a master cannot and should not be extinguished: its action is salutary, when its position is subordinate; but the supreme authority should not lie in human hands.

An event stands in distinct outline on the field of my memory, far distant in the otherwise dim back-ground of early childhood, relating to a certain little hammer which I lifted from its place without leave, and broke by unskilful handling. Dismayed at the sight of the damage which I had done, and dreading the retribution which might succeed discovery, I hid the fragments under a chest of drawers in the room, and retired into a corner to meditate a plan of defence. When the case came on, I emitted a declaration to the effect that I knew nothing of the hammer or its fate. Experienced eyes easily read guilt in my countenance. The broken hammer was dragged from its hiding-place as a witness against me. The fragments, flourished in my face, choked my utterance, and refuted my flimsy plea. I was summarily convicted. When I expected smart correction, my sister, who presided at the inquiry, gravely pronounced, from a hymn which we all knew well, the words–

> "He that does one fault at first,
> And lies to hide it, makes it two."

She paused, looked solemnly sorrowful in my face, and went away. I received no punishment; but my sister, acting a mother's part, although only thirteen years older than myself, was grieved because I had told a lie. My sister's silent grief that day went deeper in and took a firmer hold than any correction by a material rod that I ever received. She gently introduced the instrument, and, not by violence, but by a sort of lever power and inclined plane, lifted the child's spirit up from the fear of man, where it was insnared, and set it on the fear of the Lord, where it was safe. For reward, she had from beneath the gratitude of a motherless boy, and from above the blessing of the orphan's God.

For Servants, too, this snare is thoughtlessly spread, and servants thoughtlessly step in. In maintaining discipline among servants, as in all other human things, there are two opposite extremes, which are both dangerous, and one path in the middle which is safe. There is a measure of strictness which is in effect, as it is in design, a hedge planted by kindness along their path to keep them from wandering; and there is a measure of strictness which, whatever may be intended, actually becomes a snare for their feet. There is a tendency in our nature to permit the power of things unseen to wane like Saul's house, while the power of things seen waxes like David's. If wheat and chaff are mixed in a vessel, and the whole mass shaken violently from side to side, the chaff gradually comes to the surface, and the wheat lies unseen at the bottom. It is thus that, in the jostlings of human life, trust in the Lord goes down out of sight, while the fear of man comes up, and exerts the supreme control. Where grace is in active operation, this dreadful law may be held in check by constant prayers and constant pains in the opposite direction. But external forces, instead of being employed to check, are, by a perverse ingenuity, exerted to augment the power of evil already too strong in nature. Servants are too apt to magnify, as an object of terror, the discovery of a fault by a master, and proportionally to make light of the faulty act as a sin against God. Thus the fear of man becomes a snare. It is the duty of a master or a mistress in this respect to treat servants wisely and tenderly. Beware lest, by inconsiderate harshness, you make their path more slippery, and hasten their fall. If you successfully train them to fear God first, the service which they render to you will be more valuable, even in the market of the world, than service rendered by persons who have no higher master than yourself, and no greater fear than a fear of your displeasure. This fear of man, when it overrides the fear of the Lord, is both a snare which entraps the servant into sin, and a misfortune which injures the interests of the master. When the fear of a mistress is more powerful in a servant's heart than a trust in the Lord, the desire to do what is right is thrust down into a subordinate place, and the desire to conceal what she has done wrong becomes the governing motive. This is disastrous alike to the moral character of the dependant and the material interests of the chief. Godliness is profitable unto all things, having the promise of the life that now is and also of that which is to come. A servant who fears God but not you, will in your absence and in your presence alike endeavour to do well; a servant who fears you but not God, will study by all means, and at any sacrifice, to conceal from your knowledge whatever would displease you. It may be demonstrated from the nature of the case, and observed in the history of the world, that in this department of life the fear of man bringeth a snare, and a trust in the Lord is safety to the interests of all. The Lord reigneth, let the earth be glad.

It is to Ministers of the gospel that this many-sided proverb is most readily and most frequently applied. So be it. Those of them who know their Master and themselves, instead of putting in a plea of exemption, confess their need of the reproof, and claim the benefit of the warning. When they endeavour to act on Paul's advice to the ministers of Ephesus,—"Take heed unto yourselves, and to all the flock,"—they find this word of God peculiarly profitable. It is given to strengthen a weak point, where the enemy too frequently effects a breach.

When a minister is publicly preaching the word, two fears, both connected with man, but very different in character and consequences, flutter out and in and around his heart. The one may be described as a fear *of* man, and the other as a fear *for* man. They lie near each other, and in some aspects present almost the same appearance; but in nature they are opposite as good and evil. A fear for man—an old, a young, a rich, a poor, a proud, or a timid man, may and should possess the preacher's heart while he proclaims the gospel;—a fear lest, from defects in the preacher, or peculiarities in the hearer, or both, any one should have his prejudices offended, and be driven off from the truth and the Saviour: a fear of man,—influential by station, by wealth, or by numbers, may and often does knock for entrance at the preacher's heart, and bid him please the powerful. The one fear is an angel of light, and the other an angel of darkness. Sometimes it is difficult to distinguish their outward forms and secret forces: the angel of darkness puts on the garments of an angel of light. Fear of man that leads to unfaithfulness may successfully personate the prudence that would take him by guile for his good; and fear for man, which is really the wisdom of the serpent wielded by a disciple of Christ, may seem to be selfishness pandering to power. The two lie as near to each other as the sparkling eye of Tell's living child and the apple that lay on his head; he who would, with an arrow, cleave the one without hurting the other must have a clear eye and a steady hand. It is only in very obvious and outstanding cases that man is able to judge; to his own Master every servant in this work standeth or falleth. A minister must draw his supplies from the fulness of the Godhead treasured up in Christ: seeking there, he will find grace at once to speak boldly as he ought to speak, and be all things to all men, that he may gain some.

The press as well as the pulpit is liable to be unworthily affected by the fear of man. This mighty tree, whose branches afford a lofty perch for the fowls of heaven, and far-spreading shade for the beasts of the earth, has in modern times sprung gradually and unexpectedly from a very small mustard-seed, dropped into the ground by our fathers. It is an instrument of immeasurable reach and inexpressible power. Already it has done much for the religious, and more for the civil liberty of men. It is probable that this engine is destined to great uses hereafter in preparing the way of the Lord. Men are busy girdling the globe with a network of electric wires. Each State covers its own territory for its own purposes; but when the machinery is all ready, the Supreme Monarch may see meet to appropriate the whole, and thereby circulate his own message in every language and in every land. The press has in its nature great capability; but in the meantime a twofold weakness practically cripples its power: It has too much fear of man, and too little trust in the Lord. When it obtains a faith in God as its fountain of life, and shakes off the fear of man which impedes its motion, the power of that instrument may yet beneficially affect the world, to an extent of which we cannot now form any adequate conception. When all things work together for good, this one will work mightily.

To these and to other classes the principle of this proverb is applicable; but its meaning may be still more clearly illustrated by specific instances in which the operation of the principle is historically exhibited.

The Jewish rulers " straitly threatened" Peter and John, and " commanded them not to speak at all nor teach in the name of Jesus." Here the fear of man was woven into a snare, and spread across the path of the messengers who after Pentecost went forth to preach the gospel to every creature. But these bands were broken asunder by the faith of the Galilean fishermen like threads of tow before the flame : " Whether it be right in the sight of God to hearken unto you more than unto God, judge ye; for we cannot but speak the things which we have seen and heard" (Acts iv. 17–22). In the same strength have the martyrs of every age borne the cross, and thereby reached the crown. The steadfast step of these trustful witnesses easily breaking through the snare might, indeed, serve indirectly to illustrate the lesson of the text, but that lesson may be more vividly taught by the hopeless struggle or miserable end of those who have stumbled and fallen.

Herod the king was one notable example (Mark vi. 14–29). A woman with a fair skin over a black heart threw the foolish man off his guard, bound him hand and foot, and led him captive. " Give me here John Baptist's head in a charger," said this female fiend. This unexpected demand, like a peal of thunder, awakened the effeminate drunkard from his cups. There was a sharp conflict in the king's breast. Two opposite principles, the fear of man and the fear of God, struggled for the mastery within him. Before men he feared the reproach of vacillation if he should break his promise; before God he feared the torment of a guilty conscience if he should murder the innocent. The struggle was sharp and short. The fear of man was too much for the king, and he had no trust in the Lord to protect him from its onset. Ah! these "lords, high captains, and chief estates of Galilee," had heard him say it, and he feared their scorn if he should draw back. He gave the executioner his order, and saw the ghastly dish delivered to the damsel. Often afterwards did the wretched king flee from that gory head when no living man pursued him.

Pilate fell into the snare, and Felix after him. Through fear of a mob and their leaders, the one governor crucified the Lord, and the other imprisoned his disciple. Time would fail to tell of the snares that were spread, and the victims whom they caught in the days of old.

The latest and greatest example is now running its course in the East, with a continent for its theatre, and for spectators the civilized world. Our Government in India has through fear of man fallen into a snare, and the nation has paid the price in tears and blood. The Government has propagated heathenism, and repressed Christianity; made the teaching of the Koran imperative in all public institutions for the Moslem natives, and forbidden the reading of the Bible in any; constituted their army in a large measure of a heathen priestly caste, and sternly prohibited the missionaries from approaching the soldiery with the name of Christ. Idolatry was authoritatively maintained in the army of Bengal, and Christianity forcibly excluded. Such are the melancholy facts, and the motives are more melancholy still. This disastrous course was not a principle, but a policy. The ruling powers supported idolatry and excluded the Bible, not because they thought that course right, but because they expected it to be profitable; the grand design was to keep the people quiet. The chief aim of the governing power was to fish the pearls of India's wealth, and therefore they desired above all things to fish in smooth water. They feared the tumults of the people more than God. The British Government practically denied God in the heathen's sight, in order to keep the favour of the heathen. The policy was certainly not godly, but was it gainful? Read the answer in the events of the day. The events point distinctly to their cause in the just displeasure of God. The rebellion has been raised by the soldiery from whom Christian missionaries were excluded, and not by the people to whom the missionaries had access. Of the army, moreover, the portion that has rebelled is precisely the portion whose false religions the Government protected and pampered. So plainly do our disasters point to our sins, that men of all ranks and parties, with unwonted unanimity, have read the same lesson from the history : no voice is raised now to defend our past policy. At present, in the time of our distress, it appears to be the unanimous demand of the nation, that while absolute freedom of conscience shall be accorded to all, henceforth the superstitions of India shall be left to themselves, and the gospel of Christ owned, protected, and encouraged. May this mood of mind remain when the calamities which produced it shall have passed away. For the future the rulers of India may select from the Bible and hang up in their council hall the motto of a policy older and better than their own : " The fear of man bringeth a snare; but *whoso trusteth in the Lord shall be safe*."

The fear of man leads you into a snare; and will the fear of God make you safe? No ; if the character of the affection remain the same, you will gain nothing by a change of object. If you simply turn round and fear God as you feared man, you have not thereby escaped : the fear of the greater Being is simply a greater fear. The weight presses in the same direction, and it is heavier by all the difference between the finite and the infinite. When this terror of the Lord bursts in upon the unclean conscience, the man instinctively begins to reform his life with a view to the judgment. The Ethiopian falls a washing at his skin. It grows no whiter under the operation; but he washes on. He has a terrible presentiment that if he cannot make it white he will perish. He experiences a secret hatred of God for being so holy, but he conceals the enmity and continues his struggle. His life is spent in painful alternations between partial external efforts to please the God whom he dreads, and heart dread of the God whom he is unable to please.

It is not a transference of fear from man to God that makes a sinner safe : the kind of the affection must be changed, as well as its object. Safety lies not in terror, but in trust. Hope leads to holiness. He who is made nigh to God through the death of his Son, stands high above the wretched snares that entangled his feet when he feared men. The sovereign's son is safe from the temptation to commit petty thefts. A greater interval divides the tortuous courses of the world from the serene peacefulness of a redeemed and trustful soul, waiting the signal for his exodus, and rejoicing in the anticipation of rest. When you know in whom you have believed, and feel that any step in life's journey hereafter may be the step into heaven, the fear of this man and the favour of that will exert no sensible influence in leading you to the right hand or to the left.

Philosophy and Faith

(Proverbs 30:1-9)

" The words of Agur the son of Jakeh, even the prophecy: the man spake unto Ithiel, even unto Ithiel and Ucal, Surely I am more brutish than any man, and have not the understanding of a man. I neither learned wisdom, nor have the knowledge of the holy. Who hath ascended up into heaven, or descended? who hath gathered the wind in his fists? who hath bound the waters in a garment? who hath established all the ends of the earth? what is his name, and what is his son's name, if thou canst tell? Every word of God is pure: he is a shield unto them that put their trust in him. Add thou not unto his words, lest he reprove thee, and thou be found a liar. Two things have I required of thee; deny me them not before I die: Remove far from me vanity and lies: give me neither poverty nor riches; feed me with food convenient for me: lest I be full, and deny thee, and say, Who is the Lord? or lest I be poor, and steal, and take the name of my God in vain.".

THIS last portion of the book is distinguished from all the rest by several strongly marked peculiarities. It suggests some difficult but interesting questions in criticism. The chief difficulty lies in the first verse, and refers to the four terms which the translators have taken as the names of four persons. It is still uncertain whether these should be read as proper names, or as ordinary Hebrew words, expressing a specific meaning. It is well known that Hebrew names are always significant, and therefore it is not surprising that such an ambiguity should occur. The interpretation of the subsequent discourse, however, is not at all dependent on the solution of a philological difficulty in the introduction; and, accordingly, we adhere to our rule of avoiding exegetical discussions, and occupying ourselves exclusively with the lessons that come easily, like ripe fruit when the branch is slightly shaken. If Ithiel and Ucal are proper names, the record commemorates the persons, otherwise unknown, who sat as scholars at the sage's feet: if not, the words, like the heading of a chapter, indicate that the prophet's subject for the moment is an inquirer's search after God. Whether the first verse, which constitutes the title, be intended to name the audience or intimate the preacher's theme, the discourse itself remains the same. It is its own interpreter. The meaning is obvious, the form elegant, and the matter grave.

At the entrance of the temple, this worshipper of the Truth stoops very low: "Surely I am more brutish than any man, and have not the understanding of a man. I neither learned wisdom, nor have I the knowledge of the holy." It is truly spoken, thou ancient seer; this attitude becomes thee well! This man has already worshipped oft within Truth's awful dome, and hence the sweet humility that clothes him. Those who have never been within, hold their heads higher at the threshold. It was Sir Isaac Newton who, in respect to the knowledge of physical laws, felt himself a little child picking up a pebble on the ocean's shore: since his day, some who have learned less have boasted more. The same law rules in the spiritual hemisphere. Paul was, in his department, as eminent as Newton, and therefore as humble. They who know most, feel most their want of knowledge, whether the subject be the covenant of grace or the laws of nature. The secret—if a matter so obvious can be called a secret—lies here: Those heroes who, in their several lines, march foremost, do not compare themselves with other men. They do not look backward to measure themselves with those who are coming up behind; by habit, they keep their faces forward and upward. The sense of lowliness which sits so seemly on a great man's brow, is produced by the heights of knowledge or holiness yet unscaled, which tower to the heavens always in his sight. "Who hath ascended up into heaven?" This question explains how a philosopher counts himself ignorant, a saint counts himself unclean. It is a precious practical rule, to look towards heaven while we measure ourselves. To keep the eye, not on the little which a neighbour knows, but on the much of which ourselves are ignorant, is the surest method of repressing pride and cherishing humility. God will raise up those who thus keep themselves down, for "He resisteth the proud, but giveth grace unto the humble."

This observer deliberately measures himself against the magnitude of God's works in creation, that he may experience, in the fullest measure, a sense of his own low estate. Humility is sweet to the taste of the humble. Those who get a little of this gentle grace desire more. Like other appetites of an opposite kind, it grows by what it feeds on

Having thus, for personal profit, introduced the subject, he displays both accuracy and comprehensiveness in his method of handling it. These few words sketch, in three departments, an outline of the mundane system. After suggesting, in general terms, the whole question of the Divine work and government—"Who hath ascended up into heaven, or descended?"—he proceeds to specify the departments in detail:

The air, atmosphere,—"Who hath gathered the wind in his fists?"

The sea,—"Who hath bound the waters in a garment?"

The earth,—"Who hath established all the ends of the earth?"

There is an obvious and interesting relation between this reverential acknowledgment of God's governing power and the subsequent request,—"Feed me with food convenient for me" (verse 8). He intends afterwards to ask "daily bread," and therefore he begins with the invocation, "Our Father who art in heaven." Before he utters the specific request for the supply of nature's need, he looks up to the Father of lights, from whom every good gift comes down. He ascribes the power to God, and enumerates the agencies in nature whereby he works his will. The discourse is philosophically accurate, as well as religiously devout. It is through the mutual relations of air, earth, and water, that the Supreme Ruler gives or withholds the food of man. These three, each in its own place and proportion, are alike necessary to the growth of grain, and, consequently, to the sustenance of life; it is by the agency of these three working together for good that the Father of all supplies his creatures' wants.

The Earth is the basis of the whole operation. From its fertile bosom it brings forth fruit sufficient to sustain all the living creatures that move upon its surface. It is wisely constructed to serve the purposes of God and satisfy the wants of men. "Who hath established the earth?" Its hills and valleys, echoing to each other, answer, God. Its cohesive mass and its waving outline, its soft surface and its solid frame, are well-defined marks of its Maker's hands. Alike in its creation and its arrangement, its material and its form, the final cause of the earth has obviously been the growth of vegetation and the support of life.

But the earth could not bear fruit at any portion of its surface without the concurrence of Water; and how shall the supply of this necessary element be obtained? "Who hath bound the waters in a garment?" Again the clouds and showers, the springs and streams, with one voice answer, God. So wide is the dry land, and so low lies the water in its ocean store-house, that we could not even conceive how the two could be made to meet, unless we had seen the cosmical hydraulics in actual operation from day to day, and from year to year. Here lies the earth, rising into mountains and stretching away into valleys, but absolutely incapable, by itself, of producing food for any living thing. There lies the sea, held by its own gravity helpless in its place, heaving and beating on the walls of its prison-house, but unable to arise and go to the help of a barren land. Even although these struggling waves should at last beat down the barriers and roll over the earth, the flood would not fertilize any place, but desolate all. The brine would scorch the world like a baptism of fire. Unless a gentler, sweeter, sprinkling can be contrived, the earth might as well have been, what the moon is thought to be, a waterless world.

In this strait,—when the land could not come to the water, and the water could not come to the land,—a mediator was found perfectly qualified for the task. "Who hath gathered the wind in his fists?" The Air goes between the two, and brings them together for beneficent ends. The atmosphere softly leans on the bosom of the deep, and silently sucks itself full. The portion so charged then moves away with its precious burden, and pours it out partly on the plains, but chiefly on vertebral mountain ranges Thus the continents are watered from their centres to the sea. The fertility of the earth depends absolutely on the mechanical aid of the air in the process of irrigation.

When I stood beside Niagara, listening to its low but awful hum, and gazing on its gathered waters rushing impetuously toward the sea, I saw one of the larger veins through which the world's life-blood flows back into the world's mighty, ever-throbbing heart. Looking upward from the same spot, I saw white clouds careering in close succession, in the opposite direction, through the bright blue sky,—the purified blood going outward by the arteries to repair waste and maintain vitality in every portion of the complex frame. How different, and yet how similar are the mechanical arrangements whereby, in the larger and lesser systems, the pure blood is carried outward for use on one line, and the used blood carried back for purification on another, without any risk of collision on the way! No two things can be more like each other in character than the river system of a continent, as represented on a map, and the veins of a human hand as seen through the skin. The Author of the mundane system is also the Author of organic life.

He who holds the winds in His hand controls directly the world's supply of food. Famine scourges a land, or plenty gladdens it, according as these cloudy chariots with their load are sent in this direction or in that. Some portions of the earth, such as the Sahara in the interior of the African continent, are so situated with respect to the atmospheric currents, that the winds waft no rain-clouds over them; and, as a consequence, they lie in unmitigated and perpetual barrenness. These belts of dry, barren sand, show men what the world would have been if its Maker had not commanded his winds to water it. In the progress of modern art, certain unprofitable and unpromising moors have been rendered fertile by a manure which is imported at great expense from tropical climes. In these cases the operators take care to leave a strip of the field untouched by the fertilizer; and the barrenness of this bit in contrast with the rank growth of the rest proves to the owner the value of the agent. On the same principle, the deserts which occur here and there on the globe prove to forgetful men their dependence on Him who binds the waters in a garment and gathers the wind in his fists.

The laws which regulate the land and the water lie much more within the reach of our observation than those which the winds obey. We can predict the time of the tides, and measure the breadth of a continent; but we cannot tell when a shower will fall and when the sun will shine. Rain depends directly on the wind, and the wind to us is very uncertain. Air, whether in motion or at rest, is under law to God as much as earth and water. Every blast is under law as strictly as the steady swell of the tidal wave; but the causes in operation are so far removed, so numerous, and so varied, that the calculation of the results baffles all human skill. The majestic door of plenty stands in our sight upon the earth. Wind is the key which opens or shuts it. The hand which holds that key is kept high in heaven, and covered with a cloud; but every movement on the earth's surface is absolutely controlled by that unseen hand.

But this student of Nature is a worshipper of God. When philosophy fails him, he falls back on faith. He seems, indeed, to have commenced his physical researches with the conviction that he could not carry them far, and does not conceal his satisfaction when the obscurity of creation affords him an opportunity of magnifying the word. By a series of seven consecutive questions without a single answer, he shows that the evolutions of nature are not a sufficiently articulate revelation of God. Against that disappointment, as a dark ground to set off their beauty, lean the short and simple lines of light, "Every word of God is pure." This inquirer, like the writer of the nineteenth Psalm, skilfully employs even the glories of creation as a foil to the "glory that excelleth" them in a more perfect law. After a painful and unsuccessful search for God in nature, he turns round to the word, and through that pure medium beholds the light which otherwise is "inaccessible and full of glory."

The transitions are quick; and yet the steps are obviously connected and consecutive. Those who discover experimentally that God's word is pure, will find out also that "He is a shield unto them that put their trust in him." This learner is far in advance of his starting-point now. He set out in quest of knowledge to gratify a curious intellect: he ends by finding rest for a troubled soul. He addressed his question successively to the air, and the water, and the earth; but they were all dumb; they sent back to him only the echo of his own cry. Turning next to the Scriptures, he finds what he sought, and more. His darkness vanishes, and his danger too. No sooner has he learned that the word is pure, than he feels that the Speaker is gracious. He has traversed this path before: he knows it well. He goes over it again, in pity for those who are still groping without, that he may lead them "into that which is within the veil."

Having obtained a privilege, he is not slow to take advantage of it. Having found God to be a Father, he quickly exercises the rights of a child: "Two things have I required of thee: deny me them not before I die." A remarkable precision of conception and expression may be observed in this ancient prophecy. As in the observation of nature, so also in the reflex examination of his own spiritual state, the survey of the whole is comprehensive, and the distribution of parts exact. Measuring carefully the weakness that lay within, and the dangers that lay before him, he perceived that the two extremes were the points of exposure, and pleaded accordingly for support there. He saw one set of temptations pressing on the wealthy, and another set of temptations pressing on the poor; he feared that if he should be exposed to either stream, he would be carried down like a withered leaf on the water. Desiring to "live righteously," he dreaded the extreme of poverty; desiring to "live humbly," he dreaded the extreme of prosperity. He pleaded, therefore, for a safer place between the two. He who so seeks will certainly find. He may not, indeed, obtain the medium between poverty and riches which he counts so favourable to spiritual safety; but he will obtain the spiritual safety on which his heart is set. He will obtain his end, which is good, either through the means which he specifies, or others which God judges better. The Captain of his salvation will either keep the weak safe in the centre, or strengthen him to fight on the flanks.

Three distinguishing features in this prayer supply corresponding lessons for present use; the requests are specific and precise; the temporal interests are absolutely subordinated to the spiritual prosperity of the suppliant; and a watch is set against the danger to a soul which lies in extremes either of position or of character.

1. Prayer should consist of specific requests, proceeding on grounds that are known and felt by the suppliant. None of us would dare to go into the presence of an earthly sovereign with bundles of unmeaning words, fashioned to sound like a petition. Petitioners who stand there experience a pressing want, cherish a hope of relief, and present a definite request. Go and do likewise when you pray. Survey your own and your neighbour's need; consider the ground on which your plea may rest; express your request, whether for two things or for ten; and when you have expressed it, cease. The precision of this antique collect is a sharp reproof of every dim word-cloud that floats above men's heads, and calls itself a prayer.

2. The chief desire should be set upon the chief good; seek first the kingdom of God and his righteousness. The grand aim of this ancient Israelite was to keep the relations of his soul right towards God; and he made his material condition subservient to

his spiritual attainments. The aim of this anxious heart comes articulately out in the prayer: "Lest I be full and deny thee, and say, Who is the Lord? or lest I be poor and steal, and take the name of my God in vain." Wealth is desired or dreaded, not for its own sake, but as it might serve to help or to hinder the progress of grace in his soul. It is especially worthy of notice, that while he sees in the fore-ground two opposite temptations, pride on this side, and dishonesty on that,—ungodliness, to which both errors equally lead, is the ultimate object of his fear. More than wealth or poverty, more than even pride and dishonesty, he feared and loathed in thought beforehand the possible issue to which by either line an unstable heart might be led,—sin against God. The Lord will preserve those who so fear him: when we are jealous for him, he will be a shield to us. The common method of men is to set this world's good silently in the centre of their aim, and cram in as much religion at the edges as the space will hold. The method adopted here is the reverse: it is first, How shall I please God? and then let my relations to the world take shape accordingly. If we make Christ the Master, he will make the world wait upon his children; but if we permit the world to be master, we have no part in Christ. If we put either object out of its proper place, we thereby destroy for ourselves its value. The wealth which is ranked first will not satisfy; the religion which is dragged in second will not save.

3. This suppliant observed the danger of extremes, and set a watch against it on either side. Riches and destitution, as to temporal possessions, are not the only extremes which threaten the safety of a soul. They are as various as human character and condition. The Church of the Reformation was intensely doctrinal, but it was not practically missionary; it searched the Scriptures for life, but did not occupy the world for work. The legs of the lame are unequal: that revived Church was crippled even in the vigour of its youth. It is too early yet to pronounce whether the Evangelical Church of the present will stumble as much on the other side. We have acknowledged the world as our field, and are spreading ourselves over it for labour. If we maintain the truth and live on it as the Reformers did, and work for the whole world as they did not, it may be that the Lord will do great things for us and great things by us in the coming days.

Much good is effected in the world by earnest men fixing on chosen objects, and prosecuting them with all their might. I do not, I dare not, bid any such enthusiast in the Lord's service retire from the work; but I advise him to watch and pray lest he get damage from the exclusiveness and intensity of his pursuit. A miner has fallen faint under the effect of foul air in the pit; another generously descends to the rescue. The act is right; but the rightness of the act will not prevent the foul air from choking the devoted man, if he abide too long under its influence. You may be absorbed in a good thing, and yet suffer spiritual damage by the absorption. Much devotion may become a snare, if it take you from work; much work, if it take you from devotion. I do not say that any one should flee from the extremes because they are dangerous; the danger does not lie in being on the edge but in being unwatchful there. Go wherever the Lord in his providence calls you; abide wherever congenial work lies to your hand; but in every place watch and pray that ye enter not into temptation.

Lemuel and His Mother

(Proverbs 31:1)

" The words of king Lemuel, the prophecy that his mother taught him. What, my son?
and what, the son of my womb? and what, the son of my vows?".

ANOTHER appendix to the book, in the words of a certain king Lemuel. Like Agur of the preceding chapter,
he is personally and historically unknown. The mark
of the mother's faith is left in the name of the son, for it signifies
one dedicated to God. There would be nothing contrary to the
analogy of ancient practice in supposing that Solomon gave some
of his lessons under this significant designation; but the circumstances otherwise do not suit his character and history. It is
pleasant to cherish the hypothesis—in itself by no means impro-
bable—that Lemuel was the king of some neighbouring country,
and that his mother was a daughter of Israel. We know that
idolatrous practices were imported into Jerusalem by daughters
of heathen princes admitted by marriage into the royal house of
Judah: it is probable, on the other hand, that glimpses of light
sometimes fell on those heathen lands through the marriage of
their princes to Hebrew women who worshipped the living God.
The instructions given to the heir-apparent, with special reference
to his future reign, have already come under our notice in preceding chapters; and therefore, passing over the substance, we call
attention only to the circumstances of the lesson here.

The monarch, in the very act of publishing the prophecy, proclaims that he received it from his mother. Two memorable
things are joined together here in most exquisite harmony. It is
not, on the one hand, the bare historical fact that a godly mother
wisely trained her son; nor is it, on the other hand, merely
another instance of a young man acting his part well in the
world. The peculiar value of the lesson consists in the union of
these two. We know not only the good counsels which the

mother gave, but also the effect which they produced on the character of her son. Again, we know not only the practical wisdom of the son, but also the source of it in the godly counsels of the mother. The fountain is represented visibly supplying the stream, and the stream is distinctly traced to the fountain.

The mother has departed from the stage; but her son arises and blesses her. She did not personally publish her instructions in the assembly of the people, but her instructions reached the people in a more becoming and more impressive form. She knew her own place, and kept it. Whatever questions might divide the court or agitate the multitude, she remained beside her child, dropping wisdom, like dew, into his soul. She had seed in her possession, and knew that God "gives seed to the sower." By sowing it in the soft soil, and in the time of spring, she made the return larger and surer. Her honour is greater as published by the life of her son than if it had been proclaimed by her own lips.

The prophecy recorded here is an honour to Lemuel as well as to his mother. The king is not ashamed to own his teacher. His frank ascription of the credit to his parent is the highest credit also to himself. He began to set a higher value on the lessons when the lips that taught them were silent in the grave. Knowing that the stream would no longer flow from the living fountain, he constructs a reservoir in which he may hoard his supply Thus did Lemuel, with filial affection, collect and reproduce the lessons of his mother. He was not on that account less dignified in council or less bold in war. Young men frequently fall into great mistakes in determining, for practical purposes, what is mean and what is manly; very many of them, in making a spring for the sublime, plunge into the ridiculous.

There was a certain three-fold cord of maternal love which this parent was wont to employ, and which remained, in its form as well as its power, in the memory of her son: "My son, the son of my womb, the son of my vows." "My son" is the outmost and uppermost aspect of the relation. This is a bond set in nature, felt by the parties and obvious to all; on this she leans first when she makes an appeal to his heart. But at the next step she goes deeper in; she recalls the day of his birth. She goes back to that hour when nature's greatest sorrow is dispelled by nature's gladdest news,—"A man-child is born into the world." By the pains and the joys of that hour she knits the heart of her son to her own, and thereby increases her purchase upon the direction of his life. But still one step further back can this mother go; he is the "son of her vows." Before his birth she held converse, not with him for God, but with God for him; she consecrated him before he saw the light. The name given to the infant was doubtless the result of a previous vow. In this channel, and at this time, a believing mother's prayers often rise to God; and surely his ear is open to such a cry. Why should it be thought a thing incredible with you, that God should cast the character of the man in the mould of the mother's faith before the child is born? It is a fact, indisputable though inscrutable, that mental impressions of the mother sometimes imprint themselves on the body of the infant unborn, in lines that all the tear and wear of life cannot efface from the man. When we are among the mysteries either of nature or of grace, it does not become us to say what can and what cannot be. What gift is so great that faith cannot ask—that God cannot bestow it?

Dedication of an infant before or after birth may be misunderstood and abused. As a general rule, it is not safe to determine the capacity in which the man shall serve the Lord before the character of the child has been manifested. Such a dedication to the ministry of the gospel has in some cases become a snare and a stumbling-block. It is presumptuous in a parent so to give a child for the ministry as to leave no room for taking into account his bent and qualifications. For aught that you know, the Lord may have need of a Christian seaman or emigrant in a distant land, and there may lie in embryo within your infant the faculty which in these capacities might be more wisely laid out, and bring in a more abundant return. The sure and safe method is to offer them to God, and plead that he would save and use them for himself, but leave the special sphere to be determined by events. It is known to some extent already, and when the books are opened it will be better known, that sons of believing mothers' vows have been the chosen instruments of the greatest works for the kingdom of Christ and the good of the world. Dedicate them to the Lord; but ask the Master to determine the servant's sphere, and watch for indications of his will.

A Heroine

(Proverbs 31:10-31)

" Who can find a virtuous woman? for her price is far above rubies."

THE last page of the Proverbs displays the full-length portrait of a heroine. There is an extraordinary fulness in this description; it is a model character, brought out in high relief, and finished with elaborate minuteness. In the original, the peculiar resources of Hebrew poetry are all employed to beautify the picture and fasten it on the memory.

Verses 10–12 serve to introduce the theme. They constitute a stately porch through which we enter the gorgeous galleries within. The interrogation, "Who can find a virtuous woman?" seems to intimate that few of the daughters of men attain or approach the measure of this model. As usual with rare things, the price is high; it is "above rubies." The meaning obviously is, that a virtuous woman is above all price. Woman is the complement of man—a necessary part of his being. As no man would name a price for his right arm or his right eye, woman shoots over all the precious things of earth; and there is no standard by which her value can be expressed. "The heart of her husband trusts in her;" and he is not deceived, for he trusts " safely." A woman's nature and gifts are provided by the Creator as a pillow for man to rest his head upon when it is weary with the journey. An help-meet designed and bestowed by our Father in heaven, " she will do him good and not evil all the days of his life."

At the 13th verse the details begin. The design of the picture is to display the practical virtues that operate day by day in the common affairs of life. Many leafy branches, bearing useful fruit in abundance, wave before us in the wind all through the chapter; and not till the very close do we reach the root of godliness that nourishes them all. Look at some leading features of the portrait—some of the larger jewels in this woman's crown.

Industry.—Her hands are full of useful occupation. Nor is this the eulogy of a woman in a lowly condition of life; these are not the qualifications of a menial servant, but the accomplishments of a noble matron. Lemuel learned this poem from his mother's lips, and delighted to rehearse it after he became a king. People make egregious mistakes in regard to the qualifications which go to constitute a lady. In a wealthy mercantile community these mistakes are at least as rife as in families that are related to royalty. It is generally observed, indeed, that the shorter the period of time which separates a rich family from daily labour the more careful they are to obliterate all its marks. Although there are outstanding exceptions, in which sound common sense has put conventional falsehood to flight, we need not attempt to conceal the fact, that a numerous class of females practically count uselessness an essential constituent of ladyhood.

I do not frown upon refinement—I do not counsel rudeness; but I warn womankind that error on one extreme is as common and as great as error on the other. Here, as in other regions of human duty, there is a path of safety in the midst, and a dangerous pit on either side of it. Some females, in the effort to avoid vulgarity, are bound body and spirit in swaddling-clothes, and blanched into a sort of full-grown infancy. Their greatest dread seems to be lest others should suspect them of being able to put their hands to any useful employment. They may dismiss their fears, for generally the matter is made so plain, that there is very little risk of misconception. I most earnestly counsel mothers to throw off artificial trammels, and dare to be sensible and free in judging how their daughters should be trained. The power of helping themselves, besides affording a line of retreat in the event of disaster, will double the enjoyment of life, although prosperity should continue to the end. The lady who has lost, or never acquired, the faculty of performing occasionally with her own hands an ordinary operation about her house or her person, has bartered independence for ease. We smile at Chinese notions of feminine refinement; but if all the elements were fairly valued, the balance in our favour would perhaps not be great.

The form of the industry is primitive. The spindle and the distaff are its instruments; wool and flax its raw material. In the rural districts of our own land, this species of skill continued till very lately to be considered an essential feminine accomplishment. In my younger years, when the goods of a richly dowered bride were conveyed on the evening before the marriage to her future home, it was still the custon to set a spinning wheel, fully rigged with its " rock " of flax and its thread begun, aloft on the top of the hindmost cart in the glad procession. I have seen this significant symbol, and it is quite possible I may have joined in the joyous hurra that greeted the emblem of industry as it passed. My mother, whom I never saw, span with both hands every afternoon; and as her eyes were not fully occupied with the work, she kept a Bible lying open on the " stock " of the wheel, that by a glance now and then she might feed her soul while she was employed in clothing her household.

This form of female industry, we may presume, is now conclusively superseded amongst us. It is not necessary, it is not expedient, that industrious mothers in this country should now handle the distaff or ply the wheel. Human nature is pliant, and fitted for progress : we are constituted capable of accommodating ourselves to changes. Other lines lie open for enterprise and effort : some line should be chosen by each, and prosecuted with vigour. The future of the country will be dark indeed if indolence take possession of its homes. When the progress of art drives out one form of industry, others should be admitted to occupy the space; if the space stand empty in our homes, our progress in art will be a declension in happiness.

Activity.—She is an early riser. This is a great victory over a great enemy. Slothful habits make a family miserable. Early hours appointed, and appointed hours punctually kept, cause the economic arrangements to move softly and easily, like well oiled machinery, without noise and without jars.

Benevolence.—" She stretcheth out her hand to the poor." Industry and activity would only make a female character more harsh and repulsive, if it wanted this. The presence of the poor is, like the necessity of labour, a blessing to mankind : it provides a field for the exercise of affections which are necessary to the perfection of human character. When material acquisitions are great, and benevolent efforts small, the moral health cannot be maintained : when much flows in, and none is permitted to flow out, wealth becomes a stagnant pool, endangering the life of those who reside upon its brim. The sluice which love opens to pour a stream upon the needy, sweetens all the store. The matron who really does good to her own house, will also show kindness to the poor : and she who shows kindness to the poor, thereby brings back a blessing on her own dwelling.

Forethought.—" She is not afraid of the snow for her household," because she foresaw its approach, and prepared to meet it. While the summer lasted, she laid up stores of food and clothing for the winter's need. Miserable is that family whose female head is destitute of forethought. It is a common and a great evil : in a land of plenty such as this, ten homes are made unhappy by want of method, for one that is made unhappy by want of means. Look forward, and so provide that you shall not be obliged to run for the covering after the snow has come.

Elegance.—When she has provided all the necessaries of life for her family, and contributed to relieve the wants of the poor, she puts on ornaments suited to her station and her means: " Her clothing is silk and purple." She deserves and becomes it. It is precisely such a woman that should wear such garments ; the silk hangs all the more gracefully on her person, that it was wound and spun by her own hands. There is a legitimate place for ornamental female attire; but it is not easy either to define what its limits should be or to keep it within them. Perhaps there is no department of human affairs for which it is more difficult to lay down positive law : we shall venture, however, to give a few simple suggestions, which, if taken by those interested, may be of use as supports on our weaker side.

The dress should, in the first place, be modest. In pure eyes, nothing is aesthetically beautiful which is morally awry. It should not be in form so peculiar, or in bulk so great, as to attract attention from the wearer to the robe. It should not be oppressive to the finances of the family ; as a luxury, it should only come in after works of necessity and mercy have been suplied. If it cannot, as in this example, be fabricated by the wearer's hand, it ought at least to be paid from her purse. Dames who sail along the street in silk and purple which is not their own, have no right in any respect to the honour which belongs to women who work with their hands and pay their own way. By the common practice of the country, the man who distributes cotton cloth in cart loads from a wholesale warehouse is of higher rank in commercial heraldry than his neighbour who measures off the same cotton cloth by yards across the counter. On the same principle, women who wear mountains of silk for which other people must pay, should be reckoned greater operators in their line, than the bare-footed, half-naked, shaggy-haired girl, who has snatched a handkerchief from a passenger's pocket and discounted it at the "wee pawn." The same principle which gives the whole-sale merchant the higher honour, should consign the wholesale swindler to deeper disgrace. Finally, those who hang purple on their shoulders should have a change at hand : the silk that must be worn every day will soon grow shabby. This matron is not limited to the silk and purple;—"strength and honour are her clothing" too. She may safely wear elegant garments, who in character and bearing is elegant without their aid. If honour be your clothing, the suit will last a life-time; but if clothing be your honour, it will soon be worn thread-bare.

Discretion and Kindness.—"She openeth her mouth." Ah! this is the sorest strain to which her character has been subjected yet. But if a wife's words are habitually sensible and prudent, her husband's heart learns to trust her, and he experiences no mis-giving when she begins to speak. Another lovely feature of feminine excellence is added, "The law of kindness is on her lips." This is one grand constituent of woman's worth. They call her sometimes in thoughtless flattery an angel, but here an angel in sober truth she is,—a messenger sent by God to assuage the sorrows of humanity. The worn traveller, who has come through the desert with his life and nothing more; the warrior faint and bleeding from the battle; the distressed of every age and country, long instinctively for this heaven-provided help. Deep in the sufferer's nature, in the hour of his need, springs the desire to feel a woman's hand binding his wound or wiping his brow,—to hear soft words dropping from a woman's lips. The women who, during the late war, smoothed the sick soldier's pillow in the hospital, have as high a place this day in the esteem and affection of the nation as the heroes who led the assaulting column through the breach. Woman was needed in Eden; how much more on this thorny world outside ! Physically the vessel is weak, but in that very weakness her great strength lies. If knowledge is power in man's department, gentleness is power in woman's. Nor is it a fitful, uncertain thing; it is a law. When the heart within is right, the kindness is constitutional, and flows with the softness and constancy of a stream. Among the things seen and temporal it is the best balm for human sorrows.

Moral Discipline.—" She looketh well to the ways of her household." This is the key-stone which binds all the other domestic virtues into one. A watchful superintendence of children and servants, with a view to encourage good and restrain evil in their conduct, is a cardinal point in the character of a mother and mistress : a serious defect here is sufficient to dislocate the whole machinery of home. Servants have in their nature all the instincts of humanity : the affections and capacities which find scope in the relations of the family circle are ingredients in their constitution. When by the pressure of poverty they are compelled in early youth to leave their own homes, these instincts, bereft of their objects, are paralyzed for want of exercise. Young persons suddenly separated from all that glued their hearts to home, are like branches cut from the parent tree : if they are not permitted to grow like grafts into a master's family, the best emotions of their nature will wither for want of sap, or seek the dangerous sweetness of stolen waters. It is disastrous to the interests of all, when love is not bestowed on the one side, or expected on the other. Some measure of a mother's care will, as a general rule, produce a corresponding measure of a daughter's devotion. A portion of the time and energy devoted to expensive entertainments, turned into the channel of consistent, considerate kindness and faithfulness toward the servants, would greatly augment the usefulness and happiness of many families. Servants severed from home by the poverty of their parents, and through the neglect of a mistress not ingrafted into a new moral relationship, become avenging thorns in the transgressor's side; opulent families can neither live without them nor be happy with them. There is only one way of relief, and that is the way of confession and amendment. The thorns will continue to prick, as long as the law of the Lord in that matter is despised. The Father of the fatherless is mighty, and the orphans cannot with impunity be defrauded of their right. While a mistress looks well to the work which the servants do, and ill to the way in which the servants go, the economy of the house will halt painfully through all its complicated movements. There are two classes who do not look well to the ways of their households ;—those who do not look to them at all, and those who look to them with a stern, unsympathizing, indiscriminating stringency. For the bones of its strength let the moral superintendence exact obedience from the subordinate, and maintain untarnished the dignity of the chief ; but cover these bones deeply with the warm living flesh of human love, so that, while all their force is exerted, none of their hardness shall be felt.

In general, as to the education of females, let parents beware of sacrificing solid attainments for superficial polish. From the time when Salome won her hideous prize by dancing well before Herod and his lords, down to our own day, the world's history teems with examples to teach us that seven devils may hide under the ample folds of all the fashionable accomplishments in a hollow female heart. Sow the vital seed of God's word betimes, and fill their hands with useful employment. Beware of emptiness. As the rich owner of a ship who sails for his own pleasure, and does not need to carry merchandise for profit, loads his ship notwith-standing, for her safety in the sea; so, parents who do not need a daughter's winnings for their own sake, should for her sake make her skilful and keep her busy. Empty hours, empty hands, empty companions, empty words, empty hearts, draw in evil spirits, as a vacuum draws in air. To be occupied with good is the best defence against the inroads of evil.

Faith and Obedience, Work and Rest
(Proverbs 31:30, 31)

" A woman that feareth the Lord, she shall be praised. Give her of the fruit of her hands, and let her own works praise her in the gates.".

THE lessons end, where they began, " in the fear of the Lord ;" obedience is traced up to faith. In this last chapter the doctrine of the whole book is illustrated by a bright example. As we traverse the various phases of her character, we seem to be making our way over a well-watered and fruitful region, until we reach at last the fountain of its fertility. She "feareth the Lord :" here we look into the very eye of the well which clothed with verdure the landscape of this woman's life ; her faith sent forth these virtues, and then these virtues published her praise. Her good works flowed like a stream to refresh a desert neighbourhood ; but the fountain which fed it was her heart's trust in God. Those who are partakers of her precious faith will imitate her abundant labours. When you are led by the Spirit, and strive lawfully, faith and obedience do not jostle each other in your heart and life. To each its own place has been assigned it in the covenant of grace, and in true saints each keeps its own place silently and steadfastly, as if regulated by the laws of nature.

The concluding feature of this pattern character is a graceful and congruous termination to the Book of Proverbs as a whole. The key-note of all the hymn is found in the close : its theme throughout is, Righteousness the fruit of faith. We who live under the Christian dispensation should beware of a fatal mistake in our conception of its distinguishing characteristic. The gospel is not a method of bringing men to heaven without righteousness, or with less of it than was demanded in ancient times. The actual holiness of his creatures is the end of the Lord in all his dispensations, as certainly as fruit is the object of the husband-man when he plants, and waters, and grafts his trees. The death of Christ for sin is the divine plan, not for dispensing with obedi-ence from men, but for effectually obtaining it. Reconciliation is the road to righteousness. God proclaims pardon and bestows peace, that the rebels may submit and serve him. They who feel more at ease in their alienation because they have heard that Christ gave himself for sinners, are trampling under foot the blood of the covenant. Alas! even God's dear Son is made the stumbling-block over which men fall blindfold. A vague impres-sion comes in and possesses a corrupt heart, that personal holiness is in some way less needful under the reign of grace. God is my witness, I have not in these pages taught that men should try their own obedience, instead of trusting in the Saviour for the free pardon of sin : but I have taught often, and once more tenderly repeat the lesson here, that those who do not like the obligation to obedience, have no part yet in the forgiving grace.

Throughout these expositions it has been assumed that human life on earth is a life of labour. The world that man stands on is not a rest for man : ever since it became the abode of sin, it is like the troubled sea that cannot rest. Toil and suffering are the lot alike of the evil and the good in this life. It is a poor portion for those who have no other. Ah! it is a sad thing to be weary, and have no rest in store ! Jesus wept over wearied men, labour-ing in the fire for nought, and refusing to lay their aching heads on his loving breast. Labouring, sin-laden men, He still says, "Come unto me." If you refuse Him that speaketh, the universe will offer no resting-place, and eternity no resting-time.

But a rest remaineth for the people of God. The coming rest already casts the gentle foretastes of morning twilight over the dark surface of life's labour here. Present toil will give zest to the joy of future rest, and the hope of rest softens and sweetens the labour while it lasts. What may be the enjoyments of those who were never weary we cannot tell, as a man born blind cannot appreciate the pleasures of sight. Those "flames of fire," the angels who do God's pleasure, are happy, doubtless, as they are holy ; but they cannot share the rest of the redeemed from among men, for they were never weary. Only the weary rest; and the greater the weariness the sweeter the rest. Heaven to the saved will be better than paradise to the unfallen. The effects of the fall are removed by Christ, and more; grace will abound more than sin abounded. God is greater than the author of evil. At the winding up of the world, it will not be a drawn battle between the introducer of sin and the Saviour of sinners; we shall be *more* than conquerors through Him that loved us. The saved shall not only escape from bondage and hold their own, but spoil adverse principalities and powers. The enemy, when subdued, will be constrained to serve the children of the Conquerer; out of the eater shall come forth meat. The memory of sin will enhance the joy of holiness: the pain of labour will make rest more sweet.

The whole world consists of two classes, different in many things from each other but alike in this, that both are obliged to labour all their days: they are those who serve sin, and those who fight against it. Both experience pain and weariness; sin is a hard master, and a formidable foe. If you do its bidding, you are a miserable drudge; if you war against it, you will receive many wounds in the conflict. It would be hard to tell whether of the two is the more wearied—the carnal who obeys the flesh, or the spiritual who crucifies it. Both are compelled to labour. Both are weary: the one is weary by sinning, and the other weary of sin. One of these strifes will soon be over: the other will never cease. If sin be your antagonist, there will soon be peace; for if sin cannot be taken wholly away from you, you will ere long be taken away from sin. But if sin be, and till death abide, your master, there is no deliverance from the yoke.

On the whole, for moral and immortal creatures there are only two masters, and no man can serve both; the one is sin, the other is the Saviour. Either we serve sin against Christ, or we serve Christ against sin. Both masters put their servants to labour. Let not disciples expect what their Lord has neither provided nor promised; He gives them many pleasures in this life, but these are the pleasures of labour, not the pleasures of rest. This world cannot be their rest, expressly " because it is polluted." It may and should become their meat and drink to do their Lord's will; but still it is a doing, a working, a bearing. They may—they will love the work; but still it is work. They who love the Lord that bought them, are in haste to do something for Him while they are in this distant world ; for at home in heaven no such work is needed. Work is very joyful in the prospect of rest, rest will be very joyful when the work is done.

" Let the children of Zion be joyful in their King." Heaven and earth are both beautiful when God gives a shining light, and man possesses a seeing eye. Faith and obedience run sweetly into one.

Near the base of a mountain range, early in the morning of the day and the spring of the year, you may have seen, in your solitary walk, a pillar of cloud, pure and white, rising from the earth to heaven. In the calm air its slender stem rises straight like a tree, and like a tree spreads out its lofty summit. Like an angel tree in white, and not like an earthly thing, it stands before you. You approach the spot and discover the cause of the vision. A well of water from warm depths bursts through the surface there, and this is the morning incense which it sends right upward to the throne. But the water is not all thus exhaled; a pure stream flows over the well's rocky edge, and trickles along the surface, a river in miniature, marked on both sides by verdure, while the barrenness of winter lies yet on the other portions of the field.

Such are the two outgoings of a believer's life. Upward rises the soul to God in direct devotion ; but not the less on that account does the life flow out along the surface of the world leaving its mark in blessings behind it wherever it goes. You caught the spring by surprise at the dawn, and saw its incense ascending; at mid-day, when the sun was up, and the people passing, that incense was still rising, but then it rose unseen. It is thus in the experience of living Christians in the world. At certain times, when they think that none are near, their intercourse with heaven may be noticed ; but for the most part it is carried on unseen. The upright pillar is seldom visible ; but the horizontal stream is seen and felt, a refreshment to all within its reach. True devotion is chiefly in secret ; but the bulk of a believer's life is laid out in common duties, and cannot be hid. These two, alternate and yet simultaneous, separate and yet combined—these two fill up a Christian's life. Lift up your heart to God, and lay out your talents for the world ; lay out your talents for the world, and lift up your heart to God.